中国研究
China Studies

文化和旅游部国际交流与合作局
中外文化交流中心 编

"汉学与当代中国"
座谈会文集 2018

Symposium on China Studies 2018:
a Collection of 37 papers

中国社会科学出版社

图书在版编目(CIP)数据

"汉学与当代中国"座谈会文集.2018/文化和旅游部国际交流与合作局，中外文化交流中心编.——北京：中国社会科学出版社，2020.5
ISBN 978-7-5203-7193-3

Ⅰ.①汉… Ⅱ.①文…②中… Ⅲ.①汉学—文集 Ⅳ.①K207.8-53

中国版本图书馆 CIP 数据核字（2020）第 171843 号

出 版 人	赵剑英
责任编辑	孙砚文
责任校对	沈丁晨
责任印制	王 超

出　　版	中国社会科学出版社
社　　址	北京鼓楼西大街甲 158 号
邮　　编	100720
网　　址	http://www.csspw.cn
发 行 部	010-84083685
门 市 部	010-84029450
经　　销	新华书店及其他书店

印刷装订	北京君升印刷有限公司
版　　次	2020 年 5 月第 1 版
印　　次	2020 年 5 月第 1 次印刷

开　　本	710×1000　1/16
印　　张	33
字　　数	573 千字
定　　价	219.00 元

凡购买中国社会科学出版社图书，如有质量问题请与本社联系调换
电话：010-84083683
版权所有　侵权必究

2018年7月23日，"汉学与当代中国"座谈会嘉宾合影
Group photo of the "Symposium on China Studies" on July 23, 2018

2018 "汉学与当代中国" 座谈会开幕式前并行圆桌会议
The parallel round table sessions held before the opening ceremony of the "Symposium on China Studies"

2018"汉学与当代中国"座谈会开幕式前并行圆桌会议
The parallel round table sessions held before the opening ceremony of the "Symposium on China Studies"

2018"汉学与当代中国"座谈会现场
At the "Symposium on China Studies"

2018 "汉学与当代中国"座谈会分议题讨论现场
At the Sub Panel of the "Symposium on China Studies"

2018 "汉学与当代中国"座谈会现场交流
Sinologists communicating during the "Symposium on China Studies"

2018年7月23日下午，国家博物馆专场座谈现场
The meeting in the National Museum of China in the afternoon of July 23, 2018

2018年7月23日下午，国家博物馆专场座谈学者代表发言
Representative speaking at the meeting in the National Museum of China in the afternoon of July 23, 2018

2018年7月25日，赴杭州考察的汉学家一行与浙江省政府代表座谈
Sinologists on a visit to Hangzhou and discussing with representatives of Zhejiang Provincial Government on July 25, 2018

2018年7月27日，赴杭州考察的汉学家一行在访问阿里巴巴总部后合影
Group photo of Sinologists after a visit to Alibaba headquarters, Hangzhou on July 27, 2018

主办：中华人民共和国文化和旅游部　中国社会科学院
承办：中外文化交流中心

Hosts: Ministry of Culture and Tourism of the People's Republic of China
　　　　Chinese Academy of Social Sciences
Organizer: Network of International Culturalink Entities

| 目 录 |

1　理解中国文化：西方的挑战
　　荣大伟　【新西兰】
　　新西兰中国友好协会主席

9　"一带一路"倡议与拉丁美洲和加勒比地区：客观和主观方面
　　古斯塔夫·吉拉尔多　【阿根廷】
　　阿根廷拉努斯国立大学当代中国硕士研究专业负责人

29　中国的改革开放政策
　　路易斯·坎文努巴萨　【布隆迪】
　　布隆迪新闻出版局局长

39　心灵独舞
　　李莎　【加拿大】
　　翻译家

49　"一带一路"倡议为非洲和发展中国家带来机遇
　　梅拉库·穆鲁阿勒姆　【埃塞俄比亚】
　　埃塞俄比亚外交关系战略研究所对外政策研究室主任

54　文化教育与"一带一路"倡议
　　韦塞林·武科蒂奇　【黑山】
　　黑山波德戈里察大学校长、教授

75　阿拉伯特色中国学学术问题初探
　　穆赫辛·法尔加尼　【埃及】
　　艾因·夏姆斯大学语言学院中文系教授

80　白俄罗斯与中国文化联系及命运共同体的概念
　　斯维特洛夫·鲍里斯　【白俄罗斯】
　　白俄罗斯文化部前部长

94	"一带一路"倡议与共同发展：新丝路花开巴尔干地区	
	艾立山 【保加利亚】	
	索非亚大学教授	
106	文化资源匹配中国的新发展理念——"一带一路"倡议：欧亚大陆共赢合作的契机	
	奥勒·德林 【德国】	
	柏林自由大学汉学和中国研究教授	
122	哈中产能合作关系发展	
	纳比坚·穆哈穆德罕 【哈萨克斯坦】	
	哈萨克斯坦阿里—法拉比国立大学当代中国研究中心主任 / 东方学系汉学教研室主任	
137	"一带一路"倡议与韩国中国学的新前景	
	金铉哲 【韩国】	
	韩国延世大学中国研究院院长 / 孔子学院院长、中文教授	
154	中国古典诗词译成荷兰语和英语的一些思考：衡量标准、目的、押韵和对仗	
	伊维德 【荷兰】	
	哈佛大学东亚语言与文化系荣休教授	
177	中国国有企业和私营企业在全球市场上的崛起	
	柯保罗 【英国】	
	哈佛大学肯尼迪政府学院非常驻高级研究员	
211	"一带一路"倡议在尼泊尔的展望	
	萨尔波塔姆·什雷斯塔 【尼泊尔】	
	尼泊尔阿尼哥协会会长 / 加德满都示范医院神经病学家	
228	文明对话与人类命运共同体	
	普西奇·拉多萨夫 【塞尔维亚】	
	贝尔格莱德大学语言学院东方学系教授、博士 / 贝尔格莱德孔子学院外方院长	

238　中国和罗马尼亚的经济关系：从古代的联系到现在的"一带一路"
　　萨尔米扎·潘瑟卡　【罗马尼亚】
　　罗马尼亚科学院世界经济研究所经济发展模式部主任

281　传统与现代在全球化中的交融：从罗马尼亚的角度看中国
　　玛格鲁·乔治　【罗马尼亚】
　　罗马尼亚外交部长顾问 / 新战略中心科学委员会成员

305　良好的治理："一带一路"沿线基础设施建设
　　杰米·贺诗礼　【美国】
　　布鲁金斯学会约翰·桑顿中国中心访问学者 / 耶鲁大学法学院蔡中曾中国中心高级研究员、访问讲师

338　我对"一带一路"倡议的看法
　　孟什·法耶兹·艾哈迈德　【孟加拉】
　　孟加拉国国际和战略研究所主席

348　文学协同：构建人类命运共同体
　　舒明经　【印度】
　　印度文化部文化资源和培训中心高级研究员 / 印度中央邦博帕尔高等教育学院英语系教授、主任

359　中国发展新理念与国际合作新前景
　　斯巴修　【阿尔巴尼亚】
　　阿中文化协会会长

366　在"汉学与当代中国"座谈会上的发言
　　雅克·高德弗兰　【法国】
　　戴高乐基金会主席

373　在"汉学与当代中国"座谈会上的发言
　　郑永年　【新加坡】
　　新加坡国立大学东亚研究所所长、教授

380　在"汉学与当代中国"座谈会上的发言
　　罗杰·哈特　【美国】
　　德克萨斯南方大学历史与地理学系副教授 / 德克萨斯南方大学孔子学院外方校长

387　在"汉学与当代中国"座谈会上的发言
玛琳娜·吉布拉泽 【格鲁吉亚】
格鲁吉亚汉学家协会主席

394　民心相通与文明互鉴
黄平 【中国】
中国社会科学院欧洲研究所所长 / 中华美国学会会长 / 中国世界政治研究会会长

400　中国发展新理念新实践为国际广泛合作提供了新机遇
李君如 【中国】
中共中央党校原副校长，研究员、博士生导师

411　从三个数字深入理解"一带一路"倡议
李永辉 【中国】
北京外国语大学国际关系学院院长 / 中国和平统一促进会理事 / 中华美国学会常务理事

428　上海在新一轮对外开放中的桥头堡作为
王振 【中国】
上海社会科学院副院长

440　"一带一路"倡议与全球治理
张维为 【中国】
复旦大学中国研究院院长

447　"说长道短""一带一路"建设
黄仁伟 【中国】
复旦大学"一带一路"与全球治理研究院常务副院长 / 上海社会科学院智库研究中心理事长兼主任

455　是翻译成就了中国现代文学的高峰
陆建德 【中国】
原中国社会科学院文学所所长 / 学者

461 人类命运共同体与人类对话共同体
黄卓越 【中国】
北京语言大学汉学研究所所长、博导 / 中国文化对外翻译与传播研究中心主任

466 中国经济文化与全球对话的切入点
魏鹏举 【中国】
中央财经大学文化与传媒学院院长、教授

471 在开放的体系中认识中国历史文化
葛剑雄 【中国】
复旦大学资深教授 / 中央文史研究馆馆员

477 人类在 21 世纪还能走到一起吗——中国古代圣哲怎样看人类的迷失
刘梦溪 【中国】
中国艺术研究院终身研究员 / 中国文化研究所所长 / 中央文史研究馆馆员

CONTENTS

Traditional Culture and Contemporary China

4   **Understanding Chinese Culture: the Challenge to the West**
Dave Andrew Bromwich / New Zealand
President of New Zealand China Friendship Society

16   **The BRI and LAC: Objective and Subjective Aspects**
Gustavo A.Girado / Argentina
Director of Postgraduate Studies on Contemporary China at the National University of Lanús

33   **China's Reform and Opening-up Policy**
Louis Kamwenubusa / Burundi
General Director of Press Publications of Burundi (PPB)

43   **Dancing Alone**
Lisa Carducci / Canada
Translator

51   **The Benefits and Opportunities: the Belt and Road Initiative to Africa and Developing Countries**
Melaku Mulualem / Ethiopia
Head of Foreign Policy Analysis Department at Ethiopian Foreign Relation Strategic Studies Institute

62   **Culture and Education and the "Belt and Road" Initiative**
Veselin Vukotic / Montenegro
Rector of University of Donja Gorica, Professor

77   **Exploration of Academic Issues of Chinese Studies in Arabic Countries**
Mohsen Fergani / Egypt
Professor of Chinese Language, Ain Shans University

85　The Belarusian-Chinese Cultural Relations and Concept of Community with a Shared Future
Svetlov Boris / Belarus
Former Minister of Culture of the Republic of Belarus

99　New Silk Road and Common Development: Making the Balkans Bloom
Alexander B. Alexiev / Bulgaria
Professor of Sofia University

112　Aligning Cultural Resources with China's New Developmental Philosophy: The "Belt and Road" as an Opportunity for Win-Win Cooperations Across Eurasia
Ole Doering / Germany
Professor of Freie Universität Berlin/Academic Department Advisor & visiting professor of the Hong Kong Polytechnic University

128　Development of the Cooperation Between Kazakhstan and China on Production Capacity
Nabizhan Muhametkhanuly / Kazakhstan
Head of the Department of Sinology, Director of the Centre of Modern Chinese Studies, Al-Farabi Kazakh National University

144　The "Belt and Road" and New Prospects for Chinese Studies in Republic of Korea
Kim Hyun Cheol / Republic of Korea
Dean of China Research Institute, Dean of the Confucius Institute, Professor of Yonsei University

162　Some Thoughts on the Translation of Classical Chinese Poetry in Dutch and English: Meter, Purpose, Rhyme, and Parallelism
Wilt L. Idema / Holland
Professor Emeritus, the Department of East Asian Languages and Civilizations, Harvard University

190　The Emergence of Chinese Companies in Global Markets
Paul Gilmore. Clifford / Britain

Non-resident Senior Fellow at the Kennedy School of Government, Harvard University

218 **Prospects of the "Belt and Road" Initiative in Nepal**
Sarbottam Shrestha / Nepal
President of Arniko Society, Neurologist of Kathmandu Model Hospital

232 **Dialogue of Civilizations and the Community with a Shared Future for Mankind**
Radosav Pušić / Serbia
Professor of the Department of Oriental Studies, Faculty of Philology, University of Belgrade / Director of Confucius Institute in Belgrade

256 **China-Romania Economic Relations: from Ancient Connectivity to Nowadays BRI**
Sarmiza Pencea / Romania
Head of the Economic Development Models Department, Institute for World Economy, Romanian Academy

290 **Tradition and Modernity in a Globalized World: a View on China from Romania**
Magheru Gheorghe / Romania
Advisor to the Minister of Foreign Affairs of Romania/Member of the Scientific Board of New Strategy Center

315 **Building Good Governance Infrastructure along the Belt and Road**
Jamie P. Horsley / United States of America
Visiting Fellow, John L. Thornton China Center, The Brookings Institution/ Senior Fellow & Visiting Lecturer, Paul Tsai China Center, Yale Law School

342 **Belt and Road Initiative (BRI)**
Munshi Faiz Ahmad / Bangladesh
Chairman of Bangladesh Institute of International and Strategic Studies

352   **Literary Synergism: Fostering a Shared Future for Mankind**
        Shubhra Tripathi / India
        Professor and Head of Dept. of English of Govt. MVM College/Dept. of Higher Education, Govt. of Madhya Pradesh, Bhopal / Senior Fellow of the Center for Cultural Resources and Training, Ministry of Culture, New Delhi

362   **China's New Concept of Development and the Prospect of International Cooperation**
        Iljaz Spahiu/ Albania
        Chairman of the China-Albania Cultural Association

369   **Speech at the Symposium on China Studies 2018**
        Jacques Godfrain / France
        President of Foundation Charles de Gaulle

376   **Speech at the Symposium on China Studies (2018)**
        Yongnian Zheng / Singapore
        Professor and Director of the East Asian Institute at the National University of Singapore

383   **Speech at the Symposium on China Studies (2018)**
        Roger Hart/ United States of America
        Associate Professor of Department of History, Geography and General Studies/Director of Confucius Institute, Texas Southern University

390   **Speech at the Symposium on China Studies (2018)**
        Marine Jiblaze/Georgia
        Chairman of Association of Georgia Sinologists, Dean of Confucius Institute at Free University of Tbilisi

396   **People-to-People Bond and Mutual Learning Among Civilizations**
        Huang Ping/ China
        Director General of the Institute of European Studies, Chinese Academy of Social Sciences / President of the Chinese Association of American Studies / President of Chinese Association of World Politics Studies

404	**China's New Concepts of Practice of Development in Creating New Opportunities for International Cooperation**
	Li Junru / China
	Former Vice-president of Party School of the Central Committee of C.P.C, Researcher, Ph. D. Supervisor

418	**An In-depth Understanding of the Belt and Road Initiative from Three Figures**
	Li Yonghui/ China
	Director of the School of International Relations and Diplomacy, Beijing Foreign Studies University / Council Member of the China Council for the Promotion of Peaceful National Reunification / Executive Member of the Chinese Association of American Studies

433	**Shanghai: a Bridgehead in the New Round of Opening-up**
	Wang Zhen/ China
	Deputy Dean of the Shanghai Academy of Social Sciences

443	**The Belt and Road Initiative and Global Governance**
	Zhang Weiwei/ China
	Director of China Institute, Fudan University

450	**A Discussion of the Construction of the Belt and Road**
	Huang Renwei/ China
	Executive Vice-president of the Fudan Institute of "Belt and Road" and Global Governance/Director of the Center of Think Tank Studies of Shanghai Academy of Social Sciences

458	**Modern Chinese Literature Peaked in Translation**
	Lu Jiande/ China
	Former Director of the Institute of Literature , Chinese Academy of Social Sciences

463	**A Community with a Shared Future for Mankind and a Community for a Dialogue of Mankind**
	Huang Zhuoyue/ China

Director of the Institute of Sinology/Doctoral Advisor in Beijing Language and Culture University/ Director of the Center of Chinese Culture Communication and Translation

468 The Entry Point of China's Economic and Cultural Dialogues with the World

Wei Pengju/ China

Director and Professor of the School of Culture and Communication, Central University of Finance and Economics

474 Understanding Chinese History and Culture in the Perspective of Open System

Ge Jianxiong/ China

Senior Professor of Fudan University/Member of the Central Research Institute of Culture and History

490 Can Human Beings Still Come Together in the 21st Century?—— How Did Ancient Chinese Sages View Human Beings' Getting Lost?

Liu Mengxi/ China

Tenured Fellow and Director of the Institute of Chinese Culture, the Chinese National Academy of Arts / Member of the Central Research Institute of Culture and History

理解中国文化：西方的挑战

荣大伟　【新西兰】
新西兰中国友好协会主席

在过去三十年中，世界见证了中国社会、经济的重大变化和全球地位的提升。中国已成为世界舞台上不可或缺的参与者。然而西方的主流叙事仍然不能理解为何中国没有西方化。中国正在创造出西方的替代模式。

西方没能认真地理解中国视野，并且在很大程度也不希望存在替代模式。孔子曰："知之为知之，不知为不知，是知也。"很多人过度迷信西方中心论，因无知而未能理解中国，致使自身陷入被新兴世界秩序抛弃的危险。

在西方视野占主导地位的西方报纸头条新闻中经常可以读到这种无知的评论和报道。通过选择性的报道刻画负面印象，而事实往往被歪曲。西方的新闻报道缺乏批判性评价，因此媒体在加强对话和推动对中国的有效理解方面信誉很低。不可否认虚假新闻的确存在！

最近，一家新西兰报纸报道称，中国派遣120名医生前往太平洋岛国帮助他们改善社区健康水平。人们应该认为这是一项积极的行动，但是这篇报道关注的焦点在于中国在太平洋做了些什么，"我们太失败了，怎么能允许这种事情发生。"中国人在"我们的地盘"干什么？！

这种类型的媒体报道损害公众接受中国立场的潜在可能，给中国带来负面影响。中国几乎没有机会向西方展示自己的形象。

我希望从两个不同的角度探讨这一矛盾现象。

西方对中国的崛起充满敬畏,而且在很大程度上将其视为威胁而不是机遇。

"一带一路"倡议的宣传可以作为另一个案例反映对中国走向世界的不同反应。它是对目前世界各国关系的威胁,只对中国有利,还是在威胁当前全球秩序的同时也提供机遇和利益?

面临重大分歧的另一个方面在于,结果的时间框架。西方民主本质上对每个民族国家内部的稳定治理施加限制。我们目前观察到的诸多案例都可以证明来之不易的政策遭到破坏和逆转,因为这些政策可能对世界秩序产生影响。孔子提到,世界上唯一不变的是变化本身。不稳定可能被视为改变新世界秩序的诱因,而习近平在这一秩序下积极推动建设"和谐的国际社会"。危机蕴含着机遇,从长远来看,今天的破坏可能是明天的美好。但是在破坏当前世界秩序的过程中,西方是否有替代方案?

那么,西方面临的挑战是增强对"中国是什么"的理解和认识。从长远来看,中国的文化遗产如何为世界带来积极和乐观的优势?

为了理解这一问题,重要的是思考中国文化和社会的基础。中国拥有5000多年不间断的历史和文化进程。我们至少需要追溯到2500年前,研究老子和道家文化和哲学渊源,研究孔子的社会哲学以及对社会的影响。

我在这里表示抱歉,因为我不是一名学者,而是今日中国和中国起源的热心观察员。

我认为道教为我们揭示了中国文化和哲学特殊性的许多方面。阴和阳的概念在西方广为人知,但没有多少人能够完全理解或实践,包括个人和领导者。阴和阳通过对立融合为我们带来平衡。

中国具有对立带来平衡的文化基因。例如中文的"危机"一词包括"危"和"机"两个字,分别代表"危险"和"机遇"。

中医将人体视为一个整体,如果阴阳失调,冷热不均,身体就会产生疾病。治疗方案是恢复身体机能平衡,而不是孤立地针对特定症状或问题区域。中医治疗往往需要很长时间才能见效,主要关注身体的协调。这并不是说西医不完美,我仅以此为例来说明中国人解决问题的方法。

最近,我参加了在贵州举行的以"生态文明与反贫困"为主题的国际论坛。在整个演讲过程中普遍提到人与自然之间的和谐。这个概念在道教思想中有着很深的渊源。21世纪的中国,由于环境恶化而造成经济损失,中国致力于通过建立生态文明社会解决这一问题。几位国际演讲者提到对某些西方国家保持全球共识的信心正在下降。演讲者对中国决定参与领导这一共识产生越来越正面的印象。关于生态文明，中国已经在领先过渡到使用清洁能源，并且在所有国家当中，中国在全球范围内为使人们摆脱贫困做出了重大贡献。

中国饮食是我们大多数人都熟悉的中国文化的一部分。通过一系列不同食材的简单组合，中国菜背后的哲学理念是创造平衡。众所周知，酸和甜是一对明显不同的味道，但不同的结构和颜色的组合也很重要。

中国传统水墨画的表现形式简单，但蕴含模仿人性的自然环境图像。为了完全欣赏中国艺术，我们必须理解这些元素。竹子是优雅的象征，空心茎暗示着谦虚。梅花象征高贵和力量，往往在地面上还有积雪的时节盛开。

孔子的贡献也让中国社会与西方社会不同。从儒家和希腊时代开始，东西方社会在哲学方面的时间跨度相似，但两者的交叉点很少。简而言之，东方社会将社区或大家庭的概念视为社会最重要的组成部分。这样可以将社会问题的所有考虑因素置于一个主观框架中。

西方社会将个人视为构成社会的单元，与问题的客观分析相容。

我喜欢问一个问题："猴子、牛和香蕉，请问哪一个不同？"对于猴子、牛和香蕉，大多数中国人会选择牛，因为猴子和香蕉存在联系！猴子喜欢吃香蕉，香蕉是猴子的食物。西方人总是选择香蕉，因为他们都认为猴子和牛属于动物这一客观分类。考虑到这两种不同的反应以及更深层次的哲学思考，中西方的思维方式存在重大差异。中国人具有更强的社会意识，重视事物之间的相互关系，而不是个人主义。

儒家学者墨子提倡"大爱"的概念，或者更准确地说，尊重他人和事物。如果以利他的方式表达，可以轻松和积极地统合人民与国家，人与自然。拥抱生态文明以及"一带一路"倡议就是这种统合的案例。

西方面临的挑战是如何接受另一种观点。西方媒体是时候在新闻报道上追求平衡，批判西方的视野。现在是时候让西方人听到中国的声音。舆论可以开始对中国的奉献表示欣赏。中国在当今复杂的世界上发挥越来越重要的作用，因此理解中国文化已变得不可或缺。

只有这样，才能允许和谐的全球秩序自由发展，全球共识才能成为和平的共识，冲突也将减少。我们将在更长的时间框架内处于这样的状态。

Understanding Chinese Culture: the Challenge to the West

Dave Andrew Bromwich / New Zealand

President of New Zealand China Friendship Society

In the last three decades, the world has observed a major transformation of Chinese society, economy, and position on the world stage. China has become an indispensable global player. Yet in the west, the dominant narrative has failed to understand that this does not mean that China has become westernised. China is creating an alternative to the west.

The west has not made a serious effort to understand a Chinese perspective, and to a great extent has not appreciated that an alternative understanding exists. Confucius said "real knowledge is to know the extent of one's ignorance." The west, with its western-centric approach, through its ignorance and failure to understand China, has placed itself in peril of being left behind in a newly emerging world order.

We see this ignorance in headlines in Western Newspapers, in which the western perspective is dominant. There is selective reporting to portray negative impressions, and fact is often misrepresented. Too often western reporting lacks critical evaluation, leading to a very low credibility within the media to further the dialogue and promote a valid understanding of China. Fake News does exist!

Recently, a New Zealand newspaper reported that China was sending 120 medical doctors to a Pacific Island to assist with their low level of community health. A positive action, one might think, but the focus of the story was to ask what was China doing in the Pacific, how have we failed to the extent that we have allowed this to happen. What are the Chinese doing on "our patch"?!

This kind of media attention does damage to the potential for the public to appreciate what China stands for, and gives a negative impression of China.

I would like to consider some of the contradictions in the two different perspectives.

The rise of China is met with awe in the west, and to a great extent promoted as a threat, rather than as an opportunity.

The promotion of Belt and Road Initiative is another example of the different responses to China reaching out to the world. Is it a threat to existing relationships, with advantage only to China, or is it offering opportunity and benefits globally as the existing global order is threatened.

A second area where a major difference exists lies in the timeframe for outcomes. The very nature of western democracy places constraints on stable governance within each nation state, and we are currently seeing very strong examples of disruption and reversal of hard won policy that potentially impacts on the world order. Confucius observed that the only thing that does not change is change itself, so this destabilising factor could be seen as an essential part of a change to a new world order, one that Xi Jinping positively promotes as a "harmonious global community". The crisis becomes an opportunity, and what may be bad now is good tomorrow, in the longer term. But in destabilising the current world order, does the west have an alternative in place?

The challenge to the west, then, is to enhance an understanding and appreciation of "What is China"? How does China's cultural heritage present a positive and optimistic advantage to the world in the longer term?

To understand this question it is important to consider the foundations of Chinese culture and society. China has more than 5000 years of uninterrupted history and cultural development. We at least need to go back 2500 years and study Lao Zi, and Daoism, for a cultural and philosophical root, and Confucius for his social philosophy, and impact on society.

To me, Daoism provides us with many aspects of the special nature of Chinese culture and philosophy. The concept of yin and yang is well known in the west, but not fully understood or practiced by many, either individuals or leaders. Yin and Yang brings us balance through the integration of opposites.

China has a cultural heritage of opposites creating balance. For example, crisis in Chinese "危机", consists of two characters, wei and ji, to represent peril and opportunity.

In Chinese medicine, there is a holistic approach that treats the whole body, in which imbalance with yin and yang, hot and cold, are the cause of disease. The solution is to restore imbalance rather than targeting the specific symptom or problem area in isolation. The solutions offered tend to take a longer time to take effect, with a focus to work in harmony with the body. This is not to say that western medicine is imperfect, I merely use this as an example of a Chinese approach to seeking solutions to problems.

Earlier this month, I participated in an international forum titled 'Eco-civilisation and Anti-poverty' in Guizhou. Throughout the speeches was common reference to harmony between man and nature. This concept has very deep roots in Daoist thinking. In 21st century China, the economic loss through environmental degradation fits very comfortably into the Chinese approach to addressing the establishment of an eco-society. Several international speakers referred to a decreasing confidence in certain western countries to maintain a global consensus. The speakers presented an increasingly positive impression of China's determination to participate in leadership of this consensus.With reference to an eco-civilisation, China is already a leader of the transition to clean energy, and of all countries, has made the major contribution globally to lifting people from poverty.

Chinese food is a Chinese culture that most of us feel we are familiar with. Underlying the creation of dishes is the philosophy of creating balance, through a simple combination of a range of different elements. Sweet and Sour is a well-known example of apparently opposing tastes, but also different textures and colour combinations are valued.

Chinese traditional ink paintings are simple in presentation, but rich in images of the natural environment that mimic human nature. To fully appreciate Chinese art, these elements need to be understood. The bamboo is a symbol of elegance, and the hollow stem suggests modesty. Plum blossom is an element representing nobility and strength, emerging while the snow is still on the ground.

Confucius contribution to Chinese society also provides a difference to western society. Eastern and western philosophical aspects of society have a similar time span from Confucian and Greek time forward, but the confluence is minimal. Put very basically, eastern society places the community, or a concept of a big family, as the most important component of society. This can place all considerations of social issues in a subjective framework.

In western society, it is the individual that is considered to be the unit of society, compatible with an objective analysis of issues.

I like to question people, "considering a monkey, cow and banana, which is the odd one out?" Monkey, cow, banana. The vast majority of Chinese will choose the cow as the odd one out because of the relationship between the monkey and the banana! The monkey eats the banana, the banana gives sustenance to the monkey.

Western people invariably see the banana as the odd one out because they see the objective classification of the monkey and cow both being animals. Consideration of these two responses, and extension into deeper philosophical understanding present a major difference between Chinese and Western thought. Chinese have a much stronger sense of community, and the interrelationship of things compared to an individualistic approach.

Confucian scholar Mozi promotes a concept of "da ai" a big love, or more appropriately, respect for others and things. If expressed in an altruistic way, this makes for an easy, positive unification of people, countries, man and nature. Embracing an Eco-civilisation, and the Belt and Road Initiative, are examples of the potential this unification can offer.

The challenge to the west is to embrace an alternative perspective on issues. It is time for western media to seek a balance in reporting affairs, and critique the western perspective. It is time for a Chinese voice to be allowed to be heard in the west. Then public opinion can begin to adopt an appreciation of what China has to offer. Understanding Chinese culture has become indispensable to appreciate the complex world where China plays an increasingly crucial role. Leaders need this understanding.

Only then will a harmonious global order be allowed to develop freely, and the global consensus can become a peaceful one, and conflict diminished. We are in this for the longer timeframe.

"一带一路"倡议与拉丁美洲和加勒比地区：客观和主观方面

古斯塔夫·吉拉尔多 【阿根廷】
阿根廷拉努斯国立大学当代中国硕士研究专业负责人

一、引言

中国在全球的崛起直接引发激烈的辩论。大体而言，争论主要围绕与东方价值观相比，西方的自由民主价值观是否仍然有效。东方的经济体在当今世界最具有活力，虽然仍存在大量问题，但正在加快推动减贫工作。

在这场辩论中，基本观点与自由主义的特征有关，特别是在北半球的西方，自由主义制度无法对人民的需求做出适当的回应，从而导致在特定类型的反对革命框架下旧观念出现和兴起并拥有大量的追随者。迄今为止，欧洲的民主、资本主义和一体化模式似乎并不适应新的复杂性（旧大陆上出现的城市网络、银行家、恐怖分子和移民）。某些作者对此进行严厉批评，并且分析认为人们已经"背叛"使欧洲保持数十年繁荣的自由主义价值观，这种情绪化和错误见解的升级让我们没有理性辩论和协商的空间。

第二次世界大战结束后，统一、自由和民主的欧洲梦开始出现（美国权力加强的延伸和反映）。当前边缘化政党的崛起（在欧洲，他们通常被称为"民粹主义者"）主要是因为管理欧盟的机构不是由多数人选举产生，中央银行、宪法法院、监管机构以及当前的欧盟总体上似乎是由开明专家领导的体制模式所统治。有人认为自由主义已经被贪婪的银行家"绑架"或者一直是自满的滋生地，所以少数人，包括职业政客、记者、银行家和世界精英专家在内，始终在告诉大多数人什么最适合他们。通过向非通过选举的机构转移更多的权力，自由主义者剥夺选民在政治中发出声音的可能性。

有文章称，自由主义使人们迷失在强大国际市场的迷宫中。在第二次世界大战后急需制度和政治秩序重构的时期，冷战期间创建的制度（因为旧制度的支撑已经崩溃）成为大众的意志。七十年前，美国为了维护自身的利益，对当时的苏联制定了遏制政策，但未发生战争，也没有将进程和制度的民主化与安全目标混为一体。

随后的问题导致那些并不可靠政治党派的兴起，这些党派重视由全球化过程中出现的社会需求，将民主变成制度化的工程，忽略了公民的参与。而公民的参与其实非常重要。丹尼斯·斯诺尔（Dennis J. Snower）等作者认为，自文明诞生以来，人类社会逐渐形成规模更大的合作网络：首先改变观念，然后改变制度，但世界各地的民族主义势力威胁要逆转这一进步趋势。在这种情况下，作为多边主义的支持者必须证明国际合作的价值和必要性。总之，目前的情形重大的决策似乎都是由非选举的机构根据具体情况，例如包括中央银行、宪法法院和欧盟委员会本身做出的。

中国与这些问题和辩论有什么关联？太多关联。因为在北半球的西方国家，几十年来中国一直是一面镜子，用于向人民展示不应该遵循的制度。中国目前的全球心理意象将会产生影响，如果围绕欧洲建设根基的辩论仍然陷于混乱之中，这种影响会加大。

根据上面的介绍，我们揭示中国在战后多边组织中的部署以及在大多数组织中的边缘化是构建实体和机制必要的政治底线，从而允许中国与世界建立联系、制订政策并且在更加不确定的世界上保证未来。中国尝试从不同的方面指出确定性，向世界其他地方证明行为的确定性，从不同的角度进行融合，让自己的声音能够清晰地听到。事实上，最近还在修正宪法，以明确对未来时代的看法以及中国前进的方向。为了实现这一目标，中国采用了各种机制，包括"一带一路"倡议。

二、客观方面

美国政府在特朗普总统的领导下退出《跨太平洋伙伴关系协定》；北美自由贸易协定谈判过程一直很困难，单方面采取行动减少美国贸易赤字的威胁加剧，人们对世界贸易组织的争端解决程序提出批评，美国新的税制改革法案包含保护主义方案……如今，我们亲眼目睹美国与中国贸易政策的激烈碰撞。总之，一系列行动和其他行为削弱美国经济与拉丁美洲和加勒比地区之间的经济联系。许多国家与美国签订了《自由贸易协定》，同时也是当前世界贸易秩序的坚定支持者。

美国贸易保护主义泛滥，与此同时拉丁美洲和加勒比地区的产品需要市场。由于过度的技术依赖，这是该地区唯一的外汇来源。在观察到的任何时间序列中，几乎所有拉丁美洲和加勒比地区的国际收支经常项目账户都能证明这一点。为了获得新的市场，亚太地区成为人们关注的焦点。从现在开始，随着"一带一路"倡议在欧亚大陆取得进展，人们应将其视为更加紧密的联系。因此，拉美和中国的互补需求找到了另一个融合渠道："一带一路"平台将使中国能够客观地推动其金融机构以及与拉美的融合战略。本地区认为这是中国倡议所能够提供的，也会影响大多数拉美国家的物质和政治利益。

不仅仅是上述商业决策将产生影响。自第二次世界大战以来，除了二十世纪八十年代对拉丁美洲和加勒比地区的《华盛顿共识》外，随着多边金融组织的出现，拉丁美洲和加勒比地区经济依赖最终达到一定的程度，以至于本地区所需要的金融融资受到出资实体的永久控制和监督，发放资金的前提条件是拉美国家必须采取政治行动，调整经济政策以符合他们的要求。这种专门为拉丁美洲和加勒比地区设计发展方案的"限制条件"加深了依赖程度并使得结构缺陷更加明确。

中国认为"一带一路"倡议是提升中国地位和国际形象的理想政治和经济平台，拉丁美洲也不例外。由于没有设定完成倡议的具体日期，中国领导人可以在认为合适的时候宣布成功，而不必遵守严格的最后期限。考虑到经常性的政治变化正在定义中国在大多数拉美和加勒比国家共同体成员国心目中的形象，这一方面也符合拉丁美洲的要求。拉丁美洲和加勒比地区政治决策的变动和更改似乎已经成为一种规范，鉴于"一带一路"倡议没有设定具体期限，这种规范可以发挥作用。

反过来，为了摆脱幽灵，采用政治机制是合理的，因此"一带一路"倡议将不会被视为具有侵略性或单向性。换句话说，中国编织的网络和更大的相互依存关系使中国越来越难以维持旧的不干预政策。随着中国规模的增大和活跃度的提升，认为中国的行为没有危险的国家将会越来越少。中国在非洲、拉丁美洲、南亚和中亚等地的投资和经济利益面临政治和安全挑战。由于中国寻求与其他全球经济大国并驾齐驱的先进技术，中国将受到政治反对、国家安全和竞争恐惧等问题的阻碍。

但这不是唯一的观点。其他作者认为，中国在发展中经济体的布局可以被视为强迫，事实上并没有强迫。伊万（Evan Ellis）在最近的文章中称，虽然中国可能未明确寻求在拉美地区推行替代性的政治经济秩序，但对其自身经济和其他利益的关注对拉美地区的政治和经济动态产生变革性的影响，严重程度相当于强迫推行替代性的秩序。

迄今为止，指出的各个方面都是因改变当今世界格局的政治现实所决定的。这一现实界定拉丁美洲和加勒比地区与现代世界最重要的两个国家关系的某些特征。一方面，美国显然正在后退，对世界事务失去兴趣；另一方面，中国崛起以及在建立长期政治联系的政策基础上对拉美地区进行布局，其可靠和优质的供应商提供发展所需的所有投入。但这并不是全部。

三、主观方面

我们在引言部分指出一些问题，这些问题与拉丁美洲和加勒比地区的历史及其人口来源有关。该地区与北半球的西方国家存在历史文化关系和大体上相同的价值观。美洲大陆上的民族国家成立之前，欧洲人遍布整个大陆，首先通过对大片自然资源丰富的土地进行殖民。他们记录拉美地区的历史，因为除了部分国家的文化精髓外，过去的原住民几乎没有任何东西被保留下来。

目前共同的价值观（行为和文化价值模式，例如习俗、语言等），包括政府组织形式和自由民主制度，使中国通过贸易融资和投资以外的其他途径进入和布局拉丁美洲更加困难。中国用软实力对此进行补偿，但方式须与欧亚大陆不同。无论如何，中国与欧亚大陆的分歧较小，相互之间的亲和力更大，有着更多的共同历史……

总而言之，中国不仅在地理和文化上与拉丁美洲相距遥远，而且采取的方式和机制也须多样化。这是解决双方关系其他重要问题的关键所在。

显然，在技术和物质变得更加一体化的世界，传统的宗主—殖民地关系（后来的中心—外围关系）所赋予的联系不再存在，或者说与以前不同。尽管拉丁美洲与中国之间的地理和文化距离非常遥远，但备受吹捧的全球化概念所带来的变化让我们在 21 世纪增进理解，以及出乎意料，更加远离根据自己的需要随意安排拉丁美洲和加勒比地区的势力。在这个群体中，我们发现美国似乎退缩了，并且在广泛意义上对多边和一体化进程起了反应，因为共和党人不久前接管国家的管理。正如前文所述，该政策影响了拉丁美洲和加勒比地区。

让我们认真审视背景。在拉丁美洲的几个行业部门和国家中，中国的存在曾经和现在给人们留下深刻的印象，但该地区的政府、商人和民间社会并不能很好地理解中国的动机、战略和程序。同样，中国公司仍需要加深对拉丁美洲开展业务的背景以及该地区所能提供机会的了解。

"一带一路"倡议实行应考虑并非所有在拉美地区的中国项目都能成功。已经取得成就的项目在巩固方面存在困难，仍然在学习如何在与本国不同的环境下经营业务。这是理解实施问题的核心事实。这些投资在拉丁美洲和加勒比地区的发展只有十多年的时间，而且随着每个行业和经济体呈现出自身的动态变化，本地合作伙伴的作用变得尤为重要。中国人的存在几乎改变了他们试图建立业务的所有市场。

中国公司不论是在进入市场初期还是在开始运营之后，不论是过去还是现在，只要实施业务活动，可能引起人们的不信任，还会引发对劳动法规、当地人员、可能的环境后果（特别是采掘活动，涉及一定程度的补偿）对本地社区的直接影响，以及安全问题的关注和纠纷。这些方面是中国在拉丁美洲和加勒比地区经营业务的基础，并将成为支持"一带一路"框架内下可能开展活动的支撑。

简而言之，新阶段的关系意味着中国人和中国企业的实际存在为该地区带来了新的活力。这是中国政府发挥越来越大的影响力的根本，从而帮助中国的企业和人员，检验中国政府运用所谓的软实力缓解中国企业面临的政治和管理压力的能力。

孤立、政治和公民社会的期望，支付制度及其实践，不同的劳动文化……所有这些因素都会影响他们与即将开展业务所在社区的关系。

四、结论

2017年，中国提出中拉合作"3×3"模式，这是中国希望为拉丁美洲和加勒比地区铺平道路的第一步。该模式提出共同建设三大通道（物流、电力、信息），实现南美大陆互联互通[1]；遵循市场经济规律，实现三方（企业、社会、政府）的良性互动，以及第三点，围绕合作项目，拓展三条融资渠道（基金、信贷、保险）。

总之，这种"三管齐下的模式"意味着首先要满足拉丁美洲的内部需求，然后中国将遵循所谓的"市场经济规律"，实现企业、社会、政府三者良性互动，最后拓展金融渠道[2]。因此，建议拉美可以参与"一带一路"倡议，以加速实施"3×3"，进而巩固中国与拉美之间的双边关系。

这就是"一带一路"倡议最初想法的松动，开始证明其灵活性合理：如果这些国家对中国表现出更大的开放性和意愿，中国可能愿意为拉美地区的基础设施项目支付更多的融资费用。尽管欧亚大陆构成"一带一路"倡议的神经中枢，相关文件似乎考虑拉丁美洲和加勒比地区的利益，对其参与保持开放性。该地区具有若干所谓的"新兴市场"，它们是中国的主要贸易伙伴，也是其在美洲大陆的主要投资目的地。

此外，提出这一倡议的动机之一是中国制造业存在生产过剩现象，因此新的基础设施可以作为调节机制和减压阀，推动过剩产能的流动。通过合作稳定区域需求，有理由认为，从拉丁美洲的角度进行解读，这种推理应具有跨大陆性。因此，"一带一路"倡议支持其他互补性：拉丁美洲和加勒比地区在贸易领域（尤其是南美洲）与中国形成互补，物质的流动性可以证明这一点。但"一带一路"倡议也推动其他非商业互补，例如技术（知识）、资本（融资）和基础设施（工程）的需求。

在已经举办的两届中国—拉共体论坛部长级会议上，"一带一路"倡议似乎占据议程的很大一部分（特别是在智利举行的上届会议），虽然拉丁美洲和加勒比地区不是中国"一带一路"倡议部署战略第一阶段的组成部分。现在可以认为，该倡议将作为互补性交换的载体：它将为中国所倡导的"共赢"提供更多的视角，可以被理解为改变、转化拉美地区的功能性工具、输出矩阵，不再是主要依赖。借助"一带一路"倡议，拉丁美洲和加勒比地区企业可以了解是否与中国资本产

---

1 中国政府提出与拉丁美洲共同构建"1+3+6"合作和联系概念框架，包括"一个规划"（《中国与拉美和加勒比国家合作规划（2015-2019）》）、"三大引擎"（贸易、投资和金融合作）以及"六大领域"（能源、自然资源、基础设施建设、农业、制造业、科技创新和信息技术）。
2 中国已经创建并领导亚洲基础设施投资银行和金砖国家新开发银行。可以发现，在美国退出时，中国将作为拉丁美洲和加勒比地区的替代发展资金来源。中国似乎对世界银行和国际货币基金组织等国际金融机构并不信任。此外，中国的银行可以发掘整个拉丁美洲目前仍未被探究的融资机会，例如中国和墨西哥，两个国家在2016年底设立基础设施项目联合基金。

生联系。

也存在矛盾的一面。中国与拉丁美洲关系面临的困难似乎已经不存在并且具有偿付能力，例如加强商业和投资联系。实际上在过去的三十年中，中国和拉美从几乎没有任何联系，到如今在这些领域建立非常重要的关系，甚至已签订自由贸易协定和联系协定。非常有意义的整体战略。在那个时期，贸易往来能证明中国资本在拉美的直接投资规模，今天的中国已成为拉美三大主要外部投资来源国之一。

然而，中国可以为拉丁美洲提供融资也为这种关系的不断发展带来了动力。需要考虑的方面是，如上文所述，不存在类似于发放资金的多边金融组织向拉美地区施加的条件。总之，出现了一个新的参与者，它是重要而有活力的潜在合作伙伴，它拥有拉美地区所缺乏的资金，而与拉丁美洲和加勒比地区具有相同价值观和共同历史的经济体无法提供这些资金。矛盾再次浮现。在一定程度上，拥有资本的国家没有共同的历史，并且还是更具有吸引力的资金提供者，因为融资不附加任何条件。

从理论上讲，这些难以突破的方面似乎容易解决，产生联系的机制源自其中一方拥有相对丰富的要素（中国资金）。然而，文化上的距离似乎能够削弱所有这些优势。这不仅妨碍人际关系的发展，也阻碍企业之间关系的实质性发展。

在这种情况下，中国似乎已经做好充分准备，利用其公共能力（软实力）与该地区的机构建立更紧密的联系，以推动"一带一路"倡议在拉美地区的进展，从而降低因缺乏对拉美地区的文化和价值观的了解而带来的风险。虽然中国资本及其全球布局与拉美地区多种多样的需求距离遥远，但与中国过剩的基础设施、技术和资金开发能力直接相关。

更为广泛的关系可以构成当前和预期自由贸易协定的基础，深化中国与拉美国家的战略伙伴合作并且保障政治和经济关系，让中国拥有高品质投入的可靠供应商。伴随着这些转变，"一带一路"倡议在拉美地区的部署水平将提升并成为真正的全球项目，将考虑拉美地区的利益，超越当前多边金融组织的融资附加条件。

通过中国资本在全球价值链中的增加，不依赖于西方技术的中国项目将引领拉美地区的企业参加，在中国的羽翼下，具有类似于中国的发展能力。

The BRI and LAC: Objective and Subjective Aspects

Gustavo A.Girado / Argentina

Director of Postgraduate Studies on Contemporary China at the National University of Lanús

Introduction

There is an interesting debate that is gaining momentum, directly related to the Chinese emergency worldwide. More broadly, the controversy is associated with the validity of the values held by the western liberal democracies, placed in compared perspective to those values in force in the East, where the world's most dynamic economies are today, and which reduce their poverty levels accelerated despite the large number of problems that remains.

In this discussion, the basic argument has to do with the liberal institution's character that, particularly in the Western North hemisphere, are not being able to give adequate responses to the demands of the population, giving rise to the appearance and rise of old ideas with new protagonists in the framework of certain kind of counterrevolution. So far, the European models of democracy, capitalism and integration do not seem to be in tune with the new complexities (networks of cities, bankers, terrorists and migrants that appear in the old continent). There are authors[1] who are severe about it and analyze that the liberal values that allowed Europe to prosper for many decades may have been "betrayed", so that the escalation of emotions and myths left little room for reason, debate and agreements.

In the Post Second World War, the dream of a united, liberal and democratic Europe (by extension and as a reflection of the consolidation of US power) appears, and hence the current rise of parties that were on the margin of politics (in the EU they are often called "populist") it is attributed to the fact that the institutions that govern the EU were not elected by majority, nor the members of the central banks, the constitutional courts, the regulatory bodies and, in general, the current EU appears governed by an institutional model led by enlightened experts. There are authors who argue that liberalism has been "kidnapped" by greedy bankers or has been the breeding ground of complacency, so it is the minorities -professional politicians, journalists, bankers and experts of the world elite- who are telling to the majorities what is best for them. By transferring more and more power to institutions that nobody has chosen, the liberals would have taken from the voters the possibility of having a voice in politics.

It is also often read that the liberal project has left people lost in the labyrinth of powerful international markets, to which we say that institutions created in the heat of a need for institutional and political reordering (because the institutional pillars of representation are they would have collapsed) in the Post Second World War, in the middle of the cold war, they became of the popular will, an aspect that was not questioned while the social ascent was common currency for the European people. Seven decades ago, the USA developed a policy of containment on the Soviet Union to safeguard their interests, but without war and mixing democratization of processes and institutions with security objectives.

Subsequent problems bring as emerging to shady political parties that place on

---

1 Jan Zielonka, "Counter-Revolution, Liberal Europe in Retreat", Oxford, (2018).

their shoulders the social demands originated in the supposed problems that appear in globalization, turning democracy into an institutional engineering style with little margin for the citizen's participation. The concern is important. Authors such as Dennis J. Snower argue that since the dawn of civilization, humanity has gradually formed ever larger cooperative networks, first changing minds and then institutions, but with nationalist forces around the world threatening to reverse that progress. In this we are: the supporters of multilateralism must show why international cooperation is not only valuable, but also necessary.In sum, the scenario seems to be that of a place where the fundamental decisions are taken by non-elected bodies, such as central banks, constitutional courts and the European Commission itself, as the case may be[1].

And what does China have to do with all these issues and debate? Much, because it is the mirror that for decades was used in the western northern hemisphere to show the population which way they should not follow. Its current global projection has consequences, and even more so if a strong discussion around the fundamental pillars of European construction is in turmoil.

With this introduction we intend to show that the Chinese deployment on the post-war multilateral organizations, as well as the under-representation that has in most of them, is the political floor necessary for the creation of entities and mechanisms that allow China to link with the world, develop its policies and secure the future in a much more uncertain world. From different places he tries to present certainties, provide certainty to the rest of the world about his actions and integrate himself from a different place, making his voice heard more clearly. In fact, until recently he has modified his constitution to make clear what his vision of the times to come is, and from where China will try to progress. For all this uses various mechanisms, among which is the "Belt and Road Initiative" (BRI).

---

1 "Reclaiming Multilateralism", in Project Syndicate.

Objectively

With President Trump, the US administration leaves the Trans-Pacific Partnership Agreement (TPP); the NAFTA renegotiation process has been difficult, intensified threats of unilateral action to reduce US trade deficits, criticized the WTO dispute settlement process and the new US tax reform bill includes several protectionist proposals ... and today we are witnessing its strong encounters with China in terms of trade policy. In sum, the set of these and other actions weaken the economic ties between the US economies and Latin America and the Caribbean (LAC). Many have a Free Trade Agreement with the United States and they are at the same time firm supporters of the current world trade order (Deorukhkar et al., 2018)[1].

This greater protectionism in the United States is going head-to-head with the needs of Latin America and the Caribbean to obtain markets for its products, almost the only source of foreign exchange due to its extensive technological dependence. The result of the Current Account of the Balance of Payments of almost all LAC shows it clearly in any time series observed. The need, then, to get new markets puts Asia Pacific in the spotlight, which from now on should be seen more interconnected as the BRI progresses in Eurasia. The complementary needs of LAC and China thus find another channel of convergence: the BRI platform would allow China -objectively- to promote more and better its financial institutions and its integration strategy with LAC, while they perceives that a large part of the offer with which the Chinese initiative is presented, it is functional to the material and political interests of a large part of its members.

And not only the aforementioned commercial decisions have an impact. Since the 2WW and with the emergence of multilateral financial organizations, in addition to the implementation of the Washington Consensus on LAC during the eighties, economic dependence ended up being sealed to the extent that the financing

---

[1] China has signed bilateral free trade agreements with Chile, Peru and Costa Rica, has others in management and has signed cooperation agreements with multiple regional countries, which reach different degrees and status.

required by LAC was subject to permanent control and monitoring by the granting entities, conditioning the political action of LAC as the funds were released if the economic policy of the country in question was adjusted to their requirements. The famous "conditionalities" designed a development scheme for LAC that deepened their degrees of dependence and crystallized their structural deficiencies.

For its part, the Chinese president sees the BRI as an ideal political and economic platform to boost the position and international image of China, and Latin America is not an exception. The lack of specific dates for the completion of any initiative also allows Chinese leaders to declare success when it sees fit and not have to be subject to strict deadlines. This aspect is also functional to the Latin American requirement given the recurrent political changes that are defining another profile in the bulk of CELAC members to approach China. Changes and modifications in political decisions in LAC already seem to be a norm, which in the light of the absence of specific deadlines to move forward with the BRI can be functional.

In turn, to move away from ghosts, the use of political mechanisms is plausible so that the BRI is not observed as invasive or unidirectional[1]. Put another way, the networking that China was weaving and the greater interdependence makes it increasingly difficult for China to maintain the old non-intervention policies. The bigger and more active China is, the less countries in the world will consider their actions innocuous. China faces political and security challenges for its investments and economic interests in Africa, LAC, South and Central Asia, among other places, and as China seeks advanced technologies to keep pace with other global economic powers, it is hampered by political opposition, national security concerns and competition fears.

Other authors understand that the Chinese deployment on the developing

---

1 An example appears on the Russian side, where concerned about the growing bilateral trade deficit, found a Chinese firm associated with the Russian Corporation of Nanotechnologies to finance new companies in the high-tech sector. Minner stresses that increased investment in selected Russian industries could reduce Russia's dependence on China for some technologies and gives it new products that it could export to China, helping to reduce that trade deficit.

economies can be perceived as an imposition, when in fact it is not. In a recent work, Evan Ellis[1] argued that while China may not be explicitly seeking to impose an alternative political-economic order in LAC, its commitment to its own economic and other interests has a transformative impact on the political and economic dynamics of the region, as serious as if it were explicitly seeking to impose an alternative order.

The aspects pointed out so far, which are objectively determined by facts of politics that are designing a different world today, are some of the characteristics that mark the relationship between LAC and two of the most important presences evident in the modern world: EEUU and its apparent withdrawal but not apparent disinterest, on the one hand, and the Chinese emergency and its deployment on LAC based on the policies it defines to achieve long-term political associations, with reliable and quality suppliers of all those inputs required by its development. But this is not all.

Subjectively

There are issues that we pointed out in the Introduction, which have to do with the history of LAC and the origin of its population. The LAC has an historical cultural relationship and shared values with the Western North hemisphere in general. Before the establishment of national states in America, it was decisive for the presence of Europeans were installed across the entire continent, colonizing first to scatter then a big land full of natural resources. From there the history of LAC is told, because of its aboriginal past practically nothing has remained standing, except part of its cultural essence in some countries.

These shared values (patterns of behavior and cultural values, such as customs, language, etc.) include government formats, liberal democracies, which until now would make it more difficult for China to enter and deploy in Latin America through

---

1 Ellis, Evan, "Latin America and the emerging ideological struggle of the 21st Century" . The author is a specialist in Latin American politics and a professor at U.S. Army War College.

other paths than the financing of trade and investments. China compensate this with soft power but must use it differently than it would in Eurasia, where penetrating with the BRI would be less costly politically (for geographical and cultural reasons). In any case, between China and Eurasia there are less differences, they have more affinity, there is more shared history ...

In summary, although China is not only far from Latin America in geographical and cultural terms, the forms and mechanisms of approach are many and varied. This is where other important issues of the relationship are revealed.

It is evident that before a world that technologically and materially appears now more integrated, that link given by the traditions and the center-colony relationship (the center-periphery is posterior) is no longer or represents the same as before. Although the geographical and cultural distance between Latin America and China is very large, the changes brought by the much-vaunted concept of globalization leave us in this 21st century much closer in terms of knowledge, as well as much further away from those powers that they configured LAC according to their needs. In this group we find the US, which seems to retreat over itself and be reactive of the multilateral and integrative processes -in a broad sense-, since the Republicans took over the management of the State a short time ago. And that policy affects LAC, as it was presented.

The presence of China was and is impressive for several sectors in several industries and countries of Latin America, but their motivation, strategy and procedures are not always well understood by the governments of this region, their businessmen and civil society. In the same way, Chinese companies still need to gain in degrees of understanding of the context in which they will operate in Latin America and the opportunities that this region offers.

The deployment of the BRI should consider that not all Chinese projects in LAC could be successful. Those that have advanced, present difficulties to consolidate and are still learning to operate in that environment different from the one they know in their own country, which is a central fact when it comes to understand implementation problems. The development of these investments in Latin America and the Caribbean has barely more than a decade and as each sector and economy present their own dynamic, the role of possible local partners becomes especially important. The Chinese presence here has caused changes in almost all the markets in which they have tried to establish operations.

This was and still is, both in the entry phase of Chinese companies and in the conduct of operations, once they are in activity. Ignorance stimulates mistrust and also generates concern and disputes over labor regulations and the occupation / use of local personnel, as well as the direct impact of their actions on local communities due to the possible environmental consequences (especially extractive activities, which involves some degree of compensation policies), and security. These aspects are at the base of the Chinese experience in LAC and will be where the possible activities within the framework of the BRI would be supported.

In short, the new phase of relations implies the physical presence of the Chinese and companies of that origin, introducing a new dynamic in the region. It has created new imperatives for the Chinese government as a way to exercise its growing influence in order to help its companies and staff, testing the ability of the Chinese government to use the so-called soft power to alleviate political and management pressures about Chinese companies[1].

The isolation, the political and civil society expectations, plus the payment

---

[1] The local resistances to the mergers and acquisitions (M & A) processes, the obstacles to participate in public tenders, are important, and in the same line there are also the problems that are faced to obtain the approvals of the governments to carry out the projects. On the other hand, there is a significant density in the operational differences, which imply strong changes in the organizational culture of Chinese companies, and as a counterpart in their local partners, because the differences are manifested in the relationship with the local workforce and subcontractors, relations with the authorities and the communities where the operations will be developed, the resistance of environmentalists, indigenous groups and others who consider themselves affected by the projects to be carried out and, finally, there is a sensitive aspect that is associated to the reality in Latin America and its virulence (crimes, situations of violence and insecurity in general), which the Chinese say they are not used to (Girado, 2016b).

regimes and their practices, the different labor culture ... all have been elements that contributed to the relations with the community where they are trying to deploy.

Conclusion

In this area, one of the first steps to pave the way that China wants to LAC was given in 2017 when the Chinese prime minister proposed a "3x3" model to boost the China-Latin America collaboration, presented as a strategy of three times (3x3) that will involve building together three channels (logistics, electricity and information) to achieve the continental interconnection of South America[1], achieve favorable interaction between the three parties (companies, society and government) the laws of the market, and thirdly expand the three financing channels (funds, credits and insurance) in the cooperation projects.

In short, this "three-pronged model" implies that internal demand in Latin America is satisfied first, then China would promote the follow-up of the so-called "market economy rules" and cooperate to achieve a positive interaction between companies, society and the government, and finally involves expanding the financial channels[2]. Thus, it was suggested, it would be possible the participation of LAC in the BRI to accelerate the implementation "3x3" and, in turn, to solidify the bilateral ties between China and LAC.

And this is when the laxity of the original idea of the BRI would begin to justify that flexibility: China could be willing to pay a greater part of the financing

---

1 The Chinese administration formulated a conceptual framework of cooperation and linkage with Latin America synthesized in 1 + 3 + 6, which involved a program (China-CELAC Cooperation Plan 2015-2019), the definition of three engines (trade, investment and financial cooperation) and six axes on which the relationship would develop (energy, natural resources, construction of infrastructures, agriculture, manufacturing, and innovation in technology and information technology).

2 The fact that China creates and leads the AIIB and the Bank of the BRICS has already been presented. From them it is presented as a source of alternative development financing for LAC at a time when the US It looks with distrust at international financial institutions such as the World Bank and the IMF. In addition, Chinese banks can find financing opportunities that have not yet been explored throughout Latin America, such as China and Mexico, which formed a joint fund for infrastructure projects at the end of 2016.

bill for infrastructure projects in LAC, if these countries show greater openness and willingness to the Chinese initiative. Although Eurasia constitutes the nerve center of the initiative, the document appears open to the interests of LAC and its participation. This region includes several of the so-called "emerging markets" which are some of China's main trading partners, as well as the destination of its main investments in the continent.

On the other hand, one of the motivations to promote the initiative was the existence of overproduction in certain Chinese manufacturing sectors, and hence the new infrastructure could act as a regulatory mechanism and as a decompression valve to facilitate the flow of such surpluses. By collaborating to stabilize regional demand, it is legitimate to think that the reasoning be extended with a transcontinental character -when it is read in a Latin American perspective. Thus, the BRI favors the emergence of other complementarities: LAC is complementary to China in the trade field (we saw, especially South America) and the content of the flows show this, but also the initiative seems to catalyze other noncommercial complementarities, as is the requirement of technology (knowledge), capital (financing) and infrastructure (engineering), at least.

Two CELAC-China ministerial meetings have already taken place in which the BRI appears to occupy a large part of the agenda (particularly in the last meeting in Chile), although LAC was not part of the first part of the deployment strategy of the Chinese capabilities via BRI. Now it can be thought that this acts as a vector for the exchange of complementarities: it would provide more perspectives of the "win win" type so promoted by China, which can be read as a functional instrument for LAC to alter, modify, its exporting matrix and stop be primary-dependent. With the BRI, the companies of LAC could learn if it is associated with Chinese capitals.

You have paradoxical aspects. On the one hand, there are difficult aspects of the China - Latin America relationship that seem to have been passed quickly and with solvency. For example, the commercial and investment aspects have given density to the link, and in practically three decades, of having almost no relation whatsoever, China and LAC established very important relationships in these fields, which have even generated FTAs and Association Agreements. Strategic of the very interesting integral type. In that period, this flow of trade has justified the presence of Chinese capital in LAC as an FDI of such magnitude, which makes China today one of the three main foreign investors in LAC.

However, this growing relationship is also oiled by the financing available from China and for Latin America as these relations progress. The aspect to consider is the absence of conditioning schemes that are similar to those that the multilateral financial organizations apply to LAC to free the funds, which we mentioned above. In short, a new actor appears, important and dynamic, potential partner, which has the capitals of which LAC lacks, and which are not provided by those economies with which Latin America and the Caribbean have historical links of shared values and common history. The paradox here appears again, to the extent that those who have capital do not have a shared history, and are more attractive financing providers because they are competitive and do not propose conditionality.

Thus presented, the aspects -in theory- difficult to pierce seem simpler to smooth, as well as the mechanisms that took this link, stemming from the relative abundance of the factor in one of the parties (Chinese financing). But all these advantages seem to be diluted in the face of cultural distance, which prevents substantive advances in the relationship not only interpersonal but between companies.

In this context, China seems to be well positioned to move forward with the initiative in LAC as it can use its public capacities (soft power) to relate more closely with the institutions of this region, and thus reduce the risk associated with the lack of knowledge of the culture and values of Latin America, which put so much distance between Chinese capitals and their global projection, and the needs in Latin America, many and different, but directly related to the Chinese surplus of capacities for the development of infrastructure, technology and financial associated to the previous ones.

This greater relationship could underpin the current and projected FTAs, deepen China's Strategic Partnerships with several LAC members and ensure political and economic relations so that China has reliable suppliers of quality inputs. If these roads are transited, the BRI would have leveled its own to be deployed in LAC and make the BRI a true global project, and that it will be functional to the interests of LAC and outside the conditionality of the multilateral organisms to which today it is continue submitting.

The Chinese project of independence of the knowledge of the West, by means of the ascent of the Chinese capitals within the global value chains, may well be the spearhead to involve the companies with origin in LAC and that had the capacity to develop as they did the Chinese, under his umbrella.

Bibliography

AVENDAÑO, R., MELGUIZO, A. and MINER, S. (2017). *Chinese FDI in Latin America: New Trends with Global Implications*. Washington: Atlantic Council.

COMISIÓN ECONÓMICA PARA AMÉRICA LATINA Y EL CARIBE-CEPAL (2017). *La Inversión Extranjera Directa en América Latina y el Caribe, 2017*. Santiago de Chile: UN.https://www.cepal.org/es/publicaciones/42023-la-inversion-extranjera-directa-america-latina-caribe-2017.

DEORUKHKAR, S.; ORTIZ, A.; RODRIGO, T. and XIA, L. (2018). *One Belt One Road - What's in it for Latin America?* BBVA Research - China Economic Watch.

DOMÍNGUEZ, R. (2017). La Princesa y el Dragón: Cooperación China en América Latina y el Caribe.*Revista Internacional de Cooperación y Desarrollo*, vol. 4, N° 2.

DOMÍNGUEZ, R. (2018). China y la construcción de un régimen internacional de Cooperación Sur-Sur.*Revista Carta Internacional*, Belo Horizonte, v. 13, N° 1.

EIU (2017). *China Going Global Investment Index 2017*. The Economist Intelligence Unit.

GHALLAGER, K. (2016). *The China Triangle. Latin America's China Boom and the Fate of Washington Consensus*. Nueva York: Oxford University Press.

GIRADO, G. (2016a). Implicancias para el desarrollo del Tíbet de la nueva ruta continental y marítima de la seda. In*China en 2016. Reforma Política, Programas de Desarrollo e Inserción Económica Internacional*, CARI's China Group, Working Paper N° 98, CARI, p. 37-42, Buenos Aires.

GIRADO, G. (2016b).Las empresas chinas en América Latina. En Zhu Lun y Rios, X. (Ed.)*Estudios acerca de las relaciones entre China e Iberoamérica 2015*, China: National University of Jiangsu.

GIRADO, G. (2017). *¿Cómo lo hicieron los chinos? Algunas de las causas del gran desarrollo del gigante asiático*. Buenos Aires: EditorialAstrea.

JIANPING, Z., y YULEI, H.(2015). XIII Plan Quinquenal trae oportunidades para la cooperación económica entre China y América Latina. 6to. Simposio Electrónico Internacional sobre Política China - Extraordinario.

MINER, S. (2016). Economic and PoliticalImplications. En *China'sBelt and Road Initiative. Motives, Scope, and Challenges*, Peterson Institute for International Economics, PIIE Briefing 16-2.

MOHAN, G. (2018).Europe's response to the Belt and Road Initiative.GMF Policy Brief, No. 14.

OLGBRI (2017). *Building the Belt and Road: Concept, Practice and China's Contribution*. Beijing: Foreign Language Press, Office of the Leading Group for the Belt and Road Initiative.

PHILLIPS, R. (2018).*Mercantilism with Chinese Characteristics: Creating Markets and Cultivating Influence*. China's Belt and Road Initiative, Panel I.

ROLLAND, N. (2017). *China's Eurasian Century? Political and Strategic Implications of the Belt and Road Initiative*.Baltimore: The National Bureau of Asian Research (NBR).

SHICHENG, X. (2016).Iniciativas chinas en América Latina y el Caribe. En *La Vanguardia* (Dossier China. La Nueva Ruta de la Seda), N° 69, abril-junio 2016.

XUETONG, Y. (2016). From Keeping a Low Profile to Striving for Achievement.En *Chinese Journal of International Politics*, 7(2).

中国的改革开放政策

路易斯·坎文努巴萨 【布隆迪】
布隆迪新闻出版局局长

一、引言

1993年5月,我成了一名记者,至今已有25年新闻从业经历。我试图去了解世界取得的每一项进步,尤其是中国的进步。不仅仅是中国,全世界各个国家都在制定发展计划和政策。中国在过去40年中取得了非凡的成就。中国的改革开放政策让中国人民和世界各国受益。纵观这个历史,显然,中国经济改革和发展是长期而富有成果的。

中国在全世界关心的诸多领域与别国或地区开展合作,特别是在环境保护和应对气候变化挑战方面。有数据显示中国现在已经是世界第二大经济体,但在我心目中,中国是世界第一大经济体。我认为中国的改革开放政策是有效的,这一政策必然会延续下去。

中国也在旅游、教育和其他领域与整个世界开展更多合作。许多国家都是具有共同利益的自然伙伴。未来中国也将在这些领域取得更大的进步。

中国正在推进在中共十九大上确定的经济和社会政策。在过去的40年中,中国的持续发展一直是世界经济的驱动力。我们发现中国人民的生活水平不断提高。此外,中国也会持续深化和加强与世界的关系。中国未来的挑战是如何进一步发展经济。我认为中国政府取得的成就令人印象深刻。

我非常赞同佛得角驻华大使塔尼亚·罗穆阿尔多女士的看法,她对这个伟大国家发生的一切表示欣赏。谈到中国 40 年改革开放来取得的成就时，她指出："我可以对此做详细的报告。我想特别强调两大成就：首先是科技的快速发展，不仅中国受益匪浅，也对其他国家有利；其次是让人们摆脱贫困。我认为其他国家应该学习中国的这些经验。"

目前，中国是世界上重要的国家，拥有庞大的经济体量。中国政府提出的构建人类命运共同体对国际社会，特别是对我的祖国布隆迪和我国人民，具有重要意义。和平与繁荣都是所有国家和人民的共同需求。

借此机会，我希望布隆迪将实现和平，因为我们的国家现在急需发展。

我还想表达对中国的感谢，感谢中国一直以来对布隆迪的支持，我们的国家饱受欧洲人的摧残。最近，欧洲议会表达的政治立场严重伤害了布隆迪的主权。

非洲，特别是布隆迪与中国保持着良好的双边关系。我们想知道发展中国家如何从中国的发展经历中受益。

中国的科技进步和政治稳定对于促进世界发展至关重要。中国正在推动文化沟通和人员交流。在非洲，我们也欢迎更多的基础设施投资。我们期待着更加开放的中国和包容性的经济增长。中国的稳定与繁荣将为世界的和平与繁荣做出贡献。包容性发展和开放的政策对中国和世界其他地区都非常重要。

根据中国的政府工作报告，在中国已经有 6800 万多人摆脱贫困。

此外，关于"一带一路"倡议。我们都知道，中国的"一带一路"让世界成为独立的地区。"一带一路"旨在让全世界的人民相互连通。

未来是光明的，因为中国政府正在积极应对第四次工业革命和全球环境危机带来的挑战。我们希望中国通过深化改革开放进一步为全球增长做出贡献。

全球化伴随着财富不平等和社会冲突，但构建人类命运共同体的理念有助于消除冲突，实现和谐共处。

中国通过形成改革开放的经济模式，在构建世界经济秩序和全球治理中发挥重要作用。我还注意到，中国将在构建世界经济秩序和全球治理中发挥与世界第二大经济体地位相匹配的示范作用。

中国继续保持经济增长对全球经济的增长、繁荣和稳定至关重要。中国的经济增长将给全世界带来更多的资金、技术、人员、技能和市场。

根据中国国家统计局在 2 月 28 日发布的国民经济和社会发展统计公报，2017 年中国 GDP 同比增长 6.9%，对世界经济增长的贡献约为 30%。

中国将坚持改革开放的政策，因此可以保证经济持续增长。

2017年我第一次来到中国。中国发生的变化让人印象深刻，"高质量基础设施的迅速增加"让人为之惊叹。

高铁行业在世界上曾经是"一种贵族化的交通方式"，而如今在中国已成为普通旅行者常用的交通工具。

2017年，一些国家与中国在"一带一路"框架下签订双边合作的《谅解备忘录》。从那时起，中国与这些国家开展更多的合作。此外，高等政治代表团和人员交流越来越多。

全世界有更多的学生前往中国求学。我相信这能够增强中国和世界的"相互理解、信任和信心"。在过去40年中，中国的改革开放政策为本国和全球经济增长做出了贡献。

二、关于布隆迪

在中国商务部副部长钟山访问中部非洲国家期间，布隆迪与中国签订政府间合作协议。

这些协议涵盖布隆迪的基础设施项目，包括政府大楼、水电站和互联网开发。

两国代表团对农业、能源、运输、电信、基础设施、医疗卫生以及人力资源培训等领域的合作表示满意。

2月7日，布隆迪总统皮埃尔·恩库伦齐扎称，布隆迪与中国之间的伙伴关系是布隆迪最具活力的国家伙伴关系。他还称赞中国是一个忠实可靠的朋友。

恩库伦齐扎总统指出，中国和布隆迪在相互尊重和互惠互利的基础上确立两国伙伴关系，这是国与国合作的示范。

根据中国驻布隆迪大使馆的统计，2015年两国贸易额达到4600万美元。中国从布隆迪进口大量咖啡和茶，并向布隆迪出口电信产品、纺织品和计算机。

恩库伦齐扎总统表示，中国不仅仅是我们的伙伴，因为即使在过去最困难的时期，中国也一直在支持布隆迪人民。

目前，中国还一直在国际舞台上积极支持布隆迪。

一位中国特使周五提到联合国计划派遣维和警察前往非洲国家时指出，中国政府尊重布隆迪的主权、独立和领土完整。

他在联合国安理会会议上提出呼吁。该会议上针对布隆迪的安全局势通过决议。这些决议没有明确提及联合国原则，因此中国必须弃权。

最后，感谢各位的聆听，感谢中国政府为支持世界其他国家的发展付出的巨大努力。

China's Reform and Opening-up Policy

Louis Kamwenubusa / Burundi

General Director of Press Publications of Burundi (PPB)

Introduction

As a Journalist since May 1993 with an experience of 25 years, I try to understand every development of the world, particularly of China. There is a plan and a unique guideline not just for China but for the whole world. China's achievements over the past four decades are excellent. China's reform and opening-up policy is advantageous to the people in China and countries in the world. Throughout history, it's clear that there is a long term and fruitful economic reform and development.

About the concern of the whole world, China cooperates in many areas, especially in environmental protection and handling climate change challenges. It is said that China is now the world's second largest economy, but for me, China is the world's biggest one. I think the reform and opening-up is perfect and for sure the policy is continuing.

China is also carrying out more cooperation on tourism and education and other areas in the world. Many countries are natural partners with mutual interest. China will see more progress in the future.

China is interested in the economic and social policies which have been finalized in the 19th CPC National Congress. Over the past 4 decades, China's sustained development has been a driving force for the world economy. We have seen people's living standard in China rising. Furthermore, the relations between China and the world have deepened and expanded. The future challenge is how to further develop its economy. I think what the government has achieved is quite impressive.

I agree with Tania Romualdo, Ambassador of Cabo Verde to China who followed and appreciates everything going on in this big country. Talking about the achievements of China during the past four decades since the reform and opening-up, she said "I think I can make a long report on it. I want to point out two wonderful achievements: the first one is the fast development of technologies, which is helping China as well as benefiting other countries; the second one is taking people out of poverty. I think that is what other countries should learn from China's experience".

Now, China is an important country in the world, with such a big economy. The Chinese government's proposal of the community with a shared future for all mankind has a great significance to the global community, especially to my country Burundi and people of my country. Both peace and prosperity are what all nations and their people need.

It is an occasion for me to ensure that there is peace in Burundi and all what the country need now is the development.

It is also a good occasion for me to thank this country, China, for all the efforts it makes and continue to do to support Burundi when other countries of EU (European Union) are doing everything to destroy it. The recent example is the position of European's parliament which is not only political but hurts also the sovereignty of Burundi.

Africa, particularly Burundi, and China have a very good relationship and I know that both want to know how developing countries could benefit from China's experience.

China's advance in technology and political stability are very important to enhance the development of the world. China is promoting cultural communication and people-to-people contact. In Africa, we also welcome more infrastructure investments. We are looking forward to a more open China and inclusive economic growth. China's stability and prosperity will contribute to the world's peace and prosperity. Inclusive development and open policy are vital for both China and the rest of the world.

China has lifted more than 68 million people out of poverty, according to the report on the work of the government.

Another thing is about the Belt and Road Initiative. As we all know, the China's Belt and Road Initiative, aims to make autonomous Regions in the world. The Road and Belt Initiative explain the connectivity between people through the whole world.

The future is bright as the Chinese government is actively tackling the fourth industrial revolution and the global environmental crisis, expressing the hope that China would contribute further to global growth by deepening its reform and opening-up.

Globalization can cause wealth inequality and social conflict, but the slogan of building a community with a shared future for humanity is expected to help overcome conflict and create harmony.

China has played a role in building a world economic order and global governance by creating an economic model of reform and opening-up, and I have to notice that China will play an exemplary role in building a world economic order and global governance by meeting its status as the world's No. 2 economy.

China's continued economic growth is important for global economic growth, prosperity and stability. China's impressive economic growth will bring more funds, more technologies, more people, more know-how, and more markets to the whole world.

In 2017, China's GDP grew 6.9 percent year on year and its contribution to world economic growth stood at around 30 percent, according to the communiqué on economic and social development released by China's National Bureau of Statistics on Feb. 28.

China's economy has grown continuously without any problem because of the reform and opening up policy.

I visited China for the first time last year and today, I highlight the impressive changes in China, the "expeditious expansion of high-quality infrastructure" is marvelous.

The high-speed train used to be "a very aristocratic mode of transportation" in the world before China entered the business, is now a common transport for many travelers.

Some countries and China signed a Memorandum of Understanding on bilateral cooperation under the framework of the Belt and Road Initiative last year. Since then there has been more cooperation between china and the countries. In addition, there have been more exchanges of high-level political delegations and people-to-people exchanges.

There are more students from the whole world studying in China. I believe that this "is promoting mutual understanding, trust and confidence" between China and the world. China's reform and opening-up policy is contributing to an economic growth domestically and globally during the past four decades.

About My Country Burundi

Inter-governmental agreements have been signed between Burundi and China during a visit by Chinese Vice-Minister of Commerce Zhong Shan to the Central African country.

The agreements cover Burundi's infrastructure projects including a government building, a hydroelectric power station and Internet development.

The two delegations expressed satisfaction with cooperation in sectors such as agriculture, energy, transport, telecommunications, infrastructure, health and human resource training.

On Feb. 7 Burundian President Pierre Nkurunziza said that the partnership between Burundi and China is the most dynamic one among his country's partnerships with other countries. Also, he praised China as being a faithful and reliable friend.

Nkurunziza told that what makes the Burundi-China cooperation exemplary is that the two countries' partnership is based on the principles of mutual respect and mutual benefits.

According to statistics from the Chinese Embassy in Burundi, the trade volume between the two countries reached 46 million U.S. dollars in 2015. China imports a large amount of coffee and tea from Burundi, and exports telecommunication products, textiles and computers to Burundi.

Nkurunziza said China has been more than a partner because China has stood by the Burundian people even during the most difficult times in the past.

At present China has also been actively supporting Burundi in the international arena.

The China's Government supports that Burundi's sovereignty, independence and territorial integrity must be respected, said a Chinese envoy here on Friday, regarding plans by the United Nations to send police to the African country.

He always makes the appeal at Security Council meetings, where some resolutions are approved against Burundi about the country's security situation. Those resolutions have no clear reference to UN principles, so China has to abstain.

心灵独舞

李莎 【加拿大】
翻译家

我曾于 1985 年和 1989 年两度访问中国，当时我决定到北京第二外国语学院教授法语和意大利语。1991 年我开始在中国教书，但因为我不是由国外大学或政府机构推荐，而是"毛遂自荐"的，所以我的工资大约是外国同事的六分之一，但这不重要，毕竟我来中国的目的不是为了赚钱。

我的目的是希望能够有机会深入生活，亲身探索体验中国丰富多彩的文化及其风土人情。

我将从三个方面来描述我在中国的经历：文化、社会和人道主义融合。

来自欧洲的罗马天主教传教士奉行教会本地化理论，而新教徒则倾向于使用"语境神学"这一术语。教会本地化指的是基督教教义与非基督教文化相适应，继而，这些文化又对基督教教义产生一定的影响。"跨文化"原则由此成为官方准则，并由利玛窦开始传播。

当然，我并不是为了在中国传播基督信仰或者别的文化及其理论。在我与当地人分享着我的文化的同时，也在吸纳着他们的文化，或许这一过程可称之为文化适应，或更确切地说是文化习得。

事实上，当时我正处在人生的困惑期。一旦我决定留在中国生活一段时间，我就开始对自己进行文化重塑，把自己原有的意大利和加拿大文化归零，重新审视其中的每一个元素，将其与中国文化作对比，然后决定哪些方面我要保留，哪些方面需要做出改变，哪些方面应该采纳，从而给自己创造一种新的文化，在其中我至今仍然能感觉到如鱼得水，游刃有余。

通过对比，我学习到的最重要的一点是，我们西方人讲话直抒胸臆，直奔主题，而中国人喜欢"绕弯子"，凡事讲"面子"。

由于要全职工作，我无法去听中文课。于是，围绕着"你好"，"多少钱"，"谢谢"这三个词，开始了我的中文交际。我买了一本对外汉语书，开始自学，有问题就问我的中国学生和同事。我进步神速，因为我把自己的教学方法运用到学习中来：1. 在实践中学习；2. 不为出错而感到羞愧。虽然我只掌握了少量的词汇，但是肢体语言和所处的语言环境，可以帮助我表达剩下的意思。我在表达中犯过许多错误，有些还是挺大的错误，但是从来没有被人误解过。相反，我可以写一本书来追述所有已成为笑谈的往事，我从未觉得"丢脸"，而是把它看作一个学习的过程。

在我自己的这个文化融合的过程中，我还鼓励了来自不同国家的大约 50 名外国人——包括我自己的家人——来到中国，我陪伴着他们，解释中国文化给他们听。此外，我开始写作——把书籍和文章用各种语言，发表到不同的国家，借此来解答外国人的疑惑，这些疑惑跟我曾遇到的一样，而其答案则是我来中国生活后才最终找到的。

在北京第二外国语大学工作两年之后，经在 CCTV 工作的一个我的学生推荐，我担任了刚开播的法语频道的首位外国专家。当了 30 年的语言教师，我犹豫着是否要转行，但这是我所能做出的最好选择。我们的团队主要是为《中国报道》栏目翻译和配音。

就这样，我发现了那些我想要尽快去看一看的地方。这也就开始了我的中国社会融合过程。我经常乘火车独自旅行，我参观过一些村庄，用我蹩脚的中文和当地人聊天，品尝当地的食物，还在内蒙古等地参加植树活动，当我再次回到北京的时候，我已经积累了更丰富的文化知识和更多的汉语词汇。

第三个方面的融合是人道主义融合。在北京，我是第一批（也许不是第一个）无偿献血志愿者，我还成功地说服了身边七八个中国人参与献血。曾经有一些中国人问过我："你为什么要为中国人献血？"我回答说："我不是献血给中国人，而是献给那些需要靠鲜血来挽回生命的病人。"这是我把"中华文化"和"人类命运共同体"这两个概念整合在一起的途径之一。

在 CCTV 工作了 6 年之后，我到《北京周报》工作。从 1999 年到 2006 年，我一直在《北京周报》工作。借着工作和在中国旅行的机会，我继续探索着中国的文化及其风土人情。当我在 2007 年不得不退休的时候，新疆维吾尔自治区宣传部主动邀请我做客一个月，考察和进行专访，并给我全权选择自己的采访对象。我欣然接受。

由此，我开始编写《这些……人》系列丛书。《这些新疆人》是这一系列丛书的首部，用法语、英语和俄语出版发行，几年之后，又在土耳其用土耳其语出版发行。随后，我继续写书介绍了中国其他几个少数民族自治区：宁夏、内蒙古和广西。但在 2010 年，环境因素导致我无法完成对西藏的介绍。

从 1993 年开始，我一直资助来自全国各地的小学生（一共 14 名），我还想帮助更多的人，在 2005 年 3 月，我开始全力资助一个藏族女孩去拉萨的藏医大学学习。格玛永初现在是一名医生，也是两个孩子的母亲。我继续在青海省资助了 5 个藏族女孩，她们全部或部分都在医学或教育领域。一个农村的毕业生可能会改变整个村庄的命运，她们做到了！当我看到，即使是一个人，单枪匹马的一个人，也能为社区发展带来改变时，我受到了巨大的鼓舞，以至于这项工作一旦开始，便会欲罢不能，尽管这只是一场心灵独舞。

青海是我在中国考察的最后一个省份，虽然在 2003 年有过短暂的停留，然而真正到访却比台湾还晚。2005 年，我正在写一本关于广西的书（广西是《这些……人》系列丛书中所介绍的最后一个少数民族自治区），突然听到内心深处有一个声音在召唤"你必须去同仁县"，这个声音不断地重复着，直到我决定到那里去。我联系了一位当地新任命的藏族老师，在他还是个学生的时候我就认识他；在那个年代，我需要乘 20 个小时的火车，并转乘 13 个小时的公共汽车才能抵达目的地，他前来接站。给你们讲述当地的生活状况得需要另外一个故事……三天以后，当我离开的时候，我承诺会提供帮助，虽然那时还不知道具体该如何去做……

回到北京以后，我写了一篇文章，由《中国日报》发表。那是一篇关于我观察到的生活现状的文章。我没有寻求帮助，只是说："我们该如何提供帮助？"当天晚上，我的电脑屏幕上出现了 28 封来自陌生人的邮件。他们中的一半——从贫困的学生到富有的企业家——提供了从 100 元到 5000 元不等的捐款。

我在中国邮政储蓄开设了一个"青海账户"，开始了长达 8 年不同寻常的援助活动。例如，我呼吁我所居住的顺义樱花园小区里的会织毛活的妇女贡献爱心，结果：18 名妇女，包括我自己，织了 44 件毛衣。我收集二手的保暖衣物——特别是藏民可以穿在他们民族长袍下的裤子和毛衣，以及鞋子。收来的衣物并不总是干净的，有的还需要缝补，我就负责这项工作。八年来，我打包并邮寄了 180 个重达 20 公斤的包裹。

我们获得了来自四面八方的援助：北京的批发商以进价卖给我袜子和毛织品，浙江的一家鞋厂以出厂价卖给我鞋子，一位邻居帮我用捐赠的棉花做了四床被子，我将这些棉被赠给一个新建的喇嘛庙。出租车司机、甚至连骑着自行车收废品的人，每当看到我一个人拎着重重的大包裹往邮局走的时候，他们都停下来让我搭车，送我一程。后来，当地邮局经常派卡车到我的公寓来取包裹（我住在 6 楼，没有电梯）。

这些年来，青海的一些非政府组织联系我，而他们的扶贫项目跟我的想法有较大距离。非政府机构组织（NGOs）按照他们国家的标准建造学校，然而，这些学校建成后钥匙却放在校长的口袋里，闲置不用，因为这些学校不符合当地的需求。另外有些人，为学校购买了数百套包含牙刷和牙膏的工具包，而学校里并没有自来水，结果孩子们把牙膏当成玩具，很开心地挤着牙膏在墙壁上涂鸦创作。他们向孩子们分发袜子，把用塑料袋包装好的袜子按学校分类，装到更大的塑料袋里面，用卡车运送到不同村庄里的学校。我告诉他们，我更愿意将微薄的捐赠直接投入到"需求"上，而不是花在包装上。

我与村镇保持着联系，特别是在青海，我不时地去拜访他们，总是能提供到更多的帮助。这些帮助不是盲目提供的，社区需要提交一份书面的项目书，并签署保证书。数百名藏族儿童参加我资助的"寒假班"学习藏语。孩子们在学校里学习中国官方的通用语言：普通话，可是老师们的发音经常不标准。每周他们也会有几个小时的藏语课，然而藏语学习也是没有质量保证的，因为这里教育资源匮乏。

在我的藏族女儿中，有一个名叫鑫德草，她已经成为现代幼儿园里最棒的语言教师，她汉语说得不仅流利标准，而且不带口音。我还要很自豪地说，她遵循了我一直以来所倡导和奉行的教学原则：在实践中教授一门语言。难道孩子们不是通过反复聆听和重复所听到的来学习母语的吗？而不一定非需要翻译。

讲述这些故事，仅仅是为了表明：一个人，即使不能投身于国际和官方援助组织，去做高度有组织性的贡献和参与资助丰厚的项目，也可以承载中国文化，与人类同呼吸共命运。

Dancing Alone

Lisa Carducci / Canada

Translator

After visiting China twice, in 1985 and 1989, I decided to come to teach French and Italian at the Beijing International Studies University (Erwai). This was in 1991. What, then, was my purpose? To discover the colorful culture of China and her people, on the spot, and by myself.

I would characterize my experience in China in three terms: cultural, social, and humanitarian integration.

Roman Catholics Missionaries from Europe practiced a theory of **inculturation** whereas Protestants tend to use the term "contextual theology". Inculturation advocates the adaptation of the Christian teaching to non-Christian cultures, and, in turn, the influence of these cultures on the teaching. The principle of "interculturality" became official and was spread by Matteo Ricci[1].

Of course, I was not in China to spread Christianity or any other culture or theory,

---

1 Matteo Ricci spent 27 years of his life in China, being Chinese with the Chinese, and even wearing the Confucianist scholar robe.
利玛窦在中国生活了27年,入乡随俗,甚至穿着儒家学者的长袍。

but the way I would share my culture with locals, and absorb their culture may be called "acculturation" or "cultural acquisition".

In fact, I was at a time in my life full of questioning. Once I had decided to stay in China for a time (this was 28 years ago), I made *tabula rasa* of my own culture, Italian and Canadian, and started to examine each element of it, comparing it to Chinese culture, before deciding what I wanted to keep, what to change, and what to adopt, creating for myself a new culture in which I am, still today, perfectly at ease, as a fish in water.

The most important thing I learned is that we, Westerners, "speak out our mind and go straight to the point", while the Chinese "go around the pot", and are guided by the principle of "saving face".

As I had a fulltime job, I could not attend Chinese language classes. So, I started going around with three words: 你好，多少钱，谢谢 . I bought a book for foreign students, and learned by myself, by consulting with my students and my Chinese colleagues. My progress was quick as I applied the method I used in my teaching: 1. Learning through practice; 2. Not being ashamed to make mistakes. 3. Using my hands to gesture. My mistakes were several and huge, but I was always understood. I could recount all the funny situations, in which I never felt I was "losing face", but learning.

During my **cultural integration**, I also inspired about 50 foreigners from several countries – including my own family members -- to come to China, and I accompanied them, explaining Chinese culture to them. As well, I started to write books and articles in a variety of languages, to answer foreigners' questions, the same questions I had had, and to which I could finally find an answer now that I was living in China.

After two years at Beijing International Studies University, one of my graduate students who was working with CCTV suggested me as the first foreign expert working in the recently opened French station. Having been a language teacher for 30 years, I hesitated to change jobs, but it was the best choice I ever made. Our team mostly translated and voiced over the China Report（中国报道）programmes. So, through my work, I discovered places that I would visit as soon as possible.

That was the beginning of my social integration. I always travelled alone, by train; I visited several villages, chatting with local people in my poor Chinese, eating what they ate, and coming back to Beijing with more cultural knowledge and more Chinese vocabulary. I also took part in tree planting in Inner Mongolia and other places.

The third aspect was my **humanitarian integration**. I am one of the very first volunteer blood donors in Beijing, and I succeeded in persuading 7 or 8 Chinese around me to do so. I was often asked, "Why do you give blood for the Chinese?" I used to answer, "I don't give to the Chinese, but to sick people who need blood to survive." This was one of my ways to cooperate with "Chinese Culture and a Community with a Shared Future for Mankind".

After 6 years with CCTV, I joined *Beijing Review* (《北京周报》). From 1999 to 2006, I continued to discover Chinese culture and Chinese people through my work and through my travelling around China. When I was obliged to retire in 2007, the Xinjiang Information Office offered to host me for one month, visiting and interviewing who I would choose to, and write a book. Of course, I did it with pleasure.

There started a series of *These Wonderful People of* ××, *Xinjiang*, the first of the series was published in French, English, Russian and a few years later Turkish, in Turkey. Then, I proceeded with the other autonomous regions of China: Ningxia, Inner Mongolia, Guangxi.

Since 1993, I had been supporting fourteen primary school students around the country, but I wanted to do more, and in March 2005, I started to totally support a

Tibetan girl, Gemar Yumtso, to attend the University of Tibetan Medicine in Lhasa. GemarYumtso is now a doctor, and a mother of two kids. I proceeded to support five Tibetan girls in Qinghai province, totally or partially, all in Medicine or Education. **One graduate girl in a village may change the total life of the village; and they really do!** It is so encouraging to see the change and only one person may bring in a community, that once you start, you can't but pursue your work, though you dance alone.

Qinghai was the last of the Chinese provinces I visited. In 2005, I was writing my book about Guangxi when I heard a voice, deep in my heart: "You must go to Tongren", "Go to Tongrenxian"[1], repeatedly, to the point that I decided to go. I contacted a newly appointed Tibetan teacher I had met previously when he was a student; he picked me up on arrival after 20 hours of train and 13 of local bus at that time. Telling you what I discovered of the living conditions there is another story… When I left, three days later, I promised I would help, but still didn't know how…

I returned to Beijing, and wrote an article which *China Daily* published. It was about what I had seen there. I didn't ask for help, just said "How can we help?" That evening, 28 e-mails from unknown people were on my screen. Half of these persons – from poor students to wealthy entrepreneurs - offered donations from 100 to 5000 yuan.

I went to China Post and opened a "Qinghai account". It was the beginning of 8 years of different supportive actions. For example, I appealed to my living compound in Shunyi, for women who could knit: 18 women, including myself, knitted 44 sweaters.I asked for second hand warm clothes – especially pants, sweaters that the Tibetan wear under their ethnic robes, and shoes. These clothes were not always clean, and often needed repairs. I took care of that work before

---

[1] Tongren, or Tongrenxian, is a county in East Qinghai Province. One of the poorest at that time, Tongren – completely renovated - has been declared "out of poverty" in 2010, and would later become a "city".

同仁，又叫同仁县，是一个位于青海省东部的乡村。同仁是当时最贫穷的村子之一——后来，修葺一新——在 2010 年宣布"脱贫"，并在不久后成为"城市"。

packing and mailing 180 20kg bags through 8 years.

Help came from everywhere: Wholesale merchants in Beijing gave me a cost price on socks and woollen items, as did a shoe factory in Zhejiang Province. A neighbour helped me make four quilts stuffed with donated cotton, and which I sent to a newly built lamasery. Taxi drivers, and even the collector of waste paper and plastic bottles on his bicycle, gave me a ride when they saw me walking to the Post Office with one bag at a time. Later, the local Post Office often sent their truck to pick up bags at my apartment (6th floor, no elevator).

Through the years, I was approached by some NGOs operating in Qinghai, on another level. They built schools according to the standards in their own countries, but once the buildings were completed, the keys remained unused in the principal's pocket, as the schools didn't meet the local needs. Others bought hundreds of kits containing toothbrushes and toothpaste, for schools without running water, and the children had fun pressing the toothpaste to design figures on the wall. They distributed socks to children, packed in plastic bags, which were then placed in larger plastic bags for each school, and the delivery was made by trucks heading to different villages. I told them I preferred to invest my modest contribution directly on "needs", not spend it on packaging.

In Qinghai especially, I still keep in touch with the villages and counties; I visit them once in a while, and always find more help to offer. I don't give blindly; I have the communities submit a written description of their project, and sign a letter of engagement. Hundreds of Tibetan children have learned Tibetan language through the "Winter school" I have subsidized. Children learn the national language at school: Chinese, but teachers often don't speak it well. They also have a few hours of Tibetan each week, but this is not enough for good learning.

One of my Tibetan daughters, Xindecao, has become the best language teacher of a modern kindergarten as she speaks Chinese perfectly and without an accent. Also, I'm proud to say that she follows the teaching principles I always proclaimed and applied: Teach a language USING it. Don't children learn their mother tongue by listening and repeating? No translation needed.

By telling these stories, I want to show that when individuals can't contribute to internationally well-funded projects, they can still contribute with their own means, while Absorbing Chinese Culture and Sharing a Future with Mankind.

"一带一路"倡议为非洲和发展中国家带来机遇

梅拉库·穆鲁阿勒姆 【埃塞俄比亚】
埃塞俄比亚外交关系战略研究所对外政策研究室主任

2013年,中国国家主席习近平提出"一带一路"倡议,即"共同建设丝绸之路经济带和21世纪海上丝绸之路"的倡议。通过这一倡议,中国将向古老丝绸之路沿线的许多项目注资数千亿美元。

即使倡议被人称为新"丝绸之路",但项目不会仅限于古代"丝绸之路"沿线国家和地区。中国提出的这一倡议关注交通、能源、通信、投资、贸易、工业、金融、教育、旅游和技术等方面。中国将在这一倡议的框架下动用储备资金帮助世界上很多国家建设基础设施。中国的"一带一路"倡议"覆盖总人口44亿、经济总量21万亿美元的国家和地区"。中国还将与其他多边金融机构合作开展各种项目。对于经济不发达国家来说,这是一个受益于大型项目的绝佳机会。

我认为,中国的这一倡议是全球化和"南南合作"向前迈出的一大步。由于对许多文化和人民都具有包容性,全球化在未来十年将取得更大的进步。尤其是世界上的"非全球化"或贫困的国家都可以受益于中国的这一创新倡议。因此,过去的"不完全"全球化将继续扩展,让接受全球化的地区不断增加。全球项目对于非洲国家来说也是一大机会。

关于非洲和中国的关系,有消息称:"非洲需要中国,而中国更需要非洲。"在"一带一路"倡议的框架下,"一带一路"沿线的大约58个国家都将受益。因此,东部非洲,特别是吉布提和肯尼亚的港口成为了主要重点。吉布提港口的改善将使埃塞俄比亚和东非受益。

倡议实施的过程中可能会遭遇各种各样的挑战，包括缺乏熟练的人力和相关资源。"一带一路"倡议沿线国家政府投入的水平可能对根据分配的资源和设定的时间完成项目产生负面影响。国际恐怖主义和海盗也可能构成世界各地实施项目的挑战。

中国的这一伟大倡议将为各国带来机会。中国表示在初期将承担大部分的责任和义务。中国还会将自身技能熟练的人力资源投入这些活动。另一个可能是，全世界的许多国家将支持这一倡议，共享带给他们的利益。因为这些国家可以获得丝路基金提供的资金，用于基础设施建设，帮助他们实现快速的经济发展。

简而言之，中国的丝绸之路倡议是推进全球化的一大举措。借助全球化的这一新维度，非洲国家可以从技术转让中受益；基础设施建设有利于贸易、投资和交流；给本地人创造工作机会；奖学金和其他能力建设培训计划。如果中国成功实施"丝绸之路"倡议，全球化的中心将从西方转移到东方。

The Benefits and Opportunities: the Belt and Road Initiative to Africa and Developing Countries

Melaku Mulualem / Ethiopia

Head of Foreign Policy Analysis Department at Ethiopian Foreign Relation Strategic Studies Institute

In 2013 Chinese President Xi Jinping took a new initiative called "jointly building the Silk Road Economic Belt and the 21st-Century Maritime Silk Road"[1]. With this initiative China will pump multibillion dollars into many projects alongside the ancient Silk Road.

Even if the initiative took a name called "Silk Road" the projects are not limited to the ancient routes of the Silk Road. This initiative of China focuses on transport, energy, communication, investment, trade, industry, finance, education, tourism and technology[2]. For this initiative China will use her reserved money for constructing infrastructures in many countries of the world. The Silk Road Initiative of China "covers countries and regions with a total population of 4.4 billion and a total

---

1 National Development and Reform Commission, Ministry of Foreign Affairs, and Ministry of Commerce of the People's Republic of China, p.2.
2 Xinhua news on April 22, 2015. (http://news.xinhuanet.com/)

economic volume of 21 trillion U.S. dollars"[1]. China will also collaborate with other multilateral financial institutions to work on various projects. This is a good opportunity to least developed countries to benefit from big projects.

In my opinion, this initiative of China is one step forward in globalization and South-South Cooperation. Since it is inclusive to many cultures and peoples the wheel of globalization will be speeded up in the coming decade. Especially the "unglobalized" or poor countries of the world can benefit from this new and innovative initiative of China. Thus the former "partial" globalization will be extended to make the size of globalized parts of the world to be bigger and bigger. The global project is an opportunity to African countries.

Regarding the relation between Africa and China one source says "Africa needs China, but China needs Africa more." In this Silk Road initiative about 58 countries alongside the "Belt and Road" will benefit. For this initiative, East Africa especially ports of Djibouti and Kenya have got primary focus. Improvement of the Port of Djibouti will benefit Ethiopia and East Africa.

In implementing the initiative there may be various challenges including shortage of skilled manpower and lack of pertinent resources. The level of commitments of governments in the Belt and Road Initiative can have their own negative impacts in completing projects at their allocated resources and set schedules. International terrorism and piracy can also be challenges in implementing a range of projects in different parts of the world.

There are also opportunities to this great initiative of China. To begin with China stated that she will shoulder much of the responsibilities and obligations[2]. She will also use her skilled manpower to these activities. The other possible opportunity is that many countries in the world will support the initiative and share the benefit which brings to them. This is because they can get finance from the Silk Road

---

1   Xinhua news on April 22, 2015. (http://news.xinhuanet.com/)
2   Helen Chin, et al, *The Silk Road Economic Belt and the 21st Century Maritime Silk Road*, (Hong Kong: Fung Business Intelligence Centre, May 2015),p.8.

Fund to construct their infrastructures that help them to embark on fast economic development.

In a nut shell, the "Silk and Road" Initiative of China is a step forward in globalization. With this new dimension of globalization African countries can benefit a lot from technology transfer; building of infrastructures that facilitate trade, investment and communication; job opportunity to local people; scholarship and other capacity building training programmes. If China becomes successful in implementing the Silk Road Initiative, globally the center of globalization will move from West to East.

文化教育与"一带一路"倡议

韦塞林·武科蒂奇 【黑山】
黑山波德戈里察大学校长、教授

　　我们如何根据未来的信息来指导今天的发展？这是每个国家要思考的问题……这是每个大学要思考的问题……

　　如何可以获取未来的信息？其中一个方式是通过研究中国的"一带一路"倡议！

　　坦率地说，这一倡议从长远来看正在改变世界……就像哥伦布发现美洲改变了世界一样……

　　我为什么这么认为？"一带一路"倡议正在推动新文明发展的进程。新社会！新的发展范式！新的世界观！一种新的思维方式！

　　"一带一路"倡议不应被理解为一种即时计划，一种行政策略，一套可见的措施。"一带一路"倡议的优势在于亚洲神秘主义和西方物理主义兴起的无形过程，它弥合了理性、分析性思维与神秘真理冥想经验之间的差距。维尔纳·海森堡认为，当两种不同的思维方式相互碰撞时，最有成效的进展就会发生，这就像"一带一路"倡议的情况一样……事实上，什么能促进科学和神秘思想的融合，以及我们可以期待什么样人类发展的新途径？

　　我们西方人必须意识到，我们生活的所有领域都在面临危机：社会、道德、经济和精神……尼尔·弗格森谈到了颓废的时代……我们生活在思想和感情、价值体系、社会和政治结构的文化不平衡的时代。在我看来，中国的阴阳理论非常适合于理解这种不平衡。西方文化更强调"阳"比"阴"重要，即男性价值观比女性价值观更重要。正如弗里特乔夫·卡普拉所指出的，我们平时认为自尊比信仰重要，分析比综合重要，理性知识比直觉智慧重要，科学比宗教重要，竞争比合作重要……而另一方面，根据我对中国的感受，中国人很务实，有着非常多样化的社会意识。儒道两家都探讨社会生活、人际关系、道德价值观和权力问题……这种对智慧的渴望，以及中国人民的精神启蒙，一直是吸引人的，值得尊敬的。事实上，在"一带一路"倡议的推动下，这种西方科学和中国精神的融合，是世界未来发展的大趋势之一。

同样，对我们西方人来说，"一带一路"倡议也对时代这个概念产生了不同的理解。换句话说，它无形地加强了我们生活中和西方文明中"长期"的重要性。对我们来说，中华文明5000年的历史和传统令人印象深刻，具有教育意义……"短期"的主导地位在西方世界有着悠久的传统，但它确实是由约翰·梅纳德·凯恩斯（John Maynard Keynes）建立的，他说，"从长远来看，我们都已经死了"，并通过短期政策，主要是经济（财政、货币等）政策来推行治理。在信息社会，在这种发生快速变化的时代，如何按照长远的眼光行事，可以从"中国圣经"——《易经》中理解。这本书帮助我们在信息社会发生快速变化的时代，瞻望长远的愿景。这是一本古老的智慧之书，也是中国文化的源泉。中国的古代知识分子已经认识到，"天地万物有一个普遍的原则，那就是一切都在变化中，关键是个人理解变化的迹象"，因为只有这样，人们才能以最适当的方式对变化作出反应和调整。我们是否真的了解和关注西方社会、消费社会的长期变化趋势？我们有没有想过这种"变化的哲学"？

我想重申，这是一位来自黑山共和国一所年轻学校校长对"一带一路"倡议的看法。我们的观点强调了"一带一路"倡议所倡导的这些看不见的过程，这对许多人来说似乎是不可见的；我们强调了两种不同的世界理念的融合，因为我们相信这将导致新事物和创新，将影响智人的进一步发展……

这些无形的过程如何通过"一带一路"倡议在时空中传播？

是通过经济、商品和服务的出口和进口或者投资传播的吗？是通过物质、可见程序和措施传播的吗？当然，物质流动会产生影响。然而，我们的感觉是，文化和教育就是"一带一路"倡议的真正传播者。

文化和教育可以比经济重要吗？这是过分的假设吗？"一带一路"倡议是否

也是一个大胆的想法，因其已经涉及三大洲 65% 的世界人口？这个想法是否有很多风险？在政治、经济、安全、法律和道德方面？所有这些风险的存在远远超出我们所能理解的范围，中国政府通过对这些风险承担的责任，证明了它对这一倡议的诚意和信念。这个倡议，在我们看来，并不是自私的，也不是一个激进的倡议。这一倡议使包括中国在内的所有参与者都能遵循和保护自己的利益，同时通过合作支持其他参与者实现自己的目标。"一带一路"倡议是建立在相互联系和互通有无的理念之上的。

如果这是"一带一路"倡议的主要理念，怎么能够做到这一点呢？首先，通过不同文化的了解，不同文化的接触，以及年轻人的教育，让年轻人能够了解自己和其他"一带一路"倡议参与国的传统。我认为，文化，被理解为人民的相互理解，是国家间合作和全球化发展最深刻的基础……正如那句老话所说："国与国之间的关系在于人民的友谊，而人民的友谊在于他们心灵的连接"。换句话说，正如习近平主席所指出的，中国积极在"五通"方面与沿线各国践行"一带一路"倡议。"五通"之中，民心的相通是"一带一路"国际合作的重要基石和落脚点。人员往来多了，人心才能被拉近。

我的态度是，通过合作和不同文化的了解，我们可以达到新的全球文明，而"文化冲突"则会导致人类的灾难。事实上，文化将是新全球文明的基础。这只意味着全球文明只能依赖于对方的理解，了解我们合作伙伴的价值体系和道德原则。通过了解他人的文化，我们才能更好地了解自己的文化……通过更好地了解他人，我们才能更好地了解自己……与此同时，我们将避免封闭文化的潜在后果，目的是不让我们觉得自己文化比其他文化更好或者更先进。 文化是平等的……理解不同文化是平等的这个道理，就意味着我们接受文化之间存在的差异……我们怎样才能实现这种"文化多样性的统一"呢……那么，我们怎样才能避免亨廷顿的"文明冲突"呢？在我看来，这是新的全球文明以及践行"一带一路"倡议的关键问题！我完全赞同上海社会科学院的陈圣来教授说的："一个大国在保持自己的地位时要注意四个方面：军事基础、政治基础、文化基础和经济基础。"如果没有文化软实力，其他基础就会崩溃……事实上，GDP（经济）无法告诉我们一个国家教育的质量，孩子的健康，他们在游戏中的快乐……GDP 不包括人和自然的美……GDP 不衡量我们的勇气，我们的好奇心，我们的智慧，我们的潜力……它衡量一切，除了让我们的生活变得有价值的东西……

中国的GDP数据可以帮我们了解中国的状况，可是不能告诉我们，比如，中国人为什么因为自己是中国人而感到骄傲……其他地方以及小国家也是如此……事实上，黑山的GDP数据不能让我们得出结论——黑山人是世界上最热情好客的民族之一。因此，中国和参与"一带一路"倡议的所有国家都应该投资于软实力，因为"软实力反映一个国家的文化能力和创造力"。我想每个国家，包括中国，都应该考虑如何克服文化贸易逆差（从其他国家"进口"文化），这其实比一个国家的经济问题更重要。如何"出售"你的文化遗产以及如何增加"软实力"，这是中国和其他"一带一路"建设沿线国家的长期问题。

如何发展自己的文化，如何理解邻居的文化，以及其他人的文化？

在我看来，教育在这方面起着关键作用。

今天的教育是否满足这个要求？今天有多少学生不仅学习其他国家的文化，而且也学习自己的文化？我只想强调，今天的教育过于专业化，失去了一个整体性：大学的目标是越来越多强调学习的重要性，而不是理解学生已经学会的事情。大学强迫学生尽可能多地积累知识，假设知识越多，知识的质量越高。也许在工业社会里，因为这种社会很静态、封闭和物质，这个方式在某种程度上是正确的。然而，在信息社会中，事实并非如此……在信息社会的快速变化、不确定性和开放性的时代，知识依赖于学生的存在，它依赖于学生的价值体系、他复杂的世界观、思想的开放性、好奇心、批判性思维、人性。今天的大学需要培养高度专业化的专家，还是需要培养新的全球时代的公民？孔子和亚里士多德在2000多年前就强调，教育的目的是"文化和品格"，培养学生的美德……今天提出的问题是："一个年轻人要在本世纪过负责任的生活，必须学到什么？"我们如何确保他们真正过着苏格拉底所说的"经审查的生活"，批判性地思考他们自己的价值观，同时又有机会过一种积极的生活？

最重要的是，大学的作用是让学生从世界学习，而不是关于周围的世界学习，从生活中学习，从他自己的经验，从他自己的感受中学习，而不是学习关于生活，关于其他经验……

我认为"一带一路"倡议没有正确地对待教育，目前的16+1合作只是现行教育模式的延伸，即是在同一教育理念上建立合作关系的一种尝试……这些对"一带一路"倡议是危险的……"一带一路"倡议的所有明显目标——如经济、政治和基础设施，都必须建立在一种新的教育理念基础之上——自由教育，理解生命完整性的教育，基于过程思维、批判性思维、人类的美德……基于孔子和老子所写的特点……如何做到这一点，我没有一个具体的解决方案……我们大学正在找这种操作模式……

我们的大学建立了一个学习公式：$S = Z \cdot I$，在这里，"S"是学生的能力，它是"Z"——知识（事实，定义）和"I"——学生在学习过程中的生活强度这两个概念的产物。生命的强度可以从最广泛的意义上理解为经验。换句话说，"Z"是对知识的投资，而"I"是对学生存在的投资。正如在爱因斯坦的公式 $E = m \cdot c^2$ 中，光速（c）将质量（m）转换为能量，而在我们的公式中，学生在学习期间的经验（生活），将他的知识转化为解决问题的能力，以及学生创造性、创新和创业能力。我们的经验表明，这种模式要求很高，首先需要新一代的教授，未来的一代教授……马克斯的问题："谁教育教育者"越来越重要。人们不应该问"学生是谁"这样一个问题，而应该问"教授是谁？"……教授正在"塑造"社会，所以在发展国家精神的过程中，他们比政治家更重要……而政治家之前也做过教授的学生……这些都是理解社会进程的重要道理……

考虑到教育的重要性，我认为在"16+1"之内应该开始一种关于教育的概念和哲学的辩论；这场辩论将包括专业人员、专家、诗人、作家等等……但它应该排除政治家和教育机构管理人员……教育应该从"官僚主义"中解放出来，我们决不能允许教育成为今天思维方式的再生产（保留）工具。

我属于那些相信古典民族国家会有未来的人。确实，在过去的 300 年里，民族国家为发展做出了一定贡献，但已经耗尽了其内在的力量。在我看来，尽管有所有的弱点，欧盟还是代表一个高贵的想法，也就是取消边界，保持合作与和平。同样，东南亚的东盟也有差不多的目的，我认为未来全球治理也会使用类似的一个解决方案。1648 年由威斯特伐利亚和平创立的民族国家作为一个组织概念，有助于克服部落、宗教、部族和阶级之前的分裂……今天，在融合的时代，正如新加坡教授马凯硕说的，民族国家正在失去它的优势。虽然以前的民族国家是海上的特殊船只，经常在坠毁，今天我们都在同一条船上……有人想整理好他自己的船舱，并不能帮助全球的船只。2008 年的金融危机没有告诉我们，我们都在同一条船上吗？我们 70 亿人都受到了金融危机的影响？再也不说"不了解"国家边界的气候变化？

我知道这是令人震惊的，特别是对于那些只有从选举到选举有时间概念的政治家，他们可能只在乎自己民族国家的选举结果。在"一带一路"倡议中，我认为民族国家的作用必须改变，因为它可以促进趋同……我们不应该对这种变化和民族国家的作用感到悲伤，并为此增加"一带一路"倡议这个重要的文明理念的政治风险，以保存它。我们需要明白，中国的"一带一路"倡议正在改变民族国家的作用，但它对"国家社会"产生了非常积极的影响。"一带一路"倡议对我来说是可以接受的，因为它"打破"了"社会属于国家"的观点，也打破了一切都取决于民族国家的观点。"一带一路"正好为每一个人、公司、城市、地区提供了机会，让他们能够在"一带一路"倡议的范围内独立地采取行动。正因为如此，我认为文化的重要性是"一带一路"倡议的核心。

总之，我强调的是，理解东方神秘主义和西方科学的密切关系和相互渗透非常重要，同时要认为文化，即文化的交融，是"一带一路"倡议的基础。这方面的关键工具是教育，这一倡议的载体是一个社会，即个人、公司、城市和地区。官僚和官僚程序的影响越小，"一带一路"倡议的成功越大。

如何让来自西方的年轻人，尤其是来自 16+1 国家的年轻人，在了解中国的历史、文化、宗教、科学方面摆脱许多偏见？我已经许多次访问过中国，并跟中国有很好的合作。我研究中国的结果是，根据我个人的经验，中国代表一个独立的文明。我不会更详细地解释这一点。我要指出的是，西方文明的核心是民族国家和威斯特伐利亚组织的政治制度，而中国的基础在于五千年文明。所有中国知名专家都表示，中国是一个"文明国家"而不是"民族国家"。我知道中国是建立在文化、儒家和道德原则的基础上的，而西方的基础在于经济和科学。如果没有对中国文化的更深入了解，16+1 的任何国家以及整个世界都不会从与中国的合作中获益最大。这就是我强调要了解中国文化的原因。当然，中国需要了解 16+1 每个国家的文化，这意味着中国主要应该根据世界的要求调整好自己，而不是帝国主义的态度——根据自己的要求去调整世界。用"历史的眼镜"来看，中国是唯一一个强国在其文化和历史上尊重这种根据世界调整自己的原则，而不是反过来的。这就让我明白"一带一路"理念的意义和前景。

从这些观点出发，黑山的一所年轻大学——下戈里察大学，已经开始与中国、中国的大学和中国的公司进行密切的合作。我们的目标很简单：唤醒学生，让他们感受未来发展的大趋势，因为这些趋势已经对他们的生活有不少的影响，将来这些 21 世纪的大趋势肯定会有更大的影响。这个过程的第一步是让年轻人摆脱任何意识形态。意识形态与宗教是一样的：它捕捉到思想，构成世界观，构成偏见……我们在下戈里察大学没有任何直接反对意识形态化的程序。我们只是在自己的历书专门强调了两个信念："地球是我们的母亲"以及"这个地球上所有的人都来自非洲——我们都是兄弟！"……我校大多数学生和教授都有国际经验，尤其是在西欧和美国。几乎所有人都在那里学习或工作并生活过。我们已经把英语选择为大学的第二官方语言。如果我们大学的发展愿景是建立一个全球负责任的公民，那么这个愿景必须与全球发展的愿景联系起来……

作为一所私立大学，我们对中国"进入全球舞台"的反应更迅速。我们首先组织了一系列关于中国经济的讲座……然后很快意识到，如果不了解中国的历史、文化和哲学，我们就无法理解中国的经济……从此，好几个学生正式选择了关于中国相关问题的本科、硕士以及博士论文主题……在中华人民共和国驻黑山大使馆的支持下，尤其是崔志伟大使的支持下，我们与四川和北京的大学建立了合作关系，目前我校大约40名学生正在中国学习一个或者两个学期。同时，来自中国的约40名学生也访问过黑山……请不要忘记，下戈里察大学是一所拥有2500名学生的大学。此外，我们已与中国的公司和银行开展合作，从今年开始，我们的学生在中国实习，包括在四川公路桥梁建设集团有限公司，在银行等；另一方面，来自中国的10名学生在我们安排的黑山公司实习了1-2个月。此外，来自中国的教授正在UDG访问和教学，以及我们的教授去中国的大学讲课。下戈里察大学于2017年9月在采蒂涅组织了一次关于"全球化与'一带一路'倡议"主题的重要国际论坛。论坛有来自东欧和全国各地的200多名参与者，以及来自中国的约60名参与者。中国驻黑山大使崔志伟阁下作了主旨发言。来自中国的教授和商人在几个分论坛中发言。论坛在该地区得到了很大的推动，为推广"一带一路"倡议及其理念做出了重要贡献……论坛有助于与中国朋友建立新的联系。下戈里察大学为学生开设中文课多年。从2018年起，该大学将设立汉学硕士专业，目的是让年轻人有机会更好地研究中国、中国的历史、文化和文明。

在我们大学有一个项目叫"想法和性格"比赛，即，每位学生每个学期可以申请一个新的研究项目或工作主题，并在学期结束时以公开演讲的形式展示他们的研究结果。学生们被分成小组，每个小组有3到5名学生，比赛的时候所有的学生和老师都成为听众和评委。观众有权在演讲结束时提出问题和讨论。上个学期比赛的主题就是"中国、历史、文化、宗教、哲学"……大约1300名学生被分成 280 个小组。演讲在 5 个圆形剧场（学习室）进行，"评委"在每个学习室投票并任命获奖者……最后，圆形剧场的获奖者参加了决赛，中华人民共和国大使和黑山的所有中国公司的代表出席了比赛。冠军获得了中国大使馆的奖励，而每家中国公司都为 2-4 名学生提供了实习机会。通过这种方式，我们宣传了中国，增进了学生对中国的了解，提高了他们对"远方亚洲"的兴趣……

Culture and Education and the "Belt and Road" Initiative

Veselin Vukotic / Montenegro

Rector of University of Donja Gorica, Professor

How can we guide today's development based on the information from the future? That is the question for every country... That is the question for every university...

How to get information from the future?

Among other things, by studying the initiative of China: Belt and Road!

Frankly speaking, this initiative changes the world in the long run ... As Columbus changed the world by discovering America ...

Why do I think so?

"Belt and Road" is driving the process of development of the new civilization.

The Belt and Road Initiative should not be understood as some instant program, as an administrative strategy, as a set of visible measures. Belt and Road is essentially what is least visible. The strength of the Initiative lies in the invisible processes of the rise of Asian mysticism and Western physicism, in bridging the gap between rational, analytical thinking and the meditative experience of the mystical truth. Verner Heisenberg argued that the most fruitful progress occurs when two different directions of opinion are met[1], as is the case with the "Belt and Road" Initiative ... Indeed, what can encourage the fusion of scientific and mistical thought, and what new ways of homo-sapiens development can we expect?

We, people from the West must realize that we have come to a crisis in all areas of life: social, moral, economic and spiritual... Niel Ferguson speak about the age of decadence... We live in the age of cultural imbalance in our thinking and feelings, in our system of values, in our social and political structures... It seems to me that the Chinese symbols Yang and Jin are extremely suitable for understanding this imbalance. The Western culture preferes Yang in relation to Yin; male values compared to female values... As Fritjof Capra[2] pointed out, we put self-esteem ahead of adherence, analysis in front of synthesis, rational knowledge ahead of intuitive wisdom, science before religion, competition in front of cooperation... On the other side, as I experience China, the Chinese are a practical people with a very diverse social consciousness. Both Confucianism and Thaosim have dealt with life in society, in human relations, in moral values and in power... But, this practicality is complemented by the mystical side of Chinese thought - rising above everyday life and attaining a high level of awareness ... The aspiration to wisdom, to the spiritual enlightening of Chinese people has always been attractive and respectable. Indeed, this blend of Western science and Chinese spirituality, spurred by the "Belt and Road" Initiative, is one of the megatrends of the future development of the world.

Likewise, the "Belt and Road" Initiative for us Westerners also launches a

---

1 "It is probably true quite generally that in the history of human thinking the most fruitful developments frequently take place at those points where two different lines of thought meet. These lines may have their roots in quite different parts of human nature, in different times or different cultural environments or different religious traditions: hence if they actually meet, that is, if they are at least so much related to each other that a real interaction can take place, then one may hope that new and interesting developments may follow." (Werner Heisenberg)
2 Fritjof Capra "The Tao of Physics", 1991.

different understanding of the times. In other words, it invisibly sthrengthen the importance of long term in our lives and in Western civilization. For us, the fact that Chinese civilization is continually evolving for 5000 years and impressive and educational... The dominance of short-run has long tradition in the Western world, but it was truly established by John Maynard Keynes, who said "In the long run we are all dead" and introduced governance through short run policies, primarily economic (fiscal, monetary...) policies. How to behave according to the vision of a long-run in the time of rapid changes occuring in the information society can be understood from the "Chinese Bible": *The Book of Changes* (The Complete I Ching)[1] help us to follow the vision of long term in the time of fast changes which take place in information society... It is a book of ancient wisdom and a source of Chinese culture. The Chinese sages have realized that "there is a universal principle in the heavens and the earth that says that everything is always in the course of change... The key is that the individual understands the signs of change,"because only then can he respond and adjust to the changes in the most appropriate way"... Do we really understand and pay attention to the long-run trends of change in the consumer society of the Western society today? Do we even think about the "philosophy of change"?

I repeat, this is a look at the "Belt and Road" from a small country and from a small and young University. Our view emphasizes these invisible processes initiated by the "Belt and Road Initiative", which seems invisible for many; it emphasizes this blend of two different philosophies of understanding the world, as we believe that will lead to new events and inventions that will influence the further development of homo sapiens ...

How these invisible processes promoted through "The Belt and Road Initiative" disperse through the space and time?

Are they dispersed through economy, exports and imports of goods and services,

---

1　Alfred Huang: "Ji Ding, (The Complete I Ching)" .

investments? Is it connecting through material, visible programs and measures? Certainly, material flows have an impact. However, our assumption is that culture and education are true transmitters of the "Belt and Road" idea.

Culture and education are put ahead economy!?... Was it too much of an assumption? But, is "The Belt and Road" Initiative also courageous idea, which already involves 65% of world population from three continents? Does not this idea have a lot of risks: political, economic, safety, legal, moral...? All these risks are existing much more than we can understand them, and by taking responsibility for these risks, the Government of China proved that its sincerity and faith in this idea. The idea that, as it seems to us, is not selfish, as it was the ideas of colonialism of Great Britain from the 19th century or the USA in the 20th century, nor is a militant idea. It is the idea which enable all participants, including China to follow and protect their interests, but at the same time, through cooperation, they support other participant to achieve their goals. The "Belt and Road" is founded on the idea of interconnecting and interpenetrating.

If this is the founding base of the Belt and Road, how can all of this be achieved? First of all, through understanding of cultures, their permeation and education of young people to be able to understand tradition of both their own and other participating countries in the "Belt and Road". I think that culture, understood as the mutual understanding of people is the deepest foundation for the cooperation between countries and the development of globalization... As the wise, old saying points out "The relationship between countries lies in the friendship of people and friendship of people lies in the connectivity of their hearts"... In other words, the "Belt and Road Initiative" is based on five factors of connectivity, as President Yi Jinping pointed out. One of these five factors is "strengthening cultural and people-to-people cooperation, achieving understanding among people".[1]

My thesis is that we can reach new global civilization through cooperation

---

[1] Wang Yiwei: *The Belt and Road Initiative*, New Word Press, 2016, p. 132.

and understanding of cultures, while the "clash of cultures" would lead us to the disaster of homo-sapiens. Indeed, culture will be in the foundation of the new global civilization. This only means that global civilization can be leaned only on understanding of the other, on understanding the system of values and moral principles of the one we cooperate with. By understanding the culture of others we better understand our own culture... By better understanding of others, we better understand ourselves... At the same time we will avoid the potential consequences of closed culture which can be understood as the belief that our culture was superior to other cultures. Cultures are equal... Understanding culture as equal means that we accept the differences that exist between them... How can we reach this "unity of diversity of culture"... So, how can we avoid Hungtington "clash of civilizations"?[1] In my opinion, it is the key issue of the new global civilization, as well as the "Belt and Road Initiative"! I fully agree with professor Chen Shenglai from Shangai Academy of Sciences and Arts who says: "The position of a big country should be maintained in four ways: a military foundation, a political foundation, a cultural foundation and an economic foundation. Without cultural soft power, the other foundations will collapse"... Indeed, GDP (economy) can not tell us much about e.g. the quality of education, the health of children, their joy in the game... It does not include the beauty of individual, nature, people... GDP does not measure our courage, our curiosity, our wisdom, our potential... It measures everything, but what makes our life worthwhile...

The GDP figures of China can tell us everything about China, but not why the Chinese are proud of the fact that they are Chinese ... The same holds true for the others, and small nations... Indeed, the data on the GDP of Montenegro can not makes us conclude that the Montenegrins are one of the most hospitable people in the world ... Therefore, China and all countries of the Belt and Road should invest in SOFT POWER, because "soft power reflects the cultural capability and creativity of a country". I think every country, including China, should think about how to

---

[1] Hungtinton, Samuel P., *The Clash of Civilizations and the Remaking of World Order*, Simon & Schuster, 1996.

overcome the cultural trade deficit ("importing" cultures from other countries), even more than about economic deficits. How to "sell" your cultural heritage and how to increase "soft power" - this is for China and other countries of "The Belt and Road" the long-term issue.

How to develop your own culture and how to understand the culture of neighbors, the culture of other people?

In my opinion, education plays a key role in this.

Does today's education fulfill this role? How many students today learn not only about the culture of other nations, but also about their own? It is not necessary to repeat that education is in crisis, especially university education... I would just stress that today's education is too specialized oriented, that a whole has been lost: the goal of the university is more and more learning, rather than understanding the facts learned by students. Universities force students to accumulate as much knowledge as possible, assuming that a greater amount of knowledge leads to a higher quality of knowledge ... Perhaps in the industrial society, which is static, closed and material society it is true to some extent ... However, in the information society, this is not true... In the time of rapid changes, uncertainty and openness, which characterize information society, knowledge becomes dependent on the student's being $(Z = f(B))$ – it depends on the value system of the student, his complex view of the world, openness of mind, curiosity, critical thinking, humanity... Does today's university need to produce highly-specialized experts or citizens for a new global era? Confucius and Aristotle, more than two thousand years ago, emphasized that education aims at "culture and character" and the development of virtues of a student... The question that is raised today is "What must a young person learn in order to lead a responsible life in this century?" How do we ensure that they actually live what Socrates called the "examined life", thinkingly critical about their own values, and at the same time have the opportunity for an active life?

The role of the university is, above all, that a student learns from the world, not about the world around him, to learn from life, from his own experience, from his own feelings, not to learn about life, about other experiences ...

I think that education is not treated properly in "The Belt and Road", current cooperation within 16+1 cooperation is just an extension of the current model of education, that is, an attempt to establish cooperation on the same concept of education ... It is dangerous for "Belt and Road Initiative"... All visible goals of the Belt and Road – economic, political and infrastructural must be based on a new concept of education - liberal education, education that understands the wholity of life, based on process thinking, critical thinking, on the attributes which are rich in human virtues ... On the characteristics of which were written by Confucius and Lao Ce ... How to do it - I do not have a general solution ... We are looking this solution at our University ...

Our University develops a model of studies: $S = z \cdot i^2$, where S is a student's ability which is the product of z - knowledge (fact, definition) and i - the intensity of a student's life during studies. The intensity of life can be understood as experience in the broadest sense. In other words, z is an investment in knowledge, and i is investment in a student's Being. As in Einstein's equation $E = m \cdot c^2$, where the speed (c) converts the mass (m) into energy, in our model the student's experience (life) during studies, converts his knowledge into the ability to solve problems, to be creative, innovative, and entrepreneurial. Our experience shows that this model is highly demanding and requires, first of all, a new generation of professors, a generation of professors from the future... Marks' question: "Who educates the educators" is becoming very important. One should never ask the question: "Who are the students?", but "Who are the professors?" ... The professors are "shaping" the society, so they are much more important than politicians for developing the spirit of the state... And politicians were pupils or students of the professors ... These are long-term lessons in understanding the process in society ...

Having in mind the importance of education, I believe a debate on the concept and philosophy of the education should be opened within 16+1; debate which would involve all the profiles of professionals, experts, poets, writers ... But it should exclude politicians and educational bureaucracy ... Education should be liberated from "bureaucratic fittings" and we must not allow that education becomes the tool of reproduction (retention) of today's way of thinking.

I belong to people who do not believe in the future of a classical national state ... The truth, over the last 300 years, the nation-state has contributed to the development, but has exhausted its inward strength. In my opinion, despite all the weaknesses, the idea of the EU has a noble goal – to eliminate borders, strengthen cooperation and the struggle for peace. The ASEAN has similar orientation in Southeast Asia. In this I see the future solution of the governance on a global scale. The national state created by the Westphalian Peace in 1648, as the organizational concept of society, has contributed to overcoming old divisions of tribes and religious communities, clans and classes ... Today, at the time of convergence, as Kishar Mahbubani, a Singapore professor says, the nation state is losing advantages it had. While the former national states were special ships at sea and often crashed, today we are all on the same boat ... The fact that somebody is trying to rearrange his cabin will not save a global ship. Didn't the crisis from 2008 confirm this, because it hit all 7 billion people on the Planet? What to say about climate changes which "disclaim" state borders?

I know this is shocking for politicians, for whom there is only a time horizon from elections to elections, and who understand the whole at the level of their electoral circles in their national states ... In the "Belt and Road" Initiative, I see that the role of national states must change, so as it can encourage convergence... We should not grieve about this change of place and the role of the national state, and raise political risk of the "Belt and Road" Initiative, this important civilization idea, in order to preserve it. We need to understand that the Chinese initiative "Belt and Road" is changing the role of the nation state, but it has a very positive impact on the "national society" .... The "Belt and Road Initiative" is acceptable to me because it "breaks" the present opinion that "the state is the owner of the society"... It break the opinion that everything depends on the nation-state... The "Belt and Road" just provides the opportunity for every individual, company, city, region, independently take initiatives within the "Belt and Road"... For this very reason, I consider that the importance of culture is fundamental to the "Belt and Road"...

In short, I emphasized the importance of understanding the closeness and interpenetration of the mysticism of the East and the science of the West, and that culture, interpenetration of cultures, is the foundation of the "Belt and Road". The key tool for this is education, and the carrier of this initiative is a society, that is, individuals, companies, cities, regions. The smaller the impact of bureaucrats and bureaucratic procedures - the "Belt and Road" will make more success ...

How to make young people from the West, especially from the 16+1 countries, free from many prejudices when it comes to understanding China: its history, culture, religion, science? Perhaps it is one of the most influential prejudices that China will follow the Western model of development, and according to Fukuyama's statement from 1989 after the fall of the Berlin Wall that "the end of history" came. Does China bring Western universalism - the Western model of democracy into question? My opinion and experience, which is the result of many visits, cooperation and research about China is that China is a civilization for itself. I would not explain that in more details. I will just point out that the heart of the Western civilization is the nation-state state and the Westphalian organized political system, while the foundation of China lies in the thousand-year civilization. All China's better-known experts say China is a "civilization state" and not a "national state". I understand that China was based on the development of culture, Confucian and moral principles, and the foundation of the West lie in economy and science. Without deeper knowledge of Chinese culture, any country from 16+1, as well as the whole world, will not reach the maximum benefit from cooperation with China. That's why I insist on getting to know Chinese culture. Of course, China needs to learn about the culture of the 16+1 countries, which means that China must dominantly adapt to the world and not have an imperialist attitude – to adjusts the world to itself. Viewed through the "glasses of history," China is the only great force that in its culture, its history, has this approach to adapting to the world, not the other way around. In this I see the significance and perspective of the "Belt and Road" idea.

Starting from these views, one young University in Montenegro - the University of Donja Gorica has started intensive cooperation with China, Chinese universities and companies. Our goal is very simple: to awaken students to feel the future megatrends of development that already shape the world in which they live and in which they will live in the 21st century. The initial step in this is to make young people free from any ideologies. Ideology is the same as religion: it captures the mind, frames the view of the world, creates prejudices ... We did not have any kind of deideologization program at UDG. Simply, the Almanac of our studies is based on two myths: "Planet Earth is our mother"; "All the people on the planet are from Africa—we are all brothers!" ... Most of our students and professors and students has experience from the Western Europe and especially United States. Almost all of them studied or worked and lived there. We have introduced English as the official language of the University. If the vision of the development of our University is to create a globally responsible citizen, then this vision must be linked to the vision of global development ...

As a private university, we reacted more quickly to China's "arrival in the global scene". We started with a series of lectures on China, first of all, about the economy of China... Soon we realized that without the knowledge of Chinese history, culture and philosophy, we can not understand the Chinese economy... Several students started working for graduate and master thesis on topic related to China, some of them are working on their PhD thesis about China... Thanks to the understanding of the Embassy of the People's Republic of China in Montenegro, especially the Ambassadors, HE. Cui Zhiwei, we have established cooperation with the universities from Sichuan, from Beijing and about 40 students are staying a semester or two in China. On the other hand, about 40 students from China came to Montenegro ... Do not forget, UDG is a

University with 2,500 students. Also, we have opened cooperation with companies and banks from China and since this year our students have internship in China, for example, in SBRC, at the Sichuan Tianfu Bank .... On the other hand, already 10 students from China had 1-2 months internship in Montenegrin companies, organized by. Also, professors from China are visiting and teaching at UDG, as well as our professors who go to and teach at Chinese universities. UDG organized a major international conference on the topic "Globalization and the Belt and Road Initiative" in Cetinje, in September 2017. Conference had over 200 participants from all over the region and Eastern Europe, and we had about 60 participants from China. The keynote address was given by the Ambassador of China to Montenegro, HE Cui Zhiwei. Professors and businessmen from China were speakers at several panels. The conference had a great promotion in the region and significantly contributed to popularizing the "Belt and Road Initiative" and its idea... The conference served to establish new contacts with Chinese friends. The Chinese language is being taught at UDG for several years. From this year, the study program of Chinese studies will be established at the University, with the goal to give young people the chance to become more familiar with China, its history, culture, religion ...

At our University there is a project "Ideas and Character" – students get the topic which they research and work on during one semester, and present their results at the end of semester in the form of public presentation. Students are divided into small groups, 3-5 students and the final presentation is made in front of their colleagues, several hundred students and teaching staff. The audience has the right to ask questions and discuss at the end of presentation. The general topic of the project in the last semester was "China - History, Culture, Religion, Philosophy" ... About 1300 students were divided into 280 groups. The presentations took place in 5 Amphitheaters (study rooms) the "jury" voted and appointed the winners in each Amphitheater... In the end, the winners of the Amphitheater competed in the final, with the presence of the Ambassador of the People's Republic of China and representatives of all Chinese companies active in Montenegro. The winners received a reward from the Chinese Embassy, while each Chinese company provided internships for 2-4 students. In this way, we popularized China and increased the knowledge of our students about China, awakened their interest in that "far Asia"...

I want to emphasize that all these activities and other activities from our vision are carried out without any state aid, without any intervention by the state, with minimal bureaucratic procedures and without any financial assistance.

Why we invest so much in cooperation with China, and the "Belt and Road Initiative"!

I have already emphasized many issues we consider important, however I would like to point out several more things:

1. China is an upcoming economic or political great power - around 2050 China will be the world's first economy, with a GDP that will be equal to today's GDP of the world economy;

2. China is not a classical national state but a more "civilization state". This facts break the opinion which is imposed to young people today that the "nation state" was from God and it will be eternal;

3. It is also important for a student to realize that it is possible to have one country with multiple systems, to have "one country - two systems". I see this as necessary mental assumption of young people to understand the importance of the region, to understand the differences between "systems" in the regions, and to understand the upcoming organization of Europe as a "Europe-region-state". It will be something similar to the current provinces-based organization of China;

4. It is becoming increasingly clear that the world of 21st will be shaped not by the most developed countries, as in the 20th century, but by the countries which are in the process of rapid development ... Of course, China is one of the most developed, but we must not forget Brazil, South Africa, India, Nigeria ...

5. If the West is synonymous for the development and fast developing processes, do not forget that China is west of the West! At the end, I think that understanding China, its history, culture, religion and philosophy will be one of the greatest challenges of the 21st century. If so, why not prepare young people for it?

阿拉伯特色中国学学术问题初探

穆赫辛·法尔加尼 【埃及】
艾因·夏姆斯大学语言学院中文系教授

　　笔者在创立"阿拉伯特色中国学"方案中，值得深思的学术问题为数不少。其中最重要的一点是，这门学科似乎没有固定的、众所周知的客观定义。

　　笔者相信为了把"阿拉伯特色中国学"当做一门学术，就要有特定的研究方法，但是这里出现了一个问题：是否不同民族在研究"中国学"的时候创立了其本土化的"中国学"概念和研究方法。这也不奇怪，因为"汉学"或者说"中国学"跟其他的人文学科有一些共性，也就是说，此门学科，从大体上来讲，除了遵循人类社会（无论是东方社会，还是西方社会）的共同规律以外，还有一些对某些国家与民族的特殊看法的总结。

　　在此，可能有人提出这样的问题：为什么要创立"阿拉伯特色中国学"？换句话说，阿拉伯在研究汉学所采取的方法、目的和概念跟其他民族的有什么差别？如今，我们正处于经济全球化的世界，也免不了受到世界上强势文化的影响。事实证明，长期处于殖民化的阿拉伯民族的文化已沦为弱势文化，以至于在阿拉伯和中国之间的对话中，双方文化所构建的话语权力很难引起彼此之间的斗争，从而在做"阿拉伯特色中国学"研究时，不太可能停留在研究两种文化中僵化的二元对立这种偏极化的立场上。

　　这并不意味着这门学科的方案遵循的是"独立独行"、远离世界上其他民族以及各个学术流派给"汉学"或"中国学"长期以来提供丰富的、取之不尽的资料和有价值的启发。

在这里，笔者更不意味着中东地区专门研究中国的学者要建立一门完全不同于西方在 300 多年时间里所建立的知识体系。此外，有不少结论证明欧洲汉学的根源发源于中国本土。确切来讲，西方汉学根源于 17—19 世纪入华耶稣会士们的中国研究。那么，我们在某种意义上可以进一步说，这种"汉学"仍是源自中国本土，然后向欧洲大陆发展。于 19 世纪在法国学术中奠定基础。而这个外扩的西方汉学可定位为欧美学者的首次汉学研究。欧洲很早以前所制定的"传统汉学"久而久之变为"汉学传统"，以至于任何一个要为这门学科拟建学术框架的人，都应该视之为现成的、稳定的探究方式和有价值的知识结构。

所谓"传统汉学"最大的缺陷在于，由于诸多方面的原因，它对当代中国研究相对薄弱。再就是，有不少研究评论沦为置后性、局限性和片面性，与快速发展和急剧变迁的当代中国现实存在一定的距离。

中国改革开放以来，在经济和社会等方面都发生了深刻的变化。而为了客观地了解到快速发展和不断变化的中国，把研究中国古代历史和文化视为重要学术的阿拉伯特色中国学要避免局限性、片面性和欠缺的解释力。

客观认识中国政治、经济和社会生活，会在某种意义上有助于推动阿中关系友好发展，也能对全面认识当代中国起到积极的作用。

笔者相信，阿拉伯特色中国学的建立标志着中国学研究在阿拉伯国家的良好孕育及发展，同时也体现了其客观学术的历史性责任。

基于此，为建立"阿拉伯特色的中国学"，笔者建议首先为其建立一个基本定义及科学研究方法。

阿拉伯特色中国学是研究古代和当代中国文化的一门学科，而文化本身是个综合性的人文学科。其研究范围包括中国与其他民族的文化交流，还涉及西方"传统汉学"。

此外，这种学科体系所采取的研究方法要从实际情况出发。而为了达到这一目的，笔者建议采用"假说演绎推理"（Hypothetic Deductive Method），即要根据假说进行演绎推理，再通过实验检验所推理的结论，达到自然规律的过程。

Exploration of Academic Issues of Chinese Studies in Arabic Countries

Mohsen Fergani / Egypt

Professor of Chinese Language, Ain Shans University

There are too many academic issues worth pondering when creating the program of "Chinese Studies in Arabic Countries". The most important point is that this subject does not seem to have a fixed, well-known objective definition.

In my opinion, to be academic, "Chinese Studies in Arabic Countries" must have specific research methods, but there is a problem: whether different ethnic groups have their localized concepts and research methods for "Chinese Studies". This is not surprising because "Sinology" or "Chinese Studies" has some points in common with other humanities studies, that is to say, this subject, generally speaking, has summaries of special views by certain countries and ethnic groups, in addition to the common laws of the human society (either Oriental or Western).

Here, some people may ask a question: Why should we found the subject of "Chinese Studies in Arabic Countries"? In other words, what are the differences between the methodologies, goals and concepts adopted by Arabs in studying

Sinology with those applied by other ethnic groups? Today, in a world of economic globalization, we are inevitably influenced by powerful cultures in the world. Facts have proven that the culture of Arabian peoples who have been colonized for a long period has become a vulnerable culture so that in the dialogue between the Arab world and the Chinese world, the power of discourse built up by the two cultures can hardly cause a struggle between them, thus "Chinese Studies in Arabic Countries" is unlikely to stay on the polarized view of binary opposition between the two cultures.

This does not mean that the program of this subject is "isolated" and far from the abundant and inexhaustible information and valuable inspirations contributed by other ethnic groups and academic genres in the world to "Sinology" or "Chinese Studies".

Here, I do not mean that scholars specializing in Chinese Studies in the Middle East need to establish a system of knowledge that is completely different from that established by the West over more than three hundred years. Besides, there are many conclusions that have been reached saying that European Sinology originated in China. To be exact, Western Sinology began from Chinese Studies by Jesuits who entered China between the seventeenth and the nineteenth centuries. In a sense, this kind of "Sinology" derived from China, then developed to the European continent and laid a solid foundation in French scholarship in the nineteenth century. This extended Western Sinology can be positioned as the first Sinology study by European and American scholars. The "traditional Sinology" that was developed long ago in Europe has gradually become a "sinological tradition" so that anyone who wants to develop an academic framework for this subject should regard it as a ready-made, stable way of inquiry and valuable knowledge structure.

The biggest flaw of the so-called "traditional Sinology" is that it does not perform well in studying contemporary China for many reasons. Furthermore, there is a great deal of research that is lacking, limited and one-sided, thus being unable to keep pace with rapidly developing and drastically changing contemporary China.

Ever since the reform and opening-up of China, profound economic and social changes have taken place. In order to objectively understand China in fast growth and constant changes, Chinese Studies in Arabic Countries, which focuses on the study of ancient Chinese history and culture, should avoid limitations, one-sidedness and lack of explanatory power.

An objective understanding of China's political, economic and social life can be helpful for promoting the friendly development of the Arab-Chinese relationship in a certain sense, and also for playing a positive role in comprehensively understanding contemporary China.

I presume that the establishment of "Chinese Studies in Arabic Countries" marks the gestation and development of China studies in Arab countries and reflects the historical responsibility of objective academics.

On this basis, in order to found "Chinese Studies in Arabic Countries", I suggest first establishing a basic definition of it and scientific methods of research for it.

Definition: "Chinese Studies in Arabic Countries" is a subject that studies the ancient and contemporary Chinese culture, but culture itself is an integrated branch of the humanities. Its research scope covers cultural exchanges between China and other ethnic groups, as well as the Western "traditional Sinology".

In addition, the methods of research adopted by this disciplinary system should proceed from the actual situation. In order to achieve this goal, I propose to adopt the "Hypothetical Deductive Method", that is, to carry out deductive reasoning according to the hypothesis, then test the conclusions of the reasoning by experiments and finally achieve the process of natural law.

白俄罗斯与中国文化联系及命运共同体的概念

斯维特洛夫·鲍里斯 【白俄罗斯】
白俄罗斯文化部前部长

"把跨越时空、超越国界、富有永恒魅力、具有当代价值的文化精神弘扬起来。"

——习近平

如今白俄罗斯共和国的文化是维持社会稳定、国家完整和独立的强大基础,也是加强与中国的相互了解和友谊的支点。

尽管彼此在地理上相距甚远,白俄罗斯和中国在世界历史的时空发展上具有许多共同点。

在白俄罗斯与中国的交往历史上有几个重要的里程碑。

第一个里程碑发生在公元 8 世纪左右,与一条经过白俄罗斯领土的古老贸易路线有关,被称作"希腊的瓦兰吉人"之路。即"大丝绸之路"的北方路线,将拜占庭与斯堪的纳维亚半岛相连。这条贸易路线加强人民之间的贸易往来并使文化相互渗透。

由于贸易的发展,现代白俄罗斯境内的古老城市和公国开始崛起,例如波洛茨克、明斯克、图罗夫和平斯克。与东方的商业往来是其成功发展的关键。最赚钱的收入项目之一是中国丝绸贸易。丝绸衣服是一种奢侈的商品,还会作为主人的陪葬品。在连接黑海和波罗的海的河流沿线墓葬中都发现过陪葬的丝绸衣服。

从东方输入大量的银币，城市开始繁荣，人口也在增长。与东方国家的贸易利润达到数千万甚至上亿银币。目前，仅波洛茨克一地已经发现 40 座 9 世纪或 11 世纪的银币宝藏。

白俄罗斯和中国文化互动第二个重要的里程碑发生在 13 世纪上半叶，即所谓的金帐汗国的形成时期。

我们都知道，古代俄罗斯和中国在同一时期都被强大的蒙古人所统治，覆盖欧亚大陆的大部分领土，并且在那个时代从根本上改变了世界地缘政治形势。

金帐汗国的出现为在现代白俄罗斯领土上传播中国文化价值创造了机会。这不是在蒙古人统治时期实现的，而是作为立陶宛大公国的组成部分。

几乎在同一时期，中国和俄罗斯摆脱蒙古人的统治。当时人民起义被称作是"红巾军"，随后中国人进入明朝时期。在欧亚大陆的另一端爆发了库利科沃战役，这为从金帐汗国的统治下解放俄罗斯奠定了基础。然而，金帐汗国的覆灭使中国和白俄罗斯之间再次拉开了距离。数百年后，两国文化才能开始直接的对话。

这片领土名称的起源，"白色俄罗斯"随后成为国名，与鞑靼蒙古人白俄罗斯领土的独立性有关。

因此，蒙古人曾经征服的位于俄罗斯西边的旧俄罗斯公国领土未被金帐汗国统治。由于在中国西部地区偏好白色，鞑靼蒙古人借用了这种颜色的象征，将金帐汗国西边的领地命名为"白俄罗斯"。也就是说，我们国家的名字来源于中国的文化传统。

15 世纪或 16 世纪，商人、旅行者和传教士的活跃将中国与白俄罗斯以及整个欧洲联系起来。对异国情调的喜爱，对中国产品的渴望，导致 18 世纪中国文化元素风靡整个欧洲。这种风格被称为"shinuazra"（源自法国的中国艺术风格）。白俄罗斯人也偏爱中国文化，包括大量宫殿、城堡和庄园的装饰。首先是涅斯维日的宫殿和公园建筑群和米尔城堡建筑群。白俄罗斯领土上的中国文化渗透在许多方面与杰出的历史人物安娜·卡塔尔吉纳·拉德齐维尔有关。代表欧洲最大的权贵家族，在白俄罗斯领土上推广中国的瓷器制作技术和艺术作品。

这是白俄罗斯和中国文化关系发展道路上的第三个里程碑。

当今世界的重要趋势是，国家之间的关系越来越密切，不仅是因为贸易和经济，还要感谢不断扩大的文化交流。

目前白俄罗斯和中国人文沟通的活跃发展，首先是因为两国之间不存在根本矛盾，且遵循相同的国内和外交政策。

人文交流的各个方面已签订的合约正在推动这一趋势的发展。

白俄罗斯和中国于 1992 年 11 月签订关于文化合作的《政府间文化合作协定》，鼓励在文化和艺术领域开展交流。

2013 年白俄罗斯和中国签订博物馆、图书馆、影视创作、文字写作和电视频道等领域的合作协定。

2015 年 5 月，两国在明斯克签署《中华人民共和国政府和白俄罗斯政府关于互设文化中心协定》。

2015 年 10 月，在白俄罗斯举办的"中国文化日"期间召开中白政府间合作委员会文化合作分委会第一次会议。

2017 年 5 月，在中国举办的"白俄罗斯文化日"期间召开中白政府间合作委员会文化合作分委会第二次会议。

2016 年 12 月，中国文化中心揭牌仪式在白俄罗斯首都明斯克举行。

2017 年的"白俄罗斯文化日"期间，在北京市隆重地举办了白俄罗斯共和国文化中心揭牌仪式。

交流文化日：两国之间文化交流的传统形式之一。文化日活动自 1999 年起连续举办。文化日活动的数量和种类逐年增加。因此，在 2017 年的中华人民共和国文化日期间，白俄罗斯共和国歌剧和芭蕾舞团在国家莫斯科大剧院进行表演，由国家现代艺术中心出资举办现代白俄罗斯画展，并组织"白俄罗斯艺术家联盟"大师课程。

白俄罗斯和中国的艺术家积极开展合作交流。白俄罗斯国家美术馆和故宫皇家博物院签订合作协议。来自白俄罗斯的艺术大师已经成为中国举办的各种艺术论坛和展览的常客和参与者。白俄罗斯和中国艺术家的联合展览在两国首都和省会城市举行。大多数活动均得到两国大使馆的资助。

最近还有系列文化活动举办，如：

—在中国现代文学馆联合举办的艺术展览中展示白俄罗斯作家 **Janka Kupala** 的古典文学作品；

—在白俄罗斯国家美术馆举办画展"白俄罗斯和中国艺术中的女性形象"；

—白俄罗斯国家历史博物馆举办"中国电影 110 年展览"；

—在白俄罗斯国家图书馆举办的书展"龙的翅膀"，纪念两国建立外交关系

25周年。

还在白俄罗斯首都明斯克建立白俄罗斯共和国伟大的卫国战争历史博物馆。

中国主席习近平对白俄罗斯共和国正式访问期间参观该博物馆。

白俄罗斯国家图书馆与中国国家图书馆积极合作。

如今，白俄罗斯国家图书馆珍藏五千本关于中国文化、历史、地理和政策的文献。

中国国家图书馆通过"中国之窗"项目捐赠大量的图书。

在过去的两年中已采取以下行动：

——"欢乐春节给白俄罗斯带来欢乐"；

——在白俄罗斯国家爱乐音乐厅举行中国钢琴家音乐会；

——中国学生合唱团在白俄罗斯国立音乐学院和白俄罗斯学生合唱团在上海音乐学院演出；

——江苏女子民族乐团在白俄罗斯国立音乐学院演出；

——致敬白俄罗斯诗人雅库布·科拉斯（Yakub Kolas）和中国作家鲁迅的文学音乐会。

中国舞蹈演员参加在维捷布斯克举行的国际现代舞蹈节。

中国音乐家参加索列丁斯基国际音乐节。

当然，还有其他一些活动，比如：

在首都明斯克的电影院，中国大使馆在白俄罗斯共和国文化部的协助下定期组织中国电影周活动。

2017年5月，白俄罗斯文化部与中国国家新闻出版广电总局达成电影摄影领域合作协议。

同年，白俄罗斯电影《寻亲记》（Tum-Pabi-Dum）获得上海合作组织国家电影节评委会特别奖。

2016年，在敦煌市举办的首届"丝绸之路国际文化博览会"上，白俄罗斯宣布一项提议，要求丝绸之路上的每个国家将中国的敦煌市视为丝绸之路的象征性文化大门。

白俄罗斯城市格罗德诺是一个美丽的古老城市，具有悠久的历史和传统。

现阶段，不仅在艺术文化领域，而且在经济、教育、旅游等诸多其他领域，白俄罗斯和中国也在加强国际合作。白俄罗斯与中国的教育合作发展迅速。两国签署的双边协定构成合作基础，特别是：政府间关于相互承认学历证书的协议，政府间关于互相承认学位证书的协议，白俄罗斯教育部和中国教育部关于教育领域合作的协议。在白俄罗斯，汉语学习逐渐流行。在白俄罗斯的许多学校中，汉语是第一外语。在高等教育机构中开展汉语、翻译理论和实践、跨文化交流等学科教学，除了白俄罗斯专家外，还有来自中国的老师培养白俄罗斯学生了解汉语的细节。白俄罗斯设有三家孔子学院，在大连理工大学校领导和专家的全力支持下，2006年招收第一批"汉学"专业学生。

在教育方面，两国领先的高等教育机构之间签订合作协定，在此基础上进行学生和教师交流。白俄罗斯的高等教育机构与中国的高等教育和研究机构签订了一百多项双边协议。由于白俄罗斯国内教育水平高以及社会治安良好，每年大约有2000名中国公民在白俄罗斯的高等教育机构就读。

根据白俄罗斯国家统计委员会的最近十年移民相关数据，在白俄罗斯的华人人数增长了二十倍以上。

全方位合作使中国驻白俄罗斯大使馆和白俄罗斯驻中国大使馆能提供必要的帮助。

在白俄罗斯与中国建立外交关系后的二十六年中，两国的双边合作取得了良好的成果，堪称其他国家合作的典范。由于彼此之间形成强大的战略信任，白俄罗斯与中国的关系变得更加成熟和稳定。两国的关系不受国际环境的影响，也不针对任何第三方。白俄罗斯与中国的合作脚踏实地，因为两国都需要对方。现在，白俄罗斯与中国的关系经历了稳定发展的时期，每一年都变得越来越密切。

The Belarusian-Chinese Cultural Relations and Concept of Community with a Shared Future

Svetlov Boris / Belarus

Former Minister of Culture of the Republic of Belarus

"It is necessary to glorify spirit of culture which is capable to overcome space, time and borders of the states which has eternal bewitching force and has modern value" [1].

——Xi Jinping

Today the culture of Republic of Belarus, is a strong basis of maintaining stability of society, integrity and independence of the state, a stronghold of development of mutual understanding and friendship with People's Republic of China.

Despite geographical remoteness from each other, Belarus and China have a lot of common ground on the way of world history which is developed in space and time.

The first milestone belongs, approximately, by the eighth century of our era and is connected with a trade way widely known in the ancient time which passed through the territory of Belarus and called in sources as a way "from the Varangian in Greeks".

It was a northern branch of the Great Silk Road and connected Byzantium to Scandinavia. This way promoted strengthening of trade contacts between the people and to interpenetration of cultures. Thanks to it such ancient cities and, respectively, principalities, in the territory of modern Belarus as Polotsk, Minsk, Tourov, Pinsk and others arose and developed. Business with the East was the main key to their successful development. And one of the most profitable income items, was trade in the Chinese silk. Silk clothes buried together with their owners as luxury goods in ancient times. It is found in burials along the river ways connecting the Black and Baltic seas. From the East a large number of silver coins also arrived, the called cities grew, and their population increased.

Profit on trade with east countries made up to tens, and sometimes and hundreds of millions of silver coins.

Only in the territory of the Polotsk earth nearly forty treasures of silver coins of the ninth or eleventh of centuries are found now.

The second significant milestone on the way of interaction of the Belarusian and Chinese cultures belongs to the first half of the thirteenth century, by the period of formation of the so-called Golden Horde.

It is known that Ancient Russia and China practically at the same time were a part of the Mongolian power – the huge territorial education covering a considerable part of Eurasia and radically changed during that era a geopolitical situation in the world.

Emergence of the Golden Horde created an opportunity for broadcast of cultural values from China on the territory of modern Belarus which was not won by Mongols, but was a part of Grand Duchy of Lithuania. Liberation of China and Russia from the Mongolian dominion, happened too almost at the same time. The people's movement known in the history of China as a revolt of "red troops", brought the Chinese Ming dynasty to power. On other end of the Eurasian space there was a Battle of Kulikovo which laid the foundation for liberation of Russia from the Golden Horde.

However, elimination of the Golden Horde distanced China and Belarus from each other again and for centuries removed the beginning of rather direct dialogue between our cultures.

But it is curious that one of hypotheses of origin of the name of the territory, and subsequently and the country, "White Russia" is connected with independence of the Belarusian lands of Tataro- Mongols.

So, the territory of Old Russian principalities which was to the west from Russia conquered by Mongols was not included into the Golden Horde.

As the West in China was associated with white colour, and this symbolism of colour was borrowed by Tataro-Mongols, lands to the west from the Golden Horde could receive the name "White Russia".

That is, it is quite admissible that sources of the name of our country could be defined by the Chinese cultural tradition.

Interest in China, in the territory of Belarus, as well as in the whole Europe, in the fifteenth or sixteenth was supported centuries by vigorous activity of merchants, travellers and missionaries.

Hobby for exotic objects, desire to have the Chinese products, brought in the eighteenth century to distribution of elements of the Chinese culture across the whole Europe.

There was a whole direction which received the name of a shinuazra (from the French chinoiserie).

In the territory of Belarus confirm hobby for the Chinese culture, interiors of numerous palaces, castles, estates.

First of all, it is the Nesvizh Palace and Park Complex and Mir Castle Complex.

Penetration of the Chinese culture on the territory of Belarus is connected in many respects with a name of the outstanding historic figure Anna Katarzhina Radzivill.

This representative of a family of the largest European magnates promoted distribution, including, technologies of creation and art painting of the Chinese porcelain in the territory of Belarus.

Such is the third milestone on the way of development of the Belarusian-Chinese cultural relations.

Today the main tendency is that our countries become closer every year, thanking not only trade and economy, but also dynamically extending cultural exchange.

Now the Belarusian-Chinese humanitarian communications dynamically develop that, first of all, is caused by lack of basic contradictions, community of the principles of domestic and foreign policy.

It is also promoted by existence of the developed contractual base in various directions of humanitarian activity.

Contacts in the sphere of culture and art are regulated by the Intergovernmental Agreement between Republic of Belarus and People's Republic of China on cultural cooperation signed in Beijing in November, one thousand nine hundred ninety second.

Since two thousand thirteenth cooperation agreements between the Belarusian and Chinese museums, libraries, bodies of cinematography, the Writers' Unions of two countries, television channels work.

In May, two thousand fifteenth in Minsk the Agreement between the Government of Republic of Belarus and the Government of People's Republic of China on mutual establishment of the cultural centres was signed.

In October, two thousand fifteenth the first joint sitting of the commission which took place during Culture Days of People's Republic of China in Republic of Belarus took place.

The second joint sitting of the commission took place in May, two thousand seventeenth within Culture Days of Republic of Belarus in People's Republic of China.

In December, two thousand sixteenth the ceremonial opening of the Centre of culture of People's Republic of China in Minsk was held.

The next year opening of the Centre of culture of Belarus in Beijing within Culture Days of Republic of Belarus in People's Republic of China followed.

Culture Days take place serially since one thousand nine hundred ninety ninth. Every year they become more and more volume and various according to the program. So, during last year's Culture Days in People's Republic of China the performance of troupe of the National academic Bolshoi Theatre of the opera and ballet of Republic of Belarus, holding an exhibition of modern Belarusian graphics from funds of the National centre of the modern arts and the organization of master classes of "The Belarusian union of artists" took place.

Cooperation on the line of artists of Belarus and China actively develops.

The agreement between the State art museum and the State museum of the imperial Gugun palace is signed.

The Belarusian masters already became constant guests and participants of various art forums and the exhibitions held in China.

Joint exhibitions of the Belarusian and Chinese artists take place both in the capitals of both countries, and in provincial towns.

The majority of actions takes place under patronage of embassies of our countries.

The followings are actions lately took place:

- joint art exhibition in State the literary museum of the classic of the Belarusian literature Janka Kupala;

- painting exhibition within the International festival of arts "A Slavic market in Vitebsk";

- painting exhibition "Images of women in art of Belarus and China" in National art museum of Republic of Belarus;

- the "Hundred Eleven Years to the Chinese Cinema" exhibition organized by National History Museum of Belarus;

- the book exhibition "Under Wings of a Dragon" devoted to the twenty-fifth anniversary of establishment of diplomatic relations in National library of Belarus.

In Minsk the unique modern Museum of history of the Great Patriotic War of Republic of Belarus is created. During the official visit of the leadership of China to Republic of Belarus he was visited by the Chairman of People's Republic of China mister Xi Jinping. Within the international document exchange the National library of Belarus actively cooperates with National library of China.

Today funds of National library of Belarus contain about five thousand documents concerning the Chinese culture, history, geography, policy. The considerable array of these documents was transferred by National library of China within the Window to China project.

For last two years such actions as took place:

- "The Cheerful holiday of spring brings joy to Belarus";

— Concerts of piano music of the Chinese performers in the Belarusian state philharmonic hall;

— The Chinese student's choruses in the Belarusian state academy of music and the Belarusian student's choruses in the Shanghai conservatory;

— Female national orchestra of the Province of Jiangsu in the Belarusian state academy of music;

— The literary musicale devoted to the Belarusian poet Yakub Kolas and the Chinese writer Lu Xin.

The Chinese dancers participated in the International festival of modern choreography in Vitebsk. The Chinese musicians participated in the International musical festival of Sollertinsky. Some other actions took place.

In the sphere of cinematography in Minsk regularly there pass the Weeks of the Chinese cinema organized by Embassy to People's Republic of China with assistance of the Ministry of Culture of Republic of Belarus.

In May, two thousand seventeenth the Cooperation agreement in the sphere of cinematography between the Ministry of Culture of Republic of Belarus and the Head public administration for the press, publishing houses, broadcasting, cinematography and television of the People's Republic of China is signed.

In the current year the Belarusian movie "Tum-Pabi-Dum" is awarded a special prize of jury of a film festival of the countries of the Shanghai Cooperation Organization.

In two thousand sixteenth in the city of Dunhuang on the First International cultural the EXPO of the Silk way, from Belarus announced an initiative to define in each country of the Silk way the city which, as Dunhuang in China, could become symbolical cultural gate of the Silk way.

In Belarus as such city Grodno which is one of the most beautiful ancient cities of Belarus with rich history and traditions is offered. [slide]

At the present stage enhancing international cooperation of Republic of Belarus and People's Republic of China not only in the sphere of art culture, but also in many other directions is observed: economic, educational, tourist.

Cooperation between Belarus and China in education develops very dynamically.

A number of bilateral agreements is its cornerstone, in particular: the intergovernmental Agreement on mutual recognition of documents on education, the intergovernmental Agreement on mutual recognition of academic degrees, the Agreement between the Ministry of Education of Republic of Belarus and the Ministry of Education of People's Republic of China on cooperation in the field of education.

In Belarus studying of Chinese gains the increasing popularity.

In a number of schools of Belarus Chinese language is learned as the first foreign.

In higher educational institutions teaching such disciplines as Chinese, theory and practice of translation, cross-cultural communication and so on, carry out, except the Belarusian experts, teachers from People's Republic of China who train the Belarusian students in Chinese subtleties.

The first release of students majoring in "Sinology" took place in two thousand and sixth year thanks to full support of the management and specialists of the Dalian university of technologies.

In Belarus three Institutes of Confucius work.

In education there are also contracts on cooperation between the leading higher education institutions of two countries on the basis of which there is an exchange of students and teachers.

Institutions of formation of Belarus concluded more than hundred bilateral agreements with higher education institutions and research establishments of the People's Republic of China.

Thanks to high domestic standards of education and also a good social situation annually in higher education institutions of Belarus about two thousand Chinese citizens study.

According to data of National statistical committee of Republic of Belarus for the last ten years in connection with migration processes the number of Chinese in the territory of Belarus grew more than by twenty times.

The necessary help with all directions of cooperation render Embassy of People's Republic of China in Belarus and Embassy of Republic of Belarus in China.

In twenty six years of diplomatic relations between Belarus and China dynamics of bilateral cooperation achieved good results that can be considered as a sample for other states.

The Belarusian-Chinese relations become more mature and stable thanks to formation of strong strategic trust to each other.

Reference

1   Си Цзиньпин. О государственном управлении. – Пекин: Издательство литературы на иностранных языках, 2014. – С. 225.

2   Франкопан Питер. Шелковый путь. Дорога тканей, рабов, идей и религий. – Москва, 2017.

3   Су Фэнлинь. История культурных отношений Китая с Россией до середины XIX в. Автореф. дисс. д. ист. наук в форме науч. докл. 07.00.03. – Москва, 2000.

"一带一路"倡议与共同发展：新丝路花开巴尔干地区

艾立山 【保加利亚】
索非亚大学教授

保加利亚位于欧洲东南部巴尔干半岛地区（东南欧）。南欧有三大山脉半岛：比利牛斯、亚平宁和巴尔干。巴尔干半岛地区位于黑海、爱琴海、爱奥尼亚海和亚得里亚海四海之间的欧洲东南部。地区面积约 50 万平方公里，人口约有 5500 万人。地区名称来自于从保加利亚东西中线到东塞尔维亚的一条叫做巴尔干的大山脉的名称。

欧洲历史上"巴尔干"这个名称首次于 1490 年在给罗马教皇写的一封信中提到。巴尔干半岛作为地理名称最初是由德国地理学家 Johann August Zeune（1778—1853）在 1808 年使用的。其后也有人使用其他名称，如"东南欧半岛"，但都没有传播并保留下来。[1]

在地理方面，东南欧巴尔干半岛包括 12 个国家：罗马尼亚、保加利亚、塞尔维亚、科索沃、黑山、克罗地亚、斯洛文尼亚、波斯尼亚和黑塞哥维那（波黑）、马其顿、阿尔巴尼亚、希腊和土耳其的欧洲一侧，包括伊斯坦布尔以及博斯普鲁斯海峡以西的欧洲部分。欧洲的西巴尔干地区包括 6 个非欧盟国家：塞尔维亚、科索沃、马其顿、波黑、黑山、阿尔巴尼亚。

东南欧历史悠久曲折。巴尔干（东南欧）国家有 6 个用斯拉夫语族的语言：保加利亚语、马其顿语、塞尔维亚语、克罗地亚语、波黑语、黑山语。保加利亚

---

[1] Todorova, Maria. *Imagining the Balkans*. Oxford University Press, 2009. pp.22-28.

语和马其顿语相当接近，像方言。前南斯拉夫的塞尔维亚语、克罗地亚语、波黑语、黑山语、塞尔维亚语也同样互相接近，但跟保语、马其顿语为母语的人互相交流时困难一些。虽然斯洛维尼亚语作为斯拉夫语系的语言一样也有很多相似之处，但斯洛维尼亚一般归入中欧，不属巴尔干国家。巴尔干半岛人民和国家的复杂共性、互惠和互补性，在学术文献中经常被描述为一个特定的"语言联盟"，也被称为"文化联盟"。[1]

中国巴尔干丝绸之路与巴尔干半岛的连通议程

中国 21 世纪"走出去"战略[2] 越来越发挥着中国对全球新发送的引力波。东欧的第一次引力冲动在 2012 年"16+1"合作框架创建时发生，然后随着 2013 年中国国家主席习近平落实"一带一路"倡议，就变成后者的组成部分。中国在欧洲对"16 加中国"合作平台采取更广泛的连通性方式，将欧盟成员国和非欧盟国家汇集在一起：11 个欧盟成员国和 5 个非欧盟成员的巴尔干国家。[3]

东欧国家和中国 16+1 合作框架包括：爱沙尼亚、拉脱维亚、立陶宛（波罗的海国家）、波兰、捷克、斯洛伐克、匈牙利、斯洛文尼亚（中欧国家）、罗马尼亚、克罗地亚、黑山、塞尔维亚、保加利亚、波斯尼亚和黑塞哥维那、马其顿、阿尔巴尼亚（东南欧国家）。巴尔干丝绸之路包括 8 个巴尔干半岛国家，即 16+1 合作平台中所有国家的一半：5 个非欧盟国家（阿尔巴尼亚、马其顿、塞尔维亚、波黑、黑山）和 3 个欧盟成员国（保加利亚、罗马尼亚和克罗地亚）。首届 16+1 峰会在波兰华沙（2012 年）举行。第 2 届在罗马尼亚布加勒斯特（2013 年），第 3 届在塞尔维亚贝尔格莱德（2014 年），第 4 届在中国苏州（2015 年），第 5 届在拉脱维亚首都里加（2016 年）举行。2017 年峰会于 11 月在匈牙利首都布达佩斯举行。

"16+1 合作"平台与中欧合作议程密切相关，客观上有助于推动欧洲一体化进程。这一重要讯息于 2018 年 7 月在保加利亚首都索非亚举行的第 7 次 16+1 合作峰会上得到重申。

1　Daskalov, R.D., Mishkova, D., Marinov, T., Vezenkov, A. Entangled Histories of the Balkans-Volume Four: Concepts, Approaches, and(Self-) Representations. Balkan Studies Library. BRILL, 2017.
2　https://baike.baidu.com/item/走出去战略, 2018.7.14.
3　CIFE. China's Balkans Silk Road: Does it pave or block the way of Western Balkans to the European Union? At:http://www.cife.eu/Ressources/FCK/files/publications/policypaper/2018/CIFE_Policy_Paper_ChinaBalkansSilkRoad_Stumvoll_Flessenkemper_February2018. pdf, 2018.7.14.

第 7 届 16+1 峰会于 2018 年 7 月在保加利亚索非亚举行

中国总理李克强在会晤开始开宗明义表示，16+1 合作不仅有利于中国与中东欧 16 国，有利于欧洲一体化，也有利于世界[1]。

保加利亚总理鲍里索夫说，中国与中东欧国家的合作，会帮助一些发展速度较慢的国家加快发展进程，追上其他欧洲国家的脚步，不是反对欧盟一体化，而是促进欧盟以内国家，以及欧盟以外中东欧国家与中国的经贸人文交流，是完全基于市场原则的务实合作。[2]

李克强与保总理一致表示，"16+1"不是地缘政治平台，而是经贸人文合作平台。[3]

第 7 届 16+1 峰会的重要通知，是巴尔干丝绸之路将在逾期填补东欧和西欧经济发展差距方面发挥重要作用。众所周知，没有基础设施就没有经济发展，而基础设施投资就是巴尔干地区新丝绸之路 16+1 项目的核心。巴尔干和西欧国家之间在高速公路、铁路、能源生产和强大电力供应线等基础设施方面，还存在着巨大的差距。只有在信息和通信技术基础设施方面例如互联网接入，东欧和西欧似乎差距还小一点。[4]

中东欧互利互惠的"一带一路""16+1 合作"

中东欧 16 国地处联通欧亚非的枢纽地带，普遍重视发展对华互利互惠合作，均与中国签署了"一带一路""16+1 合作"文件。中国的巴尔干丝绸之路项目将为中东欧带来长期的经济增长，因为它也迫使欧盟接受中国的挑战，改善自己的规则，以便更好地与中国进行合作，协调欧盟标准，简化程序规则，提高项目执行效率，全面改善中欧之间的协同效应。[5]

巴尔干国家经济规模相对较小，但通过巴尔干丝绸之路，中国也可以与欧盟

---

1 李克强总理与保总理一致表示："16+1"不是地缘政治平台，而是经贸人文合作平台。2018-07-06. 中国政府网：http://www.gov.cn/guowuyuan/2018-07/06/content_5304161.htm,2018.7.14.
2 同上。
3 同上。
4 参见：Grübler, Julia.China's Out reach to CEE Could Be Win-Win. WIIW. April 23, 2018. In:https://emerging-europe.com/voices/chinas-outreach-cee-win-win, 2018.7.14.
5 参见：Michal Makocki. China in the Balkans: The battle of principles. 06thJuly, 2017. At: https://www.ecfr.eu/article/commentary_china_in_the_balkans_the_battle_of_principles_7210, 2018.7.11.

手增加本地供应链，提高本地区连通性，促进该地区的整体发展，从而有助于开发 5500 万消费者的新大市场。

2018 年上半年保加利亚欧盟理事会主席国：恢复实行巴尔干地区一体化进程

除了举办"16+1 合作"峰会之外，今年直至 2018 年 7 月，保加利亚还担任欧洲联盟理事会轮值主席国。结果 2018 年成为对巴尔干地区兴趣复兴的一年。西巴尔干地区的入盟前景和连通性，是 2018 年上半年保加利亚当欧盟理事会主席的首要任务，2018 年 5 月在索非亚举办了 15 年来的欧盟——西巴尔干国家的首次峰会。

2018 年 2 月，欧盟委员会发布新的欧盟扩大战略，旨在振兴欧盟与巴尔干地区的相互关系。2018 年 4 月，欧盟委员会发布了关于西巴尔干地区每个欧盟候选国和潜在欧盟候选国情况的年度报告。欧洲理事会将于 2019 年 6 月，在改革继续取得具体成果的情况下，与马其顿和阿尔巴尼亚开始进行入盟谈判。[1]

欧洲东南部对了解中国文化的滞后需要赶上

要积极推动保中之间的文化交流，促进中国与巴尔干地区国家在"一带一路"倡议"16+1"框架下发挥作用，开展文化交流。目前，保加利亚对中国文化和语言人才资源虽然比以往多得多，但毕竟普通了解程度还远远不够。

保加利亚和东南欧的巴尔干地区是中国沿着新巴尔干丝路跟欧洲扩展经济协作的重要组成部分，虽然最近 20 年来经济和文化比以前开放得多，但毕竟还不如西欧国家历史悠久的对外开放程度，所以欧洲东南部对于中国文化的了解需要迅速地从平面走到立体，包括电影、文学、体育、娱乐。

成立中东欧国家索非亚"16+1"的中国与中东欧国家全面合作研究中心

2018 年 7 月 6 日下午，在第 7 次中国——中东欧国家领导人会晤跟李克强总理会见时，保加利亚总统拉德夫的一项提议——建立索非亚"16+1"研究中心，

---

[1] Gotev, G. EU begins screening Macedonia, Albania formid-2019 accession talks. At:https://www.euractiv.com/section/enlargement/news/eu-begins-screening-macedonia-albania-for-mid-2019-accession-talks, 2018.7.18.

探讨各方规划规则，寻找欧盟政策与"16+1合作"的多赢[1]，与李克强总理"一拍即合"。李克强说，成立这一研究中心是衔接"16+1合作"与欧盟法律法规的重要途径，不仅有助于向外界"解疑释惑"，还可以向"16+1合作"有关机制提供咨询报告，以便有针对性地讨论和解决各方面的问题。[2] 然后李克强总理与保加利亚总理鲍里索夫达成协议，成立了中国与中东欧国家全面合作研究中心。[3]

庆祝2019年保中建交70周年，促进中国与中东欧合作进入新时代

最后但并非最不重要的是，明年——2019年10月2日是中国与保加利亚建交70周年的确切日子。保加利亚是世界上第二个承认新中国的国家。我们要把这个大周年纪念日作为新机遇，加强传统友谊，不仅更加稳定地推进双边关系，而且对整个巴尔干地区发挥积极作用，进一步增进互信，为推动"16+1合作"深入发展提供新动力，促进中国与中东欧合作进入新时代。

---

1 President Rumen Radev and the Prime Minister of the People's Republic of China Li Keqiang Discussed the Establishment in Sofia of a Center for Coordinating Joint Projects and the Norms between the EU and China. 6 July 2018. At:https://www.president.bg/news4513/tsentar-za-koordinirane-na-obshtite-proekti-i-na-normite-mezhdu-es-i-kitay-da-bade-izgraden-v-sofiya-obsadiha-prezidentat-rumen-radev-i-ministar-predsedatelyat-na-knr-li-katsyan.html, 2018.7.14.
2 保加利亚总统这项提议与李克强"一拍即合".2018-07-07. 中国政府网:http://www.gov.cn/premier/2018-07/07/content_5304429.htm, 2018.7.15.
3 Global Partnership Centre of CEEs and China was Agreed by Prime Ministers Boyko Borissov and Li Keqiang.07.07.2018.At:http://www.government.bg/en/Press-center/News/GLOBAL-PARTNERSHIP-CENTRE-OF-CEECS-AND-CHINA-WAS-AGREED-BY-PRIME-MINISTERS-BOYKO-BORISSOV-AND-LI-KEQIANG,2018.7.14.

New Silk Road and Common Development: Making the Balkans Bloom

Alexander B. Alexiev / Bulgaria

Professor of Sofia University

Bulgaria is a Balkan country situated in southeastern Europe, on the Balkan Peninsula. There are three major peninsulas on large mountain ranges in Southern Europe, West to East: the Pyrenees, the Apennines and the Balkans. The Balkan Peninsula borders four seas: Black, Aegean, Ionian and Adriatic. It has an area of about 500,000 square kilometres and population of about 55 million people. The name of the area comes from that of the Balkan Mountain range that spans along the East-West Central Line of Bulgaria and in Eastern Serbia.

The name "Balkan" was first mentioned in European history in 1490 in a letter to the Pope. The geographical location of the Balkan Peninsula was originally named by the German geographer Johann August Zeune (1778-1853) in 1808. Since then people have tried to use other names for it, like Southeast European Peninsula, but with no success[1].

---

[1] For full treatment of the subject see: Todorova, Maria. *Imagining the Balkans*. Oxford University Press, 2009. pp.22-28.

In geographical terms Southeast Europe's Balkan Peninsula consists of 12 countries: Romania, Bulgaria, Serbia, Kosovo, Montenegro, Croatia, Slovenia, Bosnia and Herzegovina, Macedonia, Albania, Greece, and the European part Turkey west of the Bosphorus, including Istanbul. The term Western Balkans refers to six non-EU countries: Serbia, Macedonia, Bosnia, Montenegro, Albania, and Kosovo.

Southeastern Europe is a place with long history of twists and turns. A common Slavic language is spoken in six countries in the Balkans (southeastern Europe): Bulgarian, Macedonian, Serbian, Croatian, Bosnian-Herzegovinian, and Montenegrin. Bulgarian and Macedonian languages are quite close, much like dialects. The languages of Croatia, Bosnia and Herzegovina, Montenegro and Serbia, of former Yugoslavia are also closely related to each other, but oral communication with native speakers of Bulgarian and Macedonian languages is more difficult. Slovenian, although also a Slavic language with many similarities, is usually associated with Central Europe, since the country is typically not considered a Balkan state. The specific complexity of commonalties, reciprocities and complementarities of peoples and nations in the Balkan Peninsula is often characterized in academic literature as a "language union" and "cultural union".[1]

China's engagement in the Balkans and the connectivity agenda of the Balkan Silk Road

China's international cooperation plan started to exert new and strong gravitational waves at global level in the 21st century. The first big gravitational impulse in Eastern Europe was felt in 2012, when the "16+1" cooperation framework was created, and then in 2013 it became a part of the New Silk Road or Belt and Road Initiative after it was launched by Chinese President Xi Jinping. In SE Europe China took a broader connectivity approach, bringing together EU

---

1 For full treatment of the subject see: Daskalov, R.D., Mishkova, D., Marinov, T., Vezenkov, A. Entangled Histories of the Balkans - Volume Four: Concepts, Approaches, and (Self-) Representations. Balkan Studies Library. BRILL, 2017.

member states and non-EU countries: there are 11 EU Member States and another 5 Balkan countries in the 16-plus-China cooperation platform. [1]

The 16 Countries of Central and Eastern Europe from North to South are: Estonia, Latvia, Lithuania (Baltic states), Poland, Czech Republic, Slovakia, Hungary, Slovenia (CE states), and Romania, Croatia, Montenegro, Serbia, Bulgaria, Bosnia and Herzegovina, Macedonia, Albania (Balkan states).

The New Silk Road in the Balkans, often called the Balkan Silk Road includes eight Balkan countries – half of all countries in the "16+1" platform: five non-EU Members (Albania, Bosnia and Herzegovina, Montenegro, Serbia, and Macedonia) and three EU Members (Bulgaria, Romania, and Croatia). The First 16+1 Summit took place in Warsaw, Poland (2012). The second was in Bucharest, Romania (2013), the third was in Belgrade, Serbia (2014), the fourth Summit – in Suzhou, China (2015) and the fifth in Riga, Latvia (2016). The sixth Summit was held Nov. 2017, in Budapest, Hungary.

It should be noted that the "16+1" cooperation goes hand in hand with China-EU cooperation agenda and objectively helps promote the process of European integration. This important message was reiterated on the 7th Summit of the 16+1 format, held about in July 2018 in Bulgaria's capital, Sofia.

The 7th Summit of 16+1 in July 2018, Sofia, Bulgaria

At the very beginning of the meeting Chinese Premier Li Keqiang clearly pointed out that "16+1 cooperation is not only beneficial to China and the 16 countries of Central and Eastern Europe, but also to European integration and the world." [2]

Bulgarian Prime Minister Borisov said that China's cooperation with Central and Eastern Europe will help EU integration of countries with slower pace, accelerate

---

1 CIFE. China's Balkans Silk Road: Does it pave or block the way of Western Balkans to the European Union?. At: http://www.cife.eu/Ressources/FCK/files/publications/policypaper/2018/CIFE_Policy_Paper_ChinaBalkansSilkRoad_Stumvoll_Flessenkemper_February2018.pdf, 14.7.2018
2 http://www.gov.cn/guowuyuan/2018-07/06/content_5304161.htm, 2018.7.14.

their development and catching up with the other European countries. It is not against EU integration, but promotes economic and trade exchanges between countries within the EU and Central and Eastern European countries outside the EU. It stands for pragmatic cooperation based entirely on market principles.[1]

Li Keqiang and Premier Borisov both reiterated that "16+1" is not a geopolitical platform, but a stage for economic and trade cooperation.[2]

The important announcement from the 7th 16+1 Summit was that the Balkan Silk Road will be of crucial help in the overdue filling of the economic development gap between Eastern and Western Europe. It is common knowledge that there can be no economic development without infrastructure, which is exactly the core venture of the New Silk Road projects in the Balkan region. There is a big divide between Balkan and Western European countries for it to mend, especially in the development of infrastructure, like motorways, railways, also energy production and powerful electric supply lines. Only in information and communications technology infrastructure – such as internet access – does the gap between Eastern and Western Europe seem to be smaller[3].

CEEC welcome a win-win cooperation between China and Europe

The 16 countries of Central and Eastern Europe are strategically located in the hub of Europe, Asia and Africa. They attach importance to the development of mutually beneficial cooperation with China, and all have signed cooperation documents with China on the "Belt and Road" Initiative. China's Balkan Silk Road project is expected to hopefully boost CEEC's economies, because it makes the EU want to take up the China challenge and improve its own rules of project implementation to be able to better cooperate with China's offers. This process

---

1 http://www.gov.cn/guowuyuan/2018-07/06/content_5304161.htm, 2018.7.14.
2 Ibid.
3 For more on the subject see: Grübler, Julia. China's Outreach to CEE Could Be Win-Win. WIIW. April 23, 2018. In: https://emerging-europe.com/voices/chinas-outreach-cee-win-win, 14.7.2018.

is about streamlining EU and Chinese standards, dovetailing procedural rules to improve the swiftness of execution of projects, enhancing China – EU's cooperation synergy.[1]

Balkan economies are relatively small, but through the Balkan Silk Road China they have the potential to grow, catch up with the rest of EU, develop better connectivity and supply chains, achieve overall regional advance and thereby help develop a new big market of 55 million consumers for its products.

Bulgaria's EU Council Presidency in the first half of 2018: reviving the Balkan integration process

Besides the 7th Summit of the 16+1 cooperation, Bulgaria also held the rotating presidency of the Council of the European Union (EU) in the first half of this year. As a result 2018 is a year of revived EU interest in the Balkan region. Thus, the European perspective and connectivity of the Western Balkans was placed at the top of priorities of Bulgaria's EU Council Presidency in the first half of 2018, which organised the first EU-WB summit in 15 years – the EU-Western Balkans Summit in Sofia in May 2018.

Before the May EU-Western Balkans Summit in Sofia, this February, the European Commission published a new EU enlargement strategy that aims to revitalise relations with the Balkan region. In April, it released its annual reports of the situation in each of the EU candidate and potential EU candidate countries in the Western Balkans. The European Council has thus reached an agreement on opening accession talks with Macedonia and Albania to begin in June 2019, if reforms continue to deliver concrete results.[2]

---

[1] See also: Michal Makocki. China in the Balkans: The battle of principles. 06th July, 2017. At: https://www.ecfr.eu/article/commentary_china_in_the_balkans_the_battle_of_principles_7210, 11.7.2018

[2] Gotev, G. EU begins screening Macedonia, Albania for mid-2019 accession talks. At: https://www.euractiv.com/section/enlargement/news/eu-begins-screening-macedonia-albania-for-mid-2019-accession-talks, 18.7.2018.

South-Eastern Europe needs catching up on Chinese culture

The framework of the Belt and Road Initiative is a great new opportunity to actively promote cultural exchanges between China and Bulgaria through cultural cooperation between China and the Balkan countries. At present, although Bulgaria has much more people with a certain degree of understanding of Chinese language and culture than ever before, the common level of appreciation is still far from enough.

Bulgaria and the Balkan countries in South-Eastern Europe are an important part of China's expanding economic synergy with Europe along the New Balkan Silk Road. Although Chinese economy has been much more open in the past 20 years, its culture is still far less available in our region, compared to the long-established tradition of contacts with the Western European countries. Therefore, South-Eastern Europe needs to start catching up on Chinese culture, including films, literature, sports, and entertainment.

Establishing a 16+1 CEEC and China Global Partnership Centre based in Sofia

While meeting Premier Li in the afternoon of July 6, 2018 during the 7th 16+1 Summit in Sofia, Bulgarian President Radev proposed establishing a research centre based in Sofia, in order to study the planning and find win-win conditions between EU policy and "16+1 cooperation" platform.[1] Chinese Premier Li welcomed its founding and said that such a research hub is an important way to link "16+1 cooperation" with EU laws and regulations, and that it could not only help to "dispel doubts and confusion" to the outside world, but also provide advisory reports to the "16+1 cooperation" mechanism, targeting and discussing all aspects of any problem

---

[1] President Rumen Radev and the Prime Minister of the People's Republic of China Li Keqiang Discussed the Establishment in Sofia of a Center for Coordinating Joint Projects and the Norms between the EU and China. 6 July 2018. At: https://www.president.bg/news4513/tsentar-za-koordinirane-na-obshtite-proekti-i-na-normite-mezhdu-es-i-kitay-da-bade-izgraden-v-sofiya-obsadiha-prezidentat-rumen-radev-i-ministar-predsedatelyat-na-knr-li-katsyan.html, 14.7.2018.

that arises.[1] An agreement on the establishment of the CEEC and China Global Partnership Centre was later finalised between the Chinese Premier Li Ke Qiang and the Bulgarian Prime minister Borisov.[2]

2019 marks the 70th anniversary of the establishment of diplomatic relations between China and Bulgaria

Last, but not least, it should also be noted that next year – 2nd October 2019 marks the 70th anniversary of the establishment of diplomatic relations between China and Bulgaria – the second country in the world to recognize New China. We should take this anniversary as an opportunity to strengthen traditional friendship and advance more steadily not only bilateral relations, but also activate relations throughout the whole Balkan region, further enhance mutual trust, provide new impetus to promote in-depth development of "16+1 cooperation", and usher in a new era of cooperation between China and Central-and-Eastern Europe.

1　http://www.gov.cn/premier/2018-07/07/content_5304429.htm, 2018.7.15.
2　GLOBAL PARTNERSHIP CENTRE OF CEECS AND CHINA WAS AGREED BY PRIME MINISTERS BOYKO BORISSOV AND LI KEQIANG. 07.07.2018. At: http://www.government.bg/en/Press-center/News/GLOBAL-PARTNERSHIP-CENTRE-OF-CEECS-AND-CHINA-WAS-AGREED-BY-PRIME-MINISTERS-BOYKO-BORISSOV-AND-LI-KEQIANG, 14.7.2018.

文化资源匹配中国的新发展理念——"一带一路"倡议：欧亚大陆共赢合作的契机

奥勒·德林 【德国】
柏林自由大学汉学和中国研究教授

一、文化背景

几个世纪以来，欧亚大陆被人为地分割成彼此隔离的领土。随着科技和思想的流动，人类的创新和合作势头让全人类受益。在全球化的第三个阶段，国家、民族和意识形态认同的文化构建导致出现新的、持久的边界。如今，中亚地区所谓的"伟大的游戏"肇始后两个世纪，是时候纠正这一路线，为欧亚大陆的繁荣开辟新的道路。我们是否应该考虑进入西方探险家在"同一"的名义下热心征服世界和塑造一切打开的大门？

考虑到经济是"适当内政管理"的扩展，当我们采取经济全球化方法时，也可以探索其他方法，例如人文全球化。经济是一种整体性的治理方法，包含可持续性、公平和合作等内涵，具有社会价值文化，利用劳动者的表达创造力、社会交易、科学（认识）、伦理道德和法律，最终达到和平的目标。在这一概念性的方法下，外部边界不起作用，因为价值源自人类的基本贡献。

这种经过深思熟虑的实用方法可以培养合作精神，释放创造性的人文主义资源，从而全面阻止意识形态和单边主义。此外，哲学思想构成欧亚大陆古典人文的骨架，从雅典到曲阜，从魏玛到岳麓，从康德到孔子。凭借最初的指称，为了理解和规定极端混乱状态下的可持续人类关系结构，古典的社会凝聚力编织模式以能力作为经线，人文作为纬线将人类联结起来。

二、创新的叙事

当今世界人口远远多于过去，人类拥有无限的潜能。我们的当务之急是克服仍然存在于伟大叙事中的帝国殖民主义思想观念和组织框架，从赫尔德到魏源，从拉迪亚德·吉卜林到康有为，从施本格勒到严复等，他们在继续限制当前世界人类进步的选择。

毫无疑问，在人类的经典模式中没有任何形式的对抗、剥削、歧视、排斥、社会达尔文主义或种族主义，这些在人类中没有任何根基。人类经典是对其历史背景的表达，虽然可能存在模糊不清，但不能否认其主要观点和成就，也就是说，对我们引入真理、美好和善良的前景和呼吁提供强大的叙事。

人类拥有共同理念和人类历史上的丰富经验，为全球化创造适当的发展条件。对于欧洲而言，我们的任务是诚实地修正文化偏见和有缺陷的自我观念，克服在非理性的亲近中国和恐惧中国之间摇摆的节奏。

为了自身利益的最佳选择，我们必须重新审视取代长期单一中心和文化叙事主导地位的文化多样化选项，以便根据当前和未来世代的需要正确表达和转换价值。另一方面，在探索明德价值的基础上成功地构建真正无偏见的"格物致知"方法后，中国将推动这一伟大事业。

三、中国发起的游戏：谁来加入？

如今，通过中国及时提出的"一带一路"倡议，至少将为欧亚大陆国家的健康发展提供新的动力。广阔的地区保持开放并不是一件坏事。例如，尤其是必要的"软"监管和多样的社会适用条款没有在硬基础设施、安全和金融的战略关注下给予积极的定义。物有本末，事有终始，知所先后，则近道矣。显然，在指挥家的舞台上仍然有空缺的席位，使得监管体系的设计以及终极精神和目标的确定仍然处于灰色地带——只要尝试有益于人类生活向着高品质的方向发展，这种情况是可以接受的。

因此，卫生、教育、职业和社会保障体系等基础部门的共同发展仍然有待定义和塑造。首先，最重要的是澄清实现跨文化的理论基础，消除合作方向和合法性方面的分歧。对于西欧而言，将自身在这些领域的信念和既有优势转化为文化适应性矩阵，既是机遇也是挑战。通过学习和纠正内在的概念和历史上的缺陷可以获益。中国需要对欧洲保有耐心，因为欧洲没有迎接全球化的挑战可持续的资源（如在人文科学方面），特别是在接受重大变革的机会方面。具有讽刺意味的是，如今的欧洲长期受到亚洲简化的、物质的、商业和技术营销策略便利带来的困扰。尽管欧洲为了企业的利益制定大量监管制度，甚至在教育和文化领域，还未能适当关注为全人类开创开放和建设性发展道路的人文资源和框架。

这是深入、务实、深思熟虑和精心策划的合作战略。经历多个世纪的分隔、疏离和动荡后，欧亚大陆文化开始重新找回尊严，设计出一种全新的"游戏"，本着适当参与的精神在联合过程中设定目标、策略和规则。显然，欧洲仍需要采取循序渐进和持续相互学习的方法实现和谐共处，确保人类以义为利。

最后，我们需要克服后殖民时代的单一文化，尤其是采取嵌入形式。实现这一点尤为困难，因为：（1）中国已经进入一个至今尚未明确的混合文化状态，由于对其文化遗产的不确定性，可能会传递不适合的规范性概念；（2）欧洲对可持续文化多样性的错误观念已根深蒂固，倾向于在宏大的叙事中重复单一模式，但实际上仅适用于中观而不是宏观扩展。欧洲仍在构成东西方鸿沟的跨大西洋保护范围内保持预先设定的态度。对东方立场的不确定性导致维持傲慢自大和僵化胆怯的姿态，结果可能适得其反。

四、文化方面合作的方法论

这些问题也有自身的解决办法，尤其在结合自我批评和给予真诚的尊重时，可以从他人那里学习和共同探索目前未知的一切。理想的出发点可能是（尽管只是假设）适当地引入文化。双方需要尽最大努力真诚地表现自我，并激发好奇心和保持开放性。尽管我们相信自己了解一切，但我们不能期待自己无所不知，或者我们已经足够清楚地说明了自己的方式和意图。当我们为了相互理解和学习而在自身的文化视野中了解多样性的时候，适当的相互联系将成为可能。这是根本的常识，但并非无关紧要。因为在向对方介绍的时候，可能会发生变化。它可以作为指导，为满足我们时代的需要打下坚实的基础。这是可持续和平与合作的基础。

从方法论的角度而言，转化能力必须重新定义基本能力并进行系统梳理，以促进理解与合作。这意味着一种双重方法：首先，通过对经典知识和历史研究的分享重新确认人文学科的视野；其次，如何合理、秉持稳重的团队精神，各方尽最大努力在精心安排的过程解决当今世界面临的共同挑战（例如，欧亚大陆）。

在有关转换问题的概念层面上，分别支配我们视野的伟大叙事结构需要进行最细致的审视。维持理解过程始于转换，也以转换为结尾。我们应该准备好接受探索，如在黑暗中走钢丝。我们可以做到这一点，但不能认为任何事情都是理所当然的。因此，我们可以利用其优势而克服其劣势。例如，错误地将"中"理解为"单一中心"，而不是多元中心的视角，从而模糊了一元论（例如，一神论）和关系目的论（例如儒家）思想层级之间的根本差异；我们甚至无法欣赏和探索某种特定文化财富，更不用说学习或利用理性的分辨和解决矛盾，虽然我们知道自己能做到。在这种特殊情况下，终极与终极的并列反映出文化模式（尤其是语言）中理性的二律背反结构。这为理论化和组织跨文化和跨语言的哲学探索提供了一个宏伟的框架。

在这个世界上最重要资产是：因为它根植于两种活跃的文化，每种文化都包含与另一种文化交往的经验。最明显的是，中国在关于"无极"或"太极"的辩论中，欧洲在神学或亚里士多德的"不动的推动者"争论，而占主导地位的叙事显然是截然不同的。同时，它是经过深思熟虑后对各自传统中引起深入和广泛争议事项的回应。这种配置也出现在社会经济中。在直接积极承诺、法律或道义上的义务以外，将我们如何对他人承担责任视为一种康德式的框架，代表一个人的人性。这与历史上的基督教慈悲或怜悯的不完美感相互呼应，使社会纽带成为转瞬即逝的念头、机会、道德感或审判，而不是社会经济理性，因为对"仁"的主流解释是指集体义务，而不加选择地关注每一个人（兼爱）提供正式的关系承诺，以造福所有人。简单而直接地概括：康德对理性二律背反的回应证明他是一位真正的中国哲学家，而墨子的"兼爱"理念则表明他是一位真正的德国社会经济伦理学家（参见"Solidarität"）。

五、项目框架确定

这一概念框架转化为涵盖经济、科技、社会稳定与安全等各个领域，在各个层面上的组织和监管实践潜在策略。相对于其他合作主体，"一带一路"的欧亚大陆部分是我们限定的学习和合作范围。如果我们接受正义与和平作为指导目标，那么适当的全球化意味着采用"全球在地化"的方法。这种方法克服传统的文化相对论与文化统一论的传统对抗，这两种理论都受到关系自我中心和多边殖民的支配。它接受先验（非活跃、语义前的）理性基本规律作为一种规章启发，将仪式化或教条式的确信转变为程序化的逻辑（目的论）。简单概括："全球在地化"作为一种方法，要求我们从渐进比对的视角对组织规范进行情境化和重新评估，保持品质缺陷的产生，并以此作为激励因素使其变得更好。

作为全球参与者，中国在战略上运用并根据其他文化背景进一步发展自身的知识基础，同时努力适应可以受益的重要方面。中国目前正有效地进入自我依赖的阶段，而且在越来越多的关键领域领先，尤其是科技领域。值得注意的是，系统相关管理能力的根本进步，例如，生产质量控制（即医学/生物科技等）、环境可持续能力、尖端的信息科技和人工智能开发，在国际上被完全忽视或低估。然而，想象一下，在三个战略目标领域，中国和欧洲都无法独自实现可能和期望的利益，但通过共同努力和资源可以取得成功。

欧亚大陆全局完善：所有的相关经济交易应结合起来，以在公正的居住环境中回归健康本源。这适用于个人和家庭在工作场所、公共和私人领域降低健康风险、健康行为教育以及获得必要的最佳医疗保健和健康防护。欧亚大陆地域广阔，方便需要综合治理制度的各种物质流动，例如，伴随着非法买卖路线的复兴，预防和早期应对大规模流行病。在适当的"全球在地化"组织框架下，完善的市场价值和社会效益将随着时间的流逝而逐渐融合并累积，为所有人维持美好生活的前景。作为支撑的人类学应在关系和非简化主义健康决定因素方面予以澄清。这将严重影响传统经济中从致病产品或行为中获利的几个领域。欧亚大陆足够广阔，可以作为一个充满活力的实验和学习场所，为当世楷模。

欧亚大陆全面团结：团结是一个抽象的概念，它让所有人有义务去照顾陌生人。在组建社会和卫生健康系统时，原则上没有任何边界。照顾他人是一种额外的利益策略，首先不支持自我考虑的风险计算，但不是不利效益计算，原则上是德国团结的一部分：因此，受益人不会想要进入自身有权受益的状态。没有人希望生病或依赖他人。该运作设定采用审慎的默认模式，能够让他人受益，自身也能受益于他人，尤其是除了抽象的社会经济体系之外没有任何生活联系的人。在社会经济价值与劳动力组织结构之间存在有力的联系。通过团结的概念，中国和欧洲可以在不沦为"发展援助"框架的情况下，激发和鼓励实现可持续社会经济和互助的本地化模式。因此，生活、工作和业务的品质随着时间的流逝而逐渐融合并累积。

欧亚大陆全体：人口结构、职业领域、系统需求的多样性以及欧亚社会开放视野的原始动机价值可以有机地结合，从而在教育、劳工组织和流动性方面加强边界以内和跨边界的人力资源战略发展。也就是说，老龄化社会与孤儿社会之间的失衡可以通过跨边界的合作，提升价值螺旋（双赢）而使所有人受益。另一方面，欧洲需要对中国在治理或信息技术/人工智能社会价值应用方面的进步给予建设性的回应，允许"丝绸之路"沿线受影响的社会进行模式试验。多样性应作为资源加以利用，调动和提升人口尊严，增加工作产生的价值。人的价值可以在各个国家之间融合并随着时间的流逝而累积，不是仅以商品和有形物质服务于单一的市场，而是支持贡献的多样性。

当我们迈出第一步克服文化主义的关注和既定的仪式时，就可以实现这一进步。我们将超越对"东方"或"西方"的错误期待、偏见和恐惧，避免通过不合理的推理导致歪曲。这要求我们将逐渐落下的功课补上。为了实现理智的政策，我们需要哲学、转换能力、健全制度和基础设施。当我们将当前状态与跨大西洋连接现有基础设施的丰富程度进行比较时，我们将获知巨大的动力。这一行动越早开始越好。

六、实践的意义

这将最终形成全球多边和跨区域合作的真正全球化和务实的表观殖民理解。这与"愚蠢的经济"无关，而是人文的经济，与商业无关，而是将公平正义作为家庭、国家和整个世界受益的通用规则：以义为齐家国治天下平。

整个欧亚大陆将携手进行社会、经济、文化和科学创新，这是人类真正希望的源泉。当前，中国的发展正在推动这一趋势。让我们鼓励欧洲也跟着效仿，同时我们将重新审视这些变化。

Aligning Cultural Resources with China's New Developmental Philosophy: The "Belt and Road" as an Opportunity for Win-Win Cooperations Across Eurasia

Ole Doering / Germany

Professor of Freie Universität Berlin/Academic Department Advisor & visiting professor of the Hong Kong Polytechnic University

Culture History

Over centuries, Eurasia had been artificially divided into isolated realms. Just when mobility of technologies and minds could have benefitted humanity with an innovative and collaborative momentum of human ingenuity, during the third phase of globalization[1], cultural constructions of national, ethnic and ideological identities erected new, lasting frontiers. Now, two centuries after the beginning of what was

---

[1] Eurasia-perspectives on globalization comprise first antiquity-civilic imperialism, second, medieval-mercantile imperialism, third industrialized imperialism and 4th promethean imperialism, after 1989 began what may in retrospect become the turning point for humanistic globalization; the term globalization as coined by Naisbitt, Megatrends, 1982, is historically and structurally biased. Therefore, the term will be used here only in an broad, pragmatic and inclusive sense.

euphemistically coined, the "Great Game" in Central Asia[1], it is time to correct that course and open a new avenue towards prosperity, across Eurasia. Shall we consider entering the gate that Western explorers passed by in their zeal to conquer the world and shape all under the image of the One?

Potential for some other kind of, humanistic globalization, can be explored, when we take an economic approach, considering that, *economy* is the widest extension of "proper housekeeping". Economy is, a holistic application of governance. It embraces sustainability, justice and cooperation, it harbors cultures of social value, and employs the value from labour in expressive creativity, social transactions, science (epistemics), ethics and law, in order to furnish a realm of peace. Within this conceptual approach, external borders play no role, because value is derived from elementary contributions of human beings.

Such a deliberated pragmatic focus will foster a spirit of collaboration and liberate resources of creative humanism, in a comprehensive sense, keeping ideologies and unilateralism at bay. Moreover, these philosophies form the humanistic backbone of the classics across Eurasia, between Athens and Qufu, Weimar and Yuelu, Kant and Confucius. By virtue of their original designation, to understand and prescribe the structure of sustainable human relations under conditions of ultimate chaos, these classical weaving patterns of social coherence connect us as threads with competence and cord with humaneness.

Narratives for Innovation

The world is now populated as never before, with human potential in abundance. It is imperative and overdue for us, to surmount the mindsets and organizational frames of imperial colonialism that still permeate our great narratives, from Herder or Wei Yuan, Rudyard Kipling or Kang Youwei, Oswald Spengler or Yan Fu, and

---

[1] Ironically, as a figure of speech regarding the rivalry of European political powers over dominion in Central Asia, the "Great Game", was initially rendered an advance humanitarianism, albeit, notably, as "the noble part that the first Christian nation of the world ought to fill", that is, in a peculiar skewed truncated notion of "humanism", in 1840.

many others, as they continue to limit our options for human advancement within the present world.

There should be no doubt about it: in the classical canons of humanity, there is no room, for confrontation, exploitation, discrimination, exclusion, social darwinism or racism, in any form and on any grounds among people. It is true that our classics have been expressions of their historical setting, but these could only blur, not negate their major points and achievements, that is, to provide powerful narratives on our ways to introducing truth, beauty and goodness as a prospect and call, beyond phenotypical boundaries.

We own a robust, universal framework and a host of experience from human histories, to build proper developmental conditions for globalization. For Europe, this implies the task, to honestly revise culturalistic prejudice and flawed self-conception, overcoming the rigor that fueled the pacemaker of the irrational pendulum between Sino-philia and Sino-phobia.

It is in our own best interest, to revisit the options within the cultural diversity that preceded the long phase of dominance of mono-centric and culturalistic narratives, so as to capture and translate its value according to the needs of our times and future generations. On the other hand, China will help this cause when it succeeds in building a truly unbiased, that is, scientifically (in the sense of 格物致知[1]) grounded approach in exploring the value of her genuine enlightenment (明德) tradition, which has been buried among the rubble of ill-advised iconoclasm and the ignorance of well-meaning Western instructors.

China Plays – Who Joins?

Now, with its new Silk Road strategy, China has set in motion a timely initiative that may very well unfold dynamics towards a wholesome development for, at least, the Eurasian countries, with obvious implications for 天下. It is not a downside,

---

1   The original Chinese technical terms used in this paper are taken from the 大学 in the version of the 礼记 and as interpreted in my own research.

that large areas of details of application are left open, because this is a sketch delivered to be worked out. For example and especially, the essential "soft" regulatory and diverse socially applied provisions are not defined in positive terms under this strategic focus, that prudently sets on with the roots, that is, hard infrastructures, security and finances. Notably, there are still vacant seats at the conductors' table, leaving the design of the regulatory system and the determination of the ultimate spirit and purpose in the grey - this situation could be tolerated for as long as the tentative direction supports development of the quality of human livelihood.

Therefore, foundational sectors remain open to be defined and moulded, such as the co-development of health-education-vocational and social security systems. First and foremost, trans-cultural rationales for solidarity need to be clarified, so as to disambiguate the direction and legitimacy of the entire venture. Here lie both, the opportunity and the challenge for Western Europe, to translate her very own convictions and established strengths in these areas into a culturally adaptive matrix. To benefit from learning and correction of intrinsic, conceptual and historical flaws. The Chinese part will be asked for patience, because Europe has not maintained the resources (such as in the humanities) to cater for a globalized challenges, especially to appreciate opportunities for serious change. Ironically, Europe now suffers from the long period of convenience of a reduced, materialistic, commercial and technological marketing strategy in Asia. While it initiated much of the regulatory systems in order to benefit European business interests, even in the areas of education and culture, it failed to pay due attention to the proportional development of humanistic resources and frameworks that would enable open and constructive developmental paths for all.

This is an opportunity for deep, pragmatic, well considered and orchestrated collaborative strategies. Eurasian cultures can reclaim their dignity, after centuries of separation, alienation and turmoil, to devise a decidedly new "game", with purpose, strategy and rules set up in joint processes in a spirit of due participation.

It will obviously take a step-by-step and continued mutual learning approach, to get along, and integrity to make sure we stay on the course of benefit from justice.

Eventually, it means to overcome the post-colonial monocultures, especially in their embedded forms. This is genuinely difficult because, (a) China has acquired an as yet unexplained hybrid culture state that might transport ill-suited normative notions while being uncertain about her cultural heritage, and, (b) Europe has consolidated a misconception of sustainable diversity of cultures, with a propensity to reiterate monological patterns in the great narratives, that are indeed only fitted for meso-, not macro-extensions. Europe still entertains attitudes pre-shaped under the transatlantic protective sphere of the East-West divide. Uncertainty in the position watching East has sustained a self-defeating posture of arrogance and sclerotic timidity.

Methodology for Collaborative Cultures

However, these problems also bear recipes for their own resolution, especially when combined with honest self-critical reflection and genuine respect, for all the yet unknown that one might learn from, and together with, the other. The ideal starting point could be, rather simply albeit hypothetically, to stage a proper introduction of cultures, as if it were the first encounter. To bring on curiosity and openness, from both sides, to perform sincerely at their best. We cannot expect that we know anything just about the other, or that we have explained our ways and intentions clearly enough, in spite of all we believe that we understand. Proper interrelation is possible, when we muster what we have learned within our cultural horizons about diversity, in order to understand one another, and learn from them. This is common knowledge, deeply embedded but not trivial. Because it changes when expressed to the other side in terms of self-introduction. It can be used as guidance to work out a solid basis for the needs of our times. There lies the matrix for sustainable peace and collaboration.

Methodologically, translational capabilities must be redefined as fundamental and addressed systematically in order to facilitate understanding and cooperation. This implies a twofold methodology: one, to reconfirm the horizons of our humanities by sharing the study of our classical knowledge and history; and two, to address shared challenges of this our present world (such as with Eurasia), together wherever it makes sense, in a deliberated team spirit, as each does what each can best, in a well orchestrated process.

On the conceptual level of the relevant translational issues, the structural patterns of the great narratives governing our horizons, respectively, will require most delicate scrutiny. Translation is the beginning and the end of understanding as an continued process. We should be prepared to operate walking on a tightrope in the dark. We can do it but cannot take anything for granted. Thus we can learn expressly from implicit patterns, use their strengths and overcome their weaknesses. Such as, misreading zhong as substantive mono-"center", instead of a perspectively pluralist centrality, blurs the fundamental differences between a monological (e.g. monotheist) and relational-teleologic (e.g. Confucian) order of thinking; we cannot even begin to appreciate and explore the wealth of each particular culture, let alone learn, or use our common reason in order to clarify and console such contradictions, as we know we can. In this particular case, the juxtaposition of ultimates versus ultimate reflects the antinomic structure of reason in cultural patterns, especially as in languages. This makes for a grand framework to theorize and organize cross-cultural and trans lingual philosophical explorations.

The most remarkable asset within this constellation is: because it is rooted in two living cultures, each includes a history of experiences in dealing with the other. China had it, most expressly, in the debate over "无极" or "太极", Europe in theological arguments or Aristoteles' "unmoved mover" - whereas the dominant narrative is quite clearly distinct, it is, at the same time, a deliberate response to a deep and broad controversy within the respective tradition. This configuration also appears in social economy. Considering, how it is that we owe to others beyond immediate positive commitment, legal or moral obligations to oneself and the other, describes a Kantian framework, as representing humanity in one's person. This echoes a sense of imperfection within a history of Christian charity or pity leaving social bonding to whim, chance, moral sense or verdict, instead of social-economic reason, as the mainstream interpretation of 仁 refers to in-group obligations, while indiscriminate concern for each human being (jian ai 兼爱) offers a formal relational commitment for the benefit of each and all[1]. To put it in an outrageously simple nutshell: the Kantian response to the Antinomies of Reason[2] prove him to be a true Chinese philosopher, whereas Mo Di's concept of jian ai shows that he is a genuinely German social-economic ethicist (cf. "Solidarität").

Framing Projects

This conceptual framework translates into potential strategies for organizational and regulatory practice on all levels, covering areas of economy, science and technology, social stability and security. Consider the Eurasia-part of the "Belt and Road" as a circumscribed sphere for learning and collaboration, among collaborating agents. Proper globalization implies a GLocal methodology approach, if we accept that justice and peace should guide our purposes. This figure of deliberation overcomes the traditional confrontation of cultural relativism versus cultural uniformity, of both, relational-self-centered and multilateral-colonial, dominions. It accepts transzendental (non-positive, pre-semantic) fundamental laws of reason as a regulative heuristic and transforms ritualized or dogmatic certainties with a procedural logic (teleology). In a nutshell: the GLocal approach, as a method, requires that we contextualize and re-evaluate the organizational code, in a progressive alignment perspective, in order to keep the quality deficits productive, as motivators to make it better.

As a global player, China strategically applies and further develops its

---

1 Carine Defoort 2008. "The Profit That Does Not Profit: Paradoxes with 'Li' in Early Chinese Texts." Asia Major 21.1: 153–181.
2 Immanuel Kant, Critique of Pure Reason: "Als bloße Erscheinung kann die Welt weder ein an sich unendliches noch ein an sich endliches Ganzes sein, da sie nur «im empirischen Regressus der Reihe der Erscheinungen», nicht als abgeschlossene Totalität gegeben ist."

knowledge base from other cultural contexts while trying to adapt what matters in terms of benefit. China is now effectively entering the stage of self-reliance or even leadership in an increasing number of key areas, especially in science and technology. Notably, the underlying advancement of system-relevant administrative competences, such as in production quality control (i.e. in medicine / biotech), or of environmental sustainability or of cutting-edge IT- and AI developments, have gone largely unnoticed or underrated internationally. Imagine, however, three strategic target areas where neither China nor Europe can mobilize the possible and desired benefit adequately on their own, but can succeed when orchestrating efforts and resources.

Global Health Eur-Asia : All relevant economic transactions should be combined, so that they contribute to the salutogenesis of a just habitat. This applies to, reduction of exposure to health risks, education of health sustaining behaviour, access to best available needed health care and health protection for individuals, families, at the workplace, in public and private domains. It recognizes Eurasia as one vast zone for migrating biro-substances of all kinds that require a comprehensive governance system, e.g., for prevention of and early response to pandemics alongside the revitalized trafficking routes. Within a properly GLocalised organizational framework, the *market value and social benefit of health converge and cumulate over time* and sustain prospects of a good life for all. The underlying anthropologies should be clarified in terms of relational and non-reductionist determinants of health. This will bear heavily on several areas of traditional economies that generate profit from pathogenic products or behaviour. Eurasia is vast enough to become a vibrant field for experiments and learning, as a model for the world.

Global Solidarity Eur-Asia: Solidarity is an abstract concept that obliges all to care for those they do not feel connected with. When organizing the constitution of a social and health care system, in principle no borders apply (though they maintain a strong role in governing their provisional constituencies). The primacy of caring for the other as an added benefit strategy will not support a self-regarding Risk Calculation, but, rather an Adverse Benefit Calculation, as it is part of Germany's solidarity fund (in principle): accordingly, the beneficiary will not want to get into a situation in which he is entitled to receive the benefit. No one wants to fall ill or become dependent. This operational setting employs a prudential default mode, to be able to benefit others and from others, especially those with whom there is no living connection except for the abstract social-economic system[1]. Here lies a powerful connection between social-economic value and the organizational fabric of labour. Through the concept of solidarity, China with Europe can inspire and encourage localized models for sustainable social economy and mutual assistance, without degenerating into a frame of "development aid". Accordingly, *quality of life, work and business converge and cumulate over time.*

Global Humanity Eur-Asia: Diversity of demographic compositions, vocational profiles, systemic needs and the raw motivational value of open horizons for development in Eurasian societies can be organized so as to deliberately strengthen the strategic development of a pool of human resources, within and across borders, in terms of education, labour organization and mobility. Namely the imbalance between aging and orphan societies can benefit all through cross-boundary-collaboration, in upscaling value spirals (win-win-win). On the other hand, Europe needs to respond constructively to China's advances in the governance or social value applications of IT/AI technologies, allowing for experimental model trials along the "Silk Route" by co-opting the affected societies. These diversities should be approached as resources, mobilizing and dignifying populations, and adding to the value-generation of the work. *Human value can converge across nations and cumulate over time*, not to serve one monolithic market, with commodities and material goods only, but to support diversity of contributions.

This advancement can be achieved when we take first steps to overcome

---

[1] With this definition, my approach to solidarity expressly rejects the similarity based approaches dominating current mainstream, such as: Nuffield Report, "Solidarity: reflections on an emerging concept in bioethics", 2012: http://nuffieldbioethics.org/report/solidarity-2/definition-of-solidarity/ .

culturalistic preoccupations and established rituals. We grow beyond wrong expectations, biases and fears, regarding "East" or "West", that effect failure not as much as misrepresentation, through unsound reasoning. This demands from us, neither more nor less than, to catch up with overdue homework. Philosophy, translational capabilities, institutional infrastructures are needed in order to inform sensible policies. When we compare the present state with the wealth of infrastructures in place for transatlantic connectivity, we get an idea about the enormity of the charge. Better, to start early.

Imperative of Practice

Eventually, a truly globalized, pragmatic epi-colonial[1] understanding of multi-lateral global and trans-regional cooperations can take shape. It is, not about "the economy, stupid", but humane economy (οἰκονομία), not about business, but: to employ justice as the general rule to benefit households, countries and the world as one.

Joining hands across Eurasia, for social, economic, cultural and scientific innovation, is a source of genuine hope for humanity. Currently, China's development is driving the momentum. Let's encourage Europe to follow suit, while we revisit the terms together.

---

1 Epi stands for being constitutionally embedded in a greater context, as in epi-genetics.

哈中产能合作关系发展

纳比坚·穆哈穆德罕 【哈萨克斯坦】
哈萨克斯坦阿里—法拉比国立大学当代中国研究中心主任 / 东方学系汉学教研室主任

哈萨克斯坦和中国合作关系中的产能合作，是两国战略伙伴关系新阶段的显著成果，且具有发展前景的合作领域和具有示范效应的合作模式，也是颇为值得关注和研究的一大课题。

一、哈中两国产能合作关系的建立

自从 1992 年哈萨克斯坦和中国建立外交关系以来，两国间各个领域的友好合作关系呈现出逐渐拓展和提升态势。2002 年哈中两国建立了睦邻友好合作关系，2005 年建立了战略伙伴关系，2011 年提升为全面战略伙伴关系。

2013 年 9 月，中国国家主席习近平首次访问中亚国家时，在哈萨克斯坦共和国提出用创新的合作模式，共同建设"丝绸之路经济带"国际倡议，不仅具有划时代的意义，亦有历史和现实地缘政治经济意义。因而哈萨克斯坦共和国立即回应了中国倡议，并于同年 11 月 11 日纳扎尔巴耶夫总统在 2014 年度国情咨文中提出了"光明之路——通往未来之路"的新经济政策，旨在促进经济结构转型、强力推动经济增长。"光明之路"新经济政策把发展交通运输基础设施、发展工业基础设施、发展能源基础设施和发展公共基础设施作为优先发展项目。因而，哈萨克斯坦的未来发展计划直接与中国倡议衔接起来了，实现了哈中两国在"一带一路"框架下的"政策沟通",使两国关系提升至新的历史高度,并为两国在产能领域的合作创造了政策基础。从此《哈中两国开始探讨产能合作》。

由于"政策沟通",两国高层更加频繁互动,在"一带一路"框架下签订了一系列的合作协议,并逐个着手实施。

2014年12月,中国总理李克强访问哈萨克斯坦共和国,两国政府签署了总额达140亿美元的30多项合作协议,《关于共同推进丝绸之路经济带建设的备忘录》,并就价值180亿美元的哈中合作框架协议达成共识。两国初步确定16个早期收获项目和63个前景项目清单,涉及水泥、钢铁、平板玻璃、矿业、化工、能源、电力等领域。

2015年3月,哈萨克斯坦共和国总理马西莫夫访华期间,两国签署加强产能与投资合作备忘录,并签署钢铁、炼油、水电、汽车、有色金属、平板玻璃等总金额为236亿美元的产能合作协议。2015年12月,哈中两国总理签署《哈萨克斯坦共和国和中华人民共和国政府联合公报》,提出《尽快启动"丝绸之路经济带,建设与光明之路"新经济政策对接规划联合编制工作》。

2015年8月31日,哈国总统纳扎尔巴耶夫访华期间,哈中两国元首签署《哈萨克斯坦共和国和中华人民共和国关于全面战略伙伴关系新阶段的联合宣言》和加强产能与投资合作政府间框架协议。表明了两国发展战略的对接。由此为中国与外国签订的首个产能合作协议。

为保证协议落实,中国还建立部门间工作机制,同时设立产能合作基金,其中确定51个项目,并签订了总金额230亿美元的25项协议。汽车组装、聚丙烯项目、阿斯塔纳市轻轨项目已开工,而钢铁、冶炼、水泥等领域十余个项目正在启动之中。

二、哈中两国产能合作关系的发展

2016年9月2日哈中两国政府签署《哈萨克斯坦共和国和中华人民共和国政府关于"丝绸之路经济带"建设与"光明之路"新经济政策对接合作规划》。该《规划》提出,在交通基础领域,加强基础设施互联互通合作,继续积极推动中国—哈萨克斯坦—西亚、中国—哈萨克斯坦—俄罗斯—西欧和中国—哈萨克斯坦—南高加索—土耳其—欧洲交通建设,优化中方西北边疆至东南沿海一线交通基础设施,提高双方公路、铁路运输能力,为新亚欧大陆桥经济走廊建设夯实基础。因此，哈国总统纳扎尔巴耶夫在 2017 年度国情咨文中，敦促政府优先实施哈中签署的合作项目。

2017 年 5 月在北京召开"一带一路"高峰会议上，哈萨克斯坦总统纳扎尔巴耶夫发表讲话，他认为："'一带一路'项目的付诸实施，必将使丝路沿线国家，其中包括中亚地区，将获得以崭新的发展模式而著称于世界的良好机遇"。他称赞"光明之路"和"一带一路"衔接而取得的成就，并建议下一步在"科技创新领域深度合作"。这是他为推进在该年度国情咨文中提出的发展科技、教育创新，增强国民竞争力政策而提出的具体建议。这表明，哈国总统有着在科技创新领域和中国深度合作的意愿。

哈萨克斯坦驻华大使努雷舍夫说："哈萨克斯坦与中国在落实'一带一路'倡议的重要组成部分——'丝绸之路经济带'的问题上保持着密切协作。目前，我们与中方在产能合作领域共同实施 51 个总价值达 260 亿美元的项目。我相信，这些计划的成功实施不仅将推动哈萨克斯坦的发展，还将推动整个地区的发展。"

哈中在产能合作方面已经取得显著成果，在铁路核电等优势装备和钢铁、有色金属、建材等产能方面有长足的发展。阿克托盖 25 万吨 / 年铜选矿厂、巴甫洛达尔州 25 万吨 / 年电解铝厂、里海 100 万吨 / 年沥青厂、梅纳拉尔 3000 吨 / 日水泥厂等 34 个项目已竣工投产；阿斯塔纳首条全部采用中国标准的全自动化无人驾驶的城市轻轨、阿拉木图钢化玻璃厂及 10 万吨大口径螺旋焊钢管厂、北哈州农产品加工企业，阿特劳炼油厂石油深加工项目、库斯塔奈江淮汽车组装企业等 43 个项目正在实施之中。

由此可见，自从哈中两国战略伙伴关系进入新发展阶段以来，两国在产能领域的合作呈现出深度发展态势。这就说明中国在新的国际形势下提出的合作共赢新理念，已被哈国所认同和积极回应，从而"光明之路"新经济政策与"一带一路"构想衔接，从而推动了两国产能合作关系的拓展和提升。所以哈国总统纳扎尔巴耶夫曾说："从外资和贷款数额以及合资企业数量方面看，中华人民共和国成为哈国的主要经济伙伴之一"。中国驻哈萨克斯坦大使张汉晖谈道："在'一带一路'框架下，哈中开展了 50 多项产能合作，合作总金额达 270 亿美元，不少项目已经完成并投入使用。"

以上事实说明，哈萨克斯坦是"一带一路"和"光明之路"契合上进行产能合作并取得丰硕成果。这在中亚地区具有一定的示范效应。

三、哈中产能合作关系的发展前景

哈中两国在产能合作的发展前景非常宽阔。因为哈中产业分工和资源禀赋上存在着极大的互补性，特别是哈中两国在基础设施及加工制造业方面的产能合作具有巨大潜力。哈萨克斯坦是以石油工业为支柱的，能源、农牧产品出口的中亚大国，又是积极推行工业化、信息化、经济多元化的国家，所以目前哈国所迫切需要的是资金和技术。而中国是拥有雄厚资金和技术的国家，而且其基础设施建设基本饱和，钢铁、水泥、电力、电解铝等大宗产品均出现产能过剩。所以中国迫切需要产能转移。这种经济上的互补性为哈中两国产能合作奠定了坚实的基础。

从政策上而言，中共总书记习近平在十九大报告中指出："中国坚持对外开放的基本国策，坚持打开国门搞建设，积极促进'一带一路'国际合作，努力实现'政策沟通、设施联通、贸易畅通、资金融通、民心相通'，打造国际合作新平台，增添共同发展新动力"。因此可以说，中国将继续推进"一带一路"建设。哈萨克斯坦认为"中国提出'一带一路'国际倡议为哈萨克斯坦乃至中亚国家提供新的发展机遇"。所以哈萨克斯坦共和国和中国在共同的国家利益基础上将会继续积极进行合作。两国的产能合作必将不仅推动哈萨克斯坦经济摆脱能源出口依赖，而且促进哈萨克斯坦工业化进程，提高哈国经济竞争力，有利于增加就业，改善民生。从近年来国际关系的变化趋势来看，哈中合作领域将会更加深度发展。

2014 年 12 月举行的哈中产能合作对话中，双方确立了合作原则，即"政府引导、企业对接、务实合作、互利共赢"。哈中两国本着这个互利共赢原则进行携手合作。"合作共赢"理念已成为当今中国奉行的新型国际关系原则，也是中国发展对外合作关系的新原则。合作共赢的外交理念，对世界各国的发展，对实现人类的和平发展，深化国际交往和合作，都具有十分重要的意义，因而赢得国际社会的广泛认同和赞许。这一理念和外交原则顺应了时代潮流。实践证明，任何一个共同发展、共同受益的国际倡议和项目都会被国际社会所接受、所认同，如果它有足够的实力和诚意引领各国实现其社会经济发展的话。

到目前为止，哈中两国在"一带一路"框架下，以"合作共赢"为基本原则的产能合作已经取得丰硕成果，促进了哈萨克斯坦社会经济的发展。哈中两国在产能合作等领域将会更加长足的发展。

哈中两国元首对双方合作已经取得的成果均加以肯定。哈萨克斯坦总统纳扎尔巴耶夫于 2018 年 6 月 7 至 8 日对中国进行国事访问，同中国国家主席习近平举行会谈，并签署《中华人民共和国和哈萨克斯坦共和国联合声明》，在声明的第二条中"双方高度评价中哈共建'一带一路'合作取得的丰硕成果，上述合作对推动双边关系发展具有重要意义。双方指出，中国建设'丝绸之路经济带'倡议和哈萨克斯坦'光明之路'新经济政策对接合作意义重大，并将本着开放、透明的精神，促进两国各个领域合作发展"。

中国总理李克强在与纳扎尔巴耶夫的会谈中指出，近年来，中哈合作取得一系列开创性成果，特别是产能合作的深入推进取得积极成果。希望双方进一步加强基础设施建设、能源、资源等领域产能合作，扩大农产品贸易、金融等合作。共同促进贸易投资与人员往来便利化，推动两国产业提质升级。加强在上海合作组织框架内的协调配合，以更多务实合作成果造福本地区国家和人民。

纳扎尔巴耶夫总统表示，哈方重视对华关系。两国各领域合作成果丰硕，经贸合作不断迈上新台阶，是互利共赢的典范。哈方是"一带一路"建设的重要伙伴，愿加强同中方发展战略对接，推进在工业、投资、创新、农业、能源、金融等各领域务实合作。

由此可以说，哈中产能合作必将会向全方位、深层次、多领域发展。希望哈中两国政府在将来的合作中更多地重视"民心相通"，营造适合于深度合作的人文环境。

参考文献

1.《哈萨克斯坦独立报》(《Egemen Kazakhstan》)，2014 年 11 月 11 日。

2. 王志民：《"一带一路"背景下中哈产能合作及其溢出效应》，《东北亚论坛》，2017 年第 1 期。

3. 哈萨克斯坦《明报》-Aikhen, 2015 年 8 月 30 日。

4.http://www.akorda.kz/kz/addresses/addresses_of_president/memleket-basshysy-nnazarbaevtyn-kazakstan-halkyna-zholdauy-2017-zhylgy-31-kantar

5. 纳扎尔巴耶夫：《使中亚焕然一新的倡议》,《明报》(Aikynbao)，2017 年 5 月 16 日，第 1 页。

6. 努雷舍夫：《"光明大道"与"一带一路"积极对接将打造合作典范》。2017 年 05 月 12 日 02:11 每日经济新闻 http://finance.sina.com.cn/roll/2017-05-12/docifyfecvz1021606.shtml.

7. 纳扎尔巴耶夫：«Aikynbao»(明报)，2017 年 5 月 16 日，第 1 页。

8.（http://kz.chineseembassy.org/chn/zhgx/t1568148.htm）

https://baike.baidu.com/item/%E4%BA%A7%E8%83%BD%E5%90%88%E4%BD%9C/17012573

9. 王志民：《"一带一路"背景下中哈产能合作及其溢出效应》，《东北亚论坛》，2017 年第一期，第 45 页。

10. 习近平：《中国共产党第十九次全国代表大会上的报告（2017 年 10 月 18 日）》，人民出版社，2017 年。

11. 纳扎尔巴耶夫：Қытай–жаңамүмкіндіктеркөзі.«Turkistanbao»,2015,09,03.;ОрталықАзияныжаңатұрпаттатаныстыруғамүмкіндікберетінбастама.«Aikynbao».-2017,05,16.

12. http://kz.chineseembassy.org/chn/zhgx/t1568148.htm。

Development of the Cooperation Between Kazakhstan and China on Production Capacity

Nabizhan Muhametkhanuly / Kazakhstan

Head of the Department of Sinology, Director of the Centre of Modern Chinese Studies, Al-Farabi Kazakh National University

The cooperation between Kazakhstan and China on production capacity is a remarkable achievement in the new stage of the strategic partnership between the two countries. Due to the sectors of cooperation with prospects for development and the model of cooperation with demonstration effects, it is a topic that is worthy of attention and research.

I. The establishment of cooperation between Kazakhstan and China on production capacity

Since the establishment of diplomatic relations between Kazakhstan and China in 1992, the two countries' friendly cooperation in various sectors has been reflecting a trend of expansion. Kazakhstan and China established good-neighborly relations and friendly cooperation in 2002, a strategic partnership in 2005 and a comprehensive strategic partnership in 2011.

In September 2013, when Chinese President Xi Jinping visited Central Asian countries for the first time, he put forward the international initiative in the Republic of Kazakhstan that advocated "jointly building the 'Silk Road Economic Belt' with an innovative model of cooperation", which was epoch-making and of historical and realistic geopolitical and economic significance. Therefore, the Republic of Kazakhstan immediately responded to the Chinese initiative. On November 11, President Nazarbayev proposed the new economic policy of "The Road to Brightness — The Road to the Future" in the State of the Union Address for 2014, aiming to facilitate economic restructuring and promote economic growth. The new economic policy of the "Road to Brightness" prioritizes the development of transportation infrastructure, industrial infrastructure, energy infrastructure and public infrastructure. Therefore, Kazakhstan's future plan of development is directly linked to the Chinese initiative and realizes the "policy coordination" of Kazakhstan and China under the Belt and Road framework so that the bilateral relations of the two countries are elevated to a new historical height and provide the basis for the policy for cooperation on production capacity. Since then, China and Kazakhstan have begun to discuss this cooperation.

For the purpose of "policy coordination", the top leaders of the two countries have interacted more frequently, have signed a series of cooperation agreements under the framework of the Belt and Road and have implemented them one by one.

In December 2014, Chinese Premier Li Keqiang visited the Republic of Kazakhstan. The two governments signed more than 30 cooperation agreements totaling 14 billion US dollars and the *Memorandum of Understanding on Jointly Promoting the Construction of the Silk Road Economic Belt,* and reached a consensus on the Kazakhstan-China agreement for a framework of cooperation with a value of 18 billion US dollars. The two countries initially identified 16 early harvest projects and 63 prospective projects, covering cement, steel, flat glass, mining, chemicals, energy, electricity and other sectors.

During the visit to China by Prime Minister Masimov of the Republic of Kazakhstan in March 2015, the two countries signed the memorandum of understanding on strengthening their cooperation on production capacity and investment, as well as cooperation agreements with a total value of 23.6 billion US dollars for steel, oil refining, hydropower, vehicles, non-ferrous metals and flat glass. In December 2015, the Prime Ministers of Kazakhstan and China signed *the Joint Communiqué of the Government of the Republic of Kazakhstan and the Government of the People's Republic of China and proposed* "to launch the joint plan for connecting the construction of the 'Silk Road Economic Belt' and the new economic policy of the 'Road to Brightness'".

On August 31, 2015, during the visit to China by Kazakh President Nursultan Nazarbayev, the leaders of Kazakhstan and China signed the *Joint Declaration on the New Stage of a Comprehensive Strategic Partnership between the People's Republic of China and the Republic of Kazakhstan* and the intergovernmental framework agreement on strengthening cooperation on production capacity and investments. This meant that the developmental strategies of the two countries were integrated, and it was the first agreement on cooperation on production capacity signed between China and a foreign country.

In order to ensure the implementation of the agreement, China also established an inter-departmental working mechanism and set up a capacity cooperation fund. A total of 51 projects were determined and 25 agreements were signed for a total amount of 23 billion US dollars. The projects have already commenced, such as vehicle assembly, polypropylene project and light rail project of Astana, and more than ten projects in steel, smelting, cement and other sectors are about to be launched.

II. Development of the cooperation between Kazakhstan and China on production capacity

On September 2, 2016, the governments of Kazakhstan and China signed the

Cooperation Plan for the Coordination of the Construction of the "Silk Road Economic Belt" and the New Economic Policy of the "Road to Brightness" between the Government of the Republic of Kazakhstan and the Government of the People's Republic of China. The Plan proposed to strengthen the connectivity and cooperation regarding infrastructure in the basic transportation sector, to actively promote the traffic build-up of the China-Kazakhstan-West Asia, the China-Kazakhstan-Russia-Western Europe and the China-Kazakhstan-South Caucasus-Turkey-Europe transportation ways, to optimize transportation infrastructure from the northwest frontier to the southeast coast of China, enhance the road and railway transportation capacity of both sides, and lay a solid foundation for the construction of the new Eurasian Land Bridge Economic Corridor. Therefore, President Nazarbayev of Kazakhstan urged his government to give priority to the implementation of cooperation projects signed by Kazakhstan and China in the State of the Union address for 2017.

At the summit of the Belt and Road held in Beijing in May 2017, President Nazarbayev of Kazakhstan delivered a speech. He thought that the implementation of the Belt and Road would surely bring well-known good opportunities to countries along the Silk Road, including Central Asia, with a new developmental model. He praised the achievements of connecting the "Road to Brightness" and the "Belt and Road" and made suggestions for in-depth cooperation in the field of scientific and technological innovation in the next step. These were suggestions for the development of science and technology, educational innovations and national competitiveness proposed by our president in the State of the Union address for this year. It revealed that the President of Kazakhstan is willing to cooperate in depth with China on technological innovations.

Nuryshev, Kazakhstan's ambassador to China, pointed out that "Kazakhstan and China maintain close cooperation on the issue of the 'Silk Road Economic Belt', an important part of the Belt and Road Initiative. At present, we are working together with China on 51 projects for a total value of 26 billion US dollars in cooperation on production capacity. I believe that the successful implementation of these plans will promote not only the development of Kazakhstan, but also that of the entire region."

Kazakhstan and China have achieved remarkable results in their cooperation on production capacity, and have made great progress in advantageous equipment such as railway and nuclear power and in their capacity for the production of steel, non-ferrous metals and building materials. A total of 34 projects, such as Aktogay copper mines, with a capacity of 250,000 tons/year, the Pavlodar electrolytic aluminum plant of 250,000 tons/year, the Caspian asphalt plant with 1 million tons/year, the Menalar cement plant with 3,000 tons/day, have been completed and put into production; 43 projects are ongoing, inclusive of the first fully automated unmanned urban light railway adopting the Chinese standards in Astana, a tempered glass factory and a large-diameter spiral welded steel pipe factory with the capacity of 100,000 tons in Almaty, companies for the processing of agricultural products in the North Kazakhstan region, an oil refinery and a deep processing project in Atyrau and the Jianghuai automobile assembly plant in Kostanay.

Thus, since the strategic partnership between Kazakhstan and China entered a new stage of development, the cooperation between the two countries in production capacity has shown a trend of profound development. This means that China's new concept of cooperation and win-win results under the new international situation has been recognized and positively responded to by Kazakhstan, and the connection of the new economic policy of the "Road to Brightness" and the Belt and Road Initiative has expanded and upgraded the cooperation of the two countries on production capacity. Therefore, President Nazarbayev of Kazakhstan once said that: "The People's Republic of China has become one of the major economic partners of Kazakhstan in terms of the amount of foreign capital and loans and the number of joint ventures". Zhang Hanhui, the Chinese ambassador to Kazakhstan, pointed out that: "Under the framework of the Belt and Road, China and Kazakhstan have carried out more than 50 projects of cooperation on capacity with a total amount of

27 billion US dollars. Many projects have been completed and put into use".

The above facts indicate that Kazakhstan has achieved fruitful results in the cooperation on production capacity by connecting the "Belt and Road" and the "Road to Brightness". This has a certain demonstration effect in Central Asia.

III. Prospects for the cooperation between Kazakhstan and China on production capacity

The cooperation between Kazakhstan and China on production capacity has very broad developmental prospects because there is great complementarity between Kazakhstan's industrial sectors and resource endowments and those of China, especially the great potential for cooperation on production capacity in infrastructure, processing and manufacturing. Kazakhstan is a large Central Asian country with the petroleum industry as the pillar and exports of energy, agriculture and animal husbandry products. It also actively promotes industrialization, informationization and economic diversification. Therefore, what Kazakhstan urgently needs is capital and technology. China has powerful capital and technology and its construction of infrastructure is basically saturated. Major products such as steel, cement, electricity and electrolytic aluminum are subject to overcapacity. Accordingly, China urgently needs a capacity transfer. This economic complementarity has laid a solid foundation for cooperation between Kazakhstan and China on production capacity.

From the perspective of policies, General Secretary Xi Jinping pointed out in the report of the 19th CPC National Congress that: "China adheres to the fundamental national policy of opening-up and pursues development with its doors open wide. China will actively promote international cooperation through the Belt and Road Initiative. In doing so, we hope to achieve policy, infrastructure, trade, financial, and people-to-people connectivity and thus build a new platform for international cooperation to create new drivers of shared development." Therefore, it can be said that China will continue to promote the construction of the Belt and Road.

Kazakhstan believes that "the Belt and Road Initiative proposed by China can provide new developmental opportunities for Kazakhstan and even for Central Asian countries". The Republic of Kazakhstan and China will continue to cooperate actively on the basis of common national interests. The cooperation between the two countries on production capacity will certainly not only unleash the Kazakhstan economy from the dependence on energy exports, but it will also promote the process of industrialization in Kazakhstan, improve the economic competitiveness of Kazakhstan, and be conducive to increasing employment and improving the livelihood of its people. According to the changing trend of international relations in recent years, the cooperation between Kazakhstan and China will be further developed.

In the China-Kazakhstan Production Capacity Cooperation Dialogue held in December 2014, the two sides established the principles of cooperation, namely, "Government Guidance, Enterprise Matching, Pragmatic Cooperation, Mutual Benefit and Win-Win Results". Kazakhstan and China are working together under these principles of mutual benefit and win-win results. The concept of "win-win cooperation" has become the new principle of international relations pursued by China today and a new principle for China in developing foreign cooperative relations. The diplomatic concept of win-win cooperation is of great significance to the development of all countries in the world, to the peaceful development of mankind, and to deepening international exchanges and cooperation, thus earning wide recognition and praise from the international community. This concept and diplomatic principle is consistent with the trend of the times. Practice has proved that any international initiative and project that develops and benefits all will be accepted and recognized by the international community if it has sufficient power and sincerity to lead other countries to achieve their socio-economic development.

So far, under the framework of the Belt and Road, Kazakhstan and China have achieved fruitful cooperation in cooperation on production capacity based on the principle of "win-win cooperation", which promotes the social and economic development of Kazakhstan. Kazakhstan and China will make more progress in that cooperation.

The leaders of Kazakhstan and China have recognized the results of the cooperation between the two sides. Kazakh President Nursultan Nazarbayev paid a state visit to China from June 7 to 8, 2018, held talks with Chinese President Xi Jinping and signed the *Joint Statement between the People's Republic of China and the Republic of Kazakhstan*. In the second section, "The two sides speak highly of fruitful results achieved in the joint construction of the Belt and Road through China-Kazakhstan cooperation. Cooperation is of great significance for the development of bilateral relations. The two sides point out that it is significant to connect China's initiative for the 'Silk Road Economic Belt' and Kazakhstan's new economic policy of the 'Road to Brightness' and will promote cooperation and development in various fields with an open and transparent spirit."

In the talks with Nazarbayev, Chinese Premier Li Keqiang pointed out that in recent years, China-Kazakhstan cooperation has made a series of groundbreaking achievements, particularly the positive results of the in-depth promotion of cooperation on production capacity. He expressed the hope that both sides could further strengthen their cooperation on production capacity in the construction of infrastructures, energy and resources, and expand cooperation on the trade and financing of agricultural products. Both sides should jointly facilitate trade with and communication among people, promote industrial upgrading in both countries, strengthen coordination and cooperation within the framework of the Shanghai Cooperation Organization, and benefit more countries and people in the region with more pragmatic cooperation results.

President Nazarbayev said that Kazakhstan attached great importance to the relations with China. The cooperation between the two countries in various sectors has yielded fruitful results, and the economic and trade cooperation have continuously advanced to new levels, thus becoming a model for mutual benefit and win-win results. Kazakhstan, an important partner for the construction of the Belt and Road, was willing to strengthen strategic integration with China and encourage pragmatic cooperation in sectors such as industry, investment, innovation, agriculture, energy and finance.

In summary, the cooperation between Kazakhstan and China on production capacity will surely develop in all directions, in depth and in many sectors. It is hoped that the governments of Kazakhstan and China will pay more attention to the "people-to-people bond" in their future cooperation and create a humanistic environment suitable for deep cooperation.

"一带一路"倡议与韩国中国学的新前景

金铉哲 【韩国】
韩国延世大学中国研究院院长 / 孔子学院院长、中文教授

前言

"一带一路"倡议不是突然从习近平政府开始的。"大国崛起"及"和谐社会"是其前兆。不论是政治还是文化,要想进入某一地区,首要条件就是"路"。2000多年前,秦国为了进入蜀地,惠王制定策略,开辟了一条被称为"金牛道"的道路。这代表着21世纪这个远大而充满野心的计划,其实是中国政府在很久以前就开始着手准备的。

"一带一路"以"路"为基本,这条路上创造历史的则是"人"。因此在"One Belt"和"One Road"这两个单词里,一定会赋予人文学领域的意义。不论经济还是政治,都和人文有着不可分割的联系。"一带一路"倡议看起来是经济用语,但是它比任何一个词语更具有政治性、战略性,而且也更具有人文性。

习近平主席所说的"人文"主要是指"一带一路"框架下这条路线上的国家和民族间的"人的交流"。但这要建立在政治和经济不与人文分开的认识基础之上。他们所说的"一带一路",涉及的"人文",是指人类社会的所有文化现象,包括科学技术、教育、文化、卫生、观光、新闻、出版、学术交流和民族间的民间文化交流等各种领域。似乎对人文的范围设定得相当广泛,但推动政治和经济发展的动力还是来源于人,所以"一带一路"倡议便成为人文学界的重要研究对象。

现在的"一带一路"倡议起源于怀抱巨大野心的一群人，他们要把不只是欧亚大陆，而且非洲大陆等地区在时间和空间上捆绑在一起。因此，"一带一路"倡议的人文学分析要聚焦在时间、空间以及"人"和"路"上。基于这一点，韩国中国研究学方面，也要把焦点放在日后如何创新之"路"上。

一、"丝绸之路"与"海上丝绸之路"的时空坐标，以及那些"人们"

1. 丝绸之路

"丝绸之路"一词来源于德国地理学家李希霍芬（Fridrich Von Richthofen，1833-1905）所著《中国——亲身旅行的成果和以之为根据的研究》第一册中的"Seidenstraβe"。尽管李希霍芬作为"丝绸之路"的命名者已家喻户晓，但大家并不知道他曾七次探访中国，留下了大量关于中国地理、地形、地貌等领域的资料。

西欧学者所指的丝绸之路最初主要指的是"绿洲"。第二次世界大战以后，"丝绸之路"的概念有所延伸，包含了"草原之路"和"海洋之路"，从而含有"三大干线"之意。

目前，中国政府推进"一带一路"建设，也是对"丝绸之路"概念的进一步延伸。

《史记》中的《大宛列传》（123卷）、《匈奴列传》（110卷），《汉书》中的《张骞李广列传》（61卷）和《西域传》（96卷），都记载了汉武帝时期和匈奴的往来。汉人张骞和匈奴的甘夫保持着密切的联系，时间长达13年，这具有跨时代的象征意义。由此看来，从汉朝起，丝绸之路就开始展现其包容、融合的特征。

在载入史册前，最先进行来往的必定是"人"。我们需要铭记，在"和亲"政策下，远嫁到乌孙的汉朝"和亲公主"解忧和随行冯嫽等人，克服重重困难，为促进汉朝和乌孙之间关系做出了重要的贡献。

事实上，匈奴要比汉朝更早涉足西域的商业。匈奴从汉景帝起就开放"关市"，使得汉朝生产的物品和牲畜产品可以进行交易。据《汉书》和《后汉书·西域传》的记载，在天山山脉北部、帕米尔高原西部、兴都库什山脉南部有多个国家进行过商业活动，匈奴从商业中获得的利益也足以成为日后发展强大军力的经济基础。

一方面，法显的《佛国记》、玄奘的《大唐西域记》，以及慧超的《往五天竺国传》也是重要的基本史料。值得一提的是，《佛国记》是自张骞以后，访问过当地的人留下的记录,可以说是十分珍贵的资料。法显离开西域时已年过花甲,当地人民无不感动。看来,可能促使法显去往西域的决定性原因,是一种对知识的好奇心——"想要知道更加准确的佛经内容"。

到了唐代,文成公主远嫁吐蕃后,出现了途径西藏和尼泊尔前往印度的人们,但是相比陆路,越来越多的人选择通过海路前往印度。唐太宗对于"佛法"并不关心,而更关注崛起的突厥势力所在的西域地区的动态。玄奘知道传播佛法还是需要唐太宗的支持,他了解唐太宗的意图,因此撰写了《大唐西域记》。

之后的宋元时期,海上丝绸之路更加活跃,陆上丝绸之路逐渐冷清。之后陆上丝绸之路上又屡发战乱,加上人口的流失,曾经的繁荣景象从大陆转移到了海上。20世纪初,位于塔克拉玛干沙漠中的绿洲王国,虽然历经了500年沧桑历史,逐渐被人遗忘,却又重新恢复了原貌。

"去了就不想再回来",究竟那片沙漠有什么魅力吸引着人们?只是出于对于文物的渴望吗?我们不能说包括张骞、法显、玄奘等人没有任何私心和贪欲,但是显而易见,是对于消失的绿洲王国的好奇心,让他们拼死踏入炎热的沙漠之中。

根据张骞、法显和玄奘留下的记录,我们发现,这条路承载的最重要的人文意义,在于世界观的扩张。他们曾来往的这条路也许很久之前就已存在。

那些克服逆境,来往于"路"上的"人们"创造了多样的"融合"。在这种"融合"的过程中,丝绸之路即是"战争之路",也是"文明融合之路"。正因为那些不屈不挠的人们对路那边的另一个世界充满了开拓进取的精神,才有了这条路。这也是我们要时刻铭记这条路上的那些"人们"的理由。

2. 海上丝绸之路

"海上丝绸之路"这一概念的出现要比"陆上丝绸之路"略晚。沙畹(Chavannes)指出"丝绸之路分为海上和路上两条路线。北线经由康居出境,南线则是一条经由印度各港口的海路。"之后,1968年日本学者三杉隆敏便开始使用"海上丝绸之路"这一用语。三杉隆敏还提到"海上丝绸之路"是在航海技术发达后形成的,从时间上来看,它的出现要比"陆上丝绸之路"晚,并在宋代以后得到了快速发展。另外,三上次南也提到在菲律宾到埃及沿途地区发现了中国的陶瓷器,因此他把那条路称为"陶瓷之路"。

海路和陆路一样,起着十分重要的作用,从9世纪到10世纪期间,曾有大量的阿拉伯、印度大型商船抵达广州、泉州、明州和杭州等地。

实际上，不同的人对这条路线有不同的叫法。好比有些人把"陆上丝绸之路"称为"白银之路"或者"玉石之路"一样，"海上丝绸之路"也有"陶瓷之路"、"香料之路"和"琉璃之路"等各种各样的名字。学者们根据来往于这条路的商品种类，把这条路称为"蜀布之路""茶叶之路"和"贝币之路"等。

通过古代文献资料，我们可以知道之所以把"海上丝绸之路"看做是连接亚欧的贸易之路，不只因为它是"传统学说"，而是因为所谓的"路"是以网状形式相互连接而成，所以使得不同的文化圈相互融合从而得到共同进步发展，从这个开放的角度来说，站在整个地球的角度来看"海上丝绸之路"，可以说是对其进行更宏观地评价。

从这一观点来看，"海上丝绸之路"的东边海路把中国、朝鲜和日本连接起来，便是合乎情理的事情了。不仅是因为唐代时便存在从大阪难波途径渤海和新罗到达唐的海路，以及存在从九州到中国东海岸扬州的路线，也是因为统一新罗和高丽时期，也和中国东岸城市有很多的贸易往来。在中国有关"海上丝绸之路"论文开头也是大同小异，即"海上丝绸之路"的第一条路线，也就是通往朝鲜和日本的"东海航路"。

唐代中期随着陆上丝绸之路的中断，朝廷开始实行海上贸易的开放政策。因此南海航路和东海航路日益发达，东海航路是经由润州、常州、苏州、杭州和明州到达朝鲜和日本的航路。据《宋史·高丽传》记载，高丽使臣曾出使宋国 38 次，宋国信使也曾出使高丽 15 次。信使们来回时的必备物品就是丝绸。

现在中国再次提到海上丝绸之路，这里中国表明的立场就是，中国作为亚洲强国，并不会对邻国进行侵略或者进行帝国主义式的掠夺，而是友好地发展贸易通商关系，共同踏上繁荣富强之路。

这一点则是建立在与东南亚等周边国家维持友好关系基础之上的。为此，中国不仅着力于贸易和投资，同时也特别强调东盟（ASEAN）间的人才交流。"海上丝绸之路"还是要以"人"为本。

二、"一带一路"倡议的时空坐标

"一带一路"倡议的空间范围可以划分为以下几个方面

1. "一带（丝绸之路经济带）"路线

① 中国→俄罗斯和中亚→欧洲（波罗的海）：草原路的扩展

② 中国→中亚→西亚→波斯和地中海：绿洲之路

③ 中国→东南亚→南亚→印度洋：南方丝绸之路

2. "南方丝绸之路"路线

① 灵关道（旄牛道，西道）

蜀（成都）→临邛（邛崃）→灵关（芦山）→笮都（汉源）→邛都（西昌）→青蛉（大姚）→大勃弄（祥云）→叶榆（大理）

② 五尺道（中道）

蜀（成都）→僰道（宜宾）→朱提（云南省昭通）→味县（曲靖）→滇（昆明）→安宁→楚雄→叶榆（大理）

（此外还有两条路，一条是从安宁南下经建水和元江，然后顺着红河入海，另一条是从大理北上经丽江、中甸，最后进入西藏）

③ 牂柯道（东道）

这是一条从成都往东的路线，途经贵州省西北地区，穿过广西广东到达南海。也称为"夜郎道"。

④ 永昌道

前文介绍的三条道中，灵关道和五尺道相交的地方就是大理。大理曾是从印度到中国的重要关口所在城市，现在也是一个留有印度文化元素的地方。

实际上，20世纪80年代就有人主张要秉承"和而不同"的精神，把承载着历史文化的丝绸之路重建为经济协作地带，90年代曹孝通主张开通"南方丝绸之路"，实现"大西南的工业化和现代化"。费孝通引用"你中有我，我中有你"的口号，创造了"多民族一体"的概念，这一条路线就适用于这个概念。"21世纪海上丝绸之路"的基本理念，是不同文化和文明之间的交流与共同利益，这也正反映了中共中央提出的"人类命运共同体"这一观念。

"一带一路"虽然是在古代丝绸之路的基础上提出的，但是超出了丝绸之路的领域，扩大了空间范围。这里包含着三个"超越"的意义，即思维模式中的时代性、先进性和开拓性。"一带一路"倡议不同于"一带"和"一路"，二者同时兴盛即海陆同盛。特别是它摒弃了长久以来秉持的"重陆地，轻海洋"的观念，而重视陆地的同时也重视海洋，这一点具有十分重要的意义，而把世界各地的不同民族联系在一起形成"命运共同体"的这一观念，更是别具特色。所谓的开拓性则是指"不追求霸权，而超越种族、信仰和文化，共同追求利益，不管是邻国还是远在非洲大陆的人们"。

与此同时，新提出的"一带一路"倡议要把"文明空间和心理空间"连接起来。从中国的周边国到全世界的海洋、陆地和天空等所有实际空间，要通过基础建设把这些都连接起来，通过微盘等互联网虚拟空间使它们连接得更加紧密。

在这里韩国起着至关重要的作用，韩国研究中国学的历史已有数千年，通过此期间的各种交流，就可以看出中韩两国的"文明空间"和"心理空间"是可以融为一体的，我认为通过这一点就可以把开放、包容、平等和协作等"现代人文主义精神"发扬光大，另外，汉字文化圈文明要相互借鉴，把世界各国各民族"可持续发展，永远和谐共生"设定为目标。

如果说中国"一带一路"倡议蕴含着"儒家思想的包容精神"，那便是"己所不欲，勿施于人"的精神。正如他们所说，为了让"一带一路"倡议成为"互尊互信，合作共赢，文明互鉴之路"，最重要的依然是丝绸之路途径的各小国之间的信任。

三、结论——"一带一路"和韩国中国学具有的人文意义

"一带一路"倡议里，韩国中国学研究所具有的意义，不只是单纯人才资源的交流。应该更加倾力关注，以医疗、观光、体育和科学技术等各领域的人才交流为中心，同时关注通过互联网平台和大众媒体进行的文化交流和文化产业。但是只有这些还是不够的。所谓"人文"的意义，如果只是单纯的"人的交流"是很危险的。这是因为为了达到经济目的和政治目的，而把人文当作手段，使其带有堕落的危险性。

人类在很久以前，就很关注"丝绸之路"那边的另一个世界。因为好奇心和热情，人类永无止境地移动着。在移动的过程中，人类开创道路，沿着道路，创造历史。并且产生各种文明。不同文明之间，有时发生冲突，有时融合，就这样发展到了今天。只要人类拥有欲望，文明不是任何时候都能共存的。文明的冲突是有理由的。任何时候都有发生冲突的潜在可能性的就是文明。况且是在不同性质的宗教、习俗和意识形态并存的"一带一路"上，则更是如此。因此"丝绸之路"作为"一带一路"的基础，对这条有着历史意义和文明史意义的古老的道路更要倾力关注。不论在意识形态方面还是在生态学方面，人类正站在一个十字路口。要认真思考"一带一路"倡议，如何才能真正地为人类历史做出贡献？随着

互联网的快速发展,在文明均质化问题令人担忧的这一时期,不同性质的事物原样保存,并相互认同将成为真正共存的起点。

中国通过"中国梦"和世界梦,要在国际舞台上致力于构建和平、发展、合作共赢的"中国梦"。向世人展现"兼济天下"的大国责任感,谱写合作,共赢的人类社会新篇章。

东逝的江水流往宽广的太平洋,现在太平洋不是排他、冲突和纷争,而是要充满包容、合作与和平。纵使青山阻挡,江水依旧流向大海,这个江水就是"中国梦",世界梦。而且这必然将成为"一带一路"倡议的最终目标。

The "Belt and Road" and New Prospects for Chinese Studies in Republic of Korea

Kim Hyun Cheol / Republic of Korea

Dean of China Research Institute, Dean of the Confucius Institute, Professor of Yonsei University

1. Introduction

The Belt and Road Initiative was not suddenly proposed by the Xi Jinping government. "The Rise of the Great Powers" and the "Harmonious Society" are its precursors. "Road" is the precondition for entering a region either politically or culturally. More than 2,000 years ago, in order to enter Shu state, King Hui built a road known as the "Golden Bull Road" (Jinniudao). This ambitious plan of the 21st century was actually prepared by the Chinese government a long time ago.

The Belt and Road is based on a "road", but the "people" on the road can make history. Therefore, the words "One Belt" and "One Road" will be definitely given specific meanings in culture. Both economics and politics are inextricably linked to culture. The "Belt and Road" seems to be an economic term, but it is more political, strategic and cultural than any other term.

The "culture" proposed by President Xi Jinping mainly refers to the "communication of people" in countries and ethnic groups along the route of the Belt and Road. But this is based on the understanding that politics and economy are not separated from culture. The "culture" they refer to in the Belt and Road means all cultural phenomena in human society, including science, education, culture, health, tourism, journalism, publishing, academic exchanges and folk cultural exchanges. It seems that the scope of culture is quite broad, but the driving force for political and economic development still comes from the people, so the Belt and Road has become an important object of research.

The current Belt and Road originates from a group of people with great ambitions. They want to bundle not only Eurasia, but also the African continent into time and space. Therefore, the cultural analysis of the Belt and Road should focus on time, space, "people" and "roads". At this point, Chinese studies in South Korea should also focus on the "road" of innovation in the future.

2. The space-time coordinates of the Silk Road and the Maritime Silk Road, as well as those of "people"

(1) The Silk Road

The term "Silk Road" originated from "Seidenstraβe" in the first volume of *China: Ergebnisse eigner Reisen und darauf gegründeter Studien* (China: The Results of My Travels and the Studies Based Thereon) written by Ferdinand von Richthofen (1833-1905), a German geographer. Although Richthofen has become a household name for the term "Silk Road", no one knows that he visited China seven times and left large amounts of information about China's geography, topography and landforms.

The Silk Road referred to by Western European scholars was originally an "oasis". After the Second World War, the concept of the "Silk Road" was extended, including the "Prairie Road" and the "Ocean Road", thus containing the meaning of "three branch routes".

At present, the Chinese government's promotion of the construction of the Belt and Road is also a further extension of the concept of "Silk Road".

In the "The Account of Dayuan" (Volume 123) and "The Account of the Xiongnu" (Volume 110) of the *Records of the Grand Historian* and "Zhang Qian and Li Guangli" (Volume 61) and "Traditions of the Western Regions" (Volume 96) of *The Book of Han*, there are records on the interaction between the Emperor Wu and the Xiongnu. Zhang Qian, a member of the Han Chinese, who kept close contact with Ganfu of the Xiongnu for 13 years, which had a symbolic significance across the times. Therefore, since the Han Dynasty, the Silk Road has shown its inclusive and integrated features.

Before going down in history, the interaction began first with the "people". We need to remember "Princess Jieyou", married Wusun, and her attendant Feng Liao, who overcame many difficulties and made important contributions to promoting the relationship between the Han Dynasty and Wusun.

In fact, the Xiongnu traded with the Western Regions earlier than the Han Dynasty. The Xiongnu opened the "market" in the period of the Emperor Jing of Han so that the produce of the Han Dynasty could be traded with livestock products. According to records in The Book of Han and The Book of Later Han · Western Regions, the Xiongnu traded with countries in the northern part of the Tianshan Mountains, in the western part of the Pamirs, in the southern part of the Hindu Kush and reaped commercial benefits that laid the economic foundation for its strong military power later.

On the one hand, Faxian's Record of Buddhist Kingdoms, Xuanzang's Great Tang Records on the Western Regions and Huichao's Memoir of the Pilgrimage to the Five Regions of India are also important basic historical materials. It is worth mentioning that the Record of Buddhist Kingdoms was a record of visiting local people after Zhang Qian, so it provided very precious information. When Faxian left the Western Regions, he was more than sixty years ago, and the local people were all moved. It seemed that the fundamental reason that Faxian had gone to the Western Regions was his curiosity about knowledge — "I want to know more accurate Buddhist scriptures".

In the Tang Dynasty, after Princess Wencheng married Tubo, there were people who passed through Tibet and Nepal and went to India, but compared with the land route, more and more people chose to travel to India by sea. Emperor Taizong of Tang did not care about the "Dharma" but paid more attention to the situation of the rising Turki forces in the Western Regions. Xuanzang knew that Buddhism still needed the support of Emperor Taizong. He understood the intentions of Emperor Taizong and wrote the Great Tang Records on the Western Regions.

Later in the Song and the Yuan Dynasties, the Maritime Silk Road was more active, and the Land Silk Road gradually became deserted. Afterward, there were wars along the Land Silk Road, and plus the loss of population, the once prosperous scene was transferred from land to sea. At the beginning of the 20th century, the oasis kingdom in the Taklimakan Desert, after five centuries of vicissitudes, was gradually forgotten, but it was restored to its original appearance.

"If you go there, you won't want to come back." What charm did the desert have to attract people? Just out of the thirst for artifacts? We couldn't say that Zhang Qian, Faxian and Xuanzang had no selfishness and greed, but it was obvious that they stepped into the hot desert due to their curiosity about the disappearing oasis kingdom.

According to the records left by Zhang Qian, Faxian and Xuanzang, we find that the most important cultural significance of this road lies in the expansion of the world view. The road they used to travel on may have existed a long time ago.

Those who overcame the adversity and traveled to and from on the "road" created a variety of "integrations". In this process of "integration", the Silk Road was the "road of war" and the "road of civilization integration." It was because those indomitable people who were full of a pioneering spirit towards the unknown world that we had this road. This is also the reason why we have to remember the "people" on this road.

(2) The Maritime Silk Road

The concept of the "Maritime Silk Road" was proposed later than the "Land Silk Road". Chavannes pointed out that the Silk Road was divided into two routes, sea and land. The northern route leaves China through Kangju, and the southern route is a sea route passing through various ports in India. In 1968, the Japanese scholar Takatoshi Misugi began to use the term "Maritime Silk Road". He also mentioned that the Maritime Silk Road came into being after the development of navigation technology. In terms of time, it appeared later than the Land Silk Roa and developed rapidly after the Song Dynasty. Moreover, another Japanese scholar also mentioned that China's ceramics were discovered along the way from the Philippines to Egypt, so he called the road the "Ceramic Road".

Like the Land Silk Road, the Maritime Silk Road also played a very important role. From the 9th century to the 10th century, a great number of large Arab and Indian merchant ships arrived in Guangzhou, Quanzhou, Mingzhou and Hangzhou.

In fact, different people have different names for this route. For example, some people refer to the "Land Silk Road" as the "Silver Road" or the "Jade Road". The "Maritime Silk Road" is also known by a variety of names, such as the "Ceramic Road", the "Spice Road" and the "Glass Road". According to the types of goods traded via this road, scholars refer to it as the "Road of Shu Clothing", the "Road of Tea" and the "Road of Currency".

Through ancient literature, we have learned that the "Maritime Silk Road" is seen as a trading route connecting Asia and Europe, not only because it is a "traditional doctrine" but because the so-called "road" is connected in the form of networks. Different cultural circles are integrated with each other to achieve common progress and development. In terms of opening-up, the "Maritime Silk Road" can be evaluated more macroscopically from the perspective of the whole earth.

At this point, it is reasonable to link China, North Korea and Japan to the eastern sea route through the "Maritime Silk Road" because there was not only a sea route from Namba, Osaka through the Bohai Sea and Silla to Tang, but also a route from Kyushu to Yangzhou on the east coast of China and an increasing amount of trading with eastern coastal cities of China by Silla and Goryeo. The research papers on the Maritime Silk Road in China also mentioned that the first route of the Maritime Silk Road was the "East Sea Route" leading to North Korea and Japan.

In the middle of the Tang Dynasty, with the interruption of the Land Silk Road, the government began to adopt the policy of opening up to maritime trade. Therefore, the South China Sea route and the East China Sea route developed increasingly. The East China Sea route is a route to North Korea and Japan through Runzhou, Changzhou, Suzhou, Hangzhou and Mingzhou. According to The History of Song · Goryeo, the ambassadors from Goryeo went to the Song Dynasty 38 times, and the messengers of the Song Dynasty went to Goryeo 15 times. The essential item for messengers to carry back and forth was silk.

Now China once again mentions the Maritime Silk Road. China's position here is that China, as a great Asian power, will not invade neighboring countries or engage in imperialist plunder, but will develop trade and trade relations amicably and travel together with all the people along the prosperous and strong road.

This is based on maintaining friendly relations with neighboring countries such as those in Southeast Asia. To this end, China not only focuses on trade and investment, but also emphasizes the exchange of talents with the ASEAN community. The Maritime Silk Road still has to be oriented by "people".

3. Time and space coordinates of the Belt and Road

The spatial scope of the Belt and Road can be divided into the following routes:

(1) The Route of the "Belt (Silk Road Economic Belt)"

China→ Russia and Central Asia→ Europe (Baltic Sea): extension of the prairie road

China→ Central Asia→ Western Asia→ Persia and the Mediterranean: The Oasis Road

China→ Southeast Asia→ Southern Asia→ Indian Ocean: South Silk Road

(2) Route of the "South Silk Road"

a) Lingguandao (Maoniudao, West Route)

Shu (Chengdu)→ Linqiong (Qionglai)→ Lingguanc(Lushan)→ Zedu (Hanyuan)→ Qiongdu (Xichang)→ Qingling (Dayao)→ Dabonong (Xiangyun)→ Yeyu (Dali)

b) Wuchidao (Middle Route)

Shu (Chengdu)→ Bodao (Yibin)→ Zhuti (Zhaotong, Yunnan)→ Weixian (Qujing)→ Dian (Kunming)→ Anning → Chuxiong → Yeyu (Dali)

(There are still two routes, one from Anning to the south, passing through Jianshui and Yuanjiang, and going to the sea along the Honghe River, and another from Dali to the north, passing through Lijiang and Zhongdian, finally entering Tibet)

c) Zangkedao (Eastern Route)

This is a route from Chengdu to the east, passing through the northwestern areas of Guizhou Province, going from Guangxi and Guangdong to the South China Sea, also known as "Yelangdao".

d) Yongchangdao

In the three routes, the intersection of Lingguandao and Wuchidao is Dali, which used to be an important gateway from India to China, and is now a city to retain Indian cultural elements.

As a matter of fact, in the 1980s, some people advocated adhering to the spirit of "harmony but not uniformity" and reconstructing the Silk Road with history and culture into an economic cooperation belt. In the 1990s, Cao Xiaotong advocated the reopening of the "South Silk Road" to realize the "industrialization and modernization of the Great Southwest". Cao Xiaotong quoted the slogan "you are among us, and we are among you" to coin the concept of "multi-ethnic integration". This route applies this concept. The basic concept of the "21st Century Maritime Silk Road" is the exchanges and common interests among different cultures and civilizations, which also reflects the concept of the "community with a shared future" proposed by the CPC Central Committee.

Although the Belt and Road Initiative was proposed on the basis of the ancient Silk Road, it is beyond the scope of the Silk Road and contains the three meanings of "transcendence", namely, the nature of the era, the advanced nature and the pioneering nature of the way of thinking. The Belt and Road is different from the common prosperity of "One Belt" and "One Road". In particular, it abandons the long-term idea of "focusing on the land while ignoring the sea", and attaches importance to the land while also paying attention to the sea. This is of great significance. The concept of "community with a shared future" that links different peoples of the world is even more distinctive. The so-called pioneering spirit means "not seeking hegemony, but transcending race, belief and culture, and pursuing common interests, whether they are neighboring countries or remote people in the African continent".

Further, the newly proposed Belt and Road should connect "civilized space and psychological space". From the neighboring countries of China to all the real spaces such as the sea, the land and the sky of the world, it is necessary to link them through infrastructures and connect them more closely through virtual Internet spaces such as microdisks.

South Korea can play a vital role because it has a history of Chinese Studies for thousands of years. Through various exchanges during this period, we can find that the "civilized spaces" and "psychological spaces" of China and South Korea can be merged into one. For my part, this can carry forward the "modern humanistic spirits", such as openness, tolerance, equality and cooperation. Also, the civilizations in the Chinese cultural circle should learn from each other and set "sustainable development and harmonious coexistence" as a goal for all nations and ethnic groups in the world.

If China's Belt and Road policy contains an "inclusive spirit of Confucianism", then it is the spirit of "do unto others as you would have others do unto you". As they pointed out, in order to make the Belt and Road become "the road of mutual respect and trust, cooperation and win-win results, and of mutual learning of civilizations", the most important thing is still to win the trust of small countries along the Silk Road.

4. Conclusions: The cultural significance of the Belt and Road and Chinese Studies in South Korea

In the Belt and Road policy, the importance of the Korean Institute for Chinese Studies lies in not just the exchange of talent resources, but it should pay more attention to the exchanges of talents in various fields such as medical care, tourism, sports, science and technology, as well as cultural exchanges and cultural industries via Internet platforms and mass media. However, these are not enough. It is dangerous to limit the "cultural" significance only to the "communications of people". This is because in order to achieve economic and political purposes, culture is used as a means bearing the risk of corruption.

Humans have been focusing on the unknown world on the other side of the road for a long time ago. Because of curiosity and enthusiasm, humans have been moving forward indefinitely. In the process of moving, humans build roads, go along the roads, make history and create various civilizations. With conflicts among and integration of different civilizations, humans have evolved until today. As long as human beings have desires, civilizations cannot coexist at all times. There are reasons for the clashes of civilizations. Civilizations have the potential for clashing at any time. It is even truer of the Belt and Road along which different religions, customs and ideologies coexist. Therefore, we must pay more attention to this ancient road of historical significance and significance in the history of civilizations because the "Silk Road" is the foundation of the Belt and Road. Humans are standing at a crossroads, both in terms of ideology and ecology. We must take the Belt and Road policy seriously and consider how we can truly contribute to human history. With the rapid development of the Internet, in the period when the issue of homogenization of civilization is worrying, things of different natures being preserved as they are and mutual recognition will become the starting points for real coexistence.

Through the Chinese dream and the world's dream, China is committed to building a peaceful, developing, cooperative and win-win Chinese dream on the international stage, it shows the sense of responsibility of a great power that "commits itself to the world's welfare", and writes a new chapter of cooperation and win-win results for mankind.

Rivers flowing east to the vast Pacific Ocean. Now the Pacific is not exclusive, conflicting and in dispute, but full of tolerance, cooperation and peace. Even if there are obstructions due to mountains, the river still flows to the sea. This river is the Chinese dream, the world's dream. And this will inevitably become the ultimate goal of the Belt and Road.

中国古典诗词译成荷兰语和英语的一些思考：衡量标准、目的、押韵和对仗

伊维德 【荷兰】
哈佛大学东亚语言与文化系荣休教授

  我在荷兰乡村长大，没有任何关于中国语言和文化的背景知识，但却对学习这些情有独钟。1963 年秋，我进入莱顿大学学习，选择中国语言和文化作为我的专业。我在莱顿大学以及后来前往札幌、京都和香港求学期间，当时我还不清楚我最终会将大部分的精力用在阅读和翻译中国古典诗词上：先翻译成荷兰语，然后改写为英语。在我早期的职业生涯，我的兴趣在当代农村社会学和古代白话文学之间摇摆不定。我的第一份工作是担任著名的莱顿大学汉学研究院新成立的当代中国文献研究中心研究员。我主要负责追寻"文化大革命"期间很难了解到的中国社会发展情况。我最早发表的文章关注 20 世纪 60 年代和 70 年代初的教育改革。然而，春季学期开学前的一个周末，本院系教古典中文（文言文）和中国文学的教师意外去世，我不得不放弃当代中国研究领域。周一早上正式授课时，我被要求从那天开始接手他的教学工作。

  在做当代中国研究的整个过程中，我继续大量阅读中国传统白话小说。我喜欢幕后政治阴谋和宫廷冒险的故事，这些与当时政府在对本国国民或外部世界所宣扬的中国社会的官方形象大相径庭。最初我尝试翻译冯梦龙在 1620 年前后收集和发表的小说。这些故事大多采用散文体，但偶尔也掺杂诗词。将这些文字翻译成荷兰语时，为了强调散文和诗词的交替出现，我在翻译中遵循格律和押韵。

可以说我在荷兰语押韵方面有一定的天赋。在课程教学过程中，我还阅读十九世纪所有荷兰诗人的押韵诗来了解押韵，为教学任务做好准备。我甚至阅读数量可观的材料，使我足以成为该领域的专家，并且与一位担任荷兰文学博物馆馆长的诗人好友合作出版两本十九世纪荷兰诗选集。然而，无论是母语天赋，还是刻苦的阅读，对于了解中文诗都没有什么用处。像之前的许多翻译者一样，我发现在绝大多数情况下，如果翻译的诗押韵，我们必须牺牲许多内容，甚至是几乎所有其他形式要素。虽然偶有巧合的押韵，但这种情况非常少见。

我出版的第一部唐代古诗选集（618-906）是寒山的诗，荷兰语书名是 *"Gedichten van de koude berg"*。在中国，寒山的文学地位可能不太高，但他的作品在日本一直很流行。20世纪五六十年代，寒山的诗被多次翻译成英文（从加里·斯奈德的译文开始）、法文和德文。我对寒山的兴趣并不是源起于他的诗，而是他作为白话诗人的声誉，因为我想加深对白话发展历程的认识。自从在优秀日本注解的帮助下开始阅读这些诗，我情不自禁地尝试将一些诗翻译成荷兰语。在成功地将部分诗翻译成荷兰语并至少达到让自己满意的程度后，我就无法停止这项工作，直到翻译了200多首诗。我很幸运能够将这些诗翻译出版。

在翻译古诗选集时，我开始意识到这种现象。当时我以为，这很可能是荷兰语言所特有的现象。按照中文语序翻译五言古诗时，在荷兰语被证明是有规律的五步抑扬格诗体。现在，如果第一行是有规律的抑扬格五音步诗行，而第二行不是，没有问题；但如果第二行碰巧也是有规律的抑扬格五音步诗行，可以建立一种模式，造成的预期是，如果第三行不是这样，读者会感到不愉快。由此得出的结论是，我必须做出选择：要么努力避免有规律的抑扬格，要么整首诗的翻译都坚持抑扬格。我选择了后者。首先，可以避免不受欢迎的倾向，即插入各种解释让一行变得过长。最重要的是，即使表现力弱，我仍然能够遵循中国古诗的严格形式限制。与现当代的诗不同，中国古代诗人从来不创作自由诗，而是遵守严格的形式规则。因此，即使译文无法在另一种语言中复现这些规则，也最好包含对这一事实的反映。虽然抑扬格五音步诗行完全不能够反映中国语言的格调，但在整首诗中，不论是绝句还是律诗，连续采用抑扬格至少能够提醒读者形式上存在限制。如果"诗人带着镣铐跳舞"，至少在译文中应以一种方式反映出这种束缚。我从未宣称无韵诗是渲染中国古诗的唯一方法。我只能说对我有用，我后来的荷兰语翻译也坚持采用这种方式。

最初不仅因为寒山的文学地位相对较低,而且实际上荷兰缺乏中国诗翻译的传统,因此做出选择非常容易。当我进入莱顿大学时,这所学校有中文教学的传统,可以追溯到一百多年以前。但这种传统源于荷兰东印度公司对中国(后来是东亚)事务的管理需求,教学课程是为了学生将来容易找到工作。很少有人从中文直接翻译中国诗。"中国诗"在 20 世纪二三十年代的荷兰颇受欢迎,但"中国诗"是德国诗人汉斯·贝特(1876-1946)和克拉邦德(1890-1928)根据朱迪特·戈蒂埃(1845-1917)的法文译本改写成德文。最著名的是荷兰诗人 J.J. 斯劳尔豪夫(1898-1936),他在亚瑟·威利(1889-1966)将中国诗翻译成英文的基础上自由改写。两次世界大战期间的一些荷兰诗人甚至自行创作大量的"中国诗"。当我开始对中国古典诗词进行未经修饰的直接翻译时,会受到不喜欢中文的荷兰评论家的批评。当然,他们的意思是译文不具有中国风格,这让他们感到惊讶。荷兰语地区也不了解其他欧洲国家的传统,即语言学家应该与知名诗人合作,向他们提供粗略的散文翻译稿,然后这些诗人将其神奇地转化为真正的诗。作为一名汉学研究者,如果希望将中国诗翻译成荷兰语,我必须身体力行。

选择将中国诗翻译成荷兰语押韵诗,我与当时的国际潮流背道而驰。中国诗自 1910 年起翻译成英语,当时亚瑟·威利开始发布他的译文,在翻译时放弃押韵和格律。在我的学生时代,葛瑞汉(A.C. Graham)发表《晚唐诗选》(Harmondsworth:企鹅出版社,1965 年),引发轰动。几年后,他发表文章《李贺诗新译》(东方和非洲学研究院学刊,1971 年第 34 期,第 560-570 页),强调意象在中国诗翻译中的重要性。这种对意象的强调虽然值得称赞,却导致相对忽略中国古诗所有的形式要素。从那时起,自由诗(或不合押韵散文,取决于翻译者的素质)一直是英语世界中最受欢迎的中国古典诗翻译手段。

通常,中文诗译者出于对诗的热爱而从事翻译工作,无论是源语言还是目标语言。虽然经常受到"诗就是在翻译中失去的东西"的嘲讽以及过于在意完美翻译的可能性,但因内心的乐趣从事翻译:找到合适的词语,与句子匹配的措辞,译出至少在某种程度上与原文相似的版本,目标语言的可读性,这些都是快乐和满足的源泉。译者当然可能会强调作品在全世界的重要性(这是事实),我在想这在多大程度上是他们的主要动机。到目前为止,我还没有遇到过以经济收入为目标的诗译者。一位中世纪的荷兰诗人抱怨说:"诗只能带来卑微的收入",但诗译者的收入更少。诗译者不可能向所翻译诗的创作诗人(不论是离世或活着)收费。译者通常需要其他收入来源来谋生。翻译目的和受众仍然可以有很大的不同，这会影响我们的翻译方式。美国汉学家宇文所安（Stephen Owen）指出，"翻译是一种取决于目的之工艺，而目的通常由目标读者决定。"《诗经》的各种译本明确地证明了这一观点。当香港传教士理雅各（1815-1897）为其他在中国的传教士翻译中国古典文献时，他提供散文版本配上中文文本和详细注释，充分利用汉字。语言学家高本汉（Bernhard Karlgren，1889-1978）根据最古老的诠释重构《诗经》中诗的原始含义时，他也只提供这些诗的散文版本，供其他语文学家欣赏。当理雅各返回英国为普通大众提供《诗经》译本时，他变身为维多利亚时代的诗人，翻译出具有格律和押韵的版本，因为当时的受众希望诗不论是原创还是翻译，必须具有格律和押韵（理雅各经常接触教堂赞美诗的格律模式，对《诗经》中诗的演绎非常出色）。然而，当亚瑟·威利出版《诗经》译本时，他的翻译毫无押韵可言，因为当时英美诗人逐渐抛弃押韵。虽然亚瑟·威利尽可能地贴近《诗经》原文，但埃兹拉·庞德（1885-1972）创作出具有特别风格的版本，被视为对原创作品的最佳理解，表现出译者作为自己喜爱诗的代表，为了迎合普通大众，从原始化到本土化的转变。自20世纪50年代以来，美国出现第三种类型的中国古诗翻译受众：学习翻译中国文学课程的本科学生，他们是"被吸引的受众"。欧洲的大学很少讲授这样的课程，长期以来欧洲汉学传统的影响导致人们强调阅读原始语言的文本。但在美国却非常受欢迎，中国语言文学系得以普及，面向更大的学生群体授课，而不是仅仅是努力学习中文的学生（与最近几十年相比，最初学生很少）。如今，对于普通受众而言，许多翻译的最终目的是作为本科生的阅读材料（出版商很高兴），或许翻译人员也应多考虑这一点。毕竟，典型的大一或大二学生很少会被认为是受过良好教育一般受众。

　　有些人喜欢强调翻译中国古典诗词的困难度。如果将译者的任务视为翻译文本的含义（用自己的语言明确表达文本包含的信息），而不是隐藏的内涵（可能无法弥补，随时间和地点而变化，并且在很大程度上取决于读者），中国古典诗词并不难。当然，的确存在非常难以翻译的诗人和诗，但这是特殊情形。如果读者经常阅读西方古典诗词，熟悉浮华的修辞语言、古代神灵和神话人物，通常会对中国古典诗词的朴素和直接所吸引。中国古典诗词往往简短，诗句的跨行连续非常罕见，甚至不存在，诗行以句号结尾。四言、五言或七言的诗行不允许存在古典拉丁和希腊诗或欧洲白话古典诗中常见的修辞手段。印欧语系的语言必须处理词形、性别和数量的变化，这并不是古代中国诗人的错。中国诗人坚持自己的语法规则，这些规则非常清晰。中国评论家在分析一首诗的时候，不论在任何时候很少觉得需要详细处理诗行的语法结构。当然，外国读者可能会为诗行感到困惑，但阅读数量越多，困惑就越少。大量注释的版本和参考著作可以帮助读者理解罕见的表达和晦涩的典故。外国译者不得不做出选择，将中文语法转换为英文或荷兰文语法，但这是由目标语言决定的实践方面，与中文诗本身无关。

如果说中国诗很难理解，那是因为它是另一种文化的产物。如果将过去看作是异国，现代中国读者和外国人一样，对唐诗肯定是陌生的。与东西方的浪漫主义和后浪漫主义诗相比，过去的诗是由不同的人，出于不同目的和针对不同读者所创作，因此主题不同，语言不同，使用的典故与现当代诗也不相同。我认为这一事实是翻译中的最大问题。许多人都知道杜甫是中国最伟大的诗人，至少在唐朝时期。戴维·霍克思（1923-2009）向西方读者介绍他的诗选集时，对律诗做出如下评论："[它们的]形式完美赋予[它们]古典的优雅，但不幸的是无法通过翻译传达。这就是最出色的诗人之一杜甫的诗在外国语言中表现不佳的原因。"宇文所安将其对杜甫全集的翻译描述为毕生学习和翻译经历的成果，以双语版本出版，作为"拥有一定中文水平，但是达不到阅读杜甫诗程度"（在无其他辅助材料的情况下阅读原创诗）的"对照译本"，他也表达了相同的想法。然而，更大的问题在于杜甫也是一位儒家诗人，作为帝国官僚机构的官员，他为无法对维持帝国秩序做出贡献而深感沮丧。虽然相对容易找到合适的词翻译杜甫在流浪岁月中的思乡情感，但在杜甫诗选集翻译成荷兰语时，我发现很难在我的母语荷兰语中找到合适的表达方式，表现出他一再表达的为皇帝和帝国服务的强烈愿望。困难和复杂之处在于，我在翻译杜甫的儒家价值观和情感时避免使用产生过于明显的基督教联想的词语。

当然，通常很难确定一首诗的内涵，但寻找诗正确解释的努力注定会失败。我也认为译者的任务是使读者能够探索翻译中呈现诗的可能内涵。译者不可避免地做出的选择，在翻译中已经呈现地够好，不应在可能的范围内对诗强行解释。译者通常作为向外国读者呈现自己所选诗人的第一关，所以译者必须要求严格。然而，我认为对于翻译活动的这一方面，我们可以提供序言和引言、后记和注解。就个人而言，我必须承认不喜欢脚注，即使我无法完全避免其使用。在《从"诗经"到清朝：中国古典诗词的一面镜子》（阿姆斯特丹：Meulenhoff，1991年）一书中，我选择诗时尽可能少使用注释，因为依赖于注释的译文就像需要详细解释的笑话。我时不时运用的策略是通过增译进行澄清：如果我希望翻译一首具有特定典故的诗，我会将典故也包括在内，希望读者能自己理解典故。但这并不容易，还会增加诗的内容，让原创的诗看起来不像一首好诗。我喜欢翻译长诗，因为它们可以自行营造气氛，暗示着对其中所包括意象的理解。但不管译者怎么做，仅仅再现诗的原始语境都是远远不够的，诗必须依靠"自身"发挥作用以及获得理解。

假如译者的目标是在阅读诗时提供附上原文的对照译本，则不必担心翻译作品的形式特征。然而，如果对象是没有能力阅读原著的普通读者，必须接受将译文以诗形式呈现的挑战。虽然葛瑞汉在四十多年前发表过观点，但中国古典诗词很少能够仅凭意象进行翻译。事实上，只有少数中国诗人像李商隐（813-858）和李贺（790-816）一样使用意象，而且在他们的作品中，这些意象也受到诗的形式约束。因此，每位译者必须对原始诗中希望保留的形式要素做出选择。从某种意义上讲，维多利亚时代的译者选择最简单的方法，除了内容经常含糊不清外，为了格律和押韵可以牺牲原始诗的任何方面。如上文所述，亚瑟·威利打破了这种做法：放弃押韵而采取"跳跃韵律"，因而经常可以重现原始诗的语序。威利的跳跃韵律在翻译五言诗时效果更好，而翻译七言诗时，通常难以跟散文区分开。刘若愚在1962年开创性的《中国诗艺术》中包含忠实地遵循原始韵律模式的押韵译文，但后来也在译文中放弃押韵，因为他逐渐意识到"不可能保留押韵而不损害语言的内涵"。此后许多译者按照葛瑞汉的模式放弃保留中国诗词和译文中诗行格律对等的任何尝试。

中国读者对中国古典诗词的英文翻译常常感到失望，因为这些译文缺乏韵律。近几十年来，几位中国古典诗词的中国译者都发表了押韵的译文。他们也不可避免地遭遇与中国古典诗词的外国译者相同的问题，即为了押韵不得不牺牲几乎所有其他形式要素，而且经常需要改写内容才能实现押韵。译文的用语非常古老。除此之外，并非所有译者意识到英语中押韵必须与格律配合使用 — 没有格律的押韵通常比较拙劣。当然，每位译者都有幸运的时候，翻译的结果令人瞩目，但大多数时候，译文缺乏技巧。就个人而言，我认为中国译者坚持使用押韵的做法让人困惑。当然必须承认，所有体裁的中国古典诗词都以一种或另一种方式押韵，甚至在中国被归类为"散文"的某些体裁也是如此，例如"赋"。因此，押韵不能算作是中国诗的独有特征。此外，如果押韵的声调对中国读者来说非常重要，人们希望采取诗词创作时代的发音读诗，但事实并非如此。自唐朝以来，入声已从标准语言中消失，许多词语的音调和发音发生改变。甚至在唐朝时期，押韵类别在某种程度上也是人工构建的。某些方言声称它们的发音仍然与唐朝时的发音接近，虽然总体上不确定，至少保留那个时期的大部分音调，但没有人建议采用这些方言作为阅读和朗诵唐诗的标准发音。最后，也很重要的一点是，传统的中国评论家很少（几乎没有）讨论诗如何使用押韵——仅假设押韵的使用构成形式上的完美。

这些评论家可以假设押韵是形式上的完美，因为押韵在中文中相对容易。押韵的数量是有限的，许多押韵类别都是"广泛使用的"，包括数百个押韵词。即使在所谓的"窄"押韵类别中，仍然有数十个押韵词。由于这种押韵容易，很少特别强调押韵词。诗句中最重要的词很少是押韵词。诗"眼"通常在不同的位置。如果愿意的话，中国诗人可以保持数十行或者更多相同的押韵。偶然还会看到一些诗歌，诗人试图在一个押韵组中尽可能多地使用押韵词，而不重复任何押韵词。然而，日耳曼语系中仅具有数量有限的押韵词，因此在押韵位置使用特定词语，通常会对下一行中可能的押韵词产生强烈的期望。押韵词的有限可用性也使十四行诗成为日耳曼语系中特别具有挑战性的诗形式，因为相同的押韵必须使用四次。在其他体裁中，押韵的重复通常受到限制和单调乏味，这恰恰是因为在日耳曼语系的诗中，押韵比在中国诗中更难"呈现"。在英文译本中保留中国古诗押韵的大多数译者也默认押韵在英文中的局限性：即使使用押韵，他们也很少努力重现源语言的押韵模式。然而，如果押韵是中国古典诗词的重要元素，难道不应该尝试呈现翻译作品的特定押韵模式吗？实现成功押韵译文的最佳体裁可能是绝句。

传统的中国评论家很少关注押韵，但对精心创作的对仗却非常着迷。当然，评论家还探讨单个诗行，但在他们看来，对仗显得更为重要。对仗的迷恋当然不仅限于诗：所有文体类型中都有对仗，甚至衍生出独立的类别——对联。对联雕刻在许多建筑物上，并在许多活动中展示。在传统教育中，学生从小接受创作复杂对仗诗行的训练。虽然在西方也有人们无法想出匹配押韵词的故事（直到有人最终发现），但在中国类似的奇闻轶事却很多，人们无法为困难的诗行找出匹配的诗行（直到神童出现）。古汉语的文字特点极大地促进了对仗的形成，并使其广受欢迎，但我认为，对仗的创作只不过是博学的技巧和嬉戏的比赛。根据传统的中国宇宙观，世界是由对立和竞争的要素组成，但也有合作的力量和要素。如同通过一组具有代表性但不同的要素创造抽象的概念，对仗的创作者试图通过对比引人注目的要素抓住整体的场景或情感。在对联中起作用的不是单一意象，而是成对的意象。自唐代以来，中国古典诗词最重要的体裁之一就是八行"律诗"，其中中间两联必须是对仗句。然而，如果不是故意破坏对仗，大多数中国古典诗词的东西方译者对于对仗采取毫不在意的态度。傅汉思（Hans H. Frenkel）是中国古典诗词的敏感读者，他在1985年对译者处理中国古典诗词形式特征的方式研究中指出：

> 对仗和对偶是中国古典诗词的重要特征，偶尔也会在英语诗中使用。但在英语中，很长的诗行以句号收尾以及过多的精准对仗听起来很糟糕。因此，一些最好的译者故意打破中国对偶句的对仗性。

傅汉思另外指出，"其他译者故意放弃再现对仗的尝试，而只专注于诗的精确散文含义。"即使傅汉思指出译者"技巧性地保留句法和语义对仗"，也很难实现原始文本的精确对仗。葛瑞汉在探讨唐诗翻译时指出在对偶联方面可能有所保留。他认为，"很明显，如果不重复词语，在英语中无法实现严格的对仗，而重复造成的对仗很快就会显得僵硬和单调。"许多译者对不能完全再现中国古诗中频繁使用的对仗，常见的理由是日耳曼语系（例如英语）的语言特征不同。西方文学很少使用精准对仗，但对偶是中国诗非常重要的要素，译者或许需要更加努力去尝试。白居易（772-846）以风格的刻意简朴著称，但他也写过许多长排律诗体现文学天赋。当我在荷兰语诗歌选集中选择他的作品，我认为有必要加入一些诗，以表现出多样性。只能说，尽可能准确地将中国古诗翻译成荷兰语，我对此感到非常高兴。当然，我也希望读者在发现作者丰富的对仗句法模式变化时，也能够享受到相同的乐趣。

文学翻译作为一个专业，需要丰富的技巧。首先，全面了解诗人身处的源语言和文化。这也意味着广泛理解诗人的作品和其他相关著作。其次，要求精通目标语言，即"拇指规则"，母语译者的译文最可能取得成功。第三，最重要的是，要求在翻译诗的过程中主动运用技巧。很少有译者能够完全具备这三种素质。我也做不到。然而，这三个要求还远远不够，我们还需要具有天赋。

Some Thoughts on the Translation of Classical Chinese Poetry in Dutch and English: Meter, Purpose, Rhyme, and Parallelism

Wilt L. Idema / Holland

Professor Emeritus, the Department of East Asian Languages and Civilizations, Harvard University

There was very little in my background when I grew up in the Dutch countryside to predispose me for the study of Chinese Languages and Cultures, which I chose as my major when I entered Leiden University in the fall of 1963. Also during my years of study at Leiden, and later in Sapporo, Kyoto, and Hong Kong, there were few indications that suggested I would end up spending a large part of my adult life reading and translating classical Chinese poetry, first in Dutch, but alter also in English. During these early years of my career my interest wavered between contemporary rural sociology and late imperial vernacular literature. My first job at Leiden University was as a researcher at the Documentation Center for Contemporary China, a newly founded section of the well-known Sinological Institute, where it was my job to follow social developments in the inaccessible People's Republic of China since the 1960s, and my earliest publications are devoted to the educational reforms of the 1960s and early 1970s. I left the contemporary China field abruptly when the Department's teacher of classical Chinese (*wenyanwen* 文言文) and Chinese literature unexpectedly died in the weekend before the beginning of the Spring semester classes: when I arrived on my job that Monday morning, I was asked to take over his classes from that very day, and that was the end of my career as a China watcher.

Throughout my years in contemporary China studies I had always continued to read traditional Chinese vernacular fiction in large quantities. I liked these sprawling narratives of back-stage political intrigues and private bedchamber adventures that were quite at difference with the official image of Chinese society projected by the authorities to their own subjects or the outside world in past or present. Some of my first attempts at translation concerned the vernacular short stories (*huaben* 话本) that had been collected and printed by Feng Menglong in the 1620s. While these vernacular stories were mostly written in prose, they also included occasional couplets, poems, and lyrics. When putting these texts into Dutch, I wanted to stress the alternation between prose and poetry in its various forms, and so I wanted to use meter and rhyme in my translations. With due modesty, I dare say that I do have a certain talent for rhyming in my native Dutch. I also tried to prepare myself even better for my self-appointed task by reading large quantities of rhymed verse from the nineteenth century when Dutch poets all used rhyme as a matter of course. I even read enough of these materials to become something of an expert in the field, publishing two anthologies of nineteenth-century Dutch poetry in cooperation with a good friend who is a practicing poet and served as the director of the Dutch Museum of Literature. But neither my native talent nor my assiduous reading proved themselves of much use. Like many translators before me I discovered that in the overwhelming majority of cases it was impossible to come up with an acceptable rhyming translation without sacrificing much of the content and almost all of the other formal elements of these poems. It is not that there were no occasions where one might hit on a lucky rhyme, but such occasions were very rare indeed.

My first collection of classical poetry of the Tang dynasty (618-906) that I published was Han Shan, *Gedichten van de koude berg* (Poems of Cold Mountain; Amsterdam: De Arbeiderspers, 1974). Han Shan may not enjoy much of a status in China, but his works have always remained popular in Japan, and in the 1950s and '60s his poems were repeatedly, in ever increasing numbers, translated into English (starting with the rendition of Gary Snyder), French, and German. My interest in Han Shan had been roused not by his poetry, but by his reputation as a vernacular poet, because I wanted to deepen my knowledge of the development of *baihua*. Once I started reading the poems with the aid of the excellent Japanese commentaries that were available, I could not help myself from trying to render some of them into Dutch. And once I had succeeded in rendering some of them into Dutch to at least my own satisfaction, I could not stop myself from doing more, until I had translated two hundred poems.

While working on this collection I became beware of a phenomenon that, I thought at that time, might well be peculiar to Dutch.[1] When translating a five-syllable line and following the Chinese word-order, many Dutch lines proved to be regular iambic lines of five feet. Now if the first line is a regular iambic line and the second one is not, there is no problem, but if the second line also happens to be a regular iambic line, one has set up a pattern that creates the expectation that the third line also will be a iambic line, and if it is not, the reader will be unpleasantly surprised. From this I drew the conclusion that I had to make a choice: I either had to make an effort to avoid regular iambics, or I had to stick to iambic lines throughout the poem. I chose for the latter option. First of all, it saved me from the unwelcome tendency to extend the lines by inserting all kind of explanatory materials. But most importantly, it allowed me to suggest, if only faintly, something of the strict formal constraints under which China's traditional poets worked. Unlike may of their modern and contemporary counterparts, Chinese poets from

---

[1] It is my impression that many Dutch words because of the differences in grammar between English and Dutch often contain more unstressed syllables than English words, and this makes for the easier generation of iambic lines.

pre-modern times did not write in free verse but adhered to strict formal rules, and a translation should preferably contain some reflection of that fact even if it is impossible to replicate these rules in a different language. While a iambic line cannot reflect the tonal aspects of the Chinese language at all, its consistent use throughout a poem, whether a quatrain (*jueju*) or a regulated poem (*lüshi*), at least reminds the reader of formal constraints. If "poets dance in their chains" they are at least still wearing some shackles in translation in this way. I have never claimed that blank verse the only way to render classical Chinese poetry. All I can say is that it worked for me, and I have stubbornly stuck to it also in my later Dutch translations.[1]

Making this choice initially was made easier not only by the relative low status of Hanshan, but also the virtual absence of a tradition of Chinese poetry translation in the Netherlands. When I entered Leiden University, Leiden University had a tradition of teaching Chinese that stretched back for over a hundred years, but that tradition was rooted in the need of the administration of the Dutch East Indies for specialists in Chinese (later, East-Asian) affairs, and the teaching program was geared toward the future job situation of the students.[2] Translation of Chinese poetry directly from the Chinese had always few and far between. "Chinese poetry" had enjoyed quite some popularity in the Netherlands in the 1920s and '30s, but these "Chinese poems" were free adaptations from the German *Nachdichtungen* (creative rewritings) by the German poets Hans Bethge (1876-1946) and Klabund (Alfred Henschke, 1890-1928), who had based their free adaptations on earlier French adaptation, for instance by Judith Gautier (1845-1917).[3] The best known author of

---

[1] After moving to the United States in 1999, I also started to translate classical Chinese poetry, especially women's works, into English. Not being a native speaker of English, I initially did not try to produce metrical translations but followed the local preference for free verse. It is only in my recent *Two Centuries of Manchu Women Poets: An Anthology* (Seattle: University of Washington Press, 2017) that I did include a sizable number of metric renditions.

[2] For a survey of Dutch studies in the Netherlands, see *Chinese Studies in the Netherlands: Past, Present and Future*, ed. Wilt L. Idema (Leiden: Brill, 2014).

[3] Discussions of translations of poetry in English and Dutch are hampered by the absence of the German distinction between *Übersetzung* (translation in a narrow sense) and *Nachdichtung* (free adaptations).

this kind of Chinese poems was the famous Dutch poet J.J. Slauerhoff (1898-1936), whose free adaptations distinguished themselves by being based on the English translations of Arthur Waley (1889-1966).[1] Some Dutch poets of the Interbellum period went so far as to produce volumes of "Chinese poems" of their own creation. When I started to produce my unadorned direct translations of classical Chinese poetry, these would on occasion be criticized for their lack of Chinese favor by Dutch critics. What they meant was, of course, that these translations surprised them because of their lack of chinoiserie. The Dutch-language area also does not know a tradition as is found in some other European countries that linguists are supposed to collaborate with established poets by providing them with rough prose drafts of translations, which are then magically transformed into true poetry by these poets. If I as a sinologist wanted to translate Chinese poetry into Dutch, I would have to do it myself.

By choosing to render Chinese poetry into metrical verse in my Dutch translations, I was going against the international trend at the time. English translators of Chinese verse had since the 1910s, when Arthur Waley started to publish his translations, increasingly abandoned the use of rhyme and meter in their renditions. In my student days A.C. Graham created quite a stir with the introduction of his *Poems of the Late Tang* (Harmondsworth: Penguin, 1965), and a few years later with his article "A New Translation of a Chinese Poet: Li Ho"[2], in which he stressed the primacy of the image in the translation of Chinese poetry. This emphasis on the image, laudable as it may be, has resulted in the relative neglect of almost all formal elements of classical Chinese poetry, and since then free verse (or lame prose, depending on the quality of the translator) has been by far the most popular vehicle for the translation of classical Chinese poetry in the Anglophone world.

---

1 W.L. Idema, "Dutch Translations of Classical Chinese Literature: Against a Tradition of Retranslation," in *One into Many: Translation and the Dissemination of Classical Chinese Literature*, ed. Leo Tak-hung Chan, 213-42 (Amsterdam/New York: Rodopi, 2003).
2 *Bulletin of the School of Oriental and African Studies* 34 (1971), 560-70.

Some Thoughts on the Translation of Classical Chinese Poetry in Dutch and English: Meter, Purpose, Rhyme, and Parallelism

Translators of Chinese poetry as a rule engage in their work because of their love of poetry, both in the source language and in the target language. Though always haunted by the sneer that "poetry is what's lost in translation" and only too aware of the impossibility of a perfect translation, they also engage in the treasonous act of translation (*traditori traduttori*) because of the inherent pleasures it brings: finding the right word, phrasing a fitting sentence, and producing a version that at least to some extent approximates the original and reads well in the target language are a source of joy and gratification. Translators may of course stress the importance of their work in a global world (which is of course true), but I wonder how often that is their primary motivation. So far I have never encountered a translator of poetry whose primary motivation was financial. "Van dichten comt mi cleine bate" (Poetry only brings small profit) complained a medieval Dutch poet, and the translation of poetry is even less profitable. Translators of poetry don't make good money at the expense of the poets they translate, whether dead or alive; as a rule translators need other sources of income to make a living. Still the purposes and audiences of their translations can be quite different, and this impacts the way one translates. In the words of Stephen Owen, "Translation is a craft that is contingent on its purpose, and the purpose is usually determined by the readers for whom it is intended."[1] This is clearly demonstrated by the various translations of the *Book of Odes* (*Shijing*). When the Hong Kong-based missionary James Legge (1815-1897) produced his translation of the Chinese Classics for the benefit of his fellow missionaries in China, he provided prose versions alongside the Chinese texts together with detailed annotations making ample use of Chinese characters. When the linguist Bernhard Karlgren (1889-1978) set out to reconstruct the original meaning of the songs in the *Book of Odes* on the basis of the earliest preserved glosses, he too only provided prose versions of these poems for enjoyment of his fellow-philologists. But when Legge produced a translation of the *Book of Odes* for a general audience back in Great Britain, he, being a good Victorian, produced metrical, rhymed versions, because that audience at the time expected its poetry, whether original or translated,

---

1 Du Fu, *The Poetry of Du Fu*, trans. and ed. Stephen Owen (New York: De Gruyter, 2016), lxxxxi.

to be metrical and rhymed (as Legge often followed the metrical patterns of church hymns, his renditions of the poems in the *Book of Odes* are eminently singable). But when Arthur Waley published his translation of the *Book of Odes*, his translations were rhymeless, because by that time British and American poets were increasingly abandoning the use of rhyme. And while Arthur Waley tried to stay as close as possible to the text of the *Book of Odes*, Ezra Pound (1885-1972) produced a highly idiosyncratic version that probably is best appreciated as an original creation, showing between the two of them the wide range from barbarization to nativization that is available to translators as they woo the general audience on behalf of the poets they love. Since the 1950s the United States have witnessed a third kind of audience for translation of classical Chinese poetry: the "captive audience" of undergraduate students who have signed up for classes in Chinese literature in translation. Such classes are only rarely taught in European universities, where the lasting influence of their Sinological tradition leads to an emphasis on reading texts in the original language, but they became quite popular in the United States where it allowed Departments of Chinese Language and Literature to reach out to a larger student body beyond those who were willing to put in the effort to learn the language (in contrast to more recent decades, initially only a very small number). As the final destination these days of many translations for the general audience is to end up as prescribed reading for undergraduates (to the delight of our publishers), this is perhaps something many translators should take more into account. After all, a typical freshman or sophomore can rarely be considered a member of the supposedly well-educated general audience.

Some people like to stress the difficulty of classical Chinese poetry. If one sees it as the translator's mission to translate the sense of a text (the explicit message of the text in its own words) and not necessarily the meaning (which may well be irrecoverable, can change over time and place, and depends very much on the reader), Chinese classical poetry is not all that difficult. Of course, there are difficult poets and difficult poems, but they tend to be exceptions. Readers who are raised on classical Western poetry with its often highly rhetorical language and panoply of ancient gods and mythical characters are often positively struck by the simplicity and directness of Chinese classical poetry. Chinese classical poems tend to be short, and, as enjambment is rare if not non-existent is *shi* 诗 poems, mostly consist of end-stopped lines. Such lines of four, five, or seven syllables do not allow for the rhetorical contortions that are commonly found in classical Latin and Greek poetry, or Classicist poetry in the European vernaculars. It is not the fault of the ancient Chinese poets that speakers of Indo-European languages have to deal with conjugations and declinations, gender and number. The Chinese poets stick to the rules of their own grammar and these are as a rule clear enough. When analyzing individual poems, Chinese critics then and now rarely feel a need to deal in detail with the grammatical structure of a line. Of course a foreign reader may be baffled by a line, but the more one reads, the less that happens. Extensively annotated edition and numerous reference works are available to help him find his way through the minefield of rare expressions and obscure allusions. The foreign translator may have to make choices to turn grammatical Chinese into grammatical English or Dutch, but that is a practical aspect determined by the target language and has nothing to do with the Chinese poem as such.

If Chinese poetry presents difficulties of understanding it is because it is the product of a different culture, but if the past is a foreign country, the Tang dynasty must be as alien to contemporary Chinese readers as to foreigners. The poetry of the past was written by different people, for different purposes, and for a different audience than Romantic and post-Romantic poetry East and West, and for that reason it was written on different topics, used a different language, and employed other allusions than modern and contemporary poetry. I am afraid that this fact causes the greatest problems in translation. Many of us may agree that Du Fu 杜甫 is China's greatest poet, at least of the Tang dynasty. When introducing a selection of his poems to Western audiences David Hawkes (1923-2209) commented as follows on his regulated poems, "[Their] perfection of form lends [them] a classical grace which unfortunately cannot be communicated in translation. That is the reason why Du Fu, one of the great masters of the form, makes so comparatively poor a showing in foreign languages."[1] When Stephen Owen describes his translations of the complete works of Du Fu, the result of a lifetime of study and experience in translation and published in a bilingual edition, as only "a crib" for "those who have some level of Chinese, but whose Chinese is not up to reading Du Fu" (in the original without assistance), that statement may well be informed by the same thought.[2] But even more of an issue may well be the fact that Du Fu is also very much a Confucian poet, deeply frustrated by his inability to contribute to the ordering of the realm as an official in the imperial bureaucracy. And while it may be relatively easy to find the right words for the translations of his feelings of homesickness during his years of wandering, I found it very hard when working on a small Dutch anthology of Du Fu to find fitting expressions in my native Dutch for the rendition of his repeatedly expressed fervent desire to serve the emperor and the realm. That difficulty was further compounded by the fact that I wanted to avoid words with too obvious Christian associations in translating Du Fu's Confucian values and sentiments.

Of course it is often difficult to ascertain the meaning of an individual poem, but then the search for the one correct interpretation of a poem is doomed anyway. I also believe that the translator has a task in enabling the reader to explore the possible meanings of the poems presented in translation. By the choices the translator unavoidably makes, he or she is already very much present in the translation, but to the extent possible he or she should not impose his or her own interpretation on the poem. Because the translator often is the first to present the poet of his or her choice to a foreign audience, he or she also has to be critic. But for that aspect of our activities, I believe, we have prefaces and introductions, postfaces and annotations. Personally I must confess that I am not a fan of footnotes, even though I have not

---

[1] David Hawkes, *A Little Primer of Tu Fu* (Oxford: Clarendon Press, 1967), p.47.
[2] Du Fu, *The Poetry of Du Fu*, trans. and ed. Stephen Owen, 6 vols. (New York: De Gruyter, 2016), lxxxi.

been able to avoid them completely. In my *Spiegel van de klassieke Chinese poëzie van het Boek der Oden tot de Qing dynastie* (A mirror of classical Chinese poetry from the Book of Odes to the Qing dynasty, Amsterdam: Meulenhoff, 1991) I have preferred poems that need as little annotation as possible, also because a translation that relies on annotation reads like a joke that is explained in detail. One strategy I have applied from time to time is clarification through more translations: If I wanted to include a poem that used allusions to a certain poem, I would include that poem too, hoping the reader would catch the allusions by her/himself. But this is tricky and increases the bulk, while the original poem may not be a good poem at all. I also have preferred longer poems which created their own atmosphere, suggesting an understanding of the images included. But whatever the translator will do, it will never be enough to recreate the original context of the poem, in which the poem functioned and was understood "by itself".

As long as the translator's aim is to provide cribs for reading the poem in its original language, he or she does not need to be concerned about the formal features of the works he or she translates. But if one aims for a general audience that is unable to read the originals, one has to take up the challenge of presenting the translations as poetry. Despite A.C. Graham's arguments of more that forty years ago, few classical Chinese poems can survive translation on the strength of their images alone. The fact of the matter is that only a few Chinese poets were as original as Li Shangyin (813-858) and Li He (790-816) in their use of imagery, and in their works too, these images gain from formal constraints of the poem. Every translator therefore has to make a choice as to which formal elements of the original poem he or she wants to maintain in his or her rendition. In a way, the Victorian translators took the easy way out by sacrificing almost any aspect of the original poem for the sake of meter and rhyme except for an often vague correspondence in content.[1]

---

1 Edward H. Sxhafer, otherwise known as a quite barbarizing translator of Chinese poetry, once provided multiple translations of a single Chinese poem in different period styles of English poetry in his "Mineral Imagery in the Paradise Poems of Kuan-hsiu," *Asia Major* New Series 10 (1963), 73-102.

Arthur Waley, as was mentioned before, broke with that practice: abandoning rhyme and adopting "sprung rhythm" he could often reproduce the word-order of the original. Waley's sprung rhythm worked out better in the translation of five-syllable lines than in the case of seven-syllable lines that often were indistinguishable from prose.[1] James J.Y Liu, who in his pioneering *The Art of Chinese Poetry* of 1962 had included rhymed translation that faithfully followed the original rhyme patterns, later abandoned rhyme in his translations as he had come to realize "the virtual impossibility of keeping the rhymes without damage to the meaning."[2] Following the model of A.C. Graham, many translators have since abandoned any attempt to maintain a metrical equivalence between the lines in the Chinese poem and in their translation.[3]

Chinese readers of English translations of Chinese classical poetry are often disappointed by the lack of rhyme in these translations, and in recent decades several Chinese translators of classical Chinese poetry have produced rhyming translations. Unavoidably, they run into the same issues as foreign translators of classical Chinese poetry, that is that they have to sacrifice almost every other formal element for the sake of rhyme, and often have to adapt the contents to the available rhymes. Moreover, the diction in such translations is often trite. On top of that, not all of these translators seem to be aware that in English rhyme only works in cooperation with meter—rhyme without meter resulting in doggerel. Of course, every translator has his lucky day when the result is striking, but more often these translations are inept. Personally I find this insistence on the use of rhyme on the side of these Chinese translators puzzling. One must of course admit that all genres of classical Chinese poetry rhyme in one way or another, but so do some genres that are classified as "prose" in China, for instance the *fu* (rhapsody). So rhyme cannot

---
1 For a recent discussion of Arthur Waley as a translator, see Zeb Raft, "The Limits of Translation: Method in Arthur Waley's Translations of Chinese Poetry," *Asia Major Third Series* 25.2:79-128.
2 Quoted in Hans H. Frankel, "English Translations of Classical Chinese Poetry Since the 1950s: Problems and Achievements," *Tamkang Review* 15 (1984-85), 308.
3 Attempts to translate classical Chinese poetry in lines of the same number of syllables as in the original have been few and far from successful.

be counted as a distinctive characteristic of poetry in China. Moreover, if the sound of the rhyme would be so important to Chinese readers, one would expect them to read poetry in the pronunciation of the time when the poems were composed, but that is not the case. Since the Tang, the *rusheng* (entering tone) has disappeared from the standard language, and many words have changed their tone and sound. And even during the Tang dynasty, the rhyme categories were to a certain degree artificial constructs. Some dialects claim that their pronunciation remains much closer to pronunciation of the Tang, and while that in general may be questionable, some of them at least maintain most of the tonal distinction of that period, but no one proposes to make these dialects the standard for reading and reciting Tang poetry. Last but not least, traditional Chinese critics rarely if ever discuss the use of rhyme of the poems they analyze—formal perfection of the use of rhymes is assumed.

These critics can assume the formal perfection in the use of rhymes because rhyming is relatively easy in Chinese. The number of rhymes is limited, and many rhyme categories are "broad", including hundreds of rhyming words. Even in the so-called "narrow" rhyming categories there are still tens of rhyming words. Because of this ease in rhyming, there rarely is a special emphasis on the rhyming word. The most important word in a line of verse rarely is the rhyming word; the "eye" (*yan*) of a verse is usually found in a different position. Chinese poets can maintain, if they wish so, the same rhyme for tens of lines if not more, and occasionally one comes across poems in which the poet tried to use as many as possible of the rhyming words in one rhyming group without repeating any of these words. In Germanic languages, however, many words only have a quite limited number of rhyming words, so using a specific word in rhyming position often creates strong expectations about the possible rhyming word(s) in the following line(s). The limited availability of rhyming words also makes the sonnet an especially challenging verse form in Germanic languages because the same rhymes have to be used four times. Such repetition of rhyme in other genres is often experienced as constrained and boring, precisely because rhyming is much more "present" in poetry in Germanic languages than in Chinese poetry. Most translators who use rhyme in their English renditions of classical Chinese poetry silently acknowledge the limitations of rhyme in that language: even when using rhyme, they rarely make an effort to reproduce the rhyming patterns of the source language. But if rhyme is such an essential element of classical Chinese poetry, shouldn't they try reproduce the specific rhyming patterns of the works they translate? The best chances for successful rhymed translations are probably provided by quatrains.

Whereas traditional Chinese critics devote little attention to rhyme, they are fascinated by the well-crafted couplet. Of course they also discuss individual lines, but it would seem that the parallel couplet is even more important in their eyes. This fascination with the parallel couplet is of course not limited to poetry: the parallel couplet is encountered in all genres of writing, and even engendered its own genre as free-standing couplets (*duilian*). Couplets are encountered as inscriptions on many buildings and are displayed at many events, and in traditional education students were trained from early on in the composition of increasingly complex parallel lines. Whereas in the West one find stories about words for which no one has ever come up with a fitting rhyme word (until someone finally does), there are many anecdotes in China about difficult lines for which no one had ever been able to come up with a matching line (until a child prodigy does). The characteristics of Classical Chinese facilitate the composition of parallel couplets greatly, which will have enhanced their popularity, but I believe that the composition of parallel lines is more than an erudite skill and a playful competition. In traditional Chinese cosmology the world is made up contrasting and competing but also cooperative forces and elements, and just as abstract concepts are often created by naming two representative but different members of a group, the author of a couplet tries to grasp the totality of a scene or an emotion by contrasting its most conspicuous elements. In parallel couplets it is not the single image that counts, but the paired image. One of the most important genres of classical Chinese poetry since the Tang dynasty has been the eight-line "regulated poem", of which the two inner couplets have to be parallel couplets. Yet the majority of translators of classical Chinese poetry East and West have treated parallel couplets in a cavalier fashion if they did not deliberately break up the parallelism. Hans H. Frenkel, otherwise a sensitive reader of classical Chinese poetry, in his 1985 survey of the ways in which translators had dealt with the formal features of classical Chinese poetry, commented as follows:

> Parallelism and antithesis are significant features in classical Chinese poetry, and they are occasionally employed in English poetry. But a long-series of end-stopped lines and too much precise parallelism tends to sound bad in English. Therefore some of the best translators deliberately break up the parallelism of Chinese couplets.[1]

And elsewhere Frankel notes, "Other translators deliberately forego the attempt to reproduce antithetical couplets and concentrate instead on the precise prose sense of the poems."[2] Even the translators who are said by Frankel to "skillfully preserve syntactic and semantic parallelism" rarely achieve the precision of their source texts. Also in A.C. Graham's discussion of the problems in translating Tang-dynasty verse one may observe the same reserve towards the parallel couplet, when he writes, "It is clear that in English strict parallelism without repeating a word is nearly impossible, while parallelism involving repetition will quickly seem rigid and monotonous."[3] This reluctance to do full justice to the frequent use of parallelism in Chinese classical poetry on the part of many translators is usually defended with an appeal to the different characteristics of Germanic languages like English, and the limited occurrence of precise parallelism in Western literature, but if the parallel couplet is such an essential aspect of Chinese poetry, translators have perhaps to try harder. Bai Juyi (772-846) may be known for the deliberate simplicity of his style, but he also wrote a number of long *pailü* poems in which he displayed

---

[1] Hans. H. Frankel, "English Translations of Classical Chinese Poetry Since the 1950: Problems and Achievements," *Tamkang Review* 15 (1984-1985): 318.
[2] Ibid., p.320.
[3] A.C. Graham, *Poems of the Late Tang*, p.27.

his magisterial virtuosity, and when working on my Dutch anthology of his works,[1] I felt a duty to include some of these poems in order to display the variety of his poetry. I can only say that I personally derived great pleasure from turning these poems into Dutch as precisely as possible, and I hope of course that some of my readers will have enjoyed some of the same pleasure as they saw the authors varying his syntactical patterns from couplet to couplet.

Literary translation as a craft requires numerous skills. First of these is a sound knowledge of the source language and of the culture in which the poet to be translated flourished. This also implies an encyclopedic knowledge of the editions of the poet's works and other relevant reference works. Secondly it requires a mastery of the target language, which results in the rule of the thumb that translations are most likely to succeed when done by a native speaker. Thirdly, and most importantly, it requires the willingness to use these skills in the service of the poetry to be translated. Few translators fully combine these three qualities in their person. I don't. But as if these three requirements were not enough, on top of them the craft also requires talent.

---

1 Bai Juyi, *Gedichten en proza (Po Tsju-I, 772-846)*, trans. Wilt L. Idema (Amsterdam: Atlas, 2001).

中国国有企业和私营企业在全球市场上的崛起

柯保罗 【英国】
哈佛大学肯尼迪政府学院非常驻高级研究员

我的整个职业生涯中一直在研究中国,最初是以学者身份,后来是以商人的身份。1966年我开始学习汉语。1973年,我作为交换生在中国学习。我写过一篇关于辛亥革命期间知识分子动向的论文,并先后在几所大学任教。再后来,"我下海了",主要在中国的银行、战略咨询和高科技领域工作30年。我帮助跨国公司进入中国市场。我为中国国有企业重组提供帮助,也帮助中国的私营企业应对迅速增长的挑战。我想让大家进一步了解,自1978年中国开始经济改革以来,中国企业通过什么方式走向世界,中国企业取得成功的关键因素是什么。

改革的历史背景

我们在了解中国企业过去四十年的崛起历程之前,有必要回顾更早的时期,从而突出改革的重要性。19世纪末,清朝政府的改革官员试图刺激工业发展,但力度太小且为时过晚,无法拯救没落的王朝。民国时期在工业基础设施建设方面取得巨大的进步,但这一进程被腐败、侵略和内战所破坏。

中华人民共和国的成立带来新的机会,但也有负面的影响。

客观来说,中国的第一个五年计划(1952–1957)确实取得了显著成绩。这一时期建成了全面的工业基础,推动改革并提升了教育、科技、医疗卫生和妇女权利方面的社会基础设施。

1949 年，中国的工农业总产值（GDP 的合理替代指标）仅为 470 亿元人民币（约合 100 亿美元），人均产值为 66 元人民币。农业占总产值的 70%，农民占人口总量的 80%—90%，许多人生活在贫困中。重工业所占比例不到 8%。

尽管在改革之前经济有所增长，但这并没有为人民创造财富。薛木桥，中国改革的设计师之一，他在 1981 年指出：

"为了使中国摆脱贫困和落后，我们三十年来一直鼓励人民努力奋斗，艰苦朴素……然而，努力奋斗和艰苦朴素意味着在生产方面取得快速进步，并为富裕和幸福的生活创造了物质条件。我们所代表的不是永远贫困。"

值得注意地是，中国的发展道路并不是一帆风顺的，有时候经历着痛苦。中国确实采取了循序渐进的改革路径，被称为"摸着石头过河"。

国有企业的转变

与许多小型国有企业被出售不同，大型国企经历了痛苦的重组过程并随后在股票市场上市。大型国有企业改革的主要目标是从根本上增加自主权，不再需要国家在工资发放和生活方面提供支持，实现"自负盈亏"，最终提高生产效率、对市场的反应能力、整体财务表现和面对外国竞争的生存能力。它们在股票市场上市募集资金，对这一进程提供支持，而中国政府保留了控股权。

国有企业自主权在"政企分开"的政策下实施。

- 自我了解，诊断问题

在外国战略顾问的帮助下，通常企业改组的首要任务是对当前情况进行全面诊断。需要数周的时间分析、找出错误、再次整理、恢复和重新处理公司账目，剔除无关紧要的因素，并从整体上和按业务领域了解公司的真实情况。诊断完成后，国有企业的高管们被这些数据所吸引，表现出诧异和惊愕。

- 国有企业拆分和放权

许多央企只不过是具有高度独立性的省级或市级子公司的拼凑，因而无法实现标准化的战略或运营，也无法为全国各地的客户提供统一的服务网络。随着重组的进行，通常很难转化地方企业，将其并入中央企业的控制下，因为地方政府依赖于它们缴纳的税收。

明智的商业战略始于"由内而外"的方法，首先着眼于市场和客户需求，然后将其与公司自身（或可以收购或构建）的能力和技能相结合。

对于国有企业领导者而言,这种改革的整体理念是具有革命性的,取消计划经济和生产配额主导方法。最重要地是,随着中央计划逐渐解除,国有企业在新一轮自由化中释放活力并进入具有盈利潜力的新业务领域。他们面临的主要问题是缺乏明确的核心业务。

为了帮助国有企业建立产权明晰的核心业务所面临的挑战在于弱化或完全退出不符合战略选择的业务。这一过程中必须面对高层领导对亲自建立的亏损或不匹配的现有业务的情感依恋。

- **新型国有企业**

改革的一个亮点是,鼓励非常成功的新型国有企业,这些企业在很大程度上不受中央计划经济的影响。

联想是这种新型国企的典范。柳传志和计算技术研究所的其他工程师于 1984 年成立联想,据报道称最初的资金来自中国科学院(CAS)。虽然国家通过中国科学院的初始投资保持股权份额,但联想管理层表示公司所有权状况和旧国有企业的所有权之间存在明显的区别。联想首席执行官杨元庆透露,有必要避免让新兴国有企业的所有权对号入座:

> "联想是一家 100% 以市场为导向的公司。有人说我们是国有企业。这是 100% 的错误。1984 年,中国科学院仅对我们公司投资了 25,000 美元。投资的目的是,他们想将研究成果商业化。中国科学院是中国政府的纯研究机构。从这一点上,你可以说我们不同于国有企业。"

他强调指出,即使通过中国国家在联想拥有股权,也不会将其视为传统的国有企业。

> "这家公司完全由创始人和管理团队经营。政府从未参与过我们的日常运营、重要决策、战略方向、首席执行官和高层管理人员的任命以及财务管理。一切都由我们的管理团队负责。"

这是关键所在。政府退居幕后,联想的治理要优于老式的国有企业。这有助于解释联想的辉煌业绩和市场声誉。相同的情形也适用于白色家电制造商青岛海尔,它最初是由地方政府拥有的国有企业。在考察中国的国有企业时发现一个清晰的模式,即国有企业的发展质量与政府/中共的分离程度密切相关。分离程度越大,发展质量越好。

● **私营企业的兴起**

随着经济改革的开始，北京急切的官员皱起眉头开始逐渐放弃中央计划并权衡改革国有企业的各种选择。这些选择都不是没有痛苦或风险。同时，在他们的视线之外，未来的私营经济从基层崛起。

那么，这样一个充满活力的中国私营部门如何与国有企业根深蒂固的经济利益协调并生存下来呢？首先，中国的私营部门只有通过与中共建立联系来削弱其独立性才能生存。其次，中共不仅学会去适应私营部门，而且还意识到私营部门的价值，因为它为经济做出了巨大贡献。这是支撑中国改革的微妙平衡的一部分。

在1978年到1993年期间，乡镇企业的惊人增长在很大程度上是自发产生的，这使中国得以摆脱困境。在中央政府有限支持的控制下，这种令人震惊的现象发生，并最终成为在艰难而危险的过渡时期帮助国民经济扭转不利形势的关键因素。一旦取得合法地位，它们成为中国私营企业的基础。

邓小平在1978年掌握全部权力后的第一个政策举措是废除人民公社，即5000—20000农户组成的农村单位，该单位自1958年起将集体农业与农村工业结合起来。土地使用权还给个体农户。许多基于小公社的集体所有制工厂和作坊开始转变为乡镇企业。

乡镇企业为地方政府松散所有，因此不被视为与国有部门直接相关，但也不是私营企业（直到1988年才合法化）。地方政府与乡镇企业之间的关系是高度共生和相互支持，这与国有企业与政府之间的关系完全不同。管理被外包给企业家，利润共享。在某些方面，乡镇企业是对清末"官督商办"制度的一种回归。

乡镇企业在20世纪80年代和90年代初短暂存在，但其影响却是惊人的。它们是实实在在的"增长引擎"。虽然江苏和浙江等沿海省份的乡镇企业最为活跃，但这也是一个全国性的现象。

然而，许多乡镇企业存在严重缺陷，最终逐渐消失或转变为私人公司。一系列的常见缺陷包括低层次的运营、过时的设备、产品质量差、效率低下、资金短缺、环境污染和危险的工作条件。它们只考虑短期思维，业务重点瞬息万变或过度多样化并且依赖与地方政府的腐败关系。

尽管如此，虽然乡镇企业有各种缺陷，但却是中国企业的重要过渡类型，为真正私营企业的兴起奠定了基础。

虽然有地方政府支持的实例，但大多数私营企业都被迫依靠自身的优势和资源。总部位于杭州的万向集团就是一个很好的案例。

万向崛起的故事开始于 1969 年，目前已经逝去的创始人鲁冠球在当时带领 6 名农民，以相当于 500 美元的资金创办宁围公社农机厂。正如万向集团对我讲述的事实，该公司从一开始就将其视为私人企业，但需要一顶"红帽子"才能够生存，因此它被称为集体企业、乡镇企业，后来才成为私人企业。如今，它已成为全球最大的汽车万向节总成生产商，在中国的市场份额为 65%，在全球的市场份额为 10%。万向集团的销售额为 240 亿美元。鲁先生的净资产估计约为 20 亿美元。该集团拥有 40 多个海外工厂，30000 名员工其中 10000 多名在中国境外。它是中国企业"走出去"的佼佼者。

在 1979 年的改革初期，万向面临的主要挑战是，作为乡镇企业，它不属于国有部门和计划经济部门。它无法获得按计划供应的原材料配额并且被迫冶炼和热处理废金属。在销售成品时，它被禁止参加国有企业的销售计划会议。由于其乡镇企业的身份，万向发现国有银行不愿意发放贷款。

如今，万向作为一家大型私营企业，发现一切开始变得简单。例如，中国国家开发银行向万向提供贷款。然而，正如万向集团对我解释的那样，即使到今天，国家银行也仅将贷款给特定项目（例如，在国家 863 高技术发展计划下支持其电池和电动汽车的开发），而不是用于一般营运资金。为筹集资金以促进其增长，万向集团已在深圳证券交易所上市。

万向集团的经营理念是"量力而行"，这反映出其痛苦的崛起历程。

鲁先生很少宣传，悄悄地建立了自己的全球公司。幸运的是，他生于浙江。几十年来，地方政府非常开明，避免干涉私人企业家的经营。但是，当成功的私营企业达到较大规模时，它们将做出务实的判断（在专制的中国），同时受到真正的爱国主义情绪的驱使，与政府和中共密切合作。在某种程度上，万向确实被纳入"中国企业"。鲁先生是全国人大代表，也是万向集团的党委书记。然而，万向的管理层自信地认为，党的影响力不像国有企业那样具有侵入性。

与万向集团相反，某些私营企业由于在经济中具有战略性作用，受到政府的特别关注。中国的电子巨头华为技术公司就是这种情况。

华为公司总部位于深圳，由任正非于 1987 年创立，注册资本 21000 元人民币，是中国最著名的国有企业之一，2015 年实现全球销售额 600 亿美元。华为融合了私营企业的企业家行为，再加上强大和公平的政府支持，被证明是一个有力的组合，例如使其超过了深圳国企竞争对手中兴，后者也是全国领先企业。

与其他中国私营企业一样，华为面临的最大挑战之一是如何管理公司的爆发式增长。在早期，华为聘请了大量聪明的中国博士生，其中许多人被任命为"总经理"，但很少关注他们所管理的事业或人员，或者职务是否重叠。但华为逐渐重塑企业的组织结构。任正非补充了他的意见，包括一种创新的方法，即首席执行官职务每六个月轮换一次，由八人执行管理团队轮流担任。任正非组建起一支经历时间考验的强大团队。我在 15 年前与之合作的四位高管仍然在职。

政府从一开始就支持华为。在 20 世纪 90 年代后期，被誉为中国电信设备行业"四朵花"的华为与其他三家公司都获得了政府的财政支持。今天，支持仍在继续。在新兴市场，华为在中国的地缘政治中扮演着关键角色，支持从非洲到拉丁美洲的大型基础设施开发计划。中国国家开发银行向华为提供了 300 亿美元的信贷额度，以通过买方信贷支持其国际扩张。这凸显一个事实，即在被认为具有国家战略价值的行业，大型中国私营企业与中国企业的利益不可避免地交织在一起。因此，当人们关注与投资阿里巴巴相关的战略风险时，居于首位的风险就是，马云与中国政府之间的关系有多牢固。即便如此，这些对中国国家安全至关重要的私营企业，也比大型老式国有企业具有更高的自治权。

诚然，某些中国私营企业已经成为无序发展的企业集团，战略重点薄弱。他们背负着银行债务，冒险涉足国际业务。中国政府担心资本外逃和系统性的金融风险束缚了安邦、复星、万达、海航等这些公司及其亿万富翁的所有者。

因此，中国的私营部门在很大程度上完全靠自身努力而崛起。许多具有改革意识的官员承认，在国有企业改革的过程中，私营部门能够保持经济运转。

从积极的方面来看，某些省市比其他省市更全面地拥抱市场化改革。正如浙江省副省长告诉我的那样，政府的作用是提供私营企业蓬勃发展的环境，听起来很像美国的州长，与中国其他地区可能会遇到的限制性"宏观经济指导"有很大不同。海尔和海信在青岛的繁荣与市政府的积极作用息息相关。同样，当我最近访问浙江、福建和广东的一系列中小企业时，他们始终观察到，这些省份的政府干预明显少于几十年前。

私营企业继续保持这种奇怪的状态。一方面，它们带来了就业、创新、利润和税收，而另一方面，它们却在统治着国家部门的强大既得利益集团的阴影下生存并处于脆弱状态。好消息是，中国许多私营企业已经发展到可以更加坚定，开始支配自身状况的地步。随着它们（以及像私营公司一样运作的新型国有企业）成为完全成熟的跨国公司，将不那么容易在中国受到干扰。

外国直接投资的影响

中国敏锐地意识到在新中国成立后的前三十年国家被孤立的灾难性后果，从而采取"对外开放"政策。该政策使外国直接投资大量流入中国，但是，应该强调的是，这些投资仅在符合国家复兴目标的范围内。

外国直接投资已被用来填补中国在技能、技术、产品和服务方面的空白。对外开放政策一直是中国"追赶"发展方法的有机组成部分。在改革之初，邓小平就反对那些对外国直接投资将会威胁到国有企业垄断地位或鼓励企业家精神将导致腐败的担心。他认为，外国直接投资将有助于改变国有部门并鼓励商业创新。

中国寻求获得海外技术和管理技能以提高生产力，促进产业升级和创新。尤其是在外国直接投资的初期，希望通过与外国公司建立合资企业，以吸收技术和技能，"影响"中方，非正式地转让给本地企业。这发生过，但是没有达到预期的程度。

在1978—1979年改革开始之初，中国投入大量资金进口工业用资本设备，这严重拖累了经济。外国直接投资鼓励外国投资者增加投资，这被正确地视为一条可持续发展的道路。

然而，如今中国公司已经可以从股票市场或国有银行获得投资资金。今天很难使大型中国公司对合资企业产生兴趣。如果愿意合作，它们通常会要求拥有多数股权和运营控制权。

外国直接投资对于创造就业机会，抵消因国有企业改组或抛售所造成的裁员等影响非常重要，因此可以在计划经济解体之际实现软着陆。

随着国有部门的精简，外国直接投资为中国提供了机会，可以为大量几乎或没有前途的小型国有企业寻找投资者或购买者。通常，这些企业没有任何可以拿得上台面的东西，包括产品或技能。充其量，它们可能会提供一些市场准入和产品经销渠道。归根结底，它们的主要价值可能是作为新工厂的场地以及与地方官员有一些联系。

学习与追赶

中国采取"学习与追赶"模式取得了超出预期的惊人结果。

美国一位著名的经济学家解释道:"中国建立了一种不可思议的制度,可以从业务培训和技术追赶中取得价值。这是一项重大的创新。"[20] 根据对中国 IT 行业的分析,有人认为:

"中国表现出色是因为将工业生产和服务业与技术前沿完美地结合在一起……它以最快的速度运行,保持在全球技术前沿的风口浪尖,而实际上并未拓展前沿。"[21]

这种模式比某些人所建议的更为复杂,涉及参与价值链的多个要素(提供商品和服务的整个过程)。通过利用全球化对生产步骤的分工,中国打造出:

"强大的竞争能力,可以在研究、开发和生产链的不同领域进行创新……中国的创新能力不仅是过程(或增量)创新,而且还包括生产组织、制造技能和技术、交付、设计以及第二代创新。这些能力允许中国通过原始创新获利后迅速进入新的利基领域。"

在汽车和半导体领域,这种模式远远无法满足推动中国提升技术水平的主要目标。中国成为制造商,但不是产品创新者。

中国能够吸引大量的外国直接投资进入汽车行业。然而,尽管中国现在是世界上最大的汽车市场,外国企业进入市场的唯一合法途径是设立 50/50 合资企业,这一规定并没有直接让中国实现催生优秀的本土汽车企业和世界级民族品牌的目标。

合资企业当然间接地为中国本土汽车行业做出贡献。首先,它们为中国合作伙伴提供大量的现金,用于建立自身独立的汽车厂。但结果无法让人满意。目前,中国合作伙伴的利润只有大约 10% 来自自己的品牌,而其他利润仍然来源于合资企业轻松赚取的收入。

其次,伴随着外资进入中国汽车行业,中国建立起一个完整的本土汽车零部件制造商供应链,包括中国的外国的制造商。这极大地降低了新的本土中国进入者的技术壁垒,例如国企奇瑞以及吉利和比亚迪等私人公司。

然而,尽管有这些优势和学习(以及剽窃)的过程,中国仍然未能建立自己强大的本土汽车产业。为什么今天的中国汽车品牌仍然主要局限于中国的低端市场，而且只拥有 40% 的市场份额？

全球汽车制造商不仅越来越多地关注底层技术，还关注设计和消费者吸引力。即使质量和功能不断改善，在美学方面，中国企业仍在努力打动中国消费者。

虽然缺乏强大的设计能力，更不用说天赋，但这并不是中国汽车制造商未能达到理想标准的唯一原因。外国汽车公司的关键能力包括建立经销商网络、售后服务和汽车金融。中国企业主要专注于汽车的制造和销售，而不是在汽车整个使用寿命期间提供服务。

鉴于这种"学习与追赶"模式未能推动中国本土汽车业向前发展，预计中国正在朝着控股或收购外国汽车公司的方向转移。2010 年，中国私营汽车制造商吉利收购沃尔沃。2014 年，中国国有企业东风汽车公司收购其合作伙伴陷入困境的法国母公司 PSA（标致和雪铁龙的制造商）的股权，允许东风参与 PSA 的研发过程，包括产品设计的软艺术。

尽管中国汽车品牌表现不佳，预计中国会将汽车出口到发达市场，而不仅仅是亚洲和非洲的新兴市场。外国收购将在这方面有所帮助。沃尔沃已经开始向美国出口某些在中国制造的汽车型号。中国极有可能回避改进传统汽车的艰巨挑战，并跃居电动汽车的主导地位。

在中国的半导体行业中也可以发现"学习与追赶"模式的局限性。20 世纪 90 年代，中国内地成功地吸引了台湾地区、日本和美国的芯片制造商在中国建立工厂。但这就是技术发展的步伐，中国一直落后，如今只能满足其半导体需求的 10%。中国每年在半导体进口上的支出高达 2000 亿美元，相当于一年的石油进口额。作为"中国制造 2025"十年计划的重要组成部分，国家半导体产业基金已成立，为该产业投入 200 亿美元。

同时，根据政府的命令，中国的半导体行业正在寻求通过大举购买来获得核心半导体设计技术的使用权，在全球市场上寻找可以收购的外国半导体设计公司。这表明中国正在从"合作、学习"模式过渡到"走出去"模式，以获取所需技术和技能。

相比之下，中国在高铁和核电"追赶"方面表现出色。

对于庞巴迪、川崎、阿尔斯通和西门子等世界高铁供应商来说，中国国内对铁路设备的巨大需求是无法抗拒的，这些供应商通过合资企业进入中国市场。根据合资协议，外国公司的专有高铁技术转让给合资企业，但受到限制，即该技术只能在中国境内使用。

中国已经崛起，拥有强大的铁路技术。合资企业的中方吸收了国外技术，用他们的话说，"重新设计"关键部件，从而使高铁可以以更高的速度运行。当中国人在发达国家注册所谓的新技术专利，准备用于出口时，警告信号发出。川崎威胁要对子弹头列车技术发起知识产权诉讼。中国政府强调，"虽然吸收国外的（铁路）技术，但也对其进行了创新"，并拥有"独立知识产权"。川崎后来撤销法律诉讼威胁，而其他外国企业则避免直接对抗，因为他们仍然希望维持在中国的销售并为其国际业务购买中国制造的零部件。

中国正在探讨在加利福尼亚、英国、哈萨克斯坦、阿根廷、卡塔尔建设高铁项目，并与17个不同国家讨论建设通过中亚地区将中国与欧洲连接起来的高铁项目。我们很可能会发现中国将赢得重要的高铁项目，这些项目不仅可以提供机车车辆，而且可以进行完整的建设。在某些情况下，中国将与当地公司合作。但是大部分工作将由中国负责。

接下来是第三代核电的案例。更安全的第三代核电新技术外国供应商，例如西屋电气和阿海珐，完全参与中国对该技术的"再创新"并希望与中国实现双赢。

西屋电气不仅签订建造核岛和核燃料的标准合同，而且还签订第三份非标准的"全面技术转让合同"，根据该合同，西屋电气将向中方提供"技术信息、设计分析和其他支持信息"，以便中国拥有所需要的一切，将来在中国建设AP1000。

西屋电气与中国客户成立技术合资企业，以使中国设备供应商符合资格并能够生产所有组件，包括对反应堆安全至关重要的组件。合资企业的既定目标不仅是为中国的核反应堆建立供应链，而且还推动中国关键核组件出口。西屋电气已向中国移交75000份文档，用于打造本地版本的第三代技术，包括中国拥有"独立"知识产权并且可以向全球客户授权的一些版本。阿海珐也经历了类似的将技术转移到中国的过程，以换取市场准入。西屋电气设计的第三代核电站（世界上第一个）即将在中国开始运行。对于中国及其外国合作伙伴将新技术真正带入全球市场而言，这是一个双赢的好兆头。

短期内，中国在核工程方面仍将依赖于外国合作伙伴。尽管有财务上的阻力和技术上的延误，但阿海珐和西屋电气牵头的中国项目很可能会完成。外国合作伙伴将继续把中国带入发达的海外市场。

中国正在打一场漫长的比赛。利用其雄厚的资金实力和国内核电市场作为自身技术的试验场，中国最终将摆脱与外国公司的合作关系，而在此之前中国将依赖于从外国公司获取技术并消除海外市场的疑虑。中外核电双赢的局面将比下重赌注的外国公司预期的更加短命，利润也会更少。

在全球市场上收购表现不佳的资产

作为新型国有企业，联想的经营方式与私营企业非常相似，是一家成功的中国跨国公司，在个人电脑和平板电脑领域全球排名第一，在160个国家/地区的销售额达460亿美元。这个万众瞩目的故事核心在于2004年联想收购IBM的个人计算机（PC）业务，扭转亏损局面，实现持续和可盈利的增长。中国媒体将其描述为"蛇吞象"，即联想收购亏损的外国业务，该业务的规模是其自身规模的许多倍。收购一年后，其总收入从29亿美元增长到133亿美元。

联想在业务合并后的整合非常成功。IBM仍然是少数股东。联想总部迁移到纽约州。IBM和联想的产品线互补性很强。文化摩擦得到巧妙处理。联想有能力扭转亏损的IBM业务，实现可持续的盈利。

同样，前面提到的杭州万向集团也能让美国业绩差的工厂变好。这些案例证明，中国企业可以战胜批评并在全球市场取得卓越成就。

新兴市场上的中国企业

中国在全球市场上的第三种模式是中国的三大关键参与方——政府、金融机构和企业，他们步调一致，以从与非洲、亚洲、加勒比海和拉丁美洲等新兴市场的政治关系中获利。

这种模式与中国向新兴国家提供的援助密切相关。在援助计划的支持下，中国国有和私营企业获得大部分的合同。最初的合同主要涉及道路、桥梁、学校、医院、海港、铁路、机场和政府大楼，随后进入铝土矿、钻石、铜、石油和天然气等采矿业。但中国也在建设制造业项目，例如水泥和汽车组装。中国的战略目标视具体情形而定 – 例如在赤道几内亚，石油和天然气领域非常突出，但援助冈比亚可以改变该国与台北的外交关系。在吉布提，重点是"一带一路"倡议的物流基地以及通往埃塞俄比亚内陆的新运输通道。

由于引进中国人开展工作、污染以及合同授予缺乏透明度，中国面临着来自受援国的压力。但大多数批评针对腐败的地方政府，而不是针对中国本身。同时，中国正在从这种新模式中学习并调整其工作方式以适应当地舆论。在非洲，拥有强大公民社会和新闻自由的国家在批评方面比专制政权更为尖锐。尽管情况因国家/地区而异，但我们可以发现一种行为模式。一方面，欧洲列强离开后，中国的援助和企业活动填补了发展援助方面的空白。另一方面，中国通过地方精英以不透明手段行事的方法引发批评。

结 论

中国的发展模式被证明是一个成功的模式。它之所以行之有效，是因为变革的力量，企业家精神和创新与政府处于生产平衡状态。

虽然在过去40年中混合模式也确实有缺点，但是它继承了中国的政治遗产，允许有序、逐步地废除旧的经济模式。中国欢迎外国的技术和商业创意，同时牢牢握住中国社会的政治生活。

然而，考虑到全球变化的步伐，任何国家都不可能宣布在技术获取或开发上永久获胜。今天可以实现自给自足，明天可能会发现自己已经落后。现在不是宣布经济改革取得胜利，然后保持原地踏步的时候。必须继续进行改革，以使中国进一步融入全球经济。

那么，中国治理相关的事项如何在商业界逐步铺开？从积极的一面来看，中国政府将继续在重要领域保持重要角色，将继续加快技术"追赶"的步伐并培养创新，为长期投资提供丰厚的资金。

对于联想和海尔这样的新型国有企业，情形则截然不同。从小生意开始逐步发展壮大或拯救濒临死亡国企的优秀首席执行官已经实现高度的自主权，这是不容置疑的。他们有很大的机会将政府置于后台。这些企业将个人和政府所有权结合，表面上和行为上看起来更像私营公司。由于它们的管理技能可以与全球同行相媲美，因此将继续在国际舞台上竞争。

当政府弄清楚如何对待国有企业后，中国的私营企业走出阴影，帮助支撑经济。虽然具有战略角色的某些企业，例如在高科技领域，将逐渐成为中国企业的实际组成部分，但仍有许多其他企业建立起强大的独立文化。当然，私营企业仍然会担惊受怕，保持警惕，同时象征性地参与政治进程。但是它们可以自立自主。国有银行现在愿意为其提供资金。它们表现出整合并让收购的外国企业扭亏为盈的能力。所有这些预示着未来的发展。

研究指出，中国公司的业绩不完全取决于或在很大程度不由所有权决定，与企业是国有、私有还是介于二者之间无关。业绩和未来潜力与两个密切关联的因素有关。首先，需要强大、专注、战略驱动的公司领导层，有深度的中层管理者可以根据事实共同参与决策。其次，需要实力和远见，与国家官僚机构保持一定距离，这种立场与爱国主义并不矛盾，但能够提供自治的新鲜空气并高度掌控自身的命运。

私营部门和新型国有企业的强劲表现和持续发展将弥补笨重和耗竭财富的国有部门。从长远来看，我们可能会发现新经济的增长以旧经济为代价。一个积极的方面是，政府接受力量的再平衡，从而让政治在企业中居于幕后地位。这将重新启发和点亮改革进程，从而对混合模式进行微调和大修，以适应新的情况。

中国已多次表示必须加强应对国内或全球经济逆境的能力。中国的商业已经成熟，可以在不担心中国治理变化的情况下稳步前进。然而，中国准备在人工智能、物联网方面（包括新型移动解决方案的突破）在全球范围内发挥重要作用。当前中国加强对企业的政治控制以及互联网管制的趋势将使中国企业在寻求提升技术水平并全面参与全球知识经济时，难以发挥最大潜力。

The Emergence of Chinese Companies in Global Markets

Paul Gilmore. Clifford / Britain

Non-resident Senior Fellow at the Kennedy School of Government, Harvard University

My career has been focused on China, first as an academic and later as a businessman. I first learnt Chinese in 1966. I studied in China as an exchange student in 1973. I wrote a thesis on intellectual trends during the 1911 revolution and taught at several universities. After that "I went into the sea" and worked in banking, strategy consulting and high technology for 30 years and mainly in China. I saw the extraordinary forty years of economic reforms and opening up. I helped multinationals entering the China market. I assisted state-owned Chinese firms as they restructured and private Chinese firms as they handled the challenges of breakneck growth.

Having spent my career at the front line of China's economic transformation, I felt I had plenty to tell which would complement more academic or theoretical approaches. I want to explain what are the factors which account for Chinese corporate success.

The Historical Backdrop to the Reforms

Before discussing the emergence of Chinese enterprises during the last four decades, it is instructive to look back at earlier eras since this serves to highlight the significance of the reforms. During the late 19th century, reforming officials of the Qing dynasty sought to spur industrial development but it was too little and too late to save the dynasty. During the Republican period progress was made in creating an industrial infrastructure but this was dissipated by corruption, invasion and civil war.

The establishment of the People's Republic of China(PRC) opened up new opportunities, but unfortunately the perhaps inescapable choice of "leaning to one side" and embracing Soviet Union's aid and the centrally planned economy had extremely negative consequences.

To be fair, the First Five Year 1952-1957 did achieve significant results. It created a comprehensive industrial base. It drove reforms and upgraded the social infrastructure in education, science and technology, education, health, and in women's rights.

In 1949, China's gross output of industry and agriculture (a reasonable proxy for GDP) was only RMB 47 BN (about US$10 BN) with per capita output at RMB 66. Agriculture accounted for 70% of output and 80-90% of the population was farmers, many living in poverty. Heavy industry was less than 8%.

Xue Muqiao, one of the architects of the reforms who wrote in 1981 that:

"To free China from poverty and backwardness, we have for 30 years encouraged people to work hard and lead a simple life.... But hard work and a simple life are meant to achieve speedy progress in production and create the material conditions for a rich and happy life. Perpetual poverty is not what we stand for."[1]

It is worth considering what has been China's trajectory been during this complex

---

1 Xue Muqiao, *China's Socialist Economy*, Beijing 1981, p.236.

and at times painful process. It is perfectly true that China adopted a gradual, step-by-step path to the reforms, commonly referred to as "crossing the river by feeling for the stones". But though China may not have had a detailed master plan, that should in no way imply that it did not have specific goals.

The Transformation of the SOE Sector

While many smaller SOEs were sold off to the highest bidder, the largest SOEs went through a painful process of restructuring, often followed by a stock market listing.

The principal goal was to radically increase the large SOEs autonomy, get them off the State payroll, off life-support and make them "responsible for profit and loss" (zifu yingkui), thus enhancing their productivity, responsiveness to the market, overall financial performance and survivability in face of foreign competition. The stock market listings raised cash to support this process while the Chinese State retained a controlling equity position.

SOE autonomy was implemented under the banner of "separation of government and enterprise."(zhengqi fenkai).

- **Diagnosing the issues: knowing oneself**

Usually with the help of foreign strategy consultants, the first task of the restructuring was a full diagnosis of the current situation. It took weeks to analyze, pull apart, re-order, repair and re-work the firm's accounts to make sense of them, to strip out extraneous factors and to undercover the true picture of the firm, overall and by business line. When the diagnosis was finished, the SOE top executives became riveted on the data revealed. There were expressions of surprise and consternation. It was a revelation, a critical moment of shock, truth and enlightenment.

- **Fragmented and decentralized SOEs**

Many central SOEs were little more than a patchwork quilt of high independent provincial or city subsidiaries that made it impossible to standardize strategy or operations or to provide a consistent network of services for customers across China. As the restructuring proceeded, it was often difficult to transform the local entities and integrate them under central corporate control since they were closely linked into their respective local governments which relied on them for tax revenues.

This holistic concept was quite revolutionary to SOE leaders brought up on Stalinist engineering and production quota-led approaches which paid scant regard to what the customer really wanted. On top of that, as central planning was slowly unwound, SOEs delighted in their new found freedom and jumped into new business areas that appeared to have profit potential. The absence of a clear business focus became a major issue.

To help an SOE create a clear and differentiated business focus, the challenge often became building the case for de-emphasizing or completely exiting from business lines that did not fit the selected strategic option. Often we had to deal with the sentimental attachment to a loss-making or ill-fitting existing business line which had been built by one of the senior leaders of the firm.

- **A new breed of SOE**

One bright aspect of the reforms is that they have permitted a new breed of highly successful SOEs to emerge, largely un-encumbered by the legacy of central planning.

Lenovo is an excellent example of this new breed of SOE. It was established in 1984 by Liu Chuanzhi and other engineers from the Institute of Computer Technology with initial capital from the Chinese Academy of Sciences (CAS) to which it reported. Though the State maintains an equity share through the original CAS investment, its management draws a clear distinction between its ownership status and that of the old SOEs. Lenovo's CEO Yang Yuanqing revealed the need to avoiding pigeon-holing the ownership of these newly-emerged State-sponsored companies:

> "Lenovo is a 100% market-oriented company. Some people have said we are a State-owned enterprise. It's 100% not true. In 1984 the Chinese Academy of Sciences only invested $25,000 in our company. The purpose… to invest…was that they wanted to commercialize their research results. The Chinese Academy of Sciences is a pure research entity in China, owned by the government. From this point, you could say we're different from State-owned enterprises."[1]

He stressed that even through the Chinese State has an equity interest in Lenovo, it is not treated like a traditional SOE.

> "This company is run totally by the founders and management team. The government has never been involved in our daily operation, in important decisions, strategic direction, nomination of the CEO and top executives and financial management. Everything is done by our management team."[2]

This is a key point. Based on government taking a back seat, Lenovo's governance is superior to that of old-style SOEs. This can help explain Lenovo's stellar track record and market reputation. The same can be said about white goods maker Qingdao Haier which started out as a local government owned SOE. In looking at China's SOEs, a clear pattern emerges, a close correlation between their degree of separation from the government/CCP and the quality of the SOE. The greater the separation, the better the quality.

The Emergence of the Private Sector

As the economic reforms began, anxious officials in Beijing with furrowed brows were embarking on the slow unwinding of central planning and weighing up the various options for reforming the SOEs, none of which were painless or risk free.

---

[1] Terril Yue Jones, *Q&A: Chinese computer giant: Chairman of Lenovo, which acquired IBMs PC unit, says the firm has few government ties,* In *Los Angeles Times*, May 4, 2006.

[2] Ibid.

Meanwhile, far from their gaze, the future private economy was emerging at the grass roots.

How then do we reconcile the existence of such a vibrant private sector in China alongside the dominant entrenched economic interests of the SOEs? Firstly the private sector in China only survives by diluting its independence through forging links to the CCP. Secondly, the CCP has learnt not only to live with but also to appreciate the private sector since it contributes so much to the economy. This is part of the delicate equilibrium which underpins China's reforms.

In the period 1978-1993 it was the amazing growth of Township and Village Enterprises (TVEs), which occurred largely spontaneously, that keep China afloat. This stunning phenomenon that occurred under the radar with limited support from central government, ultimately turned out to be a key element that helped turn the national economy around during that difficult and risky transitional period. In turn they became the foundation block of the China privately-owned enterprises (POEs) once they became legally permitted.

One of Deng Xiaoping's first policy moves after gaining full power in 1978 was to abolish the People's Communes, rural units of 5,000-20,000 households which since 1958 had combined collective farming with rural industry. Land use was given back to individual farmer households. Numerous small commune-based collectively-owned[1] factories and workshops began transforming themselves into TVEs.

TVEs were loosely owned by local government and did not count as directly linked into the State-sector. Nor were they POEs (they only became legal in 1988) This relationship between local government and TVEs was highly symbiotic and mutually supportive, quite unlike that between that between SOEs and government. Management was contracted out to entrepreneurs, and profits were shared. In some

---
1 Collective means owned jointly by the local farmers or local government. Considered part of the "socialist" economy, but not part of the State sector.

respects, TVEs were a throwback to the late-Qing system of "Official Supervision, Merchant Management."

The age of the TVEs in the 1980s and early 1990s was short but stunning in its impact. They were truly the "engine of growth."[1] Although the coastal provinces of Jiangsu and Zhejiang saw the most feverish TVE activity, it was a nationwide phenomenon.

However, many TVEs were highly flawed and ultimately faded away or transformed themselves into private firms. The litany of common defects included subscale operations, out-of-date equipment, poor product quality, low levels of efficiency, shortage of capital, environmental pollution and dangerous working conditions. They were given to short-term thinking, with abrupt shifts in business focus or excessive diversification, and were dependent on corrupt relationships with local government.

Nonetheless, despite all their weaknesses, TVEs were a crucial transitional breed of Chinese enterprise that laid the foundation for the emergence of truly private enterprises.

Despite instances of a supportive local government, most POE's have been forced to rely on their own strengths and resources. Hangzhou-based Wanxiang Group, is an excellent example of this

The story of Wanxiang's stellar rise began in 1969 when its recently deceased leader, Lu Guanqiu, and six other farmers used capital equivalent to US$ 500 to establish the Ningwei People's Commune Agricultural Machinery Repair Factory. As Wanxiang explained to me, from the outset the firm saw itself as a private concern, but needed a "Red Hat" to survive, so it was called a collective enterprise, a TVE, and only later became a private enterprise. Today it is the world largest producer of universal joint assemblies for the auto industry with market shares of

---

[1] Yingyi Qian and Jinglian Wu, *China's Transition to a market economy: How Far Across the River*, p.9.

65% in China and 10% globally. Wanxiang has sales of US$ 24 BN. Lu's net worth was estimated at about US$ 2 BN. It has over 40 overseas factories and over 10,000 of its 30,000 employees are outside China. It is a leader among Chinese firms "going out into the world."

In 1979 at the dawn of the reforms, Wanxiang's key challenge was that, as a TVE, it lay outside the State-sector and the planned economy. It lacked access to quotas of raw materials supplied under the Plan and it was forced to smelt and the heat-treat scrap metal. When it came to selling its finished products it was barred from participating in sales planning meetings attended by SOEs. Wanxiang found the State-owned banks unwilling to lend, given its TVE status.

Today Wanxiang, as a major private company, finds things easier. For instance China Development Bank provides loans to Wanxiang. But, as Wanxiang explained to me, as even today the State banks will lend only for specific projects (for instance to support its battery and electric vehicle development program as part of the State's high tech Plan 863) but not for general working capital uses. To raise capital to fuel its growth Wanxiang has listed on the Shenzhen Stock Exchange.

Reflecting its painful emergence, Wanxiang, encapsulates its business philosophy in the traditional Chinese saying "moving forward relying on one's own strengths" (liangli erxing).

Lu quietly built his global firm with very little publicity. He has also had the good fortune to be located in Zhejiang which for decades has had a highly enlightened government which is not inclined to interfere in private entrepreneurship. But when successful POEs reach significant scale they are driven both by pragmatic good sense (in autocratic China) and genuine patriotic feelings into a closer embrace with the government and CCP. To a degree Wanxiang is certainly incorporated into "China Inc." Lu was a delegate to the National People's Congress and also Secretary of Wanxiang's CCP Committee However Wanxiang's management argue convincingly that the influence of the CCP is not as intrusive as that in SOEs.

In contrast to Wanxiang, some POEs, due to their highly strategic role in the economy, have received special attention from the government. This is the case with China's electronics giant, Huawei Technologies.

Huawei, based in Shenzhen, and established in 1987 by Ren Zhenfei with registered capital of RMB 21,000, is one of China's most celebrated SOEs achieved global sales in 2015 of US$ 60 BN. Huawei's blend of private enterprise entrepreneurial behavior, coupled with strong but arms-length government support has proved to be a powerful combination, for instance allowing it to outpace its Shenzhen SOE competitor ZTE, also a national champion.

As with other Chinese POEs, one of Huawei's biggest challenges has been managing the firm's explosive growth. In the early days Huawei hired large numbers of smart Chinese Ph.Ds. many of whom were appointed as "general managers" with little attention given to what or whom they were managing or whether there were overlapping roles. But step-by-step they reshaped their organizational structure. Ren added his input which including an innovative approach whereby the CEO role rotated every six months to a different member of eight person executive management team. Ren built a strong team which had stood the test of time. Four of the top executives I worked with 15 years ago are still in place.

Government support for Huawei was there from the outset. In the late 1990s, Huawei and three other firms described as China's "four flowers" of the telecom equipment industry received financial support from the government. Today the support continues. In emerging markets Huawei plays a key role in China's geo-political plays, supporting major infrastructure development programs from Africa to Latin America. China Development Bank provided Huawei with a US$ 30 BN line of credit to support its international expansion through buyer credits. This underlines the fact that those large Chinese POEs in sectors deemed to be of national strategic value are inevitably intertwined with the interests of China Inc. Thus when people looks at the strategic risks associated with investing in Alibaba, the risk of the top of the list is how strong the relationship is between Jack Ma and the Chinese government. Nonetheless, even these POEs which are critical to China's national security are permitted a far higher degree of autonomy than large old style SOEs.

It is true that some Chinese private firms have become sprawling conglomerates with a weak strategic focus. Loaded with bank debt, they have made risky forays into international business. The Chinese government worried about capital flight and systemic financial risk has reined in these firms, such as Anbang, Fosun, Wanda and HNA, and their billionaire owners.

While other private firms such Wanxiang and Huawei and new style SOEs such as Lenovo and Haier with better corporate governance are able to maintain a high degree of autonomy, the fundamental point remains that the private sector exists at the whim of the CCP and the government.

So China's private sector emerged largely by dint of its own efforts. Many reform-minded officials acknowledged the ability of the private sector to keep the economy afloat while the SOEs was being patched up and rebuilt.

On the positive side, some provinces and cities have embraced market-driven reforms more comprehensively than other. As a Vice Governor of Zhejiang told me, the role of government is to provide the environment in which POEs can flourish, sounding much like a the governor of a US State and quite difference from the restrictive "macro-economic guidance' you may meet in other parts of China. The flourishing of Haier and Hisense in Qingdao has much to do with the positive role played by the city government. Likewise when I recently visited a series of small and medium sized enterprises in Zhejiang, Fujian and Guangdong they consistently observed that government in those provinces were notably less interfering than they had been several decades before.

POEs continues to have this curious status. On the one hand they create jobs, innovation, profits and tax revenues, while on the other hand they live exposed and vulnerable, in the shadow of the formidable vested interests that rule the State sector. The good news is that many of China's private enterprises have grown to a point where they can be more assertive and begin to dictate their own terms. As they (and the new-style SOEs which operate like private firms) become fully fledged multinationals they will also be less easily interfered with in China.

The Impact of Foreign Direct Investment

China was acutely aware of the disastrous result of the nation's isolation during the first thirty years of the PRC and launched the "Open Door" (duiwai kaifang) policy which has enabled the massive flow of Foreign Direct Investment (FDI) into China, but, it should be stressed, only to the extent that it served its goals of national revival.

FDI has been used to fill China's gaps in skills, technology, products and services. The Open Door policy has been integral to China's "catch up" approach. At the beginning of the reforms, Deng Xiaoping pushed back against colleagues who feared that FDI would threaten the monopolies enjoyed by SOEs or, by encouraging entrepreneurial attitudes, lead to corrupt behavior. He took the view that FDI would help transform the State sector and encourage business innovation.

China sought access to overseas technology and management skills to drive productivity, industrial upgrading and innovation. Especially in the early days of FDI, there was the hope that, through engagement in JVs with foreign firms, technology and skills would be absorbed, "rub off" onto the Chinese side, be informally transferred to local firms. This has occurred, but not to the extent envisaged.

At the beginning of the reform process in 1978-1979 China spent heavily on imports of capital equipment for industry, severely straining the economy. FDI, which encouraged foreign investors to pony up some of the investment, was rightly seen as a more sustainable route.

However, today Chinese firms have ready access to investment funds from the stock market or from State banks. It is hard today to get major Chinese firms interested in a JV. If they are willing to partner, then they will typically demand majority equity and operating control.

FDI was important in creating jobs, in offsetting the impact of layoffs resulting from the restructuring or selling-off of SOEs, thus permitting a softer landing during the pain of unwinding the planned economy.

In the wake of the slimming down of the State-sector, FDI offered China an opportunity to find investors or buyers for countless smaller SOEs that had little or no viable future. Typically these firms brought nothing to the table in way of products or skills. At best, they might provide some market access and product distribution. At the end of the day, their main value might be as land that could be cleared for a new factory, plus some residual connections to local officials.

Learn and Catch up

China, using the "learn and catch-up" model, has achieved stunning results beyond what had been anticipated.

As a leading US economist explains, "China has developed a marvelous system for extracting value for business training and playing catch-up in technology. This is significant innovation."[1] Based on analysis of China's IT industry, it is argued that;

> "China shines by keeping its industrial production and service industries in perfect tandem with the technological frontier… It runs as fast as possible in order to remain at the cusp of the global technology frontier without actually advancing the frontier itself."[2]

This model is also more complex than some would suggest, involving participation

---

1 Confidential interview with US government economist specializing in the Chinese economy, Sept. 2013.
2 Dan Breznitz and Michael Murphee, *Run of the Red Queen, Government, Innovation, Globalization, and Economic growth in China*, Yale, 2011, p.3.

in multiple elements of the value chain (the entire process through which goods and services are delivered). China, through taking advantage of the way globalization has fragmented the production steps, has created;

> "A formidable competitive capacity to innovate in different segments of the research, development and production chain.... China's innovation capability is not just process (or incremental) innovation but also in the organization of production, manufacturing techniques and technologies, delivery, design and second generation innovation. Those capabilities enable China to move quickly into new niches once they have proved profitable by the original innovator." [1]

In the automotive and semiconductor sectors this model has fallen fell frustratingly short of the key goals of propelling China up the technology ladder. China became a manufacturer but not the product innovator.

China was able to attract massive FDI into its auto industry. But although China is now the largest auto market in the world, the 50/50 JVs that were legally the only market entry route for foreign players did not directly achieved China's goal of spawning its own outstanding indigenous auto industry and world-class national brands.[2]

The JVs have of course indirectly contributed to China's local auto sector. Firstly, they have provided the Chinese partners with huge piles of cash which have been used to establish their own separate auto plants. But the results have been unimpressive. Today only about 10% of the profits of these Chinese partners come from their own brands while the rest is still easily-earned money from the JVs.

Secondly, with the foreign entrants to the Chinese auto industry came the

---

1　Dan Breznitz and Michael Murphee, *Run of the Red Queen, Government, Innovation, Globalization, and Economic growth in China*, Yale, 2011, p.4.
2　Liang Xionghui, CPO, Lifan Group, quoted in Tian Ying, *China's Plan for its Own Car brands Stall*, Businessweek, Aug 30, 2012.

establishment in China of a comprehensive locally-based supply chain of auto components manufacturers – some foreign, some Chinese. This has dramatically lowered the technological barriers for a new breed of local Chinese entrants such as the SOE Chery and private firms Geely and BYD.

But despite these advantages and the process of learning (and theft) China has failed to create its own strong indigenous auto industry. Why do Chinese auto brands remain today confined mainly to the low end of the Chinese market and have a 40% market share?

The focus of global auto makers is increasingly not just on the underlying technology but also on design and consumer appeal. This aesthetic aspect is an area where Chinese players struggle to impress Chinese consumers, even as quality and functionality continues to improve.

The lack of strong design capability, let alone flair, is not the only reason why Chinese auto makers have failed to make the grade. The key competency of foreign auto firms includes how to establish dealer networks, after-sales service and auto financing.[1] Chinese players focused mainly on getting cars made and sold, rather than on providing service for the life of the vehicle.

Given the failure of this "learn and catch-up" model to propel China's indigenous auto industry forward, China's is predictably migrating towards taking holdings in or acquiring foreign auto firms. In 2010 private Chinese auto maker Geely acquired Volvo. In 2014 China's SOE car firm Dongfeng acquired an equity stake in its partner's ailing French parent company PSA (makers of Peugeot and Citroen) permitting Dongfeng's participation in PSA's R&D process including the soft art of product design.

Despite the poor showing of Chinese auto brands, we can expect Chinese to export vehicles into developed markets and not just emerging markets of Asia and

---

1 Paul Clifford, August Joas, Frank Leung, *A New Vroom for China's Auto market.* In Mercer *Management Journal*, Number 19, 2004.

Africa. The foreign acquisitions will help in this respect. Volvo have already begun exporting certain China-built models to the USA. There is also the strong likelihood that that China will sidestep the tough challenge of improving the traditional car and will leapfrog into dominance in electric vehicles.

The limitations of the "learn and catch up" model can also be seen in China's semiconductor industry. In the 1990s China was successful in enticing Taiwan, Japanese and US chip manufacturers to establish plants in China. But such is the pace of technology development that China has fallen behind and today can only supply 10% of its semiconductor needs. China annually spends as much as US$200 BN on semiconductor imports, equivalent to a year of oil imports. As a key part of China's ten year "Made in China 2025"plan, a National Semiconductor Industry Fund has been established to plough US$ 20 BN into this industry.

At the same, on orders from the government, China's semiconductor industry is seeking to gain access to core semiconductor design technology through going on a buying spree, scouring the global market for foreign semiconductor design firms that it can acquire. [1] This is part of China's transitioning from the "partner, learn" model to one which involves "going out into the world" to acquire the technology and skills needed.

In contrast, China has performed strongly in "catch-up" in high speed rail (HSR) and in nuclear power.

China's massive domestic demand for railway equipment proved to be irresistible to the world's HSR suppliers such as Bombardier, Kawasaki, Alstom and Siemens who piled into the China market through JVs. Under the JV agreements, the foreign firms' proprietary HSR technology was transferred to the JV but with the restriction that it was only for use within China.

China has emerged as a powerful force in railway technology. The Chinese

---

1 Paul G. Clifford, Confidential interview with senior leader of a major global PE firm, October 23, 2014.

side to the JVs took the foreign technology and, in their words, "re-designed" key components which permitted the HSR to run at higher speeds. Warning signals went off when the Chinese began registering patents on this supposedly new technology in the developed countries in preparation for export. Kawasaki threatened to sue for IPR infringement on its bullet rain technology. The Chinese government stressed that it had "absorbed foreign [rail] technology but also innovated it" and that they owned the "independent intellectual property rights." Kawasaki later backed off of their threat of legal action, while the other foreign players avoided direct confrontation since they still hoped to sustain their sales in China and also to purchase China-made components for their international business.

China is exploring HSR projects in California, UK, Kazakhstan, Argentina, Qatar, and is holding discussions with 17 different countries about a HSR linking China with Europe, through central Asia. We shall likely see China winning major HSR projects in which they not only supply rolling stock but also undertake the complete construction. In some cases China will partner with local firms. But the bulk of the work will go to China.

Next the case of Generation III nuclear power. In this case the foreign suppliers of the new safer Generation III nuclear power technology, such as Westinghouse and Areva, were fully complicit in the Chinese "re-innovation" of the technology and looked to have achieved a remarkable win-win with China.

Westinghouse signed not only the standard contracts for the construction of the nuclear island and for nuclear fuel, but also a third non-standard "comprehensive technology transfer contract" under which they provided the Chinese side with "technical information, design analysis and other supporting information so that they have everything that they need to go ahead and build AP 1000's themselves in China in the future."[1]

---

1 William Poirier, Westinghouse VP for Nuclear Plants, China, quoted in *Nuclear power in China. How the Red Dragon will lead the World*, www.powerengineerinmgint.com, Jan 10, 2000.

Westinghouse formed a technical JV with its Chinese customer to qualify Chinese equipment suppliers and to enable them to produce all the components including those highly critical to the safety of the reactor. The stated goal of the JV was not only to create a supply chain for Chinese reactors but also to facilitate the export of critical nuclear components from China. Westinghouse handed over 75,000 documents to China which have been used to create a local versions of the Generation III technology including several for which China owns the "independent" property rights and can therefore license to its global customers. Areva have been through a similar process of transferring their technology to China, in return for market access. A Generation III nuclear plant designed by Westinghouse is close to beginning operations in China (the first one in the world). This bodes well for China and its foreign partners to take this new technology into global market, as a true win-win.

In the short term, China will still rely on foreign partners in nuclear engineering. The China projects led by Areva and Westinghouse, despite the financial headwinds and technical delays, will likely be completed. The foreign partners will continue to shoe horn China into developed overseas markets.

China is playing a long game. Using its financial muscle and its domestic nuclear power market as a test bed for its own technology, China will ultimately outgrow its partnerships with foreign firms which it had earlier relied on to acquire technology and to allay concerns in overseas markets. The win-win from the China-foreign link-up in nuclear power will have been shorter lived and less lucrative than had been anticipated by the foreign firms that placed such heavy bets.

Acquiring underperforming assets in global markets

Lenovo, as one of a new breed of SOEs run much like a private firm, is a successful Chinese multinational firm, the world's No 1 in personal computers and tablets with sales of US$ 46 BN in 160 countries. A the heart of this remarkable story is how in 2004 Lenovo acquired IBM's Personal Computer (PC) business, turned it around and creating sustained and profitable growth. The Chinese press described it as the "snake that swallowed the elephant." Here was Lenovo acquiring a loss-making foreign business many times its own size. One year after the acquisition its total revenues had grown from US$ 2.9 BN to US$ 13.3 BN.

Lenovo's post-merger integration was highly successful. IBM remained as a minority shareholder. Lenovo's head office was moved to New York state. The IBM and Lenovo product lines were extremely complementary. Cultural frictions were handled cleverly. Lenovo was able to turnaround the loss-making IBM business and achieve sustainable profitability.

Likewise the above mentioned Hangzhou Wangxiang, also turned around underperforming factories in the USA. These examples serve to demonstrate that China firms can confound the critics and achieve excellent in global markets.

China Inc. in emerging markets

The third model of China in global market is how three key sets of Chinese players - the government, financial institutions and companies operating in lockstep to reap benefits from political relationships with emerging markets from Africa and Asia to the Caribbean and Latin America.

This model is closely entwining with Chinese aid provide to these emerging countries. Chinese firms, both state owned and private, receive most of the contracts on the back of the aid programs. The initial contracts were typically for roads, bridges, schools, clinics, seaports, railways, airports and government building. Access to minerals followed, such as bauxite, diamonds, copper and oil and gas. But China is also creating manufacturing capabilities such as in cement and car assembly. China's strategic goals vary – for instance in Equatorial Guinea oil and gas figures prominently. But the aid The Gambia was linked to that nation's switch of diplomatic allegiance from Taipei to Beijing. In Djibouti the focus a logistics base for the Belt and Road Initiative and new transportation links into Ethiopia in the interior.

China has faced some push-back from recipient countries, over Chinese being brought into do the work, pollution and over lack of transparency in contract awards. But most of the criticism is directed at corrupt local governments rather than against China itself. Meanwhile China is learning from this new model and adjusting the way it works to accommodate local public opinion. Countries in Africa which have a strong civil society and free press are more strident in their criticisms than more authoritarian regimes in that continent. Though situations vary from country to country, we can see a pattern of behavior. On the one hand Chinese aid and entrepreneurial activity fills a gap in developmental aid after the departure of the European powers. On the other hand China's modus operandi of working in an opaque manner through local elites attracts criticism.

Conclusions

China's hybrid developmental model has so proven to be a winning formula. It has worked well because the forces of change, of entrepreneurialism and innovation have enjoyed a productive equilibrium with the governing by CCP.

Though the hybrid model during the last four decades did have its weaknesses, it fitted China's political legacy and permitted an orderly and gradual dismantling of the old economic model. China welcomed foreign technology and business ideas while holding the lid on the Chinese pressure cooker of a society.

But given the pace of global change one can never declare victory in the acquisition or development of technology. Today one may achieve self-sufficiency, but tomorrow one may find oneself left behind. This is not the time to declare victory in the economic reforms and to hunker down. The reforms must continue so that China is further integrated into the global economy.

So how will the issues with China's governance play out in China's business world? On the positive side, the Chinese government will continue to play its valuable role as sponsor of "national champions" in key sectors. It will continue to force the pace of technological "catch up" and to foster innovation, providing deep pockets for long-term investment.

When it comes to new-style SOEs such as Lenovo and Haier the story is refreshingly different. Strong CEOs, who had built their firms from humble beginnings or rescued them from oblivion, have achieved a high degree of autonomy which should be unassailable. They have a good chance of keeping the government in the background. With their blend of personal and government ownership, they look and act more like private firms. Given their management skills that compare favorably with those of their global peers, they will continue to compete strongly on the world stage.

Chinese POEs came out the shadows and helped prop up the economy while the government worked out what to do with the SOEs. Although some with a strategic role, such as in high-tech, will find themselves increasingly a de facto part of China Inc, there is a raft of others which have established a strong culture of independence. They will of course look over their shoulders, watchful and playing a visible game of token participation in the political process. But they can stand on their own feet. State banks are now willing to finance them. They show the ability to integrate and turn-around foreign firms they have acquired. All this bodes well for the future.

The findings are that the Chinese corporate performance cannot solely or largely be defined by ownership, by whether the firm is state-owned or private, or something in between. Performance and future potential are linked to two closely related factors. Firstly it requires a strong, focused, strategically driven corporate leadership and below that a depth of middle management that shares in the decision-making based on facts. Secondly it requires the strength and vision to create and sustain a distance between it and the nation's bureaucracy, a position that is not incompatible with patriotism but which provides the fresh air of autonomy and a high degree of control over ones destiny.

The strong performance and sustainability of the private sector as well as of the new-style SOEs will counterbalance the ponderous and wealth-draining State sector. Longer term, we shall likely see the new economy grow at the expense of the old one. A positive scenario would be one in which there the government accepts a rebalancing of the equilibrium of forces whereby politics take more of a back seat in enterprises. That would represent an enlightened re-igniting of the reform process whereby the hybrid model is fine-tuned and overhauled to fit new conditions.

China has demonstrated repeatedly that it has to strength to weather economic adversity which domestic or global. China's businesses have a reach a maturity which permits them to forge ahead without concern over shifts in China's governance. However, China is poised to plays a fundamental global role in artificial intelligence, in the Internet of Things including breakthroughs in new mobility solutions. The current trend in China to increase political control over enterprises coupled with restrictions on the internet will make it less easy for Chinese firms to maximize their potential as they seek to move up the technology ladder and participating fully in the global knowledge economy.

"一带一路"倡议在尼泊尔的展望

萨尔波塔姆·什雷斯塔 【尼泊尔】

尼泊尔阿尼哥协会会长 / 加德满都示范医院神经病学家

一、背景

2018年是中国国家主席习近平提出"一带一路"倡议的第五年。目前,全世界已经有60多个国家参与到"一带一路"的倡议中来。位于中国西藏南边的邻国尼泊尔在参与"一带一路"倡议方面反应比较迟缓。在中国正式出台"一带一路"倡议后一年的时间内,尼泊尔没有做出任何回应。2015年3月,中国国家主席会见访华并参加博鳌论坛的尼泊尔总统亚达夫,当时亚达夫总统第一次表示尼泊尔坚定地支持"一带一路"倡议和"亚投行"建设,但是尼泊尔政府没有正式表态。直到2017年初,尼泊尔才开始了解"一带一路"倡议,当地媒体也开始介绍"一带一路",逐渐形成"一带一路"倡议对尼泊尔来讲是一个难得的发展机会的共识。2017年5月,尼泊尔政府表示愿意参与"一带一路"建设,并与中国签署了"一带一路"框架协议。2018年6月19—24日,尼泊尔总理奥利访华,在14项合作意向书、备忘录和项目上签字。但并没有明确指出,这14项中哪些属于"一带一路"倡议下的项目。

二、中国提出"一带一路"倡议后中国和尼泊尔之间的合作

中国和尼泊尔是世代友好邻邦,1955年正式建交以来两国合作不断。在中国出台"一带一路"倡议后的五年时间里,中尼之间的合作更多,但到目前还没有

确定哪些属于"一带一路"倡议下的合作项目。下面我们从"一带一路"倡议提出的"五通"五个方面分别阐述一下中国和尼泊尔的合作。

1. 设施连通方面：中国和尼泊尔之间的设施连通方面以"跨喜马拉雅多元连接网络框架"（Trans-Himalaya Multi Dimensional Connectivity Network Framework）新概念，在开通关口、修建和利用公路、光纤连接、电路连接、航线连接和铁路的修建和连接等方面在做一些工作，分别如下：

（1）关口：吉隆口岸目前是正在运转之中的唯一的尼中关口。几十年前开通的樟木口岸在 2015 年的大地震中受到严重破坏，至今仍未修复。今年 6 月尼泊尔总理奥利访问中国期间，双方同意将于 2019 年 5 月重新开通樟木口岸。除此之外还将开通其他 7 个新的关口，以便从中国西藏向尼泊尔北部与西藏接壤的地区供应日用品。准备开通的 7 个关口短期内不会发展成边贸口岸，因此也不会设立两国海关等设施。

（2）公路：在中国境内已经有许多通往尼泊尔边境的公路。但尼泊尔镜内只有一条通往中国西藏边境吉隆的公路。通往樟木口岸的阿尼哥公路在大地震中受到破坏后部分路况不好，因为樟木口岸尚未开放，这条公路靠近中国西藏的部分行驶车辆很少。这次尼泊尔总理访华时，双方同意尼泊尔的货车可以使用中国西藏境内的公路前往尼泊尔的另外一个北部边境城镇。

（3）光纤：2018 年 1 月中国和尼泊尔之间在光纤联络方面有了实质性的进展。尼泊尔通讯公司与中国环球通讯公司的合作项目成功地在吉隆 Rasuwagadhi 关口完成了光纤连接工作，从此结束了尼泊尔网络完全依赖印度的局面。

（4）电路：今年 6 月在尼泊尔总理访华签署的项目中包括"尼泊尔中国跨境电网互联项目"。这是尼泊尔国家供电局和中国国家电网公司之间签署的项目。该项目中吉隆将跟尼泊尔的 Rasuwagadhi, Galchhi, Ratmate 通过 400kV 传输线连接起来。

（5）航线：尼泊尔首都加德满都目前与中国的 6 个城市，即拉萨、成都、西安、昆明、广州和香港有直航。直航班次已经恢复到尼泊尔大地震前时期。两国仍在强调增加直航城市数目和航班次数，但最近几年并没有实现。

（6）铁路：铁路是近期尼泊尔媒体的一个热门话题，也是尼泊尔议会上经常议论的内容。一年前中国相关部门派遣一个专家组到尼泊尔，进行尼泊尔铁路修建的可行性调查，并提交了调研报告。报告称，在尼泊尔修建中等速度的电动火车技术上是可行的。今年6月份，尼泊尔总理奥利访问中国，在会见中国国家主席习近平时，总理先生重点提出在尼泊尔修铁路，并跟在中国境内的吉隆日喀则铁路相连的合作项目。尼泊尔媒体上出现的报道称，中国国家主席当场承诺，中国的火车一定会通到尼泊尔加德满都。虽然两国在理论上都同意修建这条铁路，但实现这个目标还有漫长的路要走。按照现在的计划，2018年8月进一步完善尼泊尔铁路项目的可行性调查，从2018年8月起，一年半时间内完成"项目详细报告"（DPR），之后开始修建，如果一切顺利整个项目将在5年内完成。

2. 贸易畅通：中国和尼泊尔之间的跨喜马拉雅边境贸易目前只有吉隆关口在进行中。该关口于2014年11月正式开通，目前每日运输量为250辆集装箱。2015年尼泊尔大地震中受到严重破坏的樟木口岸至今没有恢复运行。

3. 货币融通：尼泊尔国内目前没有任何外国银行的分行，只有外国银行跟尼泊尔银行的合作银行，因为尼泊尔还没有允许外国银行在尼泊尔设立分行的法律条款。因此尼泊尔和中国之间实行货币融通的基础还没有建成。目前，尼泊尔甚至还没有中国跟尼泊尔合作开办的银行。近年来，中国游客在尼泊尔中国人经营的旅行社、宾馆、餐厅使用支付宝、微信支付等网络支付，中国游客在尼泊尔的许多交易不需要经过货币了，但是尼泊尔政府还没有将这种网上支付方式合法化。

4. 政策沟通方面：尼泊尔政府在中国广州已经设立了领事馆，在成都设立尼泊尔领事馆的计划也正在讨论之中。两国同意各自设立一个高级机构来监督实施和管理两国之间签署项目的进展情况。

5. 民心相通方面：民心相通方面可以从两国之间的旅游、人员互访、举办文化活动和文化产品互译等几个方面讲述。

中国政府把尼泊尔列入国外旅游目的地之列，尼泊尔相应地也给中国游客提供落地免费签证之便，同时因为尼泊尔旅游本身并不昂贵等因素，到尼泊尔旅游的中国游客数目不断在增加。2015年尼泊尔大地震后，中国游客数突降，近来，在中国政府和其他相关部门的正面宣传下逐渐恢复。

近几年受邀访问中国的尼泊尔人比过去多，同样访问尼泊尔的中国各界人士也比过去多。尼泊尔是设立中国文化中心比较早的一个国家，近来与中国文化有关的画展、书法展、音乐舞蹈节目、中国武术表演等活动在尼泊尔越办越多，相信参与活动的人数会不断增加。

尼泊尔一些民间组织把中国优秀的文化产品介绍到尼泊尔，但还比较有限，也没能在尼泊尔开发出中国文化产品的市场。近几年有些学者把尼泊尔的一些文学作品翻译成中文并在中国出版发行，也有中国作家访问尼泊尔回国后，将在尼泊尔的所见所闻以文学作品呈现，但这种交流在两国媒体上的报道很少，社会影响较小。

三年前，中国的"一带一路"民间组织论坛在尼泊尔成立了尼泊尔分支，这是尼泊尔带有"一带一路"字眼的唯一的组织。但论坛成立后没有实质性的工作进展。

三、"一带一路"倡议在尼泊尔的展望

世界很多地区在"一带一路"倡议下已经成功地完成了许多项目，并且一些项目开始产生经济效益。尼泊尔加入"一带一路"倡议迟缓，由于当时尼泊尔国内政治任务繁重，政府没有能够重视"一带一路"倡议。现在尼泊尔已经完成推行联邦制度，成功举行全国三级（地方级、邦级和联邦级）选举，成立了三级政府。今年 2 月份，由奥利总理领导的新内阁组成，并逐渐在议会获得了三分之二的支持。这个尼泊尔历史上比较强大的、由共产党领导的尼泊尔政府，会如何参与"一带一路"倡议？"一带一路"倡议在尼泊尔的展望，或者前景如何？现从以下几个方面思考。

1. 尼泊尔政府的重视程度

尼泊尔政府在签协议方面比较积极，但实施协议里的项目方面不够积极，尤其是尼泊尔国家自己投资的项目，这是国内外观察者的判断。

尼泊尔的第二个国际机场，Nijgadha 国际机场建设项目，已经启动 17 年。11 年前尼泊尔政府将这个项目列为"民族自豪"项目，但因为尼泊尔政府不够重视，机场建设进度非常缓慢，到现在只完成了很少的工作。加德满都饮水工程 Melamchi 项目启动也已经 20 多年，到现在还没有完成，据说今年年底竣工，但一再地推迟。

奥利第一次担任尼泊尔总理时，于 2016 年 3 月在国家处于非常困难的时期

访问了中国。当时他在北京签订了有关双方贸易、交通、石油运输等重要内容的协议。但他回国以后的两年内，这些项目的实施方面没有任何进展。奥利回国后不久就下台，政府重组，新政府对奥利签订的协议兴趣不大。除此之外，当时国内也正在进行联邦议会和邦议会选举。但是实际上，就像奥利新政府的外交部长这次访华前后接受媒体采访时所讲的那样，印度解除了对尼泊尔的边境封锁以后，与中国签订的协议就不在尼泊尔政府优先考虑的事项之中了。所以这种态度始终让人怀疑，奥利政府这次到底会不会重视与"带一路"倡议有关的项目。

2. 尼泊尔政府的准备工作

近期尼泊尔政府虽然对跟中国进行"一带一路"合作表现得士气高昂，但并没有做好迎接"一带一路"合作项目的准备工作。目前，最有可能成为"一带一路"倡议下合作项目的吉隆—加德满都铁路，在尼泊尔各大媒体的宣传特别多。尼泊尔政府的出发点是，对一个内陆山区国家来说，铁路是最便宜最划算的运输方式，所以尼泊尔应该修建铁路。

修建此铁路的技术问题、投资、用途和经济效益等，只有技术问题得到解决。勘察吉隆-加德满都铁路的中国专家组认为，该地段海拔高、坡道长、地质情况复杂、环保要求高，但这些困难都是可以努力克服的。

尼泊尔向中国提出，希望中国无偿援助修建这条铁路。如果中国无偿援助来修建，它的投资、用途甚至经济效益都不成为问题。但中国政府已经表示不可能全部援助，必须有尼泊尔自己的投资。虽然政府准备两年后项目详细报告出台后再考虑它的投资问题，但该项目在民间已经成为热门话题。吉隆和加德满都之间的直线距离为 72 公里，专家组说，在这里修建铁路长度将是 75-100 公里，按每公里造价为 2.4 亿元人民币估算，整条铁路造价可达 240 亿元人民币。

通常情况下，某个地区生产过剩，或者新项目上马后有望生产过剩，这时才会想到在这个地区搞运输项目。尼泊尔目前没有什么大量的产品可以出口中国，每年中国尼泊尔贸易逆差高达 78.08 亿元人民币。尼泊尔近期也没有可能会大规模增加生产的发展项目。尼泊尔学者和智库能够想到的这条铁路的经济效益只有两个方面：第一，2020 年以后西藏将引进两千万游客到西藏旅游，这样西藏的新鲜蔬菜水果的需求量会大增，修建这条铁路后，尼泊尔可以向西藏供应新鲜蔬菜水果。为此，今年 6 月份尼泊尔总理访华时签署的协议中，就有在尼泊尔境内建立一个生产蔬菜水果尤其是有机蔬菜水果农场。第二，修建这条铁路以后，来加德满都和蓝毗尼的中国游客会新增 250 万人（次），以通过旅游业增加国家收入。但不难看出，向中国西藏出口部分新鲜蔬菜水果是无法达到贸易平衡的。同样仅靠这条铁路就能如此大规模地增加中国游客数量也不现实，因为尼泊尔的中国游客当中，来自西藏自治区的不是最多，还是内地游客占多数。内地游客考虑到西藏的高海拔、路程时间等因素，不一定愿意经由西藏来尼泊尔，而且从中国到尼泊尔的航线航班那么多，对想来尼泊尔旅行的中国人来说，目前的交通已经很方便了。

  修建这条铁路，它对国家经济的影响是多方面的，但铁路运输费的收入是很低的。有一个专家组近期对连接加德满都和尼泊尔中南部靠近印度边境城市的铁路经济效益做了调研，根据他们的调研结果，按照现在的价格，铁路每年的运输费收入仅占投资的 1.466%。而且修建铁路周期长，个人或公司不会愿意在这种项目中投资。

  现在对修建铁路做过度的宣传，执政的尼泊尔政府已经获得短暂的政治利益，而且该计划可能成为当前执政党在下次全国大选中的重点宣传内容。另外，如果将来无论任何原因，万一铁路项目不成，老百姓不会责怪尼泊尔政府，反而会对中国产生不好的印象，因为现在的宣传是，中国已经承诺将中等速度的电动铁路从吉隆修建到加德满都。

  3. 尼泊尔、中国和印度的关系

  因南亚的特殊地缘政治关系，尼泊尔发生的每件大事都受着来自印度不同程度的影响。印度认为，尼泊尔是它特殊关系的国家，两国人民在宗教、文化、语言上有相似性，印度和尼泊尔边境是开放的，人民在两国之间往来不需要护照，更不需要签证。同时，尼泊尔是一个还没有被中国影响很多的南亚国家，所以印度不希望中国增加对尼泊尔的影响。印度学者把中国在尼泊尔不断增加的影响也看成印中矛盾的重点之一。印度绝对不会希望在尼泊尔上马"一带一路"倡议下的任何大型项目，因为这样的项目无疑会提高中国在尼泊尔的影响力。

  因为国际政治的复杂因素，近期中国和印度的关系有一些好转。习近平和莫迪 5 月份在武汉的非正式会晤，可以说是印度和中国关系史上新的高度。尽管印度和中国在许多国际问题和发展理念上开始产生很多共识，但是印度仍然对"一带一路"倡议持否定态度，中国也明确表示，中国不强迫印度加入"一带一路"建设，并表示不加入"一带一路"倡议也可以合作。这样一来，尼方和中方曾经提出的建设"中国、尼泊尔、印度经济走廊"的可能性就很小。如果今后印度和中国的关系变得密切，中国和印度也不一定经由尼泊尔促进双方的贸易，因为虽然中国和尼泊尔之间的边境有 1400 公里，但印度和中国之间的共同边境更长，而且大量大型的贸易是通过海路进行的，因此尼泊尔更是被排除在外。

尼泊尔市场小、人口少，如果印度对建设"中尼印经济走廊"没有兴趣，修建铁路的意义对中国就不大。中国可以提议尼泊尔自己投资修建尼泊尔境内的铁路，但是中国也要在自己境内修建 400 多公里的铁路才能连接到尼泊尔，中国也会重新考虑这笔投资的意义。中国提出在尼泊尔修建铁路的同时，印度也提出修建连接印度边境和加德满都的铁路。不在"中尼印经济走廊"建设的框架下，印度政府提出修建这条铁路，其目的只能是加强印度和尼泊尔之间的传统贸易。

展望未来，中国和尼泊尔在"一带一路"倡议下的合作，其飞跃性发展将面临许多挑战。

Prospects of the "Belt and Road" Initiative in Nepal

Sarbottam Shrestha / Nepal

President of Arniko Society, Neurologist of Kathmandu Model Hospital

I. Background

This year marks the fifth year after the Belt and Road Initiative was proposed by Chinese President Xi Jinping. At present, more than 60 countries around the world have participated in the Belt and Road Initiative. Nepal, a neighboring country located to the south of China's Tibet, acted slowly to this initiative. It had no response within one year after China officially launched the Belt and Road Initiative. In March 2015, the Chinese President met with Nepalese President Yadav, who visited China to attend the Bo'ao Forum for Asia. At that time, President Yadav expressed for the first time that Nepal firmly supported the Belt and Road Initiative and the Asian Infrastructure Investment Bank, but the Nepalese government failed to officially make an announcement. It was not until the beginning of 2017 that Nepal began to understand the Belt and Road Initiative. The local media also began to introduce the Belt and Road Initiative and gradually reached a consensus that it was a rare opportunity for the development of Nepal. In May 2017, the Nepalese government expressed its willingness to participate in the construction of the Belt and Road, and signed the Belt and Road framework agreement with China. From June 19 to 24, 2018, Nepalese Prime Minister Oli visited China and signed 14 letters of intent, memoranda and projects. However, it was not clear which of the 14 projects belonged to the Belt and Road Initiative.

II. Cooperation between China and Nepal after the Belt and Road Initiative

China and Nepal have been friendly neighbors from generation to generation. Since the official establishment of diplomatic relations in 1955, the cooperation between the two countries has continued. In the five years after China proposed the Belt and Road Initiative, there has been more cooperation between China and Nepal, but so far it is still not clear which cooperation projects belong to the construction of the Belt and Road. Here, I would like to talk about the cooperation between China and Nepal according to the "five connections" put forward by the Belt and Road Initiative.

1) Facilities connectivity: Under the new concept of the "Trans-Himalaya Framework for a Network of Multi-Dimensional Connectivity", China and Nepal cooperate on opening gateways, building and utilizing highways, optic fiber connections, electric power connections, air route connections as well as the construction and connection of railways:

Gateways: Gyirong Port is currently the only gateway under normal operations between Nepal and China. Zhangmu Port, which opened decades ago, was severely damaged in the earthquake of 2015 and has not been repaired yet. During the visit to China by Nepalese Prime Minister Oli in June this year, the two sides agreed to reopen Zhangmu Port in May 2019. In addition, seven other new gateways will be opened to supply daily necessities from China to areas bordering Tibet in northern Nepal. The seven gateways to be opened will not be developed into border trading ports in the short term, so there will no customs facilities of the two countries.

Highways: There are already many roads leading to the Nepalese border in

China. However, there is only one road in Nepal to Gyirong bordering Tibet. Araniko Highway connecting to Zhangmu Port was damaged in the big earthquake. There are few vehicles on this road near Tibet because Zhangmu Port is not open yet. During the visit to China by Nepalese Prime Minister, the two sides agreed that Nepalese trucks can use the road in Tibet to travel to another northern border town in Nepal.

Optic fibers: In January 2018, there was substantial progress in a fiber optic liaison between China and Nepal. The cooperation project between Nepal Telecom and China Global Telecommunications successfully completed the fiber-optic connection at the Rasuwagadhi gateway in Gyirong, thus ending the situation in which the Nepalese network was completely dependent on India.

Electric power: The projects signed by the Prime Minister of Nepal when visiting China in June this year included the "Nepal-China Cross-border Grid Interconnection Project". This is a project signed between the National Electricity Supply Authority of Nepal and the State Grid Corporation of China. By this project, Gyirong will be connected with Rasuwagadhi, Galchhi and Ratmate in Nepal via a 400kV transmission line.

Air routes: Kathmandu, the capital of Nepal, currently has direct flights with six Chinese cities, namely Lhasa, Chengdu, Xi'an, Kunming, Guangzhou and Hong Kong. The direct flights have been restored to the pre-earthquake period. The two countries emphasize the increase in the number of cities with direct flights and the number of flights, but this goal has not been realized in recent years.

Railways: The railway is a popular topic on Nepalese media recently, and it is frequently discussed in the Nepalese parliament. One year ago, a competent authority of China sent a team of experts to Nepal to conduct a feasibility study on the construction of the Nepal Railway and submitted a report. The report revealed that it was technically feasible to build medium-speed electric trains in Nepal. In June this year, Nepalese Prime Minister Oli visited China. When meeting with

Chinese President Xi Jinping, the Prime Minister focused on the cooperation project to build a railway in Nepal and connect with the Gyirong-Xigaze Railway in China. According to reports on Nepalese media, the Chinese President promised immediately that Chinese trains would definitely drive to Kathmandu, Nepal. Although the two countries theoretically agreed to build this railway, there is still a long way to go to achieve this goal. According to the current plan, in August 2018, the feasibility study of the Nepal Railway Project will be further improved. From August 2018, the Detailed Project Report (DPR) will be completed within one and a half years and then construction will begin. If all goes well, the project will be completed in 5 years.

2) Unimpeded trade: Trans-Himalaya border trade between China and Nepal is currently only carried out in Gyirong Port. This gateway was officially opened in November 2014 and currently has a daily throughput of 250 containers. Zhangmu Port, which was severely damaged in the 2015 Nepal earthquake, has not resumed operations.

3) Financial integration: There are currently no branches of foreign banks in Nepal, but cooperative banks with Nepalese banks, because Nepal has no legal provisions to allow foreign banks to set up branches in Nepal. Therefore, there is no basis for the financial integration of Nepal and China yet. At present, there is not even a bank operated by China in cooperation with Nepal. In recent years, Chinese tourists use online payment services such as Alipay and WeChat payment in travel agencies, hotels and restaurants operated by Chinese in Nepal. Many transactions by Chinese tourists in Nepal do not necessitate the use cash, but the Nepalese government has not legalized this online payment method.

4) Policy coordination: The Nepalese government has a consulate in Guangzhou, and another one in Chengdu is under discussion. The two countries agree to set up a high-level authority to oversee the implementation and management of projects signed between the two countries.

5) People-to-people bond: This point can be described in terms of tourism, personnel exchanges, cultural events and translation of cultural products between the two countries.

The Chinese government has included Nepal as a foreign tourist destination. Nepal has also provided Chinese tourists with the convenience of a visa upon arrival free of charge. The number of Chinese tourists visiting Nepal continues to increase because the journey to Nepal is not expensive. After the 2015 Nepal earthquake, the number of Chinese tourists plummeted but it is gradually increasing under the positive publicity of the Chinese government and other relevant departments.

In recent years, more Nepalese people have been invited to visit China than in the past. Similarly, more people from all walks of life in China have visited Nepal as well. Nepal is one of the first countries to set up a Chinese cultural center. Recently, there have been more and more exhibitions of paintings and calligraphy, music and dance programs, and martial arts performances related to the Chinese culture in Nepal. It is believed that the number of people participating in these events will continue to increase.

Some nongovernmental organizations in Nepal introduced China's outstanding cultural products to Nepal, but they were still limited in quantity and did not develop a market for Chinese cultural products in Nepal. In recent years, scholars have translated some of Nepal's literary works into Chinese and published them in China. After visiting Nepal, Chinese writers have also written literary works about Nepal. However, such a form of exchange is seldom reported on the media of the two countries, thus having a minimum of social influence.

Three years ago, the Nongovernmental Organization Forum of China's Belt and Road established the Nepalese branch, which is the only organization in Nepal with the "Belt and Road" in its name. However, there has been no substantive progress after the establishment of the forum.

III. Prospects of the Belt and Road Initiative in Nepal

Many parts of the world have successfully completed a lot of projects under the Belt and Road Initiative, and some projects have begun to reap economic benefits. Nepal was late in beginning its participation in the Belt and Road Initiative. Due to the onerous political tasks in Nepal, the government failed to pay attention to the Belt and Road Initiative. Now Nepal has adopted the federal system, successfully held the three-level (local, state and federal) elections, and established a three-tier government. In February this year, the new cabinet led by Prime Minister Oli gradually won the support of two-thirds of the parliament. How will the Nepalese government, which is relatively powerful in the history of Nepal, led by the Communist Party, participate in the Belt and Road Initiative? What are the prospects for the Belt and Road Initiative in Nepal, or how about the future? Now we will consider this from the following aspects.

1. Degree of importance attached by the Nepalese government

The Nepalese government is more active in signing agreements than implementing projects signed by these agreements, especially the projects invested in by Nepal itself. This is the judgment of observers at home and abroad.

Nepal's second international airport, Nijgadha International Airport, has been under construction for 17 years. Eleven years ago, the Nepalese government rated this project as a "National Pride", but the progress on the construction of the airport has been very slow because the government has not paid enough attention to it. Only a small amount of work has been completed so far. The Melamchi Project for water supply to Kathmandu started construction more than 20 years ago, but has not yet been completed. It is said that it will be completed by the end of this year, but the time of completion has been postponed repeatedly.

When Oli served as the Prime Minister of Nepal for the first time, he visited China in March 2016 during a very difficult period for Nepal and signed agreements in Beijing on important contents such as bilateral trade, transportation and oil transfer. However, within two years after he returned to Nepal, there was no progress in the implementation of these projects. After Oli returned to Nepal, he stepped down and the government reorganized, but the new government was not interested in agreements signed by Oli. Of course, the elections of the federal parliament and state parliaments were also ongoing then. But in fact, as the Foreign Minister of the new government of Oli said in an interview by media before the visit to China, after India lifted the border blockade against Nepal, the agreements signed with China would not be priorities for the Nepalese government. Therefore, this attitude always raised doubts about whether the Oli government would focus on projects related to the Belt and Road Initiative.

2. Preparations of the Nepalese government

Although recently the Nepalese government has shown great enthusiasm for the cooperation on the Belt and Road together with China, it has not been well prepared for the projects of Belt and Road cooperation. At present, the Gyirong-Kathmandu Railway, which is most likely to be a cooperative project under the Belt and Road Initiative, is frequently reported on Nepal's mainstream media. The starting point of the Nepalese government is that railways are the most cost-effective means of transportation for an inland mountainous country, so Nepal should build a railway.

However, in terms of technical issues, investment, use and economic benefits for the construction of this railway, only technical issues can be solved. The Chinese team of experts investigating the Gyirong-Kathmandu Railway pointed out that although this region has a high altitude, long slopes, complicated geological conditions and high requirements for environmental protection, these difficulties could be overcome.

Nepal proposed that China should construct this railway by grant aid. If this railway is constructed by grant aid, its investment, use and even economic benefits will not be problems. However, the Chinese government has emphasized that it is impossible to provide full aid, and there must be some investment made by Nepal.

Although the government is preparing to consider investment after the release of the detailed report of the project two years later, the project has become a popular topic among Nepalese people. The straight-line distance between Gyirong and Kathmandu is 72 kilometers. The team of experts indicated that the length of the railway built here would be 75 to 100 kilometers. The estimated cost is 240 million yuan per kilometer, and the entire railway will cost 24 billion yuan.

Usually, if there is overproduction in a region, or if overproduction is expected after the launch of a new project, then the transportation project will be constructed. Nepal currently does not have a large number of products that can be exported to China. The annual trade deficit between China and Nepal is as high as 7.808 billion yuan. There is no possibility of development projects in Nepal recently that are likely to increase production on a large scale. Nepalese scholars and think tanks can think of the economic benefits of this railway in only two aspects. First, Tibet will attract 20 million tourists after 2020, so the demand for fresh vegetables and fruit in Tibet will increase greatly. After the construction of this railway, Nepal will be able to supply fresh vegetables and fruit to Tibet. To this end, agreements signed by the Prime Minister of Nepal in June this year include the construction of a farm producing vegetables and fruit, especially organic vegetables and fruit in Nepal. Second, after the construction of this railway, the number of Chinese tourists to Kathmandu and Lumbini will increase by 2.5 million, thus increasing the national income through tourism. However, it is not difficult to see that the exportation of fresh vegetables and fruit to China's Tibet cannot achieve a balance of trade. It is also unrealistic to increase the number of Chinese tourists on such a large scale by this railway alone, because the majority of Chinese tourists to Nepal come from mainland China, instead of Tibet. Mainland tourists are not necessarily willing to come to Nepal via Tibet, considering the high altitude and travel time passing through Tibet. There are so many flights from China to Nepal. For the Chinese who want to travel to Nepal, the current traffic connection is very convenient.

The construction of this railway has an influence on the national economy in many aspects, but the income from railway transportation is very low. A team of experts recently conducted a survey on the economic benefits of the railway linking Kathmandu with cities in central and southern Nepal bordering India. Their survey results showed that according to the current price, the annual income of railway transportation only accounts for 1.466% of the investment. Moreover, the railway has a long period of construction, so individuals or companies are not willing to invest in such a project.

Now the railway is over-promoted, and the ruling Nepalese government has gained short-term political benefits. The plan will be the key propaganda content of the current ruling party in the next national election. In addition, if the railway project fails in the future for any reason, the common people will not blame the Nepalese government but will have a bad impression on China, because the current propaganda is that China has promised to build a medium-speed electric railway from Gyirong to Kathmandu.

3. Relations among Nepal, China and India

Due to the special geopolitical relations in Southern Asia, almost every important event in Nepal is influenced to varying degrees by India. India believes that it has special relations with Nepal because the people of the two countries share similarities in religion, culture and languages. The border of India and Nepal is open. Neither passports nor visas are required for people moving around the two countries. Moreover, Nepal is a South Asian country that has not been much influenced by China, so India dislikes the increase in China's influence in Nepal. Indian scholars regard China's growing influence on Nepal as one of the key contradictions between India and China. India definitely refuses any large-scale projects in Nepal under the Belt and Road Initiative because such projects will undoubtedly increase China's influence in Nepal.

Because of the complexity of international politics, the relations between China and India have improved recently. The informal meeting of Xi Jinping and Modi in

Wuhan in May can be said to have reached a new height in the history of relations between India and China. Although India and China have begun to generate a lot of consensus on many international issues and developmental concepts, India still has a negative attitude toward the Belt and Road Initiative. China has also made it clear that it will not force India to join the Belt and Road and that the two countries can cooperate even if India does not join the Belt and Road. As a result, there is a faint possibility of a China-Nepal-India Economic Corridor proposed by the Nigerian side and the Chinese side. If the relations between India and China become closer in the future, China and India will not necessarily promote trade between the two sides through Nepal, because although the border of China and Nepal is 1,400 kilometers long, the common border between India and China is even longer, and a lot of large-scale trade can be realized through sea transportation. Then, Nepal would be further excluded.

Nepal has a small market and a small population. If India is not interested in building a China-Nepal-India Economic Corridor, it is meaningless for China to construct railways. China can propose investing in the construction of railways in Nepal, but China must also build more than 400 kilometers of railways in its own territory to connect Nepal, so China may reconsider the merits of such an investment. While China proposes building a railway in Nepal, India also requests building a railway connecting the Indian border and Kathmandu. Not under the framework of the China-Nepal-India Economic Corridor, the Indian government proposes to build this railway only for the purpose of enhancing traditional trade between India and Nepal.

Looking forward to the future, China and Nepal will face many challenges to the leap-forward development of their cooperation under the "Belt and Road" Initiative.

文明对话与人类命运共同体

普西奇·拉多萨夫 【塞尔维亚】
贝尔格莱德大学语言学院东方学系教授、博士 / 贝尔格莱德孔子学院外方院长

习近平主席为人类社会发展绘制了一幅美好愿景，即世界各国人民在同一个命运共同体内共同谋求生存、发展、繁荣。本人以为实现这个美好愿景的关键之一，就是不同文明不同文化间平等和积极的对话。今天就文明的多样性与对话和中华文明对命运共同体的贡献是什么，这两个问题谈一点自己的粗浅看法。

但凡社会的人，都具有进行交流的基本精神诉求，这是人类的共性。不过，这个共性背后许文明的多样性和差异性，往小里说，我们的语言不同，生活习俗也不同；往大里说，我们的是非判断标准不同，对审美的诉求不同，说到底就是价值观不同。在这个大的层次上，就是文化价值观的差异。首先，我们给"文化"下个定义，用大多数学者的看法：文化涵盖了一个族群的全部思想、行为、语言、习俗以及所创造的全部事物和创造这些事物的方式。显然，"文化"的概念内涵十分宽泛但界定又非常模糊，它涉及许多领域：语言、政治、经济、社会、宗教，等等。文化的差异性主要表现在三个方面：1. 环境差异：康德认为时空是人类理性认识周围世界的唯一方式，因此不同的时空会产生不同的文明；2. 内部张力的差异，这是说不同的文化群体中，个体与集体之间的关系也不一样；3. 自然哲学观的差异。不同的文明对宇宙起源有不同的诠释，即每个民族都有自己的创世神话、哲学和宗教。神话、哲学与宗教既具有先验性，又具有每个民族自身独特的

情感和现实性，它们是物质文明发展到最高层次的精神文明的产物。因此，总的来说，文化就是个体生命存在和人类社会创造之间的一个联系的介体。

当来自不同文化的个体试图互相传递关于周围事物的信息、认知或看法，或表达自己的思想、感情和立场时，从这一刻起便有了"文明对话"。可以这样认为，一方面，人类对话和文化分不开，只要进行对话，就与文化缠绕上千丝万缕的关系；另一方面，沟通又总是受双方文化背景的限制。要实现不同文明间真正平等、积极的对话和交流，不仅要了解一种异质文化的内容、模式，还需要了解和尊重对方的价值观。

一种文明的价值体系是该群体对世界的总的看法，也是一个民族文化传承的主要内涵。每个民族的价值标准都不可能是中立的，它既反映了各民族的不同的政治意识形态，也是不同民族间发生误解和冲突的根源。文明对话的结果是积极的还是消极的，将完全取决于交谈双方是否彼此尊重，也就是说，取决于对双方价值观的理解和尊重程度，取决于对话双方对异质文化的敏感程度。当今的文明对话有两种典型的表现：一种是以"民族文化中心主义"为特征；另一种则以"文化相对主义"为原则。民族文化中心主义主要表现为：以自我为中心，唯我独尊、封闭排他、对异质文化不敏感；而文化相对主义的特点是：具有较大的包容性、开放性，对异质文化较为敏感。我们认为，在人类共同命运体框架下的文明对话，是应该以文化相对主义为理念的一种对话，即重视个体生命的存在，并对不同文明的价值取向给予充分的理解和尊重。我们提倡对个体的尊重，因为群体或民族文化传统，是需要依托个体生命在时空的存在和延续中才能得以传承的，而世界文明间的多样性和差异性，也正是因为个体生命形式的多样性造成的。所以，从哲学意义上看，个体生命的存在比群体文化更具有本质的意义。

关于个体生命存在的本质和文化多样性，中国哲人最著名的论点就是孔子说的"性相近也，习相远也"。孔子还认为，人性就是人天生具有的自然本性。中国传统重视个体和人性，并认为人性与人的感性直接关联，由此才可能进行理性的构建。因此，虽然不同的学派为人性打上了"善"或"恶"和标签，但都赞同人性可以通过后天的教育进行改造。因此，中国的儒释道都讲究个人的"修身养性"，在提高了个人的自身修养后，才能发展一个群体文化——乃至治家治国。这点与古希腊先哲苏格拉底的观点是一致的，即"认识自己"是人性改造的前提条件，否则人将无从改变自己和世界。当人作为生物特征的存在，所有人人性相近；

当人逐渐成为社会的存在，仅与同一个群体的部分人相近，打上"民族文化"的烙印；但当人作为一个生命个体，一个具有创造性的存在并可以改造世界时，他就是独一无二的存在，异于任何人。如此说来，一个文明的价值体系里还包括了其全部个体的创造实践。我们每一个生命的诞生，都是文化的一次再创造，每一个生命的存在，都是文化的一代传承。生命在时空中发生的每一次位移，都会在文化层面产生意义和影响。从这层意义看，中国"以人为本"的传统思想，与古希腊以"认识自己"的思想不谋而合，这可以是人类命运共同体框架下东西方文明对话的一个对接点。

本文下面要谈的第二个问题是中国文明对人类命运共同体的贡献。除了上面所说的"以人为本"的思想，中国传统的自然宇宙观——"大道即大美"可以成为东西方文明对话的第二个对接点。中国古代哲学思想把大自然存在的规律称为"大道"。庄子说，"天地有大美而不言"。"不言"将天地自然、四时变化与万物之源联结为一体，它就是"道"。"道"是万物存在的具体表现形式，它无所不在，万物凭借道的力量得到生息滋养。"不言之大道"的美超越了外在的形貌，直达每一具体存在的本质。天地自然的"大美"，体现在一种天地人之间和谐与生存秩序，阴阳调和，人与自然合一。也可以说，每一种自然存在都是美的表现。美能唤起人类的激情、爱欲、本能和创造力，从这层意义上讲，对"大美"的诉求，就是对生命的诉求。

"大道"与"大美"，是中华文明对人类命运共同体奉献的一大精神财富。现代社会学家马克斯·韦伯（Max Weber）和塔尔科特·帕森斯（Talcott Parsons）等人都认为，当代社会生活里宗教元素所占的比重越来越少，科学的成分越来越重；哲学意义上自然的"大美"也越来越少见，而越来越多的是人工的庸俗的"美"。这种现象不仅表现在政治和经济生活中，还渗透到文化和文明的发展模式中。原来姿态万千的个体存在以及形态各异的生命的创造实践，如今一个个被打上国际"一体化"标签，纳入单一的"全球化"框架下，"全球文化"成为普世主义的新形式，作为高科技产物的网络和社交平台则是推行单一的"地球村文化"、在全世界实现文化"同质化"和"标准化"的有效工具。其实这是"全球化"概念的歧义以及对"全球化"进程的误读。

另一方面，当今社会还出现了一种与所谓的"一体化"进程相悖的趋势，即在同一个文化群体内部出现"零碎化"和"边缘化"的次文化圈，个体与集体间的张力也越来越大，个体企图摆脱"社会个体"的身份，成为独一无二的具有创造力的"生命个体"，以不同的生命姿态和存在方式成为人类命运共同体的一员。此外，当今社会还面临着因国家政体变革、移民问题、弱小民族身份认同问题等带来的一系列深刻迅猛的变化，这些变化也使社会群体成为一个含多次元文化圈的群体社会。

在文化"一体化"和"零碎化"这两种趋势作用下，进行积极的文明对话尤为重要。作者认为，人类命运共同体不是一个同质的、单一的文化模式，也不是推行民族文化中心语义的机制，而是实现世界多样性以及各个异质文明和谐并存的共同体。要实现积极的文明对话，应该以"文化相对主义"为前提，尊重个体生命价值和文化多样性。因为，我们的世界因文明的繁荣，才更具生命活力和创造力，才能呈现出万物归于"大道"的"大美"。要建立这样的一个人类命运共同体，需要我们有一个在全球范围内维护世界文化多样性的策略，需要我们共同努力，实现具有包容精神，相互理解和尊重、并在平等的基础上进行的文明对话。从这层意义上讲，我觉得中华文明对建设人类命运共同体的最大贡献，就是"以人为本"以及视"大道"为"大美"的最高哲学审美境界。

Dialogue of Civilizations and the Community with a Shared Future for Mankind

Radosav Pušić/ Serbia

Professor of the Department of Oriental Studies, Faculty of Philology, University of Belgrade / Director of Confucius Institute in Belgrade

President Xi Jinping has conveyed a wonderful vision for the development of mankind, that is to say, peoples of all the countries in the world seeking survival, development and prosperity together in the community with a shared future for mankind. From my own perspective, one key to realizing this great vision is the equal and positive dialogue among different civilizations and cultures. Today, I would like to share my superficial views on these two questions, namely the diversity and dialogue of civilizations and what are the contributions of the Chinese civilization to the community of common destiny?

Any socialized person has a basic spiritual desire for communication, which is a common characteristic of human beings. However, behind this commonality is the diversity and differences among civilizations. At the microscopic level, we have different languages, lifestyles and customs; at the macroscopic level, we have different views on what is right and wrong and different aesthetics; in a word, differences in values. For the latter, it is the differences in cultural values.

First of all, we provide a definition of "culture". It is universally acknolwedged that: Culture consists of the ideologies, behaviors, langauge, customs, and the things that are created and the ways to create them by a particular ethnic group. Obviously the concept of "culture" is very broad with a vague definition, and it involves many domains: language, politics, economics, society, religion and so on. Cultural differences are mainly manifested in the following three aspects: 1. Environmental differences: Kant harbors the idea that time and space are the only way for humans to rationally understand the world around them, so different times and spaces will produce different civilizations; 2. Differences in internal tension, which means in different cultural groups, the relationship between individuals and collectives is also different; 3. Differences in natural philosophy. Different civilizations have different interpretations of the origin of the universe, which is to say, each nation has its own myth regarding creation, its own philosophy and its own religion. Myths, philosophy and religion are transcendental, but each nation also has its own unique emotions and realities. They are the products of the spiritual civilization developed from the highest level of material civilization. Therefore, in general, culture is a mediator between the existence of individual life and the creation of human society.

When individuals from different cultures try to communicate information, cognitions or opinions about things around them, or express their own thoughts, feelings and standpoints, then from this moment on there is a "dialogue of civilizations". It seems that on the one hand, human dialogue and culture are inseparable. Where there is dialogue, there are inextricable relations with culture; on the other hand, communication is always subjected to the restrictions by the cultural background of the two sides. To achieve truly equal and positive dialogue and communication between two different civilizations, we must not only understand the content and model of each heterogeneous culture, but also understand and respect each other's values.

The system of values of a civilization is the group's total view of the world, and the main connotation of a nation's cultural inheritance. The values and norms of each nation cannot be neutral because they not only reflect the different political ideology of each nation, but they are also the root of misunderstandings and conflicts among different nations. Whether the dialogue of civilizations is positive or negative depends entirely on whether the two sides of the dialogue respect each other. In other words, it rests on the degree of understanding and respect of each other's values, and the sensitivity of each side to the heterogeneous culture. Today's dialogue of civilizations has two typical manifestations: One is characterized by the "national cultural centralism"; another is based on the principle of "cultural relativism". National cultural centralism is mainly manifested to be: self-centered, arrogant, closed, particularistic and insensitive to heterogeneous cultures; and cultural relativism is characterized by greater tolerance, openness and sensitivity to heterogeneous cultures. It is our view that the dialogue of civilizations within the framework of the community with a shared future for mankind should be a dialogue based on the concept of cultural relativism, that is to say, importance is attached to the existence of individual lives with full understanding and respect of the value orientations of different civilizations. The reason why the respect for individuals is advocated lies in the fact that the culture and tradition of each group or nation can be inherited by the existence and continuation of individual lives in space and time, and the diversity and differences of civilizations in the world is caused precisely by the diversity of individual life forms. Therefore, in the philosophical sense, the existence of individual life is of more essential significance than the culture of a particular group.

As far as the essence of the existence of individual life and cultural diversity are concerned, the most famous argument of Chinese philosophers is that of Confucius, "By nature, men are nearly alike; by practice, they become extremely different". Confucius also takes the attitude that human nature is the inborn nature of human beings. Chinese tradition values individuality and humanity, acknowledging that humanity is directly connected with human sensibility, and thereby it is possible to construct rationality. Although different schools label humanity as "good" or "evil", they all agree that humanity can be transformed through education. Therefore, China's Confucianism, Buddhism and Taoism lay stress on the individual's "self-cultivation". Only after improving one's own self-cultivation can one develop a group culture - and even feed the family and govern the country. This coincides with the idea of the ancient Greek sage Socrates which says that "knowing yourself" is a prerequisite for the transformation of human nature, otherwise human beings will not be able to change themselves and the world. When humans exist as biological features, all humans are similar in human nature; when humans gradually become social beings, they are only close to some people in the same group and branded with a "national culture"; when a man exists as an individual being, a creative being that can transform the world, he is unique and different from anyone else. Thus, the system of values of a civilization also includes all its individual creative practices. The birth of each of our lives is a re-creation of the culture, and the existence of each life is a generational inheritance of that culture. Every displacement of life in space and time will be of significance and have an influence at the cultural level. In this sense, China's traditional "people-oriented" idea coincides with the ancient Greek idea of "knowing yourself". This can be a connecting point for the dialogue between Oriental and Western civilizations within the framework of the community with a shared future for mankind.

The second issue to be discussed below is the contribution of Chinese civilization to the community with a shared future for mankind. In addition to the above-mentioned "people-oriented" idea, China's traditional view of the natural universe that "great way is great beauty" can become the second connecting point for the dialogue between Oriental and Western civilizations. China's ancient philosophical thoughts call the law of the existence of nature as the "great way". According to Zhuangzi, "Heaven and earth have their great beauties but do not speak of them". "Do not speak" connects the heaven, earth, nature and four seasons with the origin of all things, and it is "Tao" (the way). "Tao", the concrete manifestation of the existence of all things, is omnipresent. All things rely on the power of the Tao to grow and develop. The beauty of "the great way of not speaking" transcends the external appearance and directly reaches the essence of each concrete existence. The "great beauty" of heaven, earth and nature is reflected in a harmony among heaven, earth and mankind and the order of existence, a harmony between yin and yang, and the unity of man and nature. It can also be said that every natural existence is a manifestation of beauty. Beauty can arouse human passion, love, instinct and creativity. In this sense, the pursuit of "great beauty" is the pursuit of life.

The "great way" and "great beauty" are a great spiritual wealth that the Chinese civilization contributes to the community with a shared future for mankind. Modern sociologists Max Weber and Talcott Parsons et al. argue that there are fewer and fewer religious elements in contemporary social life, but more and more scientific elements; the natural "great beauty" in the philosophical sense becomes also increasingly rare, but there are more and more artificial and vulgar kinds of "beauty". This phenomenon is manifested not only in political and economic life, but it also penetrates into the developmental model of culture and civilization. The originally diversified individual existence and creation of life in different forms, now bearing the label of international "integration", are incorporated into a unique framework of "globalization". The "global culture" becomes a new form of universalism. The Internet and social network platforms as the products of high technology are effective tools for practicing a single "global village culture" and for achieving cultural "homogenization" and "standardization" across the world. This is actually the ambiguity of the concept of "globalization" and the misinterpretation of the process of "globalization".

On the other hand, there is also a trend in today's world that runs counter to the so-called process of "integration", that is to say, the "fragmentation" and "marginalization" of the subcultures appear within the same cultural group. Tension is also increasing between individuals and collectives. Individuals are trying to get rid of the identity of "social individual", they are attempting to transform into unique and creative "living individuals", and to become members of the community with a shared future for mankind with different life attitudes and ways of existence. Moreover, today's world is also facing a series of profound and rapid changes brought about by the reform of the state's political system, immigration issues and the identity of small ethnic groups. These changes are also transforming social groups into a group-based community made up of multiple subcultural circles.

Under the influence of the two trends, that is, the "integration" and "fragmentation" of cultures, it is particularly important to have an active dialogue among civilizations. According to the author, the community with a shared future for mankind is not a homogeneous single cultural model, nor is it a mechanism that promotes the semantics of a national cultural centralism, but it is a community that realizes the diversity of the world and the coexistence of heterogeneous civilizations. The positive dialogue among civilizations must be premised on "cultural relativism" and it must respect the values of individual life and cultural diversity, in order for our world to become more vigorous and creative with the prosperity of civilizations. Only in this way, can the "great beauty" that all things originate from the "great way" be manifested. To build such a community with a shared future for mankind, we need a strategy to safeguard cultural diversity on a global scale, and we need to work together to have a dialogue among civilizations with an inclusive spirit and mutual understanding and respect on the basis of equality. In this sense, the greatest contribution the Chinese civilization can make to the building of the community with a shared future for mankind is "people-oriented" and the supreme philosophical and aesthetic realm of regarding the "great way" as the "great beauty".

中国和罗马尼亚的经济关系:从古代的联系到现在的"一带一路"

萨尔米扎·潘瑟卡 【罗马尼亚】
罗马尼亚科学院世界经济研究所经济发展模式部主任

一、回顾过去

自人类文明出现以来,欧洲人和亚洲人一直生活在地球最大的一块陆地上。从西边命名为欧洲,从东边命名为亚洲,但现如今我们更加频繁地提及欧亚大陆——作为一整块大陆的名称——尤其是中国提出"一带一路"倡议并以现代标准重新打造古老的丝绸之路以来。这条路线在大约2000年前曾经使欧亚大陆的两端相互连接。

古代的丝绸之路对于欧亚大陆的连接至关重要,但值得铭记的是,古代人从早期开始,就在共同的大陆上来回穿梭,他们不仅带来商品的交换和沟通,还进行信息、知识、技术和观念等的交流。

1884年,罗马尼亚考古学家发掘出欧洲最古老的新石器时代文化遗址,比苏美尔人和埃及人更古老,体现了当时欧洲文化的巅峰:库库特尼文化。库库特尼文化以最早发现人工制品的罗马尼亚村庄命名,可以追溯到公元前5200-3200年。除了年代久远,该遗址引人注意的原因有很多:

(1)库库特尼人可能是欧洲最早的定居人口,他们是农民、猎人和工匠。值得注意的是,他们居住在用木头和黏土精心装饰的大房子里,上面覆盖着稻草,通常是两层楼,有许多房间设计了不同用途;

图 1　库库特尼人定居点复原图

（2）库库特尼人通常聚集在大社区中，有多达 2 万人，并为共同安全和社会生活而组织起来。房屋通常围成圈，中间有一个大型建筑物作为庇护所和社交场所，定居点周围是天然形成或人为建造的壕沟，以提供保护。整个社区附近有水源和盐；

（3）库库特尼定居点是欧洲最早的原始城镇，仅在罗马尼亚就发现 4000 多个这样的"城市"定居点；

（4）根据他们留下的大量泥塑人物来判断，这些人物从来没有愤怒的面孔，暗示他们的生活似乎是宁静与和平的。在他们的定居点没有发现任何武器，只有工具；

（5）库库特尼人也是欧洲最早从雕刻进步到抛光石头再到金属加工（主要是铜和金）的人群；

（6）库库特尼文化令人瞩目，最著名的是其独特陶艺的精美形状、图案和色彩组合。这不仅证明了这一人群的杰出艺术修养，而且还证明了其高超的技术实力（例如，他们制作弹性黏土和涂料的方法以及所使用的工具，如：陶钧的前身、特制烤箱等）和特有的技巧（例如，能够非常熟练地精确控制陶炉的温度）（图 2 和图 3）。

图 2　在罗马尼亚不同地点出土的库库特尼陶器

241　中国和罗马尼亚的经济关系：从古代的联系到现在的"一带一路"

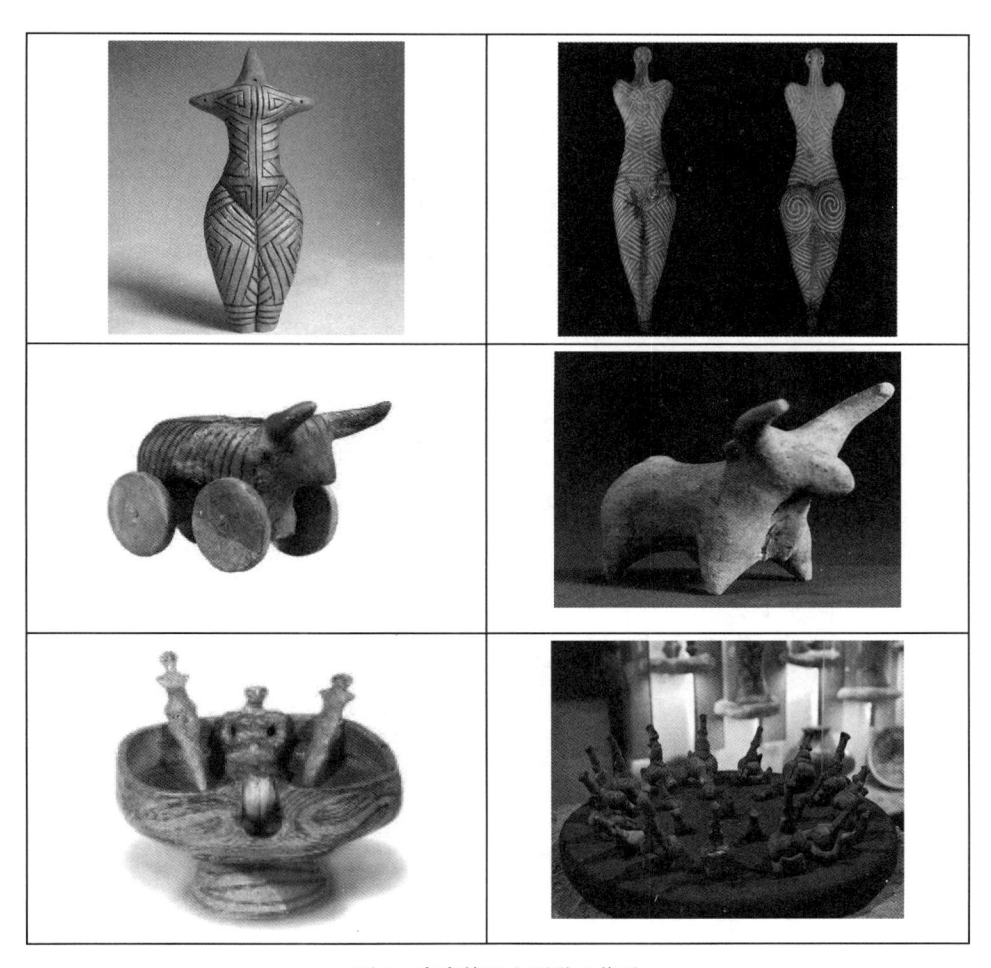

图 3　库库特尼人形黏土作品

目前，罗马尼亚拥有欧洲最大的新石器时代艺术品收藏。这些收藏品以及罗马尼亚和外国历史学家、考古学家的工作都证明了这一事实，即库库特尼文化是欧洲最古老的文化，而我们的祖先在 7000 年前发展出史前欧洲最杰出的文化，即欧洲物质和精神发展的巅峰。

虽然在欧洲是独一无二的，但库库特尼文化在整个欧亚大陆似乎并不孤单。与罗马尼亚相距数千公里的中国可能存在近亲：仰韶文化（图 4 和 5）。

仰韶文化和库库特尼文化的陶器不仅在形状、花纹、颜色和神秘符号上非常相似，而且似乎在黏土和涂料制备中采用相同的技术。有专家推测，尽管这两个人群之间的距离遥远，而且当时的交通工具并不发达，但他们可能一直保持着联系。

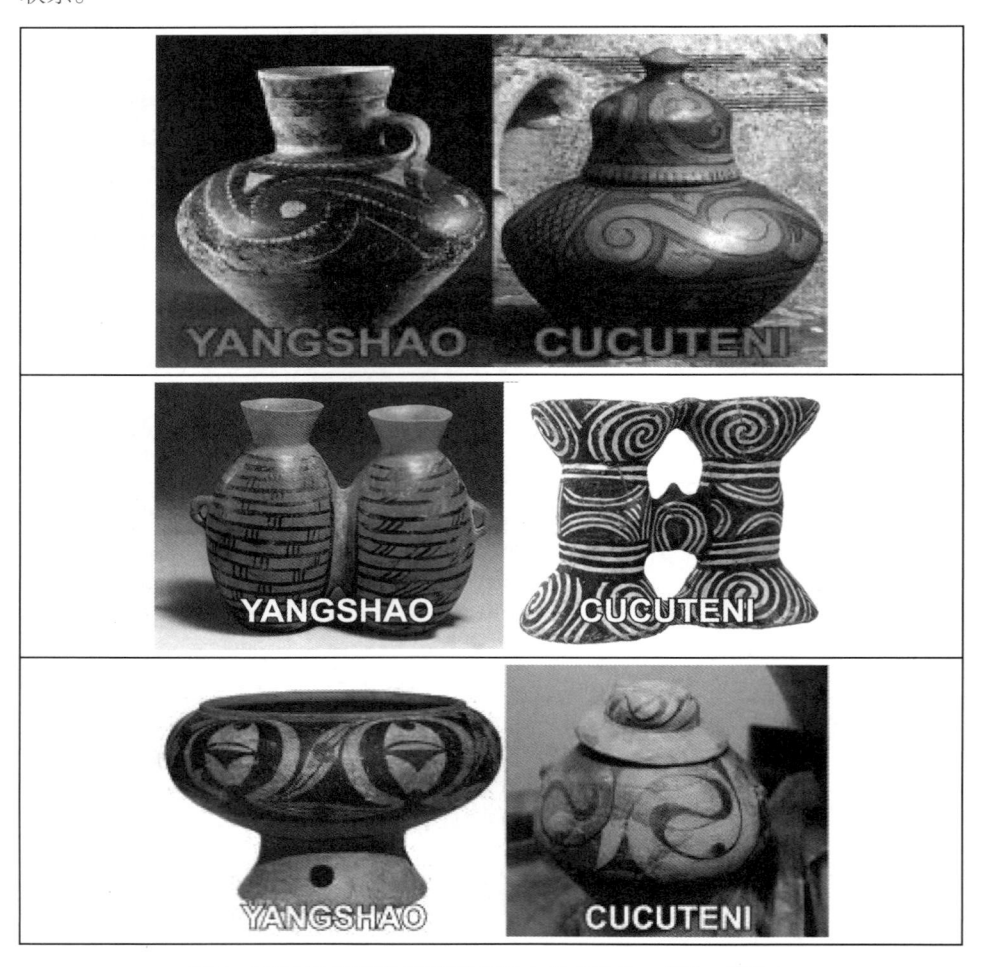

图 4　库库特尼和仰韶陶器的相似之处（形状、花纹、颜色）

特别吸引人地是，在 6000-7000 年前的库库特尼陶器上出现了两个亚洲特有的著名符号，分别是阴阳和万字记号（图 6）。

同样令人印象深刻的是，库库特尼艺术展示了欧几里得在几千年后发现的黄金矩形的完美比例。

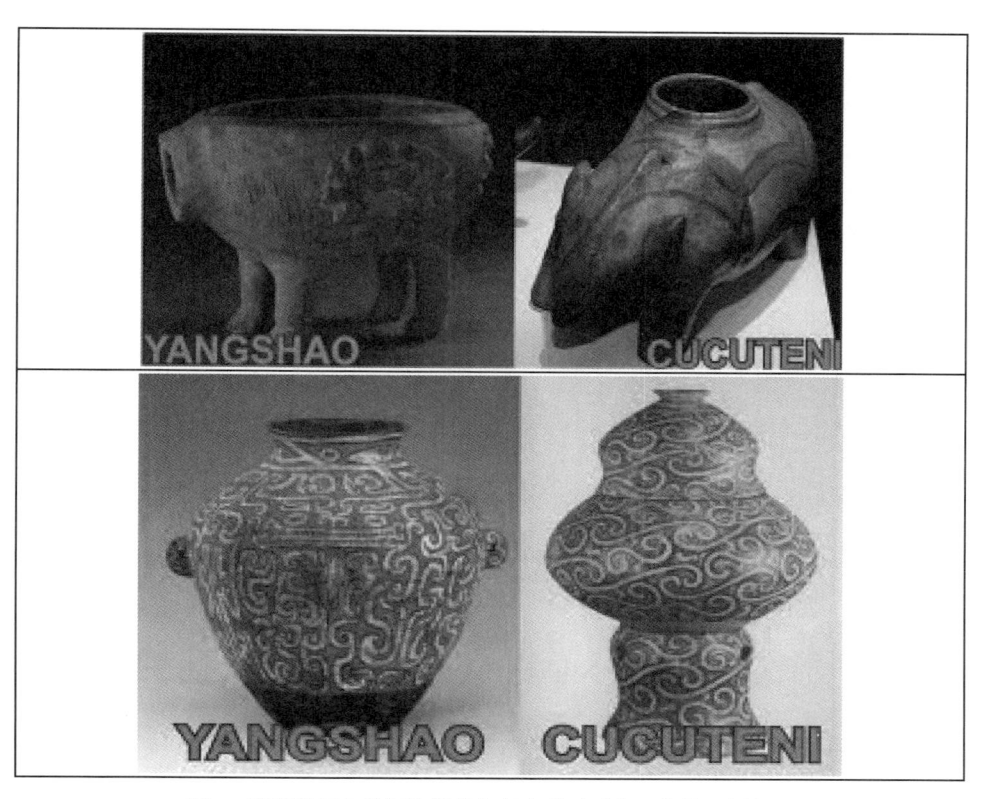

图 5 库库特尼和仰韶陶器的相似之处（形状、花纹、颜色）

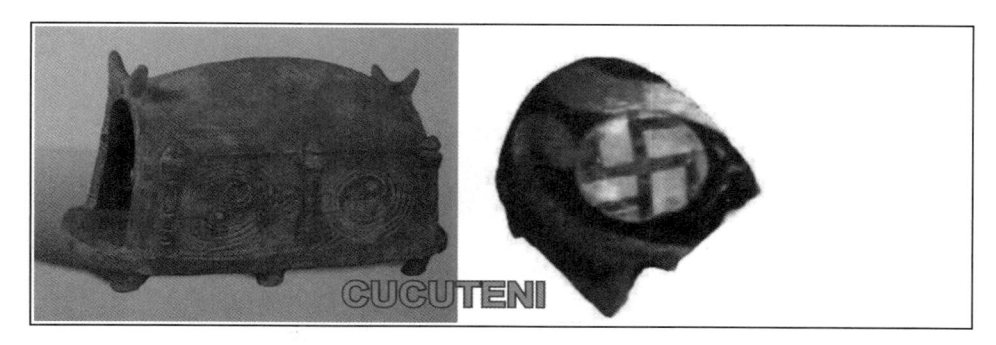

图 6 库库特尼和仰韶陶器的相似之处（阴阳、万字）

如果两种文化之间的所有这些相似性和共通性不足以证明二者的联系，那么罗马尼亚一项最新的发现无疑为这一假设提供了论据。2012 年，罗马尼亚考古学家在拜亚（Baia）村有惊人的发现：一栋 7200 年前的超大型库库特尼人早期的房屋（公元前 5200-5100 年），不仅保存了精美的陶器、独特的物品和工具、完整的壁炉等，还有谷物和其他植物。

来自剑桥大学的一组研究人员加入了罗马尼亚考古学家的行列，他们曾经在中国对谷物进行研究长达十年。在谷物生物分子考古学专家马丁·肯尼思·琼斯教授的带领下，该研究小组发现，在6000-7000年前，某些谷物从欧洲传到中国，而另一些谷物从中国传到欧洲。根据马丁·肯尼思·琼斯教授的说法，欧洲与亚洲之间的贸易首先是谷物贸易，然后是宝石贸易，直到很久以后丝绸之路才得以发展，商品种类变得丰富多样。

剑桥大学研究人员目前正在研究我们的祖先是如何做到这些。然而，他们对谷物的研究已经证明，自新石器时代以来（距今7000年前），生活在当今罗马尼亚和中国领土上的祖先之间存在商业和知识相关联系。我们还不知道我们的祖先是如何做到的，但是，如果他们可以联系和交换商品、信息、观念、知识、技术和专门技巧，那么今天我们当然可以利用当今时代的技术和能力做到这一点。

我们都拥有可以继承的完美遗产！

二、"一带一路"影响下的中国－罗马尼亚经济关系的最新进展

现在，回到我们的时代，我们想要说明2013年"一带一路"倡议启动后，对罗马尼亚和中国双边贸易和投资已经产生了哪些影响。

1. 双边贸易

（1）首先，我们注意到，在最近十年（2010-2016年）中，两国的双边贸易额有了显著的增加，甚至出现了再平衡趋势（表1）。

表1：2010-2016年罗马尼亚与中国的贸易额（单位：百万美元，%）

罗中贸易额	2010	2011	2012	2013/B&R	2014	2015	2016	2016/10 (%)	2013/10 (%)	2016/13 (%)
出口	755	947	980	1208	1517	1299	1455	+92.3	+60.0	+20.4
进口	3004	3454	2797	2823	3223	3187	3448	+14.5	-6.0	+22.1
总额(X+M)	3759	4401	3777	4031	4730	4486	4903	+30.4	+7.2	+21.6
逆差(X-M)	-2249	-2507	-1817	-1615	-1706	-1888	-1993	-11.4	-28.2%	+23.4
X:(X+M) x 100	20.1%	21.5%	25.9%	30.0%	32.1%	29.0%	29.7%			

数据来源：根据联合国商品贸易数据库的数据计算得出。

在此期间，双边贸易总额增加30%以上，罗马尼亚的出口额几乎翻了一番（+92.3%），进口增长速度明显放慢（+14.4%）。因此，罗马尼亚对中国的贸易逆差大幅下降11.4%，两国贸易开始再平衡进程；然而，比较2013年前后的发展情况，我们可以发现，2013年之后的发展比不上前些年，具体表现在：

- 贸易总额增加，实际上大部分增加发生在2013年之后（增加22%，而2013年之前仅为7%），但是2013年发起"一带一路"倡议后（+20.4%），罗马尼亚对中国的出口增幅远低于2013年之前（+60%）；2013年以后，罗马尼亚从中国的进口增幅大于出口增幅（+22.1%），并从2013年"一带一路"倡议启动之前的小幅下降（-6%）开始强劲反弹；因此，罗马尼亚的贸易逆差在2013年之后提升23%以上，而2013年之前下降-28%以上；此外，罗马尼亚出口在双边贸易总额中所占的份额从2013年之前的20%增加到30%（甚至在2014年达到32%），在2013年之后略有下降，降至29.7%；从2013年开始的罗马尼亚和中国之间的贸易再平衡进程随后被逆转，贸易逆差重新开始增长；2016年，中国直接贡献罗马尼亚总贸易逆差的28%，但也有间接贡献，因为罗马尼亚存在逆差的一些国家大量转出口中国商品（例如匈牙利、波兰）到我们的国家。

（2）2010-2016年，双边贸易的另一个重要进展是罗马尼亚对中国的出口结构有所改善（表2）。我们注意到，一方面，大多数种类的商品出口一直处于上升趋势，另一方面，出口结构已经多样化：

表2：2010年、2013年、2016年罗马尼亚对中国的出口结构（单位：百万美元）

国际标准贸易分类第3版	2010	2013/B&R	2016	2016/2010	2013/2010	2016/2013
0	1.3	0.8	17.9	13.8 x	- 38.5%	22.4 x
1	2.7	4.2	3.4	+ 26%	+ 55.6%	-19%
2	175.0	318.9	161.4	-7.8%	+ 82.2%	- 49%
3	-	0.3	3.0	new		10 x
4	-	-	1.8			new
5	89.2	72.2	45.6	- 48.9%	- 19.1%	- 36.8%
6	51,5	104.9	149.8	2.9 x	2.0 x	+ 42,3%
7	326.5	462.5	688.2	2.1 x	+41.7%	+48.8%
8	109.1	243.7	383.7	3.5 x	2.2 x	+57.4%
出口总额	755.3	1207.5	1455.2	1.9 x	1.6 x	1.2 x

数据来源：作者使用联合国商品贸易数据库的数据计算得出，https://comtrade.un.org/data。

所有国际标准贸易分类商品首次出现在罗马尼亚对中国的出口中；国际标准贸易分类（SITC）0组产品（食品和活动物）的出口增加22倍以上。猪肉（+95%）、蛋和乳制品（251%）等物品的出口明显增加。

不过，从罗马尼亚的角度更详细地考察出口情况，我们可以发现现实不太理想。例如，猪肉的出口主要是中国企业（万洲国际集团、前双汇）在罗马尼亚经营的50个农场出口，而罗马尼亚生产商的出口却遭遇中国市场的众多非关税壁垒（例如卫生认证、繁琐手续）。

（3）积极的进展是，罗马尼亚的出口结构主要在2013年以后发生了变化，并且这种变化有利于更复杂的产品（图7、8和9）。

首先是机械与运输设备（SITC 7）。该产品在罗马尼亚对中国出口总额中的比重从2005年的36%，增加到2013年的38%（9年内仅增加2个百分点）和2016年的48%（2013年后短短3年内增长10个百分点）；其次是杂项制成品（SITC 8）。该产品在罗马尼亚对中国出口总额中的比重从2005年的5%上升到2013年的20%和2016年的27%；另外是非食用原材料，燃料除外（SITC 2）。从2005年的19%增加到2013年的27%，然后在2016年下降到仅11%；还有化学制品及有关产品（SITC 5）。从9%（2005年）降至6%（2013年）和3%（2016年）。

CHINA'S IMPORT FROM ROMANIA, 2005(mil. USD)

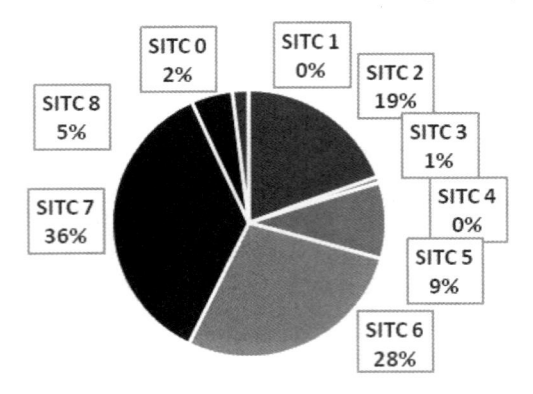

- SITC 0: 2%
- SITC 1: 0%
- SITC 2: 19%
- SITC 3: 1%
- SITC 4: 0%
- SITC 5: 9%
- SITC 6: 28%
- SITC 7: 36%
- SITC 8: 5%

图7　2005年中国对罗马尼亚的进口结构（单位：百万美元）

数据来源：作者据联合国商品贸易数据库，https://comtrade.un.org/data。

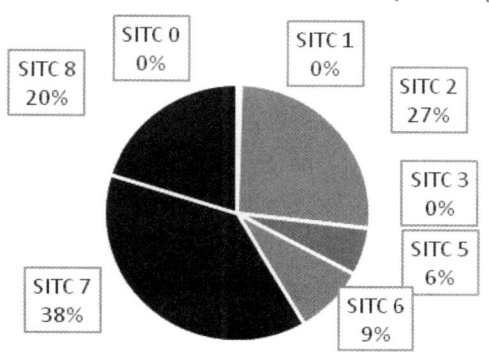

图 8 2013 年中国对罗马尼亚的进口结构（单位：百万美元）

数据来源：作者据联合国商品贸易数据库，https://comtrade.un.org/data。

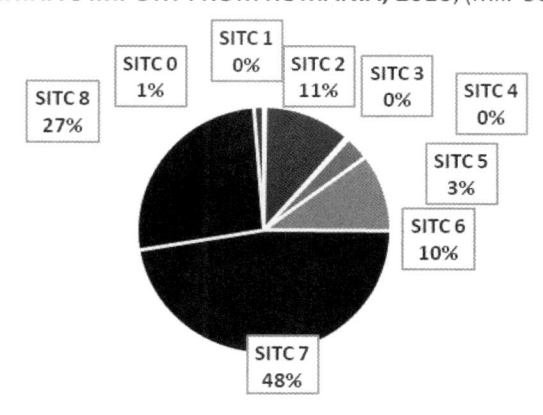

图 9 2016 年中国对罗马尼亚的进口结构（单位：百万美元）

数据来源：作者据联合国商品贸易数据库，https://comtrade.un.org/data。

（4）尽管罗马尼亚的市场规模和潜力巨大，但罗马尼亚与中国的贸易额仅排名中东欧 16 国第五位（图 10）。

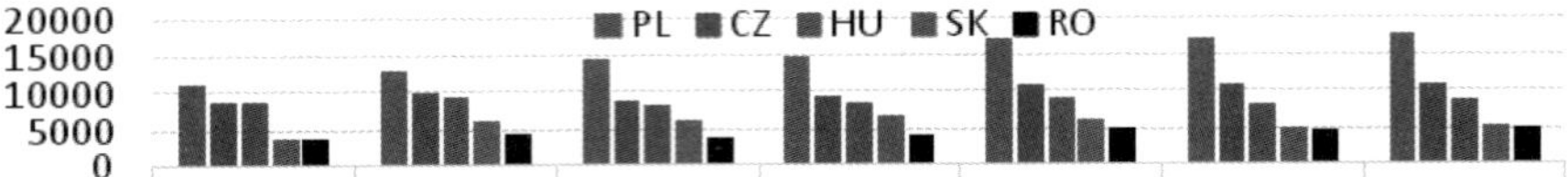

	2010	2011	2012	2013	2014	2015	2016
PL	11138	12988	14385	14807	17189	17091	17632
CZ	8850	9988	8731	9453	10979	11009	11011
HU	8716	9258	8061	8407	9024	8069	8887
SK	3749	5970	6078	6542	6204	5032	5271
RO	3759	4401	3777	4032	4740	4486	4903

图 10　2010-2016 年中东欧国家与中国贸易额排名前 5 位（单位：百万美元）

数据来源：作者据联合国商品贸易数据库，https://comtrade.un.org/data。

2010-2016 年罗马尼亚 - 中国双边贸易可总结如下：

1. 2010-2016 年，罗马尼亚 - 中国双边贸易显著增长；

2. 2010 年以后再平衡进程已经开始，罗马尼亚对中国的贸易逆差开始缩小。然而，再平衡进程自 2013 年以来已经停止，贸易逆差迅速扩大。

3. 罗马尼亚对中国的出口结构主要在 2013 年以后实现了多元化和改善，有利于更复杂的商品类别；

4. 2016 年，机械与运输设备杂项制成品合计占罗马尼亚对中国出口总额的 75%；

5. 2016 年，按原料分类的制成品占罗马尼亚对中国出口的 85%。

6. 罗马尼亚出口商进入中国市场仍然受到非关税壁垒的阻碍；

7. 尽管双边贸易额及其规模和经济潜力不断增长，但在与中国的总贸易额中，罗马尼亚仍排在中东欧 16 国的第五位。

2. 中国在罗马尼亚的投资

（1）投资额

统计数据显示，2005-2016 年，中国每年对罗马尼亚的对外直接投资（ODI）波动很大（图 11）。2013 年的投资额最低，但在"一带一路"倡议启动后的两年内，投资额出现显著的增长，但随后在 2016 年再次暴跌，仅为前一年水平的四分之一。

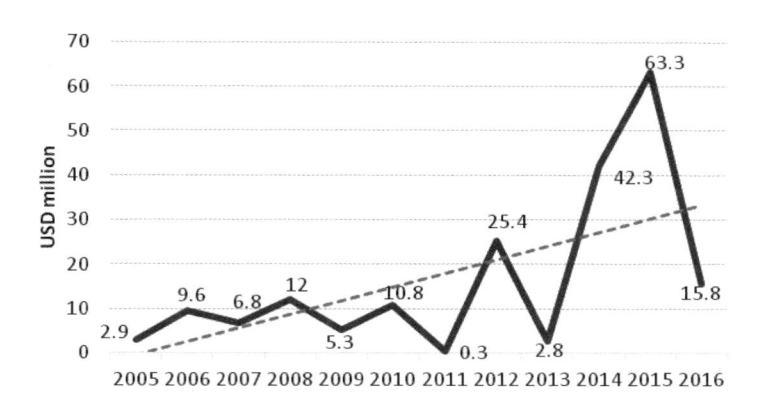

图 11　2005-2016 年中国对罗马尼亚的对外直接投资（单位：百万美元）

数据来源：作者使用中国商务部《中国对外直接投资统计公报》。

纵观全球经济危机后的整体情况，中国对外直接投资流向欧洲的动态（图11）显示，流向一半西方发达国家（欧盟17国）的投资显著增加——与2013年相比，2016年的投资增加一倍多——而流入中东欧16国，尤其是中东欧11国的投资额大幅下降。此外，中东欧16国收到的投资通常仅相当于欧盟17国的一小部分。在发起16+1和"一带一路"倡议之后（2012-2013年），虽然该倡议预计将推动新兴的中东欧经济体的发展，但中东欧16国获得的投资额更少（2016年仅相当于欧盟17国的1.2%，而2013年这一比例是2.7%）。

表 3：2005-2016 年中国对欧洲的对外直接投资（单位：百万美元）

	2010	2011	2012	2013	2014	2015	2016
欧盟 17 国	5547	7432	5970	4433	9595	5326	9934
中东欧 11 国	417	129	150	91	193	154	104
中东欧 16 国	419	130	158	118	208	174	116
中东欧 16 国与欧盟 17 国对比	7.6%	1.7%	2.6%	2.7%	2.2%	3.3%	1.2%

数据来源：根据中国商务部《中国对外直接投资统计公报》。

在2016年中国对全部中东欧16国的对外直接投资减少的背景下，以及中国商务部对之前统计公告中公布的水平进行统计修正后，中国对外直接投资存量的新水平发生变化，以至于根据这一标准，罗马尼亚在中东欧16国中排名第一（图12），回到2005年的位置（表4）。

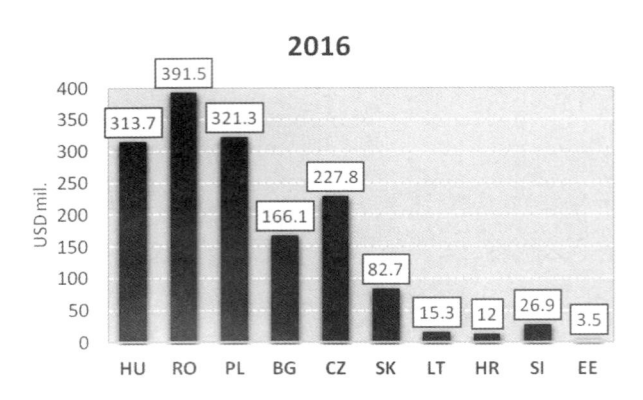

图 12 中东欧 16 国的中国对外直接投资存量前 10 名（单位：百万美元）

表 4：中东欧 16 国的中国对外直接投资存量前 5 名（单位：百万美元）

2005		2010		2013		2015		2016	
1. RO	39.4	HU	465.7	HU	523.4	HU	571.1	1. RO	391.5
PL	12.4	PL	140.3	PL	257.0	2. RO	364.8	PL	321.3
LT	3.9	3. RO	125.0	CZ	204.7	PL	352.1	HU	313.7
BG	3.0	CZ	52.3	BG	149.9	BG	236.0	CZ	227.8
HU	2.8	BG	18.6	5. RO	145.1	CZ	224.3	BG	166.1

总之，在 2012—2013 年推出 16+1 和 "一带一路" 倡议后，中国在罗马尼亚的投资增长有所放缓，但中国的对外直接投资总额仍然很低，远低于预期和潜力。

（2）中国在罗马尼亚的投资企业

罗马尼亚拥有大量有中国资本的注册公司总数超过 12000 家。但是，实际上其中只有一半保持活跃。中国驻罗马尼亚大使徐飞洪指出，拥有中国资本的公司目前占罗马尼亚外国投资者总数的 6%，仅占外国投资额的 1%。另一方面，根据罗马尼亚国家银行（NBR）的记录，中国的对外直接投资在罗马尼亚总外国投资中的比重在 2013 年可能上升到 0.2%，而在 2015 年仅上升到 0.3%。

这反映了一个事实，即罗马尼亚的主要中国投资者仍然来自第一波投资浪潮（2000 年左右），主要是中小型企业（SME），大部分是财务和投资能力差的家族企业从事中国进口商品的批发或零售。

仅一小部分早期进入的投资者成功设立一些低技术含量的制造或组装工业单位（寻求资源和市场的）并在当地和欧洲取得很大的成功：自行车组装厂

（Eurosport DHS Manufacturing、Ricky Impex）使用廉价的本地资源（劳动力、土地、低税收、原材料）并利用欧盟的单一市场准入规则；烟草单位（Friendly & Joy 集团的 Sinoroma）；低成本的家用电器单位（Friendly & Joy 集团的 Vortex）；印刷机械生产（运城制版罗马尼亚公司），建筑材料等。

在信息技术和通信领域的中国投资者中，华为（2003 年进入罗马尼亚）和中兴通讯（2002 年进入）代表成功的早期投资者的独特组成部分。与上面提到的利用本地低成本资源（通常包括低成本、低技能劳动力）的公司相反，这两家大型跨国公司是寻求资产的投资者，他们正在利用本地化的工程技能并以极具吸引力的性价比实现其专有技术的战略价值，以在欧洲范围内提供高附加值的服务。

在全球经济危机发生后，2010 年以后第二批进入罗马尼亚的中国投资者更加多元化，规模更大（表 5），其中包括建设和运营可再生能源的公司、汽车零部件制造商、房地产开发商或消费品行业的公司。这些都是资源和市场的追逐者，具有更大的投资能力，但仍未在罗马尼亚做出重大投资承诺。

表 5：在罗马尼亚的中国投资者

中国投资者	投资领域	平均投资额（单位：美元）	结果
建设和运营可再生能源的公司（2012-2017）向日葵光能、光为绿色新能源、联盛新能源、明阳风电	可再生能源	最终项目的总金额达到数亿美元	太阳能工业园和风电场；许多合同停滞（例如，明阳风电在 Vaslui-Husi 地区投资 4 亿美元的 200 MW 风电场项目）
汽车公司（2016）宁波华翔电子股份有限公司	汽车零配件	数百万美元（4500 万 + 1700 万美元）	布拉索夫 2 间工厂正在建设中
建筑公司（2016）	房地产	数百万美元	居住区（中国建筑商中途放弃克拉约瓦项目；布加勒斯特/2300 万欧元，正在建设中）；戈沃拉（20 公顷），医院 + 酒店 + 别墅 + 直升机场
消费品生产商（2016）环球照明集团，上海	照明行业	数百万美元	家用照明设备工厂（位于布勒伊拉）

数据来源：作者根据媒体新闻整理。

除了大小企业的直接投资外，由于中国最近大举收购在罗马尼亚拥有资产的西方公司，中国在罗马尼亚经济中的地位也变得更为重要（表 6）。在某种程度上说,这些第三方交易对罗马尼亚经济的影响和意义不大,仍然只是所有权交接,但只要新的中国企业进一步投资开发、产能扩大、产业升级、技能提高、应用新技术等,这些交易就可能变得很重要,在当地创造就业机会和生产更高质量的产品,以供应国内市场并增加出口。截止目前,我们仅了解到中粮集团有限公司——最近已成为黑海康斯坦察港最大的东欧谷物码头的所有者——宣布计划增设码头,以扩大其在康斯坦察的港口业务。

表6:国际收购后罗马尼亚的中国新所有者

中国投资者 (投资年)	被收购的公司 (国家)	涉及领域	平均投资额	对罗马尼亚的影响
中粮集团有限公司 (2017)	尼德拉(荷兰),一家拥有97年历史的集团,是欧洲最大的谷物贸易商	农业、农业经营、贸易	51%股权,估计价值25亿美元;总额未披露	尼德拉位于康斯坦察港的谷物码头和仓库现已归中粮集团所有;
万洲国际集团,前称双汇国际,世界最大的猪肉生产商 (2013)	史密斯菲尔德食品公司(美国)	肉类加工	超过70亿美元	在罗马尼亚的50个养猪场+2个饲料工厂+1个屠宰场目前成为中国资产
中国化工集团 (2015)	倍耐力(意大利)世界第5大轮胎生产商	汽车零部件、轮胎	77亿美元	目前位于罗马尼亚的2家工厂(斯拉迪纳轮胎厂;Bumbesti-Jiu柴油发动机滤清器厂)属于中国化工集团
宁波均胜电子股份有限公司 (2015)	Quin(德国)	汽车零件和内饰	金额未披露	布拉索夫/辛巴夫的一家工厂现已成为中国财产
宁波均胜电子股份有限公司 (2011)	Preh(德国)	汽车电子零件	收购74.9%股份	布拉索夫/辛巴夫的一家工厂现已成为中国财产
宁波均胜电子股份有限公司 (2017)	KSS/美国百利得安全系统公司(美国)	汽车安全系统	金额未披露	罗马尼亚的3家工厂现已成为中国财产
宁波均胜电子股份有限公司 (2017)	TAKATA(日本)	汽车零件	16亿美元	罗马尼亚的3家工厂(阿拉德和锡比乌)现已成为中国财产

数据来源:作者根据媒体新闻整理。

中国华信能源有限公司与 Kaz Munay Gas International 公司（哈萨克斯坦）在石油加工和汽油经销业务方面进行的最大交易是收购前罗马尼亚跨国公司 Rompetrol 51％的控股权，而该罗马尼亚公司现在是 Kaz Munay（哈萨克斯坦油气公司）的财产。这笔交易将让中国合作伙伴控制罗马尼亚的两家炼油厂（Petromidia Navodari 和 Vega Ploiesti）以及在六个欧盟国家外加摩尔多瓦和格鲁吉亚的 1000 多个加油站构成的经销网络，但最近宣布收购没有成功并最终放弃（2018 年 6 月底）。这项交易在 2016 年获得罗马尼亚国家批准。

多年来，罗马尼亚和中国官员已经在商讨或谈判大量的潜在合同，但至今尚未实现。最先谈判的有两个：一是与中国广核电力股份有限公司就 Cernavoda 核电厂的 70 亿美元扩建项目（包括 3 号和 4 号机组）进行谈判；二是与中国华电科工集团有限公司就 Rovinari 燃煤电厂扩建新的 500MW 机组进行谈判，价值 10 亿美元。在本文定稿时仍未宣布新的截止期限。两国协商的其他大多数项目也都在能源和交通基础设施领域，前景也不明确。

中国在罗马尼亚投资可总结如下：

1. 2005-2016 年，中国每年对罗马尼亚的对外直接投资额一直在剧烈波动；

2. "一带一路"倡议启动后的前两年，中国每年对罗马尼亚的对外直接投资流入发生可喜的增加，但在 2016 年，随着中国对中东欧 16 国的投资普遍减少，中国在罗马尼亚的直接投资也出现了急剧下滑；

3. 2016 年中国对罗马尼亚的投资额下降至 2015 年的 25％，但相对来说并不是中东欧 16 国最糟糕的国家，因此自 2005 年以来，罗马尼亚出人意料地重返其在中国对中东欧 16 国投资排名第一位；

4. 2013 年以后，双边联系加强，投资性质多样化，但投资额仍然很低，远低于预期和潜力；

5. 伴随着国际收购，部分中国大企业现在已成为罗马尼亚资产的所有者，它们的存在将继续投资本行业的工业发展和升级，对我们的经济有利。

6. 预计在不久的将来仍不会完成中国对能源和运输基础设施大规模投资合同融资的谈判。

三、结语

"一带一路"倡议所设想的建立更牢固的东西方联系在双方自远古以来的历史中是自然发展的趋势,而目前情况更是如此,至少是因为:

我们拥有地球上最大的一块陆地 – 亚洲和欧洲在地质上是一块拥有7000万年历史的单一陆地,欧亚大陆;在过去2000年中,尽管距离遥远且地形不好,欧亚大陆仍然拥有世界人口的大约三分之二,人口一直在从欧亚大陆的一端迁移到另一端;纵观整个历史,技术突破从欧亚大陆的一端扩散到另一端:公元16世纪之前,技术进步主要发生在亚洲,技术从东向西,从亚洲向欧洲流动;公元19世纪以后,技术进步主要发生在欧洲(工业革命),而创新又从西方向东方,从欧洲向亚洲流动;如今,欧洲和亚洲都是优秀的创新者,技术可能会双向流动。

此外,欧亚大陆目前拥有:地球上最大的工业生产区域(中国、欧盟、日本、印度、韩国等);最大的现有和潜在市场(欧盟、中国、俄罗斯、印度等);自然资源最富裕的地区(中东、中亚国家、俄罗斯、中国及领海等)和先进的经济一体化区域(欧盟)。

与古代相比,如今我们拥有高效的运输、能源、通信和信息技术网络;在历史上,进一步的创新前景也不尽相同;这种发展既是进一步加强联系的前提和激励因素,也证明全球化是一种像自然法则那样起作用的力量,不论我们是否喜欢,不论我们是否想要,抑或是反对、鼓励或试图阻止;因此,明智的态度是不要利用资源与这种不可战胜的"自然力量"作斗争,而是要明智地利用我们的资源"乘风破浪",并尽可能取得最大的利益。

"一带一路"倡议最有可能实现这一点,对中国和其他有关国家都有利,前提是各方为了共同成功而真诚行动,决策透明并让所有利益相关方参与其中,所有各方尊重彼此的利益和优先事项,允许互利互惠,减轻不平衡现象,维持公平的环境和公平竞争。

"一带一路"战略具有巨大的潜力,可以推动地区和全球经济增长并提高参与国(甚至是非参与国)人民的生活水平。然而,"一带一路"和16+1平台只有在满足以下条件的情况下,才有机会真正取得成功,即:在设计、实施、共担风险和共享利益方面实现真正的多边努力;遵守参与者已签署的国际公认的准则、规则、规范和条约;在明确和约定的规则下运作,有关各方均应完全分遵守;从决策和成本评估到项目实施和完成全过程都是透明的；考虑当地利益、借贷的需求和潜力，而避免承担违约以及给社区带来不可持续的债务负担风险；服从投资项目的经济合理性、商业可行性、社会和环境影响要求；在公平的竞争环境中推动公平竞争。

"一带一路"战略需要参与国的信任、意愿、努力和热情。如果不是所有参与国都会受益，该战略也无法实现。"一带一路"倡议本质上是一个多边计划，需要多个国家去思考、设计、协议和实施。只有一个国家，不论多么强大，即使是拥有悠久历史和卓越成就的中国，也无法独力承担。如果"一带一路"倡议不被重新制定、澄清并得到广泛接受，将不会被认为是成功的，将遭遇越来越多的反对和退缩，将步履蹒跚、引发不满、加剧局部竞争甚至敌对情绪（包括对中国在内），从而付出远远超出预期的时间和代价。另一方面，赢得其他国家的信任、意愿、参与和满意后，该战略将事半功倍，将带来巨大的影响，世界将变得更好。

China-Romania Economic Relations: from Ancient Connectivity to Nowadays BRI

Sarmiza Pencea / Romania

Head of the Economic Development Models Department, Institute for World Economy, Romanian Academy

1. A glimpse of our fascinating distant past

We, Europeans and Asians, have been living since the dawn of humankind on the largest uninterrupted landmass on Earth. We chose to name its western extremity Europe, and the eastern one, Asia, but nowadays we are speaking more about Eurasia, just one name, for one continent, not least because of China's daring BRI project of recreating, at modern standards, the ancient Silk Road that used to interlink the two extremities of our continent about 2000 years ago.

The ancient Silk Road is certainly an important point of reference in terms of Eurasian connectivity, but it is worth remembering that ancient populations travelled back and forth on our shared continent from the earliest of times, making contacts and exchanging not only goods, but also information, knowledge, technologies, ideas and believes.

This is where Romanian archaeologists unearthed in1884 amazing traces of a Neolithic culture that is the oldest in Europe, older than the Sumerian and the Egyptian ones and embodies the pinnacle of European culture of the time: the Cucuteni culture.[1] Named after the Romanian village where the first artifacts were discovered, the *Cucuteni culture* dates back to 5200-3200 B.C., and, besides its old age, it is outstanding for many reasons:

(i) *Cucutenians*, probably the first in Europe to become a sedentary population, were farmers, hunters and crasftsmen. Remarkably, they lived in big, artfully painted houses of wood and clay, covered with straw, often two-storied and having many rooms designed for different specific usages;

Fig.1: Tentative recomposition of a Cucutenian settlement

Source: Traxus Ares (2015).

(ii) *Cucutenians* usually gathered in large communities, that reached even as many as 20000 people and were organized for common protection and social life: their houses were often positioned in circles, with a bigger building in the middle serving as a sanctuary and as a socializing spot, and their settlements were surrounded by either natural, or man-made entrenchments, for protection. Nearby sources of water and salt were

---

[1] Ten years later, in 1894, in the village of Tripolie, Ukrainian archeologists made their first discoveries attesting for this culture. Ever since, the culture has also been reffered to as the Cucuteni-Trypillian culture.

provided for the whole community;

(iii) Cucutenian settlements have been the earliest proto-towns[1] in Europe. Over 4000 such "urban" settlements have been discovered only in Romania;

(iv) Judging on the numerous clay human figures they have left us, which never have furious faces, it seems that these populations were calm and peaceful. There were no arms discovered in their settlements, only tools;

(v) Cucutenians were also the first in Europe to make the leap from carved to polished stone, and then to metal processing (mainly copper and gold);

(vi) But the Cucuteni culture is singularized and best known mainly for the exquisite shapes, drawings and colour combinations in their unique art of pottery, which attest not only to an outstanding artistic refinement of this population, but also to their high technological prowess (e.g. the way they prepared resilient clay and paints, as well as the tools they used: progenitors of the potter's wheel, special ovens etc.) and know-how (e.g. they were very skillful in precisely controlling the temperature in the pottery ovens) (Figures no. 2-9 and 10-15).

---

[1] Proto-towns are the oldest ancestors of nowadays towns, organized in what urban architects call planimetry and providing the first social services for the whole community.

Fig. 2-9: Cucutenian pottery excavated in Romania, different sites

Source: See the References.

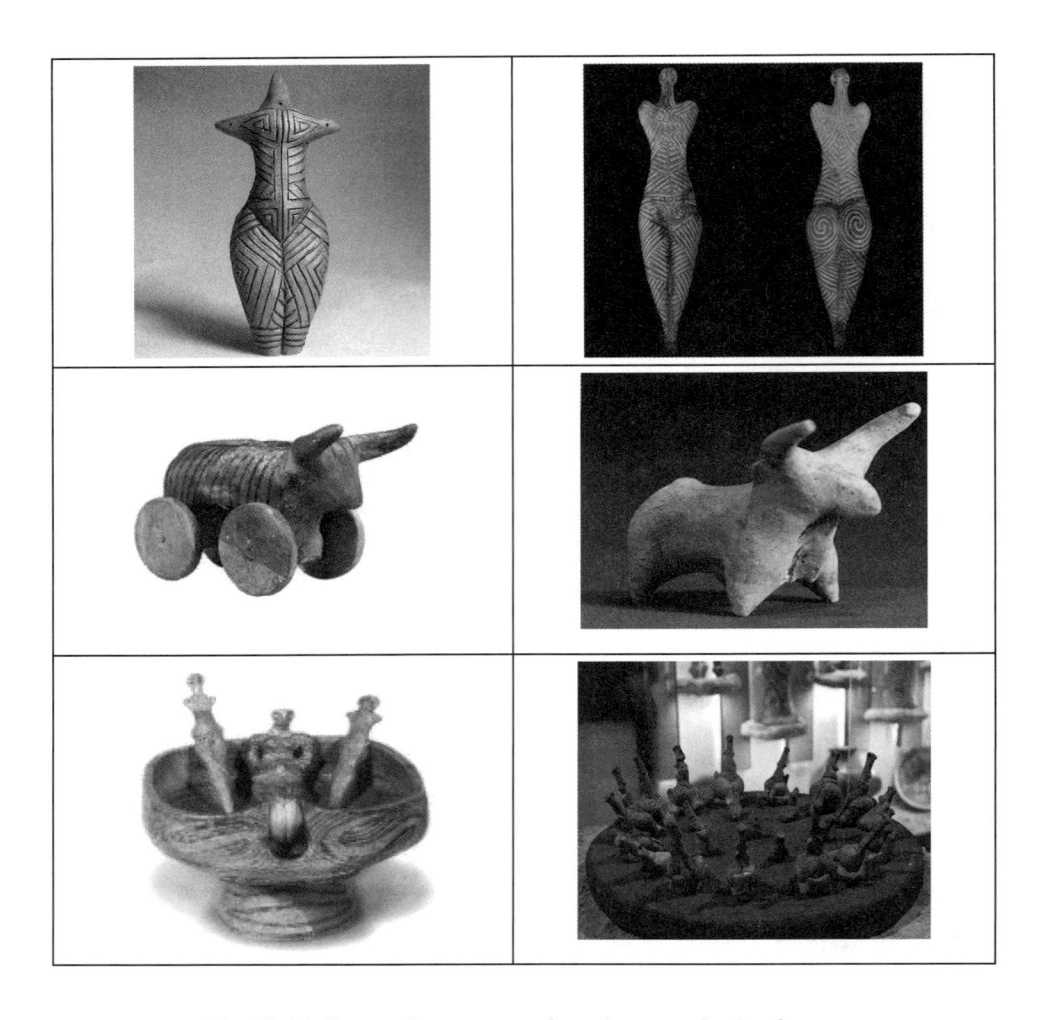

Fig. 10-15: Cucuteni antropomorfic and zoomorfic clay figures

Source: See References.

Currently, Romania has the largest collection of Neolithic art in Europe. This collection, as well as the work of the Romanian and foreign historians and archaeologists that studied it, attest to the reality that Cucuteni is the oldest culture in Europe and that our ancestors developed the most illustrious culture of prehistoric Europe, the pinnacle of the material and spiritual development of over 7000 years ago (Preoteasa, 2009).

Nevertheless, if it is unique in Europe, it seems that the Cucuteni culture is not alone in Eurasia. It may have a close relative thousands of kilometers away from Romania, in China: the Yangshao culture (Figures no. 16-21 and 22-25).

Not only that Yangshao and Cucuteni pottery look very similar in shapes, ornaments, colours and mystical signs, but they seem to have used the same technologies in clay and paint preparation. Experts consider that the two populations may have had constant contacts, in spite of the distance that separated them and of the rudimentary transport means of the time.

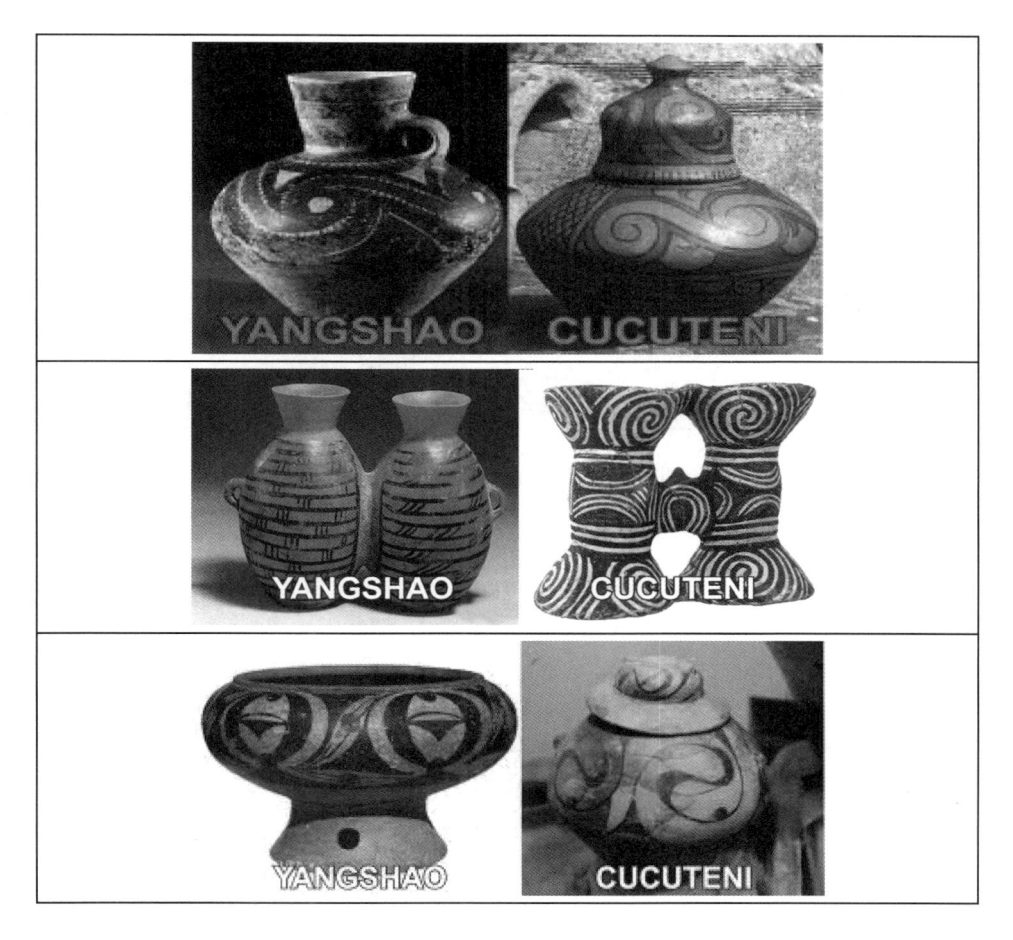

Fig. 16-21: Similitudes of Cucuteni and Yangshao pottery

Source: See References.

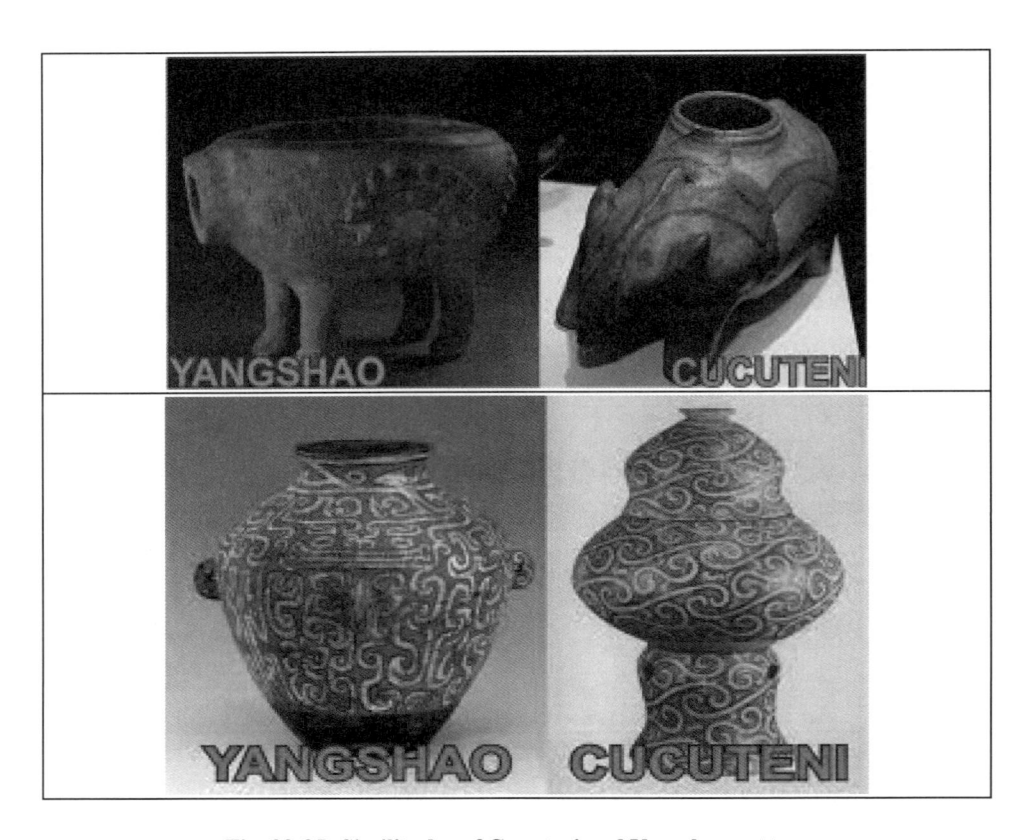

Fig. 22-25: Similitudes of Cucuteni and Yangshao pottery

Source: See References.

It is also interesting and intriguing that two of the most well-known signs, considered Asia-specific, ying and yang and the swastika, are present on Cucutenian pottery of 6000-7000 years ago (figure 26).

Also, it is very impressive that Cucutenian art displays the perfect proportions of the *golden rectangle* discovered only thousands of years later by Euclid.

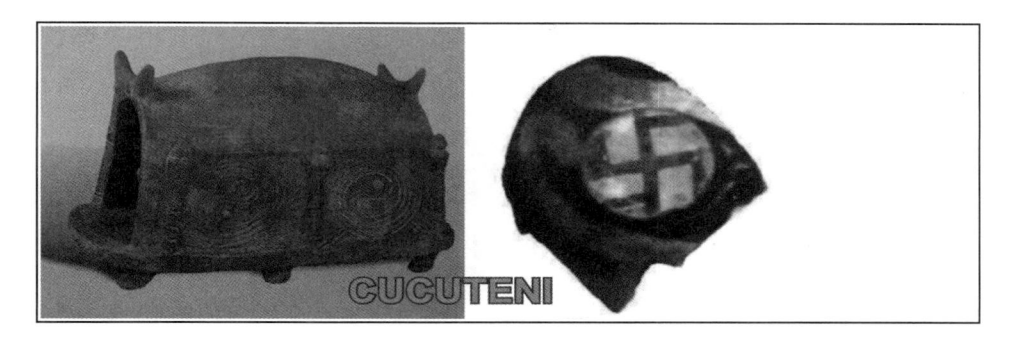

Fig. 26: Similitudes of Cucuteni and Yangshao pottery (ying and yang, swastika)
Source: See References.

If all of these similitudes and commonalities between the two cultures were not proof enough of the respective populations' connectivity, a relatively recent discovery in Romania came to offer an argument beyond any doubt to this hypothesis. In 2012, in the village of Baia, Romanian archaeologists made an outstanding discovery: a 7200 years old, unusually large pre-cucutenian house (5200-5100 B.C.), that conserved not only remarkable pottery, unique objects and tools, a complete fireplace, and so on, but also cereals and different other plants.

A team of researchers from Cambridge University, who had researched for ten years the cereals in China, joined the Romanian archaeologists. Led by professor Martin Keneth Jones, expert in the bio-molecular archaeology of cereals, this research team found out that, 6000-7000 years ago, certain cereals had been brought to China from Europe, while others had been brought to Europe from China. According to professor Martin Kenneth Jones, trade between Europe and Asia was first in cereals, then in precious stones and only much later the Silk Road developed, with its high diversity of traded goods.

Cambridge researchers are now trying to discover how exactly our ancestors could do that. However, their research on cereals has already demonstrated the existence, since the Neolithic times – 7000 years ago - of the commercial and knowledge-related links between our ancestors living in the territories of nowadays

Romania and China. We don't know yet how our ancestors did it, but, if they could connect and exchange goods, information, ideas, knowledge, technologies and know-how, we certainly can do it nowadays, with the technology and capabilities of our time.

2. Recent developments in China-Romania economic relations under the impact of BRI

Making the leap back to our times, we want to see what impact can be already discerned on the Romania-China bilateral trade and investments after the BRI launch, in 2013.

2.1 The bilateral trade

The first thing we can notice is that there is a remarkable progress and even the start of a rebalancing trend in our bilateral trade volumes, in the current decade (2010-2016) (Table 1).

Table 1: Romania trade volume with China, 2010-2016 (USD, million, %)

RO/CN TRADE	2010	2011	2012	2013 /B&R	2014	2015	2016	2016/10 (%)	2013/10 (%)	2016/13 (%)
EXPORT	755	947	980	1208	1517	1299	1455	+92.3	+60.0	+20.4
IMPORT	3004	3454	2797	2823	3223	3187	3448	+14.5	-6.0	+22.1
TOTAL (X+M)	3759	4401	3777	4031	4730	4486	4903	+30.4	+7.2	+21.6
DEFICIT (X-M)	-2249	-2507	-1817	-1615	-1706	-1888	-1993	-11.4	-28.2%	+23.4
X:(X+M)x 100	20.1%	21.5%	25.9%	30.0%	32.1%	29.0%	29.7%			

Source: Computations using UN Comtrade Database, https://comtrade.un.org/data.

- Total bilateral trade rose by over 30% during the interval considered, Romanian exports nearly doubled (+92.3%) and imports grew considerably slower (+14.4%);

- This led to a significant drop, of 11.4% in Romania's trade deficit with China and to the beginning of a rebalancing process between the two trade flows;

- But, looking comparatively at the developments in the years before and after 2013 (the year of the BRI launch), we can see that the evolution after 2013 was less favorable than that in the years before that year:

  o Total trade increased, indeed, mostly after 2013 (by nearly 22% vs. little over 7% before 2013), but

    - **Romanian exports** to China *increased considerably less after 2013 and the BRI launch* (+20.4%), than before 2013 (+60%);

    - Romanian imports from China increased more than exports after 2013 (+22,1%) and rebounded very strongly from the slight decrease recorded before the 2013 BRI launch (-6%);

    - As a result, Romanian trade deficit jumped by over 23% after 2013 vs. a decrease of over -28% before 2013;

    - Also, the share of Romanian exports in the total bilateral trade, which had grown from 20% to 30% before 2013 (and even to 32% in 2014), declined marginally to 29.7% after 2013;

    - The rebalancing process of the trade flows between Romania and China that had started before 2013 was reversed afterwards and the trade deficit has re-started growing;

    - In 2016, China contributed directly by 28%, to Romania's total trade deficit, but additionally also indirectly, as some of the countries that Romania is running deficits with, are intensely re-exporting Chinese goods to our country (e.g. Hungary, Poland).

Another significant development in our bilateral trade of 2010-2016 is that the structure of Romania's export to China has improved (Table 2). We can notice, on the one hand, that the export of most categories of goods has been on an uptrend and, on the other hand, that the export structure has diversified:

- For the first time, all the SITC groups have been present in Romanian exports to China;

Table 2: Romania's export structure to China, 2010, 2013, 2016 (mil.USD)

SITC Rev.3	2010	2013/B&R	2016	2016/2010	2013/2010	2016/2013
0	1.3	0.8	17.9	13.8 x	- 38.5%	22.4 x
1	2.7	4.2	3.4	+ 26%	+ 55.6%	-19%
2	175.0	318.9	161.4	-7.8%	+ 82.2%	- 49%
3	-	0.3	3.0		new	10 x
4	-	-	1.8			new
5	89.2	72.2	45.6	- 48.9%	- 19.1%	- 36.8%
6	51,5	104.9	149.8	2.9 x	2.0 x	+ 42,3%
7	326.5	462.5	688.2	2.1 x	+41.7%	+48.8%
8	109.1	243.7	383.7	3.5 x	2.2 x	+57.4%
TOTAL EXP.	755.3	1207.5	1455.2	1.9 x	1.6 x	1.2 x

Source: Author's computations using UN Comtrade Database, https://comtrade.un.org/data.

- Exports of group SITC 0 products (*Food and live animals*) grew over 22 times. There were significant increases in exports of items such as pork (+95%), eggs and diary (251%);

- Still, looking at some exports in more detail, we can discover a not so favourable reality, from the Romanian standpoint. For instance, the exports of pork are mainly those of the 50 farms a Chinese company (WH Group, former Shuangui) has in Romania, while the exports of Romanian producers meet numerous non-tariff barriers to China's market (e.g. sanitary certifications, red tape);

A positive development is that Romania's export structure has changed mainly after 2013 and the changes were in favour of more complex products (Graphs no. 1, 2 and 3):

- ✓ SITC 7 (Machinery & transport equipment) – Romania's export weight of SITC 7 products in its total exports to China increased from 36% in 2005, to 38% in 2013 (only +2 pp in 9 years) and to 48% in 2016 (+10 pp in just 3 years, after 2013);
- ✓ SITC 8 (Miscellaneous manufactured articles) – Romania's export weight of SITC 8 products in its total exports to China increased from 5% in 2005, to 20% in 2013 and to 27% in 2016;
- ✓ SITC 2 (Crude materials, inedible, except fuels) – increased from **19%** in 2005, to 27% in 2013 and then it decreased to only **11%** in 2016;
- ✓ SITC 5 (Chemichals and related) – kept decreasing from **9%** (2005), to 6% (2013) and to **3%** (2016).

Graph 1.

CHINA'S IMPORT FROM ROMANIA, 2005 (mil. USD)

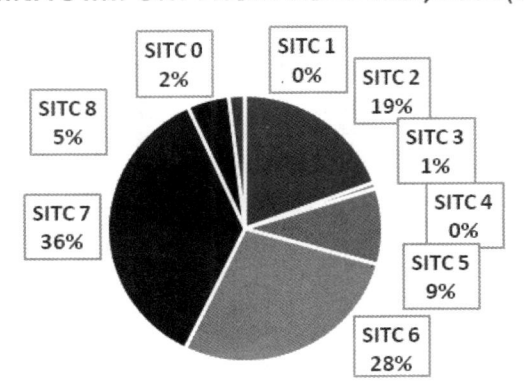

SITC	%
SITC 0	2%
SITC 1	0%
SITC 2	19%
SITC 3	1%
SITC 4	0%
SITC 5	9%
SITC 6	28%
SITC 7	36%
SITC 8	5%

Source: The author, using UN Comtrade Database, https://comtrade.un.org/data.

Graph. 2.

CHINA'S IMPORT FROM ROMANIA, 2013 (mil. USD)

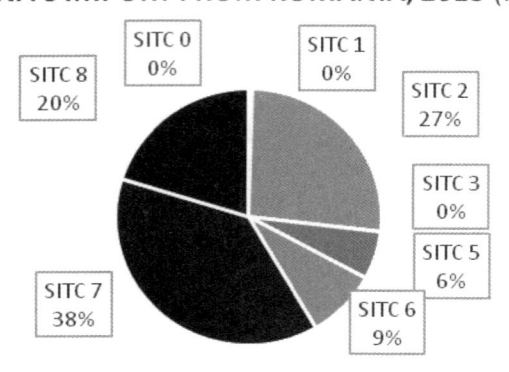

- SITC 0: 0%
- SITC 1: 0%
- SITC 2: 27%
- SITC 3: 0%
- SITC 5: 6%
- SITC 6: 9%
- SITC 7: 38%
- SITC 8: 20%

Source: The author, using UN Comtrade Database, https://comtrade.un.org/data.

Graph 3.

CHINA'S IMPORT FROM ROMANIA, 2016, (mil. USD)

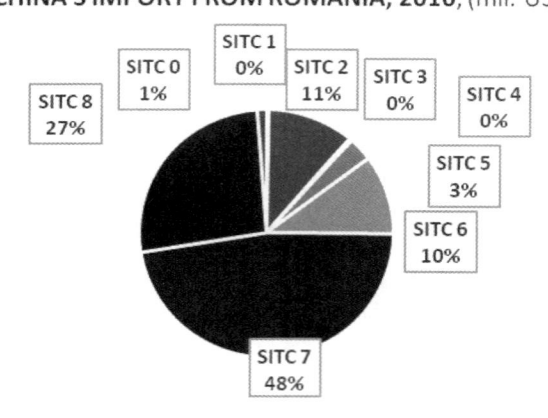

- SITC 0: 1%
- SITC 1: 0%
- SITC 2: 11%
- SITC 3: 0%
- SITC 4: 0%
- SITC 5: 3%
- SITC 6: 10%
- SITC 7: 48%
- SITC 8: 27%

Source: The author, using UN Comtrade Database, https://comtrade.un.org/data.

Romania keeps ranking only the 5th among CEE16 by trade volume with China, despite its size and potential (Graph 1).

Graph 4: Top 5 CEE by trade volume with China 2010-2016 (USD mil.)

	2010	2011	2012	2013	2014	2015	2016
PL	11138	12988	14385	14807	17189	17091	17632
CZ	8850	9988	8731	9453	10979	11009	11011
HU	8716	9258	8061	8407	9024	8069	8887
SK	3749	5970	6078	6542	6204	5032	5271
RO	3759	4401	3777	4032	4740	4486	4903

Source: The author, using UN Comtrade Database, https://comtrade.un.org/data.

The Romania-China Bilateral Trade (2010-2016) can be Concluded as the following:

CONCLUSIONS ON ROMANIA-CHINA BILATERAL TRADE 2010-2016

1. Romania-China bilateral trade has grown significantly between 2010-2016;

2. A rebalancing process had begun after 2010 and Romania's trade deficit with China had started to narrow. However, this rebalancing process has stopped since 2013 and the trade deficit has re-started advancing quite swiftly;

3. Romania's export structure to China has diversified and improved mainly after 2013, favouring more complex categories of items;

4. Groups 7 (Machinery and transport means) and 8 (Miscellaneous manufactured goods) accounted together for 75% of Romania's total exports to China, in 2016;

5. Groups 7, 8 and 6 (Manufactured goods classified by materials) accounted together for 85% of Romania's exports to China, in 2016.

6. Access to Chinese market by Romanian exporters is still hampered by non-tarriff barriers;

7. In spite of growing bilateral trade volumes and of its size and economic potential, Romania still ranks the 5th among the CEE16 by the total trade volume with China.

2.2. Chinese investments in Romania

2.2.1 The invested volumes

Statistical records show strongly fluctuating annual Chinese outbound direct investment (ODI) flows to Romania, between 2005-2016 (Graph 2). While investment flows were at a minimum in 2013, they registered a significant jump in the following two years after the BRI launch, only to plummet again afterwards, in 2016, to just one quarter of the previous year level.

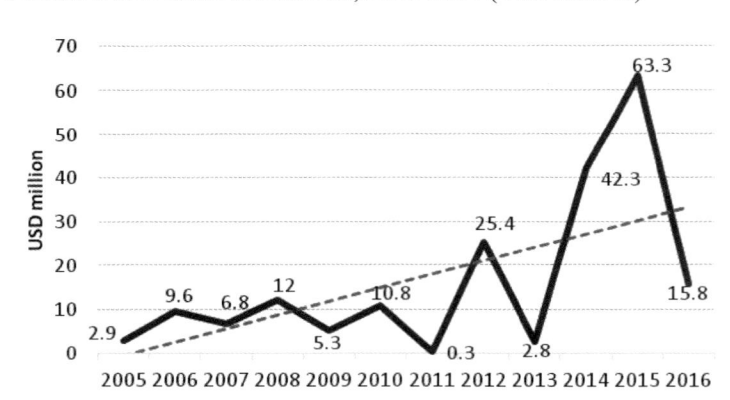

Graph 2: China's ODI flows to Romania, 2005-2016 (USD million)

Source: The author, using Statistical Bulletin of China's Outward Foreign Direct Investments, MOFCOM.

Looking at the bigger picture after the global economic crisis, the dynamics of Chinese ODI flows to Europe (Table 3) shows an impressive upswing of the investments directed to its western, highly developed half (EU17), which more than doubled in 2016 vs. 2013, coupled with a significant decline of the flows directed to the CEE16 and especially to the CEE11[1]. Also, the amounts received by the CEE16 region, which usually account for only a minor fraction of those invested in the

---

[1] In this paper we use the CEE16 acronym for the 16 CEE countries that are members of the 16+1 platform, the CEE11 acronym for the CEE that are both members of the 16+1 platform and of the European Uunion (EU) and the EU17 acronym for the other EU members besides CEE11 (EU17 + CEE11 = EU28).

EU17 group, have got, comparatively, even smaller amounts after the launch of the 16+1 and B&R initiatives (2012-2013) that were supposed to give a boost to the emerging CEE economies (only 1.2 per cent of the EU17 level in 2016 vs. 2.7 per cent in 2013).

Table 3: Chinese ODI inflows to Europe in 2005-2016 ($ million)

	2010	2011	2012	2013	2014	2015	2016
EU17	5547	7432	5970	4433	9595	5326	9934
CEE11	417	129	150	91	193	154	104
CEE16	419	130	158	118	208	174	116
CEE16 vs. EU17	7.6%	1.7%	2.6%	2.7%	2.2%	3.3%	1.2%

Source: Computations using Statistical Bulletin of China's Outward Foreign Direct Investment (various years), MOFCOM.

Against the backdrop of Chinese ODI flows declining in all of the CEE16 in 2016 and following some statistical corrections operated to the levels announced in previous statistical bulletins of MOFCOM, the new levels of the Chinese ODI stocks have changed in such a manner that Romania came to rank first by this criterion among the CEE16 (Graph 6), returning to a position it detained back in 2005 (Table 4.).

Graph 6: Top 10 CEE16 by Chinese ODI stocks (USD, Million)

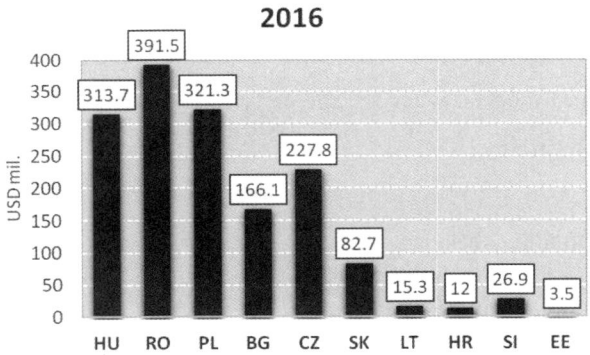

2016

Country	USD mil.
HU	313.7
RO	391.5
PL	321.3
BG	166.1
CZ	227.8
SK	82.7
LT	15.3
HR	12
SI	26.9
EE	3.5

Source: The author, using 2016 Statistical Bulletin of China's Outward Foreign Direct Investments, MOFCOM. Note: Country names abbreviations are used according to https://www.worldatlas.com/aatlas/ctycodes.htm

Table 4: Top 5 CEE16, by Chinese ODI stocks (USD, million)

2005		2010		2013		2015		2016	
1. RO	39.4	HU	465.7	HU	523.4	HU	571.1	1. RO	391.5
PL	12.4	PL	140.3	PL	257.0	2. RO	364.8	PL	321.3
LT	3.9	3. RO	125.0	CZ	204.7	PL	352.1	HU	313.7
BG	3.0	CZ	52.3	BG	149.9	BG	236.0	CZ	227.8
HU	2.8	BG	18.6	5. RO	145.1	CZ	224.3	BG	166.1

Source: The author, using 2016 Statistical Bulletin of China's Outward Foreign Direct Investments, MOFCOM. Note: country names abbreviations according to https://www.worldatlas.com/aatlas/ctycodes.htm

In conclusion, there is some modest Chinese investment growth in Romania after the 2012-2013 launch of the 16+1 and the BRI, but the total level of Chinese ODI is still very low, much under the expectations and the potential.

2.2.2 The Chinese investor companies in Romania

Romania is home to a large number of recorded companies with Chinese capital, over 12,000, but only about half of them are actually active. According to H.E. Hu Feihong, the Chinese Ambassador to Romania, the companies with Chinese capital currently account for 6% of the total number of foreign investors in Romania and for only 1% of the foreign invested value. On the other hand, according to the National Bank of Romania (NBR) records, the weight of Chinese ODI in the overall foreign investment in Romania may have raised to only 0.2% in 2013 and to slightly more, 0.3%, in 2015.

This is a reflection of the fact that the predominant Chinese investors in Romania are still the ones of the first wave (of the early 2000s), which are mainly small and medium-size enterprises (SMEs), mostly family companies of low financial and investing power, that are prevailingly involved in wholesale or retail of Chinese imported goods (market seekers).

Only a small number of the early-comers managed to set up some low-technology manufacturing or assembling industrial units (resource-seeking and market-seeking investors), that are actually quite successful locally and in Europe: bicycle assembly factories (Eurosport DHS Manufacturing, Ricky Impex) that use the cheap local inputs (labour, land, low taxation, some materials) and capitalize on the EU single market access; a tobacco unit (Sinoroma of the Friendly&Joy conglomerate) that does the same; a low-cost home appliances unit (Vortex of the Friendly&Joy conglomerate); production of printing machinery (Yuncheng Plate-Making SRL), construction materials etc.

A distinct component of this successful group of early comers is represented by the Chinese investors in the information technology and communications (ITC) sector, Huawei (since 2003 in Romania) and ZTE (since 2002). As opposed to the companies mentioned above, which are capitalizing on the local low-cost resources, often including low-cost, low-skilled labour, these two large multinational companies (MNCs) are asset-seeking investors that are using the local engineering skills and the strategic value of their know-how at a very attractive price/quality ratio, to supply high value-added services around Europe (Drahokoupil et. all, 2017).

A second group of diverse, much larger Chinese investors in Romania came in the 2010s, after the global economic crisis (Table 5) and include companies that build and operate units in renewable energy (RE), manufacturers of car components, real estate developers, or firms in the consumer goods industries. These are both resource and market seekers, that have greater investment power but still are not making big investment commitments in Romania.

Table 5: Chinese investors in Romania (2010s)

Chinese investor	Field	Average volumes invested(USD)	Outcomes
Companies building and operating RE units (2012-2017) *Sunowe, Lightway Solar, Unisun, Ming Yang Wind Power*	Renewable energy (RE)	-finalized projects add up amounts in the range of hundres of million USD	solar parks and wind farms; - many contracts stall (e.g. Ming YangWind Power USD 400 mil. 200 MW project of a wind farm in Vaslui-Husi area)

continued

Chinese investor	Field	Average volumes invested(USD)	Outcomes
Automotive companies (2016) Ningbo HuaXiang Electronic Co. Ltd	Auto parts and accesories	Tens of thousands USD (USD 45+17 mil.)	2 factories under construction in Brasov
Construction companies (2016)	Real estate	Tens of thousands of USD	Residential districts (Craiova- project abandoned half-way by the CN constructor; Bucharest / EUR 23 mil. under construction); Govora (20 ha), Hospital + hotel + villas + heliport.
Consumer goods producers (2016) Liting Universal Group, Shanghai	Lighting industry	Tens of thousands USD	factory of home lighting devices (in Braila)

Source: Author's compilation of media news.

Besides the direct investments made by smaller or larger companies, the Chinese presence in our economy has become much more significant as a result of the recent Chinese takeover spree of western companies that had assets in Romania (Table 6). To the extent that they remain just ownership handovers, such third party deals have little impact and significance for the Romanian economy, but they still can become important, provided that the new Chinese owners invest further in development, capacity expansion, industrial upgrading, improved skills, new technologies etc., generating local job creation, higher and better quality production to supply the home market and to increase exports. For now, we only know that China National Cereals, Oils and Foodstuffs Corporation (COFCO) – that has recently become the owner of the largest eastern European cereal terminal in the port of Constanza, at the Black Sea -, announced its intention of building an additional terminal in order to extend its port operations in Constanza.

Table 6: New Chinese owners in Romania following international takeovers

Chinese investors (year of investment)	Acquired companies (country)	Field	Average volumes invested	Outcomes for Romania
COFCO (2017)	NIDERA (NL), a 97 years old conglomerate, the largest cereal trader in Europe	Agriculture, agrobusiness, trade	- the first 51% stake for an est. USD 2.5 bn. - total amount undisclosed	NIDERA cereal terminal in the port of Constanza and a warehouse belong now to COFCO;
WH Group, former Shuangui International, the world's largest in pork production (2013)	SMITHFIELD FOODS (US)	Meat procesing	Over USD 7 bn.	50 active pig farms in Romania + 2 fodder factories + 1 slaughter house are now Chinese property.
ChemChina (2015)	PIRELLI (IT), 5th world tyre producer	Automotive components, tyres	USD 7.7 bn.	2 factories in RO belong now to ChemChina (Slatina, tyres; Bumbesti-Jiu, filters for diesel engines)
Ningbo Joyson Electronic Corp (2015)	Quin (DE)	Auto parts and interior ornaments	Undisclosed amount	One factory in Brasov/Ghimbav is now Chinese property
Ningbo Joyson Electronic Corp (2011)	Preh (DE)	Automotive electronic parts	Acquisition of a 74.9 % stake	One factory in Brasov/Ghimbav is now Chinese property
Ningbo Joyson Electronic Corp (2017)	KSS/Key Safety Systems (US)	Automotive safety systems	Undisclosed amount	3 factories in Romania are now Chinese property
Ningbo Joyson Electronic Corp through KSS (2017)	TAKATA (JP)	Automotive parts	USD 1.6 bn.	3 factories in Romania (Arad and Sibiu) are now Chinese property

Source: Author's compilation of media news.

The largest deal negotiated in the oil processing and petrol distribution business between CEFC China Energy Company and KazMunayGas International (KZ) for a 51% controlling stake in the former Romanian MNC Rompetrol which is now a KazMunay property, a deal that would have brought to the Chinese partner the control over two refineries in Romania (Petromidia Navodari and Vega Ploiesti) and over a distribution network of more than 1000 gas stations in six European Union countries, plus Moldova and Georgia, has been recently declared unsuccessful and abandoned (end of June, 2018). This tranzaction had obtained the approval of the Romanian state in 2016.

There is a large number of potential contracts discussed or even negotiated for quite many years between the officials of Romania and China, but none of them has materialized as yet. The most advanced negotiations are two: (i) with China Nuclear Power Corporation for the USD 7 billion extension of the Cernavoda nuclear plant with units 3 and 4; and (ii) the negotiations with China Huadian Engineering for the extension of the Rovinari coal power station with a new 500MW unit, worth USD 1 billion. No new deadline was announced for their finalization. Most of the other projects discussed between the two countries are also in the energy and transport infrastructure area and also with no clear outlook.

Regarding Chinese investments in Romania can be sum up as it follows:

1. Annual Chinese ODI flows to Romania have been strongly fluctuating between 2005-2016;

2. An encouraging jump in the annual Chinese ODI inflow to Romania took place in the first two years after the BRI launch, but in 2016, against the backdrop of a general Chinese investment plumetting in the CEE16, a new steep decline has been also registered in Romania;

3. Nevertheless, in Romania the 2016 drop to only 25% of the 2015 investment flow level was comparatively not the worst in the CEE16 region and, as such, Romania unexpectedly returned to its 1st rank position among the CEE16 recipients of Chinese ODI, as in 2005;

4. Bilateral contacts have intensified after 2013 and the nature of investments have diversified, but the invested values have remained very low, much under expectations and under the potential;

> 5. Some big Chinese actors are now asset-owners in Romania, following international takeovers, but their presence will be beneficial to our economy only to the extent that they will continue to invest in industrial development and upgrading.
>
> 6. The negotiations for large investment contracts in energy and transport infrastructure with Chinese financing are not expected to be finalized in the near future.

3.Final remarks

Establishing stronger east-west connections as envisioned by the BRI was a natural development in our distant history and it is the more so at present, at least because:

- ***We share the largest uninterrupted landmass on Earth*** – Asia and Europe are geologically a single, 70 million years old piece of land, Eurasia;

- ***During the past 2000 years Eurasia was continually inhabitted by roughly 2/3 of the world population*** and Eurasian populations have always moved from one extremity of the continent to the other, despite distance and unfriendly geography;

- ***Throughout history, technological breakthroughs difused from one extremity of Eurasia to the other***: before 1500 A.D. technological dynamism took place mostly in Asia and technologies flowed east to west, from Asia to Europe; after 1800 A.D. technological advancement took place mostly in Europe (the industrial revolutions) and innovations flew the other way round, from west to est, from Europe to Asia; nowadays, both Europe and Asia are proficient innovators and technologies may flow in both directions.

- *Also, Eurasia is now home to:*
    - *some of the largest industrial production areas on Earth* (China, European Union, Japan, India, South Korea etc.);
    - some *of the largest existing and potential markets* (EU, China, Russia, India etc.);
    - *some of the richest areas in natural resources* (The Middle East, Central Asian countries, Russia, China, their territorial waters etc.) and
    - *areas of advanced economic integration* (EU);
- As opposed to ancient times, *nowadays we can have performant transport, energy, communications and information technology networks; further innovation prospects are also without equal in history*;
- Such developments are *both prerequisites and incentives of further intensifying connectity* and they prove that *globalization is a force that acts like a law of Nature*, no matter if we like it or not, no matter if we want it, or oppose it, encourage it or try to block it;
- As such, a wise attitude would be to not exhaust resources fighting against such a *"force of Nature"*, which is invincible, but to use our resources wisely, *"riding the wave"* and trying to extract most of benefits from it;

The Belt & Road Initiative (BRI) will most probably do just that, to China's benefit and to the benefit of the other countries involved, provided that all parties act in good faith for the common success, decision making becomes transparent and involves all stakeholders, all the parties respect each others' interests and priorities, allow for reciprocity, for mitigating asymmetries, for keeping a level playing field and fair competition.

The Belt and Road strategy has a huge potential of boosting the regional and global economic growth, as well as the living standards in the participant (and even non-participant) areas. However, BRI and the 16+1 platform have a real chance of success only provided that they:

- become true multilateral endeavours in design, implementation, shared risks and benefits;

- observe the internationally recognized principles, rules and norms and the treaties previously signed by the participants;

- operate under clear, agreed-upon rules, that are fully observed by all the parties involved;

- are transparent all the way from decision making and cost assessment, to project implementation and completion;

- take into consideration the local interests, needs and potential of borrowing, without risking defaults and unsustainable debt burdens to communities;

- observe the requirements of economic rationality, commercial viability, social and environmental impact of the projects financed;

- foster fair competition in a level playing field.

The strategy needs the trust, willingness, effort and enthusiasm of the participant countries, all of which are not possible without positive results for the all of them. BRI is by its nature a multilateral endeavour and it needs multilateral thought, design, agreement and implementation. Just one country, no matter how large and strong, even China, with its long history of outstanding achievements, will not be able to carry out this endeavour by itself. If not reformulated, clarified and largely accepted, BRI will not be deemed successful, but it will meet increasing opposition and backlash, it will falter, generate discontent, reinforce local rivalries, even hostility (including towards China), it will take longer and cost considerably more than expected. On the other hand, by obtaining the trust, willingness, participation and satisfaction of the other countries, just supposing that only about half of what this strategy strives for is accomplished, the impact will be tremendous and the world will be largely changed to the better.

传统与现代在全球化中的交融：
从罗马尼亚的角度看中国

玛格鲁·乔治 【罗马尼亚】
罗马尼亚外交部长顾问 / 新战略中心科学委员会成员

  本文更多的是拷问，而不是对比来自两个不同大陆的两种文化的历史或语义。为何选择语义学？因为如果不对文化基本概念达成共识，那么对话的前提将面临难以弥合的鸿沟。在当今的地缘政治和经济现实之外，欧洲和中国之间的长期适应和互动过程仍在发展。在文化和智力对话方面，我们还有很多没有挖掘的资源，使之与长期以来对人类文明的贡献相匹配。本方法受到作者的国家感知以及面对如此广泛的主题时所掌握知识范围的限制。此外，在这个阶段提出问题比提供确定的答案的面临更大的挑战。

  孔子在《论语》中对于名正言顺有过一段评论。子路曰："卫君待子为政，子将奚先？"子曰："必也正名乎！"子路曰："有是哉，子之迂也！奚其正？"子曰："野哉，由也！君子于其所不知，盖阙如也。名不正则言不顺，言不顺则事不成，事不成则礼乐不兴，礼乐不兴则刑罚不中，刑罚不中，则民无所措手足。故君子名之必可言也，言之必可行也。君子于其言，无所苟而已矣。"

  最近在一项题为"如何在传统社会建设现代国家？"的研究中，罗马尼亚人类学家温蒂勒·米哈伊列斯库发现美国巴尔干学家特莱恩·斯托恩诺维奇的挑衅观点，称自新石器时代以来，直到19世纪初，欧洲地区的"基本上"没有发生任何改变。

如果考虑到温斯顿·丘吉尔的著名观点，即巴尔干的历史非常丰富，这些看法就是相互矛盾。然而，如果在更广阔的背景下考虑似乎也并不太矛盾，部分科学家认为地球上的人类仅在工业革命后才进入一个新的地质时代。

该罗马尼亚学者作为人类学家，认为多个世纪以来，本地区的农牧特色和社会政治关系基本上没有太大变化。另一位罗马尼亚作家、政治学家，前外交官瓦伦丁·纳乌梅斯库在 2017 年的一项研究中怀疑"在帝国的范围内和几个世界的交叉路口，我们是否有资格谈论罗马尼亚例外主义"。

这篇文章发表在《为什么罗马尼亚会这样？罗马尼亚例外主义的体现》文集，由温蒂勒·米哈伊列斯库汇集 18 名学者编撰。他们对罗马尼亚的身份进行自省和自我分析。

自 19 世纪现代罗马尼亚政治实体出现以来，部分罗马尼亚学者提出的存在问题引发罗马尼亚知识分子和政治界的激烈辩论。

在这种情况下，中国领导人以"主要矛盾"一词作为分析中国社会正在经历复杂发展过程现状的工具，可能找到让人感兴趣的运用方式。因此，纵观罗马尼亚打造现代身份的历史，可以从欧洲视角求助于中国学者在对比方法中的有利原创观点。

随着罗马尼亚人逐渐开始民族觉醒，他们不可逆转地融入西方世界的意愿已成为决定性因素。

同时，本文开头所定义的传统社会现代化的步伐和深度有时被 19 世纪后期的各种思想流派视为"表面现代化"，即"只有形式，没有本质"，或者在 20 世纪早期表现为模仿或共时社会。

实际上，罗马尼亚经历了巨大的改变过程并且仍在遵循上述基本范式。罗马尼亚人将自己视为西方的组成部分，欧盟的原则和价值观被假定为罗马尼亚存在和体制结构的必要部分。但是，在西方的广阔视野中，罗马尼亚人的故事非常复杂。

在最新文章《罗马尼亚 100 年：一个世纪的历史诠释》中，奥地利历史学家奥利弗·詹斯·施密特思考罗马尼亚国家的发展和特征以及塑造罗马尼亚社会的国家建立模板。

考虑到罗马尼亚人的意识形态建构，或称为"罗马尼亚人在罗马尼亚境内的辩论"时，他也认为自己的角色是"局外人，在一定距离外观察这一问题，没有伪装成绝对中立或客观，因为这在历史科学的诠释中是不可能的"。

本着这种承认局限性的精神，我们试图对罗马尼亚和中国历史诠释进行类比，从中汲取一些观点。

罗马尼亚悖论之一是保守主义和现代性之间的紧张状态，古代与新时代时而冲突但始终并存的维度，与地缘政治、战略和文化影响以及罗马尼亚领土毗邻的各个帝国利益带来的压力交织在一起，例如中欧的哈布斯堡王朝、南方的拜占庭人和奥斯曼人，或东北方向上的俄罗斯人。

罗马尼亚人和中国人的关系中存在着一个明显的特征，它跨越欧亚大陆的广阔区域，甚至在更广泛意义上作为东西方在全球范围内古老但仍在延续的故事的一部分，也恰好是不可阻挡的现代化潮流及其对民族和个人身份认同影响的动态紧张状态下，传统和保守主义保持不变的共同点。

诚然，文明之间存在大量的差别，其文化和政治连续性已经在自远古以来无穷无尽的考古、历史和文学记录中得到证实。喀尔巴阡山脉—多瑙河以及黑海孕育出多姿多彩且非常古老的欧洲大家庭，基本上都属于拉丁裔，以希腊-罗马和犹太教-基督教地中海文明为基础。罗马尼亚在地缘政治上是一个存在感很强的国家，既属于中欧和东南欧，也是欧洲东部向亚洲或东地中海开放的边界。它不仅是文化的十字路口，还体现出丰富的语言、种族和宗教多样性，使该地区和整个国家在欧洲具有鲜明的特色。

下面有几个很好的理由从罗马尼亚—中国的角度来看待中国人与欧洲人之间的关系：

• 第一个理由是传统的重要性，它在历史潮流的基础上构成现代进程的基石；

• 另一个理由与以下事实有关，即工业革命及其在19世纪和20世纪必然导致的各个阶段，不论主体选择什么样的治理形式，扎根于传统的民族和国家实体发生大规模社会经济和政治变革，从而引发激进、革命性的后果。

在《企鹅美国史》(企鹅出版社，2001年)中，英国历史学家休·布罗根在《凡尔赛条约》瓦解以及希特勒和斯大林的活动的背景下探讨现代工业主义主题，并指出："在亚洲甚至更强大的规矩被扭曲。现代工业主义对东方的影响是毁灭性的。例如，在19世纪，蒸汽船和铁路破坏古老中国文化的结构并对其造成严重伤害，这种文化以前一直幸存并接纳蛮族的暴力入侵。"

第三个理由是，在20世纪或艾瑞克·霍布斯鲍姆定义的"较短的20世纪"

的背景下，罗马尼亚和中国之间的关系具有非常特殊的性质，这取决于两国在冷战期间的态度，尤其是对苏联专制统治的反抗，即使名义上拥有相同的制度意识形态；

第四点是文化理由，与罗马尼亚知识分子对东方研究的持久兴趣有关。对中国文化传统的发掘和更好的理解可以响应罗马尼亚的精神特质，即寻求将罗马尼亚身份认同融入普世表现形式的类比和来源，而中国身份无疑就是这种表现形式。对中国的兴趣仍在不断增加，这是 19 世纪罗马尼亚学者和作家发现印度宇宙观与欧洲存在古老联系的必然结果。那个时代是印度—日耳曼或印度—欧洲研究的鼎盛时期，对罗马尼亚文化产生了持久的影响。我们有必要考虑到三个千年文明之间的相互交流：欧洲（希腊—罗马和犹太教—基督教）、中国和印度，因为它们之间的相互影响不对等且具有长期后果。

第五个理由将是第四次工业革命，这是 21 世纪的标志。在一百五十年的历史时间框架下，处于剧烈的命性变革中的两个社会很难进行比较，但可以评估二者之间惊人的距离，而另一方面，身份认同在此背景下如何演变。

就欧洲与东方联系的文化历史而言，通过前面提到的与拜占庭帝国、奥斯曼帝国或俄罗斯帝国的联系，罗马尼亚能够引起关注，因为我们虽然是互补的，但仍然是欧洲，尤其是西欧了解外界的大门。在这个方面的一个里程碑是具有渊博知识的摩尔多瓦贵族尼古拉·米列斯库·斯帕塔鲁（1636-1708）。除了母语罗马尼亚语外，他还精通拉丁语、希腊语、俄语、土耳其语、法语和意大利语。米列斯库是一位真正的冒险家、外交官和业余神学家，摩尔多瓦亲王的大臣、驻奥斯曼帝国和路易十四宫廷的使节，因怀疑他渴望获得王位而被逐出自己的国家。他最终成为阿列克谢·罗曼诺夫宫廷大臣，受沙皇派遣出使康熙皇帝统治下的中国，进行一次难忘的中国之旅。诚然米列斯库对中国的访问是俄罗斯领土向东方扩张和中俄关系复杂历史的一部分。我们的兴趣在于日记的价值、丰富的信息和敏锐的心理，同时详细描述两种不同传统的帝国文化是如何相互影响。

然而，我们认为，米列斯库的故事与中国发展与西方关系的广泛框架有关，超越与俄罗斯的关系，甚至达到"太阳王"路易十四的巴黎或罗马神圣教廷，更不用说葡萄牙、荷兰或英格兰。

与我们的主题相关的是作为中西方文化使者的利玛窦（Mateo Ricci）和法国汉学创始人黄加略。利玛窦于 1610 年去世，米列斯库于 1708 年去世，黄加略于

1710 年去世。在长达一个世纪的时期，中西关系经历起起伏伏，带来深远的影响。随着教宗在 1704-1705 年公布教谕（Cum Deus Optimus）和清朝雍正皇帝于 1724 年发布禁教令（天主教、佛教、道教），"礼仪之争"最终达到顶峰。

我们不会详细说明中国思想体系的神话色彩，虽然值得这样做，但在基督教世界的眼中，从七八世纪的古叙利亚传教士到 13—18 世纪的方济各会和耶稣会教士，或在不同时间到达中国的安立甘教会和东正教旅行者，他们都这样认为。这或许是另一个故事，但也是不平等的，中国和印度僧侣在敦煌和粟特之间穿越丝绸之路的沙漠小道，经过危险重重的喜马拉雅山，将恒河两岸宝贵的印度佛教经典带到长安。佛教对东亚造成长期的影响。然而，当我们深入研究类似之处和局限性时，或许可以回想起同一时代的另一个悖论，在中世纪的一次伟大的文化和语言冒险中，阿拉伯哈里发的学者复原西方拉丁文的古希腊哲学，这对欧洲的文艺复兴做出贡献。

不幸的是，随着教皇克莱门特十四世于 1773 年下达谕令解散耶稣会，不幸错过了加深中国和西方文化相互理解的机会。我们只能假设，如果在中华帝国处于鼎盛时期时继续进行下去，中西文化之间的对话将如何演变以及可能出现什么样的结合。实际上，由于地缘政治原因，19 世纪使文化之间的对话以及文化、法律或哲学原则和价值观的相互承认变得复杂，至今仍然让中国史学界深感痛心。

为了更好地评估中国与西方之间长达数百年的复杂曲折关系，我们必须回到明朝的鼎盛时期，18 世纪的割裂之前。上海政法学院何平立和周长明教授在《罗马尼亚欧亚研究述评》刊物发表的标题为"明朝的帝国巡视和郑和下西洋（印度洋）的航行"的研究论文中，将"巡狩"的概念追溯到远古时代（《晋书》中"礼"的章节），定义为对领土进行巡行视察。他们认为，这不仅体现儒家思想，例如"普天之下，莫非王土"、以礼治国、以德治国、皇帝和政府勤勉于政事，还体现保护国土和安抚边境地区的战略实施。因此，帝国巡狩是一项以军事为后盾的活动，涉及军事力量、政治、经济、文化和宗教。

在这里，我们不会过多介绍已广为世人所知，在明朝前三位皇帝统治下郑和下西洋（以及命中注定的结局）的古代故事。根据作者的观察，郑和下西洋的结局由外部世界有关的帝国文化精神所决定，而这种精神由源自古代"普天之下，莫非王土"的大一统思维逻辑和传统意识形态的命运、道德、利益和仁慈规则的解释掌控。

因此，在明清时期，如此宏伟壮观的政治和军事活动不能够打开外部世界的窗口，也无法取得成果。

由于海禁令（禁止海上活动），导致清朝皇帝无视西方敲开中国大门时世界上正在发生的一切。

诚然，从帝国的角度而言，郑和冒险的政治或经济回报似乎与所消耗的巨额费用不成比例，包括在随后的几个世纪，海盗侵犯中国海上边界的行为不断增加以及与日本的紧张关系。

因此，他们得出结论，在历史上和新时代的开放中，具有划时代意义的事件没有发生在中国，而是哥伦布的航海活动和探险。那个时代引发工业革命以及经济、技术、文化、政治和地缘政治方面的全球影响。

具有讽刺意味的是，正是在哥伦布发现美洲的背景下，钱德拉·库卡瑟斯在《牛津政治理论手册》关于"道德普遍性和文化差异"的章节中探讨"道德问题的起源和本质"。虽然自16世纪以来，亚洲、非洲和美洲发生政治和经济转变，他观察到，并未使共同的道德标准完全融合。

在该书中，这个问题与人权及其普遍性的基本问题密不可分。

同样，在广泛跨文化学术对话的背景下，深入了解产生社会和国际关系基本概念、原则和规范的历史过程，无疑会带来额外价值。

为了进一步揭示中国传统与现代概念之间的联系，上海海事大学时平教授在《中国人的文化理念：从家天下到人类命运共同体》一文中总结对罗马尼亚公众的好处。这篇文章目前正在印刷中，它确定千年传统与当前中国外交政策主要参照点之间的联系，即"一带一路"倡议和"人类命运共同体"。这篇文章涉及的概念有：天人合一；天下万民一家；长期和谐社会；34,000年的太阳崇拜等。

从这个角度来看，"构建人类命运共同体"不仅是当下和未来的任务，而且也是过去的任务：在新的背景下实现历史上波澜壮阔但尚未完成的任务和推动中西方以及其他国家之间的对话，是当代追求和平未来的组成部分。

进入当代，虽然不为普罗大众所知，在亨利·基辛格秘密访问北京，随后理查德·尼克松总统与毛泽东主席和周恩来总理诱发全球重大转变的历史性会面中，罗马尼亚扮演了重要的角色。另一个方面涉及在中美关系发生惊人的变化后，中国重新融入国际社会的过程。中华人民共和国恢复联合国安理会常任理事国席位是罗马尼亚外交史上另一个不为人知的一面，也是罗马尼亚推动多边主义的部分努力。从本文的角度来看，或许值得一提的是，中国签署《联合国宪章》和其他相关条约或契约后以及逐渐加入联合国相关的所有机构后，中国进入国际法机构和接受公认概念对中国产生的学术和法律影响。[1]

我们必须追溯 19 世纪的中国外交史，涉及大国利益在中国土地上的复杂交涉，吸收和创造的国际法概念伴随着中国加入全球秩序后的道路。这一过程与中国的全面现代化密不可分。

在法斯本德和彼得斯主编的《牛津国际法史手册》中，川岛真所著的关于中国的一章标题为"构建现代国家和万国公法"，论述中国在 19 世纪 70-80 年代的外交领域经历的重大变革。中国自认为超脱于适用于其他国家的国际法原则之外的过渡反映出清末官员对势力均衡这一痛苦现实的认识。转变体现在康有为从"一统垂裳"（分等级统治世界）到"列国并立"（世界各国共存）的思想变化。"万国公法"（公法以外的国家）被"国际法"所代替。我们不得不再次回到中国对这些概念的原始解释，对概念的承认是正在进行的文化恢复努力的一部分。

罗马尼亚公众从《中国外交：历史和精神前提》一书中受益匪浅。作者萨安娜毕业于北京大学历史系，是一位杰出的汉学家，一生经历都与中国有关。她的作品的主题从古典文献开始，有着丰富的历史数据，一直延伸到当代，对"礼"这一概念的核心作用进行探索，因为礼是中国人的基本精神/伦理特征。正是基于这个概念界定人民或民族文化生活整体的特有特征，作者建议了解几千年来中国人认识国家秩序以及个人在社会中的作用所产生的深刻力量。

当然，自我指称系统实际上并不是凭空出现。18 世纪和 19 世纪后期的外交适应和发展历史及具体而不同的交互（即欧洲在长期的战争与和平条约历史中建立起来的国际关系概念、规范和原则以及与古老的帝国，例如波斯、奥斯曼或日本），对于全球化的该阶段同样重要，表明工业革命后西方的巅峰。在这方面，亨利·基辛格或弗朗西斯·福山的作品已经是经典之作，紧随其后是著名的塞缪尔·亨廷顿，仅以几位顶尖人物为例。

中国的特别之处在于，庞大规模的转型过程仍在全面进行，并且开发出智力工具，将不同文化和文明之间呈现的对等概念融入广阔的当代知识海洋。在这种情况下，中国具有五千年不间断历史的传统，基于定义中国"世界观"的宇宙哲

---

[1] 有关冷战期间罗马尼亚外交史的更多信息，请查阅美国历史学家拉里·沃茨的最新著作《内线斗争：冷战期间的罗马尼亚安全政策》（同时由 Rao Distribution 出版公司在罗马尼亚发行，2018 年），上述事件被列为罗马尼亚当代历史上的传奇故事。

学及伦理学概念和符号，提出双重挑战：对中国人来说，这是一个挑战，因为他们必须将彼岸输入的现代模式转换为人类最前后一致和自给自足文明中的概念和语言；另一方面，理解塑造全球化和普遍主义进程的替代文化和文明共存的挑战。

考虑到上述情况，中国社会科学院将"中国文化与人类命运共同体"作为"汉学与当代中国"座谈会的议题是不合时宜的。我们认为，它实际上开辟了一个与古典方法并存的新汉学研究阵地，从而可以深入探讨现代化的影响下中国的智力转型。同时，根据具体情况，中国文化和文明中的古老概念经历时间的考验，可以应对当今的挑战的一面。

罗马尼亚受过良好教育的公众基本上了解从儒学到道教的各种知识，以及翻译成罗马尼亚语的现代和当代历史著作、世界著名小说等。即使是规模不大的汉学院，也声誉良好，覆盖各个年代，而且不断增加关于中国的新书。这是一个持续的过程，不仅应从双边角度来看，而且应作为中欧之间更广泛对话的一部分。

欧盟和中国之间深入的全面伙伴关系涵盖六十多个实质性的部门，以一种重要的结构化的方式进行对话。《中欧合作2020战略规划》是指导中欧关系的最高水平文件，规定在和平、繁荣、可持续发展和人员交流等领域开展合作。

关于人员交流，我们注意到推动跨文化间对话、促进文化多样性和民间社会参与的活动，包括教育活动。我们观察到首次中国－欧盟国家教育部长会议和首届中欧教育政策智库论坛的举行。

创新合作对话与第17届中欧国家峰会同时举行，是该领域的最新活动。

对罗马尼亚来说，中欧关系的这些篇章与我们自身的方针一致。作为欧洲与亚洲之间更广泛对话的一部分，罗马尼亚将于2019年5月担任欧盟理事会轮值主席国期间举办第七届ASEF校长会议和ASEF青年论坛以及亚欧教育部长会议。罗马尼亚还准备在2019年以16+1的方式举办教育部长会议。

我们认为，如果不把教育作为社会的优先考虑事项，就不可能解决当今世界面临的挑战。提及教育时也包括指导人类与社会联系的原则和价值观。在前面提到的"第四次工业革命"的背景下，需要考虑的另一个方面涉及在大规模地缘政治、人口、社会和文化变革的时代，历史教训如何影响教育体系，我们必须向年轻一代传授的相关知识。

最后，回到本文的主题，在我们看来，本届汉学座谈会议题涉及的主题非常具有挑战性，将不可避免地向亨利·基辛格寻求问题的答案。他在《世界秩序：

对国家的特征和历史进程的反思》一书中指出:"要实现真正的世界秩序,各个组成部分在保持自身价值的同时,还需要获取具有全球性、结构性和法律性的另一种文化 – 超越任何一个地区或国家视角和理想的秩序概念"。

Tradition and Modernity in a Globalized World: a View on China from Romania[1]

Magheru Gheorghe / Romania

Advisor to the Minister of Foreign Affairs of Romania/Member of the Scientific Board of New Strategy Center

The current essay is more of an interrogation rather than an exercise in comparative history or the semantics of two cultures from two distinct continents. Why semantics? Because without forging a common ground of understanding of the basic founding concepts, the very premises of dialogue would face a gap hard to be bridged. The long process of accommodation and interaction between Europe and China is still developing even as beyond present day geopolitical and economic realities there still are to be uncovered enormous fields of untapped resources in terms of cultural and intellectual dialogue commensurate to their durable contribution to the heritage of mankind. The approach is naturally limited by the national perception of the author and the modest scope of his knowledge confronted with such a vast subject. Moreover, the challenge of raising a question is greater at this stage than the capacity to offer the certitudes of an answer.

---
1 The views in this article are the author's only.

In the *Analects*, Confucius has a comment on the rectification of names. Zi Lu said: "The King of Wei is waiting for you to go administrate his country. What are you going to do first?" Confucius said: "To rectify names." Zi Lu said: "Why be so pedantic? Why should there be a need to rectify names?" Confucius said: "You don't understand! A gentleman will never be in a haste to present his opinions as to what he does not understand. If names are not rectified, what is said will not sound reasonable; if what is said is not reasonable, efforts cannot culminate in success; if efforts cannot culminate in success, the rites and music will not thrive; if the rites and music do not thrive, crimes cannot be punished properly; if crimes are not punished properly, the common people will have nothing to go by. Therefore, whatever a ruler says must be in accordance with the rites. He must be practical and never be casual."

In one of his recent studies entitled "How to build a modern nation with a traditional society?" (Magazin Istoric, May 2018), the Romanian anthropologist Vintila Mihailescu unearths the provocative opinion of an American Balkanologist, Traian Stoianovich, claiming that since the Neolithic revolution and till the dawn of the 19th century nothing "fundamental" had changed in this region of Europe.

This is quite a paradoxical statement if you take into account Winston Churchill's famous boutade that the Balkans had generated more history than they could digest. But it may seemingly paradoxical when some scientists, in a much wider context, consider that we have only recently entered a new geological epoch resulting from the impact of mankind on the Earth with industrial revolution, the Anthropocene.

As an anthropologist, the Romanian scholar considers that for many centuries the agro-pastoral features of the area as well as the social and political relations have not basically changed. Another Romanian author, the political scientist and former diplomat Valentin Naumescu was wondering in a study dated 2017 whether "at the confines of the empires and the crossroads of several worlds, we are entitled to speak of a Romanian exceptionalism."

This study was published in a volume entitled "Why is Romania such as it is? The Avatars of Romanian Exceptionalism", which was coordinated by the aforementioned Vintila Mihailescu and brought together eighteen scholars, who carried on a remarkable work of introspection and self-analysis on the Romanian identity.

The existential questions addressed by some Romanian authors touch upon a lively debate in Romanian intellectual and political circles, ever since the emergence in the 19th Century of a modern Romanian political entity.

In this case the term of "principal contradiction" the Chinese leaders resort to as an instrument of analysis of the current state of the Chinese society undergoing a complex development process, may also find an interesting application. Plunging into the history of the forging of the Romanian modern identity may thus render to Chinese scholars an original vantage point in a comparative demarche from a European angle.

As the process of national awakening of the Romanians was taking shape, their will to be irreversibly integrated into the Western world has become the defining element.

At the same time, the pace and depth of modernization in a traditional society as defined at the beginning of this essay was sometimes considered by various schools of thought in the late 19th century as "superficial modernization", a "form without substance" or, later on in the earlier 20th century, the expression of a mimetic or synchronic society.

In effect the process of transformation undergone by Romania has been tremendous, and it is still going on following the essential paradigm mentioned above. The Romanians definitely perceive themselves as part of the West and the principles and values of the European Union are now assumed to be structurally part of the Romanian existential and institutional fabric. But the story of the Romanians in this enlarged vision of the West is quite complex.

In his latest essay "Romania in 100 years. An account of a century of history" (Humanitas, 2018), the Austrian historian Oliver Jens Schmitt makes some considerations on the development and character of the Romanian state as well as on the manner in which the founding template of the state has shaped the Romanian society.

While taking into account the Romanians' ideological construction, or, as he calls it, "the debate of the Romanians within Romania", he also assumes his own role "as an outsider, someone tackling the subject from a certain distance, without pretending however to be absolutely neutral or objective, something anyhow impossible in the science of history, where interpretation is involved".

It is in this same spirit of acknowledged limitation that we have attempted to brush some ideas starting from possible analogies in the interpretation of Romanian and Chinese history.

One of the Romanian paradoxes has always been the tension between conservatism and modernity, the sometimes conflicting but always coexisting dimensions of the ancient and the new, mingled with the geopolitical, strategic and cultural influences and pressures resulting from the various empires whose interests abutted onto the various Romanian territories, be they the Habsburgs from Central Europe, the Byzantines and the Ottomans from the South, or the Russians from the North and East.

The one distinguishing character in the relations between the Romanians and the Chinese, a part of the old and still ongoing story between East and West across the huge expanse of Eurasia, and even more broadly between the Occident and the Orient in global terms, is precisely the common denominator of the constant of tradition and conservatism in its dynamic tension with the overwhelming tide of modernization and its impact on the identity of the peoples and individuals.

It is true that there is an ocean of difference between a civilization whose cultural and political continuity has been confirmed in inexhaustible archeological, historical and literary records since time immemorial, and the Carpathian-Danubian and Black Sea sprout of the diverse, but still very old, European family, which basically belongs to the Latin group and is based on the Greco – Roman and Judeo Christian Mediterranean civilization. Romania is geopolitically a ubiquitous country belonging both to Central Europe and South Eastern Europe, the Eastern confines of Europe opening to Asia or the Eastern Mediterranean. It is more than a crossroads of cultures, as it is a manifestation of rich linguistic, ethnic and religious diversity which gives the area and the country its distinctive features in Europe.

There are several good reasons for looking at the relations between the Chinese and the Europeans through a Romanian-Chinese lens:

- A reason is precisely the weight of heritage, which makes the seabed on which the process of modernity has been built against, or with, the tidal waves of history;

- Another is related to the fact that the Industrial Revolution and the various stages it entailed during the 19th and the 20th centuries in the socio-economic and political transformations of peoples and state entities anchored in tradition had a dramatically large magnitude, which caused radical, revolutionary consequences irrespective of the form of governance chosen by the subjects;

- In the *Penguin History of the USA* (Penguin Books, 2001) the British historian Hugh Brogan tackles the subject of modern industrialism in the context of the collapse of the Versailles treaty and the activities of Hitler and Stalin and remarks that "in Asia an even mightier rope of events was being twisted. The impact of modern industrialism on the East had been shattering. In the previous century, for example, steamboats and railways had destroyed the structure and gravely wounded the culture of that ancient China which had always previously survived and absorbed barbarian incursions, however violent".

- The third would be that, against the landscape of the 20th century, or the 'shorter 20th century' as defined by Eric Hobsbawm, the relations between Romania and China had a very particular character determined by their attitudes during the Cold War and notably their opposition to the imperial dominance by the Soviet Union even as they nominally shared the same systemic ideology as the hegemonic one;

- The fourth would be cultural, and it is related to the enduring interest of the Romanian intellectuals for Oriental studies. The discovery and better understanding of Chinese culture and tradition responds to a trait of the Romanian spirit in its quest for analogies and sources aiming to integrate the Romanian identity into the manifestations of the universal – and the Chinese identity is definitely such a manifestation. The interest for China, which is still evolving, is a natural corollary to the discovery in the 19th century by the Romanian scholars and writers of the universe of India and its ancient connections to Europe. It was the heyday of Indo-Germanic or Indo-European studies with a durable impact in Romanian culture. It is necessary to take into account the intercourse between these three millenary civilizations: European (Greco-Roman and Judeo Christian), Chinese and Indian, as their interplay was not symmetric and had long term consequences.

- The fifth would be the Fourth Industrial Revolution, which is the trademark of the 21th century and the assessment of the staggering distance covered by these two otherwise hard to compare societies in their radical revolutionary transformation, in the brief historical time frame of some one hundred fifty years and, on the other hand how the concept of identity has evolved in this context.

For the cultural history of Europe's connection to the East, the Romanian case may be interesting also through its aforementioned connections to the Byzantine, Ottoman or Russian empires as we speak here of a complementary but still European gate of knowledge to that offered by Western Europe. A landmark in this respect is the story of a Moldavian nobleman of encyclopedic knowledge, Nicolae Milescu Spatarul (1636-1708), who besides his native Romanian, was versed in Latin, Greek, Russian, Turkish, French and Italian. A true adventurer, a diplomat and an amateur theologian, Milescu was chancellor to a Moldavian Prince, envoy to the Sublime Porte and to the Court of Louis the XIV, banished from his country under suspicion of aspiring to the princely throne, to finally became a courtier of Tsar Alexei Romanov, who sent him on a memorable trip to China during the reign of Emperor Kangxi. It is true that Milescu's mission to China was part of the longer story of Russia's territorial expansion to the East and the complex history of Sino-Russian relations. Our interest here lies in the value of his journal and the wealth of information and psychological acumen while describing in detail how two imperial cultures based on distinct tradition came to deal with each other.

However, we deem that the interest of Milescu's story relates to the wider framework of China's developing its ties with the West, which go much farther than Muscovy, reaching for instance the Paris of Louis XIV, the "Roi Soleil", or Rome, The Holy See, not to speak of the Portuguese, Dutch or English.

Relevant for our topic are the cases of Mateo Ricci, as a messenger of the Western culture in China and of Huang Jialue, the founder of French sinology. Ricci died in 1610, Milescu in 1708 and Huang in 1710; during this century-long period the relations between China and the West witnessed ups and downs with far reaching consequences, the likes of the "controversy of the rites" reaching its apex in 1704−1705 with the decree "Cum Deus Optimus" and the reaction of the Qing dynasty through the edict of Emperor Yongle of 1724 concerning heterodox religious denominations (Catholicism, Buddhism, Taoism).

We shall not elaborate here, although it would certainly be worth doing it, on the mythical dimension of the Chinese universe as perceived through the eyes of the Christian world starting with the Syriac missionaries in the 7th and 8th centuries, the Franciscans and the Jesuits in the 13th to the 18th centuries, or the Anglican and the Orthodox travelers to China at various times. It is perhaps an alternative story, but again an asymmetrical one, to that of the Chinese and Indian monks crossing the passes of the Himalayas after treading the desert pathways of the Silk Road from to Dunhuang through Sogdiana, to bring to Chang'an the precious Buddhist manuscripts across the Indus from the shores of the Ganges. Or the impact of Buddhism on East Asia had long term consequences. But as we delve with analogies, and their limits, it is perhaps to recall here another paradox of those times when the scholars of the Arabian Caliphate were restituting to the Latin West the treasures of ancient Greek philosophy in one of the great cultural and linguistic adventures of the Middle Ages which contributed to the European Renaissance.

With the demolition of the order of the Jesuits by Pope Clement XIV in 1773, a chance to deeper comprehension between the Chinese and the Western culture was unfortunately missed. It is only a matter of conjecture how the dialogue between the Chinese and Western culture would have evolved if it had continued when the Chinese Empire was at the peak of its strength and what synthesis might have emerged. As it is, the 19th century has complicated the dialogue between cultures and the mutual acknowledgement of cultural, legal, or philosophical principles and values due to geopolitical reasons still resented painfully in the Chinese historiography.

To better assess this complicated and tortuous relation between China and the West spanning over centuries one must return to the heyday of the Ming dynasty, prior to the breach that was consumed in the 18th century. In a study published in the Romanian Review on Eurasian Studies (No.1-2/2008) entitled "The Imperial Inspection Tours in the Ming Dynasty and Zheng He's Voyages to the Western Ocean (Indian Ocean)", Professors He Pingli and Zhou Chiangming with the Shanghai University of Political Science and Laws trace back the concept of "xunshou" to ancient times (Chapter of Rites in *The Book of Jin*) defined as making a tour of the realm. They consider it not only a demonstration of Confucian ideas such as "a united whole under the sun", rule by rites, rule by morals and personal and diligent government by emperors, but also an implementation of the strategy for safeguarding their countries and pacifying their borders. Therefore imperial xunshou is a force-backed activity involving military force, politics, economy, culture and religion.

We shall not indulge here in the world known story of Zheng He's expeditions (and their fateful end) under the first three Ming Emperors. Suffice it to retain the observation of the authors that the outcome of Zheng He's voyages was preordained by the spirit of imperial culture in relation to the external world which was regulated by the interpretation of destiny, morals, rites and benevolent rule springing from the ancient united thinking logic and traditional ideology of "every place under Heaven belongs to me".

Hence such grand and spectacular political and military activities were unable to open a window on the outside world and come to fruition during the Ming or Qing dynasties.

This was entailed by the fateful order of Hai Jin (sea ban on maritime activities) that resulted in the Qing emperors' oblivion of what was happening in the world when the West started to knock at their door.

It is true that from the imperial perspective the political or economic rewards of Zheng He's adventures seemed disproportionate to the huge costs involved, including the increasing acts of piracy affecting China's maritime borders during the following centuries alongside the building tensions with Japan.

Thus, they conclude, it was not for China's but for Columbus's navigational activities and explorations to be an époque making event in history and the opening of a new era. And that era lead to the industrial revolution and its global consequences in economic, technological, cultural, political and geopolitical terms.

Ironically, it is precisely in the context of Columbus's discovery of America that Chandra Kukathas approaches the Origin and Nature of the Moral Problem in the chapter on Moral Universalism and Cultural difference in the Oxford Handbook of Political theory where, in spite of the political and economic transformations of Asia, Africa and the America's since the 16th century he observes that there has not been a complete convergence on common ethical standards.

This issue is also inseparable from the cardinal one on human rights and their universality dealt with in the same volume.

Likewise, enlarging the knowledge of the historical processes leading to the basic concepts, principles and norms regulating societies and international relations certainly begets added values in the context of a broad scholarly intercultural dialogue.

In order to shed more light on the underground streams connecting Chinese tradition to modern concepts, Professor Shi Ping with the Maritime University of Shanghai has summarized them for the benefit of the Romanian public in an essay entitled "The Cultural Conception of the Chinese from A Family under Heaven to the Community of Destiny of Humanity". Currently under print, this essay establishes a link between the millenary tradition and current major reference points of China's foreign policy, i.e.: the Belt and Road Initiative and The Community of Destiny of Humanity.

The essay deals with such concepts as: The Unity between Heaven and Man as a harmonious whole; Ten thousand Peoples/Nations, a Family under Heaven; A society based on long term harmony; Sun worship for 34,000 years; The will of the emperor is the Will of Heaven etc.

From this perspective, "building a community with a shared future for humanity" is not just a task for the present and the future but also for the past: for rendering in a new context the vast and as yet unfinished business of the history and substance of the dialogue between China and the West, and beyond, is part of the contemporary quest for a peaceful future.

In the contemporary era, though probably less known to the wider public, Romania had its part to play in the major global shift entailed by Henry Kissinger's secret trip to Beijing followed by that of President Richard Nixon and his famous encounters with Chairman Mao Zedong and Prime Minister Zhou Enlai. Another dimension relates to the process of China's full reinsertion in the international system following the spectacular evolution in the relations between USA and the People's Republic of China. The recovery by the PRC of its seat as permanent member of the United Nations Security Council is another less known page in the history of Romanian diplomacy and its part in promoting multilateralism. From the point of view of the present essay it is perhaps relevant to mention here the intellectual and legal impact on China's approach to the body of international law and concepts universally accepted and resulting from the PRC's signature of the UN Charter and additional relevant treaties or covenants as well as the gradual insertion in the ensemble of institutions pertaining or associated to the UN system.[1]

One has to go back to the 19th century history of Chinese diplomacy in its complicated dealings with the interests of the major powers on Chinese soil and its assimilation and creation of concepts of international law to realize the length of the road accomplished by China in its integration into the world order. This process is inseparable from the overall modernization of China.

In *The Oxford Handbook of the History of International Law*, edited by Fassbender and Peter, the chapter on China authored by Shin Kawashima is significantly named "Building of the Modern State and the Wanguogongfa" and

---

[1] More on the Romanian diplomatic history during the Cold War is found in the latest book of the American historian Larry Watts "Fighting along interior lines: Romanian Security Policy during the Cold War", 2018 (also published in Romanian by Rao Distribution, 2018), adding to his Saga on Romania's contemporary history.

deals with the big transformation undergone by Chinese diplomacy in the 1870 - 80'ies. The transition from a doctrine where China considered itself outside the realm of international law as applied to other countries reflected the awareness of the late Qing officials of the painful realities of the balance of power of the day. This transformation is reflected in Kang Youwei's transition from "yitongchuishang" (governing the world hierarchically) to "lieguobingli" (co-existence of nations of the world). "Wanguogongfa" (country outside public law) was to be replaced by "guojifa" (international law). But here again one would have to return to the original Chinese interpretation of these concepts as their acknowledgement is part of the effort of cultural restitution underway.

The Romanian public benefitted from a notable effort to synthesize "the historical and spiritual premises of Chinese diplomacy", as the title of a book by Dr. Anna Eva Budura (Editura Top Form, Colectia Geopolitica 2008) reads. The author is a graduate in history of the Beijing University and a distinguished Sinologist with a lifelong experience on and in China. What may be the theme song of her work, which starts from the classical texts and abounds in historical data to reach to present times, is the search for the central role of the concept of "li" as the basic spiritual/ethical feature of the Chinese world. It is on the basis of this concept defining the ensemble of features specific to the cultural life of a people or a nation that the author proposes to understand the intimate forces which have generated in several thousands of years the way the Chinese have conceived the order of the state and the role of the behaviour of the individual in society.

Naturally self-referential systems do not actually evolve in a vacuum. The history of the adaptation and evolution of diplomacies in the late 18th and 19th centuries and in their specific and different interaction with the concepts, norms and principles of international relations as forged during the long European history of warfare and peace treaties, of such old Empires as the Persian, Ottoman or Japanese is equally relevant for that stage of globalization indicating the high tide of the West in the aftermath of the industrial revolution. The works of Henry Kissinger or Francis Fukuyama are already classics in this respect, preceded by the no less famous Samuel Huntington, just to mention a few peaks in a large chain.

What differentiate China is the enormous size of the transformation process, which is still going on in full stride, and the special character of developing the intellectual instrument capable to render conceptual equivalents between distinct streams of culture and civilization and merge them into the vast sea of contemporary knowledge. In this case the 5,000 years long Chinese continuous tradition based on script and encapsulating basic cosmological and ethical concepts and symbols defining the Chinese 'Weltanschauung' is raising a double challenge: one for the Chinese themselves, as they have to translate the patterns of modernity imported from other shores into the concepts and language of one of the most coherent and self-sufficient civilizations produced by mankind; and on the other side, the challenge of comprehension that faces the alternative coexisting cultures and civilizations shaping the process of globalization and universalism.

Taking the above into consideration the proposal of the Chinese Academy of Social Sciences to have "Chinese Culture and its Connection to the Common Future of Mankind" as one of the main subjects of the "Symposium on Chinese Studies" is more than timely. It is our view that it actually opens a new venue for Chinese studies alongside the more classical approach in order to probe the intellectual transformation of China under the impact of modernization and, at the same time, as the case may be, the extent to which ancient concepts of the Chinese culture and civilization have stood the test of time and can respond to the challenges of the day.

The Romanian educated public has at hand a basic store of knowledge ranging from Confucianism to Taoism, modern and contemporary works on history, world-known novels etc. that were translated into Romanian. There is also a reputable even if not large school of sinologists covering all generations, and new titles keep adding to the list of books on China. This is an ongoing process and has to be perceived not only in bilateral terms but as part of the wider dialogue between Europe and China.

This dialogue is embodied in a major and structured way by the deep and comprehensive partnership between the European Union and China encompassing over sixty substantive and sectorial dialogues. The EU-China 2020 Strategic Agenda for Co-operation, the highest-level document in EU-China relations, is setting out cooperation in the areas of peace, prosperity, sustainable development and people-to-people exchanges.

Referring to people–to-people engagement we notice events fostering intercultural dialogue, promoting cultural diversity and civil society participation, including education- where we take stock of the first EU-China meeting of the ministers of education and the Sino-Europe Forum on Education Policy Think Tanks.

Also to be added here is the innovation cooperation dialogue, the latest event in the field taking place back to back with the 17th EU-China Summit.

As far as Romania is concerned these chapters of EU-China relations are consonant with its own demarche. As part of the wider dialogue between Europe and Asia, Romania will host in May 2019 during its Presidency of the EU Council, the 7th ASEF Rectors' Conference, and the ASEF Youth Forum back to back with the ASEM Conference of Ministers of Education.

Romania is also ready to host in 2019 the Conference of the Education Ministers in the 16+1 format.

In our view the challenges to the contemporary world cannot be addressed without bringing education at the forefront of societal priorities and when we speak of education we also speak of the principles and values directing human beings in relation to society. The other aspect to be taken into account, in the context of the "Fourth Industrial Revolution" mentioned before, is related to the relevance of the lesson of history in an age of massive geopolitical, demographic, societal and cultural changes affecting the educational systems and the relevant knowledge imparted to the younger generations.

But to return to our subject proper, the stakes raised by the theme of the current Symposium on China are in our view quite challenging as inevitably one is lead to search for an answer to the question formulated by Henry Kissinger in his magisterial work *World Order—Reflections on the Character of Nations and The Course of History* (Penguin Books, 2014): "To achieve a genuine world order, its components, while maintaining their own values, need to acquire a second culture that is global, structural, and juridical - a concept of order that transcends the perspectives and ideals of any one region or nation".

良好的治理:"一带一路"沿线基础设施建设

杰米·贺诗礼 【美国】
布鲁金斯学会约翰·桑顿中国中心访问学者 / 耶鲁大学法学院蔡中曾中国中心高级研究员、访问讲师

在四十年前,中国开始实行"改革开放"政策。经历数十年的外交孤立和内部动荡后,中国开始对世界开放,推动贸易、投资和全面交流。2001 年,中国开始实施"走出去"战略,鼓励中国企业对外投资,与当地合作伙伴共同利用国外资源,承包国际工程项目和提供劳务派遣。2001 年 12 月,中国正式加入世界贸易组织并承诺进一步开放经济和遵守世贸组织规则。加入世界贸易组织的中文缩写"入世",意思是"进入世界",是对这一里程碑事件象征意义的贴切描述。

除了进一步融入全球经济,中国的入世承诺还有助于推动国内"改革与开放"进入第二阶段——重构指令和管制治理模式,将其转化为适合市场经济的服务模式。这种新模式即"政务公开",旨在让中国不透明的政府官僚机构、立法机关和法院的程序和决定变得更加透明,为中国人民以及外国企业创造更多的参与机会。

如今,中国提出"一带一路"倡议,被称为"走出去"战略的升级版和"改革开放"的第三阶段。根据该倡议,中国将与全世界国家和人民携手合作,通过基础设施网络建设在 70 多个沿线国家共建"丝绸之路经济带"和"21 世纪海上丝绸之路"。中国设想"一带一路"将实现"共赢",满足接受国对基础设施的迫切需求,有助于整体经济发展;在亚洲、欧洲、非洲和周边海域实现政策沟通、贸易畅通、资金融通和民心相通,为中国创造输出过剩工业产能的机会,提供技

术和劳动力和投射"软实力",以推动"构建人类命运共同体"的愿景。

2018年7月3日,中国外交部长王毅在"一带一路"法治合作国际论坛上宣布"一带一路实际上已成为当今世界规模最大的国际合作平台,也成为国际社会最受欢迎的公共产品"。他报告一系列让人印象深刻的成就:已有近90个国家和国际组织与中方签署了共建"一带一路"的合作协议;在"一带一路"参与国共同建设了75个经济合作区;产能合作、互联互通和经济走廊建设稳步推进;中国与沿线国家的进出口总值已达到30多万亿人民币,对沿线国家的投资超过700亿美元,已经创造了20多万个就业岗位。

然而,尽管已经取得了一些成就,但"一带一路"倡议的实施也引发国际社会对中国基础设施外交的担忧,因为大部分都是受到腐败和不稳定困扰的低收入国家,破坏了全球治理规范。一些观察家担心,接受国可能会像斯里兰卡那样承受不可持续的债务;还有质疑称一带一路相关的投资和贸易是否导致某种形式的中国"殖民主义",正如一位作家对柬埔寨"一带一路"相关活动所做出的暗示。地方环境和财政冲突、腐败、沉重债务负担和停滞、项目取消或失败等相关新闻报道,让我们感觉到"一带一路"需要更好的治理机制,包括更高的环境和社会标准以及更大的透明度和地方参与度。

中国领导人发誓要推动经济全球化朝着"更加开放、包容、平衡、普惠"的方向发展,秉持"共商共建共享的全球治理观"。中国国家主席和中共总书记习近平提出一个新的全球治理理念,特点是根据"各国主权平等、权利平等、机会平等、规则平等的准则"在民族国家之间坚持"共商共建共享的原则"。"人类命运共同体"概念经常被誉为与"一带一路"倡议相关的新全球治理模式的要素,2017年2月首次纳入联合国决议,并于2018年3月写入《中华人民共和国宪法》。

这些都是值得称赞的原则,主要涉及国家之间的关系。但未能明确指出大型基础设施项目成功与否的关键因素:受影响的当地社区的支持。诚然,中国的党和国家已经认识到当地参与其雄心勃勃的发展计划的重要性。

基础设施投资非常复杂,治理不善是基础设施项目通常无法根据时间安排、预算和服务交付目标如期完成的主要原因。与许多其他国家一样,中国自身在国内建设大型基础设施项目时也遇到过复杂的情况。良好的基础设施治理不仅需要政府和企业合作,还必须与受影响的公众进行合作。由于未能征求当地居民的意见并及时向他们提供信息引起的强烈反对,导致中国许多大型基础设施项目被暂停、甚至取消，包括发电厂、化工厂、道路和垃圾处理设施。

"一带一路"框架下的跨境基础设施项目比纯粹的国内项目建设更具挑战性，因为涉及影响决策和实施的各种政治经济社会因素、监管制度和现实情况。外国融资、外国公司和外国投资的参与使典型的基础设施治理挑战变得更加复杂。对于政府提供支持和资金的大范围项目（例如"一带一路"），除了不同国家之间互动所涉及的"全球治理"事项外，还必须确保项目接受国"国内善治"，包括考虑环境社会影响以及当地受项目影响人口的关切和利益。正如中国所经历的那样，在规划过程的早期阶段，如果没有充分的信息披露和征求意见，当地的反对派可能会阻挠或破坏善意的项目。

"治理"有很多方面。例如，"经济善治"不仅仅涉及保证财务可持续性。研究表明，有效量身定制的环境社会保障措施不但有助于识别和缓解意料之外的环境社会危害，而且还可以识别和缓解可能损害项目长期财务成功的部分投资风险。根据布鲁金斯学会研究员杜大伟（David Dollar）的观察，总部位于中国的亚洲基础设施投资银行创新政策适应其他多边开发银行的通用原则，既要求财政可持续性，又要求环境社会保障，但避免对后者实行严格的"黄金标准"。目标是加强环境社会责任，同时简化特定程序，允许更及时地批准并以经济高效的方式实施急需的基础设施和其他项目。然而，杜大伟注意到，中国过去在国外的做法基本上是遵循接受国的当地法律和惯例，即使这些地方未能要求最低限度的环境社会保障。由于不好的经历，这种做法正在发生变化。

本文特别关注取得积极可持续成果要求的"项目善治"特定监管要素。中国可能在其资助和开发的海外项目中有效推动这些成果，特别是在缺乏合适的当地标准的情况下。这些要素包括：（1）开放性，允许当地和外国企业参与项目采购；（2）透明度，在整个项目周期保持透明，包括项目融资、选址、投标要求和采购过程、预期资金、环境、社会和其他影响、项目合同和项目实施有关的信息披露；（3）通过本地协商让受影响社区的公众和政府参与，从项目规划的最早阶段到环境影响评估过程、建设和运营。

中共在国内的传统治理和决策模式涉及在中共领导下的制度化合作与协商，称为"协商民主"，旨在促进社会和谐与政治稳定，同时确保有效的政策制定与实施。在项目决策和实施层面上，自上而下的传统方法将速度和可感知的经济利益优先于其他地方关切，偶尔会招致公众的反对。这种反对在某些情况下导致项目暂停、搬迁或取消，而中国的跨境和海外"一带一路"项目也遇到过这种情况。

如今，中国的决策模式正在通过合作治理和协作治理的理念进行现代化。中共领导层仍然拥有最高权力，政府起着指导性的作用，但市场参与者和社会也更多地期望参与各种配置和部门，包括环境保护、食品安全、快速发展的共享经济和社会治理。此外，二十多年来，中国领导人一直在很大程度上以"政务公开"的名义逐步引入新的治理机制。政务公开强调透明、参与、服务型和负责任的政府。2007 年通过的政府信息公开条例要求中国各级政府积极披露一系列的信息，赋予公众对政府信息的知情权以及不公开信息时起诉政府的权利。各级政府必须公开环境、执照、预算、财务、建筑项目、政府合同和其他相关信息。

法律规定的公众参与政府事务的渠道也在逐渐建立和深化。最近要求法律法规草案必须向公众征求意见（包括外国企业等）。中国中央政府也正在确定一项法规，以建立所谓的"重大行政决策"国家法定程序，包括重大政策和政府对重大项目的决策。这些程序已经通过地方法规试行十多年，重要的是要求透明度和公众参与重大项目决策。

这些法律和倡议，外加更为详细的环境等特定部门开放治理要求，正在逐渐改变中国国家和相关项目公司的态度和行为，以及公众的期望。将国内发展实践运用于国外的中国项目，不仅有助于确保项目在当地支持下可持续发展，还有利于增强中国的软实力。例如，新加坡对中国在东南亚的"一带一路"倡议相关项目的观察员发现，中国官员和项目开发商有时不能够"努力解决当地人对环境保护的担忧以及这些项目对当地社会、文化和宗教的实际影响，而且试图将有关争议项目信息对受影响人群保密"。

事实上，随着"一带一路"倡议相关项目的铺开和海外问题的出现，近年来中国中央政府机构通过制订一系列规范中国国有企业和民营企业海外融资、项目承包和投资的法规和政策，要求在海外活动中提高标准。最新的措施，包括特定行业规范在内，明确适用于"一带一路"倡议项目。一般而言，包括加强对财务、环境、社会、廉洁和其他风险因素的关注；建议聘用中国和东道国的法律、税务、会计和其他专业顾问；遵守中国和当地法律法规、国际条约和公约、行业最佳实践，尤其是在当地法律法规不完善的情况下。

2017 年中期发布的一项旨在推动对外投资持续合理有序健康发展的国家指南指出，在"一带一路"倡议的引领下，海外投资增加带来"黄金机遇"以及一系列的风险和挑战。鼓励投资带动先进产能以及优质设备和技术标准，限制不符合所在国环境保护、能源消耗和安全要求的项目。要求国有企业和私营公司考虑投资对象的国情和实际需求，与当地政府和企业合作以实现互惠互利，创造令人满意的经济和社会效益并对所有海外项目实施安全风险分析。2018 年 7 月 5 日发布指南征求公众意见稿，要求所有在海外经营的中国企业培育合规文化，无论是投资还是承包项目，均应遵守中国和当地法律、有关国际条约、企业内部的规章制度和自律规则、职业道德规范和适用的行为准则。

环境社会风险因素对中国境内的项目决策越来越重要，至少早在 2008 年就对海外活动进行规定。2008 年，中国国务院通过关于对外承包工程的国家条例，要求中国承包商注重生态环境保护，尊重当地的风俗习惯，促进当地经济社会发展。中国商务部于 2014 年发布的境外投资管理办法要求国有企业和私营企业也必须尊重当地风俗习惯，履行社会责任，做好环境、劳工保护、企业文化建设等工作，促进与当地的融合。环境和社会问题是 2012 年发布的"绿色信贷"指引关注的重点，要求银行识别和控制信贷业务活动中的环境和社会风险，该风险是指在建设、生产、经营活动中可能给环境和社会带来的危害及相关风险，确保对其提供资金的海外项目与国际良好做法以及当地法律法规保持一致。2013 年和 2015 年发布《对外投资合作环境保护指南》，涵盖参与外国项目承包的企业。2017 年 12 月发布《民营企业境外投资经营行为规范》，据报道其框架与未公开的适用于国有企业的规范相同，进一步明确要求开展环境影响评价并采取有利于东道国生态发展的环保措施，即使当地暂时没有环保法律，在这种情况下，可借鉴国际组织或多边机构的环保标准。

2018 年官方发布的《中国与世界贸易组织》白皮书中总结中国当前对海外运营公司的整体期望，指出："中国鼓励企业在海外守法经营、履行企业社会责任，支持企业按照商业原则和国际惯例在东道国经营业务和开展对外投资合作。中国将继续积极推动境外投资持续合理有序健康发展，有效防范各类风险。"此外，根据 2017 年中国各部门与 28 个国家签订的关于对对外经济合作领域严重失信主体开展联合惩戒的合作备忘，采取黑名单制度"鼓励"企业良好行为，涵盖对外投资、对外承包工程、对外金融合作和对外贸易。

中国还致力于为"一带一路"倡议相关项目提供商业争议解决服务。除了培养中国法律人才外，最高人民法院还在西安和深圳设立专门法庭，在官方英语媒体中称为国际商事法庭，专门负责调解、仲裁和处理与日益增加的涉及"一带一路"和其他国际商业纠纷的重大跨境诉讼。与"一带一路"倡议相关项目有关的投资者与国家以及国家之间贸易纠纷将继续按照相关的双边和多边条约和文书处理。

新的国际商事法庭将酌情利用中国现有的国际仲裁和调解机构以及新成立的国际商事专家委员会，协助法官确定适用的外国法律并在双方同意的情况下进行调解。中国是全球第一个成立互联网法院的先驱，国际商事法庭规则要求在线提交和听证。这表明新的法庭计划利用互联网提供"一带一路"争议解决服务，从而允许更广泛范围内的诉讼人获取他们的服务。

鉴于复杂的多管辖区项目不可避免地会发生争端，包括在尚未建立完善法律体系的国家，中国对解决"一带一路"相关争端的关注是有道理的。在中国进行裁决也能使针对中国企业的判决更加容易执行。然而，中国尚未签署相互执行民事判决的协定，因此在海外执行中国判决可能会遇到困难。目前还不清楚准备处理"一带一路"争端的外国仲裁机构是否有资格处理在中国新成立的国际法院发起的仲裁。此外，虽然批准成立国际商事法庭的中共机构要求"平等保护中外当事人的权利，营造一个稳定、公正和透明的基于法律的商业环境"，但一些观察家还是对中共领导下的中国法庭表示关切，认为不一定总是能够独立解决争端。由于涉及跨境诉讼的诸多因素，中国政府决定资助"一带一路法律合作研究与培训计划"，推动司法、执法、反腐败及其他合作，考虑有效的能力建设方案，以在"一带一路"沿线国家和地区提供司法培训和相关服务，处理海外当事方希望在本国或附近司法管辖区解决的争端。

上述关于中国不断发展和日益完善对中国企业海外经济活动和行为监管方式的探讨表明，除了财务、法律、安全、外交和其他方面的因素外，中国显然还从声誉和实践的角度意识到企业在海外（包括"一带一路"倡议框架下）开展业务时需要适当地采取行动，并被视为"优秀企业公民"。此外，据报道，在许多情况下，中国企业也在做出更好的表率，雇用和培训当地的劳动力和承包商，而且在特定情况下，更加重视当地非政府组织的关切。即使在良好的经济和基础设施治理的监管方面已取得了进展，中国还可以在以下几个方面推动"一带一路"倡议的进一步改善。

政府采购：中国已经建立完善的政府采购和竞争性招标制度，可以为了国内用途公开进行合同招标。然而，该制度并不总是对外国竞争对手开放。2018年7月3日，中国外交部副部长孔铉佑在"一带一路"法治合作国际论坛上表示，"所有符合条件的企业，不论其背景如何，均可参与一带一路建设。""一带一路"似乎没有相关的具体数据，一些研究指出，迄今为止，中国国有银行资助的项目80%是中国企业中标。根据美国国际战略研究中心（CSIS）进行的一项研究，中国在34个亚洲和欧洲国家提供资金的运输基础设施项目合同大约89%被授予中国承包商。据报道，2018年4月，欧盟28个成员国中的27个国家（不包括匈牙利）驻华大使发表一份文件批评"一带一路"倡议，要求在公开采购中对非中国企业开放，同时坚持透明和高环境社会标准的原则。

在2018年4月的在博鳌亚洲论坛上发表主旨演讲时，习近平主席承诺中国将"加快加入"世界贸易组织《政府采购协定》进程，确定开放、公平和透明国际竞争的规则。这样的表态将使东道国和非中国企业，尤其是接受国的非中国企业，更有信心在中国政府及其政策性银行资助的"一带一路"相关政府采购合同中公平竞争。加入《政府采购协定》之前，中国可能会主动面向所有合格企业，在统一的开放式数字平台上公开招标（至少提供英语和中文）。遵循国际认可的采购程序，通过包括亚投行在内的多边开发银行提供更多资金，将是增强人们对"一带一路"项目开放性和包容性信心的另一种方式。

尽管中国政府坚持认为"一带一路"倡议是透明的，一位分析师观察发现，"一带一路"倡议很可能是"正在进行中的最著名、也是最难理解的外交政策"，关于其整体进展的可靠信息很少。许多评论家指出需要获取更多关于中国国际贷款的总体信息以及获取信息、参与项目招标、取得中国融资和"一带一路"项目实施的具体程序。根据某项研究，虽然中国领导人已经确认欢迎外国企业参与"一带一路"项目，但"中国尚未提供目前直接受益于中国开发计划的外国企业确切信息。规模达400亿美元的'丝绸之路基金'于2014年成立，旨在对沿线国家进行投资，但尚不清楚谁有资格，以何种条件进行投资。"在2017年5月推动"一带一路"的首次国际会议上，据报道，欧盟官员拒绝与中国政府签署联合声明，因为不能保证透明的国际标准以及"为所有运输基础设施投资者提供平等机会"。

透明度对于中国新成立的外国援助机构"国家国际发展合作署"的成功也至关重要，据报道，该机构将管理与"一带一路"相关的融资问题。迄今为止，中国几乎没有提供任何关于其对外援助的信息。观察家呼吁提高透明度，以便各国和其他援助机构更好地了解中国如何管理其援助资金组合，资金如何使用，使用在何处，主要动机是什么，从而有助于他们制订和调整自己的计划。中国传统的捆绑援助方式也招致批评，聘请中国企业、劳工和专家从事其资助的项目，而不是发展接受国的国内产能。

中国通过十几年来推行《政府信息公开条例》和相关政策，包括有关部门建立国内投资项目和政府社会资本合作（PPP）信息公开平台等，改善政府的透明度。而且还在国内投资和 PPP 项目整个周期内实行信息披露原则，包括相关报告和评估。然而，国务院 2017 年发布的关于重大建设项目审批和实施信息公开的指南明确将海外投资和外国援助项目排除在要求之外。

就"一带一路"相关项目而言，似乎没有任何类似的全面数据库。"一带一路"中英文和其他几种语言的门户网站提供一些总体信息和（中文）汇总数据，但是关于具体项目及其实施的详细数据和报告较少。似乎不存在官方的"一带一路"中心，类似于政府和社会资本合作中心。中国商务部确实有一个中文的"走出去"公共服务平台，截至 2018 年 7 月 3 日，该平台公开将近 51500 家企业或机构并且还设有一个专门介绍"一带一路"项目一般信息的网页，包括每季度统计数据。中国商务部的另一个英文网站拥有可搜索的投资项目信息数据库，涵盖对内和对外投资以及投资意向，但迄今为止，似乎并未标明"一带一路"项目。新华丝路资讯服务提供一系列的中国项目，包括接受国、行业和相关日期的信息，但是该网站的中国企业查询数据库的英文版旨在帮助外国投资者对中国企业基本信息进行信用调查，而不是关于海外项目的信息。非中国研究组织和智囊团已经建立各种数据库追踪中国的对外投资，其中一些数据库关注"一带一路"倡议。然而，这些数据库还必须依靠假设支持的不完整信息。

中国政府最近加强对重大海外投资和对外承包工程的报告要求，以便更有效地防范风险，引导对外经济活动健康有序发展，促进"一带一路"倡议的成功实施。中国商务部负责集中整理有关海外投资的信息和维护在线平台，报告要求的信息和统计数据。据报道，中国政府还开始着手收集已经完成多少海外交易，与哪些国家进行交易以及财务条款相关信息。

中国正在努力降低国内的地方债务和金融风险，解决一些海外项目因债务增加和当地担忧而中断的问题，因此中国有必要更好地处理多层面广泛覆盖的"一带一路"项目投资组合，不仅确保项目有效和有利可图，还应保证项目最终不会破坏中国的"一带一路"倡议的外交和战略目标。考虑到公众倾向于关注负面媒体报道，因此，提高"一带一路"项目和相关数据的透明度也有助于中国应对围绕"一带一路"的不利宣传和猜测。

透明度和公众参与。提高"一带一路"项目及其实施的透明度也将有助于解决其他问题，特别是对"一带一路"项目环境和社会可持续性的关切，这直接关系到当地人口。正如经合组织一项研究得出的结论："基础设施将影响社区－如果没有妥善征求意见，再好的项目可能会止步不前"，而妥善的意见征求可以加强项目在社区内的合法性并培养一种共有意识。

中国对"一带一路"项目的融资、投资和建设应在切实可行的范围内，不仅仅要求技术上符合当地要求，还应在整个项目周期内对受影响当地社区的意见征求和信息披露保持高标准，保证适当解决当地关切，赢得公众支持。中国企业在国内需要遵守透明度和公众参与要求，包括重大项目环境影响评估和其他环境事项相关的要求。至少应鼓励中国企业在海外业务中也遵守基本的国内标准。

诚然，中国政策开始强调对海外企业行为提出更高标准。私营企业对外业务行为规范要求企业适应国外的社会环境，尊重文化传统并加强与当地工会、媒体、宗教和民族团体以及非政府组织的沟通，定期公开发布企业社会责任和可持续发展报告。同时，鼓励国有企业坚持互惠互利的原则，加强与业务所在地的媒体、企业、社会和政府的关系，积极履行企业社会责任。

关于可能适用的国际公众参与标准，亚投行《环境与社会框架》强调可以纳入"一带一路"倡议框架文件的许多相关原则。例如，不仅与政府、多边开发银行和双边发展组织，而且还鼓励与私营部门和民间社会建立合作关系，以创新方式应对亚洲基础设施挑战。环境和社会项目评估必须在最早期的"范围确定"阶段识别和征求利益相关方的意见，并遵守征求公众意见、信息披露和建立申诉机制的额外要求，这些举措有利于保证"一带一路"项目的可持续性。

采取善治最佳实践的中国领导力（例如开放和竞争性采购、透明度和公众参与"一带一路"计划和项目）将有助于说服其他国家，指出中国对全球治理做出贡献的愿望并不意味着推翻，而是坚持甚至改善全球治理和国际善治实践。所谓的领导力具体包括在中国遵守世界贸易组织《政府采购协定》的前提下，采取和执行"一带一路"项目政府采购透明度要求，面向全世界所有合格企业开放；建立统一的"一带一路"平台，收集和发布有关项目统计数据和信息，覆盖招标、参与者、价值、状态和进展；纳入适当有效的透明度和当地公众意见征求机制，作为开发和实施所有"一带一路"项目的强制要求。

"一带一路"倡议已发展成标志性的外交政策，以推进习近平主席对中国在全球治理中增强领导作用的愿景。2017 年 10 月修订后，中国共产党甚至将"一带一路"写入党章，从而强化该倡议的政治重要性。定位的提升为中国实现"一带一路"项目和全球活动的可持续性带来更大的压力。

建议中国借鉴自身丰富的国内发展和监管经验，让"一带一路"项目变得真正透明和包容。为开放的竞争性项目采购制定明确而具体的要求，提高"一带一路"和相关项目的透明度，让当地社区有效参与，更好地解决他们的关切，这些举措对建立相互信任和基础设施建设大有帮助。良好的治理改善可以确保"一带一路"倡议真正（而不是复杂化）能够在中国推动下实现共同发展、彼此连通和共同繁荣，同时促进全球和地方治理进步，同时增强中国的声誉和影响力。这才是真正的全体"共赢"局面。

Building Good Governance Infrastructure along the Belt and Road

Jamie P. Horsley / United States of America

Visiting Fellow, John L. Thornton China Center, the Brookings Institution/
Senior Fellow & visiting Lecturer, Paul Tsai China Center, Yale Law School

Forty years ago, in December 1978, China launched its ambitious "Reform and Opening" policy to open the country through increased trade, investment and comprehensive engagement with the outside world following decades of diplomatic isolation and internal upheaval. Twenty-three years later in 2001, China began to encourage its enterprises to invest abroad, exploit foreign resources with local partners, contract for international engineering projects and export labor services.[1] In December 2001, China joined the World Trade Organization (WTO), committing to further open its economy and abide by WTO rules of engagement. The Chinese acronym for WTO accession literally means "entering the world" (入世), an apt description of what that milestone event symbolized.

In addition to further integrating China into the global economy, China's WTO

---

[1] Zhu Rongji, "Report on the Outline of the Tenth Five-Year Plan for National Economic and Social Development (2001)," March 5, 2001, at: http://www.gov.cn/english/official/2005-07/29/content_18334.htm.

commitments helped spur a second phase of domestic-oriented "Reform and Opening" -- to remake its command-and-control governance style into a more service-oriented, facilitative model appropriate for a market economy. This new approach adopted an evolving "open government" (政务公开) initiative to make China's opaque government bureaucracies, legislatures and courts more transparent about their processes and decisions and to afford greater participation opportunities to the Chinese people, as well as to the foreign business community.[1]

Today, China is promoting "Belt and Road" Initiative, commonly referred to as the Belt and Road Initiative (BRI), which might be characterized as an upgrade of the "Going Out" strategy and a third stage of "Reform and Opening." This project joins China with countries and peoples around the world to construct a Silk Road Economic Belt and 21st-Century Maritime Silk Road connecting over 70 countries,[2] primarily through building physical infrastructure networks. China envisions that BRI will provide "win-win" benefits, filling a pressing need in recipient countries for infrastructure to help power overall economic development; fostering policy, trade, financial and people-to-people connectivity across Asia, Europe and Africa and their adjacent seas; and affording China greater opportunities to export industrial overcapacity, furnish technical and labor services, and project "soft power"[3] as it seeks to promote its vision of a global "community with a shared

---

1 Jamie P. Horsley, "Will engaging China promote good governance?" *Brookings Institution*, January 2017, at: https://www.brookings.edu/research/will-engaging-china-promote-good-governance.
2 The precise number of what might be termed "BRI countries" is not clear. The China State Information Center's BRI website lists some 76 countries, including India, as of July 11, 2018, at: https://eng.yidaiyilu.gov.cn/info/iList.jsp?cat_id=10076, and the Hong Kong Trade and Development Council lists 75 on its website at: https://beltandroad.hktdc.com/en/country-profiles.
3 "习近平主持召开中央全面深化改革领导小组第三十次会议" [Xi Jinping presided over the 30th meeting of the central leading group for comprehensively deepening reform], *Xinhua*, December 5, 2016, at: http://www.xinhuanet.com/politics/2016-12/05/c_1120058658.htm, mentioning approval and the main points of《关于加强 "一带一路" 软力量建设的指导意见》[Guiding Opinions on Strengthening the Construction of "Belt and Road" Soft Power] .

future for mankind."[1]

Foreign Minister Wang Yi announced on July 3, 2018 at a forum on BRI and international law cooperation that the "BRI has become the largest platform for international cooperation and the most popular public good in the world."[2] He reported an impressive list of accomplishments: nearly 90 countries and international organizations have signed BRI cooperation agreements with China; 75 economic cooperation zones have been set up in BRI participating countries; industrial capacity cooperation, connectivity and building economic corridors is steadily progressing; and China's trade with BRI countries has reached over RMB 30 trillion and investment in those countries over US$70 billion, creating more than 200,000 local jobs.[3]

Yet, in spite of its accomplishments, BRI's implementation to date has also raised international concern about the potential for China's infrastructure diplomacy, much of which is targeted at lower income countries plagued by corruption and instability, to undermine global norms of governance. Some observers worry that recipient countries may incur unsustainable debt, as has happened in Sri Lanka,[4] while others question whether BRI-related investment and trade may result in a form of Chinese "colonialism,"[5] as one writer suggested with respect to BRI-related activity in

---

1   Xi Jinping, "Secure a Decisive Victory in Building a Moderately Prosperous Society in All Respects and Strive for the Great Success of Socialism with Chinese Characteristics for a New Era," Report to the Nineteenth National Congress of the Chinese Communist Party," October 18, 2017, at: http://www.chinadaily.com.cn/china/19thcpcnationalcongress/2017-11/04/content_34115212.htm. *See, also*, "Joint Communique of the Leaders Roundtable of the Belt and Road Forum for International Cooperation," May 16, 2017, at: http://www.fmprc.gov.cn/mfa_eng/zxxx_662805/t1462012.shtml.
2   Wang Yi, "Stronger Legal Cooperation for Sound and Steady Development of the Belt and Road Initiative," July 3, 2018, at: http://www.fmprc.gov.cn/mfa_eng/zxxx_662805/t1573636.shtml.
3   Ibid.
4   Maria Abi-Habib, "How China Got Sri Lanka to Cough Up a Port," *New York Times*, June 25, 2018, at: https://www.nytimes.com/2018/06/25/world/asia/china-sri-lanka-port.html.
5   James A. Millward, "Is China a Colonial Power?," *New York Times*, May 4, 2018, at: https://www.nytimes.com/2018/05/04/opinion/sunday/china-colonial-power-jinping.html.

Cambodia.[1] Press reports of local environmental and fiscal opposition,[2] corruption,[3] heavy debt burdens and stalled, cancelled or failed projects[4] contribute to the impression that the BRI is in need of better governance mechanisms, including higher environmental and social standards[5] and greater transparency and local engagement.[6]

China's leaders vow to promote economic globalization that is "more open, inclusive, balanced and beneficial to all" and that adheres to "the principle of achieving shared growth through discussion and collaboration in engaging in

---

1 Sheridan Prasso, "Chinese Influx Stirs Resentment in Once-Sleepy Cambodian Resort," *Bloomberg*, June 20, 2018, at: https://www.bloomberg.com/news/features/2018-06-20/chinese-casinos-stir-resentment-on-cambodia-s-coast-of-dystopia ("The concentration of Chinese casinos, hotels, restaurants, factories, businesspeople, gamblers and laborers [in an area of much BRI infrastructure construction] resembles what, in another era, might have been called a colonial concession, an area carved out from sovereign territory and given over to an occupying power, much to the consternation of local residents.")
2 *See, e.g.*, "China faces resistance to a cherished theme of its foreign policy," *The Economist*, May 4, 2017, at: http://www.economist.com/news/china/21721678-silk-routes-are-not-always-appealing-they-sound-china-faces-resistance-cherished-theme?fsrc=scn/fb/te/bl/ed/thebeltandroadexpresschinafacesresistancetoacherishedthemeofitsforeignpolicy.
3 Stefania Palma, "Malaysia suspends $22bn China-backed projects," *Financial Times*, July 4, 2018, at: https://www.ft.com/content/409942a4-7f80-11e8-bc55-50daf11b720d.
4 Economist, *supra* note 11. *See, also*, James Kynge, "China's Belt and Road difficulties are proliferating across the world," *Financial Times*, July 10, 2018, at: https://www.ft.com/content/fa3ca8ce-835c-11e8-a29d-73e3d454535d, citing a study by RWR Advisory Group showing some 14%, or 234 out of 1,674, Chinese-invested infrastructure projects announced in 66 BRI countries since 2013 have hit trouble.
5 Kynge, *supra*, note 11.
6 *See, e.g.*, International Crisis Group, China-Pakistan Economic Corridor: Opportunities and Risks, June 29, 2018, at: https://www.crisisgroup.org/asia/south-asia/pakistan/297-china-pakistan-economic-corridor-opportunities-and-risks; and in Chinese at: https://www.crisisgroup.org/zh-hans/asia/south-asia/pakistan/297-china-pakistan-economic-corridor-opportunities-and-risks: "Many of these problems stem from opaque policy formulation, and the failure to heed regional and local concerns. [The China-Pakistan Economic Corridor's] Long-Term Plan (2017-2030) was formulated by the centre with little input from local leaders, business or civil society actors. It was not disclosed until December 2017 – and then only in broad strokes – after the rollout of some major elements had already begun."

global governance."[1] President Xi Jinping is credited with developing a new concept of global governance that features the "principle of extensive consultation, joint contribution and shared benefits" between and among nation states under a "norm of equality for all in terms of sovereignty, rights, opportunities and rules."[2] His "community of a shared future for mankind" concept, frequently hailed as an element of the new global governance model in connection with BRI, was incorporated for the first time into a United Nations resolution in February 2017[3] and added to the Chinese state Constitution in March 2018.

These are all laudable principles, but they involve largely state-to-state relations. They fail to expressly address a critical factor for the success of major infrastructure projects wherever located: the support of impacted local communities. Indeed, the Chinese party-state has come to recognize the importance of local engagement in its own ambitious development programs at home.[4]

Infrastructure investment is complex, and poor governance is a major reason why infrastructure projects often fail to meet their timeframe, budget, and service delivery objectives.[5] China itself, like many other countries, has experienced such complexities as it builds out major infrastructure projects at home. Good

---

1 Zhong Shan, Minister of Commerce, "An Open China and a Win-Win World -- On the Release of the White Paper 'China and the World Trade Organization,' " *Xinhua*, July 2, 2018, at: http://www.xinhuanet.com/english/2018-07/02/c_137296686.htm.
2 "Spotlight: How China's diplomatic approach is creating a more inclusive world," *Xinhua*, August 30, 2017, at: http://news.xinhuanet.com/english/2017-08/30/c_136568929.htm.
3 Xiang Bo, "China Keywords: Community with Shared Future for Mankind," *Xinhua*, January 24, 2018, at: http://www.xinhuanet.com/english/2018-01/24/c_136921370.htm.
4 Horsley (2017), *supra* note 2. Xi Jinping, in a speech given November 12, 2013, observed: "Without the people's support and participation, no reform can succeed." ["没有人民支持和参与，任何改革都不可能取得成功"]. "习近平：切实把思想统一到党的十八届三中全会精神上来" [Xi Jinping: Effectively unify thought in the spirit of the Third Plenary Session of the 18th CCP Central Committee], *Xinhua*, December 31, 2013, point 6, at: http://www.xinhuanet.com/politics/2013-12/31/c_118787463_2.htm.
5 Organization for Economic Co-operation and Development (OECD)," Getting Infrastructure Right: The Ten Key Governance Challenges and Policy Options," March 20, 2017, at: https://www.oecd.org/gov/getting-infrastructure-right.pdf; and the full report, OECD, "Getting Infrastructure Right: A Framework for better Governance," March 20, 2017, at: https://read.oecd-ilibrary.org/governance/getting-infrastructure-right_9789264272453-en#page1.

infrastructure governance must involve collaboration with not only government and business but with the impacted public as well. Strong opposition due to failure to consult local residents and provide them with timely information has led to suspension and even cancellation of many major infrastructure projects in China, including power plants, chemical plants, roads and garbage treatment facilities.[1]

Cross-border infrastructure projects under the BRI framework are even more challenging than purely domestic ventures, as they involve diverse political, economic and social factors, regulatory regimes, and on-the-ground circumstances that impact decision-making and implementation. The involvement of foreign financing, foreign companies and foreign investment makes the typical infrastructure governance challenges even more complicated. In addition to *global governance* issues involving state-to-state interaction under a wide-ranging, government-backed and financed program like BRI, attention must also be paid to ensuring *domestic good governance* in project recipient countries. This includes taking into account environmental and social impacts and the concerns and interest of the local populations affected by planned projects. As China has experienced, where adequate information is not disclosed and consultation opportunities not afforded early in the planning process, local opposition can stall or derail the best-intended of projects.[2]

"Governance" has many aspects. For example, "economic good governance" not only involves ensuring fiscal sustainability. Studies have shown that effectively tailored environmental and social safeguards can help identify and mitigate not only unanticipated environmental and social harms, but also some of the investment

---

1　See, *e.g.,* Li You, "Locals Fired Up Over China's Largest Waste Incinerator," *Sixth Tone*, June 8, 2017, at: https://www.sixthtone.com/news/1000219/locals-fired-up-over-chinas-largest-waste-incinerator; Elizabeth Economy, "China's New Governing Style: Crisis Management," *The Atlantic*, May 20, 2013, at: http://www.theatlantic.com/china/archive/2013/05/chinas-new-governing-style-crisis-management/276034.

2　See, *e.g.*, He Huifeng, "The 'Belt and Road' projects China doesn't want anyone talking about," *South China Morning Post*, August 8, 2017, at: https://www.scmp.com/news/china/economy/article/2099973/belt-and-road-projects-china-doesnt-want-anyone-talking-about.

risks that can undermine the long-term financial success of a project.[1] David Dollar of the Brookings Institution has observed that innovative policies of the China-based Asia Infrastructure Investment Bank (AIIB) adapt general principles common to other multilateral development banks to require both fiscal sustainability and environmental and social safeguards, but avoid imposing stringent "gold standard" requirements for the latter. The goal is to promote environmental and social responsibility while streamlining certain procedures to hopefully permit more timely approval and cost-effective implementation of much-needed infrastructure and other projects.[2] However, Dollar noted, China's approach abroad in the past has been to basically follow local law and practice in recipient countries, even if such localities failed to require even minimal environmental and social safeguards.[3] That approach is changing in the light of adverse experience.

This paper focuses on certain regulatory elements of "good project governance" to achieve positive, sustainable results that China might usefully promote in the projects it finances and develops abroad, especially in the absence of appropriate local standards. These consist of (1) *openness* to participation in project procurement from local and foreign companies; (2) *transparency* throughout the project life, including information disclosure relating to project financing, siting, requirements tendering and procurement processes, anticipated fiscal, environmental, social and other impacts, project contracts and project implementation; and (3) *public participation through local consultation* with impacted communities – as well as host governments -- from the earliest stage of project planning through the environmental impact assessment process, construction and operation.

The traditional CCP model of governance and decision-making at home has

---

1   Denise Leung, Yingzhen Zhao, Athena Ballesteros and Tao Hu, "Environmental and Social Policies in Overseas Investments: Progress and Challenges in China," *World Resources Institute*, May 2013, at: "http://www.wri.org/publication/environmental-and-social-policies-overseas-investments.
2   See, *e.g.*, David Dollar, "Is China's Development Finance a Challenge to the International Order?", November 9, 2017, at: https://www.brookings.edu/research/is-chinas-development-finance-a-challenge-to-the-international-order/.
3   Ibid.

involved institutionalized cooperation and consultation called "consultative democracy" under the leadership of the CCP, aimed at fostering social harmony and political stability, while ensuring efficient policy making and implementation.[1] At the level of project decision-making and implementation, traditional top-down approaches prioritized speed and perceived economic benefit over other local concerns and have occasionally given rise to public opposition. Such opposition has in some cases led to project suspension, relocation or cancellation, something China's cross-border and overseas BRI projects encounter as well.

Today, China's decision-making model is being modernized with concepts of co-governance and collaborative governance. CCP leadership remains paramount, with government playing a guiding role, but market players and society increasingly are expected also to participate in various configurations and sectors, including environmental protection, food safety, the rapidly developing sharing economy and social governance generally. Moreover, Chinese leaders have been gradually introducing new governance mechanisms largely under the rubric of "open government" (政务公开) for over two decades. This open government project emphasizes transparent, participatory, service-oriented and accountable government.[2] A nationwide information access statute adopted in 2007 requires the Chinese government at all levels proactively to disclose a broad range of information and gives the public the right to request government-held information, as well as to sue the government over non-disclosure.[3] Environmental, licensing, budget, financial, construction project, government contracts, and other relevant information must be disclosed by different levels of government.

1　Li Laifang, "Enlightened Chinese democracy puts the West in the shade," *China Daily*, October 17, 2017, at: http://www.chinadaily.com.cn/china/19thcpcnationalcongress/2017-10/17/content_33364425.htm.

2　Jamie P. Horsley, "China Promotes Open Government as it Seeks to Reinvent Its Governance Model," *Freedominfo.org*, February 22, 2016, at: https://law.yale.edu/system/files/china-law-documents/2016_horsley_china_promotes_open_government.pdf.

3　Jamie P. Horsley, "China's FOIA Turns Eight," *Freedominfo.org*, April 28, 2016, at: http://www.freedominfo.org/2016/04/chinas-foia-turns-eight/.

Legally prescribed channels for public participation in government affairs are also being established and deepened over time. Statutory requirements for making draft laws and regulations public for comment, including by foreign businesses and others, have been strengthened recently.[1] China's central government is also finalizing a regulation to establish national statutory procedures for what is called "major administrative decision-making," which includes major policies and government decisions on major projects. Those procedures, which have been piloted through local regulations for over ten years, importantly require transparency and public participation in major project decisions.[2]

These laws and initiatives, supplemented by more detailed requirements for open governance in specific sectors -- including the environment, are gradually changing the attitudes and behavior of Chinese state actors and relevant project companies, as well as public expectations. Employing these developing practices from home in Chinese projects abroad would not only help ensure sustainable projects with local support but, also help bolster China's soft power. For example, a Singaporean observer of China's BRI approach in Southeast Asia observed that Chinese officials and project developers on occasion fail to make "efforts to solve locals' worries about environmental protection and the impact of these projects on local society, culture and even religion in practice," and may attempt to keep information concerning controversial projects secret from impacted populations,"[3] thereby exacerbating various problems.

In fact, as BRI projects proliferate and problems arise overseas, China's central government agencies have in recent years have called for higher standards in overseas activities through a series of regulations and policies governing the

---

1 Jamie P. Horsley, "China Implements More Participatory Rulemaking Under Communist Party," March 15, 2018, at: https://www.theregreview.org/2018/03/15/horsley-china-implements-participatory-rulemaking/。
2 Horsley (2017), *supra* note 2.
3 See, *e.g.*, He Huifeng, "The 'Belt and Road' projects China doesn't want anyone talking about," *South China Morning Post*, August 8, 2017, at: http://www.scmp.com/news/china/economy/article/2099973/belt-and-road-projects-china-doesnt-want-anyone-talking-about.

conduct of both state-owned and private Chinese enterprises in overseas financing, project contracting and investment. More recent measures, including some sector-specific regulations, expressly apply to BRI projects. General principles include, increasingly, attention to financial, environmental, social, integrity and other risk factors; the advisability of utilizing Chinese and host country legal, tax, accounting and other professional consultants; and compliance with both Chinese and local laws and regulations, as well as with international treaties and conventions and industry best practices, especially where relevant local legal requirements are underdeveloped.

A mid-2017 national guideline aiming to promote outbound investment in a sustainable, reasonable, orderly and sound manner[1] noted that increased overseas investment, led by BRI, brings "golden opportunities" together with a series of risks and challenges. It encouraged investment that drives advanced production capacity and superior quality equipment and technology standards and restricted projects that do not conform to environmental protection, energy consumption and security requirements of destination countries. It called on both state-owned enterprises (SOEs) and private companies to consider the national conditions and actual demands in investment destinations, cooperate with local governments and enterprises for mutual benefits, create satisfactory economic and social benefits and conduct safety risk analysis for all overseas projects. A draft guideline issued for public comment on July 5, 2018, calls for fostering a culture of compliance by all Chinese enterprises operating overseas -- whether through investments or contracted projects -- with Chinese and local law, relevant international treaties, internal rules and self-disciplinary regulations, codes of professional ethics and applicable codes

---

1 Notice of the State Council General Office Forwarding the Guiding Opinions of the National Development and Reform Commission, Ministry of Commerce, People's Bank of China and Ministry of Foreign Affairs on Further Guiding and Regulating the Outbound Investment Direction [国务院办公厅转发 国家发展改革委、商务部、人民银行、外交部关于进一步引导和规范境外投资方向指导意见], August 4, 2017, at: http://www.gov.cn/zhengce/content/2017-08/18/content_5218665.htm.

of conduct.[1]

Environmental and social risk considerations, which are increasingly important to project decision-making within China, entered regulations on overseas activities at least as early as 2008. That year, the State Council adopted national regulations on contracting foreign projects that required Chinese contractors to protect the local environment, as well as respect local customs and habits and promote local economic and social development.[2] Ministry of Commerce measures on overseas investment issued in 2014 require both state-owned and private enterprises to also respect local customs, honor social responsibilities and environmental and labor protection, corporate culture-building and local culture.[3] Environmental and social concerns were the focus of "green credit" guidelines issued in 2012, which required banks to identify and control environmental and social risks, defined as possible harm and relevant risks to the environment and society in the construction, production, and business operations of their clients, in their credit business activities and ensure that overseas projects they were financing were essentially consistent with international best practices as well as local laws and regulations.[4] Guidance on environmental protection work by foreign investment and cooperation enterprises, including those engaged in contracting foreign projects, was released in 2013[5] and

---

1　National Development and Reform Commission, Announcement on Seeking Public Comments on the Guidelines for the Compliance Management of Enterprises' Overseas Operations (Draft for Comment) [关于《企业海外经营合规管理指引（征求意见稿）》公开征求意见的公告], July 5, 2018, at: http://www.ndrc.gov.cn/yjzx/yjzx_add.jsp?SiteId=150.
2　Art. 4, Administrative Regulation on Contracting Foreign Projects [对外承包工程管理条例], July 21, 2008, at:http://www.mofcom.gov.cn/article/swfg/swfgbi/201101/20110107352097.shtml.
3　Art. 20, Ministry of Commerce, Measures for the Administration of Overseas Investment [境外投资管理办法], September 6, 2014, at: http://www.mofcom.gov.cn/article/b/c/201409/20140900723361.shtml.
4　China Banking Regulatory Commission, Green Credit Guidelines [中国银监会关于印发绿色信贷指引的通知 0, 2012, at: http://www.cbrc.gov.cn/chinese/home/docView/127DE230BC31468B9329EFB01AF78BD4.html.
5　Ministry of Commerce and Ministry of Environmental Protection, Guidelines for Environmental Protection in Foreign Investment and Cooperation, February 18, 2013, at: http://english.mofcom.gov.cn/article/policyrelease/bbb/201303/20130300043226.shtml.

2015.[1] A code of conduct for overseas investments by private enterprises issued in December 2017, which reportedly has the same framework as an unpublished code that applies to SOEs, went further to specifically require conducting an environmental impact assessment and taking environmental protection measures conducive to the host country's ecological development, even in the absence of local legal requirements to do so, in which case standards of international organizations and multilateral institutions should be applied instead.[2]

The current overall approach to China's expectations of its companies operating overseas is summarized in an official 2018 White Paper on China and the WTO, which states: "China encourages its enterprises to abide by local laws, fulfill corporate social responsibilities and observe business principles and international practices when they do business in host countries and conduct outward investment cooperation. China will continue to promote the sustainable, reasonable, orderly and sound development of outward investment, and effectively prevent risks of all kinds."[3] Moreover, the "encouraged" corporate good behavior will be backed up with a blacklist system under a 2017 memorandum of cooperation among 28 state and CCP bodies concerning joint punishment of seriously dishonest entities in the field of foreign economic cooperation, including overseas investment and foreign

---

[1] Ministry of Commerce General Office, Notice on the Further Enhancement of Environmental Protection Work of Foreign Investment and Cooperation Enterprises [商务部办公厅关于进一步做好对外投资合作企业环境保护工作的通知], April 13, 2015, at: http://www.mofcom.gov.cn/article/fgsjk/201709/20170902650553.shtml.

[2] National Development and Reform Commission, Ministry of Commerce, and People's Bank of China, et al, Code of Conduct for Overseas Investment Operations by Private Enterprises (国家发展改革委、商务部、人民银行等关于发布《民营企业境外投资经营行为规范》的通知), December 6, 2017, Chapter V, at: http://www.mofcom.gov.cn/article/i/jyjl/k/201712/20171202686698.shtml. The same overall framework reportedly applies to state-owned or "central" enterprises regulated by the State-owned Asset Supervision and Administration Commission under an unpublished code of conduct. Wang Yanfei, "SOE foreign investment risk curbed," *China Daily*, December 29, 2017, at: http://www.chinadaily.com.cn/a/201712/19/WS5a383e86a3108bc8c67357f8.html.

[3] State Council Information Office, "China and the World Trade Organization," *Xinhua*, June 28, 2018, at: http://www.xinhuanet.com/english/2018-06/28/c_137286993.htm.

contracting, finance and trade.[1]

China is also undertaking to provide commercial dispute resolution services targeted at BRI projects. In addition to developing Chinese legal talent,[2] the Supreme People's Court has established specialized divisions -- called international commercial courts in official English media -- in Xi'an and Shenzhen specifically to mediate, arbitrate and handle major cross-border litigation relating to the growing number of BRI and other international commercial disputes.[3] Investor-state and state-state investment and trade disputes relating to BRI projects will continue to be handled pursuant to relevant bilateral and multilateral treaties and instruments.

These new international commercial courts will, when appropriate, utilize China's existing international arbitration and mediation institutions, as well as a new Committee of International Business Experts that will aid judges in ascertaining applicable foreign law and may mediate cases where the parties agree. China is a pioneer in establishing the world's first internet courts,[4] and the international commercial court rules call for online filings and hearings, indicating the new courts plan eventually also to utilize the internet for BRI dispute resolution services, which

---

1 Notice of the National Development and Reform Commission, People's Bank of China, Ministry of Commerce and Other Departments on Issuing the Memorandum of Cooperation on Joint Punishment of Seriously Dishonest Entities in the Foreign Economic Cooperation Field [国家发展改革委、人民银行、商务部等关于印发《关于对对外经济合作领域严重失信主体开展联合惩戒的合作备忘录》的通知], October 31, 2017, at: http://wzs.ndrc.gov.cn/zcfg/201711/t20171124_867713.html.

2 Ministry of Justice, Ministry of Foreign Affairs, Ministry of Commerce and Legislative Affairs Office of the State Council Opinions on Developing the Foreign-related Legal Service Industry [司法部、外交部、商务部、国务院法制办公室印发《关于发展涉外法律服务业的意见》], December 30, 2016, at: http://www.moj.gov.cn/index/content/2017-01/09/content_6946567.htm.

3 China International Commercial Court English-language website, at: http://cicc.court.gov.cn/html/1/219/index.html [with the sub-tittle "International Commercial Litigation and Diversified Dispute Resolution: Planning Together, Building Together and Benefit Together"]; English translation of model BRI cases as well, at: http://cicc.court.gov.cn/html/1/219/199/201/index.html.

4 Cao Yin, "World's first internet court goes online in Hangzhou," *China Daily*, August 18, 2017, at: http://www.chinadaily.com.cn/china/2017-08/18/content_30770108.htm. The plan is to establish two more in Beijing and Guangzhou, as indicated in "Xi presides over 3rd meeting of central committee for deepening overall reform," *Xinhua*, July 7, 2018, at: http://www.xinhuanet.com/english/2018-07/07/c_137306758.htm.

would make their services more accessible for far-flung litigants.

China's attention to the resolution of BRI-related disputes makes sense, given that disputes are inevitably going to arise in these complex, multi-jurisdictional projects,[1] including in states that may not yet have developed legal systems. Adjudication in China may also make it easier to enforce judgments against Chinese counterparties. However, China has not entered into many agreements for mutual enforcement of civil judgments, so enforcing Chinese judgments overseas might be problematic.[2] It is also not clear whether established foreign arbitral institutions, many of which are also gearing up to handle BRI disputes,[3] will be able to qualify to handle arbitrations for cases brought in China's new international courts.[4] In addition, although the CCP body that approved the international commercial court initiative[5] called for "equal protection of the rights of both Chinese and foreign parties to create a stable, fair and transparent law-based business environment,"[6] some observers raise a concern that courts based in China under CCP leadership might not always be

---

1 Cao Yin, "Courts handling 'a boom' of Belt and Road cases," *China Daily*, March 15, 2017, at: http://www.chinadaily.com.cn/china/2017twosession/2017-03/15/content_28559326.htm; *see, also*, Susan Finder, "Supreme People's Court & foreign-related disputes," Supreme People's Court Monitor, March 11, 2017, at: https://supremepeoplescourtmonitor.com/2017/03/11/supreme-peoples-court-foreign-related-disputes/.
2 Baker McKenzie Fen Xun, "Client Alert: SPC Launches International Commercial Courts in Shenzhen and Xi'an," July 2018, at: https://www.bakermckenzie.com/-/media/files/insight/publications/2018/07/al_china_spclaunchesinternationalcommercialcourts_july2018.pdf?la=en.
3 Jue Jun Lu, "Dispute Resolution along the Belt and Road: What does the future hold?," August 8, 2018, at: http://www.blplaw.com/expert-legal-insights/articles/dispute-resolution-along-the-belt-and-road-what-does-the-future-hold.
4 Wei Sun, "International Commercial Court in China: Innovations, Misunderstandings and Clarifications," *Kluwer Arbitration Blog*, July 14, 2018, at: http://arbitrationblog.kluwerarbitration.com/2018/07/04/international-commercial-court-china-innovations-misunderstandings-clarifications/#comment-79257.
5 Guo Liqin, "[Exclusive] China Plans International Commercial Courts for Belt and Road Dispute Resolution," *Yicai Global*, January 25, 2018, at: https://www.yicaiglobal.com/news/exclusive-china-plans-international-commercial-courts-belt-and-road-dispute-resolution.
6 PTI, "China to establish international courts to deal with BRI cases," *New Indian Express*, January 26, 2018, at: http://www.newindianexpress.com/world/2018/jan/26/china-to-establish-international-courts-to-deal-with-bri-cases-1763772.html.

able to decide disputes independently.[1] Due to the many considerations relating to bringing cross-border litigation, the Chinese government's decision to fund a "Belt and Road Legal Cooperation Research and Training Program" to boost judicial, as well as law enforcement, anti-corruption and other, cooperation,[2] might usefully consider capacity-building programs to provide judicial training and related services in BRI countries and regionally, in case overseas parties prefer to have their disputes resolved in or nearer their home jurisdictions.

The foregoing discussion of China's evolving and increasingly comprehensive regulatory approach to overseas economic activity and behaviors of Chinese enterprises indicates that, in addition to fiscal, legal, security, diplomatic, and other considerations, China clearly is cognizant of the need from both a reputational and practical perspective for its companies to act appropriately and be perceived to be "good corporate citizens" when they operate overseas, including under the BRI umbrella. Moreover, Chinese companies are reportedly stepping up their game, hiring and training local labor forces and contractors in many cases and taking the concerns of local NGOs more seriously in certain other cases.[3] While much regulatory progress in addressing the various aspects of good economic and infrastructure governance has been made, China could promote further improvements on its BRI approach in several respects discussed below.

Government Procurement: China has developed a sophisticated government procurement and competitive tender system, under which it makes such contracts publicly available, for its domestic purposes. However, this system is not always

---

1 Nyshka Chandran, "China's plans for creating new international courts are raising fears of bias," *CNBC*, February 1, 2018, at: https://www.cnbc.com/2018/02/01/china-to-create-international-courts-for-belt-and-road-disputes.html; "New Courts for the Belt and Road Initiative," *OboEurope*, February 6, 2018, at: http://www.oboreurope.com/en/bri-courts/.
2 Wang Yi, *supra* note 6.
3 Economist, *supra* note 11.

open to foreign competition.[1] Chinese Vice Foreign Minister Kong Xuanyou stated on July 3, 2018 at the BRI forum on international legal cooperation, that "all eligible enterprises, regardless of their background, can be involved in building the Belt and Road."[2] While BRI-specific data does not seem to be available, some research indicates that, to date, 80% of projects funded by Chinese state banks have been awarded to Chinese companies[3] and that, according to a study conducted by the Center for Strategic and International Studies (CSIS), roughly 89% of contracts for China-funded transport infrastructure projects in 34 Asian and European countries were awarded to Chinese contractors.[4] In April 2018, ambassadors to China from 27 of the 28 European Union member states (excluding Hungary) reportedly issued a paper criticizing the BRI and calling for openness to non-Chinese companies in public procurement, as well as adherence to principles of transparency and high environmental and social standards.[5]

In his speech to the Bo'ao Forum for Asia in April 2018, Xi Jinping promised that China will "accelerate the process of joining" the WTO Agreement on Government Procurement (GPA),[6] which establishes rules for open, fair and transparent international competition.[7] Such a move would provide greater confidence to host

---

1 American business regularly complains about their inability to participate on equal footing with domestic competitors when bidding for government procurement contracts in China and urging China to accede to the WTO GPA. AmCham China, "2017 AmCham China White Paper: American Business in China," at: file:///U:/US-China/2017%20AmCham%20White%20Paper.pdf.
2 Xu Wei, "China will work to ensure Belt, Road transparent," *China Daily*, July 4, 2018 at: http://english.gov.cn/news/video/2018/07/04/content_281476208578419.htm.
3 Chris Devonshire-Ellis, "EU Ambassadors, China Policy Advisors' Myopia Misses the Point of Belt and Road," *Silk Road Briefing*, April 25, 2018 at: https://www.silkroadbriefing.com/news/2018/04/25/eu-ambassadors-china-policy-advisors-myopia-misses-point-belt-road.
4 James Kynge, "Chinese contractors grab lion's share of Silk Road projects," *Financial Times*, January 24, 2018, at: https://www.ft.com/content/76b1be0c-0113-11e8-9650-9c0ad2d7c5b5.
5 Dana Heide, Till Hoppe, Stephan Scheuer and Klaus Stratmann, "EU ambassadors band together against Silk Road," *Handelsblatt Global*, April 17, 2018, at: https://global.handelsblatt.com/politics/eu-ambassadors-beijing-china-silk-road-912258.
6 Xi Jinping, "Openness for Greater Prosperity, Innovation for a Better Future," *China Daily*, April 10, 2018, at: http://www.chinadaily.com.cn/a/201804/10/WS5acc515ca3105cdcf6517425_1.html
7 Agreement on Government Procurement, at: https://www.wto.org/english/tratop_e/gproc_e/gp_gpa_e.htm.

countries and non-Chinese companies, especially those from recipient countries, that they can compete on a level playing field for BRI-related government procurement contracts funded by the Chinese government and its policy banks. Prior to joining the GPA, China might take the initiative to open bidding to all qualified companies, making such tenders available (in at least English as well as Chinese) on a centralized, open digital platform. Providing more funding through multi-lateral development banks including the AIIB, which follow internationally recognized procedures for procurement, would be another way to enhance confidence in the openness and inclusiveness of BRI projects.[1]

Transparency: Although the Chinese government insists that BRI is a transparent initiative,[2] one analyst has observed that the BRI may well be "the best-known, least-understood foreign policy effort underway," with little reliable information about how it is unfolding overall.[3] Many commentators cite the need for more information on China's international lending generally,[4] as well as procedures for getting information, bidding on projects, accessing Chinese financing and project implementation for BRI projects more specifically. According to one study, while Chinese leaders have confirmed that foreign firms are welcome to participate in BRI projects, "China has yet to provide exact information on which foreign firms have so far directly benefited from the Chinese development program. The $40 billion Silk Road Fund was set up in 2014 to invest in countries along the road but it is unclear who is eligible for investment, and on what terms."[5] At the first international gathering to promote BRI in May 2017, EU officials reportedly refused to sign a joint declaration with the Chinese government, because it did not guarantee international standards of transparency and "equal opportunities for all investors in

---

1 See, *e.g.*, the AIIB Procurement Policy, January 2016, at: https://www.aiib.org/en/policies-strategies/_download/procurement-policy/policy_procurement.pdf.
2 Xu Wei, *supra* note 55.
3 Jonathan E. Hillman, "China's Belt and Road Initiative: Five Years Later," *CSIS*, January 25, 2018, at: https://www.csis.org/analysis/chinas-belt-and-road-initiative-five-years-later-0.
4 Dollar, *supra* note 24.
5 Dana Heide, et al, *supra* note 58.

transport infrastructure."[1]

Transparency will also be important to the success of China's new foreign aid agency, the State International Development Cooperation Agency, which reportedly will manage BRI-related financing issues.[2] China has provided little information concerning its foreign aid to date,[3] and observers have called for more transparency so that countries and other aid agencies can better understand China manages its aid portfolio, how and where the money is spent, and what the primary motivations are, in part to help them develop and adjust their own programs. China's traditional tied aid approach has also drawn criticism for employing Chinese companies, labor and experts on its funded projects rather than developing domestic capacity in recipient countries.[4]

China has improved government transparency domestically through implementing its decade-old Regulations on Open Government Information and related policies, including establishment by relevant authorities of domestic investment project[5] and public-private partnership (PPP)[6] information disclosure platforms. It has also promoted the principle of information disclosure throughout the whole lifecycle of domestic investment and PPP projects, including of related reports and evaluations. However, a 2017 State Council guideline on information disclosure of approvals and implementation of major construction projects expressly excludes overseas

---

1 Ibid.
2 Lisa Cornish, "China's new aid agency: What we know," *Devex*, April 20, 2018, at: https://www.devex.com/news/china-s-new-aid-agency-what-we-know-92553.
3 Jenny Lei Ravelo, "DevExplains: Chinese aid," *Devex*, August 17, 2017, at: https://www.devex.com/news/devexplains-chinese-aid-90841.
4 Ibid.
5 National investment project online approval and regulation platform [全国投资项目在线审批监管平台], at: http://www.tzxm.gov.cn/.
6 The PPP Comprehensive Information Platform System in Chinese [PPP综合信息平台系统] is at: http://www.cpppc.org:8082/, with a separate accessible project database and map, expert database, and institutional database. *See, also*, Ministry of Finance, Interim Measures for the Administration of Information Disclosure for Public-Private Partnership Integrated Information Platform, February 9, 2017, at: http://www.cpppc.org/en/Guidelines/4642.jhtml.

investment and foreign aid projects from its requirements.[1]

In the case of BRI projects, there does not appear to be any comparable centralized and comprehensive database. BRI portals in Chinese, English and several other languages provide some general information and (in Chinese) aggregate data, but have little detailed data and reporting on specific projects and their implementation.[2] No official BRI center, similar to the one for PPP projects,[3] appears to exist. The Ministry of Commerce (MOFCOM) does have a Chinese language "Going Out" Public Service Platform[4] that reports nearly 51,500 enterprises or institutions recorded and as of July 3, 2018, and also hosts a webpage dedicated to general information about BRI projects, including quarterly statistics.[5] Another English language MOFCOM website hosts a searchable Investment Project Information Database on inward and outward investments as well as investment intentions, but to date it does not appear to identify BRI projects.[6] The Xinhua Silk Road Information Service provides a collection of Chinese projects,[7] which

---

1 Opinions of the State Council General Office on Advancing Public Disclosure of Government Information in the Field of Approval and Implementation of Major Construction Projects [国务院办公厅关于推进重大建设项目批准和实施领域政府信息公开的意见], December 4, 2017, at: http://www.gov.cn/zhengce/content/2017-12/15/content_5247349.htm.
2 An official government BRI portal is at: https://www.yidaiyilu.gov.cn, with links to English, https://eng.yidaiyilu.gov.cn; French, Russian, Spanish, and Arabic language websites.
3 China Public Private Public Partnerships Center, English website at: http://www.cpppc.org/en/index.jhtml.
4 " '走出去' 公共服务平台 ," at: http://fec.mofcom.gov.cn.
5 Statistics for the first quarter 2018 reveal that from January to April 2018, Chinese enterprises invested a total of US$4.67 billion in non-financial direct investment in 53 BRI countries, an increase of 17.3% over the same period of last year, accounting for 13.1% of the total amount, mainly to Singapore, Laos, Malaysia, Vietnam, Indonesia, Pakistan, Thailand and Myanmar. In terms of foreign contracted projects, Chinese enterprises newly signed 1,010 contracts for foreign contracted projects in BRI countries, which amounted to US$ 28.83 billion, accounting for 47% of the newly signed contracts for foreign contracted projects in China during the same period, down 9.5% year-on-year. The turnover was US$24.2 billion, accounting for 54% of the total period, an increase of 27.7%. http://fec.mofcom.gov.cn/article/fwydyl.
6 MOFCOM Investment Project Information Database, http://project.mofcom.gov.cn/1800000091_10000108_8.html.
7 Xinhua Silk Road [新华丝路], at: http://app.silkroad.news.cn/?app=system&controller=iframe&action=project_index

includes information on the recipient country, sector, and relevant dates, but the English version of the website's Chinese company inquiry database[1] is intended to help foreign investors conduct credit investigations of Chinese companies' basic information, not information about their overseas projects. Non-Chinese research organizations and think tanks have established a variety of databases tracking Chinese outward investment, some of which focus on BRI.[2] However, these databases also have to rely on incomplete information bolstered by assumptions.

Chinese authorities have recently strengthened reporting requirements for both major overseas investment and foreign contracting projects, in order to more effectively prevent risks, guide the healthy and orderly development of outbound economic activity, and promote successful implementation of the BRI.[3] MOFCOM is to be responsible for centralized compilation of the information on overseas investments and maintaining an online platform for reporting required information and statistical data. Chinese authorities have also reportedly started working to compile better information on how many overseas deals have already been done and with what countries, as well as their financial terms.[4]

---

1 Xinhua Silk Road, at: http://en.silkroad.news.cn/app/credit/SiteController/actionIndex, homepage at: http://en.silkroad.news.cn/.
2 See, *e.g.,* American Enterprise Institute, China Global Investment Tracker, at: http://www.aei.org/china-global-investment-tracker (the most comprehensive data set covering China's global investment and construction, which are documented both separately and together, including 2,900 large transactions across energy, transportation, real estate, and other industries, as well as 250 troubled transactions, as of mid-July 2018); Aid Data – A Research Lab at William & Mary, at: https://www.aiddata.org (extensive information on individual project, but no BRI filter); CSIS, Reconnecting Asia, at: https://reconnectingasia.csis.org (interactive map, open-source database of over 2,200 transportation projects, and expert analysis); and MERICS Belt and Road Tracker, https://www.merics.org/en/bri-tracker.
3 MOFCOM, etc., Interim Measures for the Reporting of Outbound Investments Subject to Record-filing or Approval [对外投资备案（核准）报告暂行办法], January 2018, at: http://images.mofcom.gov.cn/hzs/201801/20180125100235813.pdf; and Notice of the General Office of the Ministry of Commerce on Effectively Conducting the Recordation of Foreign Contracted Projects [商务部办公厅关于做好对外承包工程项目备案管理的通知], November 13, 2017, at: http://www.mofcom.gov.cn/article/i/jyjl/k/201712/20171202679466.shtml.
4 Keith Bradsher, "China Taps the Brakes on Its Global Push for Influence," *New York Times*, June 29, 2018, at: https://www.nytimes.com/2018/06/29/business/china-belt-and-road-slows.html.

As China strives to reduce local debt and financial risks at home, and as some overseas projects stall in the face of mounting debt and local concerns,[1] it makes sense for China to get a better handle on its widespread and multi-faceted BRI project portfolio, not only to ensure that projects are effective and profitable, but that they do not end up undermining China's diplomatic and strategic goals for BRI as well. Given that the public tends to focus on negative media reporting, greater transparency regarding BRI projects and related data might also help China counter some of the adverse publicity and speculation surrounding BRI.

Transparency and Public Engagement. Greater transparency regarding BRI projects and their implementation would also help address additional concerns the particular concerns regarding the environmental and social sustainability of BRI projects, which directly implicates local populations. As an OECD study concluded, "Infrastructure impacts communities - without well managed consultation, good projects may falter," whereas well-executed consultation processes can enhance the legitimacy of the project within the community and foster a sense of shared ownership.[2]

Chinese financing of, investment in and construction of BRI projects should, to the extent practicable, go beyond technical adherence to local requirements and instead ensure that high standards for engaging affected local communities in consultations and disclosing relevant information continuously throughout the life of projects are implemented, to ensure that local concerns are being properly addressed and public support is maintained. Chinese companies are subject to transparency and public participation requirements at home, including in connection

---

1　Yuichi Nitta and Thurein Hla Htway, "Myanmar will ask China to downsize project, minister says," *Nikkei Asian Review*, July 4, 2018, at: https://asia.nikkei.com/Politics/Myanmar-will-ask-China-to-downsize-project-minister-says; Farhan Bokhari and Kiran Stacey, "Pakistan seeks more loans from China to avert currency crisis," *Financial Times*, July 5, 2018, at: https://www.ft.com/content/1256ceaa-802c-11e8-bc55-50daf11b720d, and Adnan Aamir, "China's Belt and Road plans dismay Pakistan's poorest province," *Financial Times*, June 14, 2018, at: https://www.ft.com/content/c4b78fe0-5399-11e8-84f4-43d65af59d43.
2　OECD, "Getting Infrastructure Right: The Ten Key Governance Challenges and Policy Options," 2016, at: https://www.oecd.org/gov/getting-infrastructure-right.pdf.

with compiling environmental impact assessments and other environmental matters relating to major projects. At a minimum, they should be encouraged to adhere specifically to those basic domestic standards in their overseas business as well.

To be sure, Chinese policies are beginning to emphasize a higher standard for overseas corporate behavior. The code of conduct for private enterprises operating overseas[1] calls on companies to adapt to the overseas social environment, respect cultural traditions and strengthen communication with local trade unions, media, religious and ethnic groups and NGOs, as well as publicly release regular reports on their corporate social responsibility and sustainable development performance. Similarly, SOEs are encouraged to adhere to the principle of mutual benefit, strengthening their relationships with media, business and communities, as well as governments, where they are operating, and actively carry out their corporate social responsibility.[2]

With reference to international standards of public engagement that might be applied, the AIIB Environmental and Social Framework[3] stresses many relevant principles that might be incorporated into a BRI framework document. For example, it encourages partnership not only with governments, multilateral development banks and bilateral development organizations, but also with the private sector and civil society in devising innovative ways to meet Asia's infrastructure challenges. Required environmental and social project assessments must include stakeholder identification and consultation at the earliest "scoping" stage and additional requirements for public consultation, information disclosure and establishing grievance mechanisms would help ensure the sustainability of BRI projects.

1　*Supra*, note 39.
2　State-owned Asset Supervision and Administration Commission, Measures for the Supervision and Administration of Overseas Investments by Central Enterprises [中央企业境外投资监督管理办法], January 7, 2017, at: http://www.sasac.gov.cn/n2588035/n2588320/n2588335/c4258448/content.html.
3　AIIB, Environmental and Social Framework, January 2016, at: https://www.aiib.org/en/policies-strategies/_download/environment-framework/20160226043633542.pdf.

China's leadership in requiring good governance best practices such as open and competitive procurement, transparency and public engagement in its BRI programs and projects would also help persuade other countries that China's desire to contribute to global governance does not mean overturning but rather upholding and even improving global governance and international good governance practices. Such leadership could include, specifically, adopting and enforcing a requirement to make government procurement for BRI projects transparent and open to qualified companies from around the world, bolstered by China's adherence to the WTO Agreement on Government Procurement; establishing a centralized BRI platform for compiling and publishing statistical data and information on BRI projects, including on bid solicitations, participants, value, status and progress; and incorporating appropriate and effective transparency and local public consultation mechanisms as a requirement for the development and implementation of all BRI projects.

China would be well advised to draw on its own rich domestic developmental and regulatory experience to make BRI projects more truly transparent and inclusive. Establishing clear and specific requirements for open and competitive project procurement, greater transparency concerning BRI and its far-flung projects, and effective engagement with local communities to better address their concerns would go a long way toward building mutual trust along with physical infrastructure. Such good governance improvements can help ensure that the BRI will genuinely contribute to, rather than complicate, China's drive to achieve common development, connectivity and prosperity, while at the same time advance better global and local governance, thus also enhancing China's reputational influence. This would truly be a "win-win" situation for all.

我对"一带一路"倡议的看法

孟什·法耶兹·艾哈迈德 【孟加拉】
孟加拉国国际和战略研究所主席

一、关于"一带一路"倡议相关的数据

"一带一路"倡议有几个有趣且重要的特征。该倡议跨越 67 个国家,覆盖全球约 65% 的人口(44 亿)以及全球大约四分之三的能源资源。区域内的经济体 GDP 总量占世界的 40%。就购买力平价而言,中国已经是世界上最大的经济体,而且与"一带一路"沿线国家的年贸易额超过 1.4 万亿美元。根据世界银行的估计,"一带一路"倡议、相关倡议和机制总价值在 4 万亿到 8 万亿美元之间。考虑到所覆盖经济体的互补性,扩大区域贸易的前途光明。预计截止 2025 年,年贸易额可能增加到 2.5 万亿美元。"一带一路"沿线的主要经济体包括:1)中国 −11.23 万亿美元;2)韩国 −1.41 万亿美元;3)俄罗斯 −1.28 万亿美元;4)印尼 −0.932 万亿美元;5)土耳其 −0.863 万亿美元。

二、"一带一路"倡议由谁主导

关于"一带一路"倡议的主导权可能存在疑问。有人认为这是中国的倡议。然而,任何合作倡议都不可能完全由一个国家独自拥有。虽然在现实中是中国提出的倡议,中国境外的项目不可能由中国独自拥有。它们将由每个项目所在的国家拥有或合作伙伴共同拥有。鉴于中国可能会投资许多项目,中国将作为合作伙伴。因此,我们可以直观地看到"一带一路"倡议下的某些项目可能由特定项目

所在的参与国拥有，或者项目也可以在共同持股或双边或多边伙伴关系等其他形式的基础上共同拥有。

1. 项目选择

"一带一路"项目正在或应根据需要和可行性进行选择，同时牢记利益相关方的利益。相互平等、相互理解、相互尊重和互惠互利的原则必须用于指导共同所有权的性质以及参与的条款和条件。尽可能优先选择能够产生足够收入以覆盖成本的项目。然而，可能存在一些本身不会产生足够的收入的优先基础设施项目，但可以创造公共物品帮助社会和各个企业产生巨大的收入，分期偿还费用。

2. 投资条款和条件

"一带一路"项目的可行性在很大程度上取决于向各个国家提供项目投资 / 贷款的条款和条件。许多参与国在政治、社会和经济上都非常脆弱。因此，债务偿还问题可能非常关键。项目应尽可能充分地产生收入。必须认真考虑，避免项目成为参与国的债务陷阱。就资金 / 投资的可能来源而言，"一带一路"倡议框架下的项目可以通过不同的来源提供资金，包括主权储备基金、参与国的国内公共借款、合作伙伴国家的 G2G 贷款、国际金融机构的贷款，例如亚洲基础设施投资银行、金砖国家新开发银行、世界银行、国际货币基金组织、亚洲开发银行、伊斯兰开发银行等，以及各种来源的商业贷款。

3. 中国在"一带一路"倡议中的利益

作为发起国，中国理所当然地在"一带一路"倡议中拥有许多利益。该倡议是中国外交政策的重要组成部分。它构成补充或服务于中国的外交政策目标和优先事项，包括：确保和平的外部环境，以维持国民经济的快速增长；建立大国关系新模式，增进与邻国的友谊和合作；与其他发展中国家的合作；支持和维护全球化，加强在环境和气候变化问题上的全球合作。"一带一路"倡议可以帮助中国：最大限度地利用不断增加的储备资金；最大限度地利用制造业、建筑和基础设施等行业部门 / 产品的过剩产能；为中国进出口战略资源开辟尽可能多的替代路线；与邻国及其他国家保持友谊，影响力也随之增强。

4. 其他国家的利益

然而，中国以外的其他国家也可以从"一带一路"倡议中受益。资源相对丰富的经济体可以获得与中国类似的收益。对于资源不丰富的经济体，预计参与"一带一路"倡议可以带来以下好处：建设急需的基础设施，获取急需的资金 / 投资，获取现代科技，增强连通性以及市场准入和重要商品方面的附带利益，加强人员联系，增进与"一带一路"沿线国家在所有领域的友谊与合作。孟加拉国属于后一类国家，由于缺乏基础设施、投资资金、现代科技、市场准入等，也可能从"一带一路"倡议中获得类似的好处。

5. **一些挑战**

"一带一路"倡议并非没有挑战。虽然印度、美国、日本等国与中国已建立广泛的联系，但该倡议仍然引起各方的担心或怀疑。虚假陈述或错误包装将在人们心中产生误解。通常，问题源于"一带一路"倡议的正式表达。同时，该倡议还缺乏清晰度和充分的解释。"一带一路"倡议的批评者将其视为旨在满足中国自身利益的中国倡议/项目。通常情况下，该倡议似乎没有充分考虑其他参与者的需求和利益。尽管在中国境外有许多"一带一路"倡议的诋毁者，但也有一些中国学者、投资者、银行家敦促在保证投资回报或项目可行性方面保持谨慎。误解的方式也多种多样：许多方面仍对中国的动机持怀疑态度，他们认为"一带一路"倡议旨在保障经济和政治至上/统治地位；担心来自中国援助计划造成债务陷阱；可能强迫实施浪费/不可行的项目；也有人担心会损害主权；不同性质、规模和发展阶段的经济体之间不兼容；腐败和治理问题；参与国之间关系的变动；参与国之间缺乏协调；缺乏各种规则、规定和程序的统一。一些人将斯里兰卡的汉班托特港、中巴经济走廊等经过巴基斯坦控制克什米尔的项目视为通过国家必须在主权问题上妥协和/或陷入债务陷阱的案例。

6. **孟加拉国面临的特殊挑战**

孟加拉国实际上被印度环绕，除了在东南部与缅甸的小片边界外，包括孟加拉湾在内，四面都被印度包围。因此，印度和缅甸积极参与"一带一路"倡议是孟加拉国能够从"一带一路"倡议中获得最大利益的前提。此外，孟加拉国严重缺乏基础设施，电力和能源短缺，没有可供出口的丰富物资，需要现代化的适当科技，缺乏可投资资本，熟练人工和人力资源短缺，面临环境退化和气候变化的挑战。如果孟加拉国参与"一带一路"倡议获取最大利益，必须应对超过100万罗兴亚难民的涌入以及与缅甸关系紧张的挑战。

三、应对挑战

世界上的任何倡议几乎都会面临挑战或障碍，"一带一路"倡议也不例外。

上述对"一带一路"倡议的挑战本身就提出了相关的补救措施。然而，可能需要特别强调以下事项：应更加关注适当的叙事方式，以吸引潜在的参与者；在概念包装的同时，应更加关注所有潜在参与者的需求和利益；明确提及共同所有、共同责任、共同利益和共同繁荣；还应注意确保中国的动机和利益更加透明和清晰；注重真诚、客观和公开的谈判与协商过程；注重合作的互补性和互利；更加重视解决双边和多边成员之间悬而未决的问题；每个参与国应加强其治理并采取适当措施制止一切腐败现象，特别是在"一带一路"相关项目方面；在参与国之间逐步协调各种规则、规定和程序；在与"一带一路"项目有关的所有相关事项上加强参与国之间的协调。

四、结束语

尽管面临着各种挑战，只要能够推动各国人民实现更广泛的联系与合作，在相互平等、相互理解、相互尊重和互惠互利原则的基础上适当提出的任何倡议或努力始终是我们追求的目标并且将永远造福全人类。"一带一路"倡议也是如此。鉴于相关概念、愿景和倡议的庞大规模和深不可测，因此"一带一路"倡议有关各方所获得的利益也将是庞大和深不可测的。

Belt and Road Initiative (BRI)

Munshi Faiz Ahmad / Bangladesh

Chairman of Bangladesh Institute of International and Strategic Studies

What is BRI and Some Facts on BRI

BRI is a concept—a vision—an initiative. This is not one big/mega project, but a collection of innumerable big and small projects, some of which are already in different stages of implementation and many others that may follow; among those that have already been conceived and are at different stages of implementation are the Bangladesh-China-India-Myanmar Economic Corridor (BCIM-EC), China-Pakistan Economic Corridor (CPEC), Singapore-Kunming Rail Link, Yiwu-Madrid and Yiwu-London Rail Lines etc. There are also many maritime connectivity projects which are receiving growing importance everyday. Within the maritime connectivity dimension, there are several ports that align with this initiative, for example, Zeebrugge port in Belgium, Gwadar (Pakistan), Kyauk Pyu (Myanmar), Hambantota (Sri Lanka). Similar port facilities are also available in Greece, Spain, Italy, Morocco, and Ivory Coast etc. Although BRI is popularly viewed as a new Chinese initiative, it is in fact, neither new, nor exclusively Chinese. Many countries in the region and beyond have their own connectivity ideas, concepts and initiatives which in many ways, wholly or partially coincide with BRI.

In addition, ESCAP-ADB led Trans-Asian Railway and Trans-Asian Highway Projects seem to broadly coincide with the land-based version of the Silk Road. It is a concept that could accommodate all possible connectivity initiatives covering Asia, Europe, Africa the Indo-Pacific, and beyond. BRI has the potential to be overlapping, complementary and mutually re-enforcing with other regional, sub-regional and international cooperation endeavours, e.g., RCEP, FTAAP, SCO, SAARC, BBIN, BIMSTEC, AIIB, NDB, BRICS, IORA, ASEAN+3 etc.

One beauty of this initiative is, it has no formal structure, charter, organs or secretariat. It remains as an idea and is served by innumerable bilateral and multilateral agreements, MOUs and contracts involving various projects etc. It lends itself to a lot of flexibility which is likely to be its strength over the years.

The BRI has several interesting and important features. The initiative spans more than 67 countries. It covers around 65% of the world's population (4.4 billion people), and around ¾ of global energy resources. Economies within its borders produce 40% of GDP. The largest economy in the world in terms of PPP, i.e., China's annual trade with BRI countries already exceeds US$ 1.4 trillion. According to World Bank estimates, the BRI, related initiatives and institutions have a total value of anywhere between US$ 4 to 8 trillion. The region also has bright prospects of trade expansion given the complementary nature of the economies covered. Annual trade value may grow to US$ 2.5 trillion by 2025. Some major economies in BRI are (in trillion US$): 1) People's Republic of China—US$ 11.23, 2) ROK—US$ 1.41, 3) Russia—US$ 1.28, 4) Indonesia—US$ 0.932, 5) Turkey—US$ 0.863

Who Owns the BRI?

There may be questions regarding the ownership of BRI. Some people think it is a Chinese-owned initiative. However, no cooperation initiative can be wholly owned by one country. In reality, although a Chinese initiative, individual BRI projects, except those within China's border, cannot be exclusively owned by China.

They will be owned by countries where each project is located or jointly owned by partners. However, since China is likely to invest in many of the projects, it could be a partner in those. Therefore, we can visualise some projects under BRI could be domestically or nationally owned by any participating country where the particular project is located or such projects could also be jointly owned on the basis of equity sharing or other forms of partnerships bilaterally or multilaterally.

Selection of projects

Projects under BRI are being or should be selected on the basis of need and feasibility, keeping interests of the relevant stakeholders in mind. The principles of equality, mutual understanding, mutual respect and mutual benefit must guide the nature of joint ownerships and terms and conditions of participation. As far as possible, projects that will generate enough revenue to pay for their costs should be preferred. However, there may be priority infrastructure projects that may not generate enough revenues themselves but create public goods that help the community at large and various enterprises that generate huge revenues to repay the costs many times over.

Terms and conditions of investment

Feasibility of projects under BRI will depend largely on the terms and conditions of investment/loans to be offered to various countries for projects. Many of the participating countries are politically, socially and economically very vulnerable. Therefore, debt repayment issues may become critical. As far as possible, projects should be adequately revenue generating. Serious consideration should be given to avoid projects becoming debt traps for participating countries. When it comes to possible sources of funding/investment, projects under BRI could be funded by different sources including sovereign reserves, domestic public borrowing by participating countries, G2G loans from partner countries, loans from international financial institutions like AIIB, NDB, World Bank, IMF, ADB, Islamic Development Bank etc., as well as commercial loans from various sources.

China's interests in BRI

As the proponent country, China rightfully has many interests in the BRI. It is a major component of China's foreign policy. It complements or serves Chinese foreign policy objectives and priorities which include: ensuring a peaceful external environment to sustain fast pace of growth of national economy; new model of major power relations, improved friendship and cooperation with neighbours; cooperation with other developing countries; upholding and sustaining globalisation, increasing global cooperation on environment and climate change issues. BRI could help China in: maximising utilisation of growing reserve funds; maximising utilisation of overcapacity in various sectors/products including manufacturing, construction and infrastructure; opening up as many alternative routes as possible for Chinese imports and exports of strategic resources; a concomitant enhancement of friendship and influence with countries in the neighbourhood and beyond.

Other countries' interests

However, countries other than China can also benefit from BRI. Relatively well-endowed economies could derive benefits similar to those of China. In respect of relatively less endowed economies, the following benefits could be expected from participation in BRI: building of much needed infrastructures, access to much needed funds/investment, access to modern technology, enhanced connectivity and its concomitant benefits in terms of access to markets and vital commodities, enhanced people-to-people connectivity, enhancement of friendship and cooperation with BRI countries in all areas. Bangladesh being in the latter group, suffering from lack of infrastructures, funds for investment, modern technology, market access issues etc., could also derive similar benefits from BRI in addressing these matters.

Some challenges

The BRI has not been without challenges. It has drawn apprehension or suspicion from various parties like India, the US, Japan and others, although they have wide-ranging relations with China. Misrepresentation or faulty packaging helps create misperception in people's minds. Often, problems arise from the way the BRI is officially portrayed. Also, there is lack of clarity and adequate explanation. Critics of BRI see it as an exclusively Chinese initiative/project designed to serve exclusively Chinese interests. It often appears that the initiative does not adequately take into account other participants' needs and interests. While there are many detractors of the BRI outside China, there are also some Chinese scholars, investors, bankers who have urged caution in terms of guaranteeing return on investments or viability of projects. There are misperceptions as well which are manifold: many parties remain suspicious of China's motives viewing the BRI as aimed at securing economic and political supremacy/dominance; fear of debt traps from Chinese assistance schemes; possible imposition of wasteful/unviable projects; and there is also fear of compromising sovereignty; incompatibility among economies of different nature, sizes and stages of development; corruption and governance issues; volatility of relations among participating countries; lack of coordination among participating countries; lack of harmonisation of various rules, regulations and procedures. Some look at projects like Hambantota Port in Sri Lanka, CPEC passing through Pakistan-controlled Kashmir as examples of countries having to compromise on sovereignty issues and/or falling into debt traps.

Special challenges facing Bangladesh

Bangladesh is virtually India-locked, enclosed by India on all four sides, including in the Bay of Bengal, except for a relatively small stretch of border with Myanmar in the southeast. Therefore, proactive participation in BRI by both India and Myanmar is a precondition for Bangladesh to be able to reap maximum benefit out of the BRI; besides, serious lack of infrastructures, shortage of electricity and energy, lack of diversity of exportable items, need for modern and appropriate technology, shortage of investible capital, need for development of skilled manpower and human resources, challenges of environmental degradation and climate change; influx of more than a million Rohingya refugees and strained relations with Myanmar are some tough challenges that need to be addressed if

Bangladesh has to reap maximum benefit from participation in BRI.

Addressing challenges

There is hardly any initiative in the world that does not face challenge or obstacles and the BRI is no exception. The challenges to BRI mentioned above, themselves suggest relevant remedies. However, the following could be specially emphasized: more attention should be given to creating appropriate narratives that will appeal to prospective participants; paying more attention to the needs and interests of all prospective participants while packaging the concept; speaking clearly about shared ownership, shared responsibility, shared benefit and shared prosperity; attention should also be given to ensuring greater transparency and clarity about China's motives and interests; focusing on sincere, objective and open negotiation and consultation process; focusing on complementarities and mutual benefit of cooperation; paying greater attention to resolving outstanding issues among members, bilaterally and multilaterally; each participating country should strengthen its governance and take appropriate measures to rein in all corruption, particularly in the case of BRI related projects; incrementally harmonising various rules, regulations and procedures among participating countries; enhancing coordination among participating countries in all relevant matters connected with BRI projects.

Final words

In spite of all challenges, any initiative or endeavour that seeks to promote broader connectivity and cooperation between and amongst peoples, is always something to be pursued and something that will invariably bring benefits to all, if pursued with due diligence based on the principles of equality, mutual understanding, mutual respect and mutual benefit. The same is also true for BRI. Given the huge and almost unfathomable size of the related concept, vision and initiative, the benefits to all associated with BRI are also expected to be huge and unfathomable.

文学协同：构建人类命运共同体

舒明经 【印度】
印度文化部文化资源和培训中心高级研究员 / 印度中央邦博帕尔高等教育学院英语系教授、主任

2018 年 4 月，印度总理纳伦德拉·莫迪与中国国家主席习近平在武汉进行会晤，随后在武汉东湖乘船、品茶，中国音乐家演奏了印地语的流行歌曲。据印度《印度时报》报道，"……似乎涵盖两天的大部分时间"。其他许多报纸和分析师也有相同的看法。几天前，印度外交部部长苏诗马·斯瓦拉吉在印度大使馆组织的"印地语对印中友谊的贡献"节目中发言，强调印度人和中国人必须学习彼此的语言。她表示：当两个朋友坐在一起时，他们想要什么？他们想要彼此倾诉心声，分享各自的感受。为此，我们需要一种语言。当你说话的时候，我应该能理解你所说的中文；当我说话的时候，你能理解我所说的印度语。

由此得出的结论是，我们需要交替的外交方法和一对一的人际交往，以保持我们两个古老而伟大的国家之间的友好联系。绝对必要的是，我们必须加强人员互动和沟通。这将有利于相互了解彼此的文化、和平与和谐，为人类光辉的命运共同体铺平道路。语言、文学和书籍在这一任务中起着至关重要的作用。既然好的文学被认为是生活的反映，那么可以肯定地认为，一个国家的文学是了解其生活和文化并增进对该国理解的良好手段。

我们可以发现，印度和中国文化通过佛教进行融合是文本如何影响文化关系的一个经典案例。佛教经文对于佛教在中国的传播和发展起着不可或缺的关键作

用。另一个案例是亚洲第一位诺贝尔文学奖获得者拉宾德拉纳特·泰戈尔的文学创作。自 20 世纪初访问中国以来，泰戈尔在中国一直倍受尊敬和喜爱。他创作的文学作品非常丰富，已被全部翻译成中文。泰戈尔诞辰 150 周年在中国的许多地方都受到了与印度同样的热烈庆祝。每当印度和中国代表团为了外交目的开会时，总是会提及中国的朝圣学者，例如玄奘和法显，中国的印度僧侣菩提达摩和鸠摩罗什，当然还有泰戈尔。这就是他的文学影响和遗产。中国对印度的了解大多数来自他的著作。最近，有一段时间，中国著名作家冯唐翻译泰戈尔的《飞鸟集》引发热议。毫无疑问，泰戈尔通过文学作品与中国建立的文化纽带仍然牢固。

除了泰戈尔以外，其他著名的印度作家的作品也被翻译成中文，从而使中国读者了解印度的生活。例如，陈立新翻译塔拉桑卡尔·班德约帕迪亚（Tara Shankar Bandopadhyaya）著名的印地语小说《加纳德夫塔》（*Ganadevta*）。

最近，在过去的几年中，越来越多的中文作品被翻译成印度语言，印度作品被翻译成中文，在印度和中国这两个邻国之间扮演着文学大使的角色。一个典型的例子是将《道德经》（2017 年）翻译成印地语，这消除了印度人认为中国人缺乏宗教信仰的观念。对老子和孔子著作中所包含的伦理观念的理解有助于印度人更好地了解中国人，而共同点则使他们在文化上更加接近。例如，孔子谈论子女和统治者的责任、道德和伦理价值观等。所有这些概念也分布在各种印度教经文中。例如，《博伽梵歌》详细讲述一位战士和一个统治者（刹帝利）的责任。胡适（1891–1962 年）是新文化运动的杰出领袖，他提倡文本诠释的重要性，并在自己的文本批评实践中取得了很多成就。胡适开创性的文章《西游记考证》论证这部中国经典小说各部分的印度来源。同样，季羡林对印度文化有着持久的兴趣，几乎一生都致力于研究印度文化对中国传统的影响。因此，古代经典著作的翻译和对过去历史的了解在印度人和中国人意识到具有共同的信仰方面发挥了重要作用。印度与中国关系专家巴格姬（P. K. Bagchi）指出，这种努力"通过……将我们文化纽带的缺失联系起来，使两国团结在一起"。

与古代经典翻译类似，中国和印度现代文学的翻译有助于理解两国的现代生活。在这种情况下，值得注意的是，没有必要仅通过将中文书籍翻译成印度语言的方式传播给印度读者；英语是接受过教育的印度人的第二语言，而且读者可以接触到大量的英语翻译本。奖项和荣誉在书籍的宣传、普及和销售中也起着重要作用，并在很大程度上影响读者心目中的形象。例如，莫言获得诺贝尔奖时，全世界的注意力都集中在他身上。印度读者在突然间爱上中国的小说，尤其是莫言的作品。印度读者开始阅读他的获奖作品英文翻译本。这种阅读活动使读者在精神上有意识地或无意识地比较两种文化，自己祖国的文化和书中所描绘的文化。周小仪和童庆生在《中国比较文学》一文中将这种活动称为"一种跨文化探究的模式"。

这种心理探究被称为"跨文化探究"，在印度和中国的许多大学作为"比较文学"科目开展教学和研究。苏珊·巴斯奈特在她被广泛引用的著作《比较文学：批判性介绍》（1993）中指出，比较文学作为一门学科已经接近"死亡"。但是，周小仪和童庆生对此并不认同。他们认为：这种现象也许在不同程度上符合西方的实际情况，但是在非西方国家，包括中国在内，比较文学研究方兴未艾。特别是在中国，自70年代末开始，比较文学研究逐渐兴盛，吸引了大量的学者和学生。

不论是否为比较文学的学生，这是毋庸置疑的事实，读者在阅读另一种文化的书籍时，自然会了解该文化的思想、传统、习俗等事实（在小说中反映）。印度和中国都是如此。

译本并不是印度或中国读者了解对方国家和文化的唯一来源。即使也存在其他语言的译本，读者仍然可以阅读英文图书，尤其是小说。一些中国或印度侨民或移民后裔作家受到广泛的好评和赞誉并获得知名奖项，例如谭恩美（Amy Tan）、裘帕·拉希莉（Jhumpa Lahiri）、肖纳·辛格·鲍德温（Shauna Singh Baldwin）、基兰·德赛（Surman Rushdie）等。她们撰写作品的主题与来源国文化密切相关，因此是了解这些国家的习俗和传统社会习惯的良好来源。

一些当代作家曾经访问其他国家或短暂居住，通过事实或小说记录对这些国家的情况。郁秀女士曾经去过印度并用中英文双语记录自己的印象。她的故事扣人心弦，记录了游客可能会错过的有关印度和印度人的细微观察，展示印度文化的各个方面，例如种姓制度、嫁妆、包办婚姻与自由恋爱、印度社会中的女性地位等。同样，另一位作家，印度籍的帕拉维·艾雅尔（Pallavi Aiyar）在中国居住了几年，也通过事实以及小说记录了她的印象。她的处女作《烟雾与镜子》讲述了她在中国五年的经历。"这本书考察了喜马拉雅山两侧的人民如何看待彼此；他们的偏见和误解以及他们的相似之处和共同的情况。"接下来一本书是《中国：印度旅行者指南》，孤独星球出版的旅行指南，为游客和移民提供信息。她还写了一本小说《胡同里的猫》，背景是二十世纪初北京在混乱中发生变革的场景。

目前几位印度作家正在撰写有关中国和印度裔中国人题材的小说和纪实作品。来自孟加拉、在印度成长起来的阿米塔夫·戈什（Amitav Ghosh）是一位著名的印度英语小说家，他写了三本称为"朱鹭号三部曲"的小说。这组作品是以印度和中国在鸦片贸易中的关联为背景进行叙事的历史小说。故事发生在19世纪上半叶。主要涉及东印度公司经营的印度与中国之间的鸦片贸易以及贩卖苦力到毛里求斯。三部曲包括《罂粟海》（2008）、《烟河》（2011）和《烈火洪流》（2015）。这三部曲的名字源自"朱鹭号"船，大多数主要角色在这艘船上首次相遇。类似这样的作家还有很多。这是一个前所未有的新趋势，是移民活动的结果。

任何国家的优秀文学作品都反映了该国的文化。因此，这些作品有助于读者了解该国的生活、重大事件、大众心理、风俗和传统等。一旦读者了触这些知识并与之建立联系，就会欣赏和理解另一种文化下的人民，并在人道主义上与其建立联系。这样的文学活动促进对构建人类命运共同体必不可少的协同。

Literary Synergism: Fostering a Shared Future for Mankind

Shubhra Tripathi / India

Professor and Head of Dept. of English of Govt. MVM College/Dept. of Higher Education, Govt. of Madhya Pradesh, Bhopal / Senior Fellow of the Center for Cultural Resources and Training, Ministry of Culture, New Delhi

In April 2018, a meeting or an "informal summit" was held at Wuhan between Indian Prime Minister Narendra Modi and Chinese President Xi Jinping, followed by a boat ride in the Wuhan Lake, tea tasting ceremonies and Chinese musicians playing popular Hindi songs. This "… appeared to cover much ground over the two days" as observed by *The Times of India*, a leading national newspaper. Many other newspapers and analysts had much the same opinion. A few days earlier Sushma Swaraj, the External Affairs Minister of India, speaking during a programme, 'Contribution of Hindi in India-China Friendship', organised by the Indian Embassy, stressed upon the need for Indians and Chinese to learn each other's language. She observed:

> When two friends sit together, what do they want? They want to talk their hearts out to each other, share what they feel. And for that we need a

language. I should be able to understand Chinese when you speak, and you should be able to understand Hindi when I talk.

What emanates from this is that alternate methods of diplomacy and one to one human contacts, are required to maintain friendly ties between our two ancient and great countries. It is absolutely necessary, that we have increasing personal interactions and communication. This will promote mutual understanding of each other' culture, peace and harmony, paving the path to a glorious shared future for mankind. Language, literature and books play a vital role in this task. Since good literature is said to be a reflection of life, it can be presumed safely that literature of a country is a good means of knowing about its life and culture, and promoting a better understanding of that country.

A classic example of how texts affect cultural relations can be seen in the case of confluence of Indian and Chinese cultures through Buddhism. Buddhist texts and scriptures played an indispensible and crucial role in the spread and sustenance of Buddhism in China. Another example is the literary efforts of the first Nobel Laureate in literature from Asia, Rabindranath Tagore. He has been much revered and loved in China since he visited the country in early 1900s. All his literary works, which are quite voluminous, have been translated into Chinese. His 150th birth anniversary was celebrated in several places in China with the same fanfare as in India. Whenever Indian and Chinese delegations meet for diplomatic purposes, there are invariably references to Chinese pilgrim-scholars like Xuanzang and Fa Hien, Indian monks in China like Bodhidharma and Kumarajiva, and of course Tagore. Such is the impact and legacy of his literature. A lot of what China knew about India came from his writings. Recently, there was a loud uproar some time back against popular Chinese author Feng Tang's translation of Tagore's "Stray Birds." It proves beyond doubt that the cultural bond that Tagore had forged with China through literary works is still going strong.

Besides Tagore, there are other famous Indian writers whose works have been translated into Chinese, thus providing Chinese readers a look into life in India. For example, Chen Li Xin translated the famous Hindi novel *Ganadevta* by Tara Shankar Bandopadhyaya.

More recently, in the last few years more and more translations of Chinese works in Indian languages and Indian texts in Chinese are playing the role of literary ambassadors between the two neighbours, India and China. An example in point is the Hindi translation of *Dao De Jing* (2017) which has dispelled the belief among Indians about the absence of any religion in China. The understanding of ethical ideas enshrined in the works of Laotse and Confucious help Indians in understanding the Chinese better, and points of commonality bring them closer culturally. For example, Confucius talks about the duties of sons and rulers, moral and ethical values etc. All these concepts are found scattered in various Hindu scriptures. For example, the *Bhagvad Gita* elaborates upon the duties of a warrior and a ruler (the *Kshatriya*). Hu Shi (1819-1962), a prominent leader of the new cultural movement, advocated the importance of textual exegesis and achieved a great deal himself in his own practice of textual criticism. In his seminal article, "Xi you ji kao zheng" (*Studies of Journey to the West*), he identifies Indian sources in this classic Chinese novel. Similarly Ji Xianlin had an abiding interest in Indian culture and had devoted almost all his life to the study of its influences on Chinese tradition. Thus translations of ancient classics and knowledge of past history have played an important role in making both Indians and Chinese aware about shared common beliefs. P K Bagchi, an expert on India – China relations observes that such efforts bring the countries together "… by stringing together the lost links of our cultural ties."

Just like ancient classics, modern Chinese and Indian literatures are also being translated which help in understanding contemporary life in both countries. What is interesting to note in this case is that it is not necessary that Chinese books reach Indian readers through translations in Indian languages only; English is almost a second language all over India for educated people, and the readers reach out to

English translations in large numbers. Awards and honours also play an important role in the publicity, popularity and sales of books and affect readership profile in a big way. For example, when Mo Yan won the Nobel Prize, world attention was focused on him. There was a sudden rush for Chinese fiction among Indian readers, especially by Mo Yan. The Indian readers lapped up his award winning book in English translation. This kind of reading activity leads the reader to consciously or unconsciously compare the two cultures mentally, his own home culture and the culture the book portrays. Zhou, Xiaoyi and Tong, Q. S. in their article "Comparative Literature in China" term this kind of activity as "a mode of cross-cultural inquiry."

The kind of mental inquiry referred to as "cross-cultural inquiry" is taught and studied as an academic discipline called "Comparative Literature" in many universities of both India and China. Susan Bassnett in her widely quoted book *Comparative Literature: A Critical Introduction* (1993) suggests that comparative literature as a discipline is "dead". But Zhou, Xiaoyi and Tong, Q. S. think otherwise. They opine

> While all this may indeed be the situation of the discipline, to various degrees, in the West, in the non-Western world including China, comparative literature has enjoyed an amazing and sustained popularity. Specifically in China, since the late 1970s comparative literature has been one of the most prominent areas of research, attracting a large number of scholars and students.

Whether one is a student of comparative literature or not, it is an undoubted fact that when a reader reads a book from another culture, one is naturally acquainted with the facts (maybe interpolated with fiction) thoughts, traditions, customs etc. of that culture. This is true for India and China both.

Translated books are not the only source for Indian or Chinese readers to know about each other' countries and culture. There are books, particularly novels, written in English which the readers can access, though there may be translations in other languages available too. There are several authors of Chinese or Indian diaspora or descendants of immigrants like Amy Tan, Jhumpa Lahiri, Shauna Singh Baldwin, Kiran Desai, Salman Rushdie etc. who are widely popular, awarded and appreciated. The themes of their books are closely related to their home cultures and therefore a good source of knowing the customs, traditions social practices of these countries.

There are some contemporary writers who have either visited or have lived in each other's countries and have recorded their impressions either factually or in fiction. Yu Xiu visited India and recorded her impressions in Chinese and English simultaneously. Her stories are touching and record the minute observations about India and Indians, which a tourist might miss. They showcase aspects of Indian culture like caste system, dowry, arranged versus love marriages, status of women in Indian society etc. Similarly, another author, an Indian, Pallavi Aiyar lived in China for a few years and recorded her impressions in factual as well as fictional writings. Her debut work *Smoke and Mirrors* recounts her five-year long experience of China. "It takes a look at how people from the two sides of the Himalayas perceive each other; their prejudices and miscomprehensions as well as their similarities and shared circumstances." (back cover) Then there is her *China, for the Indian traveller*, a Lonely Planet's publication and a kind of informative guide for the tourist and immigrant. She has also authored *Chinese Whiskers* a novel set in the chaotic and ever-changing landscape of early twenty first century Beijing.

Several Indian writers are now writing fiction and non - fiction about China and Indo – Chinese subjects. Amitav Ghosh, hailing from Bengal and an established Indian English novelist, had written a set of three novels called the *Ibis Trilogy*. The set comprises of historical fictional narrative with the Indo – China opium trade links as backdrop. The story is set in the first half of the 19th century. It deals with opium trade between India and China run by the East India Company and the trafficking of coolies to Mauritius. It comprises *Sea of Poppies* (2008), *River of Smoke* (2011), and *Flood of Fire* (2015). The trilogy gets its names from the ship *Ibis*, on board which most of the main characters meet for the first time.

There are many such writers. This is a new trend, not seen before and is a result of immigrant activities.

The paper is based on the hypothesis that good literature of any country reflects the culture of that country. Therefore, it helps the reader to know and understand the life, major happenings, collective psyche, customs, traditions etc. of that country. Once the reader acquaints himself with these and identifies and co-relates with them, it is easy for him to appreciate and understand the people of another culture and relate to them on a humane level. Such literary activities lead to synergism essential for fostering a shared future for mankind.

References

Aiyar Pallavi, *Smoke and Mirrors*. (Back cover.) Harper Collins, India, 2008. Print.

---- *China, for the Indian traveller,* Lonely Planet. Print.

---- *Chinese Whiskers* **Harper** Collins, India 2010 and St Martin's Press, US 2012. Print

Bassnett, Susan. *Comparative Literature: A Critical Introduction*. Oxford: Blackwell, 1993.

Ghosh, Amitav. *Sea of Poppies*. New York: Picador.2009. Print

----- River of Smoke. New York: Picador.2011. Print

----- Flood of Fire New York: Picador. ***2015. Print***

Hu Shi. "Xi you ji kaozheng" ("Studies of a Journey to the West"). *Hu Shi Gudian Wenxue Yanjiu Lunji (Studies in Classical Literature)*. Shanghai: Shanghai guji chubanshe, 1988. 886-923.

Bagchi, Prabodh Chandra. *India and China: Interactions through Buddhism and Diplomacy: A Collection of Essays by Professor Prabodh Chandra Bagchi*. Edited by Bangwei Wang and Tansen Sen, London, New York, Delhi: Anthem Press, 2011. *JSTOR*, www.jstor.org/stable/j.ctt1gxp9zj.

Szczepanski, Kallie. "The First and Second Opium Wars." Thought Co, Jun. 14, 2017, thoughtco.com/the-first-and-second-opium-wars-195276.

Tagore, Rabindranath. *Talks in China*. New Delhi: Rupa and Co., 2002. Print.

Tan, Yun-Shan "Cultural Interchange between India and China, In the Footsteps of Xuanzang: Tan Yun-Shan and India". *Writings of Tagore, Nehru and Tan Yun-Shan,* ed. Tan Chung, New Delhi: Indira Gandhi National Centre for Arts. Print.
Swaraj. Sushma. "Need for Indians and Chinese to learn each other's language." *Times of India* PTI | Apr 23
https://timesofindia.indiatimes.com/india/sushma-swaraj-need-for-indians-and-chinese-to-learn-each-others-language/articleshow/63877293.cms

-----. "Need for Indians and Chinese to learn each other's language: Sushma Swaraj." Editorial by K J M Varma. *Free Press Journal.* PTI | Apr 23, 2018 12:18 pm
http://www.freepressjournal.in/world/need-for-indians-and-chinese-to-learn-each-others-language-sushma-swaraj/1263207.

Zhou, Xiaoyi; and Tong, Q. S. "Comparative Literature in China." CLCWeb: Comparative Literature and Culture 2.4 (2000)

中国发展新理念与国际合作新前景

斯巴修 【阿尔巴尼亚】
阿中文化协会会长

中国发展新理念作为"十三五"规划纲要的既定目标，是针对国内的创新、协调、绿色、开放、共享发展，但同时通过各种合作机制，如"一带一路"倡议，16+1等，倡导互利共赢，实现人类命运共同体，所以毫无疑问为推动国际合作具有积极作用。

当前世界形势十分混乱，不确定因素增多，因此今天我们探讨国际合作新前景，是个非常艰巨的任务。全球化面临新的障碍，单边主义和贸易保护主义趋势越来越突出，美中贸易战使大国关系和国际合作面临更大挑战。

中国提出新发展理念当然考虑自身利益，首先旨在使自己国家由"世界工厂"转变为制造强国，使国家的发展更科学化、规范化、人性化，为建设小康社会和实现"两个一百年"目标铺平道路。

然而，如今中国经济深度触入世界经济，而不仅仅只是第二经济强国，作为政治、外交、军事、文化等各方面的重量级国家，它的一举一动会引起全世界的关注，更有甚者它的新发展理念无疑也会直接或间接地影响世界，影响国际合作。新发展理念的特点是在国际关系中不仅仅强调利益，而且还重视国际合作对各自发展的意义，把世界看作是一个面临共同命运的大家庭，强调互利共赢，协调发展，缩小富国与穷国之间的差距，强调创新旨在通过技术革命来推动经济增长，强调绿色发展来创造更舒适、更好的生活环境。新发展理念所提出的目标需要投入几百亿，甚至上千亿美元的巨额资金，这就是说中国正在向世界提供一块大蛋糕请大家分享。比如说，"一带一路"倡议就是这一新发展理念在国际合作中的具体表现，是一项开放的、共享的发展机遇。

我想谈一下中国与巴尔干国家，主要是尚未加入欧盟的西巴尔干国家的合作，探讨新发展理念为这一合作带来的新机遇和所面临的问题。众所周知，这些国家的共同政治目标是加入欧盟，这要求它们建设和完善法治国家，尽快实现欧盟价值，但同时它们入盟的最大障碍之一是经济停滞不前，为了发展它们需要资金和技术。中国的 16+1 合作机制，特别是"一带一路"倡议为巴尔干国家的发展带来了难得的机遇，所以这一倡议宣布后，巴尔干国家积极响应。如今中国在塞尔维亚、黑山和马其顿的基础设施项目投资几十亿美元，不断加深同巴尔干国家的政治、经贸、文化等全面合作。而新发展理念的执行将使中国的投资更加规范，更科学，更环保。

但是另一方面中国在巴尔干的挺进还引起了布鲁塞尔的忧虑，认为中国与俄罗斯和土耳其一起正在成为该地区的"新角色"，试图分裂欧盟，拉拢那些常年等待加入欧盟而变得心灰意冷的国家。更有甚者，这些国家本身也利用中国的存在威胁欧盟，要求加快它们入盟的过程和增加投资。比如阿尔巴尼亚政府领导几次在不同场合公开提到了巴尔干的所谓新选择、新角色，也直接提到中国。另外由德国开启的"柏林进程"，强调"巴尔干属于欧洲而不属于其他地区"，也旨在提高西巴尔干国家的入盟信心和促进该地区的经济发展，强调但它优先强调的是，解决西巴尔干的关键性政治外交问题，而忽视了对该地区的投资。因此现在西巴尔干国家处在这样的局面，即，一方面在 16+1 和"一带一路"倡议背景下中国和巴尔干展开了经贸、政治、人文等领域全方位合作，另一方面是旨在处理该地区敏感问题的"柏林进程"和该地区国家加入欧盟的迫切愿望。对他们来说，最理想的是两者相结合，共同努力推进西巴尔干国家入盟和经济发展。为了保证与巴尔干国家的长期有效合作，北京必须与布鲁塞尔保持沟通，耐心地以实际行动向它解释自己的发展新理念，"一带一路"倡议等合作机制的宗旨是开放的、共享的，追根到底，中国与巴尔干的合作前景与其说取决于他们本身的意愿，还不如说取决于欧盟对此的反应和干预，即取决于欧盟与中国之间今后的合作。

中国发展新理念既有助于引领本国经济发展全局，也有助于推动世界经济转型和复苏增长。虽然西方对中国方案存有疑虑，不管彼此不信任还很深刻，不管贸易摩擦和争执、地缘政策的变数和大国关系的复杂性，各国之间的相互依赖如此之大，相互影响如此之深，以致任何国家无法陷于孤立，全球化过程是不可逆转的。

中国新发展理念为世界经济提供新的动力，提供协调发展的中国范本，为全球化提供新的选择，为世界的共享发展提供中国方案。

China's New Concept of Development and the Prospect of International Cooperation

Iljaz Spahiu/ Albania

Chairman of the China-Albania Cultural Association

China's new concept of development, as an established goal of the 13th five year plan outline, aims at domestic innovation, coordination, green, open and shared development, but at the same time, through various cooperation mechanisms, such as "one generation, one road", 16 + 1 and so on, advocates mutual benefit and win-win realization of a community of shared destiny, which undoubtedly plays a positive role in promoting international cooperation.

China's new development concept, of course, considers its own interests. First, it aims to transform its country from a "world factory" into a manufacturing power, make its development more scientific, standardized and popular, and pave the way for building a moderately prosperous society and achieving the two centenary goals.

However, today, China's economy is deeply in touch with the world economy, and not only as the second economic power, but also as a heavyweight country in politics, diplomacy, military, culture and other aspects. Its every move will attract the attention of the whole world. What's more, its new development concept will undoubtedly directly or indirectly affect the world and international cooperation. The new development concept is characterized by not only emphasizing interests in international relations, but also the significance of international cooperation for their own development. It regards the world as a big family facing a common destiny, emphasizes mutual benefit and win-win results, coordinated development, narrowing the gap between rich and poor countries, emphasizing innovation aimed at promoting economic growth through technological revolution, and emphasizing green development to create more comfort A better living environment. The goal of the new development concept requires tens of billions, or even hundreds of billions of dollars, which means that China is providing the world with a big piece of cake for everyone to share. For example, the "one generation, one road" initiative is the concrete manifestation of this new development concept in international cooperation and an open and shared development opportunity.

I would like to talk about the cooperation between China and the Balkan countries, mainly the western Balkan countries that have not yet joined the EU, and explore the new opportunities and problems that the new development concept brings to this cooperation. As we all know, the common political goal of these countries is to join the EU, which requires them to build and improve the rule of law countries and realize the value of the EU as soon as possible. But at the same time, one of the biggest obstacles for them to join the EU is that their economy is stagnant. In order to develop them, they need funds and technology. China's 16+1 cooperation one belt, especially the "one belt, one road" initiative, has brought rare opportunities to the Balkan countries. After the announcement of this initiative, the Balkan countries responded positively. Today, China has invested billions of dollars in infrastructure projects in serbia, Montenegro and Macedonia, and has continued to deepen comprehensive cooperation with Balkan countries in politics, economy, trade and culture. The implementation of the new development concept will make China's investment more standardized, scientific and environmentally friendly.

But on the other hand, China's advance in the Balkans has also caused concern in Brussels. It believes that China, together with Russia and Turkey, is becoming a "new role" in the region, trying to split the EU and bring together countries that have been waiting for EU membership for many years and become frustrated. What's more, these countries themselves take advantage of China's presence to threaten the EU and demand to speed up their accession process and increase investment. For example, the leaders of the Albanian government have publicly mentioned the so-called new choices and new roles in the Balkans on several occasions, as well as China directly. In addition, the "Berlin process" initiated by Germany emphasizes that "the Balkans belong to Europe rather than other regions", and aims to improve the confidence of the western Balkan countries in joining the league and promote the economic development of the region. It emphasizes that, however, it gives priority to solving the key political and diplomatic problems in the western Balkans, while neglecting the investment in the region. One belt, one road, is China and Balkans, which have launched an all-round cooperation in the fields of economy, trade, politics and humanities. On the other hand, they are the "Berlin advance" aimed at dealing with sensitive issues in the region and the urgent desire of the countries in the region to join the EU. The best thing for them is to combine the two and work together to promote the accession and economic development of the western Balkan countries. One belt, one road initiative, and the other, the Beijing cooperation must be maintained with Brussels. In order to ensure long-term and effective cooperation with the Balkan countries, we must be patient and take actions to explain its new development concept. The purpose of the cooperation mechanism is to open up, share and follow the end. The prospect of cooperation between China and the Balkans is not so much determined by their own will. The EU's response and intervention in this regard, frankly, depends on the future cooperation between the EU and China.

China's new concept of development is not only conducive to leading the overall development of its economy, but also to promoting the transformation and recovery of the world economy. Although the West has doubts about China's plan, no matter how deep they distrust each other, no matter trade frictions and disputes, geopolitical policy variables and the complexity of major country relations, countries rely on each other so much and influence each other so deeply that any international cannot be trapped in isolation, and the process of Globalization is irreversible.

China's new development concept provides a new impetus for the world economy, a Chinese model for coordinated development, a new choice for globalization, and a Chinese plan for the shared development of the world.

在"汉学与当代中国"座谈会上的发言

雅克·高德弗兰 【法国】
戴高乐基金会主席

戴高乐将军是首批与中华人民共和国建立外交关系的西方领导人,那是1964年。我们基金会使命所在,用一句简单的话概括,即让戴高乐的遗产继续存活和具有价值。

我主要表达两个方面的意思:

第一,戴高乐在塑造法国的政治和经济模式以及法国对外政治中的作用是什么;

第二,他的遗产对中法双边对话有何帮助。

首先,戴高乐仍然是理解法国身份认同根源的参照,因为他走上政治舞台的时刻法国正面临着严重危机。1940年,法国政权在德国军队的打击下瓦解,戴高乐当时是一名军人和政治新手,乘坐飞机前往伦敦,渴望继续战斗的法国人开始聚集在他身边。这使法国在1945年成为战争胜利者之一。戴高乐随后于1944年至1946年首次执掌政权,在国家主导政策的指导下重建国民经济。十二年后,1958年他再次执政,应对阿尔及利亚殖民地的独立战争。然后开始制定新宪法,这部宪法沿用至今,主要目的是缩短指挥链,提高效率。

到如今,法国是欧洲行政效率最高的民主国家之一。例如,在军事领域,自戴高乐以来,全体法国人民直接选举产生的国家元首统率全国军队。2013年1月,在马里决定对极端组织"博科圣地"采取"非洲山猫"作战行动时,从做出干预决定到打响第一枪仅用了几个小时。其他西方民主国家的执行速度不可能如此之快，因为其他国家需要更长时间和更加复杂的审批流程。

戴高乐的第二大贡献是在关键领域制定国家主导的战略。显然，20世纪60年代法国制造原子弹是一个很好的例子。戴高乐热衷于让高级公务员担任大型企业集团的高层，认为这是保持国家独立的战略，让大型企业直接依赖于国家。例如，戴高乐从几家石油公司中选出一家大型国有企业埃尔夫阿奎坦，以保障国家石油供应。此外，戴高乐还关心大型企业内部权力和责任的重新分配。他让工人参与企业的决策和收益，从而工人的工作更加专著，也有利于通过强劲的经济增长实现和平的社会发展。

最后但也很重要的一点是，戴高乐努力的主要目标是国家独立。在冷战期间，戴高乐渴望让法国发出自己的声音和保持独立性。因此，戴高乐采取突破性的措施，批评美国发起越南战争，将法国从北约高级指挥部撤出。他还超越意识形态分歧，与具有深厚历史背景和强大国家组织的国家（例如俄罗斯或中国）建立外交关系，自信地与在他执政期间独立的非洲国家建立信任关系：目前在教育、医疗服务和人类发展的各个领域仍however保持着这种关系。

因此，戴高乐有助于理解法国的深层政治认同，而这正是我们基金会所起到的作用。根据戴高乐的遗愿，在他人生中的最后几个月设立本基金会。首先，我们是戴高乐及其遗产的研究中心。我们当前的研究主要涉及戴高乐的政治遗产对当今时代主题的影响。我们的任务是与教育部密切合作，让年轻一代了解这一遗产。例如，我们通过教学或游戏等不同的方式在法国中等教育体系中发展国家价值观。戴高乐的遗产还通过博物馆进行展示，不论是他位于法国东部科隆贝的故居，还是著名的巴黎荣军院核心区域。

戴高乐基金会如何在法中关系中发挥作用？对于我们来说，这不是一个新课题。自2000年起，基金会就开始与中国年轻领导人进行交流。首先，基金会使人们牢记深厚的历史背景在外交政策中的重要性。一般而言，我们的研究计划试图了解1964年的决定并最终理解戴高乐的全球愿景。

此外，我们还考虑对法国和中国的政治和思维模式进行比较。此前的6月13日，在法国总理和中国驻巴黎大使的见证下，我们与上海中欧国际工商学院签署"戴高乐全球领导力"教席合作协议，对领导模型进行比较。主要目标是研究戴高乐的智力权威，而不是经典的管理模式。在通常被称为"家长式"的亚洲领导模式和戴高乐被称为"国家之父"的法国领导模式之间是否存在某种联系？

中法两国学术界在这些问题上的合作仍在进行中。戴高乐政治生涯中的一些关键时刻可能对未来的领导者都非常有价值和指导意义，因为戴高乐曾经是"叱咤风云的伟人"，我们于四年前在北京举行过该主题的展览。简言之，举一个著名的例子，1940 年 6 月 18 日他带来的突破在当时可能看起来毫无意义，如此具有反叛性，很少有人能够接受。但是，领导者的成功之处恰恰在于他的长远眼光，这使他能够在严峻的危机局势中保持冷静和清醒，即使在事情似乎相反的情况下，他也能坚持这一远见。

我们希望这一论断能够有助于设计一个新的领导模式，帮助我们的企业或政治领导人保持相同的语言，继续加强和保持双边关系。

（本文系根据座谈会速记稿整理，内容已经作者本人确认）

Speech at the Symposium on China Studies 2018

Jacques Godfrain / France

President of Foundation Charles de Gaulle

I want to particularly thank the Ministry for Culture and Tourism for his kind invitation that somehow points out the role that the Foundation Charles de Gaulle I am chairing can play in the bilateral dialogue between France and China.

It is a great honor because it echoes the vision of Charles de Gaulle, who was the first among occidental leaders to establish with People's Republic of China a relationship at the diplomatic level in 1964. It also pays tribute to our Foundation's mission that I can summarize on a short and simple motto: Keep de Gaulle's legacy alive and useful.

In a very few words, I'd like to develop two topics:

Firstly, what was the role of de Gaulle in shaping the French political and economic model, and the politics of France towards foreign continents. Secondly, how his legacy may be useful for the bilateral Franco-Chinese dialogue.

First of all, de Gaulle remains the most relevant reference to understand the

French roots of identity, as his political involvement was to face harsh crisis moments for our country. In 1940, as France was collapsing under the strikes of the German Army, de Gaulle, a military and yet a beginner into politics, flew to London, and began gathering around him French people eager to fight on. That would lead France to seat among war winners in 1945. De Gaulle would then have his first tenure in power from 1944 to 1946, reconstructing the national economy under the guidance of state driven policies. Twelve years later, in 1958, he would be called back to power to solve our harshest decolonization war, the Algerian conflict. He would then set in motion a new Constitution, which is to this day our current Constitution, under the main preoccupation to have a shorter and more efficient chain of command.

To this day, France stands as one of the most executives democracies in Europe. For example, in the military domain, the chief of State, directly elected by the whole French population, since de Gaulle, is the head of army. In January of 2013, when the Serval operation was decided, in Mali, against Boko Haram, it took only a few hours between the decision to intervene and the first shots. Such a rapidity of execution would have been impossible in another western democracy, where the chain of validation is much longer and more complex.

De Gaulle's second priority was to have, in key sectors, a state-driven strategy. The making of the French atomic bomb, during the 1960's, is of course a good example. De Gaulle was keen on having high civil servants at the head of big business groups, and considered what was strategic to national independence had to depend directly on the state. For example, de Gaulle made one big national company, Elf Aquitaine, out of several petroleum companies, in order to secure the country's supply. Moreover de Gaulle was also worried about the repartition of power and responsibilities' inside the big companies. The idea of participation, his will to have workers involved in decisions and benefits, to give meaning to their commitment into work, was also instrumental, and useful to have a rather peaceful social situation through strong economic growth. Last but not least, the main idea of de Gaulle that all those efforts were aiming to was national independence. In a cold War world, de Gaulle was eager to give back the country his own voice and independence. Hereby, De Gaulle would take breakthrough initiatives, criticizing USA for the Viet Nam War or taking France out of the High Command structure for NATO. He would also establish diplomatic relationship above ideological disagreements with countries gifted with a deep historical background and a strong state organization, such as Russia or Popular Republic of China, and secure a confident relationship with African countries he had led to independence: the inhéritage in the domains of Education, Health service and human development still colour this relationship nowadays. De Gaulle is therefore instrumental to understand French deep political identity, and there lies the utility of our Foundation, which was born was born out of de Gaulle's personal will, during the last months of his life. It is, first of all, a research center on de Gaulle and his legacy. Our current research topics deal with the defining aspect of de Gaulle's legacy for today's topics. Our task is also to share this legacy with younger generations, in a close collaboration with our Ministry of Education. For example, we develop the idea of commitment to Nation's values among the French secondary system, through different means, teaching classes or devoted games. De Gaulle's legacy is also kept alive by a museal action, both in his home of Colombey, in the East of France, and in Paris, at the heart of the prestigious Invalides Museum. Hereby, our Foundation is instrumental in the bilateral relationship.

How can the Foundation be useful to the Franco-Chinese relationship? It is an old preoccupation for us, as as soon as the beginning of the 2000's, the Foundation had already developed a young leaders exchange program with China. First of all, the Foundation is here to keep in people's mind the importance of deep historical background in foreign policy. Regularly, our research programs have tried to understand the decision of 1964, the way leading to it, but also its deep coherence with de Gaulle's worldwide vision.

Moreover, we're also thinking on a comparison of political and intellectual models between France and China. Last 13th of June, in presence of our Prime minister and of the Ambassador for Popular republic of China in Paris, a partnership was signed with Shanghai CEIBS to establish a « Charles de Gaulle Global leaderhip » chair, that will deal with a comparison of leadership models. The main idea is to question de Gaulle's intelligent authority rather than classic management model. Are there some possible connections between the Asian model of leadership, often described as « paternalistic », as the French model, where de Gaulle was often called the « father of the Nation » ?

A common work between Chinese and French Academics is yet going ahead on those matters. Several key moments in de Gaulle's political life may be useful and instructive for every future leaders, as de Gaulle was « The man inside the tempest », to refer to the exhibition our Foundation set up in Beijing four years ago. To develop in a few words a famous example, the breakthrough of 18th June of 1940 I was evoking may have appeared at the time as senseless, so transgressive very few people could handle it. But what makes a leader lies precisely among his long-term vision, that gives him some ability to stay calm and lucid among harsh crisis situations, and his ability to stick to this vision even whenever events seem opposite.

We hope this kind of assumption will contribute to design a common renewed leadership model, which could be useful to have our business or political leaders speaking the same language, and keep developing this rich bilateral relationship.

在"汉学与当代中国"座谈会上的发言

郑永年 【新加坡】

新加坡国立大学东亚研究所所长、教授

2018 年是中国改革开放的 40 周年。中国的经验可以说是世界发展经验的一个组成部分,我认为这点非常重要,中国现在是世界上第二大经济体,是世界上最大的贸易国,所以说中国对世界经济来讲是非常重要的。但是很遗憾,我认为现在还是有很多对中国的误解。为了让我们能够充分理解中国的经验,认为不光光我们要了解中国是怎么发展的,其实我们也应该了解一下中国政治体系和经济体系,是如何发展和运转的。我只有 10 分钟的时间,我希望自己能用一百分钟向大家解释,但是只有 10 分钟,我就总结一下。三个方面,三种权力、三种资本。

三种资本,指的是中国经济体系。在西方甚至在中国国内,中国的经济体系一直被认为是严格的 A 股,国家资本。西方的杂志,比如《经济学人》当中,有很多关于中国国家资本的报道。但是我认为,中国有一半的 GDP 是来自于私有领域,有一半的就业也是在私有企业,所以很难说中国实际上就是一个国有的资本。

我花了很多的时间,应该说花了 10 多年的时间,在过去 10 多年我一直在研究怎么样来概括性地总结中国的政治和经济的体系。我总结出一个概念,我称它为市场和政府的一个融合。我认为,所有的市场都应该受到监管,如果没有政府,市场是不会良好运转的。从这个角度来讲,中国的市场体系实际上是运转非常好的,所以我找到了中国经济中三个层面的资本。

首先是国家资本,然后是大量的私有企业,他们和国家及政府没有太多的关系。居于中间层级的是国家和企业进行融合，政府对企业发挥监管的作用，就是现在的 PPP，政企合作形式。我认为这三个层级构成中国的经济体系，实际上是运转非常良好的。像美国、英国这样的体系，资本主义是主导的，所以我认为资本主义是不能够完全避免危机的。但是中国的这种体系可以，因为国家也会在大型的基础设施建设方面起到重要的作用，在应对大型危机方面起到重要作用，而且企业也是具有创新的。就像我们的主席李君如先生曾经提到，如果你去深圳的话，你会发现那里有很多的私有企业，而且有很多的创新，其实创新不是说在国有企业还是在私有企业，在中间这个层级我认为也是非常重要的。我不是说在宣传自己的书，不过我有一本书马上要在 2018 年 9 月出版，大概有 500 页，书名是《政府和企业的合作》。由剑桥大学出版社出版，我花了 10 多年时间完成这本书。

如果大家有兴趣，我会给大家讲一下三个层级的资本有什么样的作用。我觉得在西方，国家一般有两个工具，第一个是财政政策，第二个是货币政策。那么这两个政策有可能在国家积累了大量的债务之后，首先财政政策就没有办法运行了。当利率变得很低，货币政策也会出乱，现在很多国家都会采取量化宽松货币政策。但量化宽松是解决问题的一种方式但不是终极的方式，在中国除了财政和货币政策之外，还有很多部分其他调节。在过去的很多年，中国内部都没有发生经济危机，我觉得以上所说的就是原因。

当然，国企也有很多需要改善的地方。中国现在向新加坡学习，这是为什么？中国经济体系总被人描述成一个混合的体系。我们看这种混合的经济体系就能够找到一些线索，可以看到三种类型的资本。再回到我们的政治体系。中国是共产党领导的多党合作政治协商制度，像习近平主席强调的一样。2017 年中共十九大，强调了监管的权力。从中国现代开始，中国从西方的政治体系里面学到了很多。中国的政治体系有人民代表大会、有政治协商会议，等等，所有的组织机构都是从西方来的，中国的过去是没有的。把三个权力纳入体系之中，这是可持续发展的体系，能够很好地协调。中国是共产党领导的国家，但是跟一党制是不一样的，在共产党体制里面有 1800 万共产党员，所以是集体的政权。但是中国共产党的权力来自于人民，在共产党内部也有监督，这是非常重要的。当然，我觉得这个系统也是能够改善的。比如权力的协调以及更好地分配，去承担不同的责任。这也是我现在着重做的项目。

我认为中国的经验对其他国家也有借鉴作用。因为在过去的 40 年中，中国的发展是在全球化的背景下完成的,在开放的体系之中完成的,中国从其他国家也学到了很多。比如从西方、从日本,也学习了很多小国的经验,比如新加坡。中国的模式对世界来说是有借鉴意义的,对自己的历史也是有借鉴作用的。

(本文系根据座谈会速记稿整理,内容已经作者本人确认)

Speech at the Symposium on China Studies (2018)

Yongnian Zheng / Singapore

Professor and Director of the East Asian Institute at the National University of Singapore

2018 year marks the 40th anniversary of China's reform and opening-up. China's experience can be said to be an integral part of the world's developmental experience. I presume that this point is very important. China is now the world's second-largest economy and the largest trading nation, so it is very important for the world economy. But unfortunately, there are still many misunderstandings about China. In order to fully understand China's experience, we must understand not only how China can achieve development, but also how the political system and economic system of China develop and operate. I have only ten minutes although the explanation could take a hundred minutes. Within ten minutes, I can only make a summary. I would like to talk about three aspects, three powers and three types of capital.

The three types of capital refer to the Chinese economic system. In the West and even in China, China's economic system has always been considered a strict A-share, state capital. In Western magazines, such as *The Economist*, there are many reports of Chinese state capital. But I think that half of China's GDP comes from the private sector and half of the employment is also in private companies, so it is not correct to say that China actually adopts a system of state-owned economic system.

I have spent a lot of time on studying China, more than ten years. Over the past ten years, I have been studying how to sum up China's political and economic system. I come up with a concept that I call a fusion of the market and the government. I suppose that all markets should be regulated. Without the government, the market would not work well. From this perspective, the Chinese system is actually working very well, so I can distinguish three levels of capital.

At the top level is state capitalism, and then there are a large number of state-owned enterprises that are not closely related to the state and the government. This is what I call liberal capital. Then there is a middle level where the state and enterprises are integrated. The government plays a regulatory role for enterprises, that is, the current PPP, public-private partnership. In my opinion, capitalism at these three levels is actually working very well. Capitalism is dominant in systems like the United States and the United Kingdom, so I presume that capitalism cannot completely avoid a crisis. But China's system can effectively cope with large-scale crises because the state plays an important role in building large-scale infrastructures. And enterprises are also very innovative. Just like what our Chairman, Mr. Li Junru once mentioned, in Shenzhen, there are many private companies and innovations there. In fact, innovation is not about state-owned enterprises or private enterprises. The middle level of capitalism is also very important. I am not promoting my own book, but I will have a book to be published in September this year. The book has about 500 pages and the title is "The Cooperation between Government and Enterprises", which will be published by the Cambridge University Press. I have spent more than ten years writing this book.

If you feel interested, I will explain the three levels of capital and what role they play in China today. In the West, a country generally has two tools, the first is *fiscal policy* and the second is *monetary policy*. Then, after too many debts owed by the country, the fiscal policy possibly becomes ineffective. If the interest rates are very low, the monetary policy will also become chaotic. Now, many countries adopt quantitative easing monetary policy. But quantitative easing monetary policy is one way of solving problems, instead of the ultimate way. In addition to the fiscal system and monetary policy, China also has some other important tools. In the past years, no economic crisis has occurred in China. I think what I mentioned above can explain this.

Of course, state-owned enterprises also have a lot to improve on. China is now learning from Singapore. Why? China's economic system is always described as a hybrid system. Looking at this hybrid economy, we can find some clues and see three types of capital. Taking a look at our political system, Of course, China's political party system is different from one-party system, it is multiparty cooperation and polittical consultation under the leadership of communist Party of China, as President Xi Jinping has emphasized. However, it is very interesting to look at China's political system. At the 19th CPC National Congress last year, the regulatory power was also incorporated into the system. Since the beginning of modern China, China has learned a lot from the Western system. This is why China has people's congresses, political consultation meetings, etc. After incorporating the powers into the system, it has become a very sustainable system that can be well coordinated. China is a country under the leadership of the Communist Party. But this is total different from the history. There are 18 million party members in the Communist system, so it is also a collective political power. The Party's power comes from the people, and there are also inner-Party Supervision within the Communist Party. This is very important. Of course, in my opinion, this system also be improved. For example, the coordination of the powers and better allocation to assume different responsibilities. This is also the project I am researching now.

In my opinion, China's experience could also be useful for other countries. Because in the past 40 years, China's development was achieved in the context of globalization and in an open system. China learned a lot from other countries, such as the West and Japan, as well as many small countries, such as Singapore. The Chinese model could be used as a reference for the world and for its own history.

在"汉学与当代中国"座谈会上的发言

罗杰·哈特 【美国】
德克萨斯南方大学历史与地理学系副教授 / 德克萨斯南方大学孔子学院外方校长

我原来不是学文科,我学理科,我是麻省理工学院数学系的宅男,当时为什么学数学?学数学是我对哲学感兴趣,在西方的传统里,往往就是从古希腊到启蒙运动,到 20 世纪,很多哲学家们开始学数学和物理,他们觉得数学是哲学的基础,就是这个原因,我选择了学数学。后来我在斯坦福上研究生数学系,我发现那里数学系的教授们非常不喜欢哲学,他们觉得跟他们的研究没有任何关系。我当时在斯坦福大学参加一个公益组织,亚洲志愿团来中国,报名一年,来了一年,我觉得我对中国文化和中国语言、哲学什么都还没有学完,所以我延长了好几次。我回美国的时候,我的汉学跟我数学差不多一个水平,这个足够说明我学数学是没有天赋的,是吧?我回去开始学中国文学,后来转到历史系,我对西方 17 世纪的《几何原本》非常感兴趣,你知道《几何原本》在西方的传统里就是公理演绎的基础,当时有人认为逻辑是数学的基础,数学是物理的基础,物理是化学的基础,等等,最重要是逻辑,所以我特别感兴趣,中国人怎么看《几何原本》的。

然后我发现很多人研究《几何原本》在中国的过程,有一点神话,不太符合历史事实。后来我写了两本书,一个叫(《现近代书的跟进》)《想象的文明体,西方中国以及他们首次相遇》。我不讲具体的细节,我就概括一下我的结论。

第一,科学技术可以非常快地循环到别的地方去,比如说(《现近代书的跟进》)。古代汉语翻译，最早的记录是在中国，可是很快在欧亚大陆，就是意大利可以发现类似的研究。所以这个循环这个扩散是比较快。可能最重要的是结论，即科学技术属于人类，不属于某一个种族、某一个国家、某一个文明。比较简单可是我觉得应该强调。

第二个部分是中国发展新理念。我主要是对科学技术发展感兴趣，比如说中国有几个招聘人才的政策，可能最重要是中国制造的计划，你们可能知道。就是在2025年，中国要在很多方面占据比较领先的地位，包括信息技术、机器人、航空航天、船舶、轨道、新能源汽车、电力、农机、新材料和医药什么的，中国有非常具体的目标、指标，我不仔细讲。

这个能不能实现？我们不知道，可是我觉得最靠谱的研究是日本科学技术厅发表一个报告，他们说如果把科学划分为八个大的领域，中国领先在四个，美国领先在四个，现在，中国排第一名，包括计算机、科学、数学、材料科学和工程，而美国是物理学、环境与地球科学基础生命科学和临床医学。比较具体的中国好像有优势包括超级计算与语音识别、石墨系、纳米技术、基因组学、量子通信，人工智能、土木工程、机器人、高铁；能源方面有火力发电，电力电动汽车，等等。我不说更多的了。

量子通信是我最感兴趣的，因为这是20世纪开始发现的量子力学的一个问题。这个来源是一个哲学题目，爱因斯坦对量子力学比较烦，因为跟相对论有矛盾，所以他发表了一篇文章，量子力学对物理实在的描述是否完备？后来一直有哲学争论。1964年被证明量子力学是完备的，可还一直是哲学的命题。到了21世纪才有人提出可能做量子计算，然后被发现的确可以做。2016年，中国领先，你可以看美国最权威的《科学和自然》杂志。

国际合作新前景这个题目，你知道现在有贸易战，美国关税、报复关税，美国在三个领域跟中国有比较紧张的关系。第一个是经济，这是比较老的消息。第二个是军事。"中国威胁论"无论怎么讲，美国是有绝对的优势在这方面。我觉得现在国际关系紧张的缘故，就是科学技术，中国已经开始超越美国。对此美国人没有任何思想准备。我们政府没有任何政策可以改变这个事实和这个趋势，所以他们是被动的，他们采取的政策是不会有任何效果的。比如说他们对学生签证管得比较严。对所谓偷窃秘密，如果中国领先这个东西是偷的吗？这不太可能，是吧。还有一种反华的情绪。所以我原来想多讲意识形态，恐怕我时间差不多了。

我就想说结论，非常简单。我觉得美国学术界是有一点对美国人民的误导，美国人民没有思想准备，对全球改变趋势。因为我们讲是西方崛起、西方优越性、西方普遍性、永恒性，包括最有名的例子是福山历史的终结。

我觉得，最重要是在学术界加强国际合作，这非常重要。包括理工科，尤其是文科和汉学的国际合作。比较具体的是我对李约瑟比较崇拜，他过去是写中国历史的科学史，那现在中国领先，我觉得我们完全可以写中国领先的这些领域的科学史，当代科学史，我自己对量子通信比较感兴趣。高铁，这些我刚刚讲过的，都可以写。

最后，用我最喜欢《论语》的一段话结束。士不可以不弘毅，任重而道远。仁以为己任，不亦重乎？死而后已，不亦远乎？谢谢！

（本文系根据座谈会速记稿整理，内容已经作者本人确认）

Speech at the Symposium on China Studies (2018)

Roger Hart/ United States of America

Associate Professor of Department of History, Geography and General Studies/ Director of Confucius Institute, Texas Southern University

I didn't study liberal arts, but science. I was a nerd who majored in mathematics at the Massachusetts Institute of Technology. Why did I study mathematics? Because I was interested in philosophy. According to the Western traditions, from ancient Greece to the Age of Enlightenment to the 20th century, many philosophers began by learning mathematics and physics. In their minds, these were the foundation of philosophy. Just for this reason, I studied mathematics. Later, I studied in the postgraduate program of mathematics at Stanford. I found that professors in the mathematics department there didn't like philosophy very much. They thought that philosophy had nothing to do with their research. I joined a non-profit organization at Stanford University, the Asian Volunteer Group, and came to China for one year. I requested extensions several times because I hadn't finished my learning of Chinese culture, language and philosophy. When I went back to the United States, maybe my Chinese was almost at the same level as my mathematics. This is enough to show that I have no talent in mathematics, right? Afterward, I began to learn

Chinese literature, and later I changed to a major in history. I was very interested in the book called Euclid's Elements in the 17th century because it was the basis for axiom deduction in the Western tradition. At that time, some people thought that logic was the basis of mathematics, mathematics was the basis of physics, physics was the basis of chemistry, and so on. The most important thing was logic, so I am particularly interested in the Chinese views on Euclid's Elements.

I found that the study of *Euclid's Elements* by many people in China was a little mysterious and could not be consistent with historical facts. Later, I wrote two books, which are entitled the *Follow-up of Modern Books* and the *Imagining Civilizations: China, the West, and Their First Encounter*. I will not talk about their details but just point to my conclusions.

First, science and technology can quickly circulate to other domains, as stated in the *Follow-up of Modern Books*. The earliest record of ancient Chinese translation was found in China, but soon similar studies were found in Eurasia, particularly in Italy. So, this circulation was very quick. Perhaps the most important conclusion is that science and technology belong to human beings, instead of one race, one country or one civilization. It's relatively simple, but I think it should be emphasized.

The second part is the new concept of China's development. I am interested in the development of science and technology. For example, China has several policies for recruiting talents. Perhaps the most important plan is "made in China". In 2025, China will take the lead in many aspects, including information technology, robotics, aerospace, shipbuilding, rail transit, new energy vehicles, electric vehicles, agricultural machinery, new materials and pharmaceutics. China has very specific goals and indicators, which I will not explain in detail.

Can this goal be realized? We don't know, but I presume that the most reliable research is a report released by the Japan Science and Technology Agency. They said that if science is divided into eight major fields, China takes the lead in four fields, and the United States leads in four fields. Now, China ranks first in computers, science, mathematics, and material science and engineering, while the United States is leading in physics, the environment and earth sciences, basic life sciences, and clinical medicine. To be specific, China seems to have advantages in supercomputing and speech recognition, graphemes, nanotechnology, genomics, quantum communication, artificial intelligence, civil engineering, robotics and high-speed railways. Also, thermal power generation, electric vehicles and so on, to name but a few.

I feel most interested in quantum communication because it was originally an issue after the discovery of quantum mechanics in the 20th century. It was sourced from a philosophical topic. Einstein was annoyed with quantum mechanics due to the contradictions with the theory of relativity. He published an article to ask whether the description of the physical reality by quantum mechanics was complete. There have always been philosophical controversies. Quantum mechanics was proven complete in 1964, but it was still a proposition of philosophy. It was only in the 21st century that quantum computing was proposed as being possible. In 2016, China took the lead, as revealed by the most authoritative magazine Science and Nature in the United States.

In terms of new prospects for international cooperation, trade wars, tariffs and retaliation tariffs, the United States has had tensions with China in three areas. The first area is the economy. This is nothing new. The second area is the military. No matter how the "China Threat Theory" illustrates it, the United States has an absolute advantage in this respect. I suppose that the reason why there are tensions in our international relations is that China has begun to surpass the United States in science and technology. According to our ideology, we Americans are not mentally prepared for this. I presume that our government does not have any policies that can change the fact and the trend, so they are passive and the policies they adopt will not have any effect. For example, they have stricter control over student visas. For the so-called theft of secrets, can China take the lead in the world by stealing? This is unlikely the fact, right? There is also an anti-China impulse. I intended to talk more about ideology, but I am afraid I do not have enough time.

It is simple to reach a conclusion. There is a little bit of misunderstanding in the American academic circle for the American people. They are not mentally well prepared for embracing global trends of change, because we are always talking about the rise of the West, the superiority of the West, and the universality and eternality of the West, including the most famous example of "the end of history" theory proposed by Francis Fukuyama.

In my opinion, it is important for us to strengthen our cooperation in the academic circle and international cooperation, including international cooperation in science and engineering, especially in liberal arts and Chinese studies. To be specific, I am an adherent of Joseph Needham. He wrote the history of science of China in ancient times. Today we can write the history of science for the fields that China has taken the lead in throughout the world, the history of contemporary science. I feel interested in quantum communication. Also, high-speed railways, as I mentioned just now, can be recorded.

Finally, I would like to end my speech with a paragraph I like most in the Analects: "One who devotes oneself to service through learning cannot but be enormously resolute, for the mission is weighty and the journey is far. Taking humaneness as the mission to which one commits oneself, is that not weighty? Only in death does one cease, is that not far?"

在"汉学与当代中国"座谈会上的发言

玛琳娜·吉布拉泽 【格鲁吉亚】
格鲁吉亚汉学家协会主席

来自阿根廷的专家强调了中国在世界上的重要性,他觉得中国是"一带一路"倡议的一面镜子,通过西方看到自己的缺点,自己一些不足的地方。西方也一样,可以把"一带一路"倡议和中国,作为自己的镜子来更好地了解自己的不足和缺点。他非常希望阿根廷也加入"一带一路"倡议,更好地发展经济贸易关系,更好地了解拉美国家,更好地了解中国。

我知道,很多人会问为什么中国对格鲁吉亚这么小的国家这么感兴趣?为什么两国关系发展得这么好?一个面积世界第三和拥有13亿人口的大国与很小的格鲁吉亚,这两国哪方面具有相同之处和契合点呢?为什么中国把格鲁吉亚看成重要的合作伙伴。

格鲁吉亚在中国国家主席习近平提出的"一带一路"倡议中,格鲁吉亚扮演着十分重要的角色。另外,中国拥有古老灿烂的文明,格鲁吉亚相较于中国是一个小国,但是同样拥有古老的语言文化和历史。

我这里想强调一点,与有些国家相比,中国虽然是强大的国家,但是中国和格鲁吉亚关系平等。两国在互相尊重主权和领土完整、互不侵犯,互不干涉内政、平等互利、和平共处五项原则的基础上建立与发展友好合作关系,发展经济和文化关系和联系,从不存在任何形式的强制性的政策。

格鲁吉亚与中国共同努力找出契合点,互相信任互相尊重,互利互惠,一切是相互的而不是单面的。中国是 1992 年承认格鲁吉亚独立的国家，也是第一批承认格鲁吉亚自主的国家之一。虽然格鲁吉亚是世界上最古老的国家之一，但拥有独立主权时间却并不长，而热爱自由的格鲁吉亚人一直以来特别珍惜来之不易的独立。格鲁吉亚独立以来，两国也一直保持着友好合作关系。回顾中华人民共和国发展历史，中国政府领导下，中国人民努力奋斗，取得伟大科学成就，中国已由一个贫穷落后的国家迅速发展成为综合国力、国际影响力不断提升的世界大国。

中国的快速发展对于国际社会有很大的影响，中国愿意完善全球治理做出更多贡献，提出的"一带一路"倡议，赢得越来越多国家积极响应。去年是中格建交 25 周年，两国政治保持较高水平，经济技术合作快速发展。"一带一路"建设合作不断深化。我相信在"一带一路"沿线国家积极参与下，中格两国友好合作关系的基础上，对"一带一路"倡议的繁荣发展将发挥重要的作用。

我这里不多说了，格鲁吉亚与中国，尤其是经济方面发展的关系签的合同比较多，两国关系发展得很顺利。

借此机会，我也想给大家介绍一下我们的政策。值得注意的是什么呢？格鲁吉亚政府就此表态发表声明，他表示格鲁吉亚不再是苏联或独联体的国家，还需要摆脱苏联这样的说法，格鲁吉亚一直被称为东欧国家，格鲁吉亚这个国名早晚会改。最近很多国家陆续做修改，调整或更改。

我想把文化方面的合作也简单介绍一下。因为最近这方面还是有很多成就。在格鲁吉亚汉学家协会的支持下，格鲁吉亚还成立了格中传媒。位于欧亚十字路口并作为"一带一路"沿线的格鲁吉亚在中国国家主席习近平提出的倡议上有非常重要的角色，我们已经强调过这一点。与此同时，投资现象越来越常见，这促进了格鲁吉亚的经济发展，使得格鲁吉亚选择中国成为它的战略伙伴。值得注意的是，中国缺乏了解格鲁吉亚的一些信息，所以通过格中传媒，格鲁吉亚人民能够更多了解中国，中国人民也可以通过用中文发布的信息了解格鲁吉亚，这也是让两国人民更好地了解彼此。

2017 年 3 月，格鲁吉亚国家议会图书馆开设了中国图书角。汉学家和中华人民共和国驻格鲁吉亚大使馆，交给图书馆很多图书材料。我们准备在中国的两所大学，北京大学和北京外国语大学开设格鲁吉亚图书角，这两所大学已经有格鲁吉亚教学，另外，我们国家图书馆馆长要来华采访，在中国国家图书馆开设格鲁吉亚图书角，我觉得这已经是很大的成就。已有不少中国人学习格鲁吉亚语，通过格鲁吉亚语更多地了解格鲁吉亚，格鲁吉亚汉学发展得也很顺利，学汉语的人越来越多，可以说比学其他东方语言多得多，这也算是一个非常重要的成就。

今年 6 月，商务印书馆和格鲁吉亚的一家出版社准备翻译文学作品、工具书、教材，等等。我们还有一个非常重要的成就是，格鲁吉亚已经有汉语系统的教学，已经编辑出版了格文版的汉语教材，在中国大使馆的支持下，汉学家开始编辑中国历史书，除了中国历史的书，还有格汉汉格辞典。另外教育部有一个新项目，就是把汉语纳入到中学外语教学体系中，等于就是说汉语以后就是作为第二外语，我们第一外语是英语，第二外语是德语、法语、俄语还准备加汉语，我觉得这个是很重要的一点，这样的话，我们格鲁吉亚的孩子从小就可以学习汉语，通过汉语了解中国，以后我觉得两国关系会发展更快，将有助于"一带一路"的实行，而这种背景将有助于很多有意义的项目的实行。

（本文系根据座谈会速记稿整理，内容已经作者本人确认）

Speech at the Symposium on China Studies (2018)

Marine Jiblaze/Georgia

Chairman of Association of Georgia Sinologists, Dean of Confucius Institute at Free University of Tbilisi

The expert from Argentina highlighted the importance of China in the world. In his opinion, China is a mirror of the Belt and Road Initiative that can reflect the shortcomings and deficiencies of the West. The West can also take the Belt and Road Initiative and China as a mirror of their defects and weaknesses. He expresses the wish that Argentina can become part of the Belt and Road Initiative to better develop economic and trade relations and better understand Latin American countries and China.

As far as I know, a lot of people feel interested in Georgia, even though it is such a small country. How come China and Georgia have developed good relations? A big country with a land area that ranks third in the world and a population of 1.3 billion, and Georgia, a very small country, what are the similarities and points of convergence between the two countries? Why does China see Georgia as an important partner?

Georgia plays a very important role in the Belt and Road Initiative proposed by Chinese President Xi Jinping. Moreover, China is a splendid, ancient civilization. Georgia is a small country compared to China, but it also has an ancient language, culture and history.

China is a big power compared with some countries, but I must emphasize one point. Georgia and China have established friendly and cooperative relations based on the five principles of mutual respect for sovereignty and territorial integrity, mutual non-aggression, non-interference in each other's internal affairs, equality and mutual benefit, and peaceful coexistence. The two countries have developed economic and cultural relations and connections without any form of policy of compulsion.

Georgia and China are working together to find the points of convergence and they both adhere to the principles of mutual trust and respect and mutual benefit. Everything is mutual rather than unilateral. China, which recognized Georgia's independence in 1992, was one of the first countries to do so. Although Georgia is one of the oldest countries in the world, it was not long ago that it managed to gain independent sovereignty. The people of Georgia, who love freedom, always cherish their hard-won independence. Since Georgia's independence, the two countries have maintained friendly and cooperative relations.Looking back on the history of the development of the People's Republic of China, under the leadership of the Chinese government, the Chinese people have worked hard and made great achievements. China has rapidly developed from a poor, backward country into a big world power with growing comprehensive national strength and international influence.

To the international community, China is willing to make more contributions to improving global governance. More and more countries have given positive responses to the Belt and Road Initiative. Last year was the 25th anniversary of the establishment of diplomatic relations between China and Georgia. The two countries continue to maintain a high level of political communication and rapid development of economic and technological cooperation. The cooperation on the construction of the Belt and Road Initiative has been continuously deepened. It is believed that the Belt and Road Initiative and the active participation of countries along the route will play an important role in the prosperity of China and Georgia as well as of the region.

Well, I have nothing more to speak of. Georgia and China have signed a lot of contracts, particularly for economic development. The relations between the two countries continue to develop very well.

I would like to take this opportunity to share our policies. What is the most important point? The Georgian government issued a statement, pointing out that Georgia is no longer a former Soviet Union or CIS (Commonwealth of Independent States) country. Furthermore, we need to get rid of the clichés of the former Soviet Union. Georgia has always been known as an Eastern European country. Sooner or later the country will change its name from Georgia, which it acquired during the period of the former Soviet Union. Recently, many countries have made changes one after another, adjusting and changing.

I would like to give a brief introduction to cultural cooperation. We have made many achievements in this aspect recently. With the support of the Society of Sinologists, Georgia has also established the Chinese Media. Located at the crossroads of Europe and Asia, Georgia plays a very important role in the initiative of Chinese President Xi Jinping. We have already emphasized this point. At the same time, more investments could boost the economic development of Georgia, and it has chosen China as its strategic partner. It is noteworthy that there is a lack of information about Georgia in China, so the Chinese media should make it possible for the Georgian people to learn more about China, and the Chinese people to learn more about Georgia through the information published by the Chinese media. This can allow the people of the two countries to know each other better.

In March 2017, the National Parliamentary Library of Georgia opened a Chinese Book Corner. The sinologists and the Chinese Embassy in Georgia handed over many books to the library. We are preparing to open Georgia Book Corners at two Chinese universities in September, namely Peking University and Beijing Foreign Studies University. The two universities already have taught the Georgian language. Moreover, the President of the National Library of Georgia will pay a visit to China and open a Georgian Book Corner at the National Library of China. I think this is already a great achievement. Many Chinese people here are learning Georgian, thus learning more about Georgia through the Georgian language. Georgian Sinology is developing very well, and more and more people are learning Chinese, much more than those who are learning other Oriental languages. This is also a very important achievement.

In June of this year, the Commercial Press and a Georgian publisher were prepared to publicize translations of literary works, reference books and textbooks. We have another very important achievement in the fact that Georgia has already taught Chinese in a systematic way, and the textbooks in Georgian have been published for the teaching of Chinese. With the support of the Chinese Embassy, sinologists have begun to edit Chinese history books, books on Chinese history, as well as Georgian-Chinese and Chinese-Georgian dictionaries. In addition, the Ministry of Education has a new project to incorporate Chinese into the foreign language teaching system in secondary schools. It is equivalent to speaking Chinese as a second foreign language. Our first foreign language is English, and the second foreign languages include German, French, Russian, as well as Chinese. For my part, this is a very important point. Thus, our Georgian children can learn Chinese when they are young and understand China through the Chinese language. In the future, I think the relations between the two countries will develop faster and facilitate the implementation of the Belt and Road Initiative. Against this macroscopic background, many interesting projects can be implemented.

Experts share their development of relations with China in the context of the Belt and Road Initiative, as well as difficulties in this process, including the influence of other big powers. I still hope that China can develop relations with all countries well.

民心相通与文明互鉴

黄平 【中国】
中国社会科学院欧洲研究所所长 / 中华美国学会会长 / 中国世界政治研究会会长

  我参加了多次或是文化部或是中国社会科学院组织的类似研讨活动，包括在座的很多同事和中外朋友，如与李君如校长在英国参加的《习近平治国理政》第二卷发行研讨会。
  目前，我们一起就中国、美国、欧洲等国家的不同发展模式进行比较和研究。即使欧洲内部，也有很多不同类型的发展模式，即使同一个国家如英国，其二三百年以来的发展，也有了很大的变化。由于时间的原因，对于这些研究我就不在此逐一地展开深谈了。
  20世纪80年代中国改革开放之初，我们就参与了中欧之间的对话，我跟着费孝通先生做了很多的调研，也曾到过甘肃、宁夏等少数民族地区。由此发现，中国的发展也不仅仅只是一种模式。当时，我们已经和欧洲学界，包括在座的法国学者，当然还有美国学者，滚动进行了一个名为"跨文化"的研究。
  "中欧跨文化对话"也已经提升到了国家的层面。今天与大家围绕这个题目进行分享，共同讨论中国发展的新理念以及与之相关的国际合作。
  我认为，"一带一路"倡议中一个很重要、但却往往被忽略的关键问题，就是"五通"中的第五通，即"民心相通"。如果没有了"民心相通"，与"一带一路"建设相关的投资、经贸交流、基础设施建设也就没有了依存。例如一座桥梁建设就算建得再好，如果没有"民心相通"，那么这座桥所在地的国家、社会、人民，也不会把它看作是自己的桥。所以,"民心相通"是第一位重要的。

第二,"民心相通"也不仅只是中国文化"走出去"的一部分。我认为,习近平主席强调的"文明互鉴"也非常重要,相互学习、取长补短,就是"文明互鉴"这个词的重要内涵,并且涵盖了必要的争论和讨论。因为,各国人民的文化认识是不一样的,包括现在使用的"思想碰撞"一词,也非常贴切。中国古代文化繁荣,不也被形容成了"百花齐放"和"百家争鸣"吗?"民心相通"是第一位特别重要的;第二就是"文明互鉴",文明要互相学习,不只是中国文化"走出去"让别人理解。"文明互鉴"中包含着思想碰撞,碰撞的结果不是斗,不是打,而是精神层面的共享。所以,重要的是新思想要跳出文明冲突的泥潭,在经济领域我们不搞零合游戏,战略领域我们不搞丛林法则,文化领域我们不搞文明冲突。

20世纪80年代,我们讲文化,自认为中国文化历史悠久,欧洲人也觉得欧洲文化非常优越,不管多么悠久,多么优越,跨越自己的文化偏见,突破傲慢的局限,我们看到了其他文明、文化的长处,这就叫取长补短,优势共享。

在今天的全球化和信息化的时代,产生了很多的挑战,如民粹主义、金融风险、地区冲突、环境气候变化以及传统和非传统的风险,越是这样,我们就越要跳出二元对立的圈子。

我是学社会学的,20世纪80年代我在英国学习,当时人类学、社会学之间没有严格的分界,欧洲的人类学家开始反思老人类学就划分落后的与先进的弊端,他们认为那种划分是不一样的。在这里,我借用费孝通老先生说的"差序格局",他讲的是中国江南,尤其是他的家乡,即"上有天堂,下有苏杭"的那个地方,苏杭便是一种差序格局,城与乡不是对立的,虽有差序但无对立,由近及远,由小到大,由我及他,推己及人。费孝通老先生举了一个例子,即将一颗石子扔到湖的中心,水波纹一点儿一点儿地往外推展,你很难说哪儿才是界限。

还有一个古老的思想,叫作"天下无外"。我认为,汉学家有一个很好的传统,他们把《水浒传》译作"四海之内皆兄弟",译成外文的时候,天下无外也有差序格局,但天下无外是一个互补,是一个和而不同,而不是同然后和。康德讲的永久和平还是同而后合,我们就要一样——和平,但和而不同的理念其实是不一样的。因此,取长补短;因此,互相借鉴;所以,是和而不同,这个不同成为和的必要条件。

所以,我们是不一样的,但我们是和而不同的。

(本文系根据座谈会速记稿整理,内容已经作者本人确认)

People-to-People Bond and Mutual Learning Among Civilizations

Huang Ping/ China

Director General of the Institute of European Studies, Chinese Academy of Social Sciences / President of the Chinese Association of American Studies / President of Chinese Association of World Politics Studies

I have participated in a number of similar seminars organized by the Ministry of Culture and Tourism or the Chinese Academy of Social Sciences before, together with many colleagues and Chinese and foreign friends present here. For example, Mr. Li Junru and I once attended the seminar on the publication of the second volume of *Xi Jinping: The Governance of China* in the United Kingdom.

Currently, we are comparing and studying the different models of development of China, the United States and Europe. In Europe alone, there are many different developmental models. Even within the same country, such as the United Kingdom, the development in the two or three hundred years has changed a lot. Due to the time limit, I will not talk about these studies one by one.

At the beginning of China's reform and opening-up in the 1980s, we took part in dialogues between China and Europe. I did a lot of research with Mr. Fei Xiaotong and often went to ethnic minority areas such as Gansu and Ningxia. Thus, we found that China's development was not just a model. At that time, we had a "cross-culture" research program with the European academic community, including French scholars here, and of course American scholars.

The "Sino-European Cross-Cultural Dialogue" has already been raised to the level of states. Today, we are making exchanges on this topic and are jointly discussing the new concept of China's development and the related international cooperation.

In my opinion, one of the most important but often overlooked key issues in the Belt and Road Initiative is the "people-to-people bond". Without the "people-to-people bond", the investment, economic and trade exchanges and construction of infrastructures related to the Belt and Road would have nowhere to take root. For example, even if a bridge is built, without the "people-to-people bond", the country, the community and the people where the bridge is located would not regard it as their own bridge. Therefore, it is our top priority to achieve the "people-to-people bond".

Furthermore, the "people-to-people bond" is not only a part of the Chinese culture "going global". From my point of view, the "mutual learning among civilizations" proposed by President Xi Jinping is equally important. Learning from each other and using others' strengths to make up for our weaknesses are the important connotations of "mutual learning among civilizations" that cover necessary debates and discussions. Because people in different countries have different cultures, a "collision of thoughts" is a very appropriate term to describe this situation. Even the prosperity of ancient Chinese culture is depicted as "a hundred flowers blossoming" and "a hundred schools of thoughts contending". The "people-to-people bond" is the most important issue, followed by "mutual learning among civilizations". Civilizations must learn from each other. It does not just mean

Chinese culture "going out" for others to understand. The "mutual learning among civilizations" contains a collision of thoughts, which result in neither a struggle nor a fight, but sharing on the spiritual level. Therefore, new thoughts should jump out of the quagmire of the clash of civilizations. We do not favor zero-sum games in the economic field, we dislike the law of the jungle in the strategic field and we are not an adherent to the clash of civilizations in the cultural field.

In the 1980s, we talked about culture. In our minds, Chinese culture has a long history. Europeans also believe that European culture is quite outstanding. No matter how long and how outstanding it is, only after crossing our own cultural prejudice and breaking through the limitations of arrogance, can we find the advantages of other civilizations and cultures. This means using others' strengths to make up for our weaknesses and share our advantages.

In the era of globalization and informatization today, there are many challenges, such as populism, financial risks, regional conflicts, environmental and climatic changes, as well as traditional and non-traditional risks. Under such circumstances, we must jump out of the vicious cycle of binary opposition.

I am a sociologist. When I was studying in the UK in the early 1980s, there was no strict demarcation between anthropology and sociology. European anthropologists began to reconsider the drawbacks of dividing the backward and the advanced by the old anthropology. They thought that that kind of division was different. Here, I would like to cite the "pattern of difference sequence" proposed by Mr. Fei Xiaotong. He mentioned the South of China, especially his hometown, that is, "above, there is heaven; below, there are Suzhou and Hangzhou". Suzhou and Hangzhou have the "pattern of difference sequence" in which urban and rural areas are not antagonistic. There are differences but no oppositions, from near to far, from small to large, from me to him, and from self to others. Mr. Fei Xiaotong gave an example. If a stone is thrown into the center of the lake, ripples will spread out little by little. It is hard to say where the boundary is.

There is also an ancient thought called "there are no external things under the Heaven". I think sinologists have a very good tradition. They translate the ancient Chinese classics *Water Margin* (literal meaning) to be "All Men Are Brothers". While being translated into foreign languages, "there are no external things under the Heaven" also has the "pattern of difference sequence", but it is a mutual complement, harmony not uniformity, instead of harmony after uniformity. Mr. Fei Xiaotong talked about permanent peace or harmony after uniformity. We just want peace, but the concept of "pursuing harmony but not seeking uniformity" is different. The "mutual learning among civilizations" means pursuing harmony but not seeking uniformity. Not seeking uniformity is a necessary condition for pursuing harmony.

Therefore, we are different, we pursue harmony but do not seek uniformity.

中国发展新理念新实践为国际广泛合作提供了新机遇

李君如 【中国】
中共中央党校原副校长，研究员、博士生导师

在中国特色社会主义进入新时代后，中国形成和提出了以人民为中心的，以创新、协调、绿色、开放、共享为主要特点的发展新理念，开始了由高速增长阶段向高质量发展阶段转型的新实践。这一发展新理念新实践，为中国和世界各国开展广泛的互利合作提供了新机遇。

单边保护主义违背时代潮流没有前途

今天的世界，出现了东欧剧变以来又一次剧烈的大动荡。东欧剧变带来的，是世界格局的变化，是东西方冷战的结束。这次动荡的结局是什么，现在还看不准，但是由于这次动荡的推手是世界上唯一的超级大国美国，他们在"美国优先"的口号下，推行单边主义、保护主义，打破了经济全球化的秩序和国际合作的格局，波及面不仅包括被美国称为战略对手的中国，还包括美国的长期盟友欧洲和日本等国，从太平洋两岸到大西洋两岸，风急浪高，到处充满挑战。

这种单边主义、保护主义，给世界带来的是什么？是福音吗？绝不是！在安全方面，单方面退出伊核协议，对中东来讲是乱上添乱；在发展方面，从退出北美自由贸易协定开始，到对中国和欧盟等国家利用关税开打贸易战，并扬言退出自由贸易组织，单方面破坏自由贸易规范，使得尚在复苏中的世界经济雪上加霜，又遭受新的打击。

这种单边主义、保护主义，给美国人民带来的是什么？是福音吗？也不是！在短期内，实施"美国优先"口号下的各项举措，对美国解决国内的就业问题、改变贸易逆差会有好处，但在经济全球化的今天，产业链已经形成全局布局的格局，美国和中国、美国和欧洲、中国与欧洲之间已经形成"你中有我、我中有你"的大局面，而贸易战一开打就会打到产业链，甚至打到金融领域，最后必定伤及美国自身的消费者和美国的跨国公司。

这种单边主义、保护主义，对美国来讲，更坏的影响是美国的道德形象。现在世界上已经出现了这样的舆论：美国"说话不算话"、"朝令夕改"、"不可信任"、"无赖"等。美国本来道德形象就不好，已故美国战略家布鲁津斯基早在上一世纪90年代初就提醒过美国领导人，美国要想抓住东欧剧变后的历史机遇，成为世界唯一的超级大国而不败落，必须改变美国在世界心目中不佳的道德形象。而美国现在的做法十分短视，把美国的道德形象搞得更糟了。这对美国的长期战略来讲，绝不是福音。

因此，我们完全可以这样说，违背时代潮流的单边主义、保护主义，是没有前途的。

在广泛的国际合作中构建共赢共享的人类命运共同体

当今世界经济的发展确实出现了许多结构性的矛盾和问题，靠单边主义、保护主义解决不了这些问题，唯有靠进一步深化和拓展国际合作，构建人类命运共同体，才能实现各国共赢共享，造福世界人民。

经济全球化是当今世界的最大特点。伴随着世界市场经济的发展，特别是生产社会化程度的提高和产业链的拉长，各个国家的经济依存度越来越大。在这样的背景下，拥有不同利益的国家之间，尽管他们的经济发展水平可以不同，历史文化可以不同，甚至社会制度和意识形态也可以不同，但在市场经济中总有利益的交汇点。这些利益交汇点就是各个不同国家之间的共同利益。在这样的基础上，就会形成各种不同层次的利益共同体。与此同时，我们也看到，在世界经济发展的过程中，各个国家之间不可避免地会有发展水平、速度和质量的差异，也不可避免地会有这样那样的竞争。应该讲，既有合作，又有竞争，是市场经济的常态。我们在合作和竞争中，应该扩大共同利益，而不是缩小共同利益，只有这样，才有利于世界经济的发展。在合作和竞争中，出现这样那样的矛盾时，我们是维护已经形成的利益共同体，还是削弱甚至解构这样的利益共同体，不仅关系到这些国家之间的前途命运，还关系到整个人类的前途命运。因此，中国的国家主席习近平提出，为了人类的进步，为了子孙后代的幸福，各个国家要相互携手，共同来构建人类命运共同体。人类命运共同体的特点是共商、共建、共赢、共享，而不是只顾自己利益而不顾他人利益的单边主义、保护主义，这是迄今为止解决世界经济问题的最佳方案。

需要指出的是，今天世界的问题很多很多，造成这些问题的原因也很多很多。不能把什么问题都归咎于经济全球化，更不能把本国的问题都归咎别的国家。比如难民潮问题，主要是地区战乱造成的，和经济全球化根本没有关系。至于在经济全球化进程中，各个国家之间会出现贸易顺差或逆差问题，以及国内就业率和国民收入增加或减少等问题。这些问题的出现，情况比较复杂，要具体分析。比如有的国家以安全为由严格控制本国的出口，势必造成贸易的逆差。又比如有的国家为了追求利润最大化，在扩大向外投资时造成本国经济空心化，就会导致本国就业率的下降和国民收入的减少。还比如在技术进步的情况下，也会出现劳动生产率提高而就业率下降的情况。也就是说，对我们面临的问题要采取实事求是的分析态度，而不是把本国经济发展中出现的问题统统归咎于别人，归咎于所谓的"不公平"。至于世界贸易规则有没有不足，这些问题是可以一起来讨论，不断解决和完善的。我们历来主张，通过协商而不是诉诸对抗来解决问题。

一句话，只有在广泛的国际合作中构建共赢共享的人类命运共同体，才是最好的选择、最佳的出路。

发展新理念引领下的中国发展是国际合作的新机遇

今年是中国改革开放40周年。众所周知，中国在对内改革和对外开放中迅速成长，不仅改变了自己落后的面貌，而且为世界经济发展做出了积极的贡献。中国虽然不是经济全球化的设计者和倡导者，但是经济全球化的积极参与者和推动者。中国不仅主张扩大国际合作，而且愿意把中国的大市场和发展经验贡献给世界，成为各国共同发展的机遇，成为深化国际广泛合作的机遇。

中国经济经过30多年快速发展，现在正在由高速增长阶段向高质量发展阶段转型。面对这种新情况，以习近平为核心的中共中央提出了创新、协调、绿色、开放、共享的发展新理念。中共十九大进一步提出，要在这样的发展新理念引领下，转变发展方式，优化经济结构，转换增长动力，建设现代化经济体系，并把这一举措作为实现经济转型的战略决策和中国长远发展的战略目标。这样的新理念，这样的新实践，这样的新发展，势必成为国际合作的新机遇。

首先是因为，高质量的发展将为中国人民提供高质量的生活，从而为世界经济发展提供 13 亿多人口构成的高需求的市场。我们讲中国特色社会主义进入了新时代，对于什么叫"新时代"，习近平主席有一个十分通俗的回答。他说，过去，我们要解决的是"有没有"的问题，现在是要解决"好不好"的问题。也就是说，"新时代"是满足人民群众对于美好生活向往的时代。13 亿多人口过上好日子，会产生多么大的需求，形成多么大的市场！当中国把这样大体量的市场贡献给世界时，对国际合作来讲不就是一个极大的发展机遇吗？！

其次是因为，创新、协调、绿色、开放、共享的发展新理念带来的是一个全面发展的中国经济，从而为世界各国企业家到中国投资创业提供了新的机遇。无论是创新，还是协调、绿色、开放、共享，每一个发展新理念都是一篇发展的大文章。而撰写这一篇篇大文章的作者，是中国人民和中国人民的朋友。每一个有眼光有作为的企业家、投资者都可以抓住机会，在这一篇篇文章中写出自己的精彩。

再次是因为，中国贯彻发展新理念是要建设一个现代化的经济体系，这也为推进广泛的国际合作提供一个大有作为的新天地。中共十九大在规划未来经济发展时，提出了一个崭新的战略目标，这就是建设中国的现代化经济体系。这个经济体系的要素，一是坚持质量第一、效益优先，以供给侧结构性改革为主线；二是着力加快建设协同发展的产业体系；三是着力构建市场机制有效、微观主体有活力、宏观调控有度的经济体制。中国将以开放的姿态来建设这样的现代化经济体系，并且在更加广泛的国际合作中让世界各国从中广为受益。

综上所述，中国共产党在中国特色社会主义进入新时代后提出的创新、协调、绿色、开放、共享的发展新理念，开始了新时代中国特色社会主义的新实践。这一发展新理念新实践，为中国和世界各国开展广泛的国际合作提供了难得的新机遇。

China's New Concepts of Practice of Development in Creating New Opportunities for International Cooperation

Li Junru / China

Former Vice-president of Party School of the Central Committee of C.P.C, Researcher, Ph. D. Supervisor

After socialism with Chinese characteristics enters a new era, China will form and propose the new concepts of development centered on the people, with innovation, coordination, green, openness and sharing as the main characteristics, and will begin the new practice of transformation from high-speed growth to high-quality development. These new concepts of and practice of development can create new opportunities for mutually beneficial cooperation between China and other countries in the world.

Unilateralism and Protectionism against the Current Trend is Hopeless

In today's world, there is another dramatic turmoil since big changes in the former Soviet Union and East Europe, which marked changes in the global landscape and the ending of the Cold War. However, no one knows what the end of this turmoil will be, but the troublemaker of this turmoil is the United States of America, the only superpower in the world. The Americans practice unilateralism and protectionism under the slogan of "America First" and break the order of economic globalization and the pattern of international cooperation. Not only China, which is called a strategic opponent by the United States, but also its long-term allies, such as Europe and Japan, are affected. From both sides of the Pacific to both sides of the Atlantic, winds are strong, the waves high and they are full of challenges.

What will this unilateralism and protectionism bring to the world? Can it bring us welfare? Not at all! In terms of security, the unilateral withdrawal from the Iranian nuclear agreement creates terrible disorder in the Middle East; in terms of development, from the withdrawal of the North American Free Trade Agreement to the trade wars against China and the European Union by means of tariffs, the United States of America threatens to withdraw from free trade organizations and unilaterally ruin free trade rules. These actions make the situation even worse and seriously affect the world economy that is still in the process of recovering.

What will this unilateralism and protectionism bring to the American people? Can it bring them welfare? Not at all! In the short term, various actions taken under the slogan of "America First" might be beneficial to the United States for increasing employment and reversing trade deficits, but in today's economic globalization, the industrial chain has already spread all over the world. Like passengers riding in the same boat, the United States and China, the United States and Europe, China and Europe, all have a stake in each other's future. The trade war will hurt the industrial chain, the financial sector, and eventually American consumers and multinational companies.

Unilateralism and protectionism will stain the reputation of the United States. There are public opinions in the world criticizing the United States for "going back on its words", "chopping and changing", "being untrustworthy" and "roguish". The

United States already has a bad moral image. American strategist Brzezinski often reminded American leaders in the early 1990s that the United States must change its tarnished moral image in the minds of the world, so as to seize the historical opportunity after drastic changes in the former Soviet Union and Eastern Europe and become the only superpower that never fails. However, the current practice in the United States is very short-sighted and stains the moral image of the United States even further. This is not good for the long-term strategy of the United States.

Therefore, it can be said that unilateralism and protectionism goes against the current trend and has no future.

Build a Community with a Shared Future for Mankind in Shared and Win-Win International Cooperation

There are many structural contradictions and problems in the development of the global economy today. These problems cannot be solved by unilateralism and protectionism. Only by further deepening and expanding international cooperation and building a community with a shared future for mankind can we achieve a win-win and shared development of all countries and benefit all people of the world.

Economic globalization is the most distinctive feature of today's world. With the development of the market economy in the world, especially a higher degree of socialization of production and the extension of the industrial chain, the economic interdependence of countries is growing. In this context, countries pursuing different interests always have intersections of interests in the market economy although their level of economic development might be different, history and culture might be different and even social systems and ideologies might be different. The intersections of interests mean the common interests of different countries. On this basis, communities with different levels of interest will be formed. Meanwhile, in global economic development, there are inevitably differences among countries with regards to the level, speed and quality of development, and there is also inevitably a great deal of competition. It is a normal situation for a market economy to have both cooperation and competition. In this process, we should enlarge rather than narrow our common interests. Only in this way, can global economic development be benefited. When contradictions arise in cooperation and competition, our choice to protect the community of shared interests or weaken or even deconstruct that community can decide not only the future of these countries, but also the future of mankind. Therefore, Chinese President Xi Jinping proposed that for the progress of mankind and the happiness of future generations, all countries should work together to build a community with a shared future for mankind. Such a community should be characterized by jointly building through consultation to achieve win-win results and meet the interests of all, rather than pursue unilateralism and protectionism which protect our own interests while ignoring the interests of others. This is so far the best solution to solving the problems existing in a global economy.

It should be pointed out that the world faces many problems today, and these problems are caused by many reasons. Economic globalization should not be blamed for whatever problem exists, and other countries should not be blamed for your own problems. For example, the refugee problems are mainly caused by regional wars, so economic globalization should not be blamed. In the process of economic globalization, there are problems of trade surpluses or deficits among countries as well as an increase or a decrease in the rate of domestic employment and national income. The reasons for these problems are very complicated and should be specifically analyzed. For example, some countries strictly control their own exports on the grounds of security, which inevitably results in trade deficits. Another example, in order to maximize profits, some countries hollow out their economies to expand outbound investments, thus leading to the decline in the employment rate and a decrease in the national income of the home country. Moreover, technological advancement can also improve labor productivity and decrease the employment rate. In other words, we must make a practical analysis of the problems we are facing, instead of blaming others or blaming the so-called "unfairness" for the problems that arise in our own economic development. As for whether there are any shortcomings in the rules of world trade, these issues can be discussed together and continuously solved and improved. We always call for solving problems through negotiation rather than resorting to confrontation.

In a word, the building of a win-win community with a shared future for mankind in a wide range of international cooperation is the best choice and path to follow.

China's Development Guided by New Concepts of Development Brings New Opportunities for International Cooperation

This year marks the 40th anniversary of China's reform and opening-up. As is known to all, China's rapid growth in internal reform and external opening-up has not only changed its backward state, but also made positive contributions to the development of the global economy. China, despite not being a designer of and an advocate for economic globalization, it is an active participant in and promoter of it. China not only advocates international cooperation, but it is also willing to share its experiences of a big market and development to the world and make them become an opportunity for the common development of all countries and for deepening international cooperation.

After more than 30 years of rapid growth, the Chinese economy is now transitioning from high-speed to high-quality development. Faced with this new situation, the CPC Central Committee with Xi Jinping as its core put forward the new concepts of development of innovation, coordination, green, openness and sharing. The 19th National Congress of the Communist Party of China further proposed that under the guidance of these new concepts of development, we should change the mode of our development, optimize our economic structure, transform the growth driver and build a modern economic system, and take these measures as strategic decisions to achieve economic transformation and strategic goals for China's long-term development. Such new concepts, practice and development are bound to become new opportunities for international cooperation.

First of all, high-quality development can provide Chinese people with a high quality of life, thus providing a high-demand market with a population of more than 1.3 billion for global economic development. Socialism with Chinese characteristics has entered a new era. President Xi Jinping has a very popular answer to what this "new era" is. He said that in the past, we had to solve the problem of "growth out of nothing", but now we face the problem of "how to become better". In other words, the "new era" is an era that meets the people's longing for a better life. If more than 1.3 billion people can live a well-off life, what a great demand and market would be created! When China contributes such a big market to the world, isn't it a great opportunity for the development of international cooperation?!

Second, the new concepts of development of innovation, coordination, green, openness and sharing can realize the development of the Chinese economy in an all-around manner, thus providing new opportunities for entrepreneurs from all over the world to invest in China. Whether it is innovation, coordination, green, openness or sharing, every new concept of development can be a big chapter for development. The authors of these chapters are the Chinese people and their friends. Every insightful entrepreneur and investor can seize the opportunity to write their own wonderful chapter.

Third, because China must build a modern economic system to implement new concepts of development, there is room for making great achievements in promoting international cooperation. When planning future economic development, the 19th National Congress of the Communist Party of China proposed a brand-new strategic goal, which is to build a modern economic system. The key elements of this economic system can be described as follows: First, insisting on quality first and benefits foremost and taking the supply-side structural reform as the main thread; second, accelerating the construction of an industrial system for coordinated development; and third, building an economic system with effective market mechanisms, prospering microscopic entities and proper macroeconomic regulations. China will build such a modern economic system with an open attitude and benefit all countries of the world in a wider range of international cooperation.

In summary, the new concepts of development of innovation, coordination, green, openness and sharing proposed by the Communist Party of China after that of socialism with Chinese characteristics entered a new era began a new practice of socialism with Chinese characteristics in that new era. The new concepts and practice of development provide rare new opportunities for international cooperation between China and other countries in the world.

从三个数字深入理解"一带一路"倡议

李永辉 【中国】
北京外国语大学国际关系学院院长 / 中国和平统一促进会理事 / 中华美国学会常务理事

首先，我谈谈中国文化很有意思的一个现象。

大家今天看中国，发现中国发展得非常快，很多东西都是新的，例如高楼大厦、高速公路、高铁、基础设施等外在的表现，可以说是日新月异。同时，大家也能够感受到现代中国人都喜欢新的东西……正是这样，中国的新时代包括了理念的创新和发展，大家到处看到的都是新、新、新！

如果回头看一下100年前，无论西方还是中国自身，人们在谈论什么呢？一位法国学者写了一本名为《停滞的帝国》的著作，认为当时中国的发展已经进入了停滞陷落期。"五四"新文化运动对中国传统文化进行无情的批判，认为这种文化是一种封闭保守的守旧文化，甚至提出了"打倒孔家店"的口号。这种百年前后的对比，反映了一个很有意思的现象。

人们都在谈创新，而今天本组论坛的主题恰恰也是"中国发展的新理念与国际合作新前景"。我简单回顾和梳理一下"中国发展新理念"提出的过程。实际上，这个理念是2015年10月在中共十八届五中全会上首次提出来的，当时的表述是这样的："全会强调实现十三五时期发展目标，破解发展难题，发挥发展优势，牢固树立并且切实贯彻创新、协调、绿色、开放、共享的发展理念。"所以，中国发展的新理念实际就是创新、协调、绿色、开放和共享。

但是，我想以自己的专业背景换一个角度来谈这个问题，主要是从新时代中国外交的创新理念谈起。自从中共十八大以后，以习近平总书记为核心的新一届中国领导集体在对外工作上便进行了一系列的重大理论和实践创新，形成了新时代中国特色社会主义的外交思想。在前不久举行的中央外事工作会议上，将此概括为"习近平外交思想"。

习近平外交思想的内容非常丰富，也有很多的具体表现。我没有办法全面地逐一进行介绍。那么我就从以下几个方面与大家共同分享我的一些了解、理解和体会。

首先，中国外交创新理念最重要的就是"人类命运共同体"的提法。作为一种理念，其本身当然是比较抽象的，但也是具体的和非常现实的。进行一个简单的梳理我们便会发现，中国外交创新理念的提出和形成实际上是有一个过程的。最早是2015年在博鳌"亚洲论坛"的年会上，习近平主席提出了推动建设"人类命运共同体"的四点主张。也是在这一年，在联合国成立70周年的系列峰会上，习近平主席系统地阐述了打造"人类命运共同体"的五大路径。2017年在日内瓦的一次演讲中，习近平主席再次讲述了构建"人类命运共同体"的五大行动。同年，在联合国安理会的会议上，构建"人类命运共同体"的理念，首次被载入联合国安理会的决议。这之后的2017年。在中国共产党十九次代表大会中，习近平总书记在其报告的第12部分，专门谈及中国外交的问题，指出中国外交主题就是"坚持和平发展道路，推动构建人类命运共同体"。2018年3月，在新一届全国人民代表大会上，推动构建"人类命运共同体"又被写入中国的《宪法》。由此我们看到其形成的一个过程，并且成为了中国外交的核心理念。

构建"人类命运共同体"概念的具体内容是什么呢？在不同时期的表述是有些差异的，可以五个方面进行概括，也就是构建"人类命运共同体"包括的五个"要"。

第一个，持久和平，要互相尊重、平等、协商、要摒弃冷战思维，强权政治，要结伴而不结盟，走国与国交往的新路。

第二个，普遍安全，要坚持以对话解决争端、以协商化解分歧，统筹应对传统和非传统安全威胁，反对一切形式的恐怖主义。

第三个，共同繁荣，要同舟共济，促进贸易和投资自由化、便利化，推动经济全球化朝着更加开放、包容、普惠、共赢的方向发展。

第四个，开放包容，要尊重世界文明的多样性，以文明交流超越文明隔阂，文明互鉴超越文明冲突，文明共存超越文明优越。

第五个，清洁美丽，要坚持环境友好，合作应对气候变化，保护好人类赖以生存的地球家园。

我认为，人类命运共同体的理念主要包含上述五个方面。

与此相联系的同样是一个新的概念，叫做建立新型的国际关系，尤其包括新型的大国关系。

新型国际关系以及包括新型的大国关系，最初是2013年3月习近平同志刚刚担任国家主席、首次出访俄罗斯的时候，提出来了要建立和推动合作共赢的新型国际关系。所以，新型国际关系理念的核心内容叫做合作共赢，这是两个理念性的思想。

在具体的路径上，一个很重要的内容是中国积极参与的全球治理。全球治理本身并不是中国提出来的新概念，但在当今世界，中国在提倡新型的全球治理方面却是非常积极的，并将其看作是中国融入世界以及与世界各国合作的一条主要路径。

在这里我再引用习近平主席的一段话，2018年4月8日，习近平主席在会见联合国秘书长古特雷斯时说："国际上的问题林林总总，归结起来就是处理好治理体系和治理能力的问题，我们需要不断推进和完善全球治理，应对好这一挑战。"所以，全球治理是应对当今世界各种挑战的非常重要的途径之一。我认为，也是中国外交的核心内容之一。中国深度参与全球治理，倡导并践行新型的全球治理观。具体的表现包括维护联合国在处理国际和平与安全事务中的核心地位和主渠道作用。支持20国集团在全球治理中发挥主要平台的作用。支持亚太经合组织等多边国际组织在国际治理中发挥作用，促使国际秩序和国际体系朝着更加合理的方向发展。推动加强"金砖国家"机制的建设。推动提升新型国家和发展中国家在国际治理体系中的作用和话语权……我认为，上述都是中国参与和推动建立新型国际治理体系的重要内容，也是新时代中国外交的重要内容。以上的种种理念、路径，相对来说可能比较宏观，有些甚至比较抽象；因为，理念本身就是抽象的。

中国外交实践操作层面有很多具体的抓手，很多可操作实践的政策和举措，其中最主要的就是大家熟悉的"一带一路"倡议，在此我顺便补充解释一下。

"一带一路"倡议在国际上被很多人称作"一带一路"战略。其实，我们从来不认为也不说"一带一路"是一项战略，我们的提法是"一带一路"倡议。对于"一带一路"倡议的出现，我做一个简单的回顾。2013年9月，习近平主席访问哈萨克斯坦的时候，最先提出了"丝绸之路经济带"的理念，这是"一带"提出的最初时间。同年10月，习近平主席访问印度尼西亚时提出了建设"海上丝绸之路"的倡议，也就是所谓的"一路"，2013年11月，将两个概念合在一起统称为"一带一路"倡议。实际上，这是在不同的时间和不同的地点被分别提出来的，现在概括为"一带一路"倡议。

在此我与大家共同分享"一带一路"的具体表述，中国官方的正式表述是这样的："加快同周边国家和区域基础设施的互联互通，推进'丝绸之路经济带''海上丝绸之路'建设，形成全方位、开放的新格局。"这就是中国官方的表述，我就该表述中很重要的两点特别地予以突出强调：

现在大家都在问"一带一路"倡议到底是什么？它的核心是什么？其实，这个表述讲得已经非常清楚了，那就是"互联互通"。

另外，"一带一路"倡议是中国新时代改革开放的体现，我称之为2.0版的开放。中国改革开放40周年，主要体现在两个方面，即对内的改革和对外的开放。但最早1.0版的开放，却是中国向外部世界开放自己，把外面先进的理念引进来，主要是西方国家的先进经验。我所在的北京外国语大学，当时将其称为"把世界介绍给中国"，这就是1.0版的开放。现在新的以"一带一路"为核心的新开放，实际上是中国自身要"走出去"，相应的说法就是"把中国介绍给世界"，不仅介绍给世界，中国更要走向世界；所以，我认为这是一个2.0版的开放，也叫全方位开放的新格局。

昨天我与一些外国朋友进行讨论，尽管这些朋友都是汉学家，也都是"中国通"，许多人研究中国数十年，可以说对中国已经非常熟悉和非常了解了，但他们仍然在问，"一带一路"到底是怎么回事？到底有哪些内容？所以，在这里我与大家做一个分享，我从下述三个数字谈谈"一带一路"倡议。

首先是"六"，即"六大经济走廊"。大家都在说的"一带一路"倡议，实际上是一个较宏观的粗线条说法，常常被分别理解为海上和陆上的一条干线。其实，所谓的"一带"，即"丝绸之路经济带"是由"六大经济走廊"构成的，具体包括：

第一，中蒙俄经济走廊，其中又包括两条支线，一是从中国腹地通过蒙古国到俄罗斯；另一条则是从中国东北到俄罗斯的传统走廊，历史上称作"草原丝绸之路"。即在我们通常所称的"丝绸之路"之外，实际上还有一个"北方丝绸之路"或叫"草原丝绸之路"，也就是现在的"中蒙俄经济走廊"。

第二，"新亚欧大陆桥"，即从中国东部沿海的连云港穿越中国北方腹地，然后直到中亚，再进一步延伸到欧洲鹿特丹港的国际大通道。

第三，"中国－中南半岛经济走廊"，该走廊东起珠三角地区，沿南广高速公路、南广高铁，经南宁、河内至新加坡，将中国的华南地区与东南亚的陆上国家连接起来。

第四，"中巴经济走廊"，具体涉及中国和巴基斯坦，其起点在中国新疆的喀什，终点在巴基斯坦的瓜达尔港。

第五，"孟中印缅经济走廊"，从中国云南省的昆明到缅甸、印度、再到孟加拉的连接中国西南地区与南亚国家，通向印度洋的国际通道。

第六，"中国－中亚－西亚经济走廊"，其起点也是从中国新疆地区开始，是通过中亚五国，到西亚和波斯湾的国际通道。从这里，还可以再进一步延伸到欧洲。

所以，"一带一路"倡议具体来说，还有上面提到的六条经济走廊。

这六大经济走廊的建设发展是不平衡的，也存在着各种各样的问题，却是中国"一带一路"建设的核心内容。

其次是"五"，即"五通"。第一个便是"政策沟通"，狭义上的"一带一路"沿线国家有 60 多个，广义上其涵盖面就更广了，如此众多的国家相互之间需要政策的协调配合，这就是"政策沟通"。第二个叫"设施联通"，是"一带一路"建设的核心概念，也就是互联互通。例如，从中国腹地四川和成都开往欧洲的班列，甚至从更长远的目标来说，还要建设从中国到欧洲的高铁，通过铁路、公路的网络，把欧亚大陆连接起来，这就叫"设施联通"。至于第三个"贸易畅通"，大家都比较容易理解，就是推动贸易自由化、便利化的建设，促进沿线国家之间的贸易合作，特别是贸易自由化。第四个则是"资金融通"，大家都知道"一带一路"倡议是一个宏大的设想，特别是基础设施的建设需要大量的资金，很多人说我们已投入的资金达到了上万亿美元的规模，而这正是"资金融通"。第五个是"民心相通"，也就是我们特别强调的人文交流，包括这次的论坛会议，实际上就是"民心相通"的重要表现之一。在中国大家经常说，"国之交在于民相亲，民相亲在于心相通"。因为心相通是其他各"通"的基础和最深刻的表现。这就是所谓的"五通"。

再次是"四",即"四个资金池"。前面说到"资金融通",其融资量是十分巨大的,因此需要动员方方面面的力量,包括从政府到企业乃至民间的投资。在最初的启动阶段,中国作为发起国,发挥了主要的作用,其中一个重要的方面就是发起和主导建立了四个"资金池",包括最著名也是大家最熟悉的"亚投行",即亚洲基础设施建设投资银行,英文缩写为AIIB。"亚投行"的注册资金是1000亿美元,是支持"一带一路"建设的主干性银行,总部设在北京。第二个是"金砖国家组织"开发银行,总部设在上海,其资金也是1000亿美元。第三个是上海合作组织开发银行,该银行仍在筹建过程中,但从长远来看,其作用和意义不可小视。第四个叫做"丝路基金",其现在的资金量是400亿美元。这4个被称作"资金池"的机构,都是银行或基金,也都是为"一带一路"建设提供融资支持的金融机构。

从上面提到的数字来看,四个"资金池"的总资本不到3000亿美元,与相关专家估计的总体约10万亿美元的资金量相比,似乎是微不足道的,但在初期的建设过程中,其发挥的启动性和种子资金的作用却是不可替代的。所以,这四个"资金池"是建设"一带一路"不可或缺的经济和金融基础。

通过"六、五、四"的具体介绍,也许大家已经感受到"一带一路"倡议不再那么抽象了,特别是有了一些数字概念。当然,其中还有很多更具体和更细节的内容,在此就无法一一介绍了。

最后,我想再回到中国文化的话题上来。其实,中国文化很重要的一个特征,就是其非常辩证。中国文化主流的儒家思想,确实具有强调等级、秩序和传统等内容的保守性,但同时,中国文化又是讲求创新的,中国最古老的诗歌集《诗经》中,便有"周虽旧邦,其命维新"的诗句,儒家经典《礼记·大学》更提出了"苟日新,日日新"的思想,说明中国文化自身也讲求与时俱进。所以,我们便会看到当今中国很有意思的一种情况,那就是100年前,西方认为中国陷入了停滞落后的封闭保守状态,但今天人们看到的却是,美国要退群了,英国要脱欧了,贸易保护主义在全世界,包括发达国家的主体——美欧都很盛行。这时候反而是中国站出来讲创新、讲贸易自由化,高举全球化的旗帜。我认为这是一个很有意思的现象,体现了中国文化中既有保守的因素,同时也不乏创新的文化基因。

另外，中国文化特别讲求辩证。这个辩证的另一个表现就是，在困难的时候，我们会看到比较乐观和光明的方面，而当处于比较顺利，特别是一帆风顺的时候，传统文化又会警示我们注意防范种种潜在的风险，不要被胜利冲昏头脑。在经历了40年的高速发展之后，中国已经成为世界第二大经济体，中国内部也有人思想有些膨胀，出现了"厉害了，我的国"等提法。但是，我想中国的主流社会对此有清醒的认识，也有反省和反思的能力。我们意识到，在这样的时候，恰恰要注意要防止骄傲自大、过于膨胀，要注意谦虚谨慎，戒骄戒躁。我认为，这正是中国文化的两面性，是其非常辩证的特点。这也是我希望与大家共同分享的一点看法。

（本文系根据座谈会速记稿整理，内容已经作者本人确认）

An In-depth Understanding of the Belt and Road Initiative from Three Figures

Li Yonghui/ China

Director of the School of International Relations and Diplomacy, Beijing Foreign Studies University / Council Member of the China Council for the Promotion of Peaceful National Reunification / Executive Member of the Chinese Association of American Studies

First of all, I would like to talk about a very interesting phenomenon in Chinese culture.

Today's China is developing very fast. Many things are new, such as high-rise buildings, highways, high-speed railways, infrastructure, etc. It can be said it is changing with each passing day. At the same time, everyone can feel that modern Chinese people like new things... Just for this reason, China's new era includes innovations to and development of ideas. Everyone sees new, new and new everywhere!

Looking back 100 years ago, either in the West or in China, what did people talk about? A French scholar wrote a book entitled "*L'Empire Immobile*", which argued that China's development had already entered a period of stagnation and collapse. The "May Fourth" Movement ruthlessly criticized the traditional Chinese culture as a conservative and old-fashioned culture, and they even called for "overthrowing Confucius". This contrast with one hundred years ago reveals a very interesting phenomenon.

Everyone is talking about innovation, and the theme of the forum today is also the "new concepts for China's development and new prospects of international cooperation". I will briefly review the process of putting forward the "new concepts for China's development". In fact, this concept was first proposed at the Fifth Plenary Session of the 18th CPC Central Committee in October 2015. The statement was: "It was stressed that China should highlight and implement the concepts of innovation-driven development, balanced development, green development, open development and development for all, in order to fulfill the goals of the 13th Five-Year period, overcoming obstacles and sharpening its edge in development." Therefore, the new concepts for China's development are actually innovation, balance, green, openness and sharing.

However, I would like to talk about this issue from a different perspective according to my professional background, that is, innovations in Chinese diplomacy in the new era. Since the 18th National Congress of the Communist Party of China, the new Chinese leadership with General Secretary Xi Jinping as the core has carried out a series of major theoretical and practical innovations in diplomacy and created the diplomatic thoughts of socialism with Chinese characteristics in the new era. At the Central Foreign Affairs Working Conference held not long ago, this was summarized as "Xi Jinping's diplomatic thoughts".

Xi Jinping's diplomatic thoughts have very abundant content with many concrete manifestations that cannot be introduced one by one. Now I will share some of my knowledge, understanding and experience from the following aspects.

First of all, the most important innovative concept of China's diplomacy is the "community with a shared future for mankind". As a concept, it is of course abstract, but it is also concrete and very realistic. After a simple review, we can find that there is a process in the formulation and formation of the innovative concept of China's diplomacy. At the annual conference of the Boao Forum for Asia in 2015, President Xi Jinping made a four-point proposal to promote the building of a "community with a shared future for mankind". In the same year, at the series of summits celebrating the 70th anniversary of the United Nations, President Xi Jinping systematically explained the five major paths for building a "community with a shared future for mankind". In a speech in Geneva in 2017, President Xi Jinping once again described the five major actions of building a "community with a shared future for mankind". In the same year, at the UN Security Council meeting, the idea of building a "community with a shared future for mankind" was first included in the UN Security Council resolution. In 2017, at the 19th National Congress of the Communist Party of China, General Secretary Xi Jinping, in the 12th part of his report, specifically talked about China's diplomatic issues and pointed out that China's diplomatic theme is "to adhere to the path of peaceful development and promote the building of a community with a shared future for mankind". In March 2018, at the new National People's Congress, the building of the "community with a shared future for mankind" was written into China's Constitution. This is the process of its formation and how it became the core concept of Chinese diplomacy.

What is the specific content of the concept of building a "community with a shared future for mankind"? The expressions in different periods are somewhat different, but the concept can be summarized in five aspects, that is, five "adherences" included in the building of a "community with a shared future for mankind".

First, for a long-lasting peace, we must adhere to mutual respect, equality and consultation, abandon the mentality of the Cold War and power politics, and take a new road of partnerships without alliances among countries.

Second, for universal security, we must adhere to resolving disputes through dialogue, overcoming differences through consultation, cope with the traditional and non-traditional security threats together and oppose terrorism in all its forms.

Third, for common prosperity, we must adhere to cooperation to promote the liberalization and facilitation of trade and investments and drive economic globalization towards a more open, inclusive and win-win direction that benefits all people.

Fourth, to become open and inclusive, we must adhere to the respect for the diversity of civilizations in the world, exchanges to transcend civilizations, learn from each other rather than by a clash of civilizations and give priority to coexistence of civilizations rather than the sense of superiority.

Fifth, to be clean and beautiful, we must adhere to environmental friendliness, cooperate to cope with climate changes and protect our home on earth in which human beings are surviving.

From my point of view, the concept of the community with a shared future for mankind mainly includes the above five aspects.

A new concept associated with this is called the building of a new model of international relations, especially including the new model of big power relations.

The new model of international relations, including big power relations, was put forward by President Xi Jinping in March 2013 when paying a first visit to Russia after his inauguration. He proposed building and promoting a new model of international relations of cooperation and a win-win situation. Therefore, the core content of the new concept of international relations is called cooperation and win-win results. These are two conceptual ideas.

In terms of a specific path, a very important content is China's active participation in global governance. Global governance itself is not a new concept proposed by China, but in today's world, China is very active in promoting a new model of global governance and regards it as a major path for China's integration into the world and cooperation with countries around the world.

Here I will quote President Xi Jinping's remarks. On April 8, 2018, when President Xi Jinping met with the United Nations Secretary-General Guterres, he said, "There are a lot of problems in the world, which come down to the governance system and capabilities. We need to continuously promote and improve global governance to cope with this challenge." Hence, global governance is one of the most important paths to follow in order to cope with the challenges faced by today's world. I presume that it is also one of the core contents of Chinese diplomacy. China is deeply involved in global governance and advocates the implementation of new concepts for global governance. Specific embodiments include maintaining the core position and channel role of the United Nations in safeguarding international peace and security, supporting the G20's role as a main platform for global governance, providing support for APEC and other multilateral international organizations to play a role in international governance, driving the development of the international order and international system in a more rational direction, strengthening the construction of the "BRICS" mechanism and enhancing the role and voice of emerging countries and developing countries in the international governance system... In my opinion, all of them are important contents of China's participation in and promotion of a new international governance system, and also important aspects of China's new international diplomacy. The above concepts and paths may be somewhat macroscopic, or even abstract; because the concepts themselves are abstract.

There are many specific actions, policies and initiatives at the operational level of China's diplomatic practice, the most important of which is the Belt and Road Initiative that we are familiar with. I would like to explain it in more detail.

The Belt and Road Initiative is called the Belt and Road strategy by many people in the world. In fact, we never consider or see it as a strategy, but the Belt and Road Initiative. Let's take a look at how this initiative was proposed. In September 2013, when President Xi Jinping visited Kazakhstan, he put forward the concept of the "Silk Road Economic Belt" for the first time. It was the "Belt". In October of the same year, when President Xi Jinping visited Indonesia, he proposed the initiative of building a "Maritime Silk Road". It was called the "Road". In November 2013, the two concepts were combined to become the Belt and Road Initiative. In fact, they were proposed separately at different times in different locations, but now summarized as the Belt and Road Initiative.

Here, I would like to clarify the specific expression of the Belt and Road. The official expression of the Chinese government is: "Accelerating the construction of infrastructure connecting China with neighboring countries and regions, and working hard to build the Belt and Road, so as to break new ground in pursuing opening-up on all fronts." This is China's official expression. I will particularly highlight the two important points in the expression:

Now many people ask, "What is the Belt and Road Initiative? What is its core?" In fact, this expression already makes it very clear, that is, "connection".

Further, the Belt and Road Initiative reflects China's reform and opening-up in the new era. I call it the version 2.0 opening. The 40th anniversary of China's reform and opening-up is mainly reflected in two aspects, namely internal reform and external opening-up. However, the version 1.0 opening was that China opened itself to the outside world and introduced advanced concepts from outside, mainly the advanced experience of Western countries. At Beijing Foreign Studies University where I work, it was called "Introducing the World to China". That was the 1.0 opening version. Now the new opening with the Belt and Road as the core is actually China's "going out". It means introducing China to the world, not only introducing to, but also going out to the world; therefore, I think it is a 2.0 opening version, also called a new pattern of all-around opening-up.

Yesterday, I had a discussion with some foreign friends. They are sinologists who are very familiar with China. Although they understand China very well after decades of study on China, they still ask me, "What is the Belt and Road? What is the content?" So, here I would like to talk about the Belt and Road Initiative from the following three figures.

First, the "six economic corridors": Everyone is talking about the Belt and Road Initiative, which is actually a macroscopic concept, or a common thread. In addition to the Belt and Road Initiative, there are actually some branches, that is, "six economic corridors". These corridors include the China-Mongolia-Russia Economic Corridor that has two branch lines, one is from the hinterland of China to Russia through Mongolia and the other is the traditional corridor from northeast China to Russia, which was known as the "Prairie Silk Road" in history. Besides the usual "Silk Road", there is also a "Northern Silk Road" or the "Prairie Silk Road", which is actually the current "China-Mongolia-Russia Economic Corridor".

Second, the "New Eurasian Land Bridge": that is, from Lianyungang on the eastern coast of China, through the hinterland of northern China, then to Central Asia, and further extending to Europe.

Third, the "China-Indochina Peninsula Economic Corridor".

Fourth, the "China-Pakistan Economic Corridor": This corridor specifically involves China and Pakistan, starting from Kashgar in Xinjiang, China, and ending at Gwadar Port in Pakistan.

Fifth, the "Bangladesh-China-India-Myanmar Economic Corridor": This refers to the economic corridor from Kunming in southwestern China to Myanmar, India and Bangladesh.

Sixth, the "China-Central Asia-West Asia Economic Corridor": This also starts from Xinjiang in China, passes through five Central Asian countries, reaches Western Asia and the Persian Gulf, and then extends to Europe.

Therefore, the Belt and Road Initiative specifically includes these six economic corridors mentioned above.

The construction and development of the six economic corridors are unbalanced with various problems, but they are still the very specific contents of the construction of China's Belt and Road.

Another figure is called "Five Connections". First, "policy coordination". More than 60 countries along the Belt and Road need to coordinate and communicate with each other's policies. Second, "facilities connectivity", which is the core concept of the construction of the Belt and Road. For example, trains run from Chengdu, Sichuan in the hinterland of China to Europe. In the long term, high-speed railways will also be constructed from China to Europe and connect Eurasia through the network of railways and highways. The third connection is "unimpeded trade", which is easier to understand. It is nothing more than promoting the liberalization and facilitation of trade and advancing trade cooperation among countries along the route. The fourth aspect is "financial integration". As is known to us, the Belt and Road Initiative is a grand vision that needs a lot of money for the construction of infrastructures. Some people claim that more than trillions of dollars have been invested. This is the reflection of "financial integration". Fifth, "people-to-people bond", that is, the cultural exchanges we pay special attention to, and our meeting on this forum is actually one of the important manifestations of the "people-to-people bond". There is a saying in China, "Friendship, which derives from close contacts among the people, holds the key to sound state-to-state relations." The most profound concept of "Five Connections" for the Belt and Road construction is the "people-to-people bond". These are the so-called "Five Connections".

"Financial integration" has a very specific meaning, that is, the investment of a lot of money. Investment requires the mobilization of all walks of life and countries. China, as the sponsor country, has made some contributions in the initial stage from the government to enterprises and private investment. Economists tell us that there are four "capital pools", the most famous one of which is the "Asian Infrastructure Investment Bank" or AIIB. The initial capital for this bank was 100 billion US dollars. The second capital pool is the "BRICS New Development Bank". The

Asian Infrastructure Investment Bank is headquartered in Beijing, and the BRICS Bank is headquartered in Shanghai also with a capital of 100 billion US dollars. The third capital pool is the Shanghai Cooperation Organization Development Bank. The fourth capital pool is called the Silk Road Fund currently with a capital of about 40 billion US dollars. These four institutions, known as "capital pools", are banks or funds providing financial support for the construction of the Belt and Road.

From the figures mentioned above, the total capital is less than 300 billion US dollars. According to the estimated amount of 10 trillion yuan, they are insufficient for meeting the huge needs of the construction of the Belt and Road. However, in the initial promotion and start-up process, they can still play a very important role. Therefore, I suppose that these four "capital pools" are very important specific contents for the the construction of the Belt and Road.

After the specific introduction of "Six, Five and Four", perhaps the Belt and Road Initiative is no longer abstract, with the especially specific content. Of course, there are a lot of more specific and more detailed contents.

Finally, I would like to look back on the topic of Chinese culture. In fact, one of the most important features of Chinese culture is dialectics. Confucianism, which is the mainstream of Chinese culture, does have some kind of conservatism because it lays stress on content with a conservative nature such as hierarchy and order; but Chinese culture also attaches importance to innovation. In the "Book of Songs", there are ideas such as "Zhou is an old state, but its mission/mandate is always renewing" and "If you can one day renovate yourself, do so from day to day". This means that Chinese culture also strives to keep up with the times. Therefore, we can observe a very interesting phenomenon in China today. That is, 100 years ago, the West argued that China was in a closed and conservative state of stagnation and backwardness, but today the United States of America intends to withdraw, the United Kingdom is leaving the European Union and trade protectionism is prevalent throughout the world, including developed countries - the United States and Europe.

Instead, China stands out in talking about innovation and trade liberalization and holding high the banner of globalization. I think this is a very interesting phenomenon because there are both conservative factors and innovative genes in Chinese culture.

Moreover, Chinese culture pays special attention to the dialectics. It means that in the times of difficulty, we will see an optimistic and bright future. In the times of rapid or even prosperous development, Chinese culture lays stress on problems to be alert to. Now China is growing fast and has become the second-largest economy. Some people in China have become too proud with the thoughts of "great, my country". However, the mainstream has a clear idea of facts and the ability of self-reflection. At this stage, we must be alert to arrogance and exaggerations and maintain an attitude of modesty and prudence. In my opinion, this is the duality of Chinese culture that reflects the very dialectical feature. This is also the point I hope to share with you.

上海在新一轮对外开放中的桥头堡作为

王振 【中国】
上海社会科学院副院长

我来自于中国上海，今天向大家介绍一下上海这座伟大城市在中国新一轮的开放中都做了一些什么？并且产生了哪些积极的作用？

众所周知，2018 年是中国改革开放 40 周年。在 40 年的迅猛发展中，中国取得了巨大的成功，而其中非常重要的一项经验，就是我们不断地实行对外开放，而且这种开放正在进入新一轮的扩大阶段。

所谓新一轮的扩大开放有什么标志呢？经过简单的梳理，我们发现了 3 个标志：第一个标志是高标准地接轨国际规则。也就是说，国际上通用什么规则，中国都是以高标准进行对接的。第二个标志是发展更高层次的开放型经济。所谓"更高层次"是指中国在更多的产业领域和市场领域的全球性开放，包括更多的中国企业"走出去"参与到各个国家的经济建设与发展之中。第三个标志是中国将深度参与全球经济治理之中，包括习近平总书记倡导的"人类命运共同体"建设。

在新一轮的对外开放中，上海若干年前就已经启动了。今天就"上海样本"我主要谈 3 点：首先是 2013 年 9 月经国务院正式批准，上海设立中国（上海）自由贸易试验区，就是上海先于全国进入新一轮对外开放阶段的标志。相信在座的各位专家对"自贸区"都已经比较了解啦。值得关注的是 2013 年 9 月份我们给出的是 1.0 版方案，2015 年 4 月份给出了 2.0 方案，2017 年又给出了 3.0 方案，而最近正在研究的是 4.0 版的方案。5 年中上海给出了 3 个版本，而且全都是升级版，说明我们的事业正在逐步地推进，而且推进的速度很快。最初是 28 平方公里先行先试，第二年便拓展至上海 120 平方公里的更大区域，同时也是上海浦东最好的地区，如陆家嘴、张江等，全部进入了"自贸区"的试验范围；更为重要的是先后在广东省、天津市、福建省再行设立了 3 个"自贸区"试验点。

到 2017 年的 3 月份，"自贸区"的新版本全国范围内又增至 7 个点的试验区，包括人们一度认为对外开放相对滞后的中西部地区如武汉、重庆等城市，也都相继推进了"自贸区"的试验。更为值得一提的是，2018 年新增的中国（海南）自由贸易试验区，并且提出了要在海南省打造自由贸易港的设想；其实，上海 2017 年底已经开始研究自由贸易港的事情了，而现在由海南省先行先试，接下来上海便会逐步地推进发展。

自由贸易区试验中值得梳理的改革措施主要有 4 项，第一项是投资管理制度的改革，主要是外商投资负面清单管理的新措施。所谓负面清单，就是外资不准入或有限制行业的名单。为什么要有这样一个负面清单呢？是因针对不断扩大的市场对外开放，几乎每年都要出台新版本的负面清单，而最早的那个版本已经长至 140 多项了。但是从 2017 年开始，我们却不断地缩小这个负面清单的范围，现在缩小到仅 50 多项了。这说明了什么呢？说明我们在更多的产业领域实行对外资的开放。另外，我们也不断地深化上市速度的改革，让外资进入中国，使之办理一系列的相关手续更加简单而便捷。再者就是贸易便利化的举措，这也是探索国际贸易单一窗口很重要的一项改革，在座的专家都是"中国通"，尤其有些专家很是知道在中国办事情是有一点儿难度的，因为部门很多，条条框框很多，对此我们都在努力地进行改革，使需要多部门办理的事情全部集中于一个窗口快速办理完成。

上述种种，说明上海不断进行的改革，其间的力度非常之大，并且不断地在更多的区域推广先进的经验。

再有一个改革就是金融创新。金融创新是变更现有的金融体制和增加新的金融工具，以获取潜在利润的改革方式，是一个为盈利动机推动、缓慢进行、持续不断的过程。重要的契机是上海较早地建立了自由贸易账户体系。也就是说，如果到"自贸区"设立企业，就可以拥有自由贸易账户，通过此账户既可以使企业的资金"走出去"，也可以使外面的资金"走进来"。当然，这个账户是需要管理的，但至少我们建立了一个资金可以进出的较为公开的渠道。

我们积极推进的第四项改革，也是最难的改革，这就是"事中事后监管"。大家知道，在中国办企业，事前要经过很多关口的审批和许可。通过改革，现在事前的审批减少了，许可放宽了，但事中、事后却要加强监管，例如企业产品的质量、安全、诚信，等等，都是需要加强监管的。也就是说，一方面让市场起决定性的作用，另一方面政府还要发挥更好的作用；而政府发挥的正是这事中、事后的监管作用。上海正在逐步地建立这个体系，如上海自贸区在这些方面都走在了前面，而且很多经验已在全国各地进行了推广。

值得提及的还有 2016 年 3 月，国家提出努力把上海自贸区建设成为符合国家"一带一路"建设、推动市场主体走出去的"桥头堡"。近年来，在国际上引发最多关注的就是中国的"一带一路"倡议，在这个倡议中，国家布局上海要起到"桥头堡"的作用。什么叫"桥头堡"？首先，桥头就是指最前沿的区域，"堡"是指城堡，也就是提供保障的区域。"桥头堡"的提法，既是上海的地理区位决定的，同时更为关键的是上海作为最大的国际金融、贸易航运中心，最为开放的城市，其贸易条件、港口条件、金融条件……在国际上都处于领先地位，尤其上海背靠长三角城市群腹地的优势是无可比拟的。长三角城市群，是世界六大城市群之一，其周边的浙江、杭州、江苏、南京的经济水平，基本与上海同步，集聚众多的优秀企业，包括大量的外资企业。可以说，该区域已经形成了若干个具有全球影响力的产业集群，包括电子信息、汽车、家电、纺织、服装、造船，等等。对上海来说，这样好的条件应该在"一带一路"建设中发挥积极的作用。而这种积极作用，则主要体现在上海为伴随国家新的对外开放，众多已经走出去和即将走出去的中国企业提供服务，如金融、贸易、航运等全方位的服务。

另外，上海集中了大量跨国公司的中国总部，包括中国本土企业的上海总部。现在很多企业都有两个总部，一个总部可能在发源地如浙江、江苏，另外一个总部可能就设在上海，当然也有总部设在北京的企业。设在上海的企业总部的基本任务就是"走出去"，进行全球布局。所以，上海在这些企业的跨国投资以及中外合作中，可以发挥更加积极的作用，如很多外资企业从中国布局，然后布局东南亚，其中的上海总部总是发挥着积极的作用。

说到基础设施的投资和建设，上海的作为也是值得自豪的。上海修高速公路、修飞机场、修高铁、修地铁、修立交桥、建造超高层大楼……现在都已是世界一流的水平。所以，上海的基础设施建筑企业"走出去"，将会发挥很好的作用，也受到了很多国家的欢迎。因为其拥有技术先进、成本低廉等重要因素。还有一个重要的因素是，上海和世界各国的很多城市建立了各种名目的非常友好的交流关系，为上海的对外开放奠定了优良的基础。

2018年4月，习近平主席在博鳌亚洲论坛上宣布了中国扩大开放的一系列重大新举措。习近平主席的讲话引起了全球的关注。当然上海也更受关注。同时，我们也很兴奋，因为上海又可以在对外开放的道路上大胆地向前迈步了。上海提出坚持开放历史、开放心思，努力把上海打造成全国新一轮全面开放的新高地，服务"一带一路"建设的桥头堡，配置全球资源的亚太门户，中国走进世界舞台的重要战略支撑……实际上就是追求更高层次的开放型经济。

2018年7月10日，上海颁布的100条行动方案，也是向全世界发声进一步扩大开放的态度，这一开放举措的力度是值得人们记住的。主要有以下几个方面。首先，是更大力度地开放金融业，提升上海国际金融中心的能力，大幅度放宽外资进入银行业、保险业、证券业，相关限制则大幅度地放宽了，包括原来功能单一的自由贸易账户服务，也进一步地扩展了，以使更多的中外企业通过这一账户更加方便地流动资金；第二是服务业、制造业的进一步开放，包括汽车、飞机、造船，原来的开放度不高，如汽车的开放曾经必须中方控股，必须达到51%的股份，但最近美国"特斯拉"在上海投资，几乎都是由美方控股的，甚至持股达到100%，如此的开放力度非常之大。这是中国下大决心更加开放，让全球外资产业能够顺利进入中国。第三是经常被各国提到的中国知识产权保护较为落后的问题，对此，上海提出了建设高标准的知识产权保护高地，保护国外知识产权，更好地保护中国本土企业的知识产权；打造更具国际市场影响力的进口新平台，还有法治化、便利化、国际化的营商环境。

而2018年11月在上海举办的首届"中国国际进口博览会"，将会吸引全世界优质的商品和服务，构建覆盖全球的进口贸易促进网络和平台。所以，中国将更加开放，让全世界的资金、产业，包括各个国家的商品和服务，都可以进入中国，都可以在中国找到各自的市场和各自的需求，由此促进各个国家的共同发展，同时表明上海始终走在中国改革开放的最前沿。对于上海开放的样本，作为上海社科院的专家团队，我们要好好研究，我们也期待世界各国的中国问题专家研究上海样本。

成立于1958年的上海社会科学院2018年恰值60周年，上海社科院共有17

个研究所，770 名工作人员，我们向来自各国的中国文化专家、汉学家们热情地开放，欢迎你们经常到上海与我们共同进行交流，或者共同开展相关课题的研究。

（本文系根据座谈会速记稿整理，内容已经作者本人确认）

Shanghai: a Bridgehead in the New Round of Opening-up

Wang Zhen/ China

Deputy Dean of the Shanghai Academy of Social Sciences

As is known to us, the year 2018 marks the 40th anniversary of China's reform and opening-up. In the 40 years of rapid development, China has achieved great success. One of the most important experiences is that we are constantly opening up to the outside world, and this kind of opening is entering a new round of expansion.

What are the signs of the new round of expansion of our opening-up? After a brief summary, three signs are revealed: The first sign is the connection with international rules in high standards. In other words, China is connected with the rules recognized in the world by high standards. The second sign is the development of a higher level of an open economy. The so-called "higher level" refers to China's global opening up in more industrial fields and market sectors, including more Chinese enterprises "going global" to participate in the economic construction and development of countries. The third sign is that China will be deeply involved in global economic governance, including the building of a "community with a shared future for mankind" advocated by General Secretary Xi Jinping.

Shanghai launched the new round of opening-up a few years ago. Today, I would like to talk about three points on the "Shanghai Sample". First, after the official approval by the State Council in September 2013, the China (Shanghai) Pilot Free Trade Zone became a sign that Shanghai had entered a new round of opening-up. Our dear experts present here may have a clear idea of the "Free Trade Zone". It is worth noting that the 1.0 version of the plan was issued in September 2013, the 2.0 version of the plan was released in April 2015, the 3.0 version of the plan was promulgated in 2017, and now we are studying the 4.0 version. In the past five years, Shanghai has contributed three versions, all of which were upgraded versions. This meant that our work gradually advanced and the speed of advancement was very fast. Initially, it was piloted in a land area of 28 square kilometers. In the second year, it expanded to a larger area of 120 square kilometers in Shanghai, also the best area in Shanghai Pudong, such as Lujiazui and Zhangjiang, both of which were included in the free trade zone. More importantly, three "pilot free trade zones" were further established in Guangdong, Tianjin and Fujian.

By March 2017, in the new version of the "Free Trade Zone", seven pilot zones were added, including the central and western regions where the opening-up had lagged behind relatively in the past, such as Wuhan and Chongqing. It is worth mentioning that the China (Hainan) Pilot Free Trade Zone added in 2018 proposed to construct a free trade port in Hainan Province. In fact, Shanghai had begun to study the free trade port at the end of 2017. Now Hainan Province will be the first pilot region, and then Shanghai will gradually achieve development.

There are four important reform measures in pilot free trade zones. First of all, the reform of the investment management system, which is mainly the management of foreign investments by a negative list. The so-called negative list is a catalogue of industries that are prohibited from entry or have restrictions for foreign investors. Why do we implement such a negative list? With the expansion of market opening, new versions of negative lists are released almost every year because the earliest version has already increased to more than 140 items. However, since 2017, we have begun to narrow the scope of this negative list, and now it has shrunk to just over 50 items. What does this mean? It means that we are opening more industrial sectors for foreign investors. Second, we are constantly deepening the reform of public listing so that more foreign capital can enter China after a series of simpler and more convenient formalities. Third, the measures for facilitating trade. This is also a very important reform to explore a single window of international trade. Our dear experts present here are all "China Hands". In particular, some experts know that it is a little difficult to do something in China because there are too many authorities with a lot of rules and regulations. We are working hard to introduce reforms, so the formalities that need to be handled by multiple authorities can be quickly completed at a single window.

The signs mentioned above mean that Shanghai is constantly reforming with great efforts and is broadening its valuable experience to more regions.

Fourth, the reform of financial innovation. Financial innovation is a reform method that changes the existing financial system and adds new financial instruments to seek potential profits. It is a process that is driven by profit motives, slow but continuous. An important opportunity is that Shanghai had established the free trade account system early on. That is to say, any enterprise set up in the "Free Trade Zone" can have a free trade account. With this account, the enterprise's fund can "go out" and external funds can "come in". Of course, this account needs to be managed, but at least we have an open channel through which funds can come in and go out.

The fourth reform we are actively pushing through is also the most difficult reform. It is the "overseeing both during and after the handling of matters". As we all know, in China, enterprises must go through many approvals and permits beforehand. After the reform, the approvals were reduced and the permits have been relaxed. However, it is necessary to strengthen overseeing both during and after the handling of matters, such as quality, safety and integrity of products, etc., the overseeing of which needs to be strengthened. That is to say, for one thing, the market plays a decisive role, and for another, the government has to play a better role; and the government is playing the role of overseeing both during and after the handling of matters. Shanghai is gradually establishing this system. For example, the Shanghai Free Trade Zone has taken the lead in these aspects, and many of its experiences are being promoted throughout the country.

It is worth mentioning that in March 2016, the state proposed to build the Shanghai Free Trade Zone into a "bridgehead" for the construction of the Belt and Road and driving market entities to go global. In recent years, the Belt and Road Initiative has attracted much attention throughout the world. In the strategic layout of this initiative, Shanghai has to play the role of "bridgehead". What does the "bridgehead" mean? First of all, the bridgehead refers to the most advanced area and the area that provides protection. The positioning of "bridgehead" depends on Shanghai's geographical location. More importantly, being the largest international financial and trade shipping center and the most open city in China, Shanghai is in an internationally leading position in terms of trade conditions, port conditions, financial conditions… In particular, the geographical advantage of Shanghai backed up by the city cluster in the Yangtze River Delta is unparalleled. The Yangtze River Delta is one of the six largest city clusters in the world. The level of economic development of Hangzhou in Zhejiang and Nanjing in Jiangsu is basically synchronized with that of Shanghai and attracts many outstanding enterprises, including a large number of foreign-funded enterprises. It can be said that the region has formed a number of industrial clusters with global influence, including electronic information, vehicles, home appliances, textiles, clothing, shipbuilding, and so on. Shanghai, blessed with such good conditions, should play an active role in the construction of the Belt and Road. This active role is mainly reflected in Shanghai's provision of services for Chinese enterprises that have already gone global or are about to go global with the new opening up of China, such as finance, trade, shipping and other comprehensive services.

Moreover, Shanghai has concentrated a large number of Chinese headquarters of multinational companies, including local Chinese companies. Many companies now have two headquarters, one may be in the birthplaces such as Zhejiang and Jiangsu, and the other may be located in Shanghai. Of course, there are also companies based in Beijing. The basic mission of companies with headquarters in Shanghai is to "go global" for global deployment. Therefore, Shanghai can play a more active role in the cross-border investment of companies and Sino-foreign cooperation. For example, many foreign-funded enterprises originated from China and entered Southeast Asia. Their headquarters in Shanghai can play an active role.

Shanghai is also proud of its investments in and construction of infrastructures. In Shanghai, the highways, airports, high-speed railways, subways, overpasses, and super high-rise buildings … all of them are now world-class. Therefore, if "going global", the infrastructure construction enterprises of Shanghai can play a very good role and be welcomed by many countries because we have advanced technology, low costs and other important factors. Another important factor is that Shanghai and many cities around the world have established very friendly relations of exchanges, which lay an excellent foundation for Shanghai's opening-up.

In April 2018, at the Boao Forum for Asia, President Xi Jinping announced a series of new initiatives for China's expansion of its opening-up. President Xi Jinping's speech aroused global attention. Of course, Shanghai was no exception. Meanwhile, we are also very excited, because Shanghai can boldly move forward on the road of opening up to the outside world. Shanghai proposes to adhere to the history of openness and keeping an open mind as well as striving to build Shanghai into a new height for a new round of opening-up, a bridgehead for the construction of the Belt and Road, an Asia-Pacific gateway for global resources, and an important strategic support for China's entry onto the world stage… In fact, it is the pursuit of a higher level of an open economy.

On July 10, 2018, the action plans with 100 items promulgated by Shanghai reflected its attitude of further opening up to the world. This initiative of opening-up is worth remembering. It mainly includes the following aspects. First of all, the financial industry must be opened broader to strengthen the capacity of Shanghai as an international financial center, greatly relax restrictions over the entry of foreign investment in the fields of banking, insurance and securities, and further extend the original free-trade account with a single function so that more Chinese and foreign companies can easily manipulate funds through this account. Second, service and manufacturing sectors must be further opened, including vehicles, aircraft and shipbuilding. Originally, these sectors were not open enough. For example, the opening of vehicle manufacturing requires a holding of at least 51% of shares by the Chinese side. However, the recent investment of "Tesla" in Shanghai is fully controlled by the American side, which holds 100% of the shares. Such openness is very broad. This demonstrates China's determination to open wider and allow foreign capital to enter China smoothly. Third, China's protection of intellectual property rights is often criticized. In this regard, Shanghai proposes to reach the heights of high-standard intellectual property protection, safeguard foreign intellectual property rights and protect the intellectual property rights of Chinese local enterprises, build a new platform for importations with greater international market influence and create a convenient rule-of-law international business environment.

The first "China International Import Expo" held in Shanghai in November 2018 attracted high-quality goods and services throughout the world and build a global import promotion network and platform. Therefore, China will become more open so that global capitals and industries, including goods and services of various countries, can enter China. They can find their own markets and their respective needs in China, thereby promoting the common development of all countries. At the same time, it proves that Shanghai is always at the forefront of China's reform and opening-up. As a team of experts from Shanghai Academy of Social Sciences, we must pay attention to the research of Shanghai, a sample for opening-up. We also look forward to the research of Shanghai by experts of Chinese studies from all over the world.

Founded in 1958, Shanghai Academy of Social Sciences celebrated its 60th anniversary in 2018. We have 17 research institutes and 770 staff members. We are open to experts of Chinese culture and sinologists from all over the world. Welcome to China for exchanging ideas or jointly doing related research with us.

"一带一路"倡议与全球治理

张维为 【中国】
复旦大学中国研究院院长

非常高兴借此机会,向大家汇报自己研究"一带一路"倡议与全球治理的体会。

我从全球化和全球治理的角度切入,首先我们要研究的是,迄今在西方模式主导下的全球化存在什么问题?因为时间有限,我仅举两个例子。一个是全球化本身,另一个是互联网革命。在西方模式主导下怎么处理这两个问题。总的来讲,就是意识形态化与零合游戏。

首先是全球化,西方主导的全球治理下它是什么呢?是自由化、市场化、私有化、民主化。但从后来的结果我们看到,为什么出现了特朗普的崛起?出现了英国的脱欧?因为贫富差距的拉大,西方国家内部的中产阶级,多数没有享受到全球化的好处。当然,全球化在非西方世界也带来很多问题,特别是2008年的国际金融危机,很多国家的财富被华尔街席卷一空。

第二是互联网的革命。互联网崛起之后,西方特别是美国明确地把互联网作为所谓政权更替的工具,将其高度地政治化了,结果导致了一场又一场所谓的"颜色革命""阿拉伯之春"。今天,我们都知道"阿拉伯之春"已经变成了"阿拉伯之冬"。2011年"阿拉伯之春"爆发时,我是较早预测"阿拉伯之春"必定变成"阿拉伯之冬"的人。因为,这个运动水土不服,运动者是在搬起石头砸自己的脚。互联网本来就是一柄双刃剑,那些赞成英国脱欧的人,支持特朗普的人,都是不看 BBC 的，他们只看推特、脸书等。

那么，中国是怎么做的呢？首先，中国是去意识形态化。第二，中国是以人民为中心，以人民为整体。对于全球化，中国看到了它的利与弊，因此趋利避害。所以，对于经济全球化中国是赞成的，基本上是拥抱的，当然也有谨慎举措的方面，例如开放资本市场就是非常谨慎地，但总体上是拥抱经济全球化的。但对于政治全球化，我们则是拒绝的，且是非常明确拒绝的。对于西方的政治模式，如果你们喜欢，就管好你们自己的事情，我们明确地画了一条线，坚定地走中国特色社会主义道路，尽管这条路并不十全十美，但是成功了。中国通过全球化变成为数不多的全球化受益者之一。

对于互联网革命，中国也没有政治化。习近平主席明确指出，互联网使人民的生活变得更为方便，以人民的整体利益为出发点和皈依点，在中国引起一场真正的互联网革命。可以说，在互联网经济大潮裹胁下，中国是走在世界最前沿的国家之一。中国移动互联网是美国的 90 倍，世界上只有中国实现了一部手机全部搞定，给人民生活带来的巨大便利是超出人们想象的，也使中国在新一代包括人工智能、大数据等方面走在了世界的最前沿，我认为这是一件很好的事情。

至于"一带一路"倡议，中国也是这样的做法。

首先在整个"一带一路"的建设过程中，我们不搞意识形态，不以意识形态画线，不管社会主义、资本主义，还是其他什么主义，我们都欢迎，大家一起来做事情。我们的主要目标是以人民利益为导向，提高人民的生活水平，中国的经验就是"要致富，先修路"，"一带一路"建设不仅修路，包括方方面面人民生活水平的整体提高，工业化的进展，等等。我去了非洲的很多国家，西方老说你们（中国）为什么帮助非洲这些专制的国家？我说，错！中国帮助非洲国家消除贫困，消除贫困在中国模式中是第一。就像国际红十字会，救死扶伤，不论敌人还是朋友。扶贫也是一个道理。

第三，中国国内广泛实现的是每个单位的协商民主，我们在"一带一路"建设中叫做"共商、共建、共享"，只要你愿意加入，我们就非常欢迎，有事大家讨论解决，最后就是共建共享。你不想加入也没关系，待在外边也是可以的，这都是非常民主的方法。

对于互联网为代表的新技术革命，包括 AI、人工智能，等等，中国的态度是要给予最好的利用，同时它可能也会有副作用，我们便趋利避害，尽量把好的用足，坏的方面尽量减少。我认为，这种思路应该值得提倡。

中国在"一带一路"建设中也推动了很多高新科技的发展。有一个与我们合作较多的公司，在"一带一路"沿线国家发展了 11 亿的客户，每到一个国家便研究这个国家的特点，例如印度，印度人识字率较低，他就开发表情包，使得其手机销售得非常成功。到了非洲，由于非洲电力供应不足，它就待机时间长，这个功能让他有很大的收益，非常之成功，各种各样的案例，我们做了调查。原来没有想到，中国企业家很有创意，即使民营企业也做得很好。

对于习近平主席提出的构建"人类命运共同体"的观念，作为学者的我们也在考虑，怎么才能真正地把它落到实处？怎么才能够做起来呢？我们的想法是要建立利益会合点，而汉学家就是一个利益会合点，要建立各种各样的共同利益会合点，最终逐步铺平一条道路。两个月前我们与耶鲁大学做了一个论坛，一天的时间我们讨论了 10 个话题，复旦和耶鲁之间竟有这么多领域的合作，如此越来越多之后，就能够使我们人类社会逐步成功构建"人类命运共同体"了。

（本文系根据座谈会速记稿整理，内容已经作者本人确认）

The Belt and Road Initiative and Global Governance

Zhang Weiwei/ China

Director of China Institute, Fudan University

From the perspective of globalization and global governance, first of all, what are the problems so far existing in globalization dominated by the Western model? Due to the time limit, I will give only two examples. One is globalization itself, and the other is the Internet revolution. How can we cope with these two problems under the leadership of the Western model? In general, with ideology and zero-sum game.

The first issue is globalization. What is it under the global governance dominated by the West? It is liberalization, marketization, privatization and democratization. But why can Mr. Trump be elected? Why does the UK desire to leave the European Union? The reason is the widening gap between the rich and the poor and that most of the middle class within the Western countries cannot benefit from globalization. Of course, globalization also causes many problems in non-Western countries. Especially in the global financial crisis of 2008, the wealth of many countries has been swept away by Wall Street.

The second issue is the Internet revolution. After the rise of the Internet, the West, especially the United States of America, explicitly uses the Internet as a tool for regime changes and highly politicizes it. As a result, one after another, the so-called "Color Revolutions" and "Arab Spring" occur. Today, as is known to us, the "Arab Spring" has turned into the "Arab Winter". When the "Arab Spring" broke out in 2011, I was one of the early predictors that the "Arab Spring" would turn out to be the "Arab Winter". Because this movement was not localized, those who launched this campaign would definitely lose. The Internet itself is a double-edged sword. Those who favored the Brexit and those who supported Trump never watched BBC, but only followed Twitter, Facebook, and Instagram.

Then, what can China do? First of all, China is never ideological. Second, China is centered on the people and regards the people as a whole. For globalization, bearing its advantages and disadvantages in mind, China draws on the advantages and avoids disadvantages. China is in favor of and embraces economic globalization, but also takes cautious measures. For example, it is very cautious about opening up to the capital market. On the whole, China embraces economic globalization. However, for political globalization, we refuse and we clearly reject it. For the Western political model, if you like it, then mind your own business. We have clearly drawn a line and firmly follow the path of socialism with Chinese characteristics. Although this path is not perfect, it has succeeded. China is one of the few beneficiaries of globalization.

For the Internet revolution, China never politicizes it. President Xi Jinping clearly pointed out that the Internet has made people's lives more convenient and there should be a real Internet revolution in China with people's overall interests as the starting point and the point of convergence. It can be said that on the tide of the Internet economy, China is one of the countries at the forefront of the world. The mobile Internet in China is 90 times that in the United States. Only China has achieved the creation of a mobile phone that can do everything in our lives. The great convenience brought to people's lives is beyond imagination. It also enables

China to take the lead in new-generation technologies such as artificial intelligence and big data. I think it is very good for us.

As for the Belt and Road Initiative, China follows the same practice.

In the entire process of the Belt and Road, we have never talked about ideology, and we have never sided with other countries on terms of ideology. We embrace all countries, either adhering to socialism, capitalism or other *isms*, to go hand in hand together. Our main goal is to improve people's living standards according to the interests of the people. China's experience is "to get rich, you must build roads first". The construction of the Belt and Road not only builds roads, but also improves the living standards of people in an all-round manner, the progress of industrialization, and so on. I have been to many countries in Africa. Western countries always ask why we (China) help autocracies in Africa. I answer that you are wrong! China helps African countries to eradicate poverty, and the Chinese model is No.1 in poverty alleviation. Just like the International Committee of the Red Cross, to save the wounded, regardless of the enemy or friends. This is also true of poverty alleviation.

Third, what has been widely realized in China is the deliberative democracy of each unit. It is known as "jointly building through consultation to meet the interests of all" in the construction of the Belt and Road. As long as you are willing to join, you are welcome. We can consult with each other and finally jointly build to meet the interests of all. It doesn't matter if you don't want to join. It's okay to stay outside of it. This is a very democratic approach.

For the new technological revolution represented by the Internet, including artificial intelligence, etc., China's attitude is making the best use of it, but it may also have side effects. We draw on the advantages and avoid disadvantages to maximize the advantages and minimize the disadvantages. In my opinion, this practice is worthy of advocation.

China also promotes the development of high technologies in the construction of the Belt and Road. A company that cooperates with us has developed 1.1 billion customers in countries along the Belt and Road. It pays attention to the characteristics of each country it enters. For example, in India, Indians have a low literacy rate, so the company develops the package of facial expressions. This action leads to its success in mobile phone sales. In Africa, due to the lack of a supply of electricity, its mobile phones are equipped with high-power batteries that can be used for a long period of time. This function makes the company profitable. We have investigated various successful cases. It is beyond my imagination that Chinese entrepreneurs can be so creative, even private enterprises can do a good job.

As for the concept of building a "community with a shared future for mankind" proposed by President Xi Jinping, our scholars are also thinking about how we can put the concept into practice and how we can achieve it. Our idea is to set a convergence point of interests, and sinologists can be a convergence point. After a variety of points of convergence of common interests are established, we can pave a road. Two months ago, we attended a forum at Yale University. We discussed 10 topics in one day. There are so many areas of cooperation between Fudan and Yale. After more and more cooperation, we, as human beings, can build a "community with a shared future for mankind" step by step.

"说长道短""一带一路"建设

黄仁伟 【中国】
复旦大学"一带一路"与全球治理研究院常务副院长 / 上海社会科学院智库研究中心理事长兼主任

我的发言是"一带一路"从第一阶段进入第二阶段的一些思考。

2013年习近平主席分别在哈萨克斯坦和印度尼西亚提出了"一带"和"一路"两个倡议后,到现在已经整整5年了。我把这5年看作是"一带一路"建设发展的第一个阶段,而今后的5年或者10年则是其即将进入的第二个阶段。

让我们先看看"一带一路"建设第一个阶段已经取得的成就:首先,"一带一路"获得了130个国家的积极反应,特别是2017年5月举行了"一带一路"国际合作高峰论坛,多达130个国家的1500位嘉宾出席了这场高峰论坛,其中30个国家的政要元首、包括联合国秘书长都积极热情地出席了论坛。这是"一带一路"倡议第一次于世界范围举办的峰会,充分表明"一带一路"倡议得到了整个国际社会的广泛承认,也说明了绝大多数国家都是从正面理解"一带一路"伟大倡议的。

第二是"一带一路"倡议建立了相关的合作机制,其中最重要的就是亚洲基础设施投资银行的创建。建立亚洲基础设施投资银行,原计划是20个国家且以亚洲国家为主,但成立时竟然吸引到了57个国家;而这57个国家中有36个是亚洲国家,18个是欧洲国家,一个美洲国家,还有两个大洋洲的国家。其中,东盟的10个国家全部参加了,欧盟28个成员国中有14个成员国参加了,G20的20

个国家中有 14 个国家参加，金砖 5 国也都全部参加。所以，"亚投行"不再仅仅只是局限于亚洲的国际银行，而是为构建"一带一路"提供重要保障的金融合作机制。即使 G7 中没有加入"亚投行"的美国、日本、加拿大等国家，其内部如美国也还是存在很大争议的，有的人认为当时不加入"亚投行"是错误的。而联合国前官员、全球民间学者及国际组织，为了宣传中国领导人提出的"一带一路"合作倡议，将每年的 12 月 16 日作为国际日，这也是第一个源于中国、代表中国文化自信的国际日。从上述事例来看，"一带一路"倡议不仅在欧亚大陆，而且在更大的世界范围，获得了广泛的积极响应。

具体而言，"一带一路"建设已有项目大约 4000 个，直接投资大约已达 250 亿美元，从 2013 年到现在，平均每年增长的投资率是 30%。当然，投资金额中只有少量的或不超过三分之一的是官方和"亚投行"的作为，更多的部分都是民营企业的投资。"一带一路"建设中很重要的一个内容是中欧班列，即中国到欧洲的货运铁路，已经开通往返大约 3000 次的班列，带动了中国和沿线国家的贸易达到 350 亿美元。所以，无论"一带一路"建设的项目也好、贸易量也好、投资总量也好，这些数字在这 5 年中有如此数目量的增长，且是在"一带一路"项目启动开始的情况下，尤其 2013 年、2014 年舆论扩大影响的时段，以及 2015 年到现在的两年半间，便已经有了如此巨大的可喜发展。

进入第二阶段，我认为应该认真思考"一带一路"建设的不足之处，"一带一路"的短板甚至其风险，以及有哪些问题是需要注意和纠正的，有哪些问题是做得还不够好的，或者有哪些问题是国际社会还不太理解的。

第一点，"一带一路"倡议的概念比较空，所有国家知道这个名词但不知道它的具体内容，特别是大部分社会中下层人士对"一带一路"倡议的不了解。所以，它给人一种大而空的感觉。

第二点，虽说"一带一路"倡议有些大而空，但其发展却非常迅猛，原来准备的是 60 个左右的沿线国家，现在一下子达到了 130 个国家，原来说是在欧亚大陆，现在非洲、拉丁美洲都包括进来了，"一带一路"建设发展的速度太快了，我认为应该放慢一些速度。

第三点，"一带一路"倡议的官方项目即政府投资或政府援助项目的宣传过多，由此造成了一种假象，就像尼泊尔朋友刚才所讲的那样，以为"一带一路"是中国政府无偿援助的建设，实际上这是不可能的，"一带一路"建设主要是市场投资的项目，而且主要是非官方投资的项目。所以，这个概念在实际操作中还是有些问题的。

第四点，"一带一路"建设的规则远远还不到位，合同、融资方式，各自要尽的义务、责任等规则还都滞后，与其投资速度和贸易速度相比，都远远地跟不上需求。发达国家特别要求"一带一路"建设增加透明度，例如什么项目、什么投标、由谁负责，等等。

第五点，"一带一路"倡议的社会文化沟通尚属欠缺。人们过多地都把注意力放在投资项目上，但对投资项目的社会、文化因素却了解不多，刚才保加利亚朋友说其对中国文化不了解，但中国朋友对保加利亚、巴尔干文化却更不了解，在整个中国几乎没有几个人懂得巴尔干，他们人口5500万，这是一个不小的数字，但我们没有几个人了解。由于各种的不了解，也产生了很多的误解，甚至很多安全问题也接踵而至。

第六点，"一带一路"倡议不仅局限于我们所讲的这些国家，很重要的是让发达国家也愿意参与"一带一路"建设。最近，日本正在考虑假如"一带一路"建设。因为他们突然发现，从连云港到鹿特丹的运输时间是20天，但走好望角到欧洲的时间却需要50天，由此他们就可以省掉30天和60%的运输成本。

第七点，"一带一路"建设不仅仅只是修路，更重要的是建设产业带和经济开发园区，对产业带和园区大家注意的却很少，但是要知道，如果没有产业带和产业园区，修路还有什么用呢？

第八点，"一带一路"倡议还应该与当地国家自己的发展战略紧密结合，这里说的不是中国的战略，也不是中国的规划，而是当地国家如俄罗斯、哈萨克斯坦、印度尼西亚、伊朗、印度、中东欧的国家，等等。因为各国都有自己的战略规划。

第九点，现在媒体有很多扭曲不真实的报道，中国自己的报道却少到了微乎其微。前两天有一个报道说"一带一路"建设有400个项目失败了，是不是400个项目真的失败了？但4000个项目中即使真有400个项目失败，还有90%的项目没有失败，还有3600个项目没有失败，但是，读者却看不到媒体正面的宣传报道。

最后，"一带一路"建设需要大量的人员培训，包括语言培训、法律培训、技术培训、管理以至保安人员的培训，而这些培训都还没有跟上。

（本文系根据座谈会速记稿整理，内容已经作者本人确认）

A Discussion of the Construction of the Belt and Road

Huang Renwei/ China

Executive Vice-president of the Fudan Institute of "Belt and Road" and Global Governance/Director of the Center of Think Tank Studies of Shanghai Academy of Social Sciences

Five years have passed since President Xi Jinping proposed two initiatives, "One Belt" and "One Road" in Kazakhstan and Indonesia in 2013. In my opinion, these five years can be regarded as the first stage of the building of the Belt and Road, and the next five or ten years will be the second stage of its development.

Let's take a look at the achievements that have been made during the first stage of the construction of the Belt and Road. First, 130 countries have responded positively to the Belt and Road. In particular, 1,500 guests from 130 countries attended the Belt and Road Forum for International Cooperation held in May 2017, including political leaders of 30 countries and the Secretary-General of the United Nations. It was the first Belt and Road forum held worldwide. This situation demonstrated that the Belt and Road Initiative has been widely recognized by the entire international community and that most of the countries have a positive understanding of the greatness of the Belt and Road Initiative.

Second, the relevant mechanisms of cooperation have been established for the Belt and Road Initiative and the most important thing is the establishment of the Asian Infrastructure Investment Bank. The bank originally planned to include 20 countries in Asia, but it finally attracted 57 countries, including 36 Asian countries, 18 European countries, 1 country in the Americas and 2 countries in Oceania. Its members included 10 countries of the ASEAN, 14 of the 28 member states of the European Union, 14 of the G20 countries and 5 BRICS countries. Therefore, the Asian Infrastructure Investment Bank is no longer just an international bank limited to Asia, but a mechanism of financial cooperation that provides important guarantees for the construction of the Belt and Road. Even if those G7 countries do not join the bank, such as the United States, Japan and Canada, there is still a lot of controversy within them because some people think that it is wrong not to join the bank. Former United Nations officials, global folk scholars and international organizations, in order to promote the initiative of Belt and Road cooperation proposed by the leader of China, determined December 16th as the International Day, which is also the first international day because of China and showing confidence in Chinese culture. According to the example, the Belt and Road Initiative has received wide and positive responses not only in Eurasia but also in a large part of the world.

Specifically, there are already 4,000 projects under the Belt and Road Initiative with the direct investments of approximately 25 billion US dollars. From 2013 until now, the average annual growth rate of investments is 30%. Of course, only a small amount or no more than one-third of the investments are made by governments and the Asian Infrastructure Investment Bank, but most of the investments come from private enterprises. A very important part of the Belt and Road construction is the China-European train, which is a freight railroad between China and Europe and it has shuttled more than 3,000 times to and fro and realized the trade of 35 billion US dollars between China and countries along the route. The tremendous increase in the Belt and Road projects, in the volume of trade and in the total amount of investments reveals satisfactory development in the past five years, particularly at the beginning of the Belt and Road and in the period when the influence was expanded and the two and half years from 2015 to now.

Entering the second stage, the shortcomings of the building of the Belt and Road should be taken seriously, including weaknesses or even risks of the Belt and Road, which problems to be noticed and corrected, what to be improved and which issues not understood by the international community.

First of all, the Belt and Road Initiative is a relatively vacuous concept. Nearly all countries know this term but rarely know its specific content, particularly the indifference of the middle and lower classes. Therefore, it leaves us an impression of being grandiose but empty.

Second, although the Belt and Road Initiative seems grandiose but empty, it achieves very rapid development. It was originally prepared for about 60 countries in Eurasia along the route. Now it has attracted 130 countries, including those in Africa and Latin America. The construction of the Belt and Road develops too fast. I think we should slow down a little bit.

Third, the government has excessive publicity of official projects under the Belt and Road Initiative, that is, those projects invested in or aided by the government. Then, there is a false impression that as mentioned by a Nepalese friend just now, the Belt and Road is mistaken as the construction with non-reimbursable assistance from the Chinese government. This is impossible. The construction of the Belt and Road mainly includes unofficial projects invested in by private enterprises on the market. Therefore, this concept is still faced with some problems in practice.

Fourth, the rules for the construction of the Belt and Road are far from adequate. The methods of contracting and financing and the rules on obligations and responsibilities of stakeholders still lag behind. Compared with the speed of the growth of investments and trade, the rules cannot meet the needs. Developed countries specifically request increasing transparency in the construction of the Belt and Road, such as what projects, what bids, who is responsible, and so on.

Fifth, there is a lack of social and cultural communication of the Belt and Road Initiative. People pay too much attention to investment projects, but they don't know much about the social and cultural factors of investment projects. A Bulgarian friend acknowledged that he had little understanding of Chinese culture, but Chinese friends also have no idea about the Bulgarian or Balkan culture. Virtually, no one in China knows much about the Balkans despite the fact that their population is 55 million. This is a large population, but few of us know them. As a result, many misunderstandings arise, and even many security issues occur.

Sixth, the Belt and Road Initiative should not be limited to the countries we are talking about. It is also important to attract the participation of developed countries in its construction. Recently, Japan has been considering joining the Belt and Road because it is aware that the transportation from Lianyungang to Rotterdam is 20 days, but 50 days are needed for transportation to Europe through the Cape of Good Hope, so they can save 30 days and 60% of transportation costs.

Seventh, the building of the Belt and Road does not just mean road construction, but more importantly, the construction of industrial belts and economic development zones, which few of us pay attention to. However, we must bear in mind that road construction will be meaningless if there are no industrial belts and parks.

Eighth, the Belt and Road Initiative should also be closely integrated with the developmental strategies of countries along the route. Here, the strategies are neither the strategies nor the planning of China, but of countries along the Belt and Road, such as Russia, Kazakhstan, Indonesia, Iran, India and countries in Central and Eastern Europe. Each country has its own strategic plans.

Ninth, there are a lot of distorted reports in the media and China's own reports are next to nothing. Two days ago, a report claimed that 400 projects had failed in the construction of the Belt and Road. Did 400 projects really fail? However, even though 400 of the 4,000 projects failed, 90% of the projects did not fail, which means 3,600 projects did not fail. However, there are no positive media reports available to readers.

Finally, the construction of the Belt and Road requires a large number of personnel training, including language training, legal training, technical training, management and even security personnel training. The training that has occurred up to now is far from enough.

是翻译成就了中国现代文学的高峰

陆建德 【中国】
原中国社会科学院文学所所长 / 学者

我准备的不很充分，但想强调一点的是，我们需要注意的一种倾向，如果用英文表达的话则叫"本质主义"。我在想，如果看不同时期的中国文学，人们会感觉其发展变化是特别巨大的。但不能认定中国的文化或者中国的文学，从开始的时候就是那样子的，认为中国文学早就形成了一种固定的特质，并且保持这种特质而一成不变，甚至不会受到历史社会发展进程的影响。我认为，这样的观点实际上就是一种"本质主义"的观点。

所以，我们观看中国文化和中国文学，就会发现它是不断发展和变化的，并且这种发展和变化是巨大的。我们发现，中国文学始终与周边国家、民族，甚至更远距离的国家、民族的文化始终拥有着积极的互动关系，例如今天上午罗马尼亚学者讲到的大量图案，都与中国文化有着密切联系的。大家也看到，佛教在中国社会的巨大影响，如印度的佛堂、图案，仿佛会旅行似地也来到了中国。我们曾经认为中国非常传统的东西，实际上其来源可能并非是本地的，而是从境外引进的。所以说，文化既是流动的，也是对外开放的。

我们看中国现代文学，便会发现一个非常有趣的现象，中国现代文学的奠基人基本上都是翻译家。我认为，中国现代文学绝对不比中国古代文学稍加逊色。因为，中国现代文学有一种新的概念，而这种文学概念与 19 世纪的文学概念是不同的，传统文学中既有诗，也有文。但自 19 世纪末以来，大量欧美的、世界的文学作品通过翻译进入中国以后，大大地提高了中国小说的地位。

小说在中国能够取得今天的地位，实在是一种新鲜的现象，是直到20世纪的10年代、20年代才开始出现的。此前人们阅读的很多中国传统小说，都是没有作者姓名的，也就是说民间记录的故事是没有作者及其版权的。之所以现代小说能够取得崇高地位，与相关翻译家的艰辛工作是密不可分的。著名翻译家林纾先生翻译了大量的外国文学作品，提供给广大的中国读者阅读，而与林纾齐名的福建人名叫严复的，也是一位伟大的翻译家，正是在他们的巨大影响下，马克思主义的学说也开始进入了中国。尽管马克思主义的三个来源与中国文化没有关系，但却证明了外来文化实际上不断地推进中国自身文化的发展和变化。那种认为中国文化自古至今一成不变的观点，我是非常不同意的。

那么，中国现代文学是怎么发生的呢？人们看到，中国现代文学巨匠鲁迅以及茅盾、巴金，当时在上海商务印书馆创办的重要文学杂志《小说月报》中，就有不少的翻译作品。其中，茅盾先生作为20世纪了不起的中国小说家，甚至亲自主编《小说月报》。而另一位著名作家、四川人巴金，最初是一位无政府主义者，曾经留学法兰西共和国，巴金也翻译了大量的外国文学作品，甚至翻译过俄罗斯的文学作品。说到中国现代文学的新诗带头人，郭沫若先生是其中之一，郭沫若先生也是翻译作品最多的作家之一，他曾任中国社会科学院的院长，不仅翻译了《战争与和平》，还翻译了不同语种的其他作品，可以说，郭沫若的翻译范围非常广泛。还有中国杰出女作家冰心，也是纪伯伦小说《先知》的翻译。老舍先生作为中国著名的小说家，曾在伦敦大学教授中文，其小说也有以世界为背景的创作；同时，老舍先生也做过翻译。中国现代文坛的这种现象，在世界文学史上都是不多见的。

由此我们看到这样的现实，即中国文学一定要敞开大门，开放疆域，最终将获得世界文学的滋养，并且与之进行积极的互动。例如古文造诣非常高的鲁迅先生，其创作小说《狂人日记》的书名，便是从俄罗斯作家果戈理处获得灵感的。可以说，中国文学与世界文学是有着积极互动过程的，中国那一代作家的创作也与世界文学是积极互动的。尽管鲁迅先生说过一些比较激进的话，但我们应该能够理解他当年时代的那种焦虑，他希望中国有新的文化，希望后人看自己民族典籍的时候，能够有一种批评的意识。正是在这样的基础上，我认为是鲁迅先生开创了中国现代文学的新天地，而这个中国现代文学的新天地与世界是相互联系着的。

我们文学所的同事如学习外国文学的小说家钱锺书先生、杨绛先生，诗人丰子恺先生、卞之琳先生，都是研究外国文学的著名学者。由此我们得知，中国现代文学得益于世界各国家、各民族文化滋养，从而形成了中国现代文学的高峰，中国当代文学是否能够超越现代文学，我还不敢肯定，这个答案则要请在座的诸位专家帮忙回答。

（本文系根据座谈会速记稿整理，内容已经作者本人确认）

Modern Chinese Literature Peaked in Translation

Lu Jiande/ China

Former Director of the Institute of Literature, Chinese Academy of Social Sciences

Although not well prepared, I want to emphasize that there is a tendency that we need to pay attention to. In English, it is called "essentialist." If we take a look at the Chinese literature in different periods, there are drastic developments and changes. However, it cannot be assumed that the Chinese culture or Chinese literature was born like that from the beginning and that Chinese literature has long formed a constant feature that remains unchanged and even cannot be influenced by the development of the historical and social process. In my opinion, this is actually an "essentialist" view.

Therefore, when observing the Chinese culture and Chinese literature, we will find that it is constantly evolving and changing, and those developments and changes are tremendous. Chinese literature has always had positive interactions with the cultures of neighboring and even distant countries and peoples. For example, a large number of patterns shown by the Romanian scholar this morning are closely linked to the Chinese culture. As is known to us, Buddhism once had a great influence on Chinese society. For example, the Buddhist temples and patterns in India traveled to China as if they could walk. Even something traditional in China might have originated from abroad. Therefore, culture is both mobile and open to the outside world.

There is a very interesting phenomenon in modern Chinese literature that the founders are also translators. In my opinion, modern Chinese literature is definitely not inferior to ancient Chinese literature because it has a new concept that is different from that of the 19th century. Traditional literature is made up of both poetry and texts. However, since the late 19th century, a large number of European and American literary works have been translated and introduced to China, hence the status of Chinese novels has been greatly enhanced.

It is a new phenomenon that novels can achieve today's status in China, and it began only in the 1910s and 1920s. The names of authors of many traditional Chinese novels that people read were unknown, in other words, no authors and copyrights for folk stories. The reason why modern novels can achieve a high status is inseparable from the hard work of translators. The famous translator, Mr. Lin Shu, translated a lot of foreign literary works and rendered them understandable to Chinese readers. Yan Fu, another Fujian celebrity, was also a great translator. It was under their great influence that the Marxist doctrines entered China. Although the three sources of Marxism had nothing to do with the Chinese culture, they proved that the foreign culture actually promoted the development of and changes in China's own culture. I strongly disagree with the view that Chinese culture remains unchanged since ancient times.

Then, how did Modern Chinese literature come into being? There were many translated literary works in the important literary magazine *Fiction Monthly* founded by the Chinese modern literary masters Lu Xun, Mao Dun and Ba Jin at the Commercial Press in Shanghai. Mr. Mao Dun, a great Chinese novelist of the 20th century, even personally edited the *Fiction Monthly*. Another famous writer Ba Jin from Sichuan, who had always been an anarchist and had studied in the French

Republic, translated plenty of foreign literary works and even those from Russia. Speaking of the new poetry leader of modern Chinese literature, Mr. Guo Moruo was one of them, and he was also a writer who had a lot of translations. He also served as the leader of the Chinese Academy of Social Sciences, and he not only translated *War and Peace*, but also other works in different languages. It could be said that Guo Moruo's translation covered a very wide range. The excellent Chinese female writer Bing Xin was the translator of Gibran's novel *The Prophet.* Mr. Lao She, another famous novelist of China, also taught Chinese at the University of London. He wrote novels with the world as the background, and he too was a translator. This phenomenon in the modern Chinese literary circle is rare in the history of world literature.

Thus, as a matter of fact, Chinese literature must open its doors, open up its territory and finally be nourished from and actively interact with world literature. For example, Mr. Lu Xun, who had a very high reputation in ancient Chinese, wrote the novel *A Madman's Diary*, the title of which was inspired by the Russian writer Gogol-Anovskii. It can be said that Chinese literature and world literature had positive interactions and that a generation of Chinese writers interacted actively with world literature. Although Mr. Lu Xun spoke some radical words, we should be able to understand the anxiety in his times. He hoped that China would have a new culture and that future generations would have a sense of criticism when reading our own classics. It was on this basis that Mr. Lu Xun opened a new world of modern Chinese literature, which was interconnected with the world.

Mr. Lu Xun's younger brother, Zhou Zuoren, also did a lot of translation work. Our colleagues in the Literature Institute, such as the novelists Qian Zhongshu and Yang Jiang, as well as the poets Feng Zikai and Bian Zhilin, were famous scholars who studied foreign literature. Therefore, it is obvious that modern Chinese literature climbed to the peak after benefiting from the nourishments of the cultures of many countries and ethnicities in the world. I am not sure whether contemporary Chinese literature can transcend modern literature. Our experts here may help us answer this question.

人类命运共同体与人类对话共同体

黄卓越 【中国】
北京语言大学汉学研究所所长、博导 / 中国文化对外翻译与传播研究中心主任

尊敬的主持人和各位代表，学者们于大会设定的框架下在两天的时间中，进行了非常精彩的发言，并且使我受益匪浅。作为最后一位发言人，我想将视野稍稍打得更开一点儿，也就是从更为漫长的历史进程的角度，谈谈我对于人类命运共同体这一重要概念的认识并与大家做一些交流。

我发言的核心词有三个，除了人类命运共同体之外，还有全球化与现代性。

大家都知道，如果我们没有对全球地形学的一个完整认识，就不可能出现人类共同体这样的观念。目前，学术界一般都赞同将 15 世纪末到 16 世纪初，看作全球化的开端。因为，只有到了这样的时间，我们才有了一个完整的全球概念，并且有了将世界联系一起的各式各样的冲动。

当然，正如我们所看到的那样，初期的全球化是以征服为主导形式展开的，无论出现的结果怎样，初期的全球化都是以一方施予、另一方被动接受的方式进行的。因此，这个过程也伴随着大量的掠夺、血腥与残暴，等等。

新的转折点可以说是出现在第二次世界大战结束之后，可以将联合国的成立看作是人类共同体概念正式诞生的标志。当然，在某种程度上这也汲取了前期现代化过程中各式各样的弊端，包括极端的民族主义等，以及与两次世界大战的教训也是密切相关的。

但是，"二战"结束之后，我们知道又发生了一场延续时间比较长的冷战，

使得整个世界再次陷入了巨大的分裂之中，尽管冷战结束后重新启动了新一轮、并且是由资本与贸易的流动所带来的全球连通过程。但因为种种原因，并没有让世界变得更加相互信任，也没有能够形成一个互惠互利、进而命运与共的世界主义观念。

通过对于这段历史的反思，我们便会考虑为什么在全球化的框架中，人们却始终无法和谐相处？反而是充满了斗争、竞争与欺诈。其实，这个原因很复杂，但这与支配全球化进程的一个核心概念，也就是现代性有着非常紧密的关系。毫无疑问，我们应该看到现代性带来的许多积极的正面意义。但现代性在向我们期许一个普遍主义的世界模式的时候，也给世界带来了重重危机，这种危机既有社会的、政治的，也有生态的。以传统自由主义，也就是从启蒙运动以来的传统自由主义为标榜的现代性理念，在推动世界的多样性与财富的大规模积累的同时，也带有另外一张面孔。这就是很强的利益内制性和占有性，进而导致国际强权主义，等等。

我们大约可以把这看作是现代性的一个悖论吧，由此也造成了希望的一次次失去，当我们看到希望的时候，失望马上伴随而来，想必认真观察与思考当今世界变化的人，都会对之有一个清醒的认识。

也就是在这样的背景下，我认为人类命运共同体概念的提出，有其历史的必然性与合理性，并且包含了一种重建全球秩序的愿景，这既可以看作是对联合国宗旨的再次重申，也包含着突出强调的更新一些的内容，对此，大家谈得也比较多了。也就是说，将一切都建立在协商的基础上，建立在彼此尊重、平等协商、互惠互利、多中心互动的前提下，由此克服现代性内涵中固有的一些悖论，并构建出一种新的国际政治话语逻辑，从原来的以征服为导向的第一期全球化模式以及以自我利益、意识形态定位、民族本位主义为导向的第二期全球化模式，走向第三期全球化。

关于人类命运共同体概念的具体内容，已有许多学者和政治家对之都做了很好的阐述，更有效的讨论也将继续进行下去，我就不在这里展开了。

最后我想补充的是：根据上述，人类命运共同体实际上首先是一个人类对话共同体；因此，人类命运共同体从来不是属于哪一个国家的，绝对不是单纯属于中国的，每一个国家、每一个民族的智慧，都会在其中发挥作用，并且也需要政治家、学者们经常聚集一起，进行思想上的切磋和交流。

（本文系根据座谈会速记稿整理，内容已经作者本人确认）

A Community with a Shared Future for Mankind and a Community for a Dialogue of Mankind

Huang Zhuoyue/ China

Director of the Institute of Sinology/Doctoral Advisor in Beijing Language and Culture University/ Director of the Center of Chinese Culture Communication and Translation

As is known to all, without a complete understanding of the global topography, there cannot be a concept of the community with a shared future for mankind. At present, the academic community generally agrees that globalization began in the late 15th century and early 16th century. Because only in that period, human beings had a complete global concept and the motivation to link the world together.

Of course, the initial globalization was realized by conquering. No matter what outcome it had, globalization during its initial period was carried out in a way that one side gave and the other side passively accepted. This process was accompanied by blood and brutality, things like that.

The new turning point emerged after the Second World War. It could be said that the establishment of the United Nations marked the official birth of the concept of a community with a shared future for mankind. Of course, to a certain extent, this was realized by drawing lessons from the previous process of modernization, including extreme nationalism, and also lessons from the two world wars.

However, after the World War, there was a Cold War lasting for a long period, which once again split the world apart. A new round of global connectivity resumed after the Cold War due to the free flows of capital and trade. But for various reasons, the world did not begin to trust one other and there was also no concept of mutual benefit and shared future.

Through reflections on history, we have a question. Why can human beings not live in harmony under the framework of globalization, but the world is full of struggle, competition and fraud? In fact, the reasons are very complicated and closely linked to modernity, a core concept that dominates globalization. Undoubtedly, modernity has a lot of positive influences, but it also causes crises to the world when we are longing for a universal global model, including social, political and ecological crises. There is another side of modernity, that is to say, when the concept of modernity represented by the traditional liberalism since the Enlightenment promotes the diversity of the world and the massive accumulation of wealth, it also shows very strong internality and possessive nature of interests, thus leading to international power politics.

This may be regarded as a paradox of modernity that results in the loss of hope again and again. Where there are hopes, there are disappointments. Those who observe and think about changes in the world today will have a clear understanding.

In this context, it is historically inevitable and reasonable to put forward the concept of a community with a shared future for mankind because it contains a vision of rebuilding the global order. This concept not only can be seen as a reaffirmation of the purposes of the United Nations, but it also contains some new content. In other words, everything will be built on the basis of negotiation and the premises of mutual respect, equal consultation, mutual benefit and multi-center interaction, thus overcoming some paradoxes inherent in the connotation of modernity, setting a new logic for international political discourse and a shift from the conquest-oriented globalization model in the first stage and the self-interest and self-positioning-oriented globalization model in the second stage to the third stage of globalization.

With respect to the specific content of the concept of a community with a shared future for mankind, many scholars and politicians have explained it clearly, and more effective discussions will continue.

Finally, I would like to add, as mentioned above, the community with a shared future for mankind is, first of all, a community for dialogue among the members of mankind; therefore, it has never belonged to only one country, it is definitely not a community of China but the wisdom of every country, and every ethnicity can play a role in such a community. Politicians and scholars also need to gather to exchange ideas.

中国经济文化与全球对话的切入点

魏鹏举　【中国】

中央财经大学文化与传媒学院院长、教授

　　关于人类命运共同体的话题，我最看中的内涵是三个即生态上的共存；经济上共融；文化上的互信。

　　我找的角度是经济与文化的结合点，由此来谈谈我对这个命题的看法。其实，这里涉及的一个问题是中国文化传统是否有效地支持现代中国的经济发展，并且能否有效地参与到全球经济伦理的对话之中。

　　我想从三个方面展开对于这个问题的思考：

　　首先，从"两个疑问"谈起。各位专家可能都清楚，德国的社会学家马克思·韦伯曾对中国为什么没有出现资本主义，进行过专门的研究，他是在一本很有名的著作——《中国的宗教儒教与道教》中提出这个命题的。我想与大家共同思考一下这个命题。马克思·韦伯的判断是否合理？从现实来看，中国的确没有像欧洲那样在近代发展出市场经济；但是，中国始于40年前的改革开放，却在非常短的时间内推动了中国市场的蓬勃发展。

　　如果中国文化历史的整个价值传统不能支持市场经济的发展，为什么会在这么短的时间内经济快速发展，并且成了全球第二大经济体。所以，在这里我提出个人的看法，我认为韦伯关于中国经济和文化传统的判断，存在着一个严重的缺陷，或者叫"关键缺陷"。因为他忽略了中国传统社会之所以没有出现市场经济意义上的资本主义，其实问题既不在儒教也不在道教，关键是法家的意识形态。

法家是真正的"重农抑商"，其对商业的抑制才是导致中国没有出现现代资本主义的关键。所以，我们称为韦伯之判断是"关键缺陷"。这是我个人的一个思考，也是我个人的一个判断。

第二个疑问是从中国自身源流来看，大量的历史学家、文化学者们一致认为，中国一直属于小农经济且具有小农经济形成的文明形态，也就是我们常说的"农耕文明"。但我还是想追问，这个判断是否合理？如果中国数千年来就是一种小农经济形态，且与小农经济相适应的就是农耕文化的话，同样没有办法解释为什么短短的三四十年内，中国经济便实现了快速的发展，而且快速发展中国经济已经和全球市场经济发生着深度的融合。所以，这也是我的第二个很重要的思考。

我个人的看法是，从人类经济史分析，实际上在大多数人类文明时期，包括当前中国整体经济都排在世界前列，而且中国世俗商业社会始终顽强地存在并且延续，例如晋商钱庄在当时没有法律和行政保障的情况下，几乎没有发生过汇兑、信用层面的风险。无论从世界看中国，还是从源流看中国，关于文化和经济关系，我个人一直认为存在很多研究意义的缺憾，可能这也是我们下一步探讨中国文化和人类命运共同体问题的时候，从经济伦理上最值得深入研究的一个话题。

最后，我想谈一点儿个人建议，即从什么角度重新梳理中国经济与文化传统？我认为从民间的立场出发，将是一个更有意思的而且更有价值的角度。我举一例，例如中国民间社会的关公崇拜。关公崇拜在中国有很长的历史，尤其到了宋代，关公崇拜越来越广泛。日本汉学家杜边一浩认为，其中最重要的原因是山西商人的快速发展，而关公是山西人。所以，山西商业的延伸和山西商人的触角所及，推动了关公膜拜的快速和广泛发展。直到今天，在中国大陆、港澳台以及全球的华人，乃至全世界中国文化影响最深远的一种现象，就是关公膜拜现象。而在关公膜拜现象的背后，我也进行了一点儿探讨，发现这种现象的产生主要是与中国传统的商业伦理、商业精神的密切结合。这种商业伦理和商业精神是什么呢？那就是诚信，或用中国人的话讲就是"信义"。

我在这里有一个建议，建议大家共同对中国这种商业伦理传统重新从民间的视角进行深入的挖掘，在此基础上才可能真正地找到中国最近三四十年经济强劲增长背后的文化基因。同时，也正是从这样的文化基因中才可能在未来建构经济一体化、文化全球化的过程中，找到一个中国经济文化与全球对话的最好切入点。

（本文系根据座谈会速记稿整理，内容已经作者本人确认）

The Entry Point of China's Economic and Cultural Dialogues with the World

Wei Pengju/ China

Director and Professor of the School of Culture and Communication, Central University of Finance and Economics

My topic is "Chinese Traditional Culture and China's Contemporary Economic Ethics". It is about Chinese culture and community with a shared future for mankind. I would like to highlight three connotations of the community with a shared future for mankind, "ecological coexistence; economic integration; mutual cultural trust".

From the perspective of the convergence point of economy and culture, I will talk about my views on this proposition. In fact, an important issue is whether the Chinese cultural tradition can effectively support the economic development of modern China and whether it can effectively participate in the dialogue on global economic ethics.

This issue may be extended from the point of view of three aspects:

Let's begin with "two doubts". As is known to our experts here, Max Weber, the German sociologist, carried out some special research on why there was no capitalism in China. He put forward the proposition in a famous book, "The Religion of China: Confucianism and Taoism". I would like to reconsider this proposition with you. Is this judgment of Max Weber's reasonable? From a realistic point of view, China did not develop a market economy in modern times like Europe did; however, after the reform and opening-up began 40 years ago, China has achieved vigorous development of the Chinese market in a very short period of time.

If the values and traditions of China's culture and history could not support the development of a market economy, then why was China able to achieve very fast economic growth in such a short period of time and become the second-largest economy in the world? In my opinion, there was a serious defect or a so-called "key defect" in Weber's judgment of the Chinese economic and cultural traditions. Because he ignored the fact that the reason why capitalism in the sense of a market economy did not emerge in the traditional Chinese society was neither Confucianism, nor Taoism, but the legalist ideology. Legalists "stressed agriculture and restrained commerce", and their suppression of commerce was the key to the absence of modern capitalism in China. Hence, there is a "key defect" in Weber's judgment. This is my personal idea and judgment.

The second doubt is that from the perspective of China's origins, a large number of historians and cultural scholars agree that China has always belonged to the small-scale peasant economy with a civilized form that made up that economy, which is what we often call "agricultural civilization". But I still want to ask, is this judgment reasonable? If China has been a small-scale peasant economy for thousands of years and the agricultural civilization is compatible with such an economic form, it is still impossible to explain why the Chinese economy is able to achieve rapid development in just 30 to 40 years. The Chinese economy has undergone a deep integration with the global market economy. So, this is my second point.

My personal opinion is that according to economic history, in most periods of human civilizations, including today's, the economic aggregate of China takes the lead in the world, and China's secular business society has always existed and continues to exist. For example, in the absence of legal and administrative guarantees, the private banks of businessmen in Shanxi Province virtually had no risk of exchange and credit. Regardless of whether China is viewed from the world or from the origins in China, I presume that there are many shortcomings of research significance in the cultural and economic relations, which may be a topic worthy of in-depth study in terms of economic ethics when we further explore the issues of Chinese culture and the community with a shared future for mankind.

Finally, I would like to talk about some personal suggestions, that is, from which perspective we can reorganize China's economic and cultural traditions? The folk perspective will be interesting and valuable, such as the worship of Guan Yu in the Chinese civil society. It has a long history in China, especially in the Song Dynasty. According to Yoshihiro Watanabe, a Japanese sinologist, the most important reason is the rapid development of businessmen in Shanxi because Guan Yu is a Shanxi native. Therefore, the extension of business by businessmen from Shanxi promoted the rapid and extensive development of the worship of Guan Yu. Until today, the worship of Guan Yu is still influential among Chinese people on mainland China, in Hong Kong, Macao and Taiwan, as well as with Chinese people around the world, and it even influences the Chinese culture throughout the world. Behind this phenomenon, I find that there is a close link with traditional business ethics and business spirit. What is this business ethic and business spirit? It is honesty, or in Chinese, "believing".

I suggest that this kind of ethical business tradition in China should be explored from the folk perspective. Only on this basis, it is possible to truly find the cultural genes behind the strong economic growth of China in the last 30 to 40 years. Meanwhile, from such cultural genes, it is possible to find the best entry point for China's economic and cultural dialogues with the world in the future process of constructing economic integration and cultural globalization.

在开放的体系中认识中国历史文化

葛剑雄 【中国】
复旦大学资深教授 / 中央文史研究馆馆员

我认为我们应该首先正确地理解中国的历史文化，才能适应改革开放和推进"一带一路"建设的需要。

中国传统的文化学者，在研究自己历史文化的过程中，往往处于一个封闭的价值体系中，并且根据这样的体系"自娱自乐"。比如长期以来我们形成了这样的观念，即中国历史上很多方面曾经是世界最先进的，或者说文明是最发达的，但却从来没有与同时在世界上存在的其他文明认真地比较过，或者将二者置于一个开放的体系中进行研究过。在中国没有开放时，这种"自娱自乐"、这种虚假的历史观念或许有利于国人的文化自信；但一旦中国走向世界了，或者世界走进中国了，我们便会发现，这种盲目夸大的自信往往适得其反，非但不会增强我们的文化自信，而且会动摇、甚至使我们丧失文化自信。而这种建立在虚假历史观上的"一带一路"建设，其作用往往也是消极的。

我们一些人对外界、对自己历史的了解，基本还停留在"自娱自乐"的阶段。从世界史的层面上讲，中国对世界的影响，其实并没有我们自我宣扬的那样大。比如说"一带一路"的概念，其实与历史上的"丝绸之路"没有什么关系，不过借用了历史上"丝绸之路"的名称罢了。但是刚刚提出"一带一路"倡议时，国内绝大多数人都以为我们要重建"丝绸之路"，于是盲目地夸大了历史上"丝绸之路"的作用。绝大多数人不知道，历史上的"丝绸之路"并不是中国主动开辟的，而其主要的动力是来自于外界。西方人对于东方的探索，比起中国人向西方探索要早得多。中国古代的很多文明都是外来的，这在"中华文明探源工程"中已经坦率地承认了。比如中国的小麦、黄牛、羊、马、青铜……都是外来的。历史上，中国没有主动利用过"丝绸之路"，也很少从"丝路"贸易中获利。又比如说，我们只看到唐朝开放，认为"丝绸之路"给中国带进了这么多东西，却不知道通过"丝绸之路"传入中国的物品可以用百位数来计算，但中国传到外国的物品却只能用个位数计算；而在这些个位数中间，大多数还是外国人主动的，而不是中国人自己主动的。

因此，至今很多地方还拼命地争说自己是"丝绸之路"的真正出发点，同时认为自己拥有今天"一带一路"的最大优势。例如，我到西安和敦煌，当地都大谈各自拥有"一带一路"倡议的最大优势。我问：你们的优势在哪儿？他们答：古代的"丝绸之路"是从我们这儿走出去的。我问他们，难道今天你们还想出口丝绸；难道今天出去的还是骆驼、马，所以不得不在敦煌你这儿采购粮食吗？比如在西安，我就坦率地批评过他们，你们今天难道还想恢复大唐时代吗？

说到所谓的大唐时代，在今天中国大多数人眼里，甚至包括历史学家，都认为唐朝的长安曾是世界的中心。这其实是一个伪命题。我曾经问他们，唐朝的长安对阿拉伯国家、对欧洲产生了什么影响？甚至对日本，唐朝也从来没有主动地影响它，都是日本人主动到长安来选择学习他们自己想要的东西。唐朝真正的影响，实际是在汉语文化圈，就只到达朝鲜，到达越南的北部，甚至都没有影响到东南亚。所以，今天我们讲文化交流，讲"一带一路"倡议，讲经济全球化，就必须实事求是地认识中国的历史，认识中国古代在世界上曾经起到过的作用。

对于"丝绸之路"，大多数中国人都存在很大误解，人们还沉浸在"自娱自乐"中没有办法解脱出来，甚至有的已成为世界常识的简单问题，居然很多中国人包括一些官员都不知道。历史上的"丝绸之路"既不是中国人兴建的，也不是中国人推行的。这条路主要不是由汉朝人，而是由中亚、西亚、甚至欧洲人建立的，动力来自他们。比如说"海上丝绸之路"的概念，也是日本学者在 20 世纪提出来的，中国泉州作为"海上丝绸之路"的出发点，是由联合国教科文组织所认定的，但我们现在大多数人居然还在讨论中国古代"海上丝绸之路"如何地发达，竟不知道这条路是如何产生的，是怎样掌握在阿拉伯人手里的。

今天，我想提醒大家包括各国的汉学家朋友，我们一起站在开放的体系里面，重新认识中国古代的历史文化，认识中国历史文化所起到的作用，看到其中哪些是值得我们今天珍惜的经验，哪些是应当我们吸取的教训，又有哪些是我们必须抛弃的包袱。

（本文系根据座谈会速记稿整理，内容已经作者本人确认）

Understanding Chinese History and Culture in the Perspective of Open System

Ge Jianxiong/ China

Senior Professor of Fudan University/Member of the Central Research Institute of Culture and History

I would like to talk from a different perspective. First of all, we must correctly understand the history and culture of China in order to adapt to the needs of reform and opening-up and advance the Belt and Road construction.

Researchers of Chinese traditional culture, when studying the history and culture of China, often "entertain" themselves in a closed value system. For example, there is a stereotype that China was once the most advanced country on earth, in other words, the civilization of China was the most developed in the world, but there is neither a serious comparison with another contemporary civilization nor any study of them in an open system. This "self-entertainment" or false historical view might have been beneficial to building up the cultural confidence of Chinese people when China was not opened up to the outside world. However, after China has embraced the world or the world has entered China, this blindly exaggerated self-confidence is actually counterproductive because it will not enhance but undermine or even lose our cultural confidence. This false historical view may have a negative impact on the Belt and Road construction.

Some people's understanding of the outside world and our own history basically stagnates into a "self-entertainment". From the broad perspective of world history, China did not have such a profound influence on the world as we often assert. For example, the concept of the Belt and Road has nothing to do with the Silk Road known in history, but it borrows the name of the ancient Silk Road. However, when the Belt and Road Initiative was first proposed, most people in China mistook it thinking that we would rebuild the Silk Road and blindly exaggerated the role of the ancient Silk Road in history. The vast majority of people do not know that the ancient Silk Road was not initiated by China, and its main driving force came from the outside world. The Westerners' exploration of the Orient was much earlier than the Chinese's exploration of the West. Many civilizations in ancient China were foreign, and this fact was candidly acknowledged by the Origin of the Chinese Civilization Exploration Project. For example, wheat, yellow cattle, pigs, sheep, horses, bronzes... all originated in foreign lands. Historically, China neither took the initiative to make use of the Silk Road nor made profit from the trade via the Silk Road. Another example, as is known to us, after the opening of the Tang Dynasty, hundreds of things were introduced into China via the Silk Road. Only several things spread from China to foreign countries by the active introduction of foreigners. China never took the initiative in spreading them.

Today, many regions in China argue that their own region was the true starting point of the Silk Road and that they have the greatest advantage of today's Belt and Road. For example, when I paid visits to Xi'an and Dunhuang, locals in both cities talked about their biggest advantages in the Belt and Road construction. I asked a question: "What are your advantages?" They answered: Our city was the starting point of the ancient Silk Road. I asked them what would you like to export today, silk on camels or horses? Must we buy food here in Dunhuang, like the businessmen in ancient times? In Xi'an, I criticized them frankly. Do you want to restore the

Tang Dynasty today?

Mentioning the Tang Dynasty, in the eyes of most people in China today, even historians, brings to mind the fact that Chang'an of the Tang Dynasty was once the center of the world. This is actually a false proposition. I once asked them what influence Chang'an of the Tang Dynasty had on Arab countries and Europe. Even for Japan, the Tang Dynasty never actively influenced the country. It was the Japanese who took the initiative in visiting Chang'an and learning what they wanted to find out. Only the Chinese cultural circle was under the influence of the Tang Dynasty, which only reached North Korea and the northern part of Vietnam and did not even reach Southeast Asia. Therefore, today when we talk about cultural exchanges, the Belt and Road Initiative and economic globalization, we must have a truthful historical view on the history of China and understand the role that ancient China has played in the world.

Most of Chinese people, who have a widespread misunderstanding of the Silk Road, are still immersed in the thoughts of "self-entertainment". Even some common sense in the world is unknown to many Chinese people, including some government officials. The Silk Road in history was neither built nor promoted by the Chinese. This road was not built by the Han Dynasty, but by Central Asia, West Asia, and even Europeans. The motivation came from them. For example, the concept of the Maritime Silk Road was proposed by Japanese scholars in the last century. Quanzhou was recognized by UNESCO as the starting point of the Maritime Silk Road, but most of us now are still discussing how the ancient Maritime Silk Road was well developed in China. They don't know how this road came into being and the fact that it was controlled in the hands of the Arabs.

Today, I would like to remind everyone, including sinologists from all over the world, that we should stand together in an open system, re-recognize the history and culture of ancient China, understand the role played by the Chinese history and culture, and find the experiences that are worth cherishing today, the lessons we should learn and the burdens we must abandon.

人类在 21 世纪还能走到一起吗——中国古代圣哲怎样看人类的迷失

刘梦溪 【中国】
中国艺术研究院终身研究员 / 中国文化研究所所长 / 中央文史研究馆馆员

一

人类在 21 世纪还能走到一起吗？中美贸易战，特朗普四处出击，美国退出一个又一个的多边合作组织，民粹主义盛行，赤裸的经济利益追求盖过了价值认同，这个世界的现实相，处处都是往反文明共存反合作共赢的方向移动。

这种粗糙的变化无定的现实相，就是人类迷失的典型形态。

人类的迷失不是第一次发生。上一个世纪的迷失，表现为疯狂，结果导致两次世界大战。这次的迷失表现为傲慢——而傲慢距离疯狂只有一步之遥。

疯狂和傲慢都是人性的异化，改变之道，在回归理性，学以成人。

中国文化的要义，就是让人改邪归正，复归人之为人的本然之善。

不久前，我曾经提出："以我多年研习中国文化的心得，于今思之，中华文化能够贡献给人类的，我认为是人之为人的、群之为群的、家之为家的、国之为国的一整套精神价值论理。这些价值理念的旨归，是使人成为健全的人，使群体成为和谐的群体，使家成为有亲有爱有敬的和睦的家，使国家成为讲信修睦、怀柔远人的文明礼仪之邦。"

人类的人与人相处、群与群相处，离不开中国古代圣哲提出的"和同"理念，以及期望"与人和同"的价值追求。

二

最早提出"和同"理念的是周幽王时期的一位叫史伯的智者。

相传史伯是西周末期人，司天文历法、典籍书史之事。一次他和封于郑的郑伯一起探讨周朝为何会走向衰亡？郑伯名伯友，系周宣王的庶弟、周幽王的叔父，封于郑，谥号桓，后来成为郑国的开国之君，是为郑桓公。跟史伯的这次对话，时当周幽王八年，当时郑伯友还是司徒。目睹衰周的状况，为了自己的家庭和郑地子民的安全，郑伯友想作一次大规模的搬迁，于是找史伯讨教此一行动的利弊得失。郑伯问道：国家的事情发展到这样的地步，周王朝本身是不是也有值得检讨的地方呢？

史伯的回答非常肯定。他说：周沦落到如此地步，完全是由于自己的错误所酿成。他分析说——

《泰誓》曰："民之所欲，天必从之。"今王弃高明昭显，而好谗慝暗昧；恶角犀丰盈，而近顽童穷固。去和而取同。夫和实生物，同则不继。以他平他谓之和，故能丰长而物归之；若以同裨同，尽乃弃矣。故先王以土与金木水火杂，以成百物。是以和五味以调口，刚四支以卫体，和六律以聪耳，正七体以役心，平八索以成人，建九纪以立纯德，合十数以训百体。出千品，具万方，计亿事，材兆物，收经入，行姟极。故王者居九畡之田，收经入以食兆民，周训而能用之，和乐如一。夫如是，和之至也。于是乎先王聘后于异姓，求财于有方，择臣取谏工而讲以多物，务和同也。声一无听，物一无文，味一无果，物一不讲。王将弃是类也而与剸同。天夺之明，欲无弊，得乎？[1]

史伯所指陈的衰周之弊，归结为一点，就是强不同以为同，而不肯和同。他使用了一个特殊的语词，叫"剸同"，"剸"字的读音作"团 tuan"，是割而断之的意思。"剸同"即专擅强制为同。其结果便走向了"和同"义理的反面。至于治国理政为什么不能剸同，只能和同，史伯作了详尽的阐述。

首先，史伯提出了关于和同观念的一个新的哲学命题，这就是"和实生物，同则不继"。其中的"生"和"继"两个动词至关重要。"生"，是指在原来的状态下生长出新的东西。"继"其实是"生"的置换词，而"不继"，则是不能新生

---

[1]《国语》下册，上海人民出版社 1988 年版，第 515—516 页。

的意思。简言之，就是"和"能生物，"同"不能生物。而"生"与"不生"，直接关系到事物的可延续和不可延续的生死攸关的问题。不能延续，就是"不继"，亦即自身陷入危机而不能调适自救，因此必然失去未来，没有前途。能够"生物"，则是可以延续生命，未来自当有继。而且"生物"一语，还思辨地揭示出生命延续的秘密，即此种延续不是旧状态的简单重复，而是旧状态下的事物发生了质的变化，诞生了新的生命或可以延续生命的新运新机。

其次，史伯给出了"和"为什么能够"生物"，"同"何以不能为继的形上理由。关键是对"和"的义理内涵需要有正确的诠解。史伯的解释是，当一种独立存在的东西和另一种独立存在的东西融合在一起的时候，这种状态可以称之为"和"，史伯称这种情形为"以他平他"。因此可以说，"和"是由不同的存在物的共存共融所达成的一种高度和谐的境界。不是指某个单一体，而是多种元素化分化合的综合体。由于内中有不同元素的交错互动，形成巨大的张力，才因彼此的相斥相激而产生新的生命体。

三

《易·系辞》说的"《易》有太极，是生两仪，两仪生四象，四象生八卦"，此种"生生"情形下的"易"之太极，其实可以视作"和"的别称。故朱子认为："太极只是一个浑沦底道理，里面包含阴阳、刚柔、奇耦，无所不有。"[1]朱子的解释，拉近了"和"与"太极"在释义学上的距离。而在张载那里，两者则变成了完全相重合的义理终极。不过他提出了一个新的和同的概念，曰"太和"。他写道：

> 太和所谓道，中涵浮沈、升降、动静、相感之性，是生絪缊、相荡、胜负、屈伸之始。其来也几微易简，其究也广大坚固。起知于易者干乎！效法于简者坤乎！散殊而可象为气，清通而不可象为神。不如野马、絪缊，不足谓之太和。语道者知此，谓之知道；学易者见此，谓之见易。不如是，虽周公才美，其智不足称也已。[2]

张载的太和论，实际上是对"和"的价值论理作了更具哲学义涵的解释。在张载看来，易道即太极，太极即太和。"浮沈、升降、动静、相感之性，是生絪缊、相荡、胜负、屈伸"等无尽藏的对立物，都包括在太和之中了。这和朱子论太极

---

[1]《朱子语类》卷七五，第五册，中华书局，第1929页。
[2]《正蒙》，《张载集》，中华书局1978年版，第7页。

如出一辙。而所谓"太和",其实就是一种新的和同论,只不过是升级了的更具有无限性的"和"的至境而已。

好了,既然"和"里面包含那么多的、无限量的物的对立体,他们之间出现相感、相汤、相生,就是再自然不过的事情了。相感、相荡,必然相生。故史伯的"和实生物"的理论,可谓颠扑不破。说开来,"和"论、"和同"论、"太和"论,也就是"易"论。张载的理论本来即来自于《易》。"太和"里面的那些个相感相荡的对立物,不过是《易·系辞》之"一阴一阳之谓道"、"生生之谓易"的变项而已。

那么,"同"呢?如何是"同"?为什么"同则不继"?同与不同,都是单一事物之间的事情。如果目标是达成"和",则同与不同都不是障碍物。但如果是史伯所批评的"去和而取同",试图"以同裨同",亦即只想用"同"来给"同"提供助益,而弃置和同的大目标,就什么都得不到了。不仅"和"的局面不能实现,"同"也会因为自己重复自己而变得索然无味,从而导致与"和同"适得其反的"剿同"。最后的结果,便是史伯所预见的"尽乃弃矣"。试想那是一种何等悲惨、落寞、无助的景象呵!

"故先王以土与金木水火杂,以成百物。"史伯说。"是以和五味以调口,刚四支以卫体,和六律以聪耳,正七体以役心,平八索以成人,建九纪以立纯德,合十数以训百体。"史伯又说。总之是集多样于一体,寓杂多于统一。这是周朝的先王获得成功的诀窍。他们"出千品,具万方,计亿事,材兆物,收经入,行姟极","居九畡之田,收经入以食兆民",繁复无尽数,道路万千条,然则"和乐如一"。史伯说,做到了这一地步,可以说是"和之至也"。

他叹美先王为了"务和同",可谓无所不用其极,包括"聘后于异姓,求财于有方,择臣取谏工而讲以多物"等等。此可知和同的理念对于治国理政是多么至关重要,真可以说败亦由是,成亦由是。

本来至此史伯已经把"务和同"、"弃剿同"的原因、理据、前因、后果,讲得一清二楚了,但他仍然感到意犹未尽,又进而请来其立论所依据的哲学原理,曰:"声一无听,物一无文,味一无果,物一不讲。"是的,这个世界,如果只有一种声音,就没法听了;所有的事物都是一样的,就单调得不能看了;用来果腹的食物都是一样的味道,还有什么吃头;世间的事物如果只有一种,没有彼此之间的比较对照,就没有什么道理好讲了。只有傻瓜、智障、低能、蠢物,才敢冒天下之大不韪，放弃大千世界的五彩缤纷，不顾人间世态的万种风情，而欲以剗同的淫威来统治丰富多彩的社会人生。

四

有意思的是，我们在《左传》里看到了与史伯之论义理全同的记载，那是在昭公二十年，齐侯和晏子的一段对话。他们所探讨的恰好是"和同"问题。齐侯问晏婴："唯据这个人与我和吗？"晏子回答说："唯据其人，与公只是同而已，哪里称得上和？"齐侯不解斯理，于是进一步追问："和与同异乎？"燕子直截了当地回答说："异。"随后又对"同"与"和"所以有区别的缘由，作了有物有则的大段阐论。晏子论述道：

  和如羹焉，水火醯醢盐梅以烹鱼肉，燀之以薪。宰夫和之，齐之以味，济其不及，以泄其过。君子食之，以平其心。君臣亦然。君所谓可而有否焉，臣献其否以成其可。君所谓否而有可焉，臣献其可以去其否。是以政平而不干，民无争心。故《诗》曰："亦有和羹，既戒既平。鬷嘏无言，时靡有争。"先王之济五味，和五声也，以平其心，成其政也。声亦如味，一气，二体，三类，四物，五声，六律，七音，八风，九歌，以相成也。清浊，小大，短长，疾徐，哀乐，刚柔，迟速，高下，出入，周疏，以相济也。君子听之，以平其心。心平，德和。故《诗》曰："德音不瑕。"今据不然。君所谓可，据亦曰可；君所谓否，据亦曰否。若以水济水，谁能食之？若琴瑟之专一，谁能听之？同之不可也如是。[1]

晏子说，"和"就如厨子所做的和羹一样，需要有水，需要掌握好火候，还需要加之以盐梅，以使鱼肉更加鲜美，甚至用什么样的薪材来烹烧，也很有讲究。而且还需要有专业人士调味，做到恰如其分，既无不够味，也不味过重。如此这般地用多种不同的材料，通过不同的程序，最后调制出美味的羹汤。由于是五味调和而成，所以《诗三百》称之为"和羹"。食用此种和羹，可以收到"以平其心"的效果。

君臣的关系也是如此。晏子说，君主认为可行的事情，其实也有不可行的部分在，经过臣僚们讲明那些不可行部分的理由，予以补充，然后变成君臣共同完成的可行方案。同样，君主认为不可行的事情，内中一定也有可行的部分，经过

---

[1] 《春秋左传集解》第四册，上海人民出版社1977年版，1463—1464页。

臣僚们献计献策，找出那些可行的部分，去掉不可行的部分，施政就宽平而少周折了。所以一定要听不同的意见，学习先王所采取的"济五味，和五声"、"平其心，成其政"的治国方略，方可有成。可是那个叫唯据的臣僚不是如此，一切都唯上是从，您认为可行的，他就说可行；您否定的，他也跟着否定。这等于是"以水济水"，做出来的东西谁还能吃？也无异于琴瑟奏一个调调，谁还肯前来一听？所以"同"与"和"是不一样的，不应该认可这种人云亦云的所谓"同"的态度，而应该是"济五味"，成"和羹"；"和五声"，"一气，二体，三类，四物，五声，六律，七音，八风，九歌，以相成"、"清浊，小大，短长，疾徐，哀乐，刚柔，迟速，高下，出入，周疏，以相济"。换言之，治国理政，如果臣僚们一律唯君主是从，谁也不出来补偏救弊，天下之人也整齐划一，没有不同的声音发出，先王所期待的"心平"、"德和"的局面，便无法实现了。

晏子的"和同论"，完全例同于史伯的"和同论"。

五

《后汉书》刘梁传，也载有该刘的一篇《辩和同之论》，则是对先秦和同思想的一次更为系统的发挥与论说。因系专论，兹将全文抄录如下，以方便对此一题义感兴趣的读者参证阅读。

夫事有违而得道，有顺而失义，有爱而为害，有恶而为美。其故何乎？盖明智之所得，暗伪之所失也。是以君子之于事也，无适无莫，必考之以义焉。

得由和兴，失由同起，故以可济否谓之和，好恶不殊谓之同。《春秋传》曰："和如羹焉，酸苦以剂其味，君子食之以平其心。同如水焉，若以水济水，谁能食之？琴瑟之专一，谁能听之？"是以君子之行，周而不比，和而不同；以救过为正，以匡恶为忠。经曰："将顺其美，匡救其恶，则上下和睦能相亲也。"

昔楚恭王有疾，召其大夫曰："不谷不德，少主社稷。失先君之绪，覆楚国之师，不谷之罪也。若以宗庙之灵，得保首领以殁，请为灵若厉。"大夫许诸。及其卒也，子囊曰："不然。夫事君者，从其善，不从其过。赫赫楚国，而君临之，抚正南海，训及诸夏，其宠大矣。有是宠也，而知其过，可不谓恭乎！"大夫众之。此讳而得道者也。及灵王骄淫，暴虐无度，芋尹申亥从王之欲，以殡于干溪，殉之二女。此顺而失义者也。鄢陵之役，晋楚对战，阳谷献酒，子反以毙。此爱而害之者也。臧武仲曰："孟孙之恶我，药石也；季孙之爱我，美疢也。疢毒滋厚，石犹生我。"此恶而为美者也。孔子曰："智之难也！有臧武仲之智，而不容于鲁国，抑有由也。作不顺而施不恕也。"盖善其知义，讥其违道也。

夫知而违之，伪也；不知而失之，暗也。暗为伪焉，其患一也。患之所在，非徒在智之不及，又在及而违这者矣。故曰"智及之，仁不能守之，虽得之，必失之"也。《夏书》曰："念兹在兹，庶事恕施。"忠智之谓矣。

故君子之行，动则思义，不为利回，不为义疚，进退周旋，唯道是务。苟失其道，则兄弟不阿；苟得其义，虽仇雠不废。故解狐蒙祁奚之荐，二叔被周公之害，勃鞮以逆文为成，傅瑕以顺厉为败，管苏以憎忤取进，申侯以爱从见退：考之以义也。故曰："不在逆顺，以义为断；不在憎爱，以道为贵。"《礼记》曰："爱而知其恶，憎而知其善。"考义之谓也。[1]

刘梁字曼山，一名岑，东平宁阳人。《后汉书》本传称其为梁宗室的子孙，但"少孤贫，卖书于市以自资"[2]。尝撰《破群论》，对世俗之"利交"和"邪曲相党"颇多讥刺，致使评者比之为"仲尼作《春秋》，乱臣知惧"，称《破群》之作当令"俗士愧心"，可惜其文未传。然此篇《辩和同之论》则完好无缺。全文结构严谨，思理清晰，比之史伯、晏婴之论，更具有论理系统完整的特点。文中所引《春秋传》一段，是为晏子的论述，不过其发明处，在于对和同概念所作的学理分疏。

刘梁给出的"和"的定义，是"可济"，即彼此之间因坦荡无私、补偏救弊而获得助益，而不是一味"顺"之而不问道义原则。所以他说："君子之行，周而不比，和而不同，以救过为正，以匡恶为忠。"他给出的"同"的定义，是"好恶不殊"，即不管是非，一味投其所好。如是的结果，必然走向"和而不同"的反面，就立国施政而言，罪莫大焉。刘梁以楚国的政事作为例证，一是楚恭王病笃之时召大夫自陈所失，表示谥号请为"灵"或"厉"。《左传》杜预注云："乱而不损曰灵，

---

[1] 《后汉书》卷八十下，文苑列传第七十下，中华国学文库版，第三册，2012年，第2118—2121页。

[2] 《后汉书》卷八十下，同前，第三册，第2118页。

戮杀不辜曰厉。"¹ 两者同为恶谥，连请五次，大夫方同意。待到恭王病没将葬，令尹子囊提出谥号的问题，大夫说，不是已有成命在先了吗？子囊表示不应照遗言来办，因历数恭王的荣光，又加之能"知其过"，因此谥为"恭"是合适的。至于有成命一事，子囊认为："事君者，从其善，不从其过。"大夫最后被说服。刘梁说，这种情况，属于"讳而得道者"。虽然违背了恭王的成命，但却符合道义。

楚国政事的另一例证，是楚灵王骄奢淫逸、暴虐不德，而申亥一意听任王之所欲，当其殡于干溪的时候，还让自己的两个女儿殉葬。刘梁说，这是"顺而失义者也"。第三个例证，是晋楚鄢陵之战，经由楚卿子反的运筹策划，楚已掌握了主动权。但关键时刻，子反的通令官阳谷却前去献酒，忘乎所以的子反喝得酩酊大醉，楚王招谋战事而不能应，致使楚军大败。子反最后自尽而死。刘梁说，这是"爱而害之者也"。第四个例证，是臧武仲不容于鲁国的故事。孟庄子和季武子是两个有势力的人物，季氏喜欢臧武仲，孟氏却讨厌他。但当孟氏死的时候，武仲前往吊唁，哭得十分悲伤。他的御者不解，说如果季氏过世，你又该如何呢。臧武仲回答道："孟孙之恶我，药石也；季孙之爱我，美疢也。疢毒滋厚，石犹生我。"刘梁认为这是"恶而为美者也"。但其所为作，属于"知而违之"，因此难免有"伪"的嫌疑。故孔子认为此人是使"智"，其"不容于鲁国，抑有由也"。

刘梁《辩和同之论》的主旨，是强调"得由和兴，失由同起"。因此对于不分"好恶"、不管是非，一律以"同"还是"不同"作为取舍标准的态度和行事方式，给予严厉警示。他反复说明，问题不在于"同"还是不同，而是要看是否合乎道义。文中以此明示："故君子之行，动则思义，不为利回，不为义疚，进退周旋，唯道是务。苟失其道，则兄弟不阿；苟得其义，虽仇雠不废。"为了使所论具有不可动摇的说服力，作者引楚国和鲁国共四个案例作为证言：一为"讳而得道者"、二为"顺而失义者"、三为"爱而害之者"、四为"恶而为美者"。此四案例，都见于《左传》以及《国语》的记载，并非僻典，难为斯刘之读史得间，使当时后世得读其"和同论"者，能生出会心默契的义理认同感。

噫！"好恶不殊"的所谓"同"，其昧心害政、伤天悖理者也大矣。而"和"则是以"可济"为标尺。所以他最后得出一个结论："君子之行，周而不比，和而不同，以救过为正，以匡恶为忠。"而千古不磨的警世之语则是："得由和兴，失由同起。"大矣哉，此鲜为人知的刘梁之《辩和同之论》也。

---

1 《春秋左传正义》中册，《十三经注疏》标点本，北京大学出版社1999年版，第911页。

六

写到这里我们可以说，从古智者史伯的和同论，到晏子的和同论，再到刘梁的《辩和同之论》，所表达的思想均与《易经》倡言的"天下同归而殊途，一致而百虑"高度吻合，也与孔子提出的"君子和而不同"若荷符契。一句话，在中国古圣哲看来，人类没有理由不走向和同，即使选择的路径不同，思考问题的方式不一样，最终还会走到一起。

但这里隐含有一个无法不予深究的学理问题：即不同为什么可以而且能够走向"和同"？说到底，是人类以及天下之物，虽然存在有种种不同，但相同之处也是有的，甚至是更加根本的规定，所以才能共处共生。正是人类和物类的相同之处，决定他们总归会走到一起，趋向大同，以至达至张载所说的太和之境。

然则人类的相同之处是什么呢？我们且看孟子的论述。

孟子就此一题义讲过的一段最著名的话是："口之于味也，有同嗜焉；耳之于声也，有同听焉；目之于色也，有同美焉。至于心，独无所同然乎？心之所同然者何也？谓理也，义也。圣人先得我心之所同然耳。故理义之悦我心，犹刍豢之悦我口。"（《孟子·告子上》）孟子所说的人类的相同之处，首先是"性"同。本来食物的味道应该是不同的，声音也应该是不一样的，颜色应该是丰富多彩的，这方面，智者史伯和齐国的谋士晏婴已经有话在先了，可我们的孟夫子为什么还说人们对于味有"同嗜"，对于声有"同听"，对于色有"同美"呢？此无他，盖喜欢好吃的，爱听美妙的音乐，喜爱色彩之美，是人类的本性使然。告子所说的"食色性也"（《孟子·告子上》），亦为斯意。此即同为生人，其人类的本性总会有相同之处，原因在于都是"人"。

荀子对生之为人的相同之处的阐述也极为系统透辟。今存《荀子》一书中，有多篇涉及此一题义。《王霸》篇云："故人之情，口好味而臭味莫美焉，耳好声而声乐莫大焉，目好色而文章致繁妇女莫众焉，形体好佚而安重闲静莫愉焉，心好利而谷禄莫厚焉，合天下之所同愿兼而有之，睪牢天下而制之若制子孙，人苟不狂惑戆陋者，其谁能睹是而不乐也哉。"[1]《荣辱》篇写道："凡人有所一同：饥而欲食，寒而欲暖，劳而欲息，好利而恶害，是人之所生而有也，是无待而然者也，是禹、桀之所同也。目辨白黑美恶，耳辨音声清浊，口辨酸咸甘苦，鼻辨芬芳腥臊，

---

[1] 《荀子·王霸》，《荀子集解》，中华书局2012年版，第213—214页。

骨体肤理辨寒暑疾养,是又人之所常生而有也,是无待而然者也,是禹、桀之所同也。"¹ 又说:"材性知能,君子小人一也。好荣恶辱,好利恶害,是君子小人之所同也,若其所以求之之道则异矣。"²《非相》篇也说:"人之所以为人者,何已也?曰:以其有辨也。饥而欲食,寒而欲暖,劳而欲息,好利而恶害,是人之所生而有也,是无待而然者也,是禹、桀之所同也。"³

质而言之,饮食男女、避寒取暖、趋利远害的生存需求,能使人的心理保持平衡的自性尊严。如好荣恶辱等,人与人之间并无不同,即使是君子和小人、圣人和常人,亦无不同,只是获得和保持的取径有所区别而已。此即"性同"之义。荀子对和同思想的结论是:"斩而齐,枉而顺,不同而一。"⁴ 此与《易》道"天下同归而殊途"毫无二致。

人之所同然者,"性同"之外是"理"同。人所不同于动物者,在人类有理性思维,故孟子说,"心之所同然者",是"理也"。而圣人所以成为我们心目中的圣人,是由于圣人所阐发的道德义理,能够深获我心,说出了我们想说而未能说出的话。此即孟子所说的"圣人先得我心之所同然"的涵义。人们常说的所谓人同此心,心同此理,即为斯义。实际上,人类原初的情感和理想期待,本来都是这个样子。只不过由于意向与行为的交错,造成了诸般的矛盾。古今贤哲启示我们,应该透过人类生活的矛盾交错的困扰,看到心理期许的一致性原理,看到不同背后的相同。这也就是孟子所说的:"舜生于诸冯,迁于负夏,卒于鸣条,东夷之人也。文王生于岐周,卒于毕郢,西夷之人也。地之相去也,千有余里;世之相后也,千有余岁。得志行乎中国,若合符节,先圣后圣,其揆一也。"(《离娄下》)"揆",是规矩、轨则、法度的意思,引申可以解释为原理、原则。亦即古代的大师巨子和后世的大师巨子,他们提出和遵循的思想义理、道德理念的规则,在本质上有相似或相同之处。

这也就是二程子所说的:"天地之间,万物之理,无有不同。"⁵ 又说:"天下万古,人心物理,皆所同然,有一无二,虽前圣后圣,若合符节。"⁶ 斯又说:"吾生所有,既一于理,则理之所有,皆吾性也。人受天地之中,其生也,具有天地之

---

1 《荀子·荣辱》,《荀子集解》,中华书局 2012 年版,第 63 页。
2 同上书,第 61 页。
3 《荀子·非相》,《荀子集解》,中华书局 2012 年版,第 78 页。
4 《荀子·荣辱》,《荀子集解》,中华书局 2012 年版,第 71 页。
5 《朱子语类》卷七五,第五册,中华书局,第 1929 页。
6 《二程集》下册,中华书局 1981 年版,第 1158 页。

德，柔强昏明之质虽异，其心之所同者皆然。特蔽有浅深，故别而为昏明；禀有多寡，故分而为强柔；至于理之所同然，虽圣愚有所不异。"[1] 兹可知程子是将"性"与"理"合一来看待和同之论的。宋代另一位思想家陆九渊也说："千万世之前有圣人出焉，同此心，同此理也；千万世之后，有圣人出焉，同此心，同此理也；东、南、西、北海有圣人出焉，同此心，同此理也。"[2] 故人之所同然者，是"性"也，"理"也。故孟子所说的"理义之悦我心，犹刍豢之悦我口"，确为不易之论。

然则在承认生之为人的性与理有所同然者的同时，如何看待就中的"同"和"不同"，亦即"同"与"异"的关系？墨子有言："其然也，有所以然也；其然也同，其所以然不必同。其取之也，有所以取之。其取之也同，其所以取之不必同。"[3] 此即所谓现象同，理由不必相同；目标相同，途径和手段不必相同。宋代的思想家程颢和程颐，他们把为人处世致力于"求同"还是"立异"，看做一个人是秉持"公心"，还是守持"私心"的分水岭。他们说："公则同，私则异。"[4] 并说"同者"是"天心"，即上天的旨意。在另一处他们还说："圣贤之处世，莫不于大同之中有不同焉。不能大同者，是乱常拂理而已；不能不同者，是随俗习污而已。"[5] 不承认人和事的不同，二程子认为是没有修养的人的胡言乱语；但如果否认"大同"，就是"乱常拂理"。就其两者的错误程度而言，显然二程子认为不能求大同的性质要更为严重。斯又有"大同"和"小同"的分别，"大同"不可违，"小同"可存异。语云："求大同，存小异。"信不诬也。

七

我国当代已故的大学问家钱锺书先生，当1948年他的《谈艺录》在上海出版的时候，其所撰之序言中有两句本人经常引证的话，曰："东海西海，心理攸同；南学北学，道术未裂。"此即在钱锺书先生看来，东西方文化虽有不同，但不论东方人还是西方人，其心理的反应特征和指向常常是相同的。而所以如此的缘故，是由于反应作用于人的主体精神世界的事物，普遍存在着物之理相同的现象。所以钱锺书先生得出一个结论："心同理同，正缘物同理同。"[6] "心同理同"是孟夫子

---

[1] 《二程集》下册，同上，第1159页。
[2] 《陆九渊集》，中华书局，1980年，第273页。
[3] 《小取》，《墨子校注》下册，中华书局，1993年，第628页。
[4] 《二程集》下册，中华书局，页1256页。
[5] 《二程集》下册，同上，第1264页。
[6] 钱锺书：《管锥编》第一册，生活·读书·新知三联书店2007年版，第85页。

的经典名言，而为宋儒等后世学者所服膺。"物同理同"则是钱先生的掘发。他援引《淮南子·修务训》的一段文字云："若夫水之用舟，沙之用鸠，泥之用輴，山之用蔂，夏渎而冬陂，因高为田，因下为池，此非吾所谓为之。圣人之从事也，殊体而合于理，其所由异路而同归。"[1] 文中的"殊体而合于理"，正是所谓"理同"也。他还征引西典作为参证："思辩之当然（Laws of thought），出于事物之必然（Laws of things），物格知至，斯所以百虑一致、殊涂同归耳。"[2] 钱先生对《易·系辞》"天下同归而殊途，一致而百虑"的诠解，可谓恰切到无须增减。钱先生的贡献在于，除了人的"性同"、"理同"之外，还增加了物的"理同"，即物理之所同然者。故钱先生结而论之曰："心之同然，本乎理之当然，而理之当然，本乎物之必然，亦即合乎物之本然也。"[3]

要之，"和"是以不同为前提的，没有不同，就无所谓和。最要不得的是"以同裨同"，其结果必然导致"剗同"。一个人如果只看到一己之私的利益，而不顾他人的利益；一国的当政者如果只顾及本国的利益，而罔顾他国的利益，甚至戕害他国的利益，在中国古圣哲看来就是强不同以为同，也就是"剗同"，用今天的话语转译则为强盗的逻辑。

人类在21世纪的环境下，已经是命运与共的共同体。刻意伤害其他国家无异于伤害自己。把自己国家的利益与意志置于全人类之上，结果必然失去自身的利益。古圣智伯所总结的衰周之失，是为不"务和同"，而痴迷"剗同"，其结果强大的周朝由衰落而走向灭亡。所谓"和实生物，同则不继"，良有以也。刘梁《辩和同之论》所总结的"得由和兴，失由同起"，也由中国和世界历史的世相无数次验证。

然则"务和同"的前提，是一个人、一个民族、一国的执政者，需要有顾及人类共同命运的胸怀，或至少需要懂得"我活也要让他人活"的浅显道理。王弼注《易经》曾援引了楚人亡弓的典例，其说见《孔子家语·弟子好生篇》，其中记载道："楚昭王出游，亡乌号之弓，左右请求之。王曰：'楚人亡弓，楚得之，又何求焉。'"这位楚昭王看来很是豁达大度了。认为弓既然是在楚国丢失的，那么拾得弓的人必定是楚人，楚弓为楚人所得，何必还要到处去找寻呢。但孔子听说后，颇不以为然，认为楚王的志量未免太小，真正的豁达大度，应该这样说：弓

---

[1] 钱锺书：《管锥编》第一册，生活·读书·新知三联书店2007年版，第84页。
[2] 同上书，第85页。
[3] 同上书，第85页。

是人丢失的，得到的也是人，人失人得，有何不好？这是试图将一事当中的价值理念和人的普遍价值联系起来，亦即"仁者，人也"。

如果不是这样，而是局限于仅仅维护一国之利益，甚至将"爱国"发挥至极点，那么其结果将是："楚人亡弓，不能亡楚，爱国愈甚，益为它灾。"这是王弼注文的原话。智哉，仅仅活了二十四岁的魏晋哲人！千古以还犹为自作聪明的后来者所不及也。

Can Human Beings Still Come Together in the 21st Century?——How Did Ancient Chinese Sages View Human Beings' Getting Lost?

Liu Mengxi/China

Tenured Fellow and Director of the Institute of Chinese Culture, the Chinese National Academy of Arts / Member of the Central Research Institute of Culture and History

1

Can human beings still come together in the 21st century? In the trade war between China and the United States, Trump provokes conflicts here and there. The United States withdraws from multilateral cooperation organizations one after another, populism prevails and the naked pursuit of economic interests defeats value identification. The reality of this world changes to the direction of anti-civilization and anti-cooperation.

This rough and capricious reality is the typical embodiment of human beings getting lost.

It is not the first time that human beings have gotten lost. In the last century, it was manifested as madness and led to two world wars. This time, it is manifested as arrogance — and arrogance is only one step away from madness.

Madness and arrogance are the alienation of human nature. The way to change is to return to principles and learn to be a human being again.

The essence of Chinese culture is to give up evil ways and return to the natural goodness of human beings.

Not long ago, I pointed out: "According to many years of the study of Chinese culture, the contribution I can think of that Chinese culture makes to human beings is the whole system of spiritual values for how can a man be a man, a group be a group, a family be a family and a state be a state. These values enable us to be a healthy man, a harmonious group, a family with love and respect, a state of civilization and ethics that can be trustworthy and harmonious and win the admiration of people from afar."

Human beings get along with each other, the groups get along with each other, so the concept of "harmony" proposed by ancient Chinese sages, and the value pursuit of "harmony with people".

2

The concept of "harmony" was first put forward by a wise man named Shibo in the period of King You of Zhou.

Shibo was a government official in the late Western Zhou Dynasty who took charge of astronomy, the calendar, classics and history. Once upon a time, he discussed with Zhengbo about why the Zhou Kingdom had begun to decline. Zhengbo, whose name was You, the youngest brother of King Xuan and the uncle of King You, was the founder of the State of Zheng and was known as the Duke Huan of Zheng. His dialogue with Shibo occurred in the eighth year of King You of Zhou when he was still the Minister of Zhou. He felt very anxious when he saw that the Zhou Kingdom was at stake. For the safety of his family and the people of Zheng,

Zhengbo consulted Shibo over the pros and cons of his relocating to a large scale. Zhengbo asked: Has the Zhou Kingdom made any mistakes that have caused the wane of the state?

Shibo answered affirmatively. He said: The situation of the Zhou Kingdom was entirely its own fault. He analyzed that —

The "Grand Oath" says: "What the populace wants is what Heave follows." Today the King abandons the bright and illustrious things; he favors the obscure and slanderous things. He dislikes the rich, plump horn of the rhinoceros, but associates with mischievous children and unproductive women. He discards harmony and seeks identicalness. Harmony is indeed productive of things, but identicalness does not advance growth. Smoothing one thing with another is called harmony. For this reason, things come together and flourish. If the one uses the same thing to complement the same thing, it leads to a dead end. Therefore, the ancient kings mixed Earth with Metal, Wood, Water, and Fire, and produced varieties of things. They balanced one's taste with the five flavors, strengthened the four limbs in order to guard the body, harmonized the six measures of sounds to improve hearing, made the seven parts of the body upright to maintain the heart/mind, balanced the eight body parts to complete the whole person, established the nine social rules to set up pure virtues, and put together the ten offices to regulate the multitude. Therefore, there came into existence thousands of categories and tens of thousands of methods used in calculating millions of things and evaluating myriads of properties. They maintained constant incomes and managed countless items. Therefore, the kings had a land of nine provinces and had incomes to raise the multitude. They taught the people adequate lessons and harmonized them as one family. Thus, it was harmony at the highest level. The wives of ancient kings were from other families, the ancient kings sought wealth in all directions and chose ministers who could remonstrate with the ruler. This way they reconciled a multitude of things. They were engaged in harmony. A single sound is nothing to hear, a single color does not make a pattern, a single taste does not satisfy the stomach, and a single item does not harmonize. The

King discards harmony and seeks identicalness. He was deprived of his by Heaven. Can the Kingdom not decline?[1]

Shibo thought that the chaos of the Western Zhou Dynasty was incurred by the fact that the rulers made light of "harmony" and focused on "being identical". He used the special word "being identical". "Being identical" is the opposite of "harmony". Shibo had a detailed explanation of why the governance of a State cannot be identical.

First of all, Shibo proposed a new philosophical proposition about the concept of harmony. This is: "Harmony is indeed productive of things, but identicalness does not advance growth". Here the two words "productive" and "growth" are very important. "Productive" refers to the producing of new things in their original state. "Growth" is actually a replacement word for "productive", and "not growth" means not being productive. In short, "harmony" is productive of things, but "identicalness" cannot be productive of things. "Productive" and "not productive" are directly related to the issue of the life-and-death of things of sustainability and unsustainability. "Unsustainability" is not productive, that is, it is in crisis and cannot rescue itself, and will inevitably have no future. Being "productive" means the continuation of life, and the future will come. The term "productive" also reveals the secret of the continuation of life, that is to say, this continuation is not a simple repetition of the old state, but with qualitative changes in the old state, a new life can be born or the new opportunity of life can continue.

Second, Shibo gave the metaphysical reason why "harmony" can be "productive", but "identicalness" cannot be sustainable. The key is to have a correct interpretation of the meaning of "harmony". Shibo's explanation is that when an independent existence is merged with another independent existence, this state can be called "harmony". Shibo calls this situation "smoothing one thing with another". Therefore, it can be said that "harmony" is a highly harmonious realm achieved

---

1 *Guoyu (Discourses of the States) Part II*, Shanghai People's Publishing House, 1988, pp.515-516.

by the coexistence and integration of different beings. It does not refer to a single existence, but a combination of multiple elements and differentiation. Because of the interlaced interaction of different elements in the interior, a huge tension is formed, and a new life is created by reciprocity.

3

The *Book of Changes* · *Xici* says, "In (the system of) the Yi there is the Grand Terminus, which produced the two elementary Forms. Those two Forms produced the four emblematic Symbols, which again produced the eight Trigrams". Tai Chi of "Yi" in the state of "production and reproduction" can be regarded as another name for "harmony". Therefore, Master Zhu claimed that: "Tai Chi is just a chaotic principle which contains yin and yang, rigid and flexible, odd and even, everything is here."[1] The explanation by Master Zhu narrowed the distance between "harmony" and "Tai Chi" in hermeneutics. However, Zhang Zai pointed out that they were the ultimate principle of complete coincidence. He proposed a new and identical concept, "Tai He". He wrote:

The Great Harmony is what is called Dao, it contains within itself the nature of floating and sinking, rising and falling, of motion, rest and mutually resonant. It produces harmonic changes, intermingling, success and failure, expansion and contraction. Subtle and minute, easy and simple are its progression; firm and resolute, wide and great its completeness. Qian is what knows through easy things, and kun is what realizes through the simple things! The dispersion of particularities that possess images is qi; what is the pure connection without images, is the spiritual dimension (shen). If it was not motion (wandering energy), and harmonic intercourse, it could not be called Great Harmony. Anyone who knows this knows the Dao; anyone who sees this while learning Yi has a clear idea of Yi. If not, even a talented man cannot be regarded as wise.[2]

---

1 *A Collection of Conversations of Master Zhu,* Volume 75, No.5, Chung Hwa Book Company Limited, p.1929.
2 Zhang Zai: "Rectifying the Obscure", in *Collections of Zhang Zai*, Chung Hwa Book Company Limited, 1978, p.7.

Zhang Zai's theory of Great Harmony (Taihe) is actually a more philosophical interpretation of the value theory of "harmony". In Zhang Zai's view, the Dao is the Tai Chi, and Tai Chi is the Great Harmony. The endless opposite pairs, including "nature floating and sinking, rising and falling, of motion, rest and mutual resonance, success and failure, expansion and contraction", are contained in the Great Harmony. This theory is exactly the same as the theory of Tai Chi by Master Zhu. The so-called "Great Harmony" is actually a new kind of theory of harmony, but it is upgraded and sublimated to the realm of infinite "harmony".

Well, since "harmony" contains so many, infinite amounts of opposite pairs, it is natural to produce mutual resonance and harmonic changes. Where there are mutual resonance and harmonic changes, there are inevitably productive things. Therefore, the theory that "harmony is indeed productive of things" can be demonstrated. To put it bluntly, all of the theory of "Harmony", the theory of "Harmony and Identicalness" and the theory of the "Great Harmony" are the theories of "Yi" (Changes). Zhang Zai's theory originated from Yi. Opposite pairs of the "Great Harmony" that are mutually resonant and harmonically changing are nothing but variants of "the successive movement of the inactive and active operations (*Yin* and *Yang*) they constitute what is called the course of things (*Dao*)" and "production and reproduction is what is called the process of change (Yi)." in the *Book of Changes · Xici*.

So, what is "identicalness"? How can we become "identical"? Why do we say "identicalness does not advance growth"? Being identical or not is a matter of a single being. If the goal is to achieve "harmony", then being identical or not identical are both obstacles. If we "discard harmony and seek identicalness", as criticized by Shibo, "if the one uses the same thing to complement the same thing" but discards the grand goal of harmony, then the result will be fruitless. Not only can the situation of "harmony" not be realized, but also "identicalness" will become useless because of self-repetition, thus leading to the opposite side, "being identical". The final result is the "dead end" as pointed out by Shibo. What a tragic, lonely and helpless scene!

"Therefore, the ancient kings mixed Earth with Metal, Wood, Water, and Fire, and produced varieties of things," said Shibo. "They balanced one's taste with the five flavors, strengthened the four limbs in order to guard the body, harmonized the six measures of sounds to improve hearing, made the seven parts of the body upright to maintain the heart/mind, balanced the eight body parts to complete the whole person, established the nine social rules to set up pure virtues, and put together the ten offices to regulate the multitude." In short, we must advocate diversity as a whole and incorporate multiplicity into unity. This is the secret for the success of the ancient kings of the Zhou Dynasty because "thousands of categories and tens of thousands of methods used in calculating millions of things and evaluating myriads of properties… maintained constant incomes and managed countless items", and "had a land of nine provinces and had incomes to raise the multitude". There are countless properties and thousands of roads, but they "harmonized them as one family". According to Shibo, by doing this, it can be said to be "harmony at its highest level".

He praised the fact that the ancient kings "were engaged in harmony" by various means and "married women from other families, sought wealth in all directions, and chose ministers who could remonstrate with the ruler … reconciled a multitude of things". Therefore, the concept of harmony is important for governing the country. It may have a direct influence on success or failure.

At this point, Shibo had already clearly explained the reasons, basis, antecedents and consequences of "seeking harmony" and "discarding identicalness", but he still had something to say, "A single sound is nothing to hear, a single color does not make a pattern, a single taste does not satisfy the stomach, and a single item does not harmonize." It is perfectly all right that in this world, if there is only one sound, there is no way to listen; if all colors are the same, it is too monotonous to see; if the food tastes the same, there is nothing to eat; if there is only one kind of object in the world, without comparison, there is no reason to talk about it. Only the foolish, the mentally retarded, the imbecile and stupid things dare to give up the colorfulness of the world, ignore the various customs and want to rule the colorful social life with identical arrogance.

4

Interestingly, the Zuo Zhuan recorded the same theory as Shibo's. It was a dialogue between the Duke Zhao of the Qi State and Yanzi in the twentieth year of his reign. What they discussed was also the issue of "harmony and identicalness". Duke Zhao asked Yanzi, "It is only Ju who is in harmony with me!" Yanzi replied, "Ju is merely identical; how can he be considered in harmony with you?" Due Zhao was confused and further asked, "Are they different, harmony and identicalness?" Yanzi bluntly replied: "They are different". Then he explained why "harmony" and "identicalness" are different. Yanzi stated that:

Harmony may be illustrated by soup. You have the water and fire, vinegar, pickles, salt, and plums, with which to cook fish. It is made to boil by means of firewood, and then the cook mixes the ingredients, harmoniously equalizing the several flavors, so as to supply whatever is deficient and carry off whatever is in excess. Then the master eats it, and his mind is made equable. So, it is in the relations of ruler and minister. When there is, in what the ruler approves of, anything that is not proper, the minister calls attention to that impropriety, so as to make the approval entirely correct. When there is, in what the ruler disapproves of, anything that is proper, the minister brings forward that propriety, so as to remove occasion for the disapproval. In this way, the government is made equal, with no infringement on what is right, and there is no quarreling with it in the minds of the people. Hence it is said in the ode (*Shi*, or Poetry),

"There are also the well-tempered soups,

Prepared beforehand, the ingredients rightly proportioned.

By these offerings, we invite his presence without a word;

Nor is there now any contention in the service."

As the ancient kings established the doctrine of the five flavors, so they made harmony of the five notes, to make their minds equable and to perfect their government. There is an analogy between sounds and flavors. There are the breath, the two classes of dances, the three subjects, the materials from the four quarters, the five notes, the six pitch-pipes, the seven sounds, the eight winds, the nine songs; [by these nine things the materials for music] are completed. Then there are [the distinctions of] clear and thick, small and large, short and long, fast and slow, solemn and joyful, hard and soft, lingering and rapid, high and low, the commencement and the end, the close and the diffuse, by which the parts are all blended together. The superior man listens to such music, that his mind may be composed. His mind is composed, and his virtues become harmonious. Hence it is said in the ode (*Shi*), "There is no flaw in his virtuous fame." Now it is not so with Ju. Whatever you say "Yes" to, he also says "Yes" to. Whatever you say "No" to, he also says "No" to. If you were to try to give water a flavor with water, who would care to partake of the result? If lutes were to be confined to one note, who would be able to listen to them? Such is the insufficiency of mere identicalness.[1]

Yanzi said, "harmony" may be illustrated by soup, which must be cooked with water and fire, and vinegar, pickle, salt and plums must be added to make the fish soup more delicious. It is also particular about what kind of firewood should be used. The several flavors must be harmoniously equalized by the cook so as to supply whatever is deficient and carry off whatever is in excess. With a variety of different ingredients and through different procedures, finally the delicious soup is cooked. Because it is a blend of five flavors, in the "Poetry Three Hundred", it is called "harmony of soup". If the master eats the soup, his mind is made equable.

---

[1] *An Interpretation to Chunqiu Zuo Zhuan,* Vol. 4, Shanghai People's Publishing House, 1977, pp.1463-1464.

The same is true of the relationship between the ruler and ministers. Yanzi said that what the ruler considered proper, there was impropriety, so that ministers must explain the reasons and correct them, and then it became a proper plan jointly made by the ruler and ministers. Similarly, what the ruler considered improper, there was propriety, so that ministers must offer suggestions, find propriety, remove impropriety and finally the government is made equal, with no infringement on what is right. Therefore, we must listen to different opinions and learn the strategy of governing the country that ancient kings adopted, such as "established the doctrine of the five flavors ... harmony of the five notes", "to make their minds equable and to perfect their government". However, the minister Ju was not the case. He was totally obedient. Whatever you said yes to, he said yes to; whatever you said no to, he said no to. This means to "give water a flavor with water", who would care to partake of the result? If lutes were to be confined to one note, who would be able to listen to them? Therefore, "identicalness" is different from "harmony". We should not recognize the "identical" attitude of this kind of person, but "establish the doctrine of the five flavors" and "make the harmony of the five notes", so that "there are breath, the two classes of dances, the three subjects, the materials from the four quarters, the five notes, the six pitch-pipes, the seven sounds, the eight winds, the nine songs; [by these nine things the materials for music] are completed", and "there are [the distinctions of] clear and thick, small and large, short and long, fast and slow, solemn and joyful, hard and soft, lingering and rapid, high and low, the commencement and the end, the close and the diffuse, by which the parts are all blended together." In other words, to govern the country, if the ministers are totally obedient to the ruler without correcting mistakes, and all the people are identical without different voices, it is impossible to achieve the situation in which "his mind is composed, and his virtues become harmonious", as expected by ancient kings.

The "theory of harmony and identicalness" of Yanzi is similar to that of Shibo.

5

In the *Biography of Liu Liang* in the *Book of the Later Han*, there is also an article entitled *On the Theory of Harmony and Identicalness*, which is a systematic summary and argument of the concept of harmony in the Pre-Qin period. This article is fully extracted below for reference.

Those who disobey but have the proper way, obey but do not go in righteousness, love but do harm and hate but do good. What are the reasons? Probably what the wise gains is what the unwise loses. Therefore, the noble man, in the world, does not set his mind either for anything or against anything; what is right he will follow.

Gain is made from harmony, but loss is the result of being identical. It is harmony to make up for the wrong by the right, and it is identicalness without a distinction between the good and the bad. The *Chunqiu Zuo Zhuan* says that: "Harmony may be illustrated by soup. Sourness and bitterness harmoniously equalize the several flavors, then the master eats it, and his mind is made equable. If you were to try to give water a flavor with water, who would care to partake of the result? If lutes were to be confined to one note, who would be able to listen to them?" Therefore, the noble man is all-embracing and not partial, harmonious and not identical; he takes the correction of mistakes as propriety of conduct and the removal of evil as loyalty. The *Xiao Jing* says, "If there are any worthy causes put forward by the leader he will be there to advance them, and if the ruler has any faults he will not hesitate to demonstrate and save the ruler from what is evil. Hence, the relationship between the superior and the subordinate is cordial and amicable."

King Gong of Chu, who was indisposed due to sickness, summoned his ministers and said that: "I am not a virtuous man, but I reigned over the country when I was young. It was my mistake to be unable to inherit the rules of the former king but instead, cause damage to the army of Chu State. If my ancestors bless me to die with my head on my body, please give me the posthumous name Ling or Li." The ministers promised. After his death, Zinang said: "No. To serve His Majesty, we must praise his virtues but forget his mistakes. He was the King of the Great Chu State who reigned the South Sea and reached the central regions. He did us big favors. With such favors, he still knew his mistakes, so we may call him King Gong!" The ministers approved. It was disobedience but it was the proper way. Later, King Ling of Chu was haughty, obscene and excessively tyrannical, but Minister Shenhai obeyed the last words and buried the king beside the stream together with his two daughters. It was obedience but did not go righteousness. In the War of Yanling between Jin and Chu, Zifan died because Yanggu drank him with delicious wine. It was love but did harm. Zang Wuzhong said: "Meng hates me, that's good medicine for my badness; Ji loves me, he flatters. Flattery is poisonous to me, but medicine can help me survive." It was hatred but it did good. Confucius said: "It is hard to be wise. There was the wise Zang Wuzhong, and yet he was not allowed to remain in Lu. And there was reason for that. He did what was not accordant with right, and did not act on the principle of reciprocity." Probably he went towards righteousness, but did not go the proper way.

If you know it but commit impropriety, it is fake; if you do not know but lose, it is confusion. Being confused and fake, there will be troubles. In troubles, although wise, you are improper. Therefore, "he who is wise but not proper will gain and eventually lose." The *Books of Xia* says: "When you think of something, you yourself must find in that thing a meaning that one's conduct should be accordant with right, and act on the principle of reciprocity." You must be loyal and wise.

Therefore, if the noble man takes action, he considers propriety. He does not commit violations on account of profit, and he does not feel remorse on account of propriety. Any moves must be done in the proper way. If his behavior is not proper, even his brothers will not agree with him; if his behavior is proper, even hatred will not discard him. So, Xie Hu was recommended by Qixi, but the Duke of Zhou executed Guan Shu and exiled Cai Shu. Bodi was tolerated by Duke Wen of Jin, but Fuxia failed due to following the Duke Li of Zheng; Guansu was hated but promoted, and Shenhou was loved but quit. The reason is propriety. So, "It doesn't matter if one obeys or disobeys, but propriety is important; it doesn't matter whether there is hatred or love, but the way is valued". The *Li Ji* says: "Love a man you should know his wickedness; while if you hate him, you must know his virtue." This is because of propriety.[1]

Liu Liang, whose courtesy name was Manshan, was alternatively known by the name Cen. He came from Ningyang, Dongping. In the *Book of the Later Han*, he was a member of the Liang Imperial House of Xiao. He was "left a poor orphan child, and sold books in the street to support his own life"[2]. He wrote the book *Against Groupism*, which satirized the worldly "friendly making" and "the gangs of evils" so that the critics said that "traitorous ministers feared the *Spring and Autumn* (Chunqiu) written by Confucius", but the *Against Groupism* made "vulgar scholars ashamed". It is a pity that this book has been lost in history. However, this article *On the Theory of Harmony and Identicalness* remains intact. The structure of the full text is rigorous and clear, and it is more complete than the theory of Shibo and Yanzi. The part quoted from *Chunqiu Zuo Zhuan* was the statement of Yanzi, but its innovation lies in the theoretical clarification of the concepts of harmony and identicalness.

The definition of "harmony" given by Liu Liang is "making up for wrong by doing right", that is to say, the candid help of each other in correcting mistakes, but never "obeying" without following the principle of propriety. Therefore, he said that: "The noble man is all-embracing and not partial, harmonious and not identical; he takes the correction of mistakes as the propriety of conduct and the removal of evil as loyalty." His definition of "identicalness" is "without a distinction between good and bad", which means bowing down to everything somebody says or does, but does not distinguish right and wrong. The result is naturally the opposite of "harmony necessarily must not be identical", which is a real mistake for the governance of a country. Liu Liang took the political affairs of the Chu State as an example. First, when King Gong of Chu was seriously ill, he called together his ministers, revealed his own mistakes and said that his posthumous name could

---

[1] *Book of the Later Han*, Volume 80 (Part 2), Biographies of Writers (No.70 Part 2), Chinese Studies Library Edition, Book 3, 2012, pp.2118-2121.
[2] *Book of the Later Han*, Volume 80 (Part 2), same as above, Book 3, p.2118.

be "Ling" or "Li". According to the annotation of Du Yu to *Chunqiu Zuo Zhuan*: "Ling means chaotic but without damage to the country, but Li means putting death to innocent ones."[1] Both of them were bad posthumous names. After making the request five times, the ministers agreed. After the death of King Gong, Prime Minister Zinang raised doubts, but the other ministers replied with the last words of the King. Zinang pointed out that the last words could not be followed because King Gong was glorious and "knew his mistakes", so it was proper to adopt the posthumous name "Gong". With regard to the last words, Zigang said: "To serve His Majesty, we must praise his virtues, and forget his mistakes." Other ministers were finally convinced. Liu Liang called this situation "disobedience but with the proper way". Although violating the last words of King Gong, it was proper.

Another example was King Ling of Chu, who was haughty, obscene and brutal, but Minister Shenhai obeyed the last words and buried the king beside the stream together with his two daughters. Liu Liang called this situation "obedience but by not going towards righteousness". The third example was the War of Yanling between Jin and Chu. After the planning by Minister Zifan, the Chu State gained the upper hand. However, at the crucial moment, but Yanggu drank him with delicious wine. Zifan got drunk and could not respond to the King, resulting in the defeat of the Chu army. Finally, Zifan committed suicide. Liu Liang called this situation "love but did harm". The fourth example was Zang Wuzhong, who was not allowed to remain in the State of Lu. Meng Zhuangzi and Ji Wuzi were two powerful figures. Ji liked Zang Wuzhong, but Meng disliked him. When Meng died, Zang Wuzhong went to mourn and cried very sadly. His rider got puzzled and asked if Ji had died, what would you do? Zang Wuzhong replied: "Meng hates me, that's good medicine for my badness; Ji loves me, he flatters me. Flattery is poisonous to me, but medicine can help me survive." Liu Liang called this situation "hatred but did good". However, he "knows it but commits an improper action", so he was inevitably suspected of being "fake". Therefore, Confucius said that this man was

---

[1] *Annotation of Chunqiu Zuo Zhuan* Part II, "Notes and Commentaries to Thirteen Classics", Peking University Press, 1999, p.911.

"wise", and yet "he was not allowed to remain in Lu, and there was a reason for it".

Liu Liang's *On the Theory of Harmony and Identicalness* highlighted the theme that "gain is made from harmony, but loss is the result of being identical". So, it is a stark warning for the attitude and behaviors that do not distinguish "good and bad" but take "being identical" or "not identical" as the principle. He emphasized that "being identical" or "not identical" did not matter, but propriety mattered. In this article, he made clear that "if the noble man takes an action, he considers it proper. He does not commit violations on account of profit, and he does not feel remorse on account of propriety. Any moves must be done in the proper way. If his behavior is not proper, even brothers will not agree with him; if his behavior is proper, even hatred will not discard him." In order to make the theory convincing and persuasive, the author cited the four examples of the Chu State and the Lu State to demonstrate "disobedience but it was done in the proper way", "obedience but by not going towards righteousness", "love but did harm" and "hatred but did good". These four examples were recorded in *Zuo Zhuan* and *Guoyu* (Discourses of the States). It is difficult for Liu Liang to propose the "Theory of Harmony and Identicalness" that can be recognized by the later generations when reading history books.

Alas! "Identicalness" without a distinction between good and bad is harmful for the government, but to "make up for wrong by doing right" is the criteria for "harmony". Finally, he arrived at the conclusion that "the noble man is all-embracing and not partial, harmonious and not identical; he takes the correction of mistakes as the propriety of conduct and the removal of evil as loyalty". The words to warn the world for thousands of years are: "gain is made from harmony, but loss is the result of being identical". This is quoted from Liu Liang's *On the Theory of Harmony and Identicalness* that is known to few people.

6

From the theory of harmony and identicalness of the ancient wise man Shibo to that of Yanzi, and then to Liu Liang's *On the Theory of Harmony and*

Identicalness, the ideas are highly coincident with "In all (the processes taking place) under heaven, what is there of thinking? What is there of anxious scheming? They all come to the same (successful) issue, though by different paths" advocated in the *Book of Changes* (I Ching) and also with "The superior man aims at harmony but not at identicalness". In a word, in the view of ancient Chinese sages, there is no reason for human beings not to go towards harmony. Even if the path is different, the way of thinking is different, eventually human beings will come together.

However, there is a theoretical problem that cannot be ignored: Why can difference move toward "harmony"? In the end, although differences exist in human beings and in all the things of the world, there are also similarities and even more fundamental laws, so we can live together on earth. It is the similarities among humans and things that determine the fact that they can always come together, tend to be identical and even reach the realm of Great Harmony as proposed by Zhang Zai.

However, what are the similarities in human beings? Let us turn to the statement of Mencius.

The most famous words that Mencius said about this topic are: "Men's mouths agree in having the same relishes; their ears agree in enjoying the same sounds; their eyes agree in recognizing the same beauty — shall their minds alone be without that which they similarly approve? What is it then of which they similarly approve? It is, I say, the principles of our nature, and the determinations of righteousness. The sages only apprehended before me that of which my mind approves along with other men. Therefore, the principles of our nature and the determinations of righteousness are agreeable to my mind, just as the flesh of grass and grain-fed animals is agreeable to my mouth." (*Mencius · Gaozi I*) What is similar in human beings, according to Mencius, first of all, is "nature". The taste of food should be different, the sounds should be different, and the colors should be diverse. In this respect, the wise man, Shibo, and the man of ideas, Yanzi, already had something to say, but why did Mencius still say that men have "the same relishes", enjoy "the same sounds" and recognize "the same beauty"? Probably it is human nature to have delicious food, listen to good music and like colorful beauty. "To enjoy food and delight in colors is the nature of men." (*Mencius · Gaozi I*) Born as men, human nature always shares similarities because we all belong to "mankind".

Xunzi also had very systematic and clear views on the similarities of mankind. In the book *Xunzi*, many articles touched on this topic. In *The True King and the Hegemon* he says: "Therefore, it is human nature that the mouth likes to eat delicious food, and no taste can be better than the king's taste; ears like to listen to euphonic sounds, and no music can be better than what the king hears; eyes like to have a look at beauty, and no one can find more colorful patterns and young women than those the king sees; the body likes ease, and nothing can be more quiet and enjoyable than what the king enjoys; the mind likes wealth, and no one can have more wealth than the king has. If a person is not crazy, confused, stupid or ignorant, then who else will not be pleased at complete ownership of all the best things in the world and control of all the people in the State like controlling children and grandchildren?"[1] The *On Honor and Disgrace* says: "People have similarities: desiring food when hungry, desiring warmth when cold, desiring rest when tired, liking the beneficial and hating the harmful — these are things people have from birth. One does not have to wait for these things, but they are already so. These are what Yu and Jie both share. Eyes can distinguish white, black, beauty and evil, ears can distinguish music, sounds, clear and chaotic sounds, the mouth can distinguish sourness, saltiness, sweetness and bitterness, noses can distinguish aroma, fragrance, fishy and bad smells, and skins can distinguish cold, hot, pain and itching — these are things people have from birth. One does not have to wait for these things, but they are already so. These are what Yu and Jie both share."[2] The book also says:

---

1 *Xunzi · The True King and the Hegemon*, Wang Xianqian, *Annotations to Xunzi* (eds. Shen Xiaohuan, Wang Xingxian), Chung Hwa Book Company Limited, 2012, pp.213-214.
2 *Xunzi · On Honor and Disgrace*, Wang Xianqian, *Annotations to Xunzi* (eds. Shen Xiaohuan, Wang Xingxian), Chung Hwa Book Company Limited, 2012, p.63.

"With regard to endowment, nature, intelligence, and capabilities, the gentleman and the petty man are one and the same. Both like honor and hate disgrace. Both like what is beneficial and hate what is harmful. In this the gentleman and the petty man are the same, but they differ in the means by which they seek these things."[1] The *Against Physiognomy* says: "What is that by which humans are distinct as human? I say: It is because they have distinctions. Desiring food when hungry, desiring warmth when cold, desiring rest when tired, liking the beneficial and hating the harmful — these are things people have from birth. One does not have to wait for these things, but they are already so. These are what Yu and Jie both share."[2]

In general, it is human nature to have food when hungry, desire warmth when cold, like the beneficial and hate the harmful, thus keeping the balanced self-esteem in mind. All men are identical in these aspects, even great men and petty men, sage men and ordinary men are no exception, but there is a distinction among men as to how they acquire and keep these things. This is the meaning of the "same nature". Xunzi's conclusion to the idea of harmony and identicalness is: "In disparity lies equality; in flexibility, smoothness; in diversity, uniformity."[3] It was identical to the "As all in the world ultimately comes to the same end, though the roads to it are different" in the *Book of Changes*.

Humans share similarities in "nature" and also in "principles". Mankind is different from animals because we have rational thinking. So, Mencius says, "What is it that is the same with people's minds?" It is "principles". Why wise men become wise in our mind is that their principles and morality can capture our mind and speak out what we desire to say but cannot. This is what Mencius called "the sage knows the sameness of our minds beforehand". As a saying goes, we have the same mind, and the mind has the same principles. In fact, it is the initial emotions and ideal

---

1 *Xunzi*, p.61.
2 *Xunzi · Against Physiognomy*, Wang Xianqian, *Annotations to Xunzi* (eds. Shen Xiaohuan, Wang Xingxian), Chung Hwa Book Company Limited, 2012, p.78.
3 *Xunzi · On Honor and Disgrace*, Wang Xianqian, *Annotations to Xunzi* (eds. Shen Xiaohuan, Wang Xingxian), Chung Hwa Book Company Limited, 2012, p.71

expectations of human beings. It is only because of the complications of intention and behavior that all kinds of contradictions are caused. Ancient and modern wise men reveal that we should find out the principle of consistency in psychological expectations through the contradictions of human life and see the same behind the differences. Mencius says: "Shun was born in Zhu Feng, removed to Fu Xia, and died in Ming Tiao — a man near the wild tribes on the east. King Wen was born in Zhou by mount Qi, and died in Bi Ying — a man near the wild tribes on the west. Those regions were distant from one another more than a thousand li, and the age of the one sage was later in time to that of the other by more than a thousand years. But when they got their wish, and carried their principles into practice throughout the Middle Kingdom, it was like uniting the two halves of a seal. When we examine those sages, both the earlier and the later, their principles (*Kui*) are found to be the same." (*Lilou Part 2*) Here, "Kui" in Chinese literally means rules and laws, but can be interpreted as principles. That is to say, the principles and morality in the thoughts of ancient masters and the masters of the later generations have similarities or are identical in essence.

The Cheng Brothers say: "Everything in the world has similarities."[1] They also say: "From ancient times until now, the minds of people and the principles of things have similarities and the sages before and now must be totally consistent."[2] They also say: "We are born to follow principles and to be rational is our nature. People are born with endowed good virtues. Although there may be differences in weakness, strength, principles and wisdom, the minds are all the same. The principles and wisdom result from different degrees of deception; the weakness and strength derive from the endowments. The principles are identical, and the sage man and petty man are no exception."[3] Therefore, the Cheng Brothers integrate "nature" and "principles" into the theory of harmony and identicalness. Lu Jiuyuan, another

---

1 *Collections of the Works of the Cheng Brothers Part 2*, Chung Hwa Book Company Limited, 1981, p.1029.
2 Ibid. p.1158.
3 Ibid. p.1159.

thinker of the Song Dynasty also says that: "The sage men during the thousands of years before have the same mind and principles; the sage men thousands of years later have the same mind and principles; the sage men in the East, South, West and North Sea also have the same mind and principles".[1] So, "nature" and "principles" are identical for all people. Mencius says "In principles and righteousness our minds are pleased, just as the flesh of beef and mutton and pork please our mouths". This is the truth.

However, when recognizing that the nature and principles that we are born with are identical, what are our views on "being identical" and "not identical", that is to say, the relationship between "identicalness" and "differences"? Mozi says: "That it is so, includes that by which it is so. When things are the same in being so, that by which they are so is not necessarily the same. When something is chosen, there is that by which it is chosen. When what is chosen is the same, that by which it is chosen is not necessarily the same."[2] This means that the phenomena are the same, but the reason may not be the same; the goals are the same, but the paths and means may not be the same. The thinkers Cheng Hao and Cheng Yi of the Song Dynasty regard "seeking identicalness" or "being different" as the dividing line for being "public" or "private". They say: "be public, be identical; be private, be different."[3] They point out that "being identical" is the "Order of the Heaven". They also say: "The wise man is different in great identicalness; not being identical is because this is not proper; not being different is because of doing as most people do."[4] They consider it as the nonsense of uncultivated men if the difference of man and things is not recognized; and not proper if denying "great identicalness". In terms of the degree of the mistake, they presume that not being identical is more serious. There is also the distinction between "great identicalness" and "minor identicalness". The "great identicalness" cannot be violated, but the "minor identicalness" may have

---

1 *Collections of Lu Jiuyuan*, Chung Hwa Book Company Limited, 1980, p.273.
2 "Mozi: Minor Illustrations", *Proofreading and Annotations of Mozi Part 2*, Chung Hwa Book Company Limited, 1993, p.628.
3 *Collections of the Works of the Cheng Brothers Part 2*, Chung Hwa Book Company Limited, p.1256.
4 Ibid. p.1264.

differences. "There should be common points in points of principle, but in incidental occurrences, differences can persist". This is really a truth.

7

Mr. Qian Zhongshu, a contemporary scholar of China, when publishing the book *On Arts* in 1948, had the sentence in the preface that I have often quoted, "Principles are the same for the Orient and the West, and the way never changes to the South and to the North". In the opinion of Mr. Qian Zhongshu, although the Oriental and Western cultures are different, the psychological characteristics and orientations of the Orientals and Westerners are often the same. The reason is that the things reacting to the spiritual world of humans have the same phenomena and principles. Therefore, he concludes that: "The same mind and principle is because of the same things and rationales."[1] "The same mind and principle" are the classic saying of Mencius followed by scholars during the Song Dynasty, but "the same things and rationales" are the invention of Mr. Qian. He quoted a paragraph from *Huainanzi · Cultivating Effort*: "It is like taking a boat in the water, taking a ride in the sand, taking a sled in the swamp, taking a basket on the mountains, dredging the ditch in the summer, excavating the pond in the winter, working the fields in the highlands, and digging rivers in low places. They are not what the men I refer to are. The sages follow the same principles although taking different actions; they have the same purposes though they reach them by different paths."[2] Here, "the same principles although taking different actions" indicates the same principles. He also quotes from the Western classics: "Laws of thought derive from the laws of things. If you study things and learn knowledge, your minds will be the same and they all come to the same issue by different paths."[3] Mr. Qian's interpretation of "They all come to the same (successful) issue, though by different paths" in the *Book of Changes · Xici* is proper without the need for addition or deletion. Mr. Qian's contribution is that

---

1 Qian Zhongshu, *Literary Criticism (Guanzhuibian)* Volume 1, SDX Joint Publishing Company, 2007, p.85.
2 Ibid. p.84.
3 Ibid. p.85.

in addition to be the "same nature" and the "same principles" of humans, he adds the "same rationales" of things, and he makes conclusions that "the identicalness of minds is the naturalness of principles; the naturalness of principles is the necessity of things, and coincides with the nature of things."[1]

In summary, "harmony" is premised on differences. If there is no difference, there is no harmony. We should not use "the same thing to complement the same thing" because it is a "dead end". If a person only cares about private interests and disregards the interests of others, if the rulers of a country only care about their own interests and ignore or even do harm to the interests of other countries, in the minds of Chinese sages, they use the same thing to complement the same thing and thus it is a "dead end". In today's words, it is the logic of robbers.

In the 21st century, there is a community with a shared future for mankind. Deliberately hurting other countries is tantamount to hurting yourself. If the interests and will of a country overtop those of all humans, the country will inevitably lose its own interests. The ancient wise man, Zhibo, told us that the decline of the Zhou Dynasty was not "engaged in harmony". It is a truth that "harmony is indeed productive of things, but identicalness does not advance growth". Liu Liang's *On the Theory of Harmony and Identicalness* highlighted the theme that "gain is made from harmony, but loss is the result of being identical", which has been verified many times throughout the history of China and of the world.

However, the premise of being "engaged in harmony" is that the people, the nation and the ruler of a country must bear the shared future of mankind in mind or at least understand the simple truth that "I survive, you survive". Wang Bi's annotations to the *Book of Changes* often quoted the example of Chu's loss of a bow. This story was recorded in the *School Sayings of Confucius · Loving Life*: "King Zhao of Chu lost his 'Ornate and Yielding' bow. His attendant asked to go find it, but the king said, 'A person of Chu lost a bow, a person of Chu will find it,

---

[1] Qian Zhongshu, *Literary Criticism (Guanzhuibian)* Volume 1, SDX Joint Publishing Company, 2007, p.85.

what need is there to go looking for it?'" King Zhao was generous. However, when Confucius heard of this, he criticized the king of the Chu State and said that if a man finds it, that is good enough; why must it be a man of Chu? This is an attempt to link the concept of value contained in the story with the universal value of mankind, that is to say, "the benevolent, the human being".

If not so, but limited to merely safeguarding the interests of one country and even arousing "patriotism" to the extreme, then the result will be: "A person of Chu lost a bow, the Chu State will not die for it. But for the more patriotic, it would become a disaster." This was what Wang Bi noted. Even the wise man who lived only for 24 years is cleverer than our later generations.